Expositions Of Holy Scripture

Alexander Maclaren

Table of Contents

Table of Contents

Expositions Of Holy Scripture

Table of Contents

Expositions Of Holy Scripture

Alexander Maclaren

Kessinger Publishing reprints thousands of hard–to–find books!

Visit us at http://www.kessinger.net

- ELIJAH COME AGAIN
- TRUE GREATNESS
- THE MAGNIFICAT
- ZACHARIAS'S HYMN
- THE DAYSPRING FROM ON HIGH
- SHEPHERDS AND ANGELS
- WAS, IS, IS TO COME
- SIMEON'S SWAN–SONG
- THE BOY IN THE TEMPLE
- JOHN THE PREACHER OF REPENTANCE
- JOHN'S WITNESS TO JESUS, AND GOD'S
- THE TEMPTATION
- PREACHING AT NAZARETH
- INSTRUCTIONS FOR FISHERMEN
- FEAR AND FAITH
- BLASPHEMER, OR—WHO?
- LAWS OF THE KINGDOM
- THREE CONDENSED PARABLES
- WORTHY–NOT WORTHY
- JESUS AT THE BIER
- JOHN'S DOUBTS AND CHRIST'S PRAISE
- GREATNESS IN THE KINGDOM
- THWARTING GOD'S PURPOSE
- A GLUTTONOUS MAN AND A WINEBIBBER
- THE TWO DEBTORS
- LOVE AND FORGIVENESS
- GO INTO PEACE
- THE MINISTRY OF WOMEN
- ONE SEED AND DIVERSE SOILS
- SEED AMONG THORNS
- A MIRACLE WITHIN A MIRACLE
- CHRIST TO JAIRUS
- BREAD FROM HEAVEN
- THE LORD THAT HEALETH THEE'
- CHRIST'S CROSS AND OURS
- PRAYER AND TRANSFIGURATION

Expositions Of Holy Scripture

- 'IN THE HOLY MOUNT'
- CHRIST HASTENING TO THE CROSS
- CHRIST'S MESSENGERS: THEIR EQUIPMENT AND WORK
- NEIGHBOURS FAR OFF
- HOW TO PRAY
- THE PRAYING CHRIST
- THE RICH FOOL
- ANXIOUS ABOUT EARTH, OR EARNEST ABOUT THE KINGDOM
- STILLNESS IN STORM
- THE EQUIPMENT OF THE SERVANTS
- THE SERVANT–LORD
- SERVANTS AND STEWARDS HERE AND HEREAFTER
- FIRE ON EARTH
- CONTENTS
- TRUE SABBATH OBSERVANCE
- THE STRAIT GATE
- CHRIST'S MESSAGE TO HEROD
- THE LESSONS OF A FEAST
- EXCUSES NOT REASONS
- THE RASH BUILDER
- 'THAT WHICH WAS LOST'
- THE PRODIGAL AND HIS FATHER
- GIFTS TO THE PRODIGAL
- THE FOLLIES OF THE WISE
- TWO KINDS OF RICHES
- THE GAINS OF THE FAITHFUL STEWARD
- DIVES AND LAZARUS
- MEMORY IN ANOTHER WORLD
- GOD'S SLAVES
- WHERE ARE THE NINE?
- THREE KINDS OP PRAYING
- ENTERING THE KINGDOM
- THE MAN THAT STOPPED JESUS
- MELTED BY KINDNESS
- THE TRADING SERVANTS
- THE REWARDS OF THE TRADING SERVANTS
- A NEW KIND OF KING
- TENANTS WHO WANTED TO BE OWNERS
- WHOSE IMAGE AND SUPERSCRIPTION?
- WHEN SHALL THESE THINGS BE?
- THE LORD'S SUPPER
- PARTING PROMISES AND WARNINGS
- CHRIST'S IDEAL OF A MONARCH [Footnote: Preached on the occasion of the death of Queen Victoria.]
- THE LONELY CHRIST

EXPOSITIONS OF HOLY SCRIPTURE

ST. LUKE

ALEXANDER MACLAREN, D. D., Litt. D.

VOLUME I: ST. LUKE *Chaps. I to XII*

ELIJAH COME AGAIN

'There was, in the days of Herod the king of Judea, a certain priest named Zacharias, of the course of Abia: and his wife was of the daughters of Aaron, and her name was Elisabeth. 6. And they were both righteous before God, walking in all the commandments and ordinances of the Lord blameless. 7. And they had no child, because that Elisabeth was barren; and they both were now well stricken in years. 8. And it came to pass, that, while he executed the priest's office before God in the order of his course, 9. According to the custom of the priest's office, his lot was to burn incense when he went into the temple of the Lord.

10. And the whole multitude of the people were praying
without at the time of incense. 11. And there appeared
unto him an angel of the Lord standing on the right
side of the altar of incense. 12. And when Zacharias
saw him, he was troubled, and fear fell upon him.
13. But the angel said unto him, Fear not, Zacharias:
for thy prayer is heard; and thy wife Elisabeth shall
bear thee a son, and thou shalt call his name John.
14. And thou shalt have joy and gladness; and many
shall rejoice at his birth. 15. For he shall be great
in the sight of the Lord, and shall drink neither wine
nor strong drink; and he shall be filled with the Holy
Ghost, even from his mother's womb. 16. And many of
the children of Israel shall he turn to the Lord their
God. 17. And he shall go before Him in the spirit and
power of Elias, to turn the hearts of the fathers to
the children, and the disobedient to the wisdom of the
just; to make ready a people prepared for the Lord.'
—LUKE i. 5–17.

The difference between the style of Luke's preface (vs. 1–4) and the subsequent chapters relating to the Nativity suggests that these are drawn from some Hebrew source. They are saturated with Old Testament phraseology and constructions, and are evidently translated by Luke. It is impossible to say whence they came, but no one is more likely to have been their original narrator than Mary herself. Elisabeth or Zacharias must have communicated the facts in this chapter, for there is no indication that those contained in this passage, at all events, were known to any but these two.

If we were considering a fictitious story, we should note the artistic skill which prepared for the appearance of the hero by the introduction first of his satellite; but the order of the narrative is due, not to artistic skill, but to the divinely ordered sequence of events. It was fitting that John's office as Forerunner should begin even before his birth. So the story of his entrance into the world prepares for that of the birth which hallows all births.

I. We have first a beautiful outline picture of the quiet home in the hill country. The husband and wife were both of priestly descent, and in their modest lives, away among the hills, were lovely types of Old Testament godliness. That they are pronounced 'blameless' militates against no doctrine of universal sinfulness. It is not to be taken as dogma at all, but as the expression of God's merciful estimate of His servants' characters. These two simple saints lived, as all married believers should do, yoked together in the sweet exercise of godliness, and helping each other to all high and noble things. Hideous corruption of wedlock reigned round them. Such profanations of it as were shown later by Herod and Herodias, Agrippa and Bernice, were but too common; but in that quiet nook these two dwelt 'as heirs together of the grace of life,' and their prayers were not hindered.

The most of the priests who appear in the Gospels are heartless formalists, if not worse; yet not only Annas and Caiaphas and their spiritual kindred ministered at the altar, but there were some in whose hearts the ancient fire burned. In times of religious declension, the few who still are true are mostly in obscure corners, and live quiet lives, like springs of fresh water rising in the midst of a salt ocean. John thus sprang from parents in whom the old system had done all that it could do. In his origin, as in himself, he represented the consummate flower of Judaism, and discharged its highest office in pointing to the coming One.

This 'blameless' pair had a crook in their lot. Childlessness was then an especial sorrow, and many a prayer had gone up from both that their solitary home might be gladdened by children's patter and prattle. But their disappointed hope had not made them sour, nor turned their hearts from God. If they prayed about it, they would not murmur at it, and they were not thereby hindered from 'walking in all God's commandments and ordinances blameless.' Let us learn that unfulfilled wishes are not to clog our devotion, nor to silence our prayers, nor to slacken our running the race set before us.

II. We are carried away from the home among the hills to the crowded Temple courts. The devout priest has come up to the city, leaving his aged wife in solitude, for his turn of service has arrived. Details of the arrangements of the sacerdotal 'courses' need not detain us. We need only note that the office of burning incense was regarded as an honour, was determined by lot, and took place at the morning and evening sacrifice. So Zacharias, with his censer in his hand, went to the altar which stood in front of the veil, flanked on the right hand by the table of shewbread, and on the left by the great lamp–stand. The place, his occupation, the murmur of many praying voices without, would all tend to raise his thoughts to God; and the curling incense, as it ascended, would truly symbolise the going up of his heart in aspiration, desire, and trust. Such a man could not do his work heartlessly or formally.

Mark the manner of the angel's appearance. He was not seen as in the act of coming, but was suddenly made visible standing by the altar, as if he had been stationed there before; and what had happened was not that he came, but that Zacharias's eyes were opened. So, when Elisha's servant was terrified at the sight of the besiegers, the prophet prayed that his eyes might be opened, and when they were, he saw what had been there before, 'the mountain full of horses and chariots of fire.' Not the Temple courts only, but all places are full of divine messengers, and we should see them if our vision was purged. But such considerations are not to weaken the supernatural element in the appearance of this angel with his message. He was sent, whatever that may mean in regard to beings whose relation to place must be different from ours. He had an utterance of God's will to impart.

It has often been objected to these chapters that they are full of angelic appearances, which modern thought deems suspicious. But surely if the birth of Jesus was what we hold it to have been, the coming into human life of the Incarnate Son of God, it is not legend that angel wings gleam in their whiteness all through the story, and angel voices adore the Lord of men as well as angels, and angel eyes gaze on His cradle, and learn new lessons there.

III. We have next the angel's message. The devoutest heart is conscious of shrinking dread when brought face to face with celestial brightness that has overflowed into our darkness. So 'Fear not' is the first word on the messenger's lips, and one can fancy the accent of sweetness and the calm of heart which followed. It has often been thought that Zacharias had been praying for offspring while he was burning incense; but the narrative does not say so, and besides the fact that he had ceased to hope for children (as is shown by his incredulity), surely it casts a slur on his religious character to suppose that personal wishes were uppermost at so sacred a moment. Prayers that he had long ago put aside as finally refused, now started to life again. God delays often, but He does not forget. Blessings may come to–day as the result of old prayers which have almost passed from our memory and our hope.

Observe how brief is the announcement of the child's birth, important as that was to the father's heart, and how the prophecy lingers on the child's future work, which is important for the world. His name, character, and work in general are first spoken, and then his specific office as the Forerunner is delineated at the close. The name is significant. 'John' means 'The Lord is gracious.' It was an omen, a condensed prophecy, the fulfilment of which stretched beyond its bearer to Him as whose precursor alone was John a token of God's grace.

His character (ver. 15) puts first 'great in the sight of the Lord.' Then there are some whom God recognises as great, small as we all are before Him. And His estimate of greatness is not the world's estimate. How Herod or Pilate or Caesar, or philosophers at Athens, or rabbis in Jerusalem would have scoffed if they had been pointed to the gaunt ascetic pouring out words which they would have thought wild, to a crowd of Jews, and been told that that was the greatest man in the world (except One)! The elements of greatness in the estimate of God which is truth, are devotion to His service, burning convictions, intense moral earnestness, superiority to sensuous delights, clear recognition of Jesus, and humble self–abnegation before Him. These are not the elements recognised in the world's Pantheon. Let us take God's standard.

John was to be a Nazarite, living not for the senses, but the soul, as all God's great ones have to be. The form may vary, but the substance of the vow of abstinence remains for all Christians. To put the heel on the animal within, and keep it well chained up, is indispensable, if we are ever to know the buoyant inspiration which comes from a sacreder source than the fumes of the wine–cup. Like John, we must flee the one if we would have the other, and be 'filled with the Holy Ghost.'

The consequence of his character is seen in his work, as described generally in verse 16. Only such a man can effect such a change, in a time of religious decay, as to turn many to God. It needs a strong arm to check the downward movement and to reverse it. No one who is himself entangled in sense, and but partially filled with God's Spirit, will wield great influence for good. It takes a Hercules to stop the chariot racing down hill, and God's Herculeses are all made on one pattern, in so far that they scorn delights, and empty themselves of self and sense that they may be filled with the Spirit.

John's specific office is described in verse 17, with allusion to the closing prophecy of Malachi. That prophecy had kindled an expectation that Elijah, in person, would precede Messias. John was like a reincarnation of the stern prophet. He came in a similar epoch. His characteristic, like Elijah's, was 'power,' not gentleness. If the earlier prophet had to beard Ahab and Jezebel, the second Elijah had Herod and Herodias. Both haunted the desert, both pealed out thunders of rebuke. Both shook the nation, and stirred conscience. No two figures in Scripture are truer brethren in spirit than Elijah the Tishbite and John the Baptist.

His great work is to go before the Messiah, and to prepare Israel for its King. Observe that the name of the coming One is not mentioned in verse 17. 'Him' is enough. Zacharias knew who 'He' was. But observe, too, that the same mysterious person is distinctly called 'The Lord,' which in this connection, and having regard to the original prophecy in Malachi, can only be the divine name. So, in some fashion not yet made plain, Messiah's advent was to be the Lord's coming to His people, and John was the Forerunner, in some sense, of Jehovah Himself.

But the way in which Israel was to be prepared is further specified in the middle clauses of the verse, which are also based on Malachi's words. The interpretation of 'to turn the hearts of the fathers to the children' is very doubtful; but the best explanation seems to be that the phrase means to bring back to the descendants of the ancient fathers of the nation the ancestral faith and obedience. They are to be truly Abraham's seed, because they do the works and cherish the faith of Abraham. The words imply the same truth which John afterwards launched as a keen-edged dart, 'Think not to say, We have Abraham to our father.' Descent after the flesh should lead to kindred in spirit. If it does not, it is nought.

To turn 'the disobedient to the wisdom of the just' is practically the same change, only regarded from another point of view. John was sent to effect repentance, that change of mind and heart by which the disobedient to the commands of God should be brought to possess and exercise the moral and religious discernment which dwells only in the spirits of the righteous. Disobedience is folly. True wisdom cannot be divorced from rectitude. Real rectitude cannot live apart from obedience to God.

Such was God's intention in sending John. How sadly the real effects of his mission contrast with its design! So completely can men thwart God, as Jesus said in reference to John's mission, 'The Pharisees and lawyers frustrated the counsel of God against themselves, being not baptized of him.' Let us take heed lest we bring to nothing, so far as we are concerned, His gracious purpose of redemption in Christ!

TRUE GREATNESS

He shall be great in the sight of the Lord.'—LUKE i. 15.

So spake the angel who foretold the birth of John the Baptist. 'In the sight of the Lord'—then men are not on a dead level in His eyes. Though He is so high and we are so low, the country beneath Him that He looks down upon is not flattened to Him, as it is to us from an elevation, but there are greater and smaller men in His sight, too. No epithet is more misused and misapplied than that of 'a great man.' It is flung about indiscriminately as ribbons and orders are by some petty State. Every little man that makes a noise for a while gets it hung round his neck. Think what a set they are that are gathered in the world's Valhalla, and honoured as the world's great men! The mass of people are so much on a level, and that level is so low, that an inch above the average looks gigantic. But the tallest blade of grass gets mown down by the scythe, and withers as quickly as the rest of its green companions, and goes its way into the oven as surely. There is the world's false estimate of greatness and there is God's estimate. If we want to know what the elements of true greatness are, we may well turn to the life of this man, of whom the prophecy went before him that he should be 'great in the sight of the Lord.' That is gold that will stand the test.

We may remember, too, that Jesus Christ, looking back on the career to which the angel was looking forward, endorsed the prophecy and declared that it had become a fact, and that 'of them that were born of women there had not arisen a greater than John the Baptist.' With the illumination of His eulogium we may turn to this life, then, and gather some lessons for our own guidance.

I. First, we note in John unwavering and immovable firmness and courage.

'What went ye out into the wilderness for to see? A reed shaken with the wind?' Nay! an iron pillar that stood firm whatsoever winds blew against it. This, as I take it, is in some true sense the basis of all moral greatness—that a man should have a grip which cannot be loosened, like that of the cuttle–fish with all its tentacles round its prey, upon the truths that dominate his being and make him a hero. 'If you want me to weep,' said the old artist–poet, 'there must be tears in your own eyes.' If you want me to believe, you yourself must be aflame with conviction which has penetrated to the very marrow of your bones. And so, as I take it, the first requisite either for power with others, or for greatness in a man's own development of character, is that there shall be this unwavering firmness of grasp of clearly–apprehended truths, and unflinching boldness of devotion to them.

I need not remind you how magnificently, all through the life of our typical example, this quality was stamped upon every utterance and every act. It reached its climax, no doubt, in his bearding Herod and Herodias. But moral characteristics do not reach a climax unless there has been much underground building to bear the lofty pinnacle; and no man, when great occasions come to him, develops a courage and an unwavering confidence which are strange to his habitual life. There must be the underground building; and there must have been many a fighting down of fears, many a curbing of tremors, many a rebuke of hesitations and doubts in the gaunt, desert–loving prophet, before he was man enough to stand before Herod and say, 'It is not lawful for thee to have her.'

No doubt there is much to be laid to the account of temperament, but whatever their temperament may be, the way to this unwavering courage and firm, clear ring of indubitable certainty, is open to every Christian man and woman; and it is our own fault, our own sin, and our own weakness, if we do not possess these qualities. Temperament! what on earth is the good of our religion if it is not to modify and govern our temperament? Has a man a right to jib on one side, and give up the attempt to clear the fence, because he feels that in his own natural disposition there is little power to take the leap? Surely not. Jesus Christ came here for the very purpose of making our weakness strong, and if we have a firm hold upon Him, then, in the measure in which His love has permeated our whole nature, will be our unwavering courage, and out of weakness we shall be made strong.

Of course the highest type of this undaunted boldness and unwavering firmness of conviction is not in John and his like. He presented strength in a lower form than did the Master from whom his strength came. The willow has a beauty as well as the oak. Firmness is not obstinacy; courage is not rudeness. It is possible to have the iron hand in the velvet glove, not of etiquette–observing politeness, but of a true considerateness and gentleness. They who are likest Him that was 'meek and lowly in heart,' are surest to possess the unflinching resolve which set His face like a flint, and enabled Him to go unhesitatingly and unrecalcitrant to the Cross itself.

Do not let us forget, either, that John's unwavering firmness wavered; that over the clear heaven of his convictions there did steal a cloud; that he from whom no violence could wrench his faith felt it slipping out of his grasp when his muscles were relaxed in the dungeon; and that he sent 'from the prison'—which was the excuse for the message—to ask the question, 'After all, art Thou He that should come?'

Nor let us forget that it was that very moment of tremulousness which Jesus Christ seized, in order to pour an unstinted flood of praise for the firmness of his convictions, on the wavering head of the Forerunner. So, if we feel that though the needle of our compass points true to the pole, yet when the compass–frame is shaken, the needle sometimes vibrates away from its true direction, do not let us be cast down, but believe that a merciful allowance is made for human weakness. This man was great; first, because he had such dauntless courage and firmness that, over his headless corpse in the dungeon at Machaerus, might have been spoken what the Regent Moray said over John Knox's coffin, 'Here lies one that never feared the face of man.'

II. Another element of true greatness that comes nobly out in the life with which I am dealing is its clear elevation above worldly good.

That was the second point that our Lord's eulogium signalised. 'What went ye out into the wilderness for to see? A man clothed in soft raiment?' But you would have gone to a palace, if you had wanted to see that, not to the reed–beds of Jordan. As we all know, in his life, in his dress, in his food, in the aims that he set before him, he rose high above all regard for the debasing and perishable sweetnesses that appeal to flesh, and are ended in time. He lived conspicuously for the Unseen. His asceticism belonged to his age, and was not the highest type of the virtue which it expressed. As I have said about his courage, so I say about his self–denial—Christ's is of a higher sort. As the might of gentleness is greater than the might of such strength as John's, so the asceticism of John is lower than the self–government of the Man that came eating and drinking.

But whilst that is true, I seek, dear brethren, to urge this old threadbare lesson, always needed, never needed more than amidst the senselessly luxurious habits of this generation, needed in few places more than in a great commercial centre like that in which we live, that one indispensable element of true greatness and elevation of character is that, not the prophet and the preacher alone, but every one of us, should live high above these temptations of gross and perishable joys, should

'Scorn delights and live laborious days.'

No man has a right to be called 'great' if his aims are small. And the question is, not as modern idolatry of intellect, or, still worse, modern idolatry of success, often makes it out to be, Has he great capacities? or has he won great prizes? but has he greatly used himself and his life? If your aims are small you will never be great; and if your highest aims are but to get a good slice of this world's pudding—no matter what powers God may have given you to use—you are essentially a small man.

I remember a vigorous and contemptuous illustration of St. Bernard's, who likens a man that lives for these perishable delights which John spurned, to a spider spinning a web out of his own substance, and catching in it nothing but a wretched prey of poor little flies. Such a one has surely no right to be called a great man. Our aims rather than our capacity determine our character, and they who greatly aspire after the greatest things within the reach of men, which are faith, hope, charity, and who, for the sake of effecting these aspirations, put their heels upon the head of the serpent and suppress the animal in their nature, these are the men 'great in the sight of the Lord.'

III. Another element of true greatness, taught us by our type, is fiery enthusiasm for righteousness.

You may think that that has little to do with greatness. I believe it has everything to do with it, and that the difference between men is very largely to be found here, whether they flame up into the white heat of enthusiasm for the things that are right, or whether the only things that can kindle them into anything like earnestness and emotion are the poor, shabby things of personal advantage. I need not remind you how, all through John's career, there burned, unflickering and undying, that steadfast light; how he brought to the service of the plainest teaching of morality a fervour of passion and of zeal almost unexampled and magnificent. I need not remind you how Jesus Christ Himself laid His hand upon this characteristic, when He said of him that 'he was a light kindled and shining.' But I would lay upon all our hearts the plain, practical lesson that, if we keep in that tepid region of lukewarmness which is the utmost approach to tropical heat that moral and religious questions are capable of raising in many of us, good−bye to all chance of being 'great in the sight of the Lord.' We hear a great deal about the 'blessings of moderation,' the 'dangers of fanaticism,' and the like. I venture to think that the last thing which the moral consciousness of England wants today is a refrigerator, and that what it needs a great deal more than that is, that all Christian people should be brought face to face with this plain truth—that their religion has, as an indispensable part of it, 'a Spirit of burning,' and that if they have not been baptized in fire, there is little reason to believe that they have been baptized with the Holy Ghost.

I long that you and myself may be aflame for goodness, may be enthusiastic over plain morality, and may show that we are so by our daily life, by our rebuking the opposite, if need be, even if it take us into Herod's chamber, and make Herodias our enemy for life.

IV. Lastly, observe the final element of greatness in this man—absolute humility of self−abnegation before Jesus Christ.

There is nothing that I know in biography anywhere more beautiful, more striking, than the contrast between the two halves of the character and demeanour of the Baptist; how, on the one side, he fronts all men undaunted and recognises no superior, and how neither threats nor flatteries nor anything else will tempt him to step one inch beyond the limitations of which he is aware, nor to abate one inch of the claims which he urges; and on the other hand how, like some tall cedar touched by the lightning's hand, he falls prone before Jesus Christ and says, 'He must increase, and I must decrease': 'A man can receive nothing except it be given him of God.' He is all boldness on one side; all submission and dependence on the other.

You remember how, in the face of many temptations, that attitude was maintained. The very message which he had to carry was full of temptations to a self−seeking man to assert himself. You remember the almost rough 'No!' with which, reiteratedly, he met the suggestions of the deputation from Jerusalem that sought to induce him to say that he was more than he knew himself to be, and how he stuck by that infinitely humble and beautiful saying, 'I am a voice'—that is all. You remember how the whole nation was in a kind of conspiracy to tempt him to assert himself, and was ready to break into a flame if he had dropped a spark, for all men were musing in their heart whether he was the Christ or not,' and all the lawless and restless elements would have been only too glad to gather round him, if he had declared himself the Messiah. Remember how his own disciples came to him, and tried to play upon his jealousy and to induce him to assert himself: 'Master, He whom thou didst baptize'—and so didst give Him the first credentials that sent men on His course—'has outstripped thee, and all men are coming to Him.' And you remember the lovely answer that opened such depths of unexpected tenderness in the rough nature: 'He that hath the bride is the bridegroom; the friend of the bridegroom heareth the voice; and that is enough to fill my cup with joy to the very brim.' And what conceptions of Jesus Christ had John, that he thus bowed his lofty crest before Him, and softened his heart into submission almost abject? He knew Him to be the coming Judge, with the fan in His hand, who could baptize with fire, and he knew Him to be 'the Lamb of God which taketh away the sin of the world.' Therefore he fell before Him.

Brethren, we shall not be 'great in the sight of the Lord' unless we copy that example of utter self–abnegation before Jesus Christ. Thomas a Kempis says somewhere, 'He is truly great who is small in his own sight, and thinks nothing of the giddy heights of worldly honour.' You and I know far more of Jesus Christ than John the Baptist did. Do we bow ourselves before Him as he did? The Source from which he drew his greatness is open to us all. Let us begin with the recognition of the Lamb of God that takes away the world's sin, and with it ours. Let the thought of what He is, and what He has done for us, bow us in unfeigned submission. Let it shatter all dreams of our own importance or our own desert. The vision of the Lamb of God, and it only, will crush in our hearts the serpent's eggs of self–esteem and self–regard.

Then, let our closeness to Jesus Christ, and our experience of His power, kindle in us the fiery enthusiasm with which He baptizes all His true servants, and let it because we know the sweetnesses that excel, take from us all liability to be tempted away by the vulgar and coarse delights of earth and of sense. Let us keep ourselves clear of the babble that is round about us, and be strong because we grasp Christ's hand.

I have been speaking about no characteristic which may not be attained by any man, woman, or child amongst us. 'The least in the kingdom of heaven' may be greater than John. It is a poor ambition to seek to be *called* 'great.' It is a noble desire to *be* 'great in the sight of the Lord.' And if we will keep ourselves close to Jesus Christ that will be attained. It will matter very little what men think of us, if at last we have praise from the lips of Him who poured such praise on His servant. We may, if we will. And then it will not hurt us though our names on earth be dark and our memories perish from among men.

'Of so much fame in heaven expect the meed.'

THE MAGNIFICAT

'And Mary said, My soul doth magnify the Lord, 47. And my spirit hath rejoiced in God my Saviour. 48. For He hath regarded the low estate of His hand–maiden: for,

11

behold, from henceforth all generations shall call me
blessed. 49. For He that is mighty hath done to me
great things; and holy is His name, 50. And His mercy
is on them that fear Him from generation to generation.
51. He hath shewed strength with His arm: He hath
scattered the proud in the imagination of their hearts.
52. He hath put down the mighty from their seats, and
exalted them of low degree. 53. He hath filled the
hungry with good things; and the rich He hath sent
empty away. 54. He hath holpen His servant Israel, in
remembrance of His mercy; 55. As He spake to our
fathers, to Abraham, and to his seed for ever.'
—LUKE i. 46–55.

Birds sing at dawn and sunrise. It was fitting that the last strains of Old Testament psalmody should prelude the birth of Jesus. To disbelievers in the Incarnation the hymns of Mary and Zacharias are, of course, forgeries; but if it be true nothing can be more 'natural' than these. The very features in this song, which are appealed to as proof of its being the work of some unknown pious liar or dishonest enthusiast, really confirm its genuineness. Critics shake their heads over its many quotations and allusions to Hannah's song and to other poetical parts of the Old Testament, and declare that these are fatal to its being accepted as Mary's. Why? must the simple village maiden be a poetess because she is the mother of our Lord? What is more likely than that she should cast her emotions into forms so familiar to her, and especially that Hannah's hymn should colour hers? These old psalms provided the mould into which her glowing emotions almost instinctively would run, and the very absence of 'originality' in the song favours its genuineness.

Another point may be noticed as having a similar bearing; namely, the very general and almost vague outline of the consequences of the birth, which is regarded as being the consummation to Israel of the mercy promised to the fathers. Could such a hymn have been written when sad experience showed how the nation would reject their Messiah, and ruin themselves thereby? Surely the anticipations which glow in it bear witness to the time when they were cherished, as prior to the sad tragedy which history unfolded. Little does Mary as yet know that 'a sword shall pierce through' her 'own soul also,' and that not only will 'all generations' call her 'blessed,' but that one of her names will be 'Our Lady of Sorrows.' For her and for us, the future is mercifully veiled. Only one eye saw the shadow of the Cross stretching black and grim athwart the earliest days of Jesus, and that eye was His own. How wonderful the calmness with which He pressed towards that 'mark' during all His earthly life!

The hymn is sometimes divided into four strophes or sections: first, the expression of devout emotion (vs. 46–48a); second, the great fact from which they arise (vs. 48b–50); third, the consequences of the fact (vs. 51–53); fourth, its aspect to Israel as fulfilment of promise. This division is, no doubt, in accordance with the course of thought, but is perhaps somewhat too artificial for our purposes; and we may rather simply note that in the earlier part the personal element is present, and that in the later it fades entirely, and the mighty deeds of God alone fill the meek singer's eye and lips. We may consider the lessons of these two halves.

I. The more personal part extends to the end of verse 50. It contains three turnings or strophes, the first two of which have two clauses each, and the third three. The first is verses 46 and 47, the purely personal expression of the glad emotions awakened by Elisabeth's presence and salutation, which came to Mary as confirmation of the angel's annunciation. Not when Gabriel spoke, but when a woman like herself called her 'mother of my Lord,' did she break into praise. There is a deep truth there. God's voice is made more sure to our weakness when it is echoed by human lips, and our inmost hopes attain substance when they are shared and spoken by another. We need not attribute to the maiden from Nazareth philosophical accuracy when she speaks of her 'soul' and 'spirit.' Her first words are a burst of rapturous and wondering praise, in which the full heart runs over. Silence is impossible, and speech a relief. They are not to be construed with the microscopic accuracy fit to be applied to a treatise on psychology. 'All that is within' her praises and is glad. She does not think so much of the stupendous fact as of her own meekly exultant heart, and of God, to whom its outgoings turn. There are moods in which the devout soul dwells on its own calm blessedness and on God, its source, more directly than on the gift which brings it. Note the twofold act—magnifying and rejoicing. We magnify God when we take into our vision some fragment more of the complete circle of His essential greatness, or when, by our means, our fellows are helped to do so. The intended effect of all His dealings is that we should think more nobly—that is, more worthily—of Him. The fuller knowledge of His friendly greatness leads to joy in Him which makes the spirit bound as in a dance—for such is the meaning of the word 'rejoice'—and which yet is calm and deep. Note the double name of God—Lord and Saviour. Mary bows in lowly obedience, and looks up in as lowly, conscious need of deliverance, and beholding in God both His majesty and His grace, magnifies and exults at once.

Verse 48 is the second turn of thought, containing, like the former, two clauses. In it she gazes on her great gift, which, with maiden reserve, she does not throughout the whole hymn once directly name. Here the personal element comes out more strongly. But it is beautiful to note that the 'lowliness' is in the foreground, and precedes the assurance of the benedictions of all generations. The whole is like a murmur of wonder that such honour should come to her, so insignificant, and the 'behold' of the latter half verse is an exclamation of surprise. In unshaken meekness of steadfast obedience, she feels herself 'the handmaid of the Lord.' In undisturbed humility, she thinks of her 'low estate,' and wonders that God's eye should have fallen on her, the village damsel, poor and hidden. A pure heart is humbled by honour, and is not so dazzled by the vision of future fame as to lose sight of God as the source of all. Think of that simple young girl in her obscurity having flashed before her the certainty that her name would be repeated with blessing till the world's end, and then thus meekly laying her honours down at God's feet. What a lesson of how to receive all distinctions and exaltations!

Verses 49 and 50 end this part, and contain three clauses, in which the personal disappears, and only the thought of God's character as manifested in His wonderful act remains. It connects indeed with the preceding by the 'to me' of verse 49; but the main subject is the new revelation, which is not confined to Mary, of the threefold divine glory fused into one bright beam, in the Incarnation. Power, holiness, eternal mercy, are all there, and that in deeper and more wondrous fashion than Mary knew when she sang. The words are mostly quotations from the Old Testament, but with new application and meaning. But even Mary's anticipations fell far short of the reality of that power in weakness, that holiness mildly blended with tenderest pity and pardoning love; that mercy which for all generations was to stretch not only to 'them that fear Him,' but to rebels, whom it would make friends. She saw but dimly and in part. We see more plainly all the rays of divine perfection meeting in, and streaming out to, the whole world, from her Son 'the effulgence of the Father's glory.'

II. The second part of the song is a lyric anticipation of the historical consequences of the appearance of the Messiah, cast into forms ready to the singer's hand, in the strains of Old Testament prophecy. The characteristics of Hebrew poetry, its parallelism, its antitheses, its exultant swing, are more conspicuous here than in the earlier half. The main thought of verses 51 to 53 is that the Messiah would bring about a revolution, in which the high would be cast down and the humble exalted. This idea is wrought out in a threefold antithesis, of which the first pair must have one member supplied from the previous verse. Those who 'fear Him' are opposed to 'the proud in the imagination of their hearts.' These are thought of as an army of antagonists to God and His anointed, and thus the word 'scattered' acquires great poetic force, and reminds us of many a psalm, such as the Second and One hundred and tenth, where Messiah is a warrior.

The next pair represent the antithesis as being that of social degree, and in it there may be traced a glance at 'Herod the King' and the depressed line of David, to which the singer belonged, while the meaning must not be confined to that. The third pair represent the same opposites under the guise of poverty and riches. Mary is not to be credited with purely spiritual views in these contrasts, nor to be discredited with purely material ones. She, no doubt, thought of her own oppressed nation as mainly meant by the hungry and lowly; but like all pious souls in Israel, she must have felt that the lowliness and hunger which Messiah was to ennoble and satisfy, meant a condition of spirit conscious of weakness and sin, and eagerly desiring a higher good and food than earth could give. So much she had learned from many a psalm and prophet. So much the Spirit which inspired psalmist and prophet spoke in her lowly and exultant heart now. But the future was only revealed to her in this wide, general outline. Details of manner and time were all still blank. The broad truth which she foretold remains one of the salient historical results of Christ's coming, and is the universal condition of partaking of His gifts. He has been, and is, the most revolutionary force in history; for without Him society is constituted on principles the reverse of the true, and as the world, apart from Jesus, is down–side up, the mission of His gospel is to turn it upside–down, and so bring the right side uppermost. The condition of receiving anything from Him is the humble recognition of emptiness and need. If princes on their thrones will come to Him just in the same way as the beggar on the dunghill does, they will very probably be allowed to stay on them; and if the rich man will come to Him as poor and in need of all things, he will not be 'sent empty away.' But Christ is a discriminating Christ, and as the prophet said long before Mary, 'I ... will bind up that which was broken, and will strengthen that which was sick; and the fat and the strong I will destroy. I will feed them with judgment.'

The last turn in the song celebrates the faithfulness of God to His ancient promises, and His help by His Messiah to Israel. The designation of Israel as 'His servant' recalls the familiar name in Isaiah's later prophecies. Mary sees in the great wonder of her Son's birth the accomplishment of the hopes of ages, and an assurance of God's mercy as for ever the portion of the people. We cannot tell how far she had learned that Israel was to be counted, not by descent but disposition. But, in any case, her eyes could not have embraced the solemn facts of her Son's rejection by His and her people. No shadows are yet cast across the morning of which her song is the herald. She knew not the dark clouds of thunder and destruction that were to sweep over the sky. But the end has not yet come, and we have to believe still that the evening will fulfil the promise of the morning, and 'all Israel shall be saved,' and that the mercy which was promised from of old to Abraham and the fathers, shall be fulfilled at last and abide with their seed for ever.

ZACHARIAS'S HYMN

'And his father Zacharias was filled with the Holy Ghost, and prophesied, saying, 68. Blessed be the Lord God of Israel; for He hath visited and redeemed His people, 69. And hath raised up an horn of salvation for us in the house of His servant David; 70. As He spake by the mouth of His holy prophets, which have been since the world began; 71. That we should be saved from our enemies, and from the hand of all that hate us; 72. To perform the mercy promised to our fathers, and to remember His holy covenant, 73. The oath which He sware to our father Abraham, 74. That He would grant unto us, that we, being delivered out of the hand of our enemies, might serve Him without fear, 75. In holiness and righteousness before Him, all the days of our life. 76. And thou, child, shalt be called the Prophet of the Highest: for thou shalt go before the face of the Lord to prepare His ways; 77. To give knowledge of salvation unto His people, by the remission of their sins, 78. Through the tender mercy of our God; whereby the day-spring from on high hath visited us, 79. To give light to them that sit in darkness and in the shadow of death, to guide our feet into the way of peace. 80. And the child grew, and waxed strong in spirit, and was in the deserts till the day of his shewing unto Israel.'—LUKE i. 67–80.

Zacharias was dumb when he disbelieved. His lips were opened when he believed. He is the last of the Old Testament prophets, [Footnote: In the strictest sense, John the Baptist was a prophet of the Old dispensation, even though he came to usher in the New. (See Matt. xi. 9–11.) In the same sense, Zacharias was the last prophet of the Old dispensation, before the coming of his son to link the Old with the New.] and as standing nearest to the Messiah, his song takes up the echoes of all the past, and melts them into a new outpouring of exultant hope. The strain is more impassioned than Mary's, and throbs with triumph over 'our enemies,' but rises above the mere patriotic glow into a more spiritual region. The complete subordination of the personal element is very remarkable, as shown by the slight and almost parenthetical reference to John. The father is forgotten in the devout Israelite. We may take the song as divided into three portions: the first (vs. 68–75) celebrating the coming of Messiah, with special reference to its effect in freeing Israel from its foes; the second (vs. 76, 77), the highly dramatic address to his unconscious 'child'; the third (vs. 78, 79) returns to the absorbing thought of the Messiah, but now touches on higher aspects of His coming as the Light to all who sit in darkness.

I. If we remember that four hundred dreary years, for the most part of which Israel had been groaning under a foreign yoke, had passed since the last of the prophets, and that during all that time devout eyes had looked wearily for the promised Messiah, we shall be able to form some faint conception of the surprise and rapture which filled Zacharias's spirit, and leaps in his hymn at the thought that now, at last, the hour had struck, and that the child would soon be born who was to fulfil the divine promises and satisfy fainting hopes. No wonder that its first words are a burst of blessing of 'the God of Israel.' The best expression of joy, when long–cherished desires are at last on the eve of accomplishment, is thanks to God. How short the time of waiting seems when it is past, and how needless the impatience which marred the waiting! Zacharias speaks of the fact as already realised. He must have known that the Incarnation was accomplished; for we can scarcely suppose that the emphatic tenses 'hath visited, hath redeemed, hath raised' are prophetic, and merely imply the certainty of a future event. He must have known, too, Mary's royal descent; for he speaks of 'the house of David.'

'A horn' of salvation is an emblem taken from animals, and implies strength. Here it recalls several prophecies, and as a designation of the Messiah, shadows forth His conquering might, all to be used for deliverance to His people. The vision before Zacharias is that of a victor king of Davidic race, long foretold by prophets, who will set Israel free from its foreign oppressors, whether Roman or Idumean, and in whom God Himself 'visits and redeems His people.' There are two kinds of divine visitations—one for mercy and one for judgment. What an unconscious witness it is of men's evil consciences that the use of the phrase has almost exclusively settled down upon the latter meaning! In verses 71–75, the idea of the Messianic salvation is expanded and raised. The word 'salvation' is best construed, as in the Revised Version, as in apposition with and explanatory of 'horn of salvation.' This salvation has issues, which may also be regarded as God's purposes in sending it. These are threefold: first, to show mercy to the dead fathers of the race. That is a striking idea, and pictures the departed as, in their solemn rest, sharing in the joy of Messiah's coming, and perhaps in the blessings which He brings. We may not too closely press the phrase, but it is more than poetry or imagination. The next issue is God's remembrance of His promises, or in other words, His fulfilment of these. The last is that the nation, being set free, should serve God. The external deliverance was in the eyes of devout men like Zacharias precious as a means to an end. Political freedom was needful for God's service, and was valuable mainly as leading to that. The hymn rises far above the mere impatience of a foreign yoke. 'Freedom to worship God,' and God worshipped by a ransomed nation, are Zacharias's ideal of the Messianic times.

Note his use of the word for priestly 'service.' He, a priest, has not forgotten that by original constitution all Israel was a nation of priests; and he looks forward to the fulfilment at last of the ideal which so soon became impracticable, and possibly to the abrogation of his own order in the universal priesthood. He knew not what deep truths he sang. The end of Christ's coming, and of the deliverance which He works for us from the hand of our enemies, cannot be better stated than in these words. We are redeemed that we may be priests unto God. Our priestly service must be rendered in 'holiness and righteousness,' in consecration to God and discharge of all obligations; and it is to be no interrupted or occasional service, like Zacharias's, which occupied but two short weeks in the year, and might never again lead him within the sanctuary, but is to fill with reverent activity and thankful sacrifice all our

16

days. However this hymn may have begun with the mere external conception of Messianic deliverance, it rises high above that here, and will still further soar beyond it. We may learn from this priest–prophet, who anticipated the wise men and brought his offerings to the unborn Christ, what Christian salvation is, and for what it is given us.

II. There is something very vivid and striking in the abrupt address to the infant, who lay, all unknowing, in his mother's arms. The contrast between him as he was then and the work which waited him, the paternal wonder and joy which yet can scarcely pause on the child, and hurries on to fancy him in the years to come, going herald–like before the face of the Lord, the profound prophetic insight into John's work, are all noteworthy. The Baptist did 'prepare the way' by teaching that the true 'salvation' was not to be found in mere deliverance from the Roman yoke, but in 'remission of sin.' He thus not only gave 'knowledge of salvation,' in the sense that he announced the fact that it would be given, but also in the sense that he clearly taught in what it consisted. John was no preacher of revolt, as the turbulent and impure patriots of the day would have liked him to be, but of repentance. His work was to awake the consciousness of sin, and so to kindle desires for a salvation which was deliverance from sin, the only yoke which really enslaves. Zacharias the 'blameless' saw what the true bondage of the nation was, and what the work both of the Deliverer and of His herald must be. We need to be perpetually reminded of the truth that the only salvation and deliverance which can do us any good consist in getting rid, by pardon and by holiness, of the cords of our sins.

III. The thoughts of the Forerunner and his office melt into that of the Messianic blessings from which the singer cannot long turn away. In these closing words, we have the source, the essential nature, and the blessed results of the gift of Christ set forth in a noble figure, and freed from the national limitations of the earlier part of the hymn. All comes from the 'bowels of mercy of our God,' as Zacharias, in accordance with Old Testament metaphor, speaks, allocating the seat of the emotions which we attribute to the heart. Conventional notions of delicacy think the Hebrew idea coarse, but the one allocation is just as delicate as the other. We can get no deeper down or farther back into the secret springs of things than this—that the root cause of all, and most especially of the mission of Christ, is the pitying love of God's heart. If we hold fast by that, the pain of the riddle of the world is past, and the riddle itself more than half solved. Jesus Christ is the greatest gift of that love, in which all its tenderness and all its power are gathered up for our blessing.

The modern civilised world owes most of its activity to the quickening influence of Christianity. The dayspring visits us that it may shine on us, and it shines that it may guide us into 'the way of peace.' There can be no wider and more accurate description of the end of Christ's mission than this—that all His visitation and enlightenment are meant to lead us into the path where we shall find peace with God, and therefore with ourselves and with all mankind. The word 'peace,' in the Old Testament, is used to include the sum of all that men require for their conscious well–being. We are at rest only when all our relations with God and the outer world are right, and when our inner being is harmonised with itself, and supplied with appropriate objects. To know God for our friend, to have our being fixed on and satisfied in Him, and so to be reconciled to all circumstances, and a friend of all men—this is peace; and the path to such a blessed condition is shown us only by that Sun of Righteousness whom the loving heart of God has sent into the darkness and torpor of the benighted wanderers in the desert. The national reference has faded from the song, and though it still speaks of 'us' and 'our,' we cannot doubt that Zacharias both saw more deeply into the salvation which Christ would bring than to limit it to breaking an earthly yoke, and deemed more worthily and widely of its sweep, than to confine it within narrower bounds than the whole extent of the dreary darkness which it came to banish from all the world.

THE DAYSPRING FROM ON HIGH

'The day–spring from on high hath visited us, 79. To give light to them that sit in darkness and in the shadow of death, to guide our feet into the way of peace.'—LUKE i. 78, 79.

As the dawn is ushered in by the notes of birds, so the rising of the Sun of Righteousness was heralded by song, Mary and Zacharias brought their praises and welcome to the unborn Christ, the angels hovered with heavenly music over His cradle, and Simeon took the child in his arms and blessed it. The human members of this choir may be regarded as the last of the psalmists and prophets, and the first of Christian singers. The song of Zacharias, from which my text is taken, is steeped in Old Testament allusions, and redolent of the ancient spirit, but it transcends that. Its early part is purely national, and hails the coming of the Messiah chiefly as the deliverer of Israel from foreign oppressors, though even in it their deliverance is regarded mostly as the means to an end, and the end one very appropriate on the lips of a priestly prophet——viz. sacerdotal service by the whole nation 'in holiness and righteousness all their days.'

But in this latter portion, which is separated from the former by the pathetic, incidental, and slight reference to the singer's own child, the national limits are far surpassed. The song soars above them, and pierces to the very heart and kernel of Christ's work. 'The dayspring from on high hath visited us, to give light to them that sit in darkness and the shadow of death, to guide our feet into the way of peace.' Nothing deeper, nothing wider, nothing truer about the mission and issue of Christ's coming could be spoken. And thus we have to look at the three things that lie in this text, as bearing upon our conceptions of Christ and His work—the darkness, the dawn, and the directing light.

I. The darkness.

Zacharias, as becomes the last of the prophets, and a man whose whole religious life was nourished upon the ancient Scriptures, speaks almost entirely in Old Testament phraseology in this song. And his description of 'them that sit in darkness and the shadow of death' is taken almost verbally from the great words from the Book of the Prophet Isaiah, who speaks, in immediate connection with his prophecy of the coming of the Christ, of 'the people that walk in darkness and them that dwell,' or sit, 'in the shadow of death, upon whom the light hath shined.'

The picture that rises before us is that of a group of travellers benighted, bewildered, huddled together in the dark, afraid to move for fear of pitfalls, precipices, wild beasts, and enemies; and so sighing for the day and compelled to be inactive till it comes. That is the picture of humanity apart from Jesus Christ, a darkness so intense, so tragic, that it is, as it were, the very shadow of the ultimate and essential darkness which is death, and in it men are sitting torpid, unable to find their way and afraid to move.

Now darkness, all the world over, is the emblem of three things—ignorance, impurity, sorrow. And all men who are rent away from Jesus Christ, or on whom His beams have not yet fallen, this text tells us, have that triple curse lying upon them.

Ignorance. Think of what, without Jesus Christ, the world has deemed of the unseen, and of the God, if there be a God, that may inhabit there. He has been to them a great Peradventure, a great Terror, a great Inscrutable, a stone–eyed Fate, a thin, nebulous Nothing, with no emotion, no attributes, no heart, no ear to hear, the nearest approach to nonentity, according to the despairing saying of a master of philosophy, that 'pure Being is equal to pure Nothing.' And if all men do not rise to such heights of melancholy abstraction as that, still how little there is of blessed certainty, how little clearness of conception of a Divine Person that turns to us with love and tenderness in His heart, apart from Christ and His teaching! If you take away from civilised men all the knowledge of God that they owe to Jesus Christ, what have you left? The ladder by which they climbed is kicked away by a great many people nowadays, but it is to Him that they owe the very conceptions in the name of which some of them turn round and deny Him.

Ignorance of God, ignorance of one's own self and of one's deepest duties, and ignorance of that solemn future, the fact of which is plain to most men, but the how of which is such a blank mystery but for Jesus Christ—these things are elements of the darkness that wraps the world. Go to heathendom if you want to see the problem worked out, as to what men know outside of the revelation which culminates in Jesus Christ. And take your own hearts, dear friends who stand aside from that sweet Lord and light of our lives, and ask yourselves, What do I know, with a certainty which is to me as valid, as—yea! more valid than that given by sense and outward perceptions? What do I know of God that I do not owe to Jesus Christ? Nothing. You may guess much, you may hope a little, you may dread a great deal, you may question more than all, but you will *know* nothing.

Well, then, further, this solemn emblem stands for impurity. And we have only to consult our own hearts to feel how true it is about us all, that we dwell in a region all darkened, if not by the coarse transgressions which men consent to call sins, yet darkened more subtly and oftentimes more hopelessly by the obscuration of pure selfishness and living to myself and by myself. Wherever that comes, it is like the mists that steal up from some poisonous marsh, and shut out stars and sky, and drape the whole country in a melancholy veil. It is white but it is poisonous, it is white but it is darkness all the same. There are other kinds of sin than the sins that break the Ten Commandments; there are other kinds of sin than the sins that the world takes cognisance of. The worst poisons are the tasteless ones, and colourless gases are laden with fatal power. We may walk in a darkness that may be felt, though there be nothing in our lives that men call sin, and little there of which our consciences are as yet educated enough to be ashamed. Rent from God, man lives to himself, and so is sunk in darkness.

And what shall I say about the third of the doleful triad of which this pregnant emblem is the recognised symbol all the world over? Surely, though earth be full of blessing, and life of possibilities of joy, no man travels very far along the road without feeling that the burden of sorrow is a burden that we all have to carry. There are blessings in plenty, there is mirth more than enough. There is 'the laughter' which is 'the crackling of thorns' under a pot. There are plenty of distractions and amusements, 'blessings more plentiful than hope'; but yet the ground tone of every human life, when the first flush of inexperience and novelty has worn off, apart from God, is sadness, conscious of itself sometimes, and driven to all manner of foolish attempts at forgetfulness, unconscious of itself sometimes, and knowing not what is the disease of which it languishes. There it is, like some persistent minor in a great piece of music, wailing on through all the embroidery and lightsomeness of the cheerfuller and loftier notes. 'Every heart knoweth its own bitterness,' and every heart *has* a bitterness of its own to know.

I do not understand how it is that men who have no religion in them can bear their own sorrows and see their neighbours' and not go mad. Sometimes the world seems to me to be moving round its central sun with a doleful atmosphere of sighs wherever it goes, and all the mirth and stir and bustle are but like a thin crust of grass with flowers upon it, cast across the sulphurous depths of some volcano that may slumber for a while, but is there all the same.

Brother! you and I, away from Jesus Christ, have to face the certainties of ignorance, of sin, of sorrow—ignorance unenlightened, sin unconquered, sorrow uncomforted.

And then comes the other tragic, and yet most picturesque emblem in the representation here: 'They *sit* in darkness.' Yes! what can they do, poor creatures? They know not where to go. The light has left them, inactivity is a necessity. And so, with folded hands, they wish for the day, or try to forget the night by lighting some little torch of their own that only serves to make darkness visible, and dies all too soon, leaving them to lie down in sorrow.

But, you say, 'What nonsense! Inactivity! look at the fierce energy of life in our Western lands.' Well, grant it all, there may be plenty of material activity attendant upon inward stagnation and torpor. But, again, I would like to ask how much of the most godless, commercial, artistic, intellectual activity of so−called civilised and Christian countries is owing to the stimulus and ferment that Jesus Christ brought. If you want to see how true it is that men without Him *sit* in the darkness, go to heathen lands, and see the stagnation, the torpor, there.

Now, dear brethren, all this is true about us, in the measure in which we do not participate by faith and love, welcoming Him into our hearts in the illumination that Jesus Christ brings. And what I want to do is to lay upon the hearts and consciences of each of us here this thought, that the solemn, tragic picture of my text is the picture of me, separate from Christ, however I may try to conceal it from myself, and to mask it from other people by busying myself with inferior knowledges, by avoiding to listen to the answer that conscience gives to the question as to my moral character, and by befooling myself with noisy joys and tumultuous pleasures, in which there is no pleasure.

II. Now, note secondly, the dayspring, or dawn.

My text, in the part on which I have just been speaking, links itself with ancient Messianic prophecy, and this expression, 'the dayspring from on high.' also links itself with other prophecies of the same sort. Almost the last word of prophecy before the four centuries of silence which Mary and Zacharias broke, was, 'Unto you that fear His name shall the Sun of Righteousness arise with healing in His beams.' There can be little doubt, I think, that the allusion of my text is to these all but the last words of the prophet Malachi. For that final chapter of the Old Testament colours the song both of Mary and of Zacharias. And it is to be observed that the Greek translation of the Hebrew uses the same verb, of which the cognate noun is here employed, for the rising of the Sun of Righteousness. The picturesque old English word 'dayspring' means neither more nor less than *sunrising*. And it is here used practically as a name for Jesus Christ, who is Himself the Sun, represented as rising over a darkened earth, and yet, with a singular neglect of the propriety of the metaphor, as descending from on high, not to shine on us from the sky, but to 'visit us' on earth.

Jesus Christ Himself, over and over again, said by implication, and more than once by direct claim, 'I am the Light of the world.' And my text is the anticipation, perhaps from lips that did not fully understand the whole significance of the prophecy which they spoke, of these later declarations. I have said that the darkness is the emblem of three baleful things, of the converse of which light is the symbol. As the darkness speaks to us of ignorance, so Christ, as the Sun illumines us with the light of 'the knowledge of the glory of God in the face of Jesus Christ.' For doubt we have blessed certainty, for a far-off God we have the knowledge of God close at hand. For an impassive will or a stony-eyed fate we have the knowledge (and not only the wistful yearning after the knowledge) of a loving heart, warm and throbbing. Our God is no unemotional abstraction, but a living Person who can love, who can pity, and we are speaking more than poetry when we say, God is compassion, and compassion is God. This we know because 'He that hath seen Me hath seen the Father.' And the solid certainty of a loving God, tender, pitying, mighty to help, quick to hear, ready to forgive, waiting to bless, is borne into our hearts, and comes there, sweet as the sunshine, when we turn ourselves to the light of Christ.

In like manner the darkness, born of our own sin, which wraps our hearts, and shuts out so much that is fair and sweet and strong, will pass away if we turn ourselves to Him. His light pouring into our souls will hurt the eye at first, but it will hurt to cure. The darkness of sin and alienation will pass, and the true light will shine.

The darkness of sorrow—well! it will not cease, but He will 'smooth the raven down of darkness till it smiles,' and He will bring into our griefs such a spirit of quiet submission as that they shall change into a solemn scorn of ills, and be almost like gladnesses. Peace, which is better than exuberant delight, will come to quiet the sorrow of the soul that trusts in Jesus Christ. The day which is knowledge, purity, gladsomeness, the cheerful day will be ours if we hold by Him. We 'are all the children of the light and of the day'; we 'are not of the night nor of darkness.'

Brother, it is possible to grope at noontide as in the dark, and in all the blaze of Christ's revelation still to be left in the Cimmerian folds of midnight gloom. You can shut your eyes to the sunshine; have you opened your hearts to its coming?

I cannot dwell (your time will not allow of it) upon the other points connected with this description of the day spring, except just to point out in passing the singular force and depth of the words—which I suppose are more forcible and deep than he who spoke them understood at the time that visitation was described. The dayspring is 'from on high.' This Sun has come down on to the earth. It has not risen on a far-off horizon, but it has come down and visited us, and walks among us. This Sun, our life-star, 'hath had elsewhere its setting, and cometh from afar.' For He that rises upon us as the Light of life, hath descended from the heavens, and was, before He appeared amongst men.

And His coming is a divine visitation. The word here 'hath *visited* us' (or 'shall visit us,' as the Revised Version varies it), is chiefly employed in the Old Testament to describe the divine acts of self–revelation, and these, mostly redemptive acts. Zacharias employs it in that sense in the earlier portion of the song, where he says that 'God hath visited and redeemed His people.' And so from the use of this word we gather these two thoughts—God comes to us when Christ comes to us, and His coming is wondrous, blessed nearness, and nearness to each of us. 'What is man that Thou shouldst be mindful of him, or the son of man that Thou shouldst visit him?' said the old Psalmist. We say 'What is man that the Dayspring from on high should come down upon earth, and round His immortal beams, should, as it were, cast the veil and obscuration of a human form; and so walk amongst us, the embodied Light and the Incarnate God?' 'The dayspring from on high hath visited us.'

III. Lastly, note the directing by the light.

'To guide our feet into the way of peace.' This Sun stoops to the office of the star that moved before the wise men and hovered over His cradle, and becomes to each individual soul a guide and director. The picture of my text, I suppose, carries us on to the morning, when the benighted travellers catch the first gleams of the rising sun and resume their activity, and there is a cheerful stir through the encampment and the way is open before them once more, and they are ready to walk in it. The force of the metaphor, however, implies more than that, for it speaks to us of the wonder that this universal Light should become the special guide of each individual soul, and should not merely hang in the heavens, to cast the broad radiance of its beams over the whole surface of the earth, but should move before each man, a light unto *his* feet and a lamp to *his* path, in special manifestation to him of his duty and his life's pilgrimage.

There is only one way of peace, and that is to follow His beams and to be directed by His preceding us. Then we shall realise the most indispensable of all the conditions of peace—Christ brings you and me the reconciliation which puts us at peace with God, which is the foundation of all other tranquillity. And He will guide docile feet into the way of peace in yet another fashion—in that the following of His example, the cleaving to Him, the holding by His skirts or by His hand, and the treading in His footsteps, is the only way by which the heart can receive the solid satisfaction in which it rests, and the conscience can cease from accusing and stinging. The way of wisdom is a path of pleasantness and a way of peace. Only they who walk in Christ's footsteps have quiet hearts and are at amity with God, in concord with themselves, friends of mankind, and at peace with circumstances. There is no strife within, no strained relations or hostile alienation to God, no gnawing unrest of unsatisfied desires, no pricks of accusing conscience; for the man who puts his hand into Christ's hand, and says, 'Order Thou my footsteps by Thy word'; 'Where Thou goest I will go, and what Thou commandest I will do.'

Brother, put thy hand out from the darkness and clasp His, and 'the darkness shall be light about thee'; and He will fulfil His own promise when He said, 'I am the Light of the world. He that followeth Me shall not walk in darkness, but shall have the Light of life.

SHEPHERDS AND ANGELS

'And there were in the same country shepherds abiding in the field, keeping watch over their flock by night. 9. And, lo, the angel of the Lord came upon them, and the glory of the Lord shone round about them; and they were sore afraid. 10. And the angel said unto them, Fear not: for, behold, I bring you good tidings of great joy, which shall be to all people. 11. For unto you is born this day, in the city of David, a Saviour, which is Christ the Lord. 12. And this shall be a sign unto you; Ye shall find the babe wrapped in swaddling clothes, lying in a manger. 13. And suddenly there was with the angel a multitude of the heavenly host praising God, and saying, 14. Glory to God in the highest, and on earth peace, good will toward men. 15. And it came to pass, as the angels were gone away from them into heaven, the shepherds said one to another, Let us now go even unto Bethlehem, and see this thing which is come to pass, which the Lord hath made known unto us. 16. And they came with haste, and found Mary and Joseph, and the babe lying in a manger. 17. And when they had seen it, they made known abroad the saying which was told them concerning this child. 18. And all they that heard it wondered at those things which were told them by the shepherds. 19. But Mary kept all these things, and pondered them in her heart. 20. And the shepherds returned, glorifying and praising God for all the things that they had heard and seen, as it was told unto them.'—LUKE ii. 8–20.

The central portion of this passage is, of course, the angels' message and song, the former of which proclaims the transcendent fact of the Incarnation, and the latter hymns its blessed results. But, subsidiary to these, the silent vision which preceded them and the visit to Bethlehem which followed are to be noted. Taken together, they cast varying gleams on the great fact of the birth of Jesus Christ.

Why should there be a miraculous announcement at all, and why should it be to these shepherds? It seems to have had no effect beyond a narrow circle and for a time. It was apparently utterly forgotten when, thirty years after, the carpenter's Son began His ministry. Could such an event have passed from memory, and left no ripple on the surface? Does not the resultlessness cast suspicion on the truthfulness of the narrative? Not if we duly give weight to the few who knew of the wonder; to the length of time that elapsed, during which the shepherds and their auditors probably died; to their humble position, and to the short remembrance of extraordinary events which have no immediate consequences. Joseph and Mary were strangers in Bethlehem. Christ never visited it, so far as we know. The fading of the impression cannot be called strange, for it accords with natural tendencies;

23

but the record of so great an event, which was entirely ineffectual as regards future acceptance of Christ's claims, is so unlike legend that it vouches for the truth of the narrative. An apparent stumbling–block is left, because the story is true.

Why then, the announcement at all, since it was of so little use? Because it was of some; but still more, because it was fitting that such angel voices should attend such an event, whether men gave heed to them or not; and because, recorded, their song has helped a world to understand the nature and meaning of that birth. The glory died off the hillside quickly, and the music of the song scarcely lingered longer in the ears of its first hearers; but its notes echo still in all lands, and every generation turns to them with wonder and hope.

The selection of two or three peasants as receivers of the message, the time at which it was given, and the place, are all significant. It was no unmeaning fact that the 'glory of the Lord' shone lambent round the shepherds, and held them and the angel standing beside them in its circle of light. No longer within the secret shrine, but out in the open field, the symbol of the Divine Presence glowed through the darkness; for that birth hallowed common life, and brought the glory of God into familiar intercourse with its secularities and smallnesses. The appearance to these humble men as they 'sat simply chatting in a rustic row 'symbolised the destination of the Gospel for all ranks and classes.

The angel speaks by the side of the shepherds, not from above. His gentle encouragement 'Fear not!' not only soothes their present terror, but has a wider meaning. The dread of the Unseen, which lies coiled like a sleeping snake in all hearts, is utterly taken away by the Incarnation. All messages from that realm are thenceforward 'tidings of great joy,' and love and desire may pass into it, as all men shall one day pass, and both enterings may be peaceful and confident. Nothing harmful can come out of the darkness, from which Jesus has come, into which He has passed, and which He fills.

The great announcement, the mightiest, most wonderful word that had ever passed angels' immortal lips, is characterised as 'great joy' to 'all the people,' in which designation two things are to be noted—the nature and the limitation of the message. In how many ways the Incarnation was to be the fountain of purest gladness was but little discerned, either by the heavenly messenger or the shepherds. The ages since have been partially learning it, but not till the 'glorified joy' of heaven swells redeemed hearts will all its sorrow–dispelling power be experimentally known. Base joys may be basely sought, but His creatures' gladness is dear to God, and if sought in God's way, is a worthy object of their efforts.

The world–wide sweep of the Incarnation does not appear here, but only its first destination for Israel. This is manifest in the phrase 'all the people,' in the mention of 'the city of David' and in the emphatic 'you,' in contradistinction both from the messenger, who announced what he did not share, and Gentiles, to whom the blessing was not to pass till Israel had determined its attitude to it.

The titles of the Infant tell something of the wonder of the birth, but do not unfold its overwhelming mystery. Magnificent as they are, they fall far short of 'The Word was made flesh.' They keep within the circle of Jewish expectation, and announce that the hopes of centuries are fulfilled. There is something very grand in the accumulation of titles, each greater than the preceding, and all culminating in that final 'Lord.' Handel has gloriously given the spirit of it in the crash of triumph with which that last word is pealed out in his oratorio. 'Saviour' means far more than the shepherds knew; for it declares the Child to be the deliverer from all evil, both of sin and sorrow, and the endower with all good, both of righteousness and blessedness. The 'Christ' claims that He is the fulfiller of prophecy, perfectly endowed by divine anointing for His office of prophet, priest, and king—the consummate flower of ancient revelation, greater than Moses the law–giver, than Solomon the king, than Jonah the prophet. 'The Lord' is scarcely to be taken as the ascription of divinity, but rather as a prophecy of authority and dominion, implying reverence, but not unveiling the deepest secret of the entrance of the divine Son into humanity. That remained unrevealed, for the time was not yet ripe.

There would be few children of a day old in a little place like Bethlehem, and none but one lying in a manger. The fact of the birth, which could be verified by sight, would confirm the message in its outward aspect, and thereby lead to belief in the angel's disclosure of its inward character. The 'sign' attested the veracity of the messenger, and therefore the truth of all his word—both of that part of it capable of verification by sight and that part apprehensible by faith.

No wonder that the sudden light and music of the multitude of the heavenly host' flashed and echoed round the group on the hillside. The true picture is not given when we think of that angel choir as floating in heaven. They stood in their serried ranks round the shepherds and their fellows on the solid earth, and 'the night was filled with music,' not from overhead, but from every side. Crowding forms became all at once visible within the encircling 'glory,' on every face wondering gladness and eager sympathy with men, from every lip praise. Angels can speak with the tongues of men when their theme is their Lord become man, and their auditors are men. They hymn the blessed results of that birth, the mystery of which they knew more completely than they were yet allowed to tell.

As was natural for them, their praise is first evoked by the result of the Incarnation in the highest heavens. It will bring 'glory to God' there; for by it new aspects of His nature are revealed to those clear–eyed and immortal spirits who for unnumbered ages have known His power, His holiness, His benignity to unfallen creatures, but now experience the wonder which more properly belongs to more limited intelligences, when they behold that depth of condescending Love stooping to be born. Even they think more loftily of God, and more of man's possibilities and worth, when they cluster round the manger, and see who lies there.

'On earth peace.' The song drops from the contemplation of the heavenly consequences to celebrate the results on earth, and gathers them all into one pregnant word, 'Peace.' What a scene of strife, discord, and unrest earth must seem to those calm spirits! And how vain and petty the struggles must look, like the bustle of an ant–hill! Christ's work is to bring peace into all human relations, those with God, with men, with circumstances, and to calm the discords of souls at war with themselves. Every one of these relations is marred by sin, and nothing less thorough than a power which removes it can rectify them. That birth was the coming into humanity of Him who brings peace with God, with ourselves, with one another. Shame on Christendom that nineteen centuries have passed, and men yet think the cessation of war is only a 'pious imagination'! The ringing music of that angel chant has died away, but its promise abides.

The symmetry of the song is best preserved, as I humbly venture to think, by the old reading as in the

Authorised Version. The other, represented by the Revised Version, seems to make the second clause drag somewhat, with two designations of the region of peace. The Incarnation brings God's 'good will' to dwell among men. In Christ, God is well pleased; and from Him incarnate, streams of divine complacent love pour out to freshen and fertilise the earth.

The disappearance of the heavenly choristers does not seem to have been so sudden as their appearance. They 'went away from them into heaven,' as if leisurely, and so that their ascending brightness was long visible as they rose, and attestation was thereby given to the reality of the vision. The sleeping village was close by, and as soon as the last gleam of the departing light had faded in the depths of heaven, the shepherds went 'with haste,' untimely as was the hour. They would not have much difficulty in finding the inn and the manger. Note that they do not tell their story till the sight has confirmed the angel message. Their silence was not from doubt; for they say, before they had seen the child, that 'this thing' is 'come to pass,' and are quite sure that the Lord has told it them. But they wait for the evidence which shall assure others of their truthfulness.

There are three attitudes of mind towards God's revelation set forth in living examples in the closing verses of the passage. Note the conduct of the shepherds, as a type of the natural impulse and imperative duty of all possessors of God's truth. Such a story as they had to tell would burn its way to utterance in the most reticent and shyest. But have Christians a less wonderful message to deliver, or a less needful one? If the spectators of the cradle could not be silent, how impossible it ought to be for the witnesses of the Cross to lock their lips!

The hearers of the story did what, alas! too many of us do with the Gospel. 'They wondered,' and stopped there. A feeble ripple of astonishment ruffled the surface of their souls for a moment; but like the streaks on the sea made by a catspaw of wind, it soon died out, and the depths were unaffected by it.

The antithesis to this barren wonder is the beautiful picture of the Virgin's demeanour. She 'kept all these sayings, and pondered them in her heart.' What deep thoughts the mother of the Lord had, were hers alone. But we have the same duty to the truth, and it will never disclose its inmost sweetness to us, nor take so sovereign a grip of our very selves as to mould our lives, unless we too treasure it in our hearts, and by patient brooding on it understand its hidden harmonies, and spread our souls out to receive its transforming power. A non−meditative religion is a shallow religion. But if we hide His word in our hearts, and often in secret draw out our treasure to count and weigh it, we shall be able to speak out of a full heart, and like these shepherds, to rejoice that we have seen even as it was spoken unto us.

WAS, IS, IS TO COME

'... The babe lying in a manger...'—LUKE ii. 16.

'... While He blessed them, He was parted from them,
and carried up into heaven...'—LUKE xxiv. 51.

'This same Jesus... shall so come in like manner as
ye have seen Him go...'—ACTS I. 11.

These three fragments, which I have ventured to isolate and bring together, are all found in one author's writings. Luke's biography of Jesus stretches from the cradle in Bethlehem to the Ascension from Olivet. He narrates the Ascension twice, because it has two aspects. In one it looks backward, and is necessary as the completion of what was begun in the birth. In one it looks forward, and makes necessary, as its completion, that coming which still lies in the future. These three stand up, like linked summits in a mountain. We can understand none of them unless we embrace them all. If the story of the birth is true, a life so begun cannot end in an undistinguished death like that of all men. And if the Ascension from Olivet is true, that cannot close the history of His relations to men. The creed which proclaims He was 'born of the Virgin Mary' must go on to say '... He ascended up into heaven'; and cannot pause till it adds '...From thence He shall come to judge the quick and the dead.' So we have then three points to consider in this sermon.

I. Note first, the three great moments.

The thing that befell at Bethlehem, in the stable of the inn, was a commonplace and insignificant enough event looked at from the outside: the birth of a child to a young mother. It had its elements of pathos in its occurring at a distance from home, among the publicity and discomforts of an inn stable, and with some cloud of suspicion over the mother's fair fame. But the outside of a fact is the least part of it. A little film of sea−weed floats upon the surface, but there are fathoms of it below the water. Men said, 'A child is born.' Angels said, and bowed their faces in adoration, 'The Word has become flesh'. The eternal, self−communicating personality in the Godhead, passed voluntarily into the condition of humanity. Jesus was born, the Son of God came. Only when we hold fast by that great truth do we pierce to the centre of what was done in that poor stable, and possess the key to all the wonders of His life and death.

From the manger we pass to the mountain. A life begun by such a birth cannot be ended, as I have said, by a mere ordinary death. The Alpha and the Omega of that alphabet must belong to the same fount of type. A divine conformity forbids that He who was born of the Virgin Mary should have His body laid to rest in an undistinguished grave. And so what Bethlehem began, Olivet carries on.

Note the circumstances of this second of these great moments. The place is significant. Almost within sight of the city, a stone's throw probably from the home where He had lodged, and where He had conquered death in the person of Lazurus; not far from the turn of the road where the tears had come into His eyes amidst the shouting of the rustic procession, as He had looked across the valley; just above Gethsemane, where He had agonised on that bare hillside to which He had often gone for communion with the Father in heaven. There, in some dimple of the hill, and unseen but by the little group that surrounded Him, He passed from their midst. The manner of the departure is yet more significant than the place. Here were no whirlwind, no chariots and horses of fire, no sudden rapture; but, as the narrative makes emphatic, a slow, leisurely, self−originated floating upwards. He was borne up from them, and no outward vehicle or help was needed; but by His own volition and power He rose towards the heavens. 'And a cloud received Him out of their sight'—the Shechinah cloud, the bright symbol of the Divine Presence which had shone round the shepherds on the pastures of

Bethlehem, and enwrapped Him and the three disciples on the Mount of Transfiguration. It came not to lift Him on its soft folds to the heavens, but in order that, first, He might be plainly seen till the moment that He ceased to be seen, and might not dwindle into a speck by reason of distance; and secondly, that it might teach the truth, that, as His body was received into the cloud, so He entered into the glory which He 'had with the Father before the world was.' Such was the second of these moments.

The third great moment corresponds to these, is required by them, and crowns them. The Ascension was not only the close of Christ's earthly life which would preserve congruity with its beginning, but it was also the clear manifestation that, as He came of His own will, so He departed by His own volition. 'I came forth from the Father, and am come into the world. Again, I leave the world and go unto the Father.' Thus the earthly life is, as it were, islanded in a sea of glory, and that which stretches away beyond the last moment of visibility, is like that which stretched away beyond the first moment of corporeity; the eternal union with the eternal Father. But such an entrance on and departure from earth, and such a career on earth, can only end in that coming again of which the angels spoke to the gazing eleven.

Mark the emphasis of their words. 'This same Jesus,' the same in His manhood, 'shall so come, in like manner, as ye have seen Him go.' How much the 'in like manner' may mean we can scarcely dogmatically affirm. But this, at least, is clear, that it cannot mean less than corporeally visible, locally surrounded by angel–guards, and perhaps, according to a mysterious prophecy, to the same spot from which He ascended. But, at all events, there are the three moments in the manifestation of the Son of God.

II. Look, in the second place, at the threefold phases of our Lord's activity which are thus suggested.

I need not dwell, in more than a sentence or two, on the first of these. Each of these three moments is the inauguration of a form of activity which lasts till the emergence of the next of the triad.

The birth at Bethlehem had, for its consequence and purpose, a threefold end: the revelation of God in humanity, the manifestation of perfect manhood to men, and the rendering of the great sacrifice for the sins of the world. These three—showing us God; showing ourselves as we are and as we may be; as we ought to be, and, blessed be His name, as we shall be, if we observe the conditions; and the making reconciliation for the sins of the whole world—these are the things for which the Babe lying in the manger was born and came under the limitations of humanity.

Turn to the second of the three, and what shall we say of it? That Ascension has for its great purpose the application to men of the results of the Incarnation. He was born that He might show us God and ourselves, and that He might die for us. He ascended up on high in order that the benefits of that Revelation and Atonement might be extended through, and appropriated by, the whole world.

One chief thought which is enforced by the narrative of the Ascension is the permanence, the eternity of the humanity of Jesus Christ. He ascended up where He was before, but He who ascended is not altogether the same as He who had been there before, for He has taken up with Him our nature to the centre of the universe and the throne of God, and there, 'bone of our bone, and flesh of our flesh,' a

28

true man in body, soul, and spirit, He lives and reigns. The cradle at Bethlehem assumes even greater solemnity when we think of it as the beginning of a humanity that is never laid aside. So we can look confidently to all that blaze of light where He sits, and feel that, howsoever the body of His humiliation may have been changed into the body of His glory, He still remains corporeally and spiritually a true Son of man. Thus the face that looks down from amidst the blaze, though it be 'as the sun shineth in his strength,' is the old face; and the breast which is girded with the golden girdle is the same breast on which the seer had leaned his happy head; and the hand that holds the sceptre is the hand that was pierced with the nails; and the Christ that is ascended up on high is the Christ that loved and pitied adulteresses and publicans, and took the little child in His gracious arms—'The same yesterday, and to-day, and for ever.'

Christ's Ascension is as the broad seal of heaven attesting the completeness of His work on earth. It inaugurates His repose which is not the sign of His weariness, but of His having finished all which He was born to do. But that repose is not idleness. Rather it is full of activity.

On the Cross He shouted with a great voice ere He died, 'It is finished.' But centuries, perhaps millenniums, yet will have to elapse before the choirs of angels shall be able to chant, 'It is done: the kingdoms of the world are the kingdoms of God and of His Christ.' All the interval is filled by the working of that ascended Lord whose session at the right hand of God is not only symbolical of perfect repose and a completed sacrifice, but also of perfect activity in and with His servants.

He has gone—to rest, to reign, to work, to intercede, and to prepare a place for us. For if our Brother be indeed at the right hand of God, then our faltering feet may travel to the Throne, and our sinful selves may be at home there. The living Christ, working to-day, is that of which the Ascension from Olivet gives us the guarantee.

The third great moment will inaugurate yet another form of activity as necessary and certain as either of the two preceding. For if His cradle was what we believe it to have been, and if His sacrifice was what Scripture tells us it is, and if through all the ages He, crowned and regnant, is working for the diffusion of the powers of His Cross and the benefits of His Incarnation, there can be no end to that course except the one which is expressed for us by the angels' message to the gazing disciples: He shall so come in like manner as ye have seen Him go. He will come to manifest Himself as the King of the world and its Lord and Redeemer. He will come to inaugurate the great act of Judgment, which His great act of Redemption necessarily draws after it, and Himself be the Arbiter of the fates of men, the determining factor in whose fates has been their relation to Him. No doubt many who never heard His name upon earth will, in that day be, by His clear eye and perfect judgment, discerned to have visited the sick and the imprisoned, and to have done many acts for His sake. And for us who know Him, and have heard His name, the way in which we stand affected in heart and will to Christ reveals and settles our whole character, shapes our whole being, and will determine our whole destiny. He comes, not only to manifest Himself so as that 'every eye shall see Him,' and to divide the sheep from the goats, but also in order that He may reign for ever and gather into the fellowship of His love and the community of His joys all who love and trust Him here. These are the triple phases of our Lord's activity suggested by the three great moments.

III. Lastly, notice the triple attitude which we should assume to Him and to them.

For the first, the cradle, with its consequence of the Cross, our response is clinging faith, grateful memory, earnest following, and close conformity. For the second, the Ascension, with its consequence of a Christ that lives and labours for us, and is with us, our attitude ought to be an intense realisation of the fact of His present working and of His present abode with us. The centre of Christian doctrine has, amongst average Christians, been far too exclusively fixed within the limits of the earthly life, and in the interests of a true and comprehensive grasp of all the blessedness that Christianity is capable of bringing to men, I would protest against that type of thought, earnest and true as it may be within its narrow limits, which is always pointing men to the past fact of a Cross, and slurs over and obscures the present fact of a living Christ who is with us, and in us. One difference between Him and all other benefactors and teachers and helpers is this, that, as ages go on, thicker and ever–thickening folds of misty oblivion wrap them, and their influence diminishes as new circumstances emerge, but this Christ's power laughs at the centuries, and is untinged by oblivion, and is never out of date. For all others we have to say—'having served his generation,' or a generation or two more, 'according to the will of God, he fell on sleep.' But Christ knows no corruption, and is for ever more the Leader, and the Companion, and the Friend, of each new age.

Brethren! the Cross is incomplete without the throne. We are told to go back to the historical Christ. Yes, Amen, I say! But do not let that make us lose our grasp of the living Christ who is with us to–day. Whilst we rejoice over the 'Christ that died,' let us go on with Paul to say, 'Yea! rather, that is risen again, and is even at the right hand of God, who also maketh intercession for us.'

For that future, discredited as the thought of the second corporeal coming of the Lord Jesus in visible fashion and to a locality has been by the fancies and the vagaries of so–called Apocalyptic expositors, let us not forget that it is the hope of Christ's Church, and that 'they who love His appearing' is, by the Apostle, used as the description and definition of the Christian character. We have to look forwards as well as backwards and upwards, and to rejoice in the sure and certain confidence that the Christ who has come is the Christ who will come.

For us the past should be full of Him, and memory and faith should cling to His Incarnation and His Cross. The present should be full of Him, and our hearts should commune with Him amidst the toils of earth. The future should be full of Him, and our hopes should be based upon no vague anticipations of a perfectibility of humanity, nor upon any dim dreams of what may lie beyond the grave; but upon the concrete fact that Jesus Christ has risen, and that Jesus Christ is glorified. Does my faith grasp the Christ that was—who died for me? Does my heart cling to the Christ who is—who lives and reigns, and with whom my life is hid in God? Do my hopes crystallise round, and anchor upon, the Christ that is to come, and pierce the dimness of the future and the gloom of the grave, looking onwards to that day of days when He, who is our life, shall appear, and we shall appear also with Him in glory?

SIMEON'S SWAN–SONG

'Lord, now lettest Thou Thy servant depart in peace, according to Thy word: 30. For mine eyes have seen Thy salvation.'—LUKE ii. 29,30.

That scene, when the old man took the Infant in his withered arms, is one of the most picturesque and striking in the Gospel narrative. Simeon's whole life appears, in its later years, to have been under the immediate direction of the Spirit of God. It is very remarkable to notice how, in the course of three consecutive verses, the operation of that divine Spirit upon him is noted. 'It was revealed unto him by the Holy Ghost that he should not see death before he had seen the Lord's Christ.' 'And he came by the Spirit into the Temple.' I suppose that means that some inward monition, which he recognised to be of God, sent him there, in the expectation that at last he was to 'see the Lord's Christ.' He was there before the Child was brought by His parents, for we read 'He came by the Spirit into the Temple, and when the parents brought in the Child Jesus ... he took Him in his arms.' Think of the old man, waiting there in the Sanctuary, told by God that he was thus about to have the fulfilment of his life–long desire, and yet probably not knowing what kind of a shape the fulfilment would take. There is no reason to believe that he knew he was to see an infant; and he waits. And presently a peasant woman comes in with a child in her arms, and there arises in his soul the voice 'Anoint Him! for this is He!' And so, whether he expected such a vision or no, he takes the Child in his arms, and says, 'Lord! Now, now !—after all these years of waiting—lettest Thou Thy servant depart in peace.'

Now, it seems to me that there are two or three very interesting thoughts deducible from this incident, and from these words. I take three of them. Here we have the Old recognising and embracing the New; the slave recognising and submitting to his Owner; and the saint recognising and welcoming the approach of death.

I. The Old recognising and embracing the New.

It is striking to observe how the description of Simeon's character expresses the aim of the whole Old Testament Revelation. All that was meant by the preceding long series of manifestations through all these years was accomplished in this man. For hearken how he is described—'just and devout,' that is the perfection of moral character, stated in the terms of the Old Testament; 'waiting for the Consolation of Israel,' that is the ideal attitude which the whole of the gradual manifestation of God's increasing purpose running through the ages was intended to make the attitude of every true Israelite—an expectant, eager look forwards, and in the present, the discharge of all duties to God and man. 'And the Holy Ghost was upon him'; that, too, in a measure, was the ultimate aim of the whole Revelation of Israel. So this man stands as a bright, consummate flower which had at last effloresced from the roots; and in his own person, an embodiment of the very results which God had patiently sought through millenniums of providential dealing and inspiration. Therefore in this man's arms was laid the Christ for whom he had so long been waiting.

And he exhibits, still further, what God intended to secure by the whole previous processes of Revelation, in that he recognises that they were transcended and done with, that all that they pointed to was accomplished when a devout Israelite took into his arms the Incarnate Messiah, that all the past had now answered its purpose, and like the scaffolding when the top stone of a building is brought forth with shouting, might be swept away and the world be none the poorer. And so he rejoices in the Christ that he receives, and sings the swan–song of the departing Israel, the Israel according to the Spirit. And that is what Judaism was meant to do, and how it was meant to end, in an *euthanasia*, in a passing into the nobler form of the Christian Church and the Christian citizenship.

I do not need to remind you how terribly unlike this ideal the reality was, but I may, though only in a sentence or two, point out that that relation of the New to the Old is one that recurs, though in lees sharp and decisive forms, in every generation, and in our generation in a very special manner. It is well for the New when it consents to be taken in the arms of the Old, and it is ill for the Old when, instead of welcoming, it frowns upon the New, and instead of playing the part of Simeon, and embracing and blessing the Infant, plays the part of a Herod, and seeks to destroy the Child that seems to threaten its sovereignty. We old people who are conservative, if not by nature, by years, and you young people who are revolutionary and innovating by reason of your youth, may both find a lesson in that picture in the Temple, of Simeon with the Infant Christ in his arms.

II. Further, we have here the slave recognising and submitting to his Owner.

Now the word which is here employed for 'Lord' is one that very seldom occurs in the New Testament in reference to God; only some four or five times in all. And it is the harshest and hardest word that can be picked out. If you clip the Greek termination off it, it is the English word 'despot,' and it conveys all that that word conveys to us, not only a lord in the sense of a constitutional monarch, not only a lord in the polite sense of a superior in dignity, but a despot in the sense of being the absolute owner of a man who has no rights against the owner, and is a slave. For the word 'slave' is what logicians call the correlative of this word 'despot,' and as the latter asserts absolute ownership and authority, the former declares abject submission. So Simeon takes these two words to express his relation and feeling towards God. 'Thou art the Owner, the Despot, and I am Thy slave.' That relation of owner and slave, wicked as it is, when subsisting between two men—an atrocious crime, 'the sum of all villainies,' as the good old English emancipators used to call it—is the sum of all blessings when regarded as existing between man and God. For what does it imply? The right to command and the duty to obey, the sovereign will that is supreme over all, and the blessed attitude of yielding up one's will wholly, without reserve, without reluctance, to that infinitely mighty, and—blessed be God!—infinitely loving Will Absolute authority calls for abject submission.

And again, the despot has the unquestioned right of life and death over his slave, and if he chooses, can smite him down where he stands, and no man have a word to say. Thus, absolutely, we hang upon God, and because He has the power of life and death, every moment of our lives is a gift from His hands, and we should not subsist for an instant unless, by continual effluence from Him, and influx into us, of the life which flows from Him, the Fountain of life.

Again, the slave—owner has entire possession of all the slave's possessions, and can take them and do what he likes with them. And so, all that I call mine is His. It was His before it became mine; it remains His whilst it is mine, because I am His, and so what seems to belong to me belongs to Him, no less truly. What, then, do you do with your possessions? Use them for yourselves? Dispute His ownership? Forget His claims? Grudge that He should take them away sometimes, and grudge still more to yield them to Him in daily obedience, and when necessary, surrender them? Is such a temper what becomes the slave? What reason has he to grumble if the master comes to him and says, 'This little bit of ground that I have given you to grow a few sugar—canes and melons on, I am going to take back again.' What reason have we to set up our puny wills against Him, if He exercises His authority over us and demands that we should regard ourselves not only as sons but also as slaves to whom the owner of it and us has given a talent to be used for Him?

Now, all that sounds very harsh, does it not? Let in one thought into it, and it all becomes very gracious. The Apostle Peter, who also once uses this word 'despot,' does so in a very remarkable connection. He speaks about men's 'denying the despot that bought them.' Ah, Peter! you were getting on very thin ice when you talked about denial. Perhaps it was just because he remembered his sin in the judgment hall that he used that word to express the very utmost degree of degeneration and departure from Jesus. But be that as it may, he bases the slave–owner's right on purchase. And Jesus Christ has bought us by His own precious blood; and so all that sounds harsh in the metaphor, worked out as I have been trying to do, changes its aspect when we think of the method by which He has acquired His rights and the purpose for which He exercises them. As the Psalmist said, 'Oh, Lord! truly I am Thy slave. Thou hast loosed my bonds.'

III. So, lastly, we have here the saint recognising and welcoming the approach of death.

Now, it is a very singular thing, but I suppose it is true, that somehow or other, most people read these words, 'Lord! now lettest Thou Thy servant depart in peace,' as being a petition; 'Lord! now *let* Thy servant depart.' But they are not that at all. We have here not a petition or an aspiration, but a statement of the fact that Simeon recognises the appointed token that his days were drawing to an end, and it is the glad recognition of that fact. 'Lord! I see now that the time has come when I may put aside all this coil of weary waiting and burdened mortality, and go to rest.' Look how he regards approaching death. 'Thou lettest Thy servant depart' is but a feeble translation of the original, which is better given in the version that has become very familiar to us all by its use in a musical service, the *Nunc Dimittis*; 'Now Thou *dost send away*' It is the technical word for relieving a sentry from his post. It conveys the idea of the hour having come when the slave who has been on the watch through all the long, weary night, or toiling through all the hot, dusty day, may extinguish his lantern, or fling down his mattock, and go home to his little hut. 'Lord! Thou dost dismiss me now, and I take the dismission as the end of the long watch, as the end of the long toil.'

But notice, still further, how Simeon not only recognises, but welcomes the approach of death. 'Thou lettest Thy servant depart in peace.' Yes, there speaks a calm voice tranquilly accepting the permission. He feels no agitation, no fluster of any kind, but quietly slips away from his post. And the reason for that peaceful welcome of the end is 'for mine eyes have seen Thy salvation.' That sight is the reason, first of all, for his being sure that the curfew had rung for him, and that the day's work was done. But it is also the reason for the peacefulness of his departure. He went 'in peace,' because of what? Because the weary, blurred, old eyes had seen all that any man needs to see to be satisfied and blessed. Life could yield nothing more, though its length were doubled to this old man, than the sight of God's salvation.

Can it yield anything more to us, brethren? And may we not say, if we have seen that sight, what an unbelieving author said, with a touch of self–complacency not admirable, 'I have warmed both hands at the fire of life, and I am ready to depart.' We may go in peace, if our eyes have seen Him who satisfies our vision, whose bright presence will go with us into the darkness, and whom we shall see more perfectly when we have passed from the sentry–box to the home above, and have ceased to be slaves in the far–off plantation, and are taken to be sons in the Father's house. 'Thou lettest Thy servant depart in peace.'

THE BOY IN THE TEMPLE

'And He said unto them, How is it that ye sought Me!
wist ye not that I must be about My Father's business?'
—LUKE ii. 49.

A number of spurious gospels have come down to us, which are full of stories, most of them absurd and some of them worse, about the infancy of Jesus Christ. Their puerilities bring out more distinctly the simplicity, the nobleness, the worthiness of this one solitary incident of His early days, which has been preserved for us. How has it been preserved? If you will look over the narratives there will be very little difficulty, I think, in answering that question. Observing the prominence that is given to the parents, and how the story enlarges upon what they thought and felt, we shall not have much doubt in accepting the hypothesis that it was none other than Mary from whom Luke received such intimate details. Notice, for instance, 'Joseph and His mother knew not of it.' 'They supposed Him to have been in the company.' 'And when they,' i.e. Joseph and Mary, 'saw Him, they were astonished'; and then that final touch, 'He was subject to them,' as if His mother would not have Luke or us think that this one act of independence meant that He had shaken off parental authority. And is it not a mother's voice that says, 'His mother kept all these things in her heart,' and pondered all the traits of boyhood? Now it seems to me that, in these words of the twelve–year–old boy, there are two or three points full of interest and of teaching for us. There is—

I. That consciousness of Sonship.

I am not going to plunge into a subject on which certainly a great deal has been very confidently affirmed, and about which the less is dogmatised by us, who must know next to nothing about it, the better; viz. the inter–connection of the human and the divine elements in the person of Jesus Christ. But the context leads us straight to this thought—that there was in Jesus distinct growth in wisdom as well as in stature, and in favour with God and man. And now, suppose the peasant boy brought up to Jerusalem, seeing it for the first time, and for the first time entering the sacred courts of the Temple. Remember, that to a Jewish boy, his reaching the age of twelve made an epoch, because he then became 'a son of the Law,' and took upon himself the religious responsibilities which had hitherto devolved upon his parents. If we will take that into account, and remember that it was a true manhood which was growing up in the boy Jesus, then we shall not feel it to be irreverent if we venture to say, not that here and then, there began His consciousness of His Divine Sonship, but that that visit made an epoch and a stage in the development of that consciousness, just because it furthered the growth of His manhood.

Further, our Lord in these words, in the gentlest possible way, and yet most decisively, does what He did in all His intercourse with Mary, so far as it is recorded for us in Scripture—relegated her back within limits beyond which she tended to advance. For she said, 'Thy father and I have sought Thee sorrowing,' no doubt thus preserving what had been the usual form of speech in the household for all the previous years; and there is an emphasis that would fall upon her heart, as it fell upon none other, when He answered: 'Wist ye not that I must be about My Father's business?' We are not warranted in affirming that the Child meant all which the Man afterwards meant by the claim to be the Son of God; nor are we any more warranted in denying that He did. We know too little about the mysteries of His

34

growth to venture on definite statements of either kind. Our sounding–lines are not long enough to touch bottom in this great word from the lips of a boy of twelve; but this is clear, that as He grew into self–consciousness, there came with it the growing consciousness of His Sonship to His Father in heaven.

Now, dear brethren, whilst all that is unique, and parts Him off from us, do not let us forget that that same sense of Sonship and Fatherhood must be the very deepest thing in us, if we are Christian people after Christ's pattern. We, too, can be sons through Him, and only through Him. I believe with all my heart in what we hear so much about now—'the universal Fatherhood of God.' But I believe that there is also a special relation of Fatherhood and Sonship, which is constituted only, according to Scripture teaching in my apprehension, through faith in Jesus Christ, and the reception of His life as a supernatural life into our souls. God is Father of all men—thank God for it! And that means, that He gives life to all men; that in a very deep and precious sense the life which He gives to every man is not only derived from, but is kindred with, His own; and it means that His love reaches to all men, and that His authority extends over them. But there is an inner sanctuary, there is a better life than the life of nature, and the Fatherhood into which Christ introduces us means, that through faith in Him, and the entrance into our spirits of the Spirit of adoption, we receive a life derived from, and kindred with, the life of the Giver, and that we are bound to Him not only by the cords of love, but to obey the parental authority. Sonship is the deepest thought about the Christian life.

It was an entirely new thought when Jesus spoke to His disciples of their Father in heaven. It was a thrilling novelty when Paul bade servile worshippers realise that they were no longer slaves, but sons, and as such, heirs of God. It was the rapture of pointing to a new star flaming out, as it were, that swelled in John's exclamation: 'Beloved, now are we the sons of God!' For even though in the Old Testament there are a few occasional references to Israel's King or to Israel itself as being 'God's son,' as far as I remember, there is only one reference in all the Old Testament to parental love towards each of us on the part of God, and that is the great saying in the 103rd Psalm: 'Like as a father pitieth his children, so the Lord pitieth them that fear Him.' For the most part the idea connected in the Old Testament with the Fatherhood of God is authority: 'If I be a Father, where is Mine honour?' says the last of the prophets. But when we pass into the New, on the very threshold, here we get the germ, in these words, of the blessed thought that, as His disciples, we, too, may claim sonship to God through Him, and penetrate beyond the awe of Divine Majesty into the love of our Father God. Brethren, notwithstanding all that was unique in the Sonship of Jesus Christ, He welcomes us to a place beside Himself, and if we are the children of God by faith in Him, then are we 'heirs of God, and joint heirs with Christ.'

Now the second thought that I would suggest from these words is—

II. The sweet 'must' of filial duty.

'How is it that ye sought Me?' That means: 'Did you not know where I should be sure to be? What need was there to go up and down Jerusalem looking for Me? You might have known there was only one place where you would find Me. Wist ye not that I *must* be about My Father's business?' Now, the last words of this question are in the Greek literally, as the margin of the Revised Version tells us, 'in the things of My Father'; and that idiomatic form of speech may either be taken to mean, as the

35

Authorised Version does, 'about My Father's business,' or, with the Revised Version, 'in My Father's house.' The latter seems the rendering most relevant in this connection, where the folly of seeking is emphasised—the certainty of His place is more to the point than that of His occupation. But the locality carried the occupation with it, for why must He be in the Father's house but to be about the Father's business, 'to behold the beauty of the Lord and to inquire in His Temple'?

Do people know where to find us? Is it unnecessary to go hunting for us? Is there a place where it is certain that we shall be? It was so with this child Jesus, and it should be so with all of us who profess to be His followers.

All through Christ's life there runs, and occasionally there comes into utterance, that sense of a divine necessity laid upon Him; and here is its beginning, the very first time that the word occurs on His lips, 'I must.' There is as divine and as real a necessity shaping our lives because it lies upon and moulds our wills, if we have the child's heart, and stand in the child's position. In Jesus Christ the 'must' was not an external one, but He 'must be about His Father's business,' because His whole inclination and will were submitted to the Father's authority. And that is what will make any life sweet, calm, noble. 'The love of Christ constraineth us.' There is a necessity which presses upon men like iron fetters; there is a necessity which wells up within a man as a fountain of life, and does not so much drive as sweetly incline the will, so that it is impossible for him to be other than a loving, obedient child.

Dear friend, have we felt the joyful grip of that necessity? Is it impossible for me not to be doing God's will? Do I feel myself laid hold of by a strong, loving hand that propels me, not unwillingly, along the path? Does inclination coincide with obligation? If it does, then no words can tell the freedom, the enlargement, the calmness, the deep blessedness of such a life. But when these pull in two different ways, as, alas! they often do, and I have to say, 'I must be about my Father's business, and I had rather be about my own if I durst,' which is the condition of a great many so-called Christian people—then the necessity is miserable; and slavery, not freedom, is the characteristic of such Christianity. And there is a great deal of such to-day.

And now one last word. On this sweet 'must,' and blessed compulsion to be about the Father's business, there follows:

III. The meek acceptance of the lowliest duties.

'He went down to Nazareth, and was subject to them.' That is all that is told us about eighteen years, by far the largest part of the earthly life of Christ. Legend comes in, and for once not inappropriately, and tells us, what is probably quite true, that during these years, Jesus worked in the carpenter's shop, and as one story says, 'made yokes,' or as another tells, made light implements of husbandry for the peasants round Nazareth. Be that as it may, 'He was subject unto them,' and that was doing the Father's will, and being 'about the Father's business,' quite as much as when He was amongst the doctors, and learning by asking questions as well as by hearkening to their instructions. Everything depends on the motive. The commonest duty may be 'the Father's business,' when we are doing manfully the work of daily life. Only we do not turn common duty into the Father's business, unless we remember Him in the doing of it. But if we carry the hallowing and quickening influence of that great 'must' into all the pettinesses, and paltrinesses, and wearinesses, and sorrows of our daily trivial lives, then we shall find, as Jesus Christ found, that the carpenter's shop is as sacred as the courts of the Temple, and that to obey Mary was to do the will of the Father in heaven.

What a blessed transformation that would make of all lives! The psalmist long ago said: 'One thing have I desired of the Lord, and that will I seek after, that I may dwell in the house of the Lord all the days of my life.' We may dwell in the house of the Lord all the days of our lives. We may be in one or other of the many mansions of the Father's house where–ever we go, and may be doing the will of the Father in heaven in all that we do. Then we shall be at rest; then we shall be strong; then we shall be pure; then we shall have deep in our hearts the joyous consciousness, undisturbed by rebellious wills, that now 'we are the sons of God,' and the still more joyous hope, undimmed by doubts or mists, that 'it doth not yet appear what we shall be'; but that wherever we go, it will be but passing from one room of the great home into another more glorious still. 'I must be about my Father's business'; let us make that the motto for earth, and He will say to us in His own good time 'Come home from the field, and sit down beside Me in My house,' and so we 'shall dwell in the house of the Lord for ever.'

JOHN THE PREACHER OF REPENTANCE

'Now, in the fifteenth year of the reign of Tiberius Cesar, Pontius Pilate being governor of Judea, and Herod being tetrarch of Galilee, and his brother Philip tetrarch of Iturea and of the region of Trachonitis, and Lysanias the tetrarch of Abilene, 2. Annas and Caiaphas being the high priests, the word of God came unto John, the son of Zacharias, in the wilderness. 3. And he came into all the country about Jordan, preaching the baptism of repentance for the remission of sins; 4. As it is written in the book of the words of Esaias the prophet, saying, The voice of one crying in the wilderness, Prepare ye the way of the Lord, make His paths straight. 6. Every valley shall be filled, and every mountain and hill shall be brought low; and the crooked shall be made straight, and the rough ways shall be made smooth; 6. And all flesh shall see the salvation of God. 7. Then said he to the multitude that came forth to be baptized of him, O generation of vipers, who hath warned you to flee from the wrath to come! 8. Bring forth therefore fruits worthy of repentance; and begin not to say within yourselves, We have Abraham to our Father: for I say unto you, That God is able of these stones to raise up children unto Abraham. 9. And now also the axe is laid unto the root of the trees: every tree therefore which bringeth not forth good fruit is hewn down, and cast into the fire. 10. And the people asked him, saying, What shall we do then? 11. He answereth and saith unto them, He that hath two coats, let him impart to him that hath none; and he that hath meat, let him do likewise. 12. Then came also publicans to be baptized, and said unto him, Master, what shall we do? 13. And he said unto them, Exact no more than that which is appointed you. 14. And the soldiers likewise demanded of him, saying, And what shall we do? And he said unto them, Do violence to no man, neither accuse any falsely; and be content with your wages.'—LUKE iii. 144.

Why does Luke enumerate so carefully the civil and ecclesiastical authorities in verses 1 and 2? Not only to fix the date, but, in accordance with the world–wide aspect of his Gospel, to set his narrative in relation with secular history; and, further, to focus into one vivid beam of light the various facts which witnessed to the sunken civil and darkened moral and religious condition of the Jews. What more needed to be said to prove how the ancient glory had faded, than that they were under the rule of such a delegate as Pilate, of such an emperor as Tiberius, and that the bad brood of Herod's descendants divided the sacred land between them, and that the very high–priesthood was illegally administered, so that such a pair as Annas and Caiaphas held it in some irregular fashion between them? It was clearly high time for John to come, and for the word of God to come to him.

The wilderness had nourished the stern, solitary spirit of the Baptist, and there the consciousness of his mission and his message 'came to him'—a phrase which at once declares his affinity with the old prophets. Out of the desert he burst on the nation, sudden as lightning, and cleaving like it. Luke says nothing as to his garb or food, but goes straight to the heart of his message, 'The baptism of repentance unto remission of sins,' in which expression the 'remission' depends neither on 'baptism' alone, nor on 'repentance' alone. The outward act was vain if unaccompanied by the state of mind and will; the state of mind was proved genuine by submitting to the act.

In verses 7 to 14 John's teaching as the preacher of repentance is summarised. Why did he meet the crowds that streamed out to him with such vehement rebuke? One would have expected him to welcome them, instead of calling them 'offspring of vipers,' and seeming to be unwilling that they should flee from the wrath to come. But Luke tells why. They wished to be baptized, but there is no word of their repentance. Rather, they were trusting to their descent as exempting them from the approaching storm, so that their baptism would not have been the baptism which John required, being devoid of repentance. Just because they thought themselves safe as being 'children of Abraham,' they deserved John's rough name, 'ye offspring of vipers.'

Rabbinical theology has much to say about 'the merits of the fathers.' John, like every prophet who had ever spoken to the nation of judgments impending, felt that the sharp edge of his words was turned by the obstinate belief that judgments were for the Gentile, and never would touch the Jew. Do we not see the same unbelief that God can ever visit England with national destruction in full force among ourselves? Not the virtues of past generations, but the righteousness of the present one, is the guarantee of national exaltation.

John's crowds were eager to be baptized as an additional security, but were slow to repent. If heaven could be secured by submitting to a rite, 'multitudes' would come for it, but the crowd thins quickly when the administrator of the rite becomes the vehement preacher of repentance. That is so to–day as truly as it was so by the fords of Jordan. John demanded not only repentance, but its 'fruits,' for there is no virtue in a repentance which does not change the life, were such possible.

Repentance is more than sorrow for sin. Many a man has that, and yet rushes again into the old mire. To change the mind and will is not enough, unless the change is certified to be real by deeds corresponding. So John preached the true nature of repentance when he called for its fruits. And he preached the greatest motive for it which he knew, when he pressed home on sluggish consciences the close approach of a judgment for which everything was ready, the axe ground to a fine edge, and lying at the root of the trees. If it lay there, there was no time to lose; if it still lay, there was time to repent before it was swinging round the woodman's head. We have a higher motive for repentance in 'the goodness of God' leading to it. But there is danger that modern Christianity should think too little of 'the terror of the Lord,' and so should throw away one of the strongest means of persuading men. John's advice to the various classes of hearers illustrates the truth that the commonest field of duty and the homeliest acts may become sacred. Not high–flying, singular modes of life, abandoning the vulgar tasks, but the plainest prose of jog–trot duty will follow and attest real repentance. Every calling has its temptations—that is to say, every one has its opportunities of serving God by resisting the Devil.

JOHN'S WITNESS TO JESUS, AND GOD'S

'And as the people were in expectation, and all men mused in their hearts of John, whether he were the Christ, or not; 16. John answered, saying unto them all, I indeed baptize you with water; but one mightier than I cometh, the latchet of whose shoes I am not worthy to unloose: He shall baptize you with the Holy Ghost, and with fire: 17. Whose fan is in His hand, and He will thoroughly purge His floor, and will gather the wheat into His garner; but the chaff He will burn with fire unquenchable. 18. And many other things, in his exhortation, preached he unto the people. 19. But Herod the tetrarch, being reproved by him for Herodias his brother Philip's wife, and for all the evils which Herod had done, 20. Added yet this above all, that he shut up John in prison. 21. Now, when all the people were baptized, it came to pass, that Jesus also being baptized, and praying, the heaven was opened, 22. And the Holy Ghost descended in a bodily shape, like a dove, upon Him; and a voice came from heaven, which said, Thou art My beloved Son; in Thee I am well pleased.'—LUKE iii. 15–22.

This passage falls into three parts: John's witness to the coming Messiah (vs. 15–17); John's undaunted rebuke of sin in high places, and its penalty (vs. 18–20); and God's witness to Jesus (vs. 21, 22).

I. Luke sharply parts off the Baptist's work as a preacher of repentance and plain morality from his work as the herald who preceded the king. The former is delineated in verses 7–14, and its effect was to set light to the always smouldering expectation of the Messiah. The people were ready to rally round him if he would say that he was the coming deliverer. It was a real temptation, but his unmoved humility, which lay side by side with his boldness, brushed it aside, and poured an effectual stream of cold water on the excitement. 'John answered' the popular questionings, of which he was fully aware, and his answer crushed them.

In less acute fashion, the same temptation comes to all who move the general conscience. Disciples always seek to hoist their teacher higher than is fitting. Adherence to him takes the place of obedience to his message, and, if he is a true man, he has to damp down misdirected enthusiasm.

Mark John's clear apprehension of the limitations of his work. He baptized with water, the symbol and means of outward cleansing. He does not depreciate his position or the importance of his baptism, but his whole soul bows in reverence before the coming Messiah, whose great office was to transcend his, as the wide Mediterranean surpassed the little lake of Galilee. His outline of that work is grand, though incomplete. It is largely based upon Malachi's closing prophecy, and the connection witnesses to John's consciousness that he was the Elijah foretold there. He saw that the Messiah would surpass him in his special endowment. Strong as he was, that other was to be stronger. Probably he did not dream that that other was to wield the divine might, nor that His perfect strength was to be manifested in weakness, and to work its wonders by the might of gentle, self-sacrificing love. But, though he dimly saw, he perfectly adored. He felt himself unworthy (literally, insufficient) to be the slave who untied (or, according to Matthew, 'bore') his lord's sandals. How beautiful is the lowliness of that strong nature! He stood erect in the face of priests and tetrarchs, and furious women, and the headsman with his sword, but he lay prostrate before his King.

Strength and royal authority were not all that he had to proclaim of Messiah. 'He shall baptize you in the Holy Ghost and fire.' We observe that the construction here is different from that in verse 16 ('with water'), inasmuch as the preposition 'in' is inserted, which, though it is often used 'instrumentaly,' is here, therefore, more probably to be taken as meaning simply 'in.' The two nouns are coupled under one preposition, which suggests that they are fused together in the speaker's mind as reality and symbol.

Fire is a frequently recurrent emblem of the Holy Spirit, both in the Old and New Testament. It is not the destructive, but the vitalising, glowing, transforming, energy of fire, which is expressed. The fervour of holy enthusiasm, the warmth of ardent love, the melting of hard hearts, the change of cold, damp material into its own ruddy likeness, are all set forth in this great symbol. John's water baptism was poor beside Messiah's immersion into that cleansing fire. Fire turns what it touches into kindred flame. The refiner's fire melts metal, and the scum carries away impurities. Water washes the surface, fire pierces to the centre.

But while that cleansing by the Spirit's fire was to be Messiah's primary office, man's freedom to accept or reject such blessing necessarily made His work selective, even while its destination was universal. So John saw that His coming would part men into two classes, according as they submitted to His baptism of fire or not. The homely image of the threshing–floor, on some exposed, windy height, carries a solemn truth. The Lord of the harvest has an instrument in His hand, which sets up a current of air, and the wheat falls in one heap, while the husks are blown farther, and lie at the edge of the floor. Mark the majestic emphasis on the Christ's ownership in the two phrases, '*His* floor' and '*His* garner.'

Notice, too, the fact which determines whether a man is chaff or wheat—namely, his yielding to or rejecting the fiery baptism which Christ offers. Ponder that awful emblem of an empty, rootless, fruitless, worthless life, which John caught up from Psalm I. Thankfully think of the care and safe keeping and calm repose shadowed in that picture of the wheat stored in the garner after the separating act. And let us lay on awed hearts the terrible doom of the chaff. There are two fires, to one or other of which we must be delivered. Either we shall gladly accept the purging fire of the Spirit which burns sin out of us, or we shall have to meet the punitive fire which burns up us and our sins together. To be cleansed by the one or to be consumed by the other is the choice before each of us.

II. Verses 18–20 show John as the preacher and martyr of righteousness. Luke tells his fate out of its proper place, in order to finish with him, and, as it were, clear the stage for Jesus. Similarly the Baptist's desert life is told by anticipation in chapter i. 80. That treatment of his story marks his subordination. His martyrdom is not narrated by Luke, though he knew of it (Luke ix. 7–9), and this brief summary is all that is said of his heroic vehemence of rebuke to sin in high places, and of his suffering for righteousness' sake. John's message had two sides to it, as every gospel of God's has. To the people he spoke good tidings and exhortations; to lordly sinners he pealed out stern rebukes.

It needs some courage to tell a prince to his face that he is foul with corruption, and, still more, to put a finger on his actual sins. But he is no prophet who does not lift up his voice like a trumpet, and speak to hardened consciences. King Demos is quite as impatient of close dealing with his immorality as Herod was. London and New York get as angry with the Christian men who fight against their lust and drunkenness as ever he did, and would not be sorry if they could silence these persistent 'fanatics' as conveniently as he could. The need for courage like John's, and plain speech like his, is not past yet. The 'good tidings' has rebuke as part of its substance. The sword is two–edged.

III. The narrative now turns to Jesus, and does not even name John as having baptized Him. The peculiarities of Luke's account of the baptism are instructive. He omits the conversation between Jesus and John, and the fact of John's seeing the dove and hearing the voice. Like Mark, he makes the divine voice speak directly to Jesus, whereas Matthew represents it as spoken *concerning* Him. The baptism itself is disposed of in an incidental clause (*having been baptized*). The general result of these characteristics is that this account lays emphasis on the bearing of the divine witness as borne to Jesus Himself. It does not deny, but simply ignores, its aspect as a witness borne to John.

Another striking point is Luke's mention of Christ's prayer, which is thus represented as answered by the opened heavens, the descending dove, and the attesting voice. We owe most of our knowledge of Christ's prayers to this Evangelist, whose mission was to tell of the Son of man. Mysteries beyond our plummets are contained in this story; but however unique it is, it has this which may be reproduced, that prayer unveiled heaven, and brought down the dove to abide on the bowed head, and the divine attestation of sonship to fill the waiting heart.

We need not dwell on the beautiful significance of the emblem of the dove. It symbolised both the nature of that gracious, gentle Spirit, and the perpetuity and completeness of its abode on Jesus. Others receive portions of that celestial fullness, but itself, as if embodied in visible form, settled down on Him, and, with meekly folded wings, tarried there unscared. 'God giveth not the Spirit by measure unto Him.'

Our Evangelist does not venture into the deep waters, nor attempt to tell what was the relation between the Incarnate Word, as it dwelt in Jesus before that descent, and the Spirit which came upon Him. We shall be wise if we refrain from speculating on such points, and content ourselves with knowing that there has been one manhood capable of receiving and retaining uninterruptedly the whole Spirit of God; and that He will fill us with the Spirit which dwelt in Him, in measure and manner corresponding to our need and our faith.

The heavenly voice spoke to the heart of the man Jesus. What was His need of it, and what were its effects on Him, we do not presume to affirm. But probably it originated an increased certitude of the consciousness which dawned, in His answer to Mary, of His unique divine sonship. To us it declares that He stands in an altogether unexampled relation of kindred to the Father, and that His whole nature and acts are the objects of God's complacency. But He has nothing for Himself alone, and in Him we may become God's beloved sons, well pleasing to the Father.

THE TEMPTATION

4 And Jesus, being full of the Holy Ghost, returned from Jordan, and was led by the Spirit into the wilderness, 2. Being forty days tempted of the devil. And in those days He did eat nothing: and when they were ended, He afterward hungered. 3. And the devil said unto Him, If Thou be the Son of God, command this stone that it be made bread, 4. And Jesus answered him, saying, It is written, That man shall not live by bread alone, but by every word of God. 5. And the devil, taking Him up into an high mountain, showed unto Him all the kingdoms of the world in a moment of time. 6. And the devil said unto Him, All this power will I give Thee, and the glory of them: for that is delivered unto me; and to whomsoever I will I give it. 7. If Thou therefore wilt worship me, all shall be Thine. 8. And Jesus answered and said unto him, Get thee behind Me, Satan: for it is written, Thou shalt worship the Lord thy God, and Him only shalt thou serve. 9. And he brought Him to Jerusalem and set Him

on a pinnacle of the temple, and said unto Him, If
Thou be the Son of God, cast Thyself down from hence:
10. For it is written, He shall give His angels charge
over Thee, to keep Thee; 11. And in their hands they
shall bear Thee up, lest at any time Thou dash Thy
foot against a stone. 12. And Jesus answering, said
unto Him, It is said, Thou shalt not tempt the Lord
Thy God. 13. And when the devil had ended all the
temptation, he departed from Him for a season.'
—LUKE iv. 1–13.

If we adopt the Revised Version's reading and rendering, the whole of the forty days in the desert were one long assault of Jesus by Satan, during which the consciousness of bodily needs was suspended by the intensity of spiritual conflict. Exhaustion followed this terrible tension, and the enemy chose that moment of physical weakness to bring up his strongest battalions. What a contrast these days made with the hour of the baptism! And yet both the opened heavens and the grim fight were needful parts of Christ's preparation. As true man, He could be truly tempted; as perfect man, suggestions of evil could not arise within, but must be presented from without. He must know our temptations if He is to help us in them, and He must 'first bind the strong man' if He is afterwards 'to spoil his house.' It is useless to discuss whether the tempter appeared in visible form, or carried Jesus from place to place. The presence and voice were real, though probably if any eye had looked on, nothing would have been seen but the solitary Jesus, sitting still in the wilderness.

I. The first temptation is that of the Son of man tempted to distrust God. Long experience had taught the tempter that his most taking baits were those which appealed to the appetites and needs of the body, and so he tries these first. The run of men are drawn to sin by some form or other of these, and the hunger of Jesus laid Him open to their power—if not on the side of delights of sense, yet on the side of wants. The tempter quotes the divine voice at the baptism with almost a sneer, as if the hungry, fainting Man before him were a strange 'Son of God.' The suggestion sounds innocent enough; for there would have been no necessary harm in working a miracle to feed Himself. But its evil is betrayed by the words, 'If Thou art the Son of God,' and the answer of our Lord, which begins emphatically with 'man,' puts us on the right track to understand why He repelled the insidious proposal even while He was faint with hunger. To yield to it would have been to shake off for His own sake the human conditions which He had taken for our sakes, and to seek to cease to be Son of man in acting as Son of God. He takes no notice of the title given by Satan, but falls back on His brotherhood with man, and accepts the laws under which they live as His conditions.

The quotation from Deuteronomy, which Luke gives in a less complete form than Matthew, implies, even in that incomplete form, that bread is not the only means of keeping a man in life, but that God can feed Him, as He did Israel in its desert life, with manna; or, if manna fails, by the bare exercise of His divine will. Therefore Jesus will not use His power as Son of God, because to do so would at once take Him out of His fellowship with man, and would betray His distrust of God's power to feed Him there in the desert. How soon His confidence was vindicated Matthew tells us. As soon as the devil departed from Him, 'angels came and ministered unto Him.' The soft rush of their wings brought solace to His spirit, wearied with struggle, and once again 'man did eat angels' food.'

This first temptation teaches us much. It makes the manhood of our Lord pathetically true, as showing Him bearing the prosaic but terrible pinch of hunger, carried almost to its fatal point. It teaches us how innocent and necessary wants may be the devil's levers to overturn our souls. It warns us against severing ourselves from our fellows by the use of distinctive powers for our own behoof. It sets forth humble reliance on God's sustaining will as best for us, even if we are in the desert, where, according to sense, we must starve; and it magnifies the Brother's love, who for our sakes waived the prerogatives of the Son of God, that He might be the brother of the poor and needy.

II. The second temptation is that of the Messiah, tempted to grasp His dominion by false means. The devil finds that he must try a subtler way. Foiled on the side of the physical nature, he begins to apprehend that he has to deal with One loftier than the mass of men; and so he brings out the glittering bait, which catches the more finely organised natures. Where sense fails, ambition may succeed. There is nothing said now about 'Son of God.' The relation of Jesus to God is not now the point of attack, but His hoped—for relation to the world. Did Satan actually transport the body of Jesus to some eminence? Probably not. It would not have made the vision of all the kingdoms any more natural if he had. The remarkable language 'showed ... all ... in a moment of time' describes a physical impossibility, and most likely is meant to indicate some sort of diabolic phantasmagoria, flashed before Christ's consciousness, while His eyes were fixed on the silent, sandy waste.

There is much in Scripture that seems to bear out the boast that the kingdoms are at Satan's disposal. But he is 'the father of lies' as well as the 'prince of this world,' and we may be very sure that his authority loses nothing in his telling. If we think how many thrones have been built on violence and sustained by crime, how seldom in the world's history the right has been uppermost, and how little of the fear of God goes to the organisation of society, even to–day, in so–called Christian countries, we shall be ready to feel that in this boast the devil told more truth than we like to believe. Note that he acknowledges that the power has been 'given,' and on the fact of the delegation of it rests the temptation to worship. He knew that Jesus looked forward to becoming the world's King, and he offers easy terms of winning the dignity. Very cunning he thought himself, but he had made one mistake. He did not know what kind of kingdom Jesus wished to establish. If it had been one of the bad old pattern, like Nebuchadnezzar's or Caesar's, his offer would have been tempting, but it had no bearing on One who meant to reign by love, and to win love by loving to the death.

Worshipping the devil could only help to set up a devil's kingdom. Jesus wanted nothing of the 'glory' which had been 'given' him. His answer, again taken from Deuteronomy, is His declaration that His kingdom is a kingdom of obedience, and that He will only reign as God's representative. It defines His own position and the genius of His dominion. It would come to the tempter's ears as the broken law, which makes his misery and turns all his 'glory' into ashes. This is our Lord's decisive choice, at the outset of His public work, of the path of suffering and death. He renounces all aid from such arts and methods as have built up the kingdoms of earth, and presents Himself as the antagonist of Satan and his dominion. Henceforth it is war to the knife.

For us the lessons are plain. We have to learn what sort of kingdom Jesus sets up. We have to beware, in our own little lives, of ever seeking to accomplish good things by questionable means, of trying to carry on Christ's work with the devil's weapons. When churches lower the standard of Christian morality, because keeping it up would alienate wealthy or powerful men, when they wink hard at sin

44

which pays, when they enlist envy, jealousy, emulation of the baser sort in the service of religious movements, are they not worshipping Satan? And will not their gains be such as he can give, and not such as Christ's kingdom grows by? Let us learn, too, to adore and be thankful for the calm and fixed decisiveness with which Jesus chose from the beginning, and trod until the end, with bleeding but unreluctant feet, the path of suffering on His road to His throne.

III. The third temptation tempts the worshipping Son to tempt God. Luke arranges the temptations partly from a consideration of locality, the desert and the mountain being near each other, and partly in order to bring out a certain sequence in them. First comes the appeal to the physical nature, then that to the finer desires of the mind; and these having been repelled, and the resolve to worship God having been spoken by Jesus, Luke's third temptation is addressed to the devout soul, as it looks to the cunning but shallow eyes of the tempter. Matthew, on the other hand, in accordance with his point of view, puts the specially Messianic temptation last. The actual order is as undiscoverable as unimportant. In Luke's order there is substantially but one change of place—from the solitude of the wilderness to the Temple. As we have said, the change was probably not one of the Lord's body, but only of the scenes flashed before His mind's eye. 'The pinnacle of the Temple' may have been the summit that looked down into the deep valley where the enormous stones of the lofty wall still stand, and which must have been at a dizzy height above the narrow glen on the one side and the Temple courts on the other. There is immense, suppressed rage and malignity in the recurrence of the sneer, 'If Thou art the Son of God' and in the use of Christ's own weapon of defence, the quotation of Scripture.

What was wrong in the act suggested? There is no reference to the effect on the beholders, as has often been supposed; and if we are correct in supposing that the whole temptation was transacted in the desert, there could be none. But plainly the point of it was the suggestion that Jesus should, of His own accord and needlessly, put Himself in danger, expecting God to deliver Him. It looked like devout confidence; it was really 'tempting God'. It looked like the very perfection of the trust with which, in the first round of this duel, Christ had conquered; it was really distrust, as putting God to proof whether He would keep His promises or no. It looked like the very perfection of that worship with which He had overcome in the second round of the fight; it wag really self-will in the mask of devoutness. It tempted God, because it sought to draw Him to fulfil to a man on self-chosen paths His promises to those who walk in ways which He has appointed.

We trust God when we look to Him to deliver us in perils met in meek acceptance of His will. We tempt Him when we expect Him to save us from those encountered on roads that we have picked oat for ourselves. Such presumption disguised as filial trust is the temptation besetting the higher regions of experience, to which the fumes of animal passions and the less gross but more dangerous airs from the desires of the mind do not ascend. Religious men who have conquered these have still this foe to meet. Spiritual pride, the belief that we may venture into dangers either to our natural or to our religious life, where no call of duty takes us, the thrusting ourselves, unbidden, into circumstances where nothing but a miracle can save us—these are the snares which Satan lays for souls that have broken his coarser nets. The three answers with which Jesus overcame are the mottoes by which we shall conquer. Trust God, by whose will we live. Worship God, in whose service we get all of this world that is good for us. Tempt not God, whose angels keep us in our ways, when they are His ways, and who reckons trust that is not submission to His ways to be tempting God, and not trusting Him.

45

'All the temptation' was ended. So these three made a complete whole, and the quiver of the enemy was for the time empty. He departed 'for a season,' or rather, until an opportunity. He was foiled when he tried to tempt by addressing desires. His next assault will be at Gethsemane and Calvary, when dread and the shrinking from pain and death will be assailed as vainly.

PREACHING AT NAZARETH

'And He began to say unto them, This day is this
scripture fulfilled In your ears.'—LUKE iv. 21.

This first appearance of our Lord, in His public work at Nazareth, the home of His childhood, was preceded, as we learn from John's Gospel, by a somewhat extended ministry in Jerusalem. In the course of it, He cast the money–changers out of the Temple, did many miracles, had His conversation with Nicodemus, and on His return towards Galilee met the woman of Samaria at the well. The report of these things, no doubt, had preceded Him, and kindled the Nazarenes' curiosity to see their old companion who had suddenly shot up into a person of importance, and had even made a sensation in the metropolis. A great man's neighbours are keen critics of, and slow believers in, his greatness. So it was natural and very prudent that Jesus should not begin His ministry in Nazareth.

We can easily imagine the scene that morning in the little village, nestling among the hills. How many memories would occupy Christ as He entered the synagogue, where He had so often sat a silent worshipper! How Mary's eyes would fill with tears if she was there, and how the companions of His boyhood, who used to play with Him, would watch Him; all curious, some sympathetic, some jealous, some contemptuous!

The synagogue service began with prayer and praise. Then followed two readings, one from the Law, one from the Prophets. When the latter point was reached, in accordance with usage, Jesus rose, thereby signifying His desire to be reader of the Prophetic portion. We can understand how there would be a movement of quickened attention as the roll was handed to Him and He turned its sheets. He 'found the place'; that looks as if He sought for it; that is to say, that it was not the appointed lesson for the day—if there was such—but that it was a passage selected by Himself.

I need not enter upon the divergences between Luke's quotation as given in our English version and the Hebrew. They are partly due to the fact that he is quoting from memory the Greek version of the LXX. He inserts, for instance, one clause which is not found in that place in Isaiah, but in another part of the same prophet. Having read standing, as was the usage, in token of reverence for the Scripture, Jesus resumed His seat, not as having finished, but, as was the usage, taking the attitude of the teacher, which signified authority. And then, His very first sentence was the most unlimited assertion that the great words which He had been reading had reached their full accomplishment in Himself. They are very familiar to our ears. If we would understand their startling audacity we must listen to them with the ears of the Nazarenes, who had known Him ever since He was a child. 'This day is this Scripture fulfilled in your ears.' Now, it seems to me that this first sermon of our Lord's to His old fellow–townsmen brings into striking prominence some characteristics of His whole teaching, to which I desire briefly to direct attention.

I. I note Christ's self-assertion.

To begin in Nazareth with such words as these in my text was startling enough, but it is in full accord with the whole tone of our Lord's teaching. If you will carefully search for the most essential characteristics and outstanding differentia of the words of Jesus Christ, even if you make all allowance that some make for the non-historical character of the Gospels, you have this left as the residuum, that the impression which He made upon the men that were nearest to Him, and that caught up most fully the spirit of His teaching, was that the great thing that differentiated it from all other was His unhesitating persistence in pushing into the very forefront, His testimony about Himself. I do not think that there is anything parallel to that anywhere else amongst the men whom the world recognises as being great religious geniuses or great moral teachers. What characterises as perfectly unique our Lord's teaching is not only the blessed things that He said about God or the deep truths that He said about men and their duty, or the sad things that He said about men and their destiny, or the radiant hopes that He unveiled as to men and their possibility, but what He said about Himself. His message was not so much 'Believe in God and do right,' as it was 'Believe in Me and follow Me.'

I need only point you to the Sermon on the Mount, which is popularly supposed to contain very little of Christ's reference to Himself, and to remind you how there, in that authoritative proclamation of the laws of the new kingdom, He calmly puts His own utterances as co-ordinate with—nay! as superior to—the utterances of the ancient law, and sweeps aside Moses—though recognising Moses' divine mission—with an 'I say unto you.' I need only remind you, further, how, at the end of that 'compendium of reasonable morality,' He lays down this principle—that these sayings of 'Mine' are a rock-foundation, on which whoever builds shall never be put to confusion. This is but a specimen of the golden thread, if I may call it so, of self-assertion which runs through the whole of our Lord's teaching.

Now, I venture to say that this undeniable characteristic is only warranted on the supposition that He is the Son of God, and His work the salvation of the world. If He is so, if 'He that hath seen Me hath seen the Father,' if the revelation of Himself which He makes is the Revelation of God, if His death is for the life of the world; and if, when we honour Him, we honour God; when we trust Him, we trust God; when we obey Him we obey God; then I can understand His persistent self-assertion. But otherwise does He not deliberately intercept emotions which are only rightly directed to God? Does He not claim prerogatives, such as forgiveness of sins, bestowal of life, answering of prayer, which are only possessed by the Divine Being?

I know that many who will not go with me in my intellectual formularising of the truth about Christ's nature do bow to Him with unfeigned reverence. But it seems to me, I humbly confess, that there is no logical basis for such reverence except the full-toned recognition that the mystery of His self-assertion is explained by the mystery of His nature, God manifest in the flesh. I, for my part, do not see how the moral perfectness of Jesus Christ is to be saved, in view of that unmistakable strand in His teaching, unless by such admission. Rather, I feel that the recognition of it brings us face to face with the tremendous alternative, and that the people who were moved to indignation by His self-assertion because they recognised not His divine origin, and said 'This man blasphemeth'; 'This deceiver said,' have more to say in defence of their conclusion than those who bow before Him with reverence, and declare Him to be the pattern of all human perfectness, and yet falter when they are

47

asked to join in the great confession, 'Thou are the Christ, the Son of the living God.'

II. Secondly, note here our Lord's sad conception of humanity.

There are, as it were, two strands running through the prophetic passage which He quotes, one in reference to Himself, one in reference to those whom He came to help. To the latter I now turn, to get our Lord's point of view when He looked upon the facts of human life.

No man will ever do much for the world whose ears have not been opened to hear its sad music. An inadequate conception of its miseries is sure to lead to inadequate prescriptions for their remedy. We must bear upon our own hearts the burdens that we seek to lift off our brothers' shoulders. There is nothing about the Master's words concerning mankind more pathetic and more plain than the sad, stern, and yet pitying view which He always took concerning them and their condition.

In the passage on which Jesus based His claims, as given by Luke, one of the clauses is probably not in this place genuine, for 'the healing of the brokenhearted' should be struck out of the true text. There are then four symbols employed: the poor, the captives, the blind, the bruised. And these four are representations of the result of one fell cause, and that is—sin.

Sin impoverishes. Our true wealth is God. No man that possesses Him, by love, and trust, and conformity of will and effort to His discerned will, is poor, whatever else he has, whatever else he lacks. And no man who has lost this one durable treasure, the loving communion with, and possession of, God, in mind and heart and will and effort, but is a pauper whatever else he possesses. Wherever a man has sold himself to his own will, and has made himself and his own inclinations and misread good his centre and his aim, which is the definition of sin, there bankruptcy and poverty have come. Thieves sometimes beset travellers from the gold mines, as they are bringing down their dust or their nuggets to market, and empty the pockets of the gold, and fill them up with sand. That is what sin does for us; it takes away our true treasure, and befools us by giving us what seems to be solid till we come to open the bag; and then there is no power in it to buy anything for us. 'Why will ye spend your labour for that which satisfieth not?' The one poverty is the impoverishment that lays hold of every soul that wrenches itself, in self–will, apart from God. Sin makes poor.

Sin not only impoverishes, but imprisons 'the captives.' Ah! you have only to think of your own experience to find out what that means. Is there nothing in the set of your affections, in the mastery that your passion has over you, in the habits of your lives, which you know as well as God knows it, to be wrong and ruinous, and of which you have tried to get rid? I know the answer, and every one of us, if we will look into our own hearts, knows it: we are 'tied and bound by the chains of our sin.' You do not need to go to inebriate homes, where there are people that would cut their right hands off if they could get rid of the craving, and cannot, to find instances of this bondage. We have only to be honest with ourselves, and to try to pull the boat against the stream instead of letting it drift with it, to know the force with which the current runs. A tiny thread like a spider's draws after it a bit of cotton a little thicker, and knotted to that there is a piece of pack–thread, and after that a two–stranded cord, and then a cable that might hold an ironclad at anchor. That is a parable of how we draw to ourselves, by imperceptible degrees, an ever–thickening set of manacles that bind our wills and make us the servants of sin. 'His slaves ye are whom ye obey.' Sin imprisons. That is, your sin—do not let us befool ourselves with abstractions—*your* sin imprisons you.

Sin blinds. Wherever there comes over a soul the mist of self–will and self–regard, sight fails; and all the greatest things are blurred and blotted. The man that is immersed in his own evil is like one plunged in the ocean. The cold, salt waters are about him, and above him; and to him the glories of the sky, and the brightness of the sun, the tenderness of the colouring, are all blotted out. He who goes through life as some of us do, never seeing God, never seeing the loftiest beauty of goodness, never beholding with any clearness of vision the radiant possibilities of the future and its awful threatenings, may indeed see the things an inch from the point of his nose; but he is blind and cannot see afar off, and can only behold, and that darkly, the insignificances that are around him. Sin blinds.

And sin bruises. It takes all the health out of us, and makes us, from the sole of the foot to the crown of the head, masses of 'wounds and bruises and putrifying sores.'

The enchantress having worked all this havoc, then gives us a cup of illusion which, when we drink, we know not that there is anything the matter with us. We are like a lunatic in a cell, who thinks himself a prince in a palace, and though living on porridge and milk, fancies that he is partaking of all the dainties of a luxurious table. The deceitfulness of sin is not the least of its tragical consequences.

III. Lastly, we have here our Lord's conception of Himself and of His own work.

Your time will not allow of my dwelling upon this as I would fain have done, but let me point out one or two of the salient features of this initial programme of His. He claims to be the theme and the fulfilment of prophecy. Now, whatever influences modern notions about the genesis of the Old Testament, and the characteristics of its prophetic utterances may have done, they have not touched, and they never will touch, this one central characteristic of all that old system, that embedded in it there was an onward–looking gaze, anticipatory of a higher fulfilment and a further development of all that it taught. To those of us to whom Christ's words are the end of all strife I need only point out that, here, He endorses the belief that prophetic utterances, however they may have had, and did have, a lower and immediate meaning, were only realised in the whole sweep and significance in Himself. So He presents Himself before His acquaintances in the little synagogue at Nazareth, and before the whole world to all time, as the centre–point and pivot on which the history of the world, so to speak, revolves; all that was before converging to Him, all that was after flowing down from Him. 'They that went before, and they that followed after, cried, Hosanna! blessed be He that cometh in the name of the Lord.'

He claims to possess the whole fullness of the divine Spirit: 'The Spirit of the Lord is upon Me.' That is a reminiscence, no doubt, of the experience by the fords of the Jordan, at the Baptism. But it also opens up a wondrous consciousness, on His part, of a complete and uninterrupted possession of the divine life in all its fullness, which involves an entire separation from the miseries and needs of men. He claims to be the Messiah of the Old Covenant, with all the fullness of meaning, and loftiness of dignity which clustered round that word and that thought. He claims not only to proclaim, but to bestow, the blessings of which He speaks. For He not only comes to 'preach good tidings to the poor,' but 'to heal the broken–hearted,' and 'to set at liberty all them that are bound.' He is the Gospel which He utters. He not merely proclaims the favour of heaven, but He brings 'the acceptable year of the

Lord.'

This, in barest outline—which is all that your time will admit—is the summary of what Jesus Christ, in that first sermon in the synagogue at Nazareth, asserted Himself to be.

He does not detail the means by which He is about to bring the golden year, the year of Jubilee, 'the acceptable year of the Lord.' But I venture to say that it is hard to find, in the life of Jesus Christ, that which fulfils Christ's own programme, as thus announced, unless you bring in His death on the Cross for the abolition of sin, His Resurrection for the abolition of death; His reign in glory for the bestowment on all sinful and bruised souls of the Spirit of healing and of righteousness.

These Nazarenes listened. Their hearts and consciences attested the magnetic power of His personality, and the truth of His word. So do the hearts and consciences of most of us. They wondered at the 'words of grace'—whose matter was grace, whose manner was gracious—that proceeded from His mouth. So do most of us. But they let the incipient movement of their hearts be arrested by the cold, carping question, 'Is not this Joseph's son?' and all the enthusiasm chilled into indifference; 'indignation' followed, and some of those who had almost been drawn to Him, in an hour's time had their hands on His robe, to cast Him from the brow of the hill on which their village was built. Every man who comes to the point of feeling some emotions towards Christ as his Redeemer, as his King, is at a fork of the road. He may either take to the right, which will lead him to full communion and acceptance; or he may go to the left, which will carry him away out into the desert. The critical hour in the alchemist's laboratory was when the lead in his crucible began to melt. If a cold current got at it, it resumed its dead solidity, and no gold could be made.

Brother! do not let the world's cold currents get at your heart and freeze it again, if you feel that in any measure it is beginning to melt into penitence, and to flow with faith. The same voice that in the synagogue of Nazareth said, 'He hath anointed Me to preach the Gospel to the poor' speaks to us to–day from heaven, saying, 'I counsel thee to buy of Me gold tried in the fire, that thou mayest be rich ... and anoint thine eyes with eyesalve that thou mayest see.'

***

A SABBATH IN CAPERNAUM

'And in the synagogue there was a man which had a
spirit of an unclean devil, and cried out with a loud
voice, 34. Saying, Let us alone; what have we to do
with Thee, thou Jesus of Nazareth? art Thou come to
destroy us? I know Thee who Thou art; the Holy One of
God. 35. And Jesus rebuked him, saying, Hold thy
peace, and come out of him. And when the devil had
thrown him in the midst, he came out of him, and hurt
him not. 36. And they were all amazed, and spake among
themselves, saying, What a word is this! for with
authority and power He commandeth the unclean spirits,

and they come out. 37. And the fame of Him went out
into every place of the country round about. 38. And
He arose out of the synagogue, and entered into
Simon's house: and Simon's wife's mother was taken
with a great fever; and they besought Him for her.
39. And He stood over her, and rebuked the fever; and
it left her: and immediately she arose and ministered
unto them. 40. Now, when the sun was setting, all they
that had any sick with divers diseases brought them
unto Him; and He laid His hands on every one of them,
and healed them. 41. And devils also came out of many,
crying out, and saying, Thou art Christ, the Son of
God. And He, rebuking them, suffered them not to speak:
for they knew that He was Christ. 42. And when it was
day, He departed, and went into a desert place; and the
people sought Him, and came unto Him, and stayed Him,
that He should not depart from them. 43. And He said
unto them, I must preach the kingdom of God to other
cities also: for therefore am I sent. 44. And He
preached in the synagogues of Galilee.'—LUKE iv.33–44.

There are seven references to Christ's preaching in the synagogues in this chapter, and only two in the rest of this Gospel. Probably our Lord somewhat changed His method, and Luke, as the Evangelist of the gospel for Gentile as well as Jew, emphasises the change, as foreshadowing and warranting the similar procedure in Paul's preaching. This lesson takes us down from the synagogue at Nazareth, among its hills, to that at Capernaum, on the lakeside, where Jesus was already known as a worker of miracles. The two Sabbaths are in sharp contrast. The issue of the one is a tumult of fury and hate; that of the other, a crowd of suppliants and an eager desire to keep Him with them. The story is in four paragraphs, each showing a new phase of Christ's power and pity.

I. Verses 33–37 present Christ as the Lord of that dark world of evil. The hushed silence of the synagogue, listening to His gentle voice, was suddenly broken by shrieks of rage and fear, coming from a man who had been sitting quietly among the others. Possibly his condition had not been suspected until Christ's presence roused his dreadful tyrant. The man's voice is at the demon's service, and only Jesus recognises who speaks through the wretched victim. We take for granted the reality of demoniacal possession, as certified for all who believe Jesus, by His words and acts in reference to it, as well as forced on us, by the phenomena themselves, which are clearly distinguishable from disease, madness, or sin. The modern aversion to the supernatural is quite as much an unreasonable prejudice as any old woman's belief in witchcraft and Professor Huxley, making clumsy fun of the 'pigs at Gadara,' is holding opinions in the same sublime indifference to evidence of facts as the most superstitious object of his narrow–visioned scorn.

Napoleon called 'impossible' a 'beast of a word.' So it is in practical life,—and no less so when glibly used to discredit well–attested facts. We neither aspire to the omniscience which pronounces that there can be no possession by evil spirits, nor venture to brush aside the testimony of the Gospels and

51

the words of Christ, in order to make out such a contention.

Note the rage and terror of the demon. The presence of purity is a sharp pain to impurity, and an evil spirit is stirred to its depths when in contact with Jesus. Monstrous growths that love the dark shrivel and die in sunshine. The same presence which is joy to some may be a very hell to others. We may approach even here that state of feeling which broke out in these shrieks of malignity, hatred, and dread. It is an awful thing when the only relief is to get away from Jesus, and when the clearest recognition of His holiness only makes us the more eager to disclaim any connection with Him. That is the hell of hells. In its completeness, it makes the anguish of the demon; in its rudiments, it is the misery of some men.

Observe too, the unclean spirit's knowledge, not only of the birthplace and name, but of the character and divine relationship of Jesus. That is one of the features of demoniacal possession which distinguish it from disease or insanity, and is quite incapable of explanation on any other ground. It gives a glimpse into a dim region, and suggests that the counsels of Heaven, as effected on earth, are keenly watched and understood by eyes whose gleam is unsoftened by any touch of pity or submission. It is most natural, if there are such spirits, that they should know Jesus while men knew Him not, and that their hatred should keep pace with their knowledge, even while by the knowledge the hatred was seen to be vain.

Observe Christ's tone of authority and sternness. He had pity for men, who were capable of redemption, but His words and demeanour to the spirits are always severe. He accepts the most imperfect recognition from men, and often seems as if labouring to evoke it, but He silences the spirits' clear recognition. The confession which is 'unto salvation' comes from a heart that loves, not merely from a head that perceives; and Jesus accepts nothing else. He will not have His name soiled by such lips.

Note, still further, Christ's absolute control of the demon. His bare word is sovereign, and secures outward obedience, though from an unsubdued and disobedient will. He cannot make the foul creature love, but He can make him act. Surely Omnipotence speaks, if demons hear and obey. Their king had been conquered, and they knew their Master. The strong man had been bound, and this is the spoiling of his house. The question of the wondering worshippers in the synagogue goes to the root of the matter, when they ask what they must think of the whole message of One whose word gives law to the unclean spirits; for the command to them is a revelation to us, and we learn His Godhead by the power of His simple word, which is but the forth-putting of His will.

We cannot but notice the lurid light thrown by the existence of such spirits on the possibility of undying and responsible beings reaching, by continued alienation of heart and will from God, a stage in which they are beyond the capacity of improvement, and outside the sweep of Christ's pity.

II. Verses 38 and 39 show us Christ in the gentleness of His healing power, and the immediate service of gratitude to Him. The scene in the synagogue manifested 'authority and power,' and was prompted by abhorrence of the demon even more than by pity for his victim; but now the Lord's tenderness shines unmingled with sternness. Mark gives details of this cure, which, no doubt, came from Peter—such as his joint ownership of the house with his brother, the names of the companions of

Jesus, and the infinitely tender action of taking the sick woman by the hand and helping her to rise. But Luke, the physician, is more precise in his description of the case: 'holden by a great fever.' He traces the cure to the word of rebuke, which, no doubt, accompanied the clasp of the hand.

Here again Christ puts forth divine power in producing effects in the material sphere by His naked word. 'He spake and it was done.' That truly divine prerogative was put forth at the bidding of His own pity, and that pity which wielded Omnipotence was kindled by the beseechings of sorrowing hearts. Is not this miracle, which shines so lustrously by the side of that terrible scene with the demon, a picture in one case, and that the sickness of one poor and probably aged woman, of the great truth that heartens all our appeals to Him? He who moves the forces of Deity still from His throne lets us move His heart by our cry.

Luke is especially struck with one feature in the case—the immediate return of usual strength. The woman is lying, the one minute, pinned down and helpless with 'great fever,' and the next is bustling about her domestic duties. No wonder that a physician should think so abnormal a case worthy of note. When Christ heals, He heals thoroughly, and gives strength as well as healing. What could a woman, with no house of her own, and probably a poor dependant on her son–in–law, do for her healer? Not much. But she did what she could, and that without delay. The natural impulse of gratitude is to give its best, and the proper use of healing and new strength is to minister to Him. Such a guest made humble household cares worship; and all our poor powers or tasks, consecrated to His praise and become the offerings of grateful hearts, are lifted into greatness and dignity. He did not despise the modest fare hastily dressed for Him; and He still delights in our gifts, though the cattle on a thousand hills are His. 'I will sup with him,' says He, and therein promises to become, as it were, a guest at our humble tables.

III. Verses 40 and 41 show us the all–sufficiency of Christ's pity and power. The synagogue worship would be in the early morning, and the healing of the woman immediately after, and the meal she prepared the midday repast. The news had time to spread; and as soon as the sinking sun relaxed the Sabbatical restrictions, a motley crowd came flocking round the house, carrying all the sick that could be lifted, all eager to share in His healing. The same kind of thing may be seen yet round many a traveller's tent. It did not argue real faith in Him, but it was genuine sense of need, and expectation of blessing from His hand; and the measure of faith was the measure of blessing. They got what they believed He could give. If their faith had been larger, the answers would have been greater.

But men are quite sure that they want to be well when they are ill, and bodily healing will be sought with far more earnestness and trouble than soul–healing. Crowds came to Jesus as Physician who never cared to come to Him as Redeemer. Offer men the smaller gifts, and they will run over one another in their scramble for them; but offer them the highest, and they will scarcely hold out a languid hand to take them.

But the point made prominent by Luke is the inexhaustible fullness of pity and power, which met and satisfied all the petitioners. The misery spoke to Christ's heart; and so as the level rays of the setting sun cast a lengthening shadow among the sad groups, He moved amidst them, and with gentle touch healed them all. To–day, as then, the fountain of His pity and healing power is full, after thousands have drawn from it, and no crowd of suppliants bars our way to His heart or His hands. He has 'enough for all, enough for each, enough for ever more.'

The reference to demoniacs adds nothing to the particulars in the earlier verses except the evidence it gives of the frequency of possession then.

IV. Verses 42–44 show us Jesus seeking seclusion, but willingly sacrificing it at men's call. He withdraws in early morning, not because His store of power was exhausted, or His pity had tired, but to renew His communion with the Father. He needed solitude and silence, and we need it still more. No work worth doing will ever be done for Him unless we are familiar with some quiet place, where we and God alone together can hold converse, and new strength be poured into our hearts. Our Lord is here our pattern, also, of willingly leaving the place of communion when duty calls and men implore. We must not stay on the Mount of Transfiguration when demoniac boys are writhing on the plain below, and heart–broken fathers wearying for our coming. A great, solemn 'must' ruled His life, as it should do ours, and the fulfilment of that for which He 'was sent' ever was His aim, rather than even the blessedness of solitary communion or repose of the silent hour of prayer.

INSTRUCTIONS FOR FISHERMEN

'Now when He had left speaking, He said unto Simon,
Launch out into the deep, and let down your nets for a
draught.'—LUKE v. 4.

The day's work begins early in the East. So the sun, as it rose above the hills on the other side of the lake, shone down upon a busy scene, fresh with the dew and energy of the morning, on the beach by the little village of Bethsaida. One group of fishermen was washing their nets, their boats being hauled up on the strand. A crowd of listeners was thus early gathered round the Teacher; but the fishermen, who were His disciples, seem to have gone on with their work, never minding Christ or the crowd. It is sometimes quite as religious to be washing nets as to be listening to Christ's teaching.

The incident which follows the words of my text, and which is called the first miraculous draught of fishes, is stamped by our Lord Himself with a symbolic purpose; for at the end of it He says: 'Fear not! from henceforth thou shalt catch men.' And that flings back a flood of light on the whole story; and not only warrants but obliges us to take it as being by Him intended for the instruction in their Christian work of these four whom He has chosen to be His workers. However many of our Lord's miracles may not come under this category of symbolism (and I, for my part, do not believe that there are any of them which do not), this one clearly does. We have His own commentary to compel us to interpret its features as meaning something beyond what appears on the surface. I take it, then, that we have here a first vivid code of instructions which our Lord gives to all His servants who do work for Him; and I wish to look at the various stages of this incident from that point of view.

If there are any of my hearers who think to themselves, 'Ah, well! he is not going to say anything that I have anything to do with,' so much the worse for you, if you are not a Christian; or, so much the worse for you if, being a Christian, you are not an active servant. Jesus Christ had four disciples who were fishermen, and out of them He made four fishers of men. The obligation is universal.

I. The Law of Service.

'Launch out into the deep, and let down your nets for a draught.' Now there is nothing more remarkable in the whole narrative than the matter–of–course fashion in which our Lord takes the disposal of these men, and orders them about. It is not explicable unless we fall back upon what Luke does not tell us, but John does, in his Gospel, that this was by no means the first time that He had come across Peter and Andrew his brother, or James and John his brother. We do not need to trouble ourselves with the chronological question how long before they had been drawn to Him at the fords of Jordan by the witness of John the Baptist, and by the witness of some of them to the others. The relationship had been then commenced which is presupposed by our Lord's authoritative tone here. It leads in the incident of my text to a closer discipleship, which did not admit of Simon and John hauling or cleaning their nets any more. They had been disciples before in a certain loose fashion, a fashion which permitted them to go home and look after their ordinary avocations. Hence–forward they were disciples in a much more stringent fashion. It was because they had already said 'Rabbi! Thou art the Son of God! Thou art the King of Israel,' that this strange imperative command, inexplicable, except by the supplement of the last of the four Gospels, came from Christ's lips and secured immediate obedience.

If we thus understand that His authority follows on our discipleship, and that the words of my text, first of all, insist upon and assert His right to command and absolutely dispose of the activities, resources, and persons of all His disciples, we have learned something that we only need to practise in order to make our lives noble with a strange nobility, and blessed and sweet with an unearthly sanctity and blessedness.

Further, the words of my text not only declare for us thus the absolute authority of Jesus Christ over all His disciples, but also reveal His sweet promise and gracious assurance that He cares to guide, to direct, to prescribe spheres, to determine methods, to lead those who docilely look to Him and wait upon Him, in paths in which their activity may most profitably be employed for Him and for His Church. If there is anything that is declared to us plainly in the Scriptures, with regard to the relationships between men and Jesus Christ, it is this, that a docile heart will always be a guided heart, partly by inward whispers, which only they disbelieve who limit God in His relation to men, beyond what they have a right to do; and partly by outward providences which only they disbelieve who limit God in His power over the external world, beyond what they have a right to do. He will guide, sometimes with His eye, to which the loving eye flashes back response; sometimes with His whispered word, when the noises of earth and the pulsations of self–will are stilled; sometimes with His rod, which the less sensitive of His sons do often need; sometimes by successes in paths that we venture upon tentatively and timidly; and sometimes by failures in paths into which we rush confidently and presumptuously; but always, the waiting heart is a guided heart, and if we listen we shall hear 'This is the way, walk ye in it.' And sometimes it is God's will that we should make mistakes, for these too help us to learn His will.

But, further, and more particularly, I do not think that I am unduly reading too much meaning into this story, if I ask you to put emphasis upon one word, 'Launch out into the *deep*.' As long as you keep pottering along, a boat's length from the shore, you will only catch little fishes. The big ones, and the heavy takes are away out yonder. Go out there, if you want to get them. Which, being translated, is this—The same spirit of daring enterprise, which is a condition of success in secular matters, is no less potent a factor in the success of Christian men in their enterprises for Jesus Christ. As long as we keep Him down, within the limits of use and wont, and are horribly afraid of anything that our great–grandfathers did not use to do, there will be very few fish in the bottom of the boat.

Oh, brethren! if one thinks of the world into which it has been God's providence to put us, a world all seething with new aspirations and unrest—if we think of the condition of the great city in which we live, which is only a specimen of the cities of England, and of the tragical insufficiency of Christian enterprise and effort, as compared with the overwhelming masses of the community, surely, surely, there is nothing more wanted to make Christian people wake up from their old jog–trot habits, and cast themselves with new earnestness, new daring and enterprise, into forms of service which conscience and sober wisdom may approve. Of course, I do not forget that any such new methods must each approve themselves at the tribunal of the Christian consciousness. It is no part of my business here to descend into details and particulars, but I do want to lay on my own heart, and especially on the hearts of the members of the church of which I have the honour to be the pastor, and also upon all other Christian people whom my voice may reach, the solemn responsibility which the conditions of life in our generation lay upon Christian men and women, 'Launch out into the deep and let down your nets.' I believe, for my part, that if all the good, God–fearing, Christ–loving men and women in Manchester were to hear this voice sounding in their ears, and to obey it, they would change the face of the city.

II. The Response.

Peter, characteristically, speaks out, and says exactly what a fisherman would be likely to say to a carpenter from Nazareth, that came down to teach him his business. The landsman would not know what the fisherman knew well enough, that it was useless to go fishing in the morning if you had not caught anything all night. There was very little chance of getting any better success when the sun's rays were glinting on the surface of the water.

'We have toiled all the night, and have taken nothing.' Experience said, 'No! do not.' Christ said, 'Yes! do.' And so when Peter has made a clean breast of his objection, founded on experience, he goes on with the consent prompted by the devotion and consecration of love, 'nevertheless.' A great word that. 'We have toiled all the night, and have taken nothing; nevertheless at *Thy* word we will let down the net. So here goes.' And away they went, breakfastless perhaps, with their nets half cleaned, and sleepy and tired with the night's work.

Here, then, we see obedience that springs delighted to obey, because it is impelled by love. That is the spirit which can be trusted to go out into the deep, which does not ask whether things are recognised and usual or not, but which, if once it is sure of the Lord's will, takes no counsel of anything else. How should it, seeing that there is nothing so delightsome to a heart that truly loves as to know and do the will of its beloved? And that, dear brethren, is the spirit that all we Christian people need—a deeper, more vivid, more continual, soul–subduing, muscle–straining consciousness that Jesus Christ 'loved me and gave Himself for me.' Then His whisper will be like thunder, and the motto of our lives will be 'At Thy word, I will!'

Further, here is obedience that was not in the least degree depressed by the recognition of past failure. All night long they had been dropping the net overboard, and drawing it in, and with horny, wet hands seeking in its meshes, and finding nothing. Then overboard with it again, and more pulling at the heavy sweeps, till the dawn began to show, and all in vain. Now the weary task must be done all over again, though in all the past hours though they were the best, there has been only failure.

I think that our Christian courage and consecration would be immensely increased, if we could learn the lesson of my text; and feel that, however often in the past I may have broken down, the word of Christ's command, which thrills into my will, is also the word of Christ's promise which should stay my heart, and give me the assurance that past defeat shall be converted into future victory.

There is an obedience which did not grudge fresh toil before the effect of past toils had been quite got over. The nets, as I said, were only half cleaned. It was a pity to begin and dirty them again. The fishers had had a very hard night's toil. If they had been like some of us they would have said, 'Oh! I have been working hard all the night. I cannot possibly do any more this morning.' 'I am so very busy with my business all the week, that it is perfectly absurd to talk about my teaching in a Sunday–school.' That was not their spirit at all. No matter how they had to rub their eyes to get the sleep out of them, they just bundled the nets into the boat once more, pushed her down the strand, and shoved her out into the blue waters at Christ's bidding. And that is the sort of workmen that He wants, and that you and I should be.

Further, we have here an obedience that kept the Master's word sounding in its heart whilst it was at work. 'At Thy word will I let down the net.'

Ah! we very often begin working with a very pure motive, and as we go on, the motive gradually oozes away, and what was begun in the spirit is continued in the flesh; and what was begun with a true devotion to Jesus Christ is continued because we were doing it yesterday, and the day before that, and the day before that, and because it is the custom to do it. So we go on. The heart having all gone out of our service, the blessing is gone out of it too. But if we will keep our hearts near that Lord and listen to His voice calling us, wearied or not wearied, beaten before or not beaten before, and do as He bids us, launch out into the deep, we shall not toil in vain.

III. The result.

Christ's command ever includes His promise. Work done for Him is never resultless. True, His most faithful servants have often to say, if they look at their few sheaves with the eye of sense, 'I have spent my strength for nought.' True, the Apostolic experience is, at the best, but too exactly repeated, 'Some believed, and some believed not.' Christ's Gospel always produces its twofold effect, being 'a savour of life unto life, or of death unto death.' If the great Sower, when He went forth to sow, expected but a fourth part of the seed to fall into good ground, His servants need look for no larger results. But still it remains true that honest, earnest work for Jesus, wisely planned and prayerfully carried out with self–oblivion and self–surrender, will not be unblessed. If our labour is 'in the Lord,' it will not be 'in vain.' Just as pain is a danger signal, pointing to mischief at work on the body, so failure in achieving the results of Christian service is, for the most part, an indication of something wrong in method or spirit.

57

But, if we are toiling in loving obedience to Christ's voice, and seeking His direction as to sphere and manner of service, we may be quite sure of this, that whether we get, immediately or no, the outward and visible results which this incident promises to all who fulfil the conditions, we shall get the results which were symbolised in the second form of this miraculous draught of fishes. For, if you remember, there was another incident at the end of Christ's life, modelled upon this one, and equally significant, though in a different fashion. On that occasion, when the disciples had been toiling all the night, and saw, in the dim twilight of the morning, the questionable figure standing on the shore there, they were bidden to bring of the fish that they had caught, and when they came to land they saw a fire of coals, and fish laid thereon, and bread; and His voice said, 'Come, and eat!' Blessed are the workers that work for the Master, for living they shall not be left without His blessing, and dying, 'they rest from their labours'—by the side of that mysterious fire, and Christ–provided food—'and their works do follow them, in that they bring of the fish which they have caught.

FEAR AND FAITH

'When Simon Peter saw it, he fell down at Jesus' knees,
saying, Depart from me; for I am a sinful man, O Lord.'
—LUKE v. 8.

'Now, when Simon Peter heard that it was the Lord, he
girt his fisher's coat unto him,... and did cast
himself into the sea.'—JOHN xxi. 7.

These two instances of the miraculous draught of fishes on the Lake of Gennesareth are obviously intended to be taken in conjunction. Their similarities and their differences are equally striking and equally instructive. In the fragment of the incident which I have selected for our consideration now, we have the same man, in the same scene and circumstances, in the presence of the same Lord, acting under the influences of the same motive, and doing two exactly opposite things.

In the first case, the miracle at once struck him with the consciousness that he was now, in some way, he knew not how, in the immediate presence of the supernatural. That was immediately followed by a quick spasm and sense of sin, and that again by a recoil of terror, and that again by the cry, 'Go out of the boat; for I am a sinful man, O Lord.'

In the other instance, as soon as he saw (or rather, by the help of his friend's clearer sight, learned) that that dim and questionable figure on the morning beach there, was the Lord, the sight brought back his sin to his mind. But this time the consciousness of sin sent him splashing over the side, and through the shallow water, to struggle anyhow to get close to his Lord, not because he thought more complacently of himself or less loftily of his Master, but because he had learned that the best place for a sinful man was as close to Christ as ever he could get. And so, if we put these two incidents together, we get two or three thoughts that it is worth our while to dwell upon.

I. I ask you to notice, first, that instinctive and swift awaking of conscience.

This was not Peter's first acquaintance with Jesus Christ, nor his first enrolment in the ranks of disciples. John's Gospel tells the very beginning, and how, long before this incident, he had recognised Jesus Christ to be the King of Israel. This was not his first experience of a miracle. There had been many wrought in Capernaum of which probably he was an observer; and he had been at the wedding of Cana of Galilee; and in many ways and at many times, no doubt had seen manifestations of our Lord's supernatural power. But here, in his own boat, with his own nets, about his own sort of work, the thing came home to him as it never had come home before. And although he had long ago recognised Jesus Christ as the Messiah, there is a new, tremulous accession of conviction in that 'O Lord!' It means more than 'Master,' as he had just called Jesus. It means more than he knew himself, no doubt, but it means at least a great, sudden illumination as to who and what Christ was. And so the consciousness of sin flashes upon him at once, as a consequence of that new vision of the divine, as manifested in Jesus Christ. The links of the process of thought are suppressed. We only see the two ends of it. He passed through a series of thoughts with lightning rapidity. The beginning was the recognition of Christ as in some sense the manifestation to him of the Divine Presence, and the end of it was the recognition of his own sinfulness. He had no new facts; but new meaning and vitality were given to the facts that had long been familiar to him. The first result of this was a new conviction of his own hollowness and evil; and then, side by side with that sense of demerit and sin, came this other trembling apprehension of personal consequences. And so, not thinking so much about the sin as about the punishment that he thought must necessarily come when the holy and the impure collided, he cried, 'Depart from me, for I am a sinful man, O Lord!'

Now I take it that you get there, in that one instance, packed into small and picturesque compass, just the outlines of what it is reasonable and right that there should always go on in a heart when it first catches a glimpse of the purity, and holiness, and nearness of God, and of the awful, solemn verity that we do, each of us for himself, stand in a living, personal relation to Him. That sudden conviction may come by a thousand causes. A sunset opening the gates to the infinite distance may do it. A chance word may do it. A phrase in a sermon may do it. Some personal sorrow or sickness may do it. Any accidental push may touch the spring, and then the door flies open, for we all of us carry, buried deep down in most of us, and not easily got at, that hidden conviction, only needing the letting in of air to flame up, that we have indeed to do with a living God; that we are sinful and He is pure, and that, that being the case, the discord between us, if we come to close quarters, must end disastrously for us.

You remember the grand vision of Isaiah, how, when he saw the King sitting on His throne, 'high and lifted up, and His train filled the Temple,' the first thought was, not of rapture at the Apocalypse, not of adoration of the greatness, not of aspiration after the purity, not of any desire to join in the 'Holy! Holy! Holy!' of the burning spirits, but 'Woe is me, for I am undone; for mine eyes have seen the King; for I am a man of unclean lips.' Ah, brethren! whenever the commonplaces of our professed religious belief are turned into realities for us, and these things that we have all been familiar with from our childhood, flame before us as true and real, then there comes something analogous to the experience of that other Old Testament character—'I have heard of Thee by the hearing of the ear, but now mine eyes see Thee; wherefore I abhor myself, and repent in dust and ashes.'

And then there comes, in like manner, and there ought to come, along with this new vision of a God in His purity, and the new sense of my own sinfulness, the apprehension of personal evil. For, although it be the lowest of its functions, it is a function of conscience, not only to say to me, 'It is wrong to do what is wrong,' but to say, too, 'If you do wrong, you will have to bear the consequences.' I believe that a part of the instinctive voice of conscience is the declaration, not only of a law, but of a Lawgiver, and that part of its message to me is not only that sin is a transgression of the law, but that 'the wages of sin is death.'

Now, let me ask you to ask yourselves whether it is not a strange and solemn and sad testimony to the reality and universality of the fact of sin that the sense of impurity and dread of its issues are the uniform results of any vivid, thrilling consciousness of nearness to God. And let me ask you to ask yourself one other question, and that is, whether it is a wise thing to live upon a surface that may be shattered at any moment; whether that is true peace which needs but a touch to melt away; whether you are wise with all this combustible material deep down in your conscience, in paying no regard to it but living and frolicking, and feasting and trafficking, and lusting and sinning on the surface, like those light–hearted, light-headed fools that build their houses on the slopes of volcanoes when the lava rush may come at any moment?

II. That brings me to note, secondly, the mistaken cry of fear.

Peter felt uneasy in the presence of that pure eye, and he also felt, and was mistaken in feeling, that somehow or other he would be safer if he was not so near the Master. Well, if it were true that Jesus Christ brought God near to him, and if it were true that the proximity of God was the revelation of his blackness and the premonition and prophecy of evil to himself, would getting Christ out of the boat help him much? The facts would remain the same. The departure of the physician does not tend to cure the disease; and thus the cry,' Go away from me because I am sinful,' was all but ludicrous if it had not been so tragical in its misapprehension of the facts of the case and the cure for them.

Now the parallel to that, with you and me, is—what? How do we commit this same error? By trying to get rid of the thoughts which evoke these uncomfortable feelings of being impure and in peril. But does ceasing to remember the facts make any difference in the facts? Surely not. Just recall for a moment the many ways in which people manage to blind themselves to these plain, and to some of us unwelcome, truths. You may do it by availing yourselves of that strange power that we all have, of not attending to things that we do not like to think about. It is a strange thing that a man should be able to do that; it is a sad thing that any man should be fool enough to do it. But there are many among my hearers, I have no doubt whatever, who know that if they were to let their thoughts dwell on the facts of their own characters and relation to God they would be uncomfortable, and who, therefore, do their best to keep such thoughts at a safe distance. So, as soon as the sermon is over, some of you will begin to criticise me, or to discuss politics, or gossip, and so get rid of the impressions that the truth might produce. Or you fling yourselves into business. One of the reasons for the fierce energy which some men throw into their common avocations is their knowledge that if they have leisure, there may come into their chambers, and sit down beside them there, these unwelcome thoughts, that kill mirth. Some of you try to get rid of the Christ out of your boat by another way. You plunge into sensualism, and live in the low, vulgar atmosphere of fleshly delight and sensuous excitements in order to drown thought. And some of you do it by the even simpler process of merely giving no heed to such thoughts when kindled. The fire, unfed and unstirred, goes out. That is one way in which people come to have consciences, to use the dreadful words of the New

Testament, 'seared as with a hot iron.' If you will only never listen to it, it will stop speaking after a while, and then you will have an exemption from all these thoughts. When Felix first heard about temperance and righteousness and judgment to come he trembled, but paid no heed to his tremor, and said, 'Go away for this time, and when I am not busy at anything else, I will have thee back again.' He did have Paul back again many a time, and communed with him, but we never read that he trembled any more. The impression is not always reproduced, although the circumstances that produced it at first may be. The most impenetrable armour in which to clothe oneself against the sword of the Spirit is hammered out of former convictions that were never acted on. A soul cased in these is very hard to get at.

But consider the folly of seeking to get rid of truth, however unwelcome, under the delusion that it ceases to be true because we cease to look at it. Christ's leaving the boat would not have helped Peter. The facts remained, however he refused to look at them. If he could have changed them by getting rid of Him who reminded him of them, it might have been worth while to send Him away—but to dismiss the physician is a new way of curing the disease. Pain is an alarm bell for the physical nature to point to something wrong there, and this sense of evil, this shrinking from God regarded as the judge, is the alarm bell in the spiritual nature to warn of something wrong there. Do you think that you banish the danger for which the alarm bell is rung because you wrap a clout round the clapper so as to prevent it from sounding? and do you think that you make it less true that 'every transgression and disobedience shall receive its just recompense of reward' by bidding your conscience hold its peace when it tells you so, or by trying to drown its voice amidst the shouts of revelry, or the whirr of spindles, or the roar of traffic? By no means. The facts remain; and nothing except what deals with the facts is the cure which a wise man will adopt.

You remember the old story of the king of Babylon who sat feasting on the night when the city was captured. When the Finger came out and wrote upon the wall, 'Mene, Mene, Tekel, Upharsin,' it did not stop the feast. They went on with their rioting, and whilst they were carousing, the enemy was creeping up the dried bed of the diverted river, 'and in that night was Belshazzar slain' amidst his wine–cups, and the flowers on his temples were dabbled with his blood. No more insane way of curing the consciousness of sin and the dread of judgment than that of stifling the voice that evokes it was ever dreamed of in an asylum.

III. Lastly, notice the right place for a sinful man.

On the second occasion to which our texts refer we have the Apostle far more deeply conscious of his sin than he was on the first. He remembered his denial, and no doubt he remembered also the secret interview that Jesus Christ had with him on the day of the Resurrection, when, no doubt, He communicated to him His frank and full assurance of forgiveness, He knows far more of Christ's dignity and character and nature after the Resurrection than he had done on that day, long ago, by the banks of the lake. The deeper sense of his own sin, and the clearer and loftier view of who and what Jesus Christ was, send him struggling to his Master, and make him blessed only at His feet.

Ah yes, brother! the superficial knowledge of my evil may drive me away from Jesus Christ; the deepest conviction of it will send me right into His arms. A partial knowledge of the divine nature as revealed in Him as judge, and punitive and necessarily antagonistic to the blackness of my sin, in the lustrous whiteness of His purity, may drive me away from Him, but the deeper knowledge of God manifested in Jesus Christ, the long–suffering, the gentle, loving, pardoning, will send me to Him in all the depth of my self–abasement and in the confidence in His love as covering over my sin and accepting me. Where does the child go when it has transgressed against its mother's word? Into its mother's arms to hide its face upon her bosom near her heart. 'Against Thee, Thee only have I sinned'; and therefore to Thee, Thee only will I go. Only in nearness to Jesus Christ can we get the anodyne that quiets the conscience—the blessed assurance of forgiveness that lightens us of our burden and dread, and the power for holiness that will change our impurity into the likeness of His own purity. He, and He only, can forgive. He, and He only, brings the loving God into the midst of unloving men. He, and He only, hath offered the sacrifice in which all sin is done away. He, and He only, by the communication of His Spirit and life to me, will make me pure and deliver me from the burden of my sin.

And so the man who knows his own need and Christ's grace will not say, 'Depart from me for I am a sinful man,' but he will say, 'Leave me never, nor forsake me, for I am a sinful man, O Lord; but in Thee I have forgiveness and righteousness.'

Dear friends! that consciousness of demerit once evoked in a man's heart, however imperfectly, as I believe it is in some of your hearts now, must issue in one of two things. Either it will send you further into darkness to get away from the light, as the bats in a cave will flit to the deepest recesses of it in order to escape the torch, or it will bring you nearer to Him, and at His feet you will find cleansing.

Oh, dear friends!—strangers many of you, but all friends—let me beseech you that, if the merciful Spirit of God is in any measure using my poor words to touch your consciences and hearts, you would not venture to seek escape from the convictions which are stirring in you by any other way than by betaking yourselves to the Cross. Let it not be, I pray you, that because you know yourselves to be in need of forgiveness, and to stand in peril of judgment, you say to God,' Depart from us, for we desire not the knowledge of Thy ways.' But rather do you cast yourselves into Christ's arms and keep near Him; saying as this same Peter did, on another occasion, 'Lord! to whom shall we go? Thou hast the words of eternal life.'

BLASPHEMER, OR—WHO?

'And it came to pass on a certain day, as He was teaching, that there were Pharisees and doctors of the law sitting by, which were come out of every town of Galilee, and Judea, and Jerusalem; and the power of the Lord was present to heal them. 18. And, behold, men brought in a bed a man which was taken with a palsy: and they sought means to bring him in, and to lay him before Him. 19. And when they could not find by what way they might bring him in because of the multitude, they went upon the house–top, and let him down through the tiling, with his couch, into the

midst before Jesus. 20. And when He saw their faith,
He said unto him, Man, thy sins are forgiven thee.
21. And the scribes and the Pharisees began to reason,
saying, Who is this which speaketh blasphemies? Who
can forgive sins but God alone? 22. But when Jesus
perceived their thoughts, He, answering, said unto
them, What reason ye in your hearts? 23. Whether is
easier to say, Thy sins be forgiven thee; or to say,
Rise up and walk! 24. But that ye may know that the
Son of man hath power upon earth to forgive sins, (He
said unto the sick of the palsy,) I say unto thee,
Arise, and take up thy couch, and go unto thine house.
25. And immediately he rose up before them, and took
up that whereon he lay, and departed to his own house,
glorifying God. 26. And they were all amazed, and they
glorified God, and were filled with fear, saying, We
have seen strange things to–day.'—LUKE v. 17–26.

Luke describes the composition of the unfriendly observers in this crowd with more emphasis and minuteness than the other Evangelists do. They were Pharisees and doctors, and they were assembled from every part of Galilee, and even from Judea, and, what was most remarkable, from Jerusalem itself. Probably the conflict with the authorities in the capital recorded in John v. had taken place by this time, and if so, a deputation from the Sanhedrim would very naturally be despatched to Capernaum, and its members would as naturally summon the local lights to sit with them, and watch this revolutionary young teacher, who had no licence from them, and apparently not much reverence for them.

One can easily imagine that these heresy–hunters would be much too superior persons to mix with the crowd about the door of Peter's house, and would, as Luke says, be 'sitting by,' near enough to see and hear, but far enough to show that they had no share in the vulgar enthusiasm of these provincial peasants. They were too holy to mingle with the mob, so they kept together by themselves, and waited hopefully for some heresy or breach of their multitudinous precepts. They got more than they expected.

We may note the contrast between their cynical watchfulness and the glorious manifestations for which they had no eyes. 'The power of the Lord'—that is, of Christ—'was' (operative) 'in His healing,' or, according to another reading, 'to heal them.' But the critics took no heed of that. There is a temper of mind which is sharp–eyed as a lynx for faults, and blind as a bat to evidences of divine power in the Gospel or its adherents. Some noses are keen to smell stenches, and dull to perceive fragrance. The race of such inquisitors is not extinct.

They contrast, too, with the earnestness of the four friends who brought the paralysed man. The former sat cool and critical, because they had no sense of need either for themselves or for others. The latter made all the effort they could to fight through the crowd, and then took to the roof by some outside stair, and hastily stripping off enough of the tiling, lowered their friend, bed and all, right down in front of the young Rabbi. The house would be low, and the roof slight, and Jesus was probably seated in an open inner court or verandah, At any rate, the description gives a piece of local colour, and presents no improbability.

Earnestness in striving to come oneself or to bring a dear one to Christ's feet seems a supremely absurd waste of energy to a cynical critic, who feels no need of anything that Christ can give. It looks rather different to the paralytic on his couch, and to the friends who long for his healing.

The first lesson from this incident is that our deepest need is forgiveness. No doubt, something in the paralytic's case determined Christ's method with him. Perhaps his sickness had been brought on by dissipation, and possibly conscience was lashing him with a whip of scorpions, so that, while his friends sought for his healing, he himself was more anxious for pardon. It is very unlikely that Jesus would have offered forgiveness unless He had known that it was yearned for. But whether that is so or not, we may fairly generalise the order of givings in this miracle, and draw from it the lesson that what Jesus then gave first is His chief gift. In most of His other miracles He gave bodily healing first. First or second, it is always Christ's chief gift in the beginning of discipleship. His miracles of bodily healing are parables of that higher miracle. This incident brings out what is always the order of relative importance, whether it is that of chronological sequence or not.

And we all need to lay that truth to heart for ourselves. No tinkering with superficial discomforts, or culture of intellect and taste, or success in worldly pursuits, will avail to stanch the deep wound through which our life−blood is ebbing out. We need something that goes deeper than all these styptics. Only a power which can deal with our sense of sin, and soothe that into blessed assurance of pardon, is strong enough to grapple with our true root of misery. It is useless to give a man dying of cancer medicine for pimples. That is what all attempts to make man happy and restful while sin remains unforgiven, are doing.

Social reformers need this lesson. Many voices proclaim many gospels to−day. Culture, economical or social reconstruction, is trumpeted as the panacea. But it matters comparatively little how society is organised. If its individual members retain their former natures, the former evils will come back, whatever its organisation. The only thorough cure for social evils is individual regeneration. Christ deals with men singly, and remoulds society by renewing the individual. The most elaborate machinery may be used for filtering the black waters. What will be the good of that if the fountain of blackness is not sealed up, or rather purified, at its hidden source? Make the tree good, and its fruit will be good. To make the tree good, you must begin with dealing with sin.

The second lesson from this incident is that Christ's claim to forgive sins is either blasphemy or the manifest token of divinity. These Pharisees scented heresy at once. They were blind to the pathos of the story, and hard as millstones towards the poor sufferer's wistful looks. But they pounced at once gleefully on Christ's words. They were perfectly right in their premises that forgiveness was a divine prerogative which no man could share. For sin is the name of evil, when considered in its relation to God. He only can forgive it, for 'against Thee, Thee only,' as David confessed, is it committed. True, the same act may be full of harmful results to men, and may be a breach of human law, but in its character as sin it refers to God only. Forgiveness is the outpouring of God's love on a sinner, uninterrupted by his sin. Only God can pour out that love.

But the cavillers were quite wrong in their conclusion. He did not 'blaspheme.' The fact that Jesus knew and answered their whispered or unspoken 'reasonings in their hearts' might have taught them that here was more than a rabbi, or even a prophet. But He goes on to reiterate His assertion that He has power to forgive sins.

Observe that He does not deny their premises. Nor does He, as He was bound in common honesty to do, set them right if they were wrong in supposing that He had claimed divine power. A wise religious teacher, who saw himself misunderstood as asserting that he could give what he only meant to assure a penitent that God would give, would have instantly said, 'Do not mistake me. I am only doing what every servant of God's should and can do, telling this poor brother that God is ready to forgive. God forbid that I should be supposed to do more than to declare his forgiveness!' Christ's answer is the strongest possible contrast to that. He knew what these Pharisees supposed Him to have meant by His authoritative words, and knowing it, He repeats them, and points to the miracle about to be done as their vindication.

Is there any possible way of escaping from the conclusion that Jesus solemnly and deliberately laid claim to exercise the divine prerogative of dispensing pardon? If He did, what shall we say of Him? Surely there is no third judgment of Him and His words possible; but either the Pharisees were right, and 'this man,' this pattern of all meekness and perfect example of humility, blasphemed, or else Peter was right when he said, 'Thou art the Christ, the Son of the living God.'

The third lesson is that the visible effects of Christ's power attest the reality of His claim to produce the invisible effects of peaceful assurance of forgiveness. It was equally easy to say, 'Thy sins are forgiven thee,' and to say, 'Take up thy bed and walk.' It was equally impossible for a mere man to forgive, and to give the paralytic muscular force to move. But the one saying could be tested, and its fulfilment verified by sight. The other could not; but if the visible impossibility was done, it was a witness that the invisible one could be.

The striking way in which our Lord weaves in His command to the palsied man to take up his bed with His words to the Pharisees is preserved in all the Gospels, and gives vividness to the narrative, while it brings out the main purpose of the miracle. It was a demonstration in the visible sphere of Christ's power in the invisible. Both were divine acts, and that which could be verified by sight established the reality of that which could not.

The same principle may be widely extended. It includes all the outward effects of Christ's gospel in the world. There are abundance of these which are patent to fair–minded observers. If one wishes to know what these are, he has only to contrast heathen lands with those in which, however imperfectly, Jesus is recognised as King and Example. The lives of His disciples are full of faults, but they should, and in a measure, do, witness to the reality of His gifts of forgiveness and conquest of sin. He has done more to restore strength to humanity paralysed for good than all other would–be physicians put together have done; and since He has visibly effected such manifest changes on outward lives, it is no rash conclusion to draw that He can change the inward nature. If He has healed the palsy, that is a work surpassing human power, and it proves that He can forgive the sin which brought the paralysis, and tied the helpless sufferer to his couch of pain.

LAWS OF THE KINGDOM

'And He lifted up His eyes on His disciples, and said, Blessed be ye poor: for yours is the kingdom of God, 21. Blessed are ye that hunger now: for ye shall be filled. Blessed are ye that weep now: for ye shall laugh. 22. Blessed are ye, when men shall hate you, and when they shall separate you from their company, and shall reproach you, and cast out your name as evil, for the Son of man's sake. 23. Rejoice ye in that day, and leap for joy; for, behold, your reward is great in heaven: for in the like manner did their fathers unto the prophets. 24. But woe unto you that are rich! for ye have received your consolation. 25. Woe unto you that are full! for ye shall hunger. Woe unto you that laugh now! for ye shall mourn and weep. 26. Woe unto you when all men shall speak well of you! for so did their fathers to the false prophets. 27. But I say unto you which hear, Love your enemies, do good to them which hate you, 28. Bless them that curse you, and pray for them which despitefully use you. 29. And unto him that smiteth thee on the one cheek, offer also the other; and him that taketh away thy cloak, forbid not to take thy coat also. 30. Give to every man that asketh of thee; and of him that taketh away thy goods ask them not again. 31. And as ye would that men should do to you, do ye also to them likewise.'—LUKE vi. 20–31.

Luke condenses and Matthew expands the Sermon on the Mount. The general outline is the same in both versions. The main body of both is a laying down the law for Christ's disciples. Luke, however, characteristically omits what is prominent in Matthew, the polemic against Pharisaic righteousness, and the contrast between the moral teaching of Christ and that of the law. These were appropriate in a Gospel which set forth Jesus as the crown of earlier revelation, while Luke is true to the broad humanities of his Gospel, in setting forth rather the universal aspect of Christian duty, and gathering it all into the one precept of love.

The fragment which forms the present passage falls into two parts—the description of the subjects of the kingdom and their blessedness, contrasted with the character of the rebels; and the summing up of the law of the kingdom in the all–including commandment of love.

1. The subjects and blessedness of the kingdom, and the rebels. It is to be well kept in view that the discourse is addressed to 'His disciples.' That fact remembered would have saved some critics from talking nonsense about the discrepancy between Luke and Matthew, and supposing that the former meant merely literal poverty, hunger, and tears. No doubt he omits the decisive words which appear

in Matthew, who appends 'in spirit' to 'poor,' and 'after righteousness' to 'hunger and thirst,' but there is no ground for supposing that Luke meant anything else than Matthew.

Notice that in our passage the sayings are directly addressed to the disciples, while in Matthew they are cast into the form of general propositions. In that shape, the additions were needed to prevent misunderstanding of Christ, as if He were talking like a vulgar demagogue, flattering the poor, and inveighing against the rich. Matthew's view of the force of the expressions is involved in Luke's making them an address *to the disciples.*, 'Ye poor' at once declares that our Lord is not thinking of the whole class of literally needy, but of such of these as He saw willing to learn of Him. No doubt, the bulk of them were poor men as regards the world's goods, and knew the pinch of actual want, and had often had to weep. But their earthly poverty and misery had opened their hearts to receive Him, and that had transmuted the outward wants and sorrows into spiritual ones, as is evident from their being disciples; and these are the characteristics which He pronounces blessed. In this democratic and socialistic age, it is important to keep clearly in view the fact that Jesus was no flatterer of poor men as such, and did not think that circumstances had such power for good or evil, as that virtue and true blessedness were their prerogatives.

The foundation characteristic is poverty of spirit, the consciousness of one's own weakness, the opposite of the delusion that we are 'rich and increased with goods.' All true subjection to the kingdom begins with that accurate, because lowly, estimate of ourselves. Humility is life, lofty mindedness is death. The heights are barren, rivers and fertility are down in the valleys.

Luke makes hunger the second characteristic, and weeping the third, while Matthew inverts that order. Either arrangement suggests important thoughts. Desire after the true riches naturally follows on consciousness of poverty, while, on the other hand, sorrow for one's conscious lack of these may be regarded as preceding and producing longing. In fact, the three traits of character are contemporaneous, and imply each other. Outward condition comes into view, only in so far as it tends to the production of these spiritual characteristics, and has, in fact, produced them, as it had done, in some measure, in the disciples. The antithetical characteristics of the adversaries of the kingdom are, in like manner, mainly spiritual; and their riches, fullness, and laughter refer to circumstances only in so far as actual wealth, abundance, and mirth tend to hide from men their inward destitution, starvation, and misery.

But what paradoxes to praise all that flesh abhors, and to declare that it is better to be poor than rich, better to feel gnawing desire than to be satisfied, better to weep than to laugh! How little the so–called Christian world believes it! How dead against most men's theory and practice Christ goes! These Beatitudes have a solemn warning for all, and if we really believed them, our lives would be revolutionised. The people who say, 'Give me the Sermon on the Mount: I don't care for your doctrines, but I can understand *it,' have not felt the grip of these Beatitudes.*

Note that the blessings and woes are based on the future issues of the two states of mind. These are not wholly in the future life, for Jesus says, 'Yours *is* the kingdom.' That kingdom is a state of obedience to God, complete in that future world, but begun here. True poverty secures entrance thither, since it leads to submission of will and trust. True hunger is sure of satisfaction, since it leads to waiting on God, who 'will fulfil the desire of them that fear Him.' Sorrow which is according to

God, cannot but bring us near Him who 'will wipe away tears from off all faces.'

On the other hand, they who in condition are prosperous and satisfied with earth, and in disposition are devoid of suspicion of their own emptiness, and draw their joys and sorrows from this world alone, cannot but have a grim awaking waiting for them. Here they will often feel that earth's goods are no solid food, and that nameless yearnings and sadness break in on their mirth; and in the dim world beyond, they will start to find their hands empty and their souls starving.

The fourth of Luke's Beatitudes contrasts the treatment received from men by the subjects and the enemies of the kingdom. Better to be Christ's martyr than the world's favourite! Alas, how few Christians wear the armour of that great saying! They would not set so much store by popularity, nor be so afraid of being on the unpopular side, if they did.

II. The second part of the passage contains the summary of the laws of the kingdom from the lips of the King. Its keynote is love. The precept follows strikingly on the predictions of excommunication and hatred. The only weapon to fight hate is love. 'The hate of hate, the scorn of scorn,' are not Christian dispositions, though Tennyson tells us that they are the poet's. So much the worse for him if they are! First, the commandment, so impossible to us unless our hearts are made Christlike by much dwelling with Christ, is laid down in the plainest terms. Enmity should only stimulate love, as a gash in some tree bearing precious balsam makes the fragrant treasure flow. Who of us has conformed to that law which in three words sums up perfection? How few of us have even honestly tried to conform to it!

But the command becomes more stringent as it advances. The sentiment is worth much, but it must bear fruit in act. So the practical manifestations of it follow. Deeds of kindness, words of blessing, and highest of all, and the best help to fulfilling the other two, prayer, are to be our meek answers to evil. Why should Christians always let their enemies settle the terms of intercourse? They are not to be mere reverberating surfaces, giving back echoes of angry voices. Let us take the initiative, and if men scowl, let us meet them with open hearts and smiles. 'A soft answer turneth away wrath.' 'It takes two to make a quarrel.' Frost and snow bind the earth in chains, but the silent sunshine conquers at last, and evil can be overcome with good.

Our Lord goes on to speak of another form of love—namely, patient endurance of wrong and unreasonableness. He puts that in terms so strong that many readers are fain to pare down their significance. Non-resistance is commanded in the most uncompromising fashion, and illustrated in the cases of assault, robbery, and pertinacious mendicancy. The world stands stiffly on its rights; the Christian is not to bristle up in defence of his, but rather to suffer wrong and loss. This is regarded by many as an impossible ideal. But it is to be observed that the principle involved is that love has no limits but itself. There may be resistance to wrong, and refusal of a request, if love prompts to these. If it is better for the other man that a Christian should not let him have his way or his wish, and if the Christian, in resisting or refusing, is honestly actuated by love, then he is fulfilling the precept when he says 'No' to some petition, or when he resists robbery. We must live near Jesus Christ to know when such limitations of the precept come in, and to make sure of our motives.

The world and the Church would be revolutionised if even approximate obedience were rendered to this commandment. Let us not forget that it *is* a commandment, and cannot be put aside without disloyalty.

Christ then crystallises His whole teaching on the subject of our conduct to others into the immortal words which make our wishes for ourselves the standard of our duty to others, and so give every man an infallible guide. We are all disposed to claim more from others than we give to them. What a paradise earth would be if the two measuring–lines which we apply to their conduct and to our own were exactly of the same length!

THREE CONDENSED PARABLES

'And why beholdest thou the mote that is in thy brother's eye, but perceiveth not the beam that is in thine own eye? 42. Either, how canst thou say to thy brother, Brother, let me pull out the mote that is in thine eye, when thou thyself beholdest not the beam that is in thine own eye? Thou hypocrite, cast out first the beam out of thine own eye, and then shalt thou see clearly to pull out the mote that is in thy brother's eye. 43. For a good tree bringeth not forth corrupt fruit; neither doth a corrupt tree bring forth good fruit. 44. For every tree is known by his own fruit: for of thorns men do not gather figs, nor of a bramble–bush gather they grapes. 45. A good man, out of the good treasure of his heart, bringeth forth that which is good; and an evil man, out of the evil treasure of his heart, bringeth forth that which is evil; for of the abundance of the heart his mouth speaketh, 46. And why call ye Me, Lord, Lord, and do not the things which I say? 47. Whosoever cometh to Me, and heareth My sayings, and doeth them, I will shew you to whom he is like: 48. He is like a man which built an house, and digged deep, and laid the foundation on a rock: and when the flood arose, the stream beat vehemently upon that house, and could not shake it; for it was founded upon a rock. 49. But he that heareth, and doeth not, is like a man that, without a foundation, built an house upon the earth; against which the stream did beat vehemently, and immediately it fell; and the ruin of that house was great.'—LUKE vi. 41–49.

Three extended metaphors, which may almost be called parables, close Luke's version of the Sermon on the Mount, and constitute this passage. These are the mote and the beam, the good and bad trees, the houses on the rock and on the sand. Matthew puts the first of these earlier in the sermon, and connects it with other precepts about judging others. But whichever order is the original, that adopted by Luke has a clear connection of thought underlying it which will come out as we proceed.

I. The striking and somewhat ludicrous image of the beam and the mote is found in Rabbinical writings, and may have been familiar to Christ's hearers. But His use of it is deeper and more searching than the rabbis' was. He has just been speaking of blind guides and their blind followers. That 'parable,' as Luke calls it, naturally images another defect which may attach to the eye. A man may be partly blind because some foreign body has got in. If we might suppose a tacit reference to the Pharisees in the blind guides, their self-complacent censoriousness would be in view here; but the application of the saying is much wider than to them only.

Verse 41 teaches that the accurate measurement of the magnitude of our own failings should precede our detection of our brother's. Christ assumes the commonness of the opposite practice by asking 'why' it is so. And we have all to admit that the assumption is correct. The keenness of men's criticism of their neighbour's faults is in inverse proportion to their familiarity with their own. It is no unusual thing to hear some one, bedaubed with dirt from head to foot, declaiming with disgust about a speck or two on his neighbour's white robes.

Satan reproving sin is not an edifying sight, but Satan criticising sin is still less agreeable. If only 'he that is without sin among you' would fling stones, there would be fewer reputations pelted than there are. Most men know less about their own faults than about their brother's. They use two pairs of spectacles—one which diminishes, and is put on for looking at themselves; one which magnifies, and is worn for their neighbour's benefit. But when their respective good qualities are to be looked at, the other pair is used in each case. That is men's way, all the world over.

Christ's question asks the reason for this all but universal dishonesty of having two weights and measures for faults. He would have us ponder on the cause, that we may discover the remedy. He would have us reflect, that we may get a vivid conviction of the unreasonableness of the practice. There is nothing in the fact that a fault is mine which should make it small in my judgment; nor, on the other hand, in the accident that it is another's, which should make it seem large. A fault is a fault, whoever it belongs to, and we should judge ourselves and others by the same rule. Only we should be most severe in its application to ourselves, for we cannot tell how much our brother has had, to diminish the criminality of his sin, and we can tell, if we will be honest, how much we have had, to aggravate that of ours. So the conscience of a true Christian works as Paul's did when he said 'Of whom I am chief,' and is more disposed to make its own motes into beams than to censure its brother's.

The reason, so far as there is a reason, can only lie in our diseased selfishness, which is the source of all sin. And the blindness to our 'beams' is partly produced by their very presence. All sin blinds conscience. A man with a beam in his eye would not be able to see much. One device of sin, practised in order to withdraw the doer's attention from his own deed, is to make him censorious of his fellows, and to compound for the sins he is inclined to by condemning other people's.

Verse 42 teaches that the conquest of our own discovered evils must precede efficient attempts to cure other people's. To pose as a curer of them while we are ignorant of our own faults is, consciously or unconsciously, hypocrisy, for it assumes a hatred of evil, which, if genuine, would have found first a field for its working in ourselves. An oculist with diseased eyes would not be likely to be a successful operator. 'Physician, heal thyself' would fit him well, and be certainly flung at him. A cleansed eye will see the brother's mote clearly, but only in order to help its extraction. It is a delicate bit of work to get it out, and needs a gentle hand.

Our discernment of others' faults must be compassionate, not to be followed by condemnation nor self–complacency but by loving efforts to help to a cure. And such will not be made unless we have learned our own sinfulness, and can go to the wrongdoer in brotherly humility, and win him to use the 'eye–salve' which our conduct shows has healed us.

II. The second compressed parable of the two trees springs from the former naturally, as stating the general law of which verse 42 gives one case, namely, that good deeds (such as casting out the mote) can only come from a good heart (made good by confession of its own evils and their ejection). It is often said that Christ's teaching is unlike that of His Apostles in that He places stress on works, and says little of faith. But how does He regard works? As fruits. That is to say, they are of value in His eyes only as being products and manifestations of character. He does not tell us in this parable how the character which will effloresce in blossoms and set in fruits of goodness is produced. That comes in the next parable. But here is sufficiently set forth the great central truth of Christian ethics that the inward disposition is the all–important thing, and that deeds are determined as to their moral quality by the character from which they have proceeded.

Our actions are our self–revelations. The words are not to be pressed, as if they taught the entire goodness of one class of men, so that all their acts were products of their good character, nor the unmingled evil of another, so that no good of any kind or in any degree is in them or comes from them. They must be read as embodying a general truth which is not as yet fully exemplified in any character or conduct.

In verse 45 the same idea is presented under a different figure—that of a wealthy man who brings his possessions out of his store–house. The application of the figure is significantly varied so as to include the other great department of human activity. Speech is act. It, too, will be according to the cast of the inner life. Of course, feigned speech of all sorts is not in view. The lazy judgment of men thinks less of words than of deeds. Christ always attaches supreme importance to them. Intentional lying being excluded, speech is an even more complete self–revelation than act. When one thinks of the floods of foul or idle or malicious talk which half drown the world as being revelations of the sort of hearts from which they have gushed, one is appalled. What a black, seething fountain that must be which spurts up such inky waters!

III. The third parable, of the two houses, shows in part how hearts may be made 'good.' It is attached to the preceding by verse 46. Speech does not always come from 'the abundance of the heart.' Many call Him Lord who do not act accordingly. Deeds must confirm words. If the two diverge, the latter must be taken as the credible self–revelation. Now the first noticeable thing here is Christ's bold assumption that His words are a rock foundation for any life. He claims to give an absolute and all–sufficient rule of conduct, and to have the right to command every man.

And people read such words and then talk about their Christianity not being the belief of His divinity, but the practice of the Sermon on the Mount! His words are the foundation for every firm, lasting life. They are the basis of all true thought about God, ourselves, our duties, our future. 'That rock was Christ.' Every other foundation is as sand. Unless we build on Him, we build on changeable inclinations, short–lived desires, transitory aims, evanescent circumstances. Only the Christ who ever liveth, and is ever 'the same yesterday, and to–day, and for ever,' is fit to be the foundation of lives that are to be immortal.

Note the two houses built on the foundations. The metaphor suggests that each life is a whole with a definite character. Alas, how many of our lives are liker a heap of stones tilted at random out of a cart than a house with a plan. But there is a character stamped on every life, and however the man may have lived from hand to mouth without premeditation, the result has a character of its own, be it temple or pig–sty. Each life, too, is built up by slow labour, course by course. Our deeds become our dwelling–places. Like coral–insects, we live in what we build. Memory, habit, ever–springing consequences, shape by slow degrees our isolated actions into our abodes. What do we build?

One storm tries both houses. That may refer to the common trials of every life, but it is best taken as referring to the future judgment, when God 'will lay judgment to the line, and righteousness to the plummet'; and whatever cannot stand that test will be swept away. Who would run up a flimsy structure on some windy headland in northern seas? The lighthouses away out in ocean are firmly bonded into living rock. Unless our lives are thus built on and into Christ, they will collapse into a heap of ruin. 'Behold I lay in Zion for a foundation a stone, a tried stone, a precious corner stone, a sure foundation: he that believeth shall not make haste.'

WORTHY–NOT WORTHY

'... They besought Him ... saying, That he was worthy
for whom He should do this:... 6. I am not worthy that
Thou shouldest enter under my roof: 7. Wherefore
neither thought I myself worthy to come unto Thee....'
—LUKE vii. 4. 6. 7.

A Roman centurion, who could induce the elders of a Jewish village to approach Jesus on his behalf, must have been a remarkable person. The garrison which held down a turbulent people was not usually likely to be much loved by them. But this man, about whom the incident with which our texts are connected is related, was obviously one of the people of whom that restless age had many, who had found out that his creed was outworn, and who had been drawn to Judaism by its lofty monotheism and its austere morality. He had gone so far as to build a synagogue, and thereby, no doubt, incurred the ridicule of his companions, and perhaps the suspicions of his superiors. What would the English authorities think of an Indian district officer that conformed to Buddhism or Brahminism, and built a temple? That is what the Roman officials would think of our centurion. And there were other beautiful traits in his character. He had a servant 'that was dear to him.' It was not only the nexus of master and servant and cash payments that bound these two together. And very beautiful is this story, when he himself speaks about this servant. He does not use the rough word which implies a bondservant, and which is employed throughout the whole of the rest of the narrative, but a much gentler one, and speaks of him as his 'boy.' So he had won the hearts of these elders so far as to make them swallow their dislike to Jesus, and deign to go to Him with a request which implied His powers at which at all other times they scoffed.

Now, we owe to Luke the details which show us that there was a double deputation to our Lord—the first which approached Him to ask His intervention, and the second which the centurion sent when he saw the little group coming towards his house, and a fresh gush of awe rose in his heart. The elders said, 'He is worthy'; he said, 'I am not worthy.' The verbal resemblance is, indeed, not so close in the original as in our versions, for the literal rendering of the words put into the centurion's mouth is 'not fit.' But still the evident antithesis is preserved: the one saying expresses the favourable view that partial outsiders took of the man, the other gives the truer view that the man took of himself. And so, putting away the story altogether, we may set these two verdicts side by side, as suggesting wider lessons than those which arise from the narrative itself.

I. And, first, we have here the shallow plea of worthiness.

These elders did not think loftily of Jesus Christ. The conception that we have of Him goes a long way to settle whether it is possible or not for us to approach Him with the word 'worthy' on our lips. The higher we lift our thought of Christ, the lower becomes our thought of ourselves. These elders saw the centurion from the outside, and estimated him accordingly. There is no more frequent, there is no more unprofitable and impossible occupation, than that of trying to estimate other people's characters. Yet there are few things that we are so fond of doing. Half our conversation consists of it, and a very large part of what we call literature consists of it; and it is bound to be always wrong, whether it is eulogistic or condemnatory, because it only deals with the surface.

Here we have the shallow plea advanced by these elders in reference to the centurion which corresponds to the equally shallow plea that some of us are tempted to advance in reference to ourselves. The disposition to do so is in us all. Luther said that every man was born with a Pope in his belly. Every man is born with a Pharisee in himself, who thinks that religion is a matter of barter, that it is so much work, buying so much favour here, or heaven hereafter. Wherever you look, you see the working of that tendency. It is the very mainspring of heathenism, with all its penances and performances. It is enshrined in the heart of Roman Catholicism, with its dreams of a treasury of merits, and works of supererogation and the like. Ay! and it has passed over into a great deal of what calls itself Evangelical Protestantism, which thinks that, somehow or other, it is all for our good to come here, for instance on a Sunday, though we have no desire to come and no true worship in us when we have come, and to do a great many things that we would much rather not do, and to abstain from a great many things that we are strongly inclined to, and all with the notion that we have to bring some 'worthiness' in order to move Jesus Christ to deal graciously with us.

And then notice that the religion of barter, which thinks to earn God's favour by deeds, and is, alas! the only religion of multitudes, and subtly mingles with the thoughts of all, tends to lay the main stress on the mere external arts of cult and ritual. 'He loveth our nation, and hath built us a synagogue'; not, 'He is gentle, good, Godlike.' 'He has built a synagogue.' That is the type of work which most people who fall into the notion that heaven is to be bought, offer as the price. I have no doubt that there are many people who have never caught a glimpse of any loftier conception than that, and who, when they think—which they do not often do—about religious subjects at all, are saying to themselves, 'I do as well as I can,' and who thus bring in some vague thought of the mercy of God as a kind of make–weight to help out what of their own they put in the scale. Ah, dear brethren! that is a wearying, an endless, a self–torturing, an imprisoning, an enervating thought, and the plea of 'worthiness' is utterly out of place and unsustainable before God.

II. Now let me turn to the deeper conviction which silences that plea.

'I am not worthy that Thou shouldest enter under my roof, wherefore neither thought I myself worthy to come unto Thee.' This man had a loftier conception of who and what Christ was than the elders had. To them He was only one of themselves, perhaps endowed with some kind of prophetic power, but still one of themselves. The centurion had pondered over the mystic power of the word of command, as he knew it by experience in the legion, or in the little troop of which he, though a man under the authority of his higher officers, was the commander; and he knew that even his limited power carried with it absolute authority and compelled obedience. And he had looked at Christ, and wondered, and thought, and had come at last to a dim apprehension of that great truth that, somehow or other, in this Man there did lie a power which, by the mere utterance of His will, could affect matter, could raise the dead, could still a storm, could banish disease, could quell devils. He did not formulate his belief, he could not have said exactly what it led to, or what it contained, but he felt that there was something divine about Him. And so, seeing, though it was but through mists, the sight of that great perfection, that divine humanity and human divinity, he bowed himself and said, 'Lord! I am not worthy.'

When you see Christ as He is, and give Him the honour due to His name, all notions of desert will vanish utterly.

Further, the centurion saw himself from the inside, and that makes all the difference. Ah, brethren! most of us know our own characters just as little as we know our own faces, and find it as difficult to form a just estimate of what the hidden man of the heart looks like as we find it impossible to form a just estimate of what we look to other people as we walk down the street. But if we once turned the searchlight upon ourselves, I do not think that any of us would long be able to stand by that plea, 'I am worthy.' Have you ever been on a tour of discovery, like what they go through at the Houses of Parliament on the first day of each session, down into the cellars to see what stores of explosive material, and what villains to fire it, may be lurking there? If you have once seen yourself as you are, and take into account, not only actions but base tendencies, foul, evil thoughts, imagined sins of the flesh, meannesses and basenesses that never have come to the surface, but which you know are bits of you, I do not think that you will have much more to say about 'I am worthy.' The flashing waters of the sea may be all blazing in the sunshine, but if they were drained off, what a frightful sight the mud and the ooze at the bottom would be! Others look at the dancing, glittering surface, but you, if you are a wise man, will go down in the diving–bell sometimes, and for a while stop there at the bottom, and turn a bull's–eye straight upon all the slimy, crawling things that are there, and that would die if they came into the light.

'I am not worthy that Thou shouldest enter under my roof.' But then, as I have said, most of us are strangers to ourselves. The very fact of a course of action which, in other people, we should describe with severe condemnation, being ours, bribes us to indulgence and lenient judgment. Familiarity, too, weakens our sense of the foulness of our own evils. If you have been in the Black Hole all night, you do not know how vitiated the atmosphere is. You have to come out into the fresh air to find out that. We look at the errors of others through a microscope; we look at our own through the wrong end of the telescope; and the one set, when we are in a cynical humour, seem bigger than they are; and the other set always seem smaller.

Now, that clear consciousness of my own sinfulness ought to underlie all my religious feelings and thoughts. I believe, for my part, that no man is in a position to apprehend Christianity rightly who has not made the acquaintance of his own bad self. And I trace a very large proportion of the shallow Christianity of this day as well as of the disproportion in which its various truths are set forth, and the rising of crops of erroneous conceptions just to this, that this generation has to a large extent lost—no, do not let me say this generation, *you and I*—have to a large extent lost, that wholesome consciousness of our own unworthiness and sin.

But on the other hand, let me remind you that the centurion's deeper conviction is not yet the deepest of all, and that whilst the Christianity which ignores sin is sure to be impotent, on the other hand the Christianity which sees very little but sin is bondage and misery, and is impotent too. And there are many of us whose type of religion is far gloomier than it should be, and whose motive of service is far more servile than it ought to be, just because we have not got beyond the centurion, and can only say, 'I am not worthy; I am a poor, miserable sinner.'

III. And so I come to the third point, which is not in my text, but which both my texts converge upon, and that is the deepest truth of all, that worthiness or unworthiness has nothing to do with Christ's love.

When these elders interceded with Jesus, He at once rose and went with them, and that not because of their intercession or of the certificate of character which they had given, but because His own loving heart impelled Him to go to any soul that sought His help. So we are led away from all anxious questionings as to whether we are worthy or no, and learn that, far above all thoughts either of undue self−complacency or of undue self−depreciation, lies the motive for Christ's gracious and healing approach in

'His ceaseless, unexhausted love,
Unmerited and free.'

This is the truth to which the consciousness of sinfulness and unworthiness points us all, for which that consciousness prepares us, in which that consciousness does not melt away, but rather is increased and ceases to be any longer a burden or a pain. Here, then, we come to the very bed−rock of everything, for

'Merit lives from man to man,
But not from man, O Lord, to Thee.'

Jesus Christ comes to us, not drawn by our deserts, but impelled by His own love, and that love pours itself out upon each of us. So we do not need painfully to amass a store of worthiness, nor to pile up our own works, by which we may climb to heaven. 'Say not, who shall ascend up into heaven,' to bring Christ down again, 'but the word is nigh thee, that if thou wilt believe with thine heart, thou shalt be saved.' Worthiness or unworthiness is to be swept clean out of the field, and I am to be content to be a pauper, to owe everything to what I have done nothing to procure, and to cast myself on the sole, all–sufficient mercy of God in Jesus Christ our Lord.

And then comes liberty, and then comes joy. If the gift is given from no consideration of men's deserts, then the only thing that men have to do is to exercise the faith that takes it. As the Apostle says in words that sound very hard and technical, but which, if you would only ponder them, are throbbing with vitality, 'It is of faith that it might be by grace.' Since He gives simply because He loves, the only requisites are the knowledge of our need, the will to receive, the trust that, in clasping the Giver, possesses the gift.

The consciousness of unworthiness will be deepened. The more we know ourselves to be sinful, the more we shall cleave to Christ, and the more we cleave to Christ, the more we shall know ourselves to be sinful. Peter caught a glimpse of what Jesus was when he sat in the boat, and he said, 'Depart from me, for I am a sinful man, O Lord!' But Peter saw both himself and his Lord more clearly, that is more truly, when, subsequent to his black treachery, his brother Apostle said to him concerning the figure standing on the beach in the grey morning, 'It is the Lord,' and he flung himself over the side and floundered through the water to get to his Master's feet. For that is the place for the man who knows himself unworthy. The more we are conscious of our sin, the closer let us cling to our Lord's forgiving heart, and the more sure we are that we have that love which we have not earned, the more shall we feel how unworthy of it we are. As one of the prophets says, with profound meaning, 'Thou shalt be ashamed and confounded, and never open thy mouth any more because of thy transgression, when I am pacified towards thee for all that thou hast done.' The child buries its face on its mother's breast, and feels its fault the more because the loving arms clasp it close.

And so, dear brethren, deepen your convictions, if you are deluded by that notion of merit; deepen your convictions, if you see your own evil so clearly that you see little else. Come into the light, come into the liberty, rise to that great thought, 'Not by works of righteousness which we have done, but by His mercy He saved us.' Have done with the religion of barter, and come to the religion of undeserved grace. If you are going to stop on the commercial level, 'the wages of sin is death'; rise to the higher ground: 'the gift of God is eternal life through Jesus Christ our Lord.'

JESUS AT THE BIER

'And when the Lord saw her, He had compassion on her,
and said unto her, Weep not. 14. And He came and
touched the bier: and they that bare him stood still.
And He said, Young man, I say unto thee, Arise.
15. And he that was dead sat up, and began to speak.
And He delivered him to his mother.'—LUKE vii. 13–15.

We owe our knowledge of this incident to Luke only. He is the Evangelist who specially delights in recording the gracious relations of our Lord with women, and he is also the Evangelist who delights in telling us of unasked miracles which Christ performed. Both of these characteristics unite in this story, and it may have been these, rather than the fact of its being a narrative of a resurrection, that found for it a place in this Gospel.

Be that as it may, it is obvious to remark that this miracle was not wrought with any intention of establishing Christ's claims thereby. Its motive was simply pity; its purpose was merely to comfort a desolate woman whose hope and love and defence were lying stretched on her boy's bier. Was that a sufficient reason for a miracle? People tell us that a test of a spurious miracle is that it is done without any adequate purpose to be served. Jesus Christ thought that to comfort one poor, sorrowful heart was reason enough for putting His hand out, and dragging the prey from the very jaws of death, so loftily did He think of human sorrow and of the comforting thereof.

Now I think we unduly limit the meaning of our Lord's miracles when we regard them as specially intended to authenticate His claims. They are not merely the evidences of revelation; they are themselves a large part of revelation. My purpose in this sermon is to look at this incident from that one point of view, and to try to set clearly before our minds what it shows us of the character and work of Jesus Christ. And there are three things on which I desire to touch briefly. We have Him here revealed to us as the compassionate Drier of all tears; the life−giving Antagonist of death; and as the Re−uniter of parted hearts.

Note, then, these three things.

I. First of all, look at that wonderful revelation that lies here of Jesus Christ as the compassionate Drier of all tears.

The poor woman, buried in her grief, with her eyes fixed on the bier, has no thought for the little crowd that came up the rocky road, as she and her friends are hurrying down it to the place of graves. She was a stranger to Christ, and Christ a stranger to her. The last thing that she would have thought of would have been eliciting any compassion from those who thus fortuitously met her on her sad errand. But Christ looks, and His eye sees far more deeply and far more tenderly into the sorrow of the desolate, childless widow than any human eyes looked. And as swift as was His perception of the sorrow, so swiftly does He throw Himself into sympathy with it. The true human emotion of unmingled pity wells up in His heart and moves Him to action.

And just because the manhood was perfect and sinless, therefore the sympathy of Christ was deeper than any human sympathy, howsoever tender it may be; for what unfits us to feel compassion is our absorption with ourselves. That makes our hearts hard and insensitive, and is the true, 'witches' mark'—to recur to the old fable—the spot where no external pressure can produce sensation. The ossified heart of the selfish man is closed against divine compassion. Since Jesus Christ forgot Himself in pitying men, and Himself 'took our infirmities and bare our sicknesses,' He must have been what none of us are—free from all taint of selfishness, and from all insensibility born of sin.

But there is another step to be taken. That pitying Christ, on the rocky road outside the little Galilean village, feeling all the pain and sorrow of the lonely mother—that is God! 'Lo! this is our God; and we have waited for Him.' Ay! waited through all the uncompassionating centuries, waited in the presence of the false gods, waited whilst men have been talking about an impassive Deity careless in the heavens, over whose serene blessedness no shadow can ever pass. This is our God. No impassive monster that no man can love or care for, but a God with a heart, a God that can pity, a God who, wonderful as it is, can and does enter, in the humanity of Jesus Christ, into a fellow–feeling of our infirmities.

If Jesus Christ in His pity was only a perfect and lovely example of unselfish sympathy such as man can exercise, what in the name of common–sense does it matter to me how much, or how tenderly, He pitied those past generations? The showers and the sunshine of this summer will do as much good to the springing corn in the fields to–day as the pity of a dead, human Christ will do for you and me. In our weaknesses, in our sorrows great and small, in our troubles and annoyances, you and I need, dear brethren, a living Jesus to pity us, there in the heavens, just as He pitied that poor woman outside the gate of Nain. Blessed be God!, we have Him. The human Christ is the manifestation of the Divine, and as we listen to the Evangelist that says, 'When He saw her He had compassion upon her,' we bow our heads and feel that the old psalmist spoke a truth when He said, 'His compassions fail not,' and that the old prophet spoke a truth, the depth of which his experience did not enable him to fathom, when he said that 'in all their afflictions He was afflicted.'

Then, note that the pitying Christ dries the tears before He raises the dead. That is beautiful, I think. 'Weep not,' He says to the woman—a kind of a prophecy that He is going to take away the occasion for weeping; and so He calls lovingly upon her for some movement of hope and confidence towards Himself. With what an ineffable sweetness of cadence in His sympathetic voice these words would be spoken! How often, kindly and vainly, men say to one another, 'Weep not,' when they are utterly powerless to take away or in the smallest degree to diminish the occasion for weeping! And how often, unkindly, in mistaken endeavour to bring about resignation and submission, do well–meaning and erring good people say to mourners in the passion of their sorrow, 'Weep not!' Jesus Christ never dammed back tears when tears were wholesome, and would bring blessing. And Jesus Christ never said, 'Dry your tears,' without stretching out His own hand to do it.

How does He do it? First of all by the assurance of His sympathy. Ah! in that word there came a message to the lonely heart, as there comes a message, dear brethren, to any man or woman among us now who may be fighting with griefs and cares or sorrows, great or small—the assurance that Jesus Christ knows all about your pain and will help you to bear it if you will let Him. The sweet consciousness of Christ's sympathy is the true antidote to excessive grief.

And He dries the tears, not only by the assurance of His sympathy, but by encouraging expectation and hope. When He said, 'Weep not,' He was pledging Himself to do what was needed in order to stay the flow of weeping. And He would encourage us, in the midst of our cares and sorrows and loneliness, not indeed to suppress the natural emotion of sorrow, nor to try after a fantastic and unreal suppression of its wholesome signs, but to weep as though we wept not, because beyond the darkness and the dreariness we see the glimmering of the eternal day. He encourages expectation as the antagonist of sorrow, for the curse of sorrow is that it is ever looking backwards, and the true attitude for all men who have an immortal Christ to trust, and an immortality for themselves to claim, is that

78

not 'backward' should their 'glances be, but forward to their Father's home.' These are the thoughts that dry our tears, the assurance of the sympathy of Christ, and the joyous expectation of a great good to be ours, where beyond those voices there is peace.

Brother! it may be with all of us—for all of us carry some burden of sorrow or care—as it is with the hedgerows and wet ploughed fields to-day; on every spray hangs a raindrop, and in every raindrop gleams a reflected sun. And so all our tears and sorrows may flash into beauty, and sparkle into rainbowed light if the smile of His face falls upon us.

And then, still further, this pitying Christ is moved by His pity to bring unasked gifts. No petition, no expectation, not the least trace of faith or hope drew from Him this mighty miracle. It came welling up from His own heart. And therein it is of a piece with all His work. For the divine love of which Christ is the Bearer, the Agent, and the Channel for us men, 'tarries not for men, nor waiteth for the sons of men,' but before we ask, delights to bestow itself, and gives that which no man ever sought, even the miracles of the Incarnation and Crucifixion of Jesus Christ our Lord. If heaven had waited until men's prayers had forced its gates ere it sent forth its greatest gift, it had waited for ever, and all mankind had perished. God's love flows out of its own expansive and diffusive nature. Its necessity is to impart itself, and its nature and property is to give. A measureless desire to bestow itself, and in itself all good, is the definition of the love of God. And Christ comes 'to the unthankful and to the evil,' bringing a gift which none of us have asked, and giving as much of Himself as He can give, undesired, to every heart, that thereby we may be led to desire these better gifts which cannot be bestowed unless we seek them.

So here we have the compassion of the human Christ, which is the divine compassion, drying all tears and giving unasked blessings.

II. Note, secondly, the further revelation of our Lord here as being the life-giving Antagonist of Death.

There is something exceedingly picturesque, and if I might use the word, dramatic, in the meeting of these two processions outside the city gate, the little crowd of mourners hurrying, according to the Eastern fashion, down the hill to the place of tombs, and the other little group toiling up the hill to the city. There Life and Death stand face to face. Jesus Christ puts out His hand, and lays it upon the bier, not to communicate anything, but simply to arrest its progress. Is it not a parable of His work in the world? His great work is to stop the triumphant march of Death—that grim power which broods like a thundercloud over humanity, and sucks up all brightness into its ghastly folds, and silences all song. He comes and says 'Stop'; and it stands fixed upon the spot. He arrests the march of Death. Not indeed that He touches the mere physical fact. The physical fact is not what men mean by death. It is not what they cower before. What the world shrinks from is the physical fact plus its associations, its dim forebodings, its recoilings from the unknown regions into which the soul goes from out of 'the warm precincts of the cheerful day,' and plus the possibilities of retribution, the certainty of judgment. All these Christ sweeps away, so that we may say, 'He hath abolished Death,' even though we all have to pass through the mere externals of dying, for the dread of Death is gone for ever, if we trust Him.

And then note, still further, we have Christ here as the Life-giver. 'Young man, I say unto thee,

Arise!'

Christ took various methods of imparting His miraculous power. These methods varied, as it would appear, according to the religious necessities of the subjects or beholders of the miracle. Sometimes He touched, sometimes He employed still more material vehicles, such as the clay with which He moistened the eyes of the blind man, and the spittle with which He touched the ears of the deaf. But all these various methods were but helps to feeble faith, and in the case of all the raisings from the dead it is the voice alone that is employed.

So, then, what is the meaning of that majestic 'I say unto thee, Arise'? He claims to work by His own power. Unless Jesus Christ wielded divine authority in a fashion in which no mere human representative and messenger of God ever has wielded it, for Him to stand by that bier and utter, 'I say unto thee, Arise!' was neither more nor less than blasphemy. And yet the word had force. He assumed to act by His own power, and the event showed that He assumed not too much. 'The Son quickeneth whom He will.'

Further, He acts by His bare word. So He did on many other occasions—rebuking the fever and it departs, speaking to the wind and it ceases, calling to the dead and they come forth. And who is He, the bare utterance of whose will is supreme, and has power over material things? Let that centurion whose creed is given to us in the earlier portion of this chapter answer the question. 'I say to my servant, Go! and he goeth; Come! and he cometh; Do this! and he doeth it. Speak Thou, and all the embattled forces of the universe will obey Thine autocratic and sovereign behest,' they 'hearken to His commandments, and do the voice of His word.'

Then note, still further, that this voice of Christ's has power in the regions of the dead. Wherever that young man was, he heard; in whatsoever state or condition he was, his personality felt and obeyed the magnetic force of Christ's will. The fact that the Lord spake and the boy heard, disposes, if it be true, of much error, and clears away much darkness. Then the separation of body and soul *is* a separation and not a destruction. Then consciousness is not a function of the brain, as they tell us. Then man lives wholly after he is dead. Then it is possible for the spirit to come out of some dim region, where we know not, in what condition we know not. Only this we know—that, wherever it is, Christ's will has authority there; and there, too, is obedience to His commandment.

And so let me remind you that this Voice is not only revealing as to Christ's authority and power, and illuminative as to the condition of the disembodied dead, but it is also prophetic as to the future. It tells us that there is nothing impossible or unnatural in that great assurance. 'The hour is coming when they that are in the graves shall hear His voice, and shall come forth.' There shall be for the dead a reunion with a body, which will bring men again into connection with an external universe, and be the precursor of a fuller judgment and an intenser retribution.

Brethren, that Voice that raised one poor bewildered boy to sit up on his bier, and begin to speak—broken exclamations possibly, and stammering words of astonishment—shall be flung, like a trumpet that scatters marvellous sounds, through the sepulchres of the nations and compel all to stand before the throne. You and I will hear it; let us be ready for it.

III. So, lastly, we have here the revelation of our Lord as the Reuniter of parted hearts.

That is a wonderfully beautiful touch, evidently coming from an eye–witness—'He delivered him to his mother.' That was what it had all been done for. The mighty miracle was wrought that that poor weeping woman might be comforted.

May we not go a step further? May we not say, If Jesus Christ was so mindful of the needs of a sorrowful solitary soul here upon earth, will He be less mindful of the enduring needs of loving hearts yonder in the heavens? If He raised this boy from the dead that his mother's arms might twine round him again, and his mother's heart be comforted, will He not in that great Resurrection give back dear ones to empty, outstretched arms, and thereby quiet hungry hearts? It is impossible to suppose that, continuing ourselves, we should be deprived of our loves. These are too deeply engrained and enwrought into the very texture of our being for that to be possible. And it is as impossible that, in the great day and blessed world where all lost treasures are found, hearts that have been sad and solitary here for many a day shall not clasp again the souls of their souls—'and with God be the rest.'

So, though we know very little, surely we may take the comfort of such a thought as this, which should be very blessed and sweet to some of us, and with some assurance of hope may feel that the risen boy at the gate of Nain was not the last lost one whom Christ, with a smile, will deliver to the hearts that mourn for them, and there we 'shall clasp inseparable hands with joy and bliss in over–measure for ever.' 'And so shall we'—they and I, for that is what *we* means—' so shall we ever be with the Lord. Wherefore comfort one another with these words.'

JOHN'S DOUBTS AND CHRIST'S PRAISE

'And the disciples of John shewed him of all these things. 19. And John calling unto him two of his disciples, sent them to Jesus, saying, Art thou He that should come? or look we for another? 20. When the men were come unto Him, they said, John Baptist hath sent us unto Thee, saying, Art Thou He that should come? or look we for another? 21. And in the same hour He cured many of their infirmities and plagues, and of evil spirits; and unto many that were blind He gave sight. 22. Then Jesus, answering, said unto them, Go your way, and tell John what things ye have seen and heard; how that the blind see, the lame walk, the lepers are cleansed, the deaf hear, the dead are raised, to the poor the gospel is preached. 23. And blessed is be, whosoever shall not be offended in Me. 24. And when the messengers of John were departed, He began to speak unto the people concerning John. What went ye out into the wilderness for to see? A reed shaken with the wind? 25. But what went ye out for to see? A man clothed in soft raiment? Behold,

they which are gorgeously apparelled, and live
delicately, are in kings' courts. 26. But what went ye
out for to see? A prophet? Yea, I say unto you, and
much more than a prophet. 27. This is he, of whom it
is written, Behold, I send My messenger before Thy
face, which shall prepare Thy way before Thee. 28. For
I say unto you, Among those that are born of women
there is not a greater prophet than John the Baptist;
but he that is least in the kingdom of God is greater
than he.'—LUKE vii. 18–28.

We take three stages in this passage—the pathetic message from the prisoner, Christ's double answer
to it, and His grand eulogium on John.

I. The message from the prisoner. Had mists of doubt crept over John's clear conviction that Jesus
was the Messiah? Some have thought it incredible that the man who had seen the descending dove,
and heard the voice proclaiming 'This is My beloved Son,' should ever have wavered. But surely our
own experience of the effect of circumstances and moods on our firmest beliefs gives us parallels to
John's doubts. A prison would be especially depressing to the desert–loving Baptist; compelled
inaction would fret his spirit; he would be tempted to think that, if Jesus were indeed the Bridegroom,
he might have spared a thought for the friend of the Bridegroom languishing in Machaerus. Above
all, the kind of works that Jesus was doing did not fill the *role* of the Messiah as he had conceived it.
Where were the winnowing fan, the axe laid to the roots of the trees, the consuming fire? This gentle
friend of publicans and sinners was not what he had expected the One mightier than himself to be.

Probably his disciples went farther in doubting than he did, but his message was the expression of his
own hesitations, as is suggested by the answer being directed to him, not to the disciples. It may have
also been meant to stir Jesus, if He were indeed Messiah, to 'take to Himself His great power.' But the
most natural explanation of it is that John's faith was wavering. The tempest made the good ship
stagger. But reeling faith stretched out a hand to Jesus, and sought to steady itself thereby. We shall
not come to much harm if we carry our doubts as to Him to be cleared by Himself. John's gloomy
prison thoughts may teach us how much our faith may be affected by externals and by changing
tempers of mind, and how lenient, therefore, should be our judgments of many whose trust may falter
when a strain comes. It may also teach us not to write bitter things against ourselves because of the
ups and downs of our religious experience, but yet to seek to resist the impression that circumstances
make on it, and to aim at keeping up an equable temperature, both in the summer of prosperity and
the winter of sorrow.

II. The twofold answer. Its first part was a repetition of the same kind of miracles, the news of which
had evoked John's message; and its second part was simply the command to report these, with one
additional fact—that good tidings were preached to the poor. That seemed an unsatisfactory reply, but
it meant just this—to send John back to think over these deeds of gracious pity and love as well as of
power, and to ask himself whether they were not the fit signs of the Messiah. It is to be noted that the
words which Christ bids the disciples speak to their master would recall the prophecies in Isaiah
xxxv. 5 and lxi. 1, and so would set John to revise his ideas of what prophecy had painted Messiah as

being. The deepest meaning of the answer is that love, pity, healing, are the true signs, not judicial, retributive, destructive energy. John wanted the lightning; Christ told him that the silent sunshine exerts energy, to which the fiercest flash is weak. We need the lesson, for we are tempted to exalt force above love, if not in our thoughts of God, yet in looking at and dealing with men; and we are slow to apprehend the teaching of Bethlehem and Calvary, that the divinest thing in God, and the strongest power among men, is gentle, pitying, self–sacrificing love. Rebuke could not be softer than that which was sent to John in the form of a benediction. To take offence at Jesus, either because He is not what we expect Him to be, or for any other reason, is to shut oneself out from the sum of blessings which to accept Him brings with it.

III. Christ's eulogium on John. How lovingly it was timed! The people had heard John's message and its answer, and might expect some disparaging remarks about his vacillation. But Jesus chooses that very time to lavish unstinted praise on him. That is praise indeed. The remembrance of the Jordan banks, where John had baptized, shapes the first question. The streams of people would not have poured out there to look at the tall reeds swaying in the breeze, nor to listen to a man who was like them. He who would rouse and guide others must have a firm will, and not be moved by any blast that blows. Men will rally round one who has a mind of his own and bravely speaks it, and who has a will of his own, and will not be warped out of his path. The undaunted boldness of John, of whom, as of John Knox, it might be said that 'he never feared the face of man,' was part of the secret of his power. His imprisonment witnessed to it. He was no reed shaken by the wind, but like another prophet, was made 'an iron pillar, and brazen walls' to the whole house of Israel. But he had more than strength of character, he had noble disregard for worldly ease. Not silken robes, like courtiers', but a girdle of camels' hair, not delicate food, but locusts and wild honey, were his. And that was another part of his power, as it must be, in one shape or other, of all who rouse men's consciences, and wake up generations rotting away in self–indulgence. John's fiery words would have had no effect if they had not poured hot from a life that despised luxury and soft ease. If a man is once suspected of having his heart set on material good, his usefulness as a Christian teacher is weakened, if not destroyed. But even these are not all, for Jesus goes on to attest that John was a prophet, and something even more; namely, the forerunner of the Messiah. As, in a royal progress, the nearer the king's chariot the higher the rank, and they who ride just in front of him are the chiefest, so John's proximity in order of time to Jesus distinguished him above those who had heralded him long ages ago. It is always true that, the closer we are to Him, the more truly great we are. The highest dignity is to be His messenger. We must not lose sight of the exalted place which Jesus by implication claims for Himself by such a thought, as well as by the quotation from Malachi, and by the alteration in it of the original 'My' and 'Me' to 'Thy' and 'Thee.' He does not mean that John was the greatest man that ever lived, as the world counts greatness, but that in the one respect of relation to Him, and consequent nearness to the kingdom, he surpassed all.

The scale employed to determine greatness in this saying is position in regard to the kingdom, and while John is highest of those who (historically) were without it, because (historically) he was nearest to it, the least *in* it is greater than the greatest without. The spiritual standing of John and the devout men before him is not in question; it is their position towards the manifestation of the kingdom in time that is in view. We rejoice to believe that John and many a saint from early days were subjects of the King, and have been 'saved into His everlasting kingdom.' But Jesus would have us think greatly of the privilege of living in the light of His coming, and of being permitted by faith to enter His kingdom. The lowliest believer knows more, and possesses a fuller life born of the Spirit, than the greatest born of woman, who has not received that new birth from above.

GREATNESS IN THE KINGDOM

'He that is least in the kingdom of God is greater than he.'—LUKE vii. 28.

We were speaking in a preceding sermon about the elements of true greatness, as represented in the life and character of John the Baptist. As we remarked then, our Lord poured unstinted eulogium upon the head of John, in the audience of the people, at the very moment when he showed himself weakest. 'None born of women' was, in Christ's eyes, 'greater than John the Baptist.' The eulogium, authoritative as it was, was immediately followed by a depreciation as authoritative, from Christ's lips: 'The least in the kingdom is greater than he.' Greatness depends, not on character, but on position. The contrast that is drawn is between being *in* and being *out* of the kingdom; and this man, great as he was among them 'that are born of women,' stood but upon the threshold; therefore, and only therefore, and in that respect, was he 'less than the least' who was safely within it.

Now, there are two things in these great words of our Lord to notice by way of introduction. One is the calm assumption which He makes of authority to marshal men, to stand above the greatest of them, and to allocate their places, because He knows all about them; and the other is the equally calm and strange assumption of authority which He makes, in declaring that the least within the kingdom is greater than the greatest without. For the kingdom is embodied in Him, its King, and He claimed to have opened the door of entrance into it. 'The kingdom of God,' or of heaven—an old Jewish idea—means, whatever else it means, an order of things in which the will of God is supreme. Jesus Christ says, 'I have come to make that real reign of God, in the hearts of men, possible and actual.' So He presents Himself in these words as infinitely higher than the greatest within, or the greatest without the kingdom, and as being Himself the sovereign arbiter of men's claims to greatness. Greater than the greatest is He, the King; for if to be barely across the threshold stamps dignity upon a man, what shall we say of the conception of His own dignity which He formed who declared that He sat on the throne of that kingdom, and was its Monarch?

I. The first thought that I suggest is the greatness of the little ones in the kingdom.

As I have said, our Lord puts the whole emphasis of His classification on men's position. Inside all are great, greater than any that are outside. The least in the one order is greater than the greatest in the other. So, then, the question comes, How does a man step across that threshold? Our Lord evidently means the expression to be synonymous with His true disciples. We may avail ourselves, in considering how men come to be in the kingdom, of His own words. Once He said that unless we *received* it as little children, we should never be *within* it. There the blending of the two metaphors adds force and completeness to the thought. The kingdom is without us, and is offered to us; we must receive it as a gift, and it must come into us before we can be in it. The point of comparison between the recipients of the kingdom and little children does not lie in any sentimental illusions about the innocence of childhood, but in its dependence, in its absence of pretension, in its sense of clinging helplessness, in its instinctive trust. All these things in the child are natural, spontaneous, unreflecting, and therefore of no value. You and I have to think ourselves back to them, and to work ourselves back to them, and to fight ourselves back to them, and to strip off their opposites which gather round us in the course of our busy, effortful life. Then they become worth infinitely more than their instinctive analogues in the infant. The man's absence of pretension and consciousness of helplessness and dependent trust are beautiful and great, and through them the kingdom of God, with all its lights and glories, pours into his heart, and he himself steps into it, and becomes a true servant and subject of the King.

Then there is another word of the Master's, equally illuminative, as to how we pass into the kingdom, when He spoke to the somewhat patronising Pharisee that came to talk to Him by night, and condescended to give the young Rabbi a certificate of approval from the Sanhedrim, 'We know that Thou art a Teacher come from God.' Christ's answer was, in effect, 'Knowing will not serve your turn. There is something more than that wanted: "Except a man be born of water, and of the Spirit, he cannot enter into the kingdom of God."' So, another condition of entering the kingdom—that is, of coming for myself into the attitude of lowly, glad submission to God's will—is the reception into our natures of a new life–principle, so that we are not only, like the men whom Christ compared with John, 'born of women,' but by a higher birth are made partakers of a higher life, and born of the Spirit of God. These are the conditions—on our side the reception with humility, helplessness, dependent trust like those of children, on God's side the imparting, in answer to that dependence and trust, of a higher principle of life—these are the conditions on which we can pass out of the realm of darkness into the kingdom of the Son of His love.

This being so, then we have next to consider the greatness that belongs to the least of those who thus have crossed the threshold, and have come to exercise joyous submission to the will of God. The highest dignity of human nature, the loftiest nobility of which it is capable, is to submit to God's will. 'Man's chief end is to glorify God.' There is nothing that leads life to such sovereign power as when we lay all our will at His feet, and say, 'Break, bend, mould, fashion it as Thou wilt.' We are in a higher position when we are in God's hand. His tools and the pawns on His board, than we are when we are seeking to govern our lives at our pleasure. Dignity comes from submission, and they who keep God's commandments are the aristocracy of the world.

Then, further, there comes the thought that the greatness that belongs to the least of the little ones within the kingdom springs from their closer relation to the Saviour, whose work they more clearly know and more fully appropriate. It is often said that the Sunday–school child who can repeat the great text, 'God so loved the world that He gave His only begotten Son, that whosoever believeth in Him should not perish, but have everlasting life,' stands far above prophet, righteous man, and John himself. This is not exactly true, for knowledge of the truth is not what introduces into the kingdom; but it is true that the weakest, the humblest, the most ignorant amongst us, who grasps that truth of the God–sent Son whose death is the world's life, and who lives, therefore, nestling close to Jesus Christ, walks in a light far brighter than the twilight that shone upon the Baptist, or the yet dimmer rays that reached prophets and righteous men of old. It is not a question of character; it is a question of position. True greatness is regulated, by closeness to Jesus Christ, and by apprehension and appropriation of His work to myself. The dwarf on the shoulders of the giant sees further than the giant; and 'the least in the kingdom,' being nearer to Jesus Christ than the men of old could ever be, because possessing the fuller revelation of God in Him, is greater than the greatest without. They who

85

possess, even in germ, that new life–principle which comes in the measure of a man's faith in Christ, thereby are lifted above saints and martyrs and prophets of old. The humblest Christian grasps a fuller Christ, and therein possesses a fuller spiritual life, than did the ancient heroes of the faith. Christ's classification here says nothing about individual character. It says nothing about the question as to the possession of true religion or of spiritual life by the ancient saints, but it simply declares that because we have a completer revelation, we therefore, grasping that revelation, are in a more blessed position, 'God having provided some better thing for us, that they without us should not be made perfect.' The lowest in a higher order is higher than the highest in a lower order. As the geologist digs down through the strata, and, as he marks the introduction of new types, declares that the lowest specimen of the mammalia is higher than the highest preceding of the reptiles or of the birds, so Christ says, 'He that is lowest in the kingdom of heaven is greater than he.'

Brethren! these thoughts should stimulate and should rebuke us that having so much we make so little use of it. We know God more fully, and have mightier motives to serve Him, and larger spiritual helps in serving Him than had any of the mighty men of old. We have a fuller revelation than Abraham had; have we a tithe of his faith? We have a mightier Captain of the Lord's host with us than stood before Joshua; have we any of his courage? We have a tenderer and fuller revelation of the Father than had psalmists of old; are our aspirations greater after God, whom we know so much better, than were theirs in the twilight of revelation? A savage with a shell and a knife of bone will make delicate carvings that put our workers, with their modern tools, to shame. A Hindoo, weaving in a shed, with bamboos for its walls and palm leaves for its roof, and a rude loom, the same as his ancestors used three thousand years ago, will turn out muslins that Lancashire machinery cannot rival. We are exalted in position, let us see to it that Abraham, and Isaac, and Jacob, and all the saints, do not put us to shame, lest the greatest should become the guiltiest, and exaltation to heaven should lead to dejection to hell.

II. Notice the littleness of the great ones in the kingdom.

Our Lord here recognises the fact that there will be varieties of position, that there will be an outer and an inner court in the Temple, and an aristocracy in the kingdom. 'In a great house there are not only vessels of gold and silver, but of wood and of clay.' When a man passes into the territory, it still remains an open question how far into the blessed depths of the land he will penetrate. Or, to put away the figure, if as Christian people we have laid hold of Jesus Christ, and in Him have received the kingdom and the new life–power, there still remains the question, how much and how faithfully we shall utilise the gifts, and what place in the earthly experience and manifestation of His kingdom we shall occupy. There are great and small within it.

So it comes to be a very important question for us all, how we may not merely be content, as so many of us are, with having scraped inside and just got both feet across the boundary line, but may become great in the kingdom. Let me answer that question in three sentences. The little ones in Christ's kingdom become great by the continual exercise of the same things which admitted them there at first. If greatness depends on position in reference to Jesus Christ, the closer we come to Him and the more we keep ourselves in loving touch and fellowship with Him, the greater in the kingdom we shall be. Again, the little ones in Christ's kingdom become great by self–forgetting service. 'He that will be great among you, let him be your minister.' Self–regard dwarfs a man, self–oblivion magnifies him. If ever you come across, even in the walks of daily life, traces in people of thinking much of themselves, and of living mainly for themselves, down go these men in your estimation at once. Whether you have a beam of the same sort in your own eye or not, you can see the mote in theirs, and you lower your appreciation of them immediately. It is the same in Christ's kingdom, only in an infinitely loftier fashion. There, to become small is to become great. Again, the little ones in Christ's kingdom become great, not only by cleaving close to the Source of all greatness, and deriving thence a higher dignity by the suppression and crucifixion of self−esteem and self−regard, but by continual obedience to their Lord's commandment. As He said on the Sermon on the Mount, 'Whoso shall do and teach one of the least of these commandments shall be called great in the kingdom of heaven.' The higher we are, the more we are bound to punctilious obedience to the smallest injunction. The more we are obedient to the lightest of His commandments, the greater we become. Thus the least in the kingdom may become the greatest there, if only, cleaving close to Christ, he forgets himself, and lives for others, and does the Father's will.

III. Lastly, I travel for a moment beyond my text, and note the perfect greatness of all in the perfected kingdom.

The very notion of a kingdom of God established in reality, however imperfectly here on earth, demands that somewhere, and some time, and somehow, there should be an adequate, a universal and an eternal manifestation and establishment of it. If, here and now, dotted about over the world, there are men who, with much hindrance and many breaks in their obedience, are still the subjects of that realm, and trying to do the will of God, unless we are reduced to utter bewilderment intellectually, there must be a region in which that will shall be perfectly done, shall be continually done, shall be universally done. The obedience that we render to Him, just because it is broken by so much rebellion, slackened by so much indifference, hindered by so many clogs, hampered by so many limitations, points, by its attainments and its imperfections alike, to a region where the clogs and limitations and interruptions shall have all vanished, and the will of the Lord shall be the life and the light thereof.

So there rises up before us the fair prospect of that heavenly kingdom, in which all that here is interrupted and thwarted tendency shall have become realised effect.

That state must necessarily be a state of continual advance. For if greatness consists in apprehension and appropriation of Christ and His work, there are no limits to the possible expansion and assimilation of a human heart to Him, and the wealth of His glory is absolutely boundless. An infinite Christ to be assimilated, and an indefinite capacity of assimilation in us, make the guarantee that eternity shall see the growing progress of the subjects of the kingdom, in resemblance to the King.

If there is this endless progress, which is the only notion of heaven that clothes with joy and peace the awful thought of unending existence, then there will be degrees there too, and the old distinction of 'least' and 'greatest' in the kingdom will subsist to the end. The army marches onwards, but they are not all abreast. They that are in front do not intercept any of the blessings or of the light that come to the rearmost files; and they that are behind are advancing and envy not those who lead the march.

Only let us remember, brother, that the distinction of least and great in the kingdom, in its imperfect forms on earth, is carried onwards into the kingdom in its perfect form into heaven. The highest point of our attainment here is the starting–point of our progress yonder. 'An entrance shall be ministered'; it may be 'ministered abundantly,' or we may be 'saved yet so as by fire.' Let us see to it that, being least in our own eyes, we belong to the greatest in the kingdom. And that we may, let us hold fast by the Source of all greatness, Christ Himself, and so we shall be launched on a career of growing greatness, through the ages of eternity. To be joined to Him is greatness, however small the world may think us. To be separate from Him is to be small, though the hosannas of the world may misname us great.

THWARTING GOD'S PURPOSE

'The Pharisees and lawyers rejected the counsel of God
against themselves, being not baptized of Him.'
—LUKE vii. 30.

Our Lord has just been pouring unstinted praise on the head of John the Baptist. The eulogium was tenderly timed, for it followed, and was occasioned by the expression, through messengers, of John's doubts of Christ's Messiahship. Lest these should shake the people's confidence in the Forerunner, and make them think of him as weak and shifting, Christ speaks of him in the glowing words which precede my text, and declares that he is no 'reed shaken with the wind.'

But what John was was of less moment to Christ's listeners than was what they had done with John's message. So our Lord swiftly passes from His eulogium upon John to the sharp thrust of the personal application to His hearers. In the context He describes the twofold treatment which that message had received; and so describes it as, in the description, to lay bare the inmost characteristics of the reception or rejection of the message. As to the former, He says that the mass of the common people, and the outcast publicans, 'justified God'; by which remarkable expression seems to be meant that their reception of John's message and baptism acknowledged God's righteousness in accusing them of sin and demanding from them penitence.

On the other hand, the official class, the cultivated people, the orthodox respectable people—that is to say, the dead formalists—'rejected the counsel of God against themselves.'

Now the word 'rejected' would be more adequately rendered '*frustrated,*' thwarted, made void, or some such expression, as indeed it is employed in other places of Scripture, where it is translated 'disannulled,' 'made void,' and the like. And if we take that meaning, there emerge from this great word of the Master's two thoughts, that to disbelieve God's word is to thwart God's purpose, and that to thwart His purpose is to harm ourselves.

I. And I remark, first, that the sole purpose which God has in view in speaking to us men is our blessing.

I suppose I need not point out to you that 'counsel' here does not mean *advice*, but *intention*. In regard to the matter immediately in hand, God's purpose or *counsel* in sending the Forerunner was, first of all, to produce in the minds of the people a true consciousness of their own sinfulness and need of cleansing; and so to prepare the way for the coming of the Messiah, who should bring the inward gift which they needed, and so secure their salvation. The intention was, first, to bring to repentance, but that was a preparation for bringing to them full forgiveness and cleansing. And so we may fairly widen the thought into the far greater and nobler one which applies especially to the message of God in Jesus Christ, and say that the only design which God has in view, in the gospel of His Son, is the highest blessing—that is, the salvation—of every man to whom it is spoken.

Now, by the gospel, which, as I say, has thus one single design in the divine mind, I mean, what I think the New Testament means, the whole body of truths which underlie and flow from the fact of Christ's Death, Resurrection, and Ascension, which in brief are these—man's sin, man's helplessness, the Incarnation of the Son of God, the Death of Christ as the sacrifice for the world's sin; Faith, as the one hand by which we grasp the blessing, and the gift of a Divine Spirit which follows upon our faith, and bestows upon us sonship and likeness to God, purity of life and character, and heaven at last. That, as I take it, is in the barest outline what is meant by the gospel of Jesus Christ.

And now I want to press upon you, dear friends, that that great and sublime body of truths made known to us, as I believe, from God Himself, has one sole object in view and none beside—viz. that every man who hears it may partake of the salvation and the hope which it brings. It has a twofold effect, alas! but the twofold effect does not imply a twofold purpose. There have been schemes of so−called Christian theology which have darkened the divine character in this respect, and have obscured the great thought that God has one end in view, and one only, when He speaks to us in all good faith, desiring nothing else but only that we shall be gathered into His heart, and made partakers of His love. He is not willing that any should perish, but that all should come to the knowledge of the truth.

If so, the question comes very sharp and direct to each of us, Is that gospel fulfilling its purpose in me? There are many subordinate good things flowing from the Christian revelation, such as blessings for social outward life, which are as flowers that spring up in its path; but unless it has effected its one purpose in regard to you and me, it has failed altogether. God meant His word to save your soul. Has it done so? It is a question that any man can answer if he—will be honest with himself.

Further, this single purpose of the divine speech embraces in its intention each of the hearers of that message. I want to gather the wide−flowing generality, 'God so loved the world that He sent His Son that whosoever believeth,' into this sharp point, 'God so loved *me*, that He sent His Son that *I*, believing, might have life eternal.' We shall never understand the universality of Christianity until we have appreciated the personality and the individuality of its message to each of us. God does not lose thee in the crowd, do not thou lose thyself in it, nor fail to apprehend that *thou* art personally meant by His broadest declarations. It is *thy* salvation that Christ had in view when He became man and died on the Cross; and it is thy salvation that He had in view when He said to His servants, 'Go into *all* the world'—there is universality—'and preach the Gospel to *every* creature'—there is individuality.

Then, further, God is verily seeking to accomplish this purpose even now, by my lips, in so far as I am true to my Master and my message. The outward appearance of what we are about now is that I am trying, lamely enough, to speak to you. You may judge this service by rules of rhetoric, or anything else you like. But you have not got to the bottom of things unless you feel, as I am praying that every one of you may feel, that even with all my imperfections on my head—and I know them better than you can tell me them—I, like all true men who are repeating God's message as they have caught it, neither more nor less, and have sunk themselves in it, may venture to say, as the Apostle said: 'Now, then, we are ambassadors for God, as though God did beseech by us, we pray in Christ's stead.' John's voice was a revelation of God's purpose, and the voice of every true preacher of Jesus Christ is no less so.

II. Secondly, this single divine purpose, or 'counsel,' may be thwarted.

'They frustrated the counsel of God.' Of all the mysteries of this inexplicable world, the deepest, the mother–mystery of all, is, that given an infinite will and a creature, the creature can thwart the infinite. I said that was the mystery of mysteries: 'Our wills are ours we know not how,'—No! indeed we don't!—'Our wills are ours to make them Thine.' But that purpose necessarily requires the possibility of the alternative that our wills are ours, and we *refuse* 'to make them Thine.' The possibility is mysterious; the reality of the fact is tragic and bewildering. We need no proof except our own consciousness; and if that were silenced we should have the same fact abundantly verified in the condition of the world around us, which sadly shows that not yet is God's 'will' done 'on earth as it is in heaven,' but that men can and do lift themselves up against God and set themselves in antagonism to His most gracious purposes. And whosoever refuses to accept God's message in Christ and God's salvation revealed in that message is thus setting himself in battle array against the infinite, and so far as in him lies (that is to say, in regard to his own personal condition and character) is thwarting God's most holy will.

Now, brethren, I said that there was only one thought in the divine heart when He sent His Son, and that was to save you and me and all of us. But that thought cannot but be frustrated, and made of none effect, as far as the individual is concerned, by unbelief. For there is no way by which any human being can become participant of the spiritual blessings which are included in that great word 'salvation,' except by simple trust in Jesus Christ. I cannot too often and earnestly insist upon this plain truth, which, plain as it is, is often obscured, and by many people is never apprehended at all, that when the Apostle says 'It is the power of God unto salvation to every one that believeth,' he is laying down no limitation of the universality or of the adequacy of that power, but is only setting forth the plain condition, inherent in the very nature of things and in the nature of the blessings bestowed, that if a man does not trust God he cannot get them, and God cannot give him them, though His heart yearns to give him them He cannot do it. How can any man get any good out of a medicine if he locks his teeth and won't take it? How can any truth that I refuse to believe produce any effect upon me? How is it possible for the blessings of forgiveness and cleansing to be bestowed upon men who neither know their need of forgiveness nor desire to be washed from their sins? How can there be the flowing of the Divine Spirit into a heart which is tightly barred against His entrance? In a word, how a man can be saved with the salvation that the Gospel offers, except on condition of his simple trust in Christ the Giver, I, for my part, fail to see. And so I remind you that the thwarting of God's counsel is the awful prerogative of unbelief.

Then, note that, in accordance with the context, you do not need to put yourselves to much effort in order to bring to nought God's gracious intention about you. 'They thwarted the counsel of God, being *not* baptized of Him.' They did not *do* anything. They simply did nothing, and that was enough. There is no need for violent antagonism to the counsel. Fold your hands in your lap, and the gift will not come into them. Clench them tightly, and put them behind your back, and it cannot come. A negation is enough to ruin a man. You do not need to do anything to slay yourselves. In the ocean, when the lifebelt is within reach, simply forbear to put out your hand to it, and down you will go, like a stone, to the very bottom. 'They rejected the counsel,' 'being *not*'—and that was all.

Further, the people who are in most danger of frustrating God's gracious purpose are not blackguards, not men and women steeped to the eyebrows in the stagnant pool of sensuous sin, but clean, respectable church–and–chapel–going, sermon–hearing, doctrine–criticising Pharisees. The man or woman who is led away by the passions that are lodged in his or her members is not so hopeless as the man into whose spiritual nature there has come the demon of self–complacent righteousness, or who, as is the case with many a man and woman sitting in these pews now, has listened to, or at all events, has *heard*, men preaching, as I am trying to preach, ever since childhood, and has never done anything in consequence. These are the hopeless people. The Pharisees—and there are hosts of their great–great–grandchildren in all our congregations—'the Pharisees ... frustrated the counsel of God.'

III. Lastly, this thwarting brings self–inflicted harm.

A little skiff of a boat comes athwart the bows of a six thousand ton steamer, with triple–expansion engines, that can make twenty knots an hour. What will become of the skiff, do you think? You can thwart God's purpose about yourself, but the great purpose goes on and on. And 'Who hath hardened himself against Him and prospered?' You can thwart the purpose, but it is kicking against the pricks.

Consider what you lose when you will have nothing to do with that divine counsel of salvation. Consider not only what you lose, but what you bring upon yourself; how you bind your sin upon your hearts; how you put out your hands, and draw disease and death nearer to yourselves; how you cannot turn away from, or be indifferent to, the gracious, sweet, pleading voice that speaks to you from the Cross and the Throne, without doing damage—in many more ways than I have time to enlarge upon now—to your own character and inward nature. And consider how there lie behind dark and solemn results about which it does not become me to speak, but which it still less becomes me—believing as I do—to suppress. 'After death the judgment'; and what will become of the thwarters of the divine counsel then?

These wounds, many, deep, deadly as they are, are self–inflicted. There do follow, on God's message and unbelief of it, awful consequences; but these are not His intention. They are the results of our misuse of His gracious word. 'Oh, Israel!' wailed the prophet, 'thou hast destroyed *thyself*' Man's happiness or woe is his own making, and his own making only. There is no creature in heaven or earth or hell that is chargeable with your loss but yourself. We are our own betrayers, our own murderers, our own accusers, our own avengers, and—I was going to say, and it is true —our own hell.

Dear friends! this message comes to you once more now, that Jesus Christ has died for your sins, and that if you will trust Him as your Saviour, and obey Him as your Sovereign, you will he saved with an everlasting salvation. Even through my lips God speaks to you. What are you going to do with His message? Are you going to receive it, and 'justify' Him, or are you going to reject it, and thwart Him?

You thwart Him if you treat my words now as a mere sermon to be criticised and forgotten; you thwart Him if you do anything with His message except take it to your heart and rest wholly upon it. Unless you do you are suicides; and neither God, nor man, nor devil is responsible for your destruction. He can say to you, as His servant said: 'Your blood be upon your own heads; I am clean.' Jesus Christ is calling to every one of us, 'Turn ye! turn ye! Why will ye die? As I live, I have no pleasure in the death of the wicked.'

A GLUTTONOUS MAN AND A WINEBIBBER

'The Son of man is come eating and drinking; and ye say, Behold a gluttonous man, and a winebibber, a friend of publicans and sinners!'—LUKE vii. 34.

Jesus Christ very seldom took any notice of the mists of calumny that drifted round Him. 'When He was reviled He reviled not again.' If ever He did allude to them it was for the sake of the people who were harming themselves by uttering them. So here, without the slightest trace of irritation, He quotes a malignant charge which was evidently in the popular mouth, and of which we should never have known if He had not repeated it; not with anger, but simply in order that He might point to the capricious inconsistency of finding fault with John and Himself on precisely opposite grounds. The former did not suit because he came neither eating nor drinking. Well, if His asceticism did not please, surely the geniality of a Christ who comes doing both will be hailed. But He is rejected like the other. What is the cause of this dislike that can look two different ways at once? Not the traits that it alleges, but something far deeper, a dislike to the heavenly wisdom of which John and Jesus were messengers. The children of wisdom would see that there was right in both courses; the children of folly would condemn them both. If the message is unwelcome, nothing that the messenger can say or do will be right.

The same kind of thing is common to–day. Never mind consistency, find fault with Christianity on all its sides, and with all its preachers, though you have to contradict yourself in doing so. Object to this man that he is too learned and doctrinal; to that one that he is too illiterate, and gives no food for thought; to this one that he is always thundering condemnation; to that one that he is always running over with love; to this one that he is perpetually harping upon duties; to that other one that he is up in the clouds, and forgets the tasks of daily life; to this one that he is sensational; to that one that he is dull; and so on, and so on. The generation that liked neither piping nor mourning has its representatives still.

But my business now is not with the inconsistency of the objectors to John and Jesus, but simply with this caricature which He quotes from them of some of His characteristics. It is a distorted refraction of the beam of light that comes from His face, through the muddy, thick medium of their prejudice. And if we can, I was going to say, pull it straight again, we shall see something of His glories. I take the two clauses of my text separately because they are closely connected with our design, and cover different ground.

I. I ask you to note, first, the enemies' attestation to Christ's genial participation in the joys and necessities of common life.

'The Son of man came eating and drinking.' There is nothing that calumny, if it be malignant enough, cannot twist into an accusation; and out of glorious and significant facts, full of lessons and containing strong buttresses of the central truth of the Gospel, these people made this charge, 'a winebibber and gluttonous.' The facts were facts; the inferences were slanders.

Notice how precious, how demonstrative of the very central truth of Christianity, is that plain fact, 'The Son of man came eating and drinking.' Then that pillar of all our hope, the Incarnation of the word of God, stands irrefragable. Sitting at tables, hungering in the wilderness, faint by the well, begging a draught of water from a woman, and saying on His Cross 'I thirst!'—He is the Incarnation of Deity, the manifestation of God in the flesh. Awe and mystery and reverence and hope and trust clasp that fact, in which prejudice and dislike could only find occasion for a calumny.

By eating and drinking He declared that 'forasmuch as the children were partakers of flesh and blood, He Himself likewise took part in the same.' If it is true that every spirit that confesseth that Jesus Christ is come in the flesh is of God,' then it is true that no miracle in His life, nor any of the supernatural glories which we are accustomed to regard as evidences of His majesty, are more blessed, or more important as revelations of His nature, than the fact that 'the Son of man came eating and drinking.'

But, still further, mark how the truth which gave colour to the slander attests that Jesus Christ presents to the world the highest type of manhood. The ideal for life is not the suppression, but the consecration, of material satisfactions and pleasures of appetite. And they are likest to the Master who, like the Master, come eating and drinking, and yet ever hold all appetites and desires rigidly under control, and subordinate them all to loftier purposes. John the Baptist could be an ascetic; the Pattern Man must not be.

The highest type of religion, as it is shown to us in His perfect life, includes the acceptance of all pure material blessings. Asceticism is second best; the religion that can take and keep secondary all outward and transitory sources of enjoyment, and can hallow common life, is loftier than all pale hermits and emaciated types of sanctity, who preserve their purity only by avoiding things which it were nobler to enjoy and to subdue.

There is nothing more striking about the Old Testament than the fact that its heroes and saints were kindly with their kind, and took part in common life, accepting, enjoying its blessings. They were warriors, statesmen, shepherds, vinedressers; 'they bought, they sold, they planted, they builded; they married and were given in marriage,' and all the while they were the saints of God. That was a nobler type of religion than the one that came after it, into which Jesus Christ was born. When devotion cools it crusts; and the crust is superstition and formalism and punctilious attention to the proprieties of worship and casuistry, instead of joyful obedience to a law, and abstinence from, instead of sanctification of, earthly delights and supplies.

So, protesting against all that, and showing the more excellent way, and hallowing the way because He trod it, 'the Son of man came eating and drinking.' Hence—forward every table may be a communion table, and every meal may be a sacrament, eaten in obedience to His dying injunction: 'This do in remembrance of Me.' If we can feel that Christ sits with us at the feast, the feast will be pure and good. If it is of such a sort as that we dare not fancy Him keeping us company there, it is no place for us. Wherever Jesus Christ went the consecration of His presence lingers still; whatever Jesus Christ did His servants may do, if in the same spirit and in the same manner.

He hallowed infancy when He lay an infant in His mother's arms; He hallowed childhood when, as a boy, He was obedient to His parents; He hallowed youth during all those years of quiet seclusion and unnoticed service in Nazareth; He hallowed every part of human life and experience by bearing it. Love is consecrated because He loved; tears are sacred because He wept; life is worship, or may be made so, because He passed through it; and death itself is ennobled and sanctified because He has died.

Only let us remember that, if we are to exercise this blessed hallowing of common things, of which He has set us the example, we must use them as He did; that is, in such sort as that our communion with God shall not be broken thereby, and that nothing in them shall darken the vision and clip the wings of the aspiring and heavenward–gazing spirit. Brethren! the tendency of this day—and one rejoices, in many respects, that it is so—is to revolt against the extreme of narrowness in the past that prescribed and proscribed a great many arbitrary and unnecessary abstinences and practices as the sign of a Christian profession. But whilst I would yield to no man in my joyful application of the principle that underlies that great fact that 'He came eating and drinking,' I do wish at this point to put in a *caveat* which perhaps may not be so welcome to some of you as the line of thought that I have been pursuing. It is this: it is an error to quote Christ's example as a cover for luxury and excess, and grasping at material enjoyments which are not innocent in themselves, or are mixed up with much that is not innocent. There is many a table spread by so–called Christian people where Jesus Christ will not sit. Many a man darkens his spirit, enfeebles his best part, blinds himself to the things beyond, by reason of his taking the liberty, as he says, which Christianity, broadly and generously interpreted, gives, of participating in all outward delights. I have said that asceticism is not the highest, but it is sometimes necessary. It is better to enjoy and to subdue than to abstain and to suppress, but abstinence and suppression are often essential to faithfulness and noble living. If I find that my enjoyment of innocent things harms me, or is tending to stimulate cravings beyond my control; or if I find that abstinence from innocent things increases my power to help a brother, and to fight against a desolating sin; or if things good and innocent in themselves, and in some respects desirable and admirable, like the theatre, for instance, are irretrievably intertwisted with evil things, then Christ's example is no plea for our sharing in such. It is better for us to cut off the offending hand, and so, though maimed, to enter into life, than to keep two hands and go into the darkness of death. Jesus Christ 'came eating and drinking,' and therefore the highest and the best thing is that Christian people should innocently, and with due control, and always keeping themselves in touch with God, enjoy all outward blessings, only subject to this law, 'whether ye eat or drink, or whatsoever we do, to do all to the glory of God,' and remembering this warning, 'He that soweth to the flesh shall of the flesh reap corruption.'

II. Now, secondly, notice the enemies' witness that Christ is the Friend of outcasts.

As I said about the other charge, so I say of this, the facts were facts, the inferences were errors. The slanderers saw, as nobody could help seeing, that there was a strange kind of mutual attraction between Jesus and publicans and sinners; that harlots as well as little children seemed to be drawn to

Him; and that He obviously delighted in the company of those at whose presence, partly from pride, partly from national enmity, partly from heartless self–righteousness, Pharisaism gathered its dainty skirts around itself in abhorrence, lest a speck should fall upon their purity. That being the fact, low natures, who always misunderstand lofty ones, because they can only believe in motives as low as their own, said of Jesus, 'Ah! you can tell what sort of a man He is by the company He keeps. He is the friend of publicans because He is a bad Jew; the friend of sinners because He likes their wicked ways.'

There was a mysterious sense of sympathy which drew Jesus Christ to these poor people and drew them to Him. It would have been a long while before any penitent woman would have come in and wept over the feet of Gamaliel and his like. It would have been a long while before any sinful men would have found their way, with tears and yet with trust, to these self–righteous hypocrites. But perfect purity somehow draws the impure, though assumed sanctity always repels them. And it is a sign, not that a man is bad, but that he is good in a Christlike fashion, if the outcasts that durst not come near your respectable people find themselves drawn to Him. Oh! if there were more of us liker Jesus Christ in our purity, there would be more of us who would deserve the calumny which is praise—'the friend of sinners.'

It was an attestation of His love, as I need not remind you. I suppose there is nothing more striking in the whole wonderful and unique picture of Jesus Christ drawn in the Gospels than the way in which two things, which we so often fancy to be contradictory, blend in the most beautiful harmony in Him—viz. infinite tenderness and absolute condemnation of transgression. To me the fact that these two characteristics are displayed in perfect harmony in the life of Jesus Christ as written in these Gospels, is no small argument for believing the historical veracity of the picture there drawn. For I do not know a harder thing for a dramatist, or a romancer, or a legend–monger to effect than to combine, in one picture—without making the combination monstrous–these two things, perfect purity and perfect love for the impure.

But, dear brethren, remember, that if we are to believe Jesus Christ's own words, that strange love of His, which embraced in its pure clasp the outcasts, was not only the love of a perfect Man, but it was the love of God Himself. 'He that hath seen Me hath seen the Father.' When we see Jesus Christ looking across the valley to the city, with tears in His sad and gentle eyes; and when we see harlots and sinners coming near Him with new hope, and a strange consciousness of a fascination which He wields; and when we see Him opening His heart to all the impure, just as He laid His clean hand on the leper's ulcers, let us rejoice to believe that the Friend of publicans and sinners is God manifest in the flesh.

Then, still further, this wondrous, seeking love of His for all the outcasts is the sign to us of His boundless hopefulness concerning the most degraded.

The world talks of races too low to be elevated, of men too hardened to be softened. Jesus Christ walks through the hospitals of this world, and nowhere sees incurables. His hope is boundless, because, first of all, He sees the dormant possibilities that slumber in the most degraded; and because, still more, He knows that He bears in Himself a power that will cleanse the foulest and raise the most fallen. There are some metals that resist all attempts to volatilise them by the highest temperature producible in our furnaces. Carry them up into the sun and they will all pass into vapour. No man or woman who ever lived, or will live, is so absolutely besotted, and held by the chains of his or her sins, as that Jesus cannot set them free. His hope for outcasts is boundless, because He knows that every sin can be cleansed by His precious blood. Therefore, Christianity should know nothing of desperate cases. There should be no incurables in our estimate of the world, but our hope should be as boundless as the Master's, who drew to Himself the publicans and sinners, and made them saints.

I need not remind you how this is the unique glory of Christ and of Christianity. Men have been asking the question whether Christianity is played out or not. What has been the motive power of all the great movements for the elevation of mankind that have occurred for the last nineteen centuries? What was it that struck the fetters of the slaves? What is it that sends men out amongst savage tribes? Has there ever been found a race of men so degraded that the message of Christ's love could not find its way into their hearts? Did not Darwin subscribe to the Patagonian Mission—a mission which takes in hand perhaps the lowest types of humanity in the world—and did he not do it because his own eyes had taught him that in this strange superstition that we call the Gospel there is a power that, somehow or other, nothing else can wield? Brethren! if the Church begins to lose its care for, and its power of drawing, outcasts and sinners, it has begun to lose its hold on Christ. The sooner such a Church dies the better, and there will be few mourners at its funeral.

The Friend of publicans and sinners has set the example to all of us His followers. God be thanked that there are signs to–day that Christian people are more and more waking up to the consciousness of their obligations in regard to the outcasts in their own and other lands. Let them go to them, as Jesus Christ did, with no false flatteries, but with plain rebukes of sin, and yet with manifest outgoing of the heart, and they will find that the same thing which drew these poor creatures to the Master will draw others to the feeblest, faintest reflection of Him in His servants.

And, last of all, dear friends, let each think that Jesus Christ is my Friend, and your Friend, because He is the Friend of sinners, and we are sinners. If He did not love sinners there would be nobody for Him to love. The universality of sin, however various in its degrees and manifestations, makes more wonderful the universal sweep of His friendship.

How do I know that He is my Friend? 'Greater love hath no man than this, that a man lay down his life for his friends,' and when we were yet enemies He was our Friend, and died for us. How shall we requite that love? 'Ye are my friends if ye do whatsoever I command you to do.' All over the Eastern world to this day the name by which the Patriarch Abraham is known is the 'Friend' or the 'Companion.' Well for us, for time and for eternity, if, knowing that Jesus is our Friend, we yield ourselves, in faith and love, to become His friends!

THE TWO DEBTORS

'There was a certain creditor which had two debtors; the one owed five hundred pence, and the other fifty. 42. And when they had nothing to pay, he frankly forgave them both. Tell Me therefore, which of them will love him most? 43. Simon answered and said, I suppose that he to whom he forgave most.'—LUKE vii.41–43.

We all know the lovely story in which this parable is embedded. A woman of notoriously bad character had somehow come in contact with Jesus Christ, and had by Him been aroused from her sensuality and degradation, and calmed by the assurance of forgiveness. So, when she heard that He was in her own town, what could she do but hasten to the Pharisee's house, and brave the cruel, scornful eyes of the eminently respectable people that would meet her there? She carries with her part of the spoils and instruments of her sinful adornment, to devote it to His service; but before she can open the cruse, her heart opens, and the hot tears flow on His feet, inflicting an indignity where she had meant an honour. She has nothing at hand to repair the fault, she will not venture to take her poor garment, which might have done it, but with a touch, she loosens her long hair, and with the ingenuity and self–abasement of love, uses that for a towel. Then, gathering confidence from her reception, and carried further than she had meant, she ventures to lay her sinful lips on His feet, as if asking pardon for the tears that would come—the only lips, except those of the traitor, that are recorded as having touched the Master. And only then does she dare to pour upon Him her only wealth.

What says the Pharisee? Has he a heart at all? He is scandalised at such a scene at his respectable table; and no wonder, for he could not have known that a change had passed upon the woman, and her evil repute was obviously notorious. He does not wonder at her having found her way into his house, for the meal was half public. But he began to doubt whether a Man who tolerates such familiarities from such a person could be a prophet; or if He were, whether He could be a good man. 'He would have known her if He had been a prophet,' thinks he. The thought is only a questionably true one. 'If He had known her, He would have thrust her back with His foot,' he thinks; and that thought is obviously false. But Simon's righteousness was of the sort that gathers up its own robes about it, and shoves back the poor sinner into the filth. 'She is a sinner,' says he. No, Simon! she *was* a sinner, but she *is* a penitent, and is on the road to be a saint, and having been washed, she is a great deal cleaner than thou art, who art only white–washed.

Our Lord's parable is the answer to the Pharisee's thought, and in it Jesus shows Simon that He knows him and the woman a great deal better than he did. There are three things to which briefly I ask your attention—the common debt, in varying amounts; the common insolvency; and the love, like the debt, varying in amount. Now, note these things in order.

I. There is, first of all, the common debt.

I do not propose to dwell at all upon that familiar metaphor, familiar to us all from its use in the Lord's Prayer, by which sin and the guilt of sin are shadowed forth for us in an imperfect fashion by the conception of debt. For duty neglected is a debt to God, which can only be discharged by a penalty. And all sin, and its consequent guilt and exposure to punishment, may be regarded under the image of indebtedness.

But the point that I want you to notice is that these two in our parable, though they are meant to be portraits of Simon and the woman, are also representatives of the two classes to one or other of which we all belong. They are both debtors, though one owes but a tenth of what the other does. That is to say, our Lord here draws a broad distinction between people who are outwardly respectable, decent, cleanly living, and people who have fallen into the habit, and are living a life, of gross and open transgression. There has been a great deal of very pernicious loose representation of the attitude of Christianity in reference to this matter, common in evangelical pulpits. And I want you to observe that our Lord draws a broad line and says, 'Yes! you, Simon, are a great deal better than that woman was. She was coarse, unclean, her innocence gone, her purity stained. She had been wallowing in filth, and you, with your respectability, your rigid morality, your punctilious observance of the ordinary human duties, you were far better than she was, and had far less to answer for than she had.' Fifty is only a tenth of five hundred, and there is a broad distinction, which nothing ought to be allowed to obliterate, between people who, without religion, are trying to do right, to keep themselves in the paths of morality and righteousness, to discharge their duty to their fellows, controlling their passions and their flesh, and others who put the reins upon the necks of the horses and let them carry them where they will, and live in an eminent manner for the world and the flesh and the devil. And there is nothing in evangelical Christianity which in the smallest degree obliterates that distinction, but rather it emphasises it, and gives a man full credit for any difference that there is in his life and conduct and character between himself and the man of gross transgression.

But then it says, on the other side, the difference which does exist, and is not to be minimised, is, after all, a difference of degree. They are both debtors. They stand in the same relation to the creditor, though the amount of the indebtedness is extremely different. We are all sinful men, and we stand in the same relation to God, though one of us may be much darker and blacker than the other.

And then, remember, that when you begin to talk about the guilt of actions in God's sight, you have to go far below the mere surface. If we could see the infinite complexity of motives—aggravations on the one side and palliations on the other—which go to the doing of a single deed, we should not be so quick to pronounce that the publican and the harlot are worse than the Pharisee. It is quite possible that an action which passes muster in regard to the morality of the world may, if regard be had (which God only can exercise) to the motive for which it is done, be as bad as, if not worse than, the lust and the animalism, drunkenness and debauchery, crime and murder, which the vulgar scales of the world consider to be the heavier. If you once begin to try to measure guilt, you will have to pass under the surface appearance, and will find that many a white and dazzling act has a very rotten inside, and that many a very corrupt and foul one does not come from so corrupt a source as at first sight might seem to be its origin. Let us be very modest in our estimate of the varying guilt of actions, and remember that, deep down below all diversities, there lies a fundamental identity, in which there is no difference, that all of us respectable people that never broke a law of the nation, and scarcely ever a law of propriety, in our lives, and the outcasts, if there are any here now, the drunkards, the sensualists, all of us stand in this respect in the same class. We are all debtors, for we have 'all sinned and come short of the glory of God,' A viper an inch long and the thickness of whipcord has a sting and poison in it, and is a viper. And if the question is whether a man has got small−pox or not, one pustule is as good evidence as if he was spotted all over. So, remember, he who owes five hundred and he who owes the tenth part of it, which is fifty, are both debtors.

II. Now notice the common insolvency.

'They had nothing to pay.' Well, if there is no money, 'no effects' in the bank, no cash in the till, nothing to distrain upon, it does not matter very much what the amount of the debt is, seeing that there is nothing to meet it, and whether it is fifty or five hundred the man is equally unable to pay. And that is precisely our position.

I admit, of course, that men without any recognition of God's pardoning mercy, or any of the joyful impulse that comes from the sense of Christ's redemption, or any of the help that is given by the indwelling of the Spirit who sanctifies may do a great deal in the way of mending their characters and making themselves purer and nobler. But that is not the point which my text contemplates, because it deals with a past. And the fact that lies under the metaphor of my text is this, that none of us can in any degree diminish our sin, considered as a debt to God. What can you and I do to lighten our souls of the burden of guilt? What we have written we have written. Tears will not wash it out, and amendment will not alter the past, which stands frowning and irrevocable. If there be a God at all, then our consciences, which speak to us of demerit, proclaim guilt in its two elements—the sense of having done wrong, and the foreboding of punishment therefor. Guilt cannot be dealt with by the guilty one: it must be Some One else who deals with it. He, and only He against whom we have sinned, can touch the great burden that we have piled upon us.

Brother! we have nothing to pay. We may mend our ways; but that does not touch the past. We may hate the evil; that will help to keep us from doing it in the future, but it does not affect our responsibility for what is done. We cannot touch it; there it stands irrevocable, with this solemn sentence written over the black pile, 'Every transgression and disobedience shall receive its just recompense of reward.' We have nothing to pay.

But my text suggests, further, that a condition precedent to forgiveness is the recognition by us of our penniless insolvency. Though it is not distinctly stated, it is clearly and necessarily implied in the narrative, that the two debtors are to be supposed as having come and held out a couple of pairs of empty hands, and sued in *forma pauperis*. You must recognise your insolvency if you expect to be forgiven. God does not accept dividends, so much in the pound, and let you off the rest on consideration thereof. If you are going to pay, you have to pay all; if He is going to forgive, you have to let Him forgive all. It must be one thing or the other, and you and I have to elect which of the two we shall stand by, and which of the two shall be applied to us.

Oh, dear friends! may we all come and say,

  Nothing in my hand I bring,
  Simply to Thy Cross I cling.

III. And so, lastly, notice the love, which varies with the forgiveness.

'Tell Me which of them will love him most.' Simon does not penetrate Christ's design, and there is a dash of supercilious contempt for the story and the question, as it seems to me, in the languid, half–courteous answer:—'I suppose, if it were worth my while to think about such a thing, that he to whom he forgave the most.' He did not know what a battery was going to be unmasked. Jesus says, 'Thou hast rightly judged.'

The man that is most forgiven is the man that will love most. Well, that answer is true if all other things about the two debtors are equal. If they are the same sort of men, with the same openness to sentiments of gratitude and generosity, the man who is let off the smaller debt will generally be less obliged than the man who is let off the larger. But it is, alas! not always the case that we can measure benefits conferred by gratitude shown. Another element comes in—namely, the consciousness of the benefit received—which measures the gratitude far more accurately than the actual benefit bestowed. And so we must take both these things, the actual amount of forgiveness, so to speak, which is conferred, and the depth of the sense of the forgiveness received, in order to get the measure of the love which answers it. So that this principle breaks up into two thoughts, of which I have only just a word or two to say.

First, it is very often true that the greatest sinners make the greatest saints. There have been plenty of instances all down the history of the world, and there are plenty of instances, thank God, cropping up every day still in which some poor, wretched outcast, away out in the darkness, living on the husks that the swine do eat, and liking to be in the pigstye, is brought back into the Father's house, and turns out a far more loving son and a far better servant than the man that had never wandered away from it. 'The publicans and the harlots' do often yet 'go into the Kingdom of God before' the respectable people.

And there are plenty of people in Manchester that you would not touch with a pair of tongs who, if they could be got hold of, would make far more earnest and devoted Christians than you are. The very strength of passion and feeling which has swept them wrong, rightly directed, would make grand saints of them, just as the very same conditions of climate which, at tropics, bring tornadoes and cyclones and dreadful thunder–storms, do also bring abundant fertility. The river which devastates a nation, dammed up within banks, may fertilise half a continent. And if a man is brought out of the darkness, and looks back upon the years that are wasted, that may help him to a more intense consecration. And if he remembers the filth out of which Jesus Christ picked him, it will bind him to that Lord with a bond deep and sacred.

So let no outcast man or woman listening to me now despair. You can come back from the furthest darkness, and whatever ugly things you have in your memories and your consciences, you may make them stepping–stones on which to climb to the very throne of God. Let no respectable people despise the outcasts; there may be the making in them of far better Christians than we are.

But, on the other hand, let no man think lightly of sin. Though it can be forgiven and swept away, and the gross sinner may become the great saint, there will be scars and bitter memories and habits surging up again after we thought they were dead; and the old ague and fever that we caught in the pestilential land will hang by us when we have migrated into a more wholesome climate. It is never good for a man to have sinned, even though, through his sin, God may have taken occasion to bring him near to Himself.

But the second form of this principle is always true—namely, that those who are most conscious of forgiveness will be most fruitful of love. The depth and fervour of our individual Christianity depends more largely on the clearness of our consciousness of our own personal guilt and the firmness of our grasp of forgiveness than upon anything else.

Why is it that such multitudes of you professing Christians are such icebergs in your Christianity? Mainly for this reason—that you have never found out, in anything like an adequate measure, how great a sinner you are, and how sure and sweet and sufficient Christ's pardoning mercy is. And so you are like Simon—you will ask Jesus to dinner, but you will not give Him any water for His feet or ointment for His head. You will do the conventional and necessary pieces of politeness, but not one act of impulse from the heart ever comes from you. You discharge 'the duties of religion.' What a phrase! You discharge the duties of religion. Ah! My brother, if you had been down into the horrible pit and the miry clay, and had seen a hand and a face looking down, and an arm outstretched to lift you; and if you had ever known what the rapture was after that subterraneous experience of having your feet set upon a rock and your goings established, you would come to Him and you would say, 'Take me all, O Lord! for I am all redeemed by Thee.' 'To whom little is forgiven the same loveth little.' Does not that explain the imperfect Christianity of thousands of us?

Fifty pence and five hundred pence are both small sums. Our Lord had nothing to do here with the absolute amount of debt, but only with the comparative amount of the two debts. But when He wanted to tell the people what the absolute amount of the debt was, he did it in that other story of the Unfaithful Servant. He owed his lord, not fifty pence (fifty eightpences or thereabouts), not five hundred pence, but 'ten thousand talents,' which comes to near two and a half millions of English money. And that is the picture of our indebtedness to God. 'We have nothing to pay.' Here is the payment—that Cross, that dying Christ. Turn your faith there, my brother, and then you will get ample forgiveness, and that will kindle love, and that will overflow in service. For the aperture in the heart at which forgiveness enters in is precisely of the same width as the one at which love goes out. Christ has loved us all, and perfectly. Let us love Him back again, who has died that we might live, and borne our sins in His own body.

LOVE AND FORGIVENESS

'Her sins, which are many, are forgiven; for she loved
much.'—LUKE vii. 47.

This story contains three figures, three persons, who may stand for us as types or representatives of the divine love and of all its operation in the world, of the way in which it is received or rejected, and of the causes and consequences of its reception or rejection. There is the unloving, cleanly, respectable, self-complacent Pharisee, with all his contempt for 'this woman.' There is the woman, with gross sin and mighty penitence, the great burst of love that is flowing out of her heart sweeping away before it, as it were, all the guilt of her transgressions. And, high over all, brooding over all, loving each, knowing each, pitying each, willing to save and be the Friend and Brother of each, is the embodied and manifested divine Love, the knowledge of whom is love in our hearts, and is 'life eternal.' So that now I have simply to ask you to look with me, for a little while, at these three persons as representing for us the divine love that comes forth amongst sinners, and the twofold form in which that love is received. There is, first, Christ the love of God appearing amongst men, the foundation of all our love to Him. Then there is the woman, the penitent sinner, lovingly recognising the divine love. And then, last, there is the Pharisee, the self-righteous man, ignorant of himself, and empty of all love to God. These are the three figures to which I ask your attention now.

I. We have Christ here standing as a manifestation of the divine love coming forth amongst sinners. His person and His words, the part He plays in this narrative, and the parable that He speaks in the course of it, have to be noticed under this head.

First, then, you have this idea—that He, as bringing to us the love of God, shows it to us, as not at all dependent upon our merits or deserts: 'He frankly forgave them both' are the deep words in which He would point us to the source and the ground of all the love of God. Brethren, have you ever thought what a wonderful and blessed truth there lies in the old words of one of the Jewish prophets, 'I do not this for your sakes, O house of Israel, but for Mine holy Name's sake'? The foundation of all God's love to us sinful men, that saying tells us, lies not in us, nor in anything about us, not in anything external to God Himself. He, and He alone, is the cause and reason, the motive and the end, of His own love to our world. And unless we have grasped that magnificent thought as the foundation of all our acceptance in Him, I think we have not yet learnt half of the fullness which, even in this world, may belong to our conceptions of the love of God—a love that has no motive but Himself; a love that is not evoked even (if I may so say) by regard to His creatures' wants; a love, therefore, which is eternal, being in that divine heart before there were creatures upon whom it could rest; a love that is its own guarantee, its own cause—safe and firm, therefore, with all the firmness and serenity of the divine nature—incapable of being affected by our transgression, deeper than all our sins, more ancient than our very existence, the very essence and being of God Himself. 'He frankly forgave them both.' If you seek the source of divine love, you must go high up into the mountains of God, and learn that it, as all other of His (shall I say) emotions, and feelings, and resolutions, and purposes, owns no reason but Himself, no motive but Himself; lies wrapped in the secret of His nature, who is all-sufficient for His own blessedness, and all whose work and being is caused by, and satisfied, and terminates in His own fullness. 'God is love': therefore beneath all considerations of what we may want—deeper and more blessed than all thoughts of a compassion that springs from the feeling of human distress and the sight of man's misery—lies this thought of an affection which does not need the presence of sorrow to evoke it, which does not want the touch of our finger to flow out, but by its very nature is everlasting, by its very nature is infinite, by its very nature must be pouring out the flood of its own joyous fullness for ever and ever!

Then, again, Christ standing here for us as the representative and revelation of this divine love which He manifests to us, tells us, too, that whilst it is not caused by us, but comes from the nature of God, it is not turned away by our sins. 'This man, if he were a prophet, would have known who and what manner of woman this is that toucheth Him,' says the unloving and self-righteous heart, 'for she is a sinner.' Ah! there is nothing more beautiful than the difference between the thought about sinful creatures which is natural to a holy being, and the thought about sinful creatures which is natural to a self-righteous being. The one is all contempt; the other, all pity. He knew what she was, and therefore He let her come close to Him with the touch of her polluted hand, and pour out the gains of her lawless life and the adornments of her former corruption upon His most blessed and most holy head. His knowledge of her as a sinner, what did it do to His love for her? It made that love gentle and tender, as knowing that she could not bear the revelation of the blaze of His purity. It smoothed His face and softened His tones, and breathed through all His knowledge and notice of her timid and yet confident approach. 'Daughter, I know all about it—all thy wanderings and thy vile transgressions: I know them all, and My love is mightier than all these. They may be as the great sea, but my love is like the everlasting mountains, whose roots go down beneath the ocean, and My love is like the everlasting heaven, whose brightness covers it all over.' God's love is Christ's love; Christ's love is God's love. And this is the lesson that we gather—that that infinite and divine loving–kindness does not turn away from thee, my brother and my friend, because thou art a sinner, but remains hovering about thee, with wooing invitations and with gentle touches, if it may draw thee to repentance, and open a fountain of answering affection in thy seared and dry heart. The love of God is deeper than all our sins. 'For His great love wherewith He loved us, when we were dead in sins, He quickened us.'

Sin is but the cloud behind which the everlasting sun lies in all its power and warmth, unaffected by the cloud; and the light will yet strike, the light of His love will yet pierce through, with its merciful shafts bringing healing in their beams, and dispersing all the pitchy darkness of man's transgression. And as the mists gather themselves up and roll away, dissipated by the heat of that sun in the upper sky, and reveal the fair earth below—so the love of Christ shines in, molting the mist and dissipating the fog, thinning it off in its thickest places, and at last piercing its way right through it, down to the heart of the man that has been lying beneath the oppression of this thick darkness, and who thought that the fog was the sky, and that there was no sun there above. God be thanked! the everlasting love of God that comes from the depth of His own being, and is there because of Himself, will never be quenched because of man's sin.

And so, in the next place, Christ teaches us here that this divine love, when it comes forth among sinners, necessarily manifests itself first in the form of forgiveness. There was nothing to be done with the debtors until the debt was wiped out; there was no possibility of other gifts of the highest sort being granted to them, until the great score was cancelled and done away with. When the love of God comes down into a sinful world, it must come first and foremost as pardoning mercy. There are no other terms upon which there can be a union betwixt the loving–kindness of God, and the emptiness and sinfulness of my heart, except only this—that first of all there shall be the clearing away from my soul of the sins which I have gathered there, and then there will be space for all other divine gifts to work and to manifest themselves. Only do not fancy that when we speak about forgiveness, we simply mean that a man's position in regard to the penalties of sin is altered. That is not all the depth of the scriptural notion of forgiveness. It includes far more than the removal of outward penalties. The heart of it all is, that the love of God rests upon the sinner, unturned away even by his sins, passing over his sins, and removing his sins for the sake of Christ. My friend, if you are talking in general terms about a great divine loving–kindness that wraps you round—if you have a great deal to say, apart from the Gospel, about the love of God as being your hope and confidence—I want you to reflect on this, that the first word which the love of God speaks to sinful men is pardon; and unless that is your notion of God's love, unless you look to that as the first thing of all, let me tell you, you may have before you a very fair picture of a very beautiful, tender, good–natured benevolence, but you have not nearly reached the height of the vigour and yet the tenderness of the Scripture notion of the love of God. It is not a love which says, 'Well, put sin on one side, and give the man the blessings all the same,' not a love which has nothing to say about that great fact of transgression, not a love which gives it the go–by, and leaves it standing: but a love which passes into the heart through the portal of pardon, a love which grapples with the fact of sin first, and has nothing to say to a man until it has said that message to him.

And but one word more on this part of my subject—here we see the love of God thus coming from

Himself; not turned away by man's sins; being the cause of forgiveness; expressing itself in pardon; and last of all, demanding service. 'Simon, thou gavest Me no water, thou gavest Me no kiss, My head thou didst not anoint: I expected all these things from thee—I desired them all from thee: My love came that they might spring in thy heart; thou hast not given them; My love is wounded, as it were disappointed, and it turns away from thee!' Yes, after all that we have said about the freeness and fullness, the unmerited, and uncaused, and unmotived nature of that divine affection—after all that we have said about its being the source of every blessing to man, asking nothing from him, but giving everything to him; it still remains true, that God's love, when it comes to men, comes that it may evoke an answering echo in the human heart, and 'though it might be much bold to enjoin, yet for love's sake rather beseeches' us to give unto Him who has given all unto us. There, then, stands forth in the narrative, Christ as a revelation of the divine love amongst sinners.

II. Now, in the second place, let us look for a moment at 'this woman' as the representative of a class of character—the penitent lovingly recognising the divine love.

The words which I have read as my text contain a statement as to the woman's character: 'Her sins, which are many, are forgiven; for she loved much.' Allow me just one word of explanation, in the shape of exposition, on these words. Great blunders have been built upon them. I dare say you have seen epitaphs—(I have)—written often on gravestones with this misplaced idea on them—'Very sinful; but there was a great deal of love in the person; and for the sake of the love, God passed by the sin!' Now, when Christ says 'She loved much,' He does not mean to say that her love was the cause of her forgiveness—not at all. He means to say that her love was the proof of her forgiveness, and that it was so because her love was a consequence of her forgiveness. As, for instance, we might say, 'The woman is in great distress, for she weeps'; but we do not mean thereby that the weeping is the reason of the distress, but the means of our knowing the sorrow. It is the proof because it is the consequence. Or (to put it into the simplest shape) the love does not go before the forgiveness, but the forgiveness goes before the love; and because the love comes after the forgiveness, it is the sign of the forgiveness. That this is the true interpretation, you will see if you look back for a moment at the narrative which precedes, where He says, 'He frankly forgave them both: tell me, therefore, which of them will love him most?' Pardon is the pre–requisite of love, and love is a consequence of the sense of forgiveness.

This, then, is the first thing to observe: all true love to God is preceded in the heart by these two things—a sense of sin, and an assurance of pardon. Brethren, there is no love possible—real, deep, genuine, worthy of being called love of God—which does not start with the belief of my own transgression, and with the thankful reception of forgiveness in Christ. You do nothing to get pardon for yourselves; but unless you have the pardon you have no love to God. I know that sounds a very hard thing—I know that many will say it is very narrow and very bigoted, and will ask, 'Do you mean to tell me that the man whose bosom glows with gratitude because of earthly blessings, has no love—that all that natural religion which is in people, apart from this sense of forgiveness in Christ, do you mean to tell me that this is not all genuine?' Yes, most assuredly; and I believe the Bible and man's conscience say the same thing. I do not for one moment deny that there may be in the hearts of those who are in the grossest ignorance of themselves as transgressors, certain emotions of instinctive gratitude and natural religiousness, directed to some higher power dimly thought of as the author of their blessings and the source of much gladness: but has that kind of thing got any living power in it?

104

I demur to its right to be called love to God at all, for this reason—because it seems to me that the object that is loved is not God, but a fragment of God. He who but says, 'I owe to Him breath and all things; in Him I live and move, and have my being,' has left out one–half at least of the Scriptural conception of God. Your God, my friend, is not the God of the Bible, unless He stands before you clothed in infinite loving–kindness indeed; but clothed also in strict and rigid justice. Is your God perfect and entire? If you say that you love Him, and if you do so, is it as the God and Father of our Lord Jesus Christ? Have you meditated on the depths of the requirements of His law? Have you stood silent and stricken at the thought of the blaze of His righteousness? Have you passed through all the thick darkness and the clouds with which He surrounds His throne, and forced your way at last into the inner light where He dwells? Or is it a vague divinity that you worship and love? Which? Ah, if a man study his Bible, and try to find out for himself, from its veracious records, who and what manner of God the living God is, there will be no love in his heart to that Being except only when he has flung himself at His feet, and said, 'Father of eternal purity, and God of all holiness and righteousness, forgive Thy child, a sinful broken man—forgive Thy child, for the sake of Thy Son!' That, and that alone, is the road by which we come to possess the love of God, as a practical power, filling and sanctifying our souls; and such is the God to whom alone our love ought to be rendered; and I tell you (or rather the Bible tells you, and the Gospel and the Cross of Christ tell you), there is no love without pardon, no fellowship and sonship without the sense of sin and the acknowledgment of foul transgression!

So much, then, for what precedes the love of Christ in the heart; now a word as to what follows. 'Her sins, which are many, are forgiven; for she loved much.' The sense of sin precedes forgiveness: forgiveness precedes love; love precedes all acceptable and faithful service. If you want to do, love. If you want to know, love. This poor woman knew Christ a vast deal better than that Pharisee there. He said, 'This man is not a prophet; He does not understand the woman.' Ay, but the woman knew herself better than the Pharisee knew himself, knew herself better than the Pharisee knew her, knew Christ, above all, a vast deal better than he did. Love is the gate of all knowledge.

This poor woman brings her box of ointment, a relic perhaps of past evil life, and once meant for her own adornment, and pours it on His head, lavishes offices of service which to the unloving heart seem bold in the giver and cumbersome to the receiver. It is little she can do, but she does it. Her full heart demands expression, and is relieved by utterance in deeds. The deeds are spontaneous, welling out at the bidding of an inward impulse, not drawn out by the force of an external command. It matters not what practical purpose they serve. The motive of them makes their glory. Love prompts them, love justifies them, and His love interprets them, and His love accepts them. The love which flows from the sense of forgiveness is the source of all obedience as well as the means of all knowledge.

Brethren, we differ from each other in all respects but one, 'We have all sinned and come short of the glory of God'; we all need the love of Christ; it is offered to us all; but, believe me, the sole handle by which you can lay hold of it, is the feeling of your own sinfulness and need of pardon. I preach to you a love that you do not need to buy, a mercy that you do not need to bribe, a grace that is all independent of your character, and condition, and merits, which issues from God for ever, and is lying at your doors if you will take it. You are a sinful man; Christ died for you. He comes to give you His forgiving mercy. Take it, be at rest. So shalt thou love and know and do, and so shall He love and guide thee!

III. Now one word, and then I have done. A third character stands here—the unloving and self–righteous man, all ignorant of the love of Christ.

He is the antithesis of the woman and her character. You remember the traditional peculiarities and characteristics of the class to which he belonged. He is a fair specimen of the whole of them. Respectable in life, rigid in morality, unquestionable in orthodoxy; no sound of suspicion having ever come near his belief in all the traditions of the elders; intelligent and learned, high up among the ranks of Israel! What was it that made this man's morality a piece of dead nothingness? What was it that made his orthodoxy just so many dry words, from out of which all the life had gone? What was it? This one thing: there was no love in it. As I said, Love is the foundation of all obedience; without it, morality degenerates into mere casuistry. Love is the foundation of all knowledge; without it, religion degenerates into a chattering about Moses, and doctrines, and theories; a thing that will neither kill nor make alive, that never gave life to a single soul or blessing to a single heart, and never put strength into any hand for the conflict and strife of daily life. There is no more contemptible and impotent thing on the face of the earth than morality divorced from love, and religious thoughts divorced from a heart full of the love of God. Quick corruption or long decay, and in either case death and putrefaction, are the end of these. You and I need that lesson, my friends. It is of no use for us to condemn Pharisees that have been dead and in their graves for nineteen hundred years. The same thing besets us all; we all of us try to get away from the centre, and dwell contented on the surface. We are satisfied to take the flowers and stick them into our little gardens, without any roots to them, when of course they all die out! People may try to cultivate virtue without religion, and to acquire correct notions of moral and spiritual truth; and partially and temporarily they may succeed, but the one will be a yoke of bondage, and the other a barren theory. I repeat, love is the basis of all knowledge and of all right–doing. If you have got that firm foundation laid in the soul, then the knowledge and the practice will be builded in God's own good time; and if not, the higher you build the temple, and the more aspiring are its cloud–pointing pinnacles, the more certain will be its toppling some day, and the more awful will be the ruin when it comes. The Pharisee was contented with himself, and so there was no sense of sin in him, therefore there was no penitent recognition of Christ as forgiving and loving him, therefore there was no love to Christ. Because there was no love, there was neither light nor heat in his soul, his knowledge was barren notions, and his painful doings were soul–destructive self–righteousness.

And so it all comes round to the one blessed message: My friend, God hath loved us with an everlasting love. He has provided an eternal redemption and pardon for us. If you would know Christ at all, you must go to Him as a sinful man, or you are shut out from Him altogether. If you *will* go to Him as a sinful being, fling yourself down there, not try to make yourself better, but say, 'I am full of unrighteousness and transgression; let Thy love fall upon me and heal me'; you will get the answer, and in your heart there shall begin to live and grow up a root of love to Him, which shall at last effloresce into all knowledge and unto all purity of obedience; for he that hath had much forgiveness, loveth much, and 'he that loveth knoweth God,' and 'dwelleth in God, and God in Him'!

GO INTO PEACE

'And He said to the woman, Thy faith hath saved thee:
go in peace.'—LUKE vii. 50.

We find that our Lord twice, and twice only, employs this form of sending away those who had received benefits from His hand. On both occasions the words were addressed to women: once to this woman, who was a sinner, and who was gibbeted by the contempt of the Pharisee in whose house the Lord was; and once to that poor sufferer who stretched out a wasted hand to lay upon the hem of His garment, in the hope of getting healing—filching it away unknown to the Giver. In both cases there is great tenderness; in the latter case even more so than in the present, for there He addressed the tremulous invalid as 'daughter'; and in both cases there is a very remarkable connection hinted at between faith and peace; 'Thy faith hath saved thee, go in peace.'

Now, there are three things that strike me about these words; the first of them is this—

I. The dismissal of the woman.

One might have expected that our Lord would have flung the shield of His companionship, for a little while, at any rate, over this penitent, and so have saved her from the scoffs and sneers of her neighbours, who knew that she was a sinner. One might have supposed that the depth of her gratitude, as expressed by her costly offering and by her tears, would have spoken to His heart, and that He would have let her stop beside Him for a little while; but no! Jesus said to her in effect; 'You have got what you wished; go away, and take care of it.' Such a dismissal is in accordance with the way in which He usually acted. For very seldom indeed, after He had gathered the first nucleus of four disciples, do we find that He summoned any individual to His side. Generally He broke the connection between Himself and the recipients of His benefits at as early a moment as possible, and dismissed them. And that was not only because He did not wish to be surrounded and hampered by a crowd of slightly attached disciples, but for two other reasons; one, the good of the people themselves, and the other, that, scattered all over northern Palestine, they might in their several circles become centres of light and evangelists for the King. He dispersed them that He might fling the seed broadcast over the land.

Jesus Christ says to us, if we have been saved by our faith, 'Go!' And He intends two things thereby. First, to teach us that it is good for us to stand by ourselves, to feel responsibility for the ordering of our lives, not to have a visible Presence at our sides to fall back upon, but to grow by solitude. There is no better way of growing reliant, of becoming independent of circumstances, and in the depths of our own hearts being calm, than by being deprived of visible stay and support, and thus drawing closer and closer to our unseen Companion, and leaning harder and heavier upon Him. 'It is expedient for you that I go away.' For solitude and self–reliance, which is bottomed upon self–distrust and reliance upon Him, are the things that make men and women strong. So, if ever He carries us into the desert, if ever He leaves us forsaken and alone, as we think, if ever He seems—and sometimes He does with some people, and it is only seeming—to withdraw Himself from us, it is all for the one purpose, that we may grow to be mature men and women, not always children, depending upon go–carts of any kind, and nurses' hands and leading–strings. Go, and alone with Christ realise by faith

107

that you are not alone. Christian men and women, have you learned that lesson—to be able to do without anybody and anything because your whole hearts are filled, and your courage is braced up and strengthened by the thought that the absent Christ is the present Christ?

There is another reason, as I take it, for which this separation of the new disciple from Jesus was so apparently mercilessly and perpetually enforced. At the very moment when one would have thought it would have done this woman good to be with the Lord for a little while longer, she is sent out into the harshly judging world. Yes, that is always the way by which Christian men and women that have received the blessing of salvation through faith can retain it, and serve Him—by going out among men and doing their work there. The woman went home. I dare say it was a home, if what they said about her was true, that sorely needed the leavening which she now would bring. She had been a centre of evil. She was to go away back to the very place where she had been such, and to be a centre of good. She was to contradict her past by her present which would explain itself when she said she had been with Jesus. For the very same reason for which to one man that besought to be with Him, He said, 'No, no! go away home and tell your friends what great things God has done for you,' He said to this woman, and He says to you and me, 'Go, and witness for Me.' Communion with Him is blessed, and it is meant to issue in service for Him. 'Let us make here three tabernacles,' said the Apostle; and there was scarcely need for the parenthetical comment, 'not knowing what he said.' But there was a demoniac boy down there with the rest of the disciples, and they had been trying in vain to free him from the incubus that possessed him, and as long as that melancholy case was appealing to the sympathy and help of the transfigured Christ, it was no time to stop on the Mount. Although Moses and Elias were there, and the voice from God was there, and the Shechinah cloud was there, all were to be left, to go down and do the work of helping a poor, struggling child. So Jesus Christ says to us, 'Go, and remember that work is the end of emotion, and that to do the Master's will in the world is the surest way to realise His presence.'

II. Now, the second point I would suggest is—

The region into which Christ admitted this woman. It is remarkable that in the present case, and in that other to which I have already referred, the phraseology employed is not the ordinary one of that familiar Old Testament leave-taking salutation, which was the 'goodbye' of the Hebrews, 'Go in peace.' But we read occasionally in the Old Testament a slight but eloquent variation. It is not 'Go in peace,' as our Authorised Version has it, but 'Go into peace,' and that is a great deal more than the other. 'Go in peace' refers to the momentary emotion; 'Go into peace' seems, as it were, to open the door of a great palace, to let down the barrier on the borders of a land, and to send the person away upon a journey through all the extent of that blessed country. Jesus Christ takes up this as He does a great many very ordinary conventional forms, and puts a meaning into it. Eli had said to Hannah, 'Go into peace.' Nathan had said to David, 'Go into peace.' But Eli and Nathan could only wish that it might be so; their wish had no power to realise itself. Christ takes the water of the conventional salutation and turns it into the wine of a real gift. When He says, 'Go into peace,' He puts the person into the peace which He wishes them, and His word is like a living creature, and fulfils itself.

So He says to each of us: 'If you have been saved by faith, I open the door of this great palace. I admit you across the boundaries of this great country. I give you all possible forms of peace for yours.' Peace with God—that is the foundation of all—then peace with ourselves, so that our inmost nature need no longer be torn in pieces by contending emotions, 'I dare not' waiting upon 'I would,' and 'I ought' and 'I will' being in continual and internecine conflict; but heart and will, and calmed conscience, and satisfied desires, and pure affections, and lofty emotions being all drawn together into one great wave by the attraction of His love, as the moon draws the heaped waters of the ocean round the world. So our souls at rest in God may be at peace within themselves, and that is the only way by which the discords of the heart can be tuned to one key, into harmony and concord; and the only way by which wars and tumults within the soul turn into tranquil energy, and into peace which is not stagnation, but rather a mightier force than was ever developed when the soul was cleft by discordant desires.

In like manner, the man who is at peace with God, and consequently with himself, is in relations of harmony with all things and with all events. 'All things are yours if ye are Christ's.' 'The stars in their courses fought against Sisera,' because Sisera was fighting against God; and all creatures, and all events, are at enmity with the man who is in antagonism and enmity to Him who is Lord of them all. But if we have peace with God, and peace with ourselves, then, as Job says, 'Thou shalt make a league with the beasts of the field, and the stones of the field shall be at peace with thee.' 'Thy faith hath saved thee; go into peace.'

Remember that this commandment, which is likewise a promise and a bestowal, bids us progress in the peace into which Christ admits us. We should be growingly unperturbed and calm, and 'there is no joy but calm,' when all is said and done. We should be more and more tranquil and at rest; and every day there should come, as it were, a deeper and more substantial layer of tranquillity enveloping our hearts, a thicker armour against perturbation and calamity and tumult.

III. And now there is one last point here that I would suggest, namely:

The condition on which we shall abide in the Land of Peace.

Our Lord said to both these women: 'Thy faith hath saved thee.' To the other one it was even more needful to say it than to this poor penitent prostitute, because that other one had the notion that, somehow or other, she could steal away the blessing of healing by contact of her finger with the robe of Jesus. Therefore He was careful to lift her above that sensuous error, and to show her what it was in her that had drawn healing 'virtue' from Him. In substance He says to her: 'Thy faith, not thy forefinger, has joined thee to Me; My love, not My garment, has healed thee.'

There have been, and still are, many copyists of the woman's mistake who have ascribed too much healing and saving power to externals—sacraments, rites, and ceremonies. If their faith is real and their longing earnest, they get their blessing, but they need to be educated to understand more clearly what is the human condition of receiving Christ's saving power, and that robe and finger have little to do with it.

The sequence of these two sayings, the one pointing out the channel of all spiritual blessing, the other, the bestowment of the great blessing of perfect peace, suggests that the peace is conditional on the faith, and opens up to us this solemn truth, that if we would enjoy continuous peace, we must exercise continuous faith. The two things will cover precisely the same ground, and where the one stops the other will stop. Yesterday's faith does not secure to–day's peace. As long as I hold up the shield of faith, it will quench all the fiery darts of the wicked, but if I were holding it up yesterday, and have dropped it to–day, then there is nothing between me and them, and I shall be wounded and burned before long. No past religious experience avails for present needs. If you would have 'your peace' to be 'as the waves of the sea,' your trust in Christ must be continuous and strong. The moment you cease trusting, that moment you cease being peaceful. Keep behind the breakwater, and you will ride smoothly, whatever the storm. Venture out beyond it, and you will be exposed to the dash of the waves and the howling of the tempest. Your own past tells you where the means of blessing are. It was your faith that saved you, and it is as you go on believing that you 'Go into peace'.

THE MINISTRY OF WOMEN

'And certain women, which had been healed of evil
spirits and infirmities, Mary called Magdalene, out
of whom went seven devils, 3. And Joanna the wife of
Chuza, Herod's steward, and Susanna, and many others,
which ministered unto Him of their substance.'
—LUKE viii. 2,3.

The Evangelist Luke has preserved for us several incidents in our Lord's life in which women play a prominent part. It would not, I think, be difficult to bring that fact into connection with the main characteristics of his Gospel, but at all events it is worth observing that we owe to him those details, and the fact that the service of these grateful women was permanent during the whole of our Lord's wandering life after His leaving Galilee. An incidental reference to the fact is found in Matthew's account of the Crucifixion, but had it not been for Luke we should not have known the names of two or three of them, nor should we have known how constantly they adhered to Him. As to the women of the little group, we know very little about them. Mary of Magdala has had a very hard fate. The Scripture record of her is very sweet and beautiful. Delivered by Christ from that mysterious demoniacal possession, she cleaves to Him, like a true woman, with all her heart. She is one of the little group whose strong love, casting out all fear, nerved them to stand by the Cross when all the men except the gentle Apostle of love, as he is called, were cowering in corners, afraid of their lives, and she was one of the same group who would fain have prolonged their ministry beyond His death, and who brought the sweet spices with them in order to anoint Him, and it was she who came to the risen Lord with the rapturous exclamation, 'Rabboni, my Master.' By strange misunderstanding of the Gospel story, she has been identified with the woman who was a sinner in the previous chapter in this book, and her fair fame has been blackened and her very name taken as a designation of the class to which there is no reason whatever to believe she belonged. Demoniacal possession was neither physical infirmity nor moral evil, however much it may have simulated sometimes the one or the other.

Then as to Joanna the wife of Chuza, Herod's steward, old Church tradition tells us that she was the consort of the nobleman whose son Christ healed at Capernaum. It does not seem very likely that Herod's steward would have been living in Capernaum, and the narrative before us rather seems to show that she herself was the recipient of healing from His hands. However that may be, Herod's court was not exactly the place to look for Christian disciples, was it? But you know they of Caesar's household surrounded with their love the Apostle whom Nero murdered, and it is by no means an uncommon experience that the servants' hall knows and loves the Christ that the lord in the saloon does not care about.

And then as for Susanna, is it not a sweet fate to be known to all the world for ever more by one line only, which tells of her service to her Master?

So I will try to take out of these little incidents in our text some plain lessons about this matter of Christian service and ministry to Christ, with which it seems to be so full. It will apply to missionary work and all other sorts of work, and perhaps will take us down to the bottom of it all, and show us the foundation on which it should all rest.

Let me ask you for a moment to look with me first of all at the centre figure, as being an illustration of—what shall I say? may I venture to use a rough word and say the pauper Christ?—as the great Pattern and Motive for us, of the love that becomes poor. We very often cover the life of our Lord with so much imaginative reverence that we sometimes lose the hard angles of the facts of it. Now, I want you to realise it, and you may put it into as modern English as you like, for it will help the vividness of the conception, which is a simple, prosaic fact, that Jesus Christ was, in the broadest meaning of the word, a pauper; not indeed with the sodden poverty that you can see in our slums, but still in a very real sense of the word. He had not a thing that He could call His own, and when He came to the end of His life there was nothing for His executioners to gamble for except His one possession, the seamless robe. He is hungry, and there is a fig–tree by the roadside, and He comes, expecting to get His breakfast off that. He is tired, and He borrows a fishing–boat to lie down and sleep in. He is thirsty, and He asks a woman of questionable character to give Him a draught of water. He wants to preach a sermon about the bounds of ecclesiastical and civil society, and He says, 'Bring Me a penny.' He has to be indebted to others for the beast of burden on which He made His modest entry into Jerusalem, for the winding sheet that wrapped Him, for the spices that would embalm Him, for the grave in which He lay. He was a pauper in a deeper sense of the word than His Apostle when he said, 'Having nothing, and yet possessing all things, as poor, and yet making many rich.' For let us remember that the great mystery of the Gospel system—the blending together in one act and in one Person all the extremes of lowliness and of the loftiness which go deep down into the very profundities of the Gospel, is all here dramatised, as it were, and drawn into a picturesque form on the very surface; and the same blending together of poverty and absolute love, which in its loftiest form is the union in one Person of Godhead and of manhood, is here for us in this fact, that all the dark cloud of poverty, if I may so say, is shot through with strange gleams of light like sunshine caught and tangled in some cold, wet fog, so that whenever you get some definite and strange mark of Christ's poverty, you get lying beside it some definite and strange mark of His absoluteness and His worth. For instance, take the illustration I have already referred to—He borrows a fishing–boat and lies down, weary, to sleep on the wooden pillow at the end of it; aye, but He rises and He says, 'Peace, be still,' and the waves fall. He borrows the upper room, and with a stranger's wine and another man's bread He founds the covenant and the sacrament of His new kingdom. He borrows a grave; aye, but He comes out of it, the Lord both of the dead and of the living. And so we have to say, 'Consider the grace of our Lord Jesus Christ, who, though He was rich, yet for our sakes became poor, that we through His poverty might become rich.'

The noblest life that was ever lived upon earth–I hope you and I think it is a great deal more than that, but we all think it is that at any rate—the noblest life that was ever lived upon earth was the life of a poor man. Remember that pure desires, holy aspirations, noble purposes, and a life peopled with all the refinement and charities that belong to the spirit, and that is ever conscious of the closest presence of God and of the innate union with Him, is possible under such conditions, and so remember that the pauper Christ is, at the least, the perfect Man.

But then what I more immediately intended was to ask you to take that central figure with this external fact of His poverty, of the depth of His true inanition, the emptying of Himself for our sakes, as being the great motive, and Oh! thank God that with all humility, we may venture to say, the great Pattern to which you and I have to conform. There is the reason why we say, 'I love to speak His name,' there is the true measure of the devotion of the consecration and the self–surrender which He requires. Christ gave all for us even to the uttermost circumference of external possession, and standing in the midst of those for whose sakes He became poor, He turns to them with a modest appeal when He says, 'Minister unto Me, for I have made Myself to need your ministrations for the sake of your redemption.' So much, then, for the first point which I would desire to urge upon you from this incident before us.

Now, in the next place, and pursuing substantially the same course of thought, let me suggest to you to look at the love—the love here that stoops to be served.

It is a familiar observation and a perfectly true one that we have no record of our Lord's ever having used miraculous power for the supply of His own wants, and the reason for that, I suppose, is to be found not only in that principle of economy and parsimony of miraculous energy, so that the supernatural in His life was ever pared down to the narrowest possible limits, and inosculated immediately with the natural, but it is also to be found in this—let me put it into very plain words—that Christ liked to be helped and served by the people that He loved, and that Christ knew that they liked it as well as He. It delighted Him, and He was quite sure that it delighted them. You fathers and mothers know what it is when one of your little children comes, and seeing you engaged about some occupation says, 'Let me help you.' The little hand perhaps does not contribute much to the furtherance of your occupation. It may be rather an encumbrance than otherwise, but is not there a gladness in saying 'Yes, here, take this and do this little thing for me'? And do not we all know how maimed and imperfect that love is which only gives, and how maimed and imperfect that love is which only receives, so that there must be an assumption of both attitudes in all true commerce of affection, and that same beautiful flashing backwards and forwards from the two poles which makes the sweetness of our earthly love find its highest example there in the heavens. There are the two mirrors facing each other, and they reverberate rays from one polished surface to another, and so Christ loves and gives, and Christ loves and takes, and His servants love and give, and His servants love and take. Sometimes we are accustomed to speak of it as the highest sign of our Lord's true, deep conviction that He has given so much to us. It seems to me we may well pause and hesitate whether the mightiness and the wonderfulness of His love to us are shown more in that He gives everything to us, or in that He takes so much from us. It is much to say, 'The Son of man came not to be ministered unto but to minister'; I do not know but that it is more to say that the Son of man let this record be written: 'Certain women also which ministered to Him of their substance.' At all events there it stands and for us. What although we have to come and say, 'All that I bring is Thine'; what then? Does a father like less to get a gift from his boy because he gave him the shilling to buy it? And is there anything that diminishes the true sweetness of our giving to Christ, and as we may believe the true sweetness to Him of receiving it from us, because we have to herald all our offerings, all our love, aspirations, desires, trust, conformity, practical service, substantial help, with the old acknowledgment, 'All things come of Thee, and of Thine own have we given Thee.'

Now, dear friends, all these principles which I have thus imperfectly touched upon as to the necessity of the blending of the two sides in all true commerce of love, the giving and bestowing the expression of the one affection in both hearts, all bears very directly upon the more special work of Christian men in spreading the name of Christ among those who do not know it. You get the same economy of power there that I was speaking about. The supernatural is finished when the divine life is cast into the world. 'I am come to fling fire upon the earth,' said He, 'and oh, that it were already kindled!' *There* is the supernatural; after that you have to deal with the thing according to the ordinary laws of human history and the ordinary conditions of man's society. God trusts the spread of His word to His people; there will not be one moment's duration of the barely, nakedly supernatural beyond the absolute necessity. Christ comes; after that you and I have to see to it, and then you say, 'Collections, collections, collections, it is always collections. This society and that society and the other society, there is no end of the appeals that are made. Charity sermons—men using the highest motives of the Gospel for no purpose but to get a shilling or two out of people's pockets. I am tired of it.' Very well; all I have to say is, first of all, 'Ye have not resisted unto blood'; some people have had to pay a great deal more for their Gospel than you have. And another thing, a man that had lost a great deal more for his Master than ever you or I will have to do, said, 'Unto me who am less than the least of all saints is this grace given, that I should preach amongst the heathen the unsearchable riches of Christ.' Ah! a generous, chivalrous spirit, a spirit touched to fine issues by the fine touch of the Lord's love, will feel that it is no burden; or if it be a burden, it is only a burden as a golden crown heavy with jewels may be a burden on brows that are ennobled by its pressure. This grace is given, and He has crowned us with the honour that we may serve Him and do something for Him.

Dear brethren! of all the gracious words that our Master has spoken to us, I know not that there is one more gracious than when He said, 'Go into all the world and preach the Gospel to every creature'; and of all the tender legacies that He has left His Church, though there be included amongst these His own peace and His own Spirit, I know not that there is any more tender or a greater sign of His love towards us and His confidence in us than when departing to the far country to receive a kingdom and to return, He gave authority to His servants, and to every man his work.'

And so, in the next place, let me ask you to look for a moment at the complement to this love that stoops to serve and delights to serve—the ministry or service of our love. Let me point to two things.

It seems to me that the simple narrative we have before us goes very deep into the heart of this matter. It gives us two things—the foundation of the service and the sphere of the service.

First there is the foundation—'Certain women which had been healed of evil spirits and infirmities.' Ah, there you come to it! The consciousness of redemption is the one master touch that evokes the gratitude which aches to breathe itself in service. There is no service except it be the expression of love. That is the one great Christian principle; and the other is that there is no love that does not rest on the consciousness of redemption; and from these two—that all service and obedience are the utterance and eloquence of love, and that all love has its root in the sense of redemption—you may elaborate all the distinct characteristics and peculiarities of Christian ethics, whereby duty becomes gladness. 'I will,' and 'I ought' overlap and cover each other like two of Euclid's triangles; and whatsoever He commands that I spring to do; and so though the burden be heavy, considered in regard to its requirements, and though the yoke do often press, considered *per se*, yet because the cords that fasten the yoke to our neck are the cords of love, I can say, 'My burden is light.' One of the old psalms puts it thus; 'O Lord, truly I am Thy servant; Thou hast loosed my bonds; and because Thou hast loosed, therefore O hear me; speak, Lord, for Thy servant heareth.'

So much then for the foundation—now for the sphere. 'Ah,' you say, 'there is no parallel there, at any rate. These women served Him with personal ministration of their substance.' Well, I think there is a parallel notwithstanding. If I had time I should like to dwell upon the side thoughts connected with that sphere of service, and remind you how very prosaic were their common domestic duties, looking after the comfort of Christ and the travel–stained Twelve who were with Him—let us put it into plain English—cooking their dinners for them, and how that became a religious act. Take the lesson out of it, you women in your households, and you men in your counting–houses and behind your counters, and you students at your dictionaries and lexicons. The commonest things done for the Master flash up into worship, or as good old George Herbert puts it—

'A servant with this clause
Makes drudgery divine;
Who sweeps a room, as for Thy cause,
Makes that and th' action fine.'

But then beyond that, is there any personal ministration to do? If any of you have ever been in St. Mark's Convent at Florence, I dare say you will remember that in the Guest Chamber the saintly genius of Fra Angelico has painted, as an appropriate frontispiece, the two pilgrims on the road to Emmaus, praying the unknown man to come in and partake of their hospitality; and he has draped them in the habit of his order, and he has put Christ as the Representative of all the poor and wearied and wayworn travellers that might enter in there and receive hospitality, which is but the lesson, 'Inasmuch as ye have done it unto one of the least of these My brethren, ye have done it unto Me.'

And there is another thing, dear friends. Do we not minister to Him best when we do the thing that is nearest His heart and help Him most in the purpose of His life and in His death? What would you think of a would–be helper of some great reformer who said: 'I will give you all sorts of material support; but I have not a grain of sympathy with the cause to which you have devoted your life. I think it is madness and nonsense: I will feed you and house you and make you comfortable, but I do not care one rush for the object for which you are to be housed and fed and made comfortable.' Jesus Christ let these poor women help Him that He might live to bear the Cross; He lets you and me help Him for that for which on the Cross He died; 'This honour have all the saints'; The foundation of our service is the consciousness of redemption; its sphere is ministering to Him in that which is nearest His heart.

And then, brethren, there is another thing that does not so immediately belong to the incident before us, but which suggests itself to me in connection with it. We have tried to show the motive and the pattern, the foundation and the sphere, of the service: let me add a last thought—the remembrance and the record of it.

How strange that is, that just as a beam of light coming into a room would enable us to see all the motes dancing up and down that lay in its path, so the beam from Christ's life shoots athwart the society of His age, and all those little insignificant people come for a moment into the full lustre of the light. Years before and years afterward they lived, and we do not know anything about them; but for an instant they crossed the illuminated track and there they blazed. How strange Pharisees, officials, and bookmen of all sorts would have felt if anybody had said to them: 'Do you see that handful of travel–stained Galileans there, those poor women you have just passed by the way? Well, do you know that these three women's names will never perish as long as the world lasts?' So we may learn the eternity of work done for Him. Ah, a great deal of it may be forgotten and unrecorded! How many deeds of faithful love and noble devotion are all compressed into those words, 'which ministered unto Him'! It is the old story of how life shrinks, and shrinks, and shrinks in the record. How many acres of green forest ferns in the long ago time went to make up a seam of coal as thick as a sixpence? But still there is the record, compressed indeed, but existent.

And how many names may drop out and not be associated with the work which they did? Do you not think that these anonymous 'many others which ministered' were just as dear to Jesus Christ as Mary and Joanna and Susannah? A great many people helped Him whose deeds are related in the Gospel, but whose names are not recorded. But what does it matter about that? With many 'others of my fellow–labourers also,' says St. Paul; 'whose names'—well, I have forgotten them; but that is of little consequence; they 'are in the Lamb's book of life.' And so the work is eternal, and will last on in our blessed consciousness and in His remembrance who will never forget any of it, and we shall self–enfold the large results, even if the rays of dying fame may fade.

And there is one other thought on this matter of the eternity of the work on which I would just touch for an instant.

How strange it must be to these women now! If, as I suppose, you and I believe, they are living with Christ, they will look up to Him and think, 'Ah! we remember when we used to find your food and prepare for your household comforts, and there Thou art on the throne! How strange and how great our earthly service seems to us now!' So it will be to us all when we get up yonder. We shall have to say, 'Lord, when saw I Thee?' He will put a meaning into our work and a majesty into it that we know nothing about at present. So, brethren, account the name of His slaves your highest honour, and the task that love gives you your greatest joy. When we have in our poor love poorly ministered unto Him who in His great love greatly died for us, then, at the last, the wonderful word will be fulfilled: 'Verily I say unto you, He shall gird Himself and make them to sit down to meat and will come forth and serve them.'

ONE SEED AND DIVERSE SOILS

'And when much people were gathered together, and were
come to Him out of every city, He spake by a parable:

5. A sower went out to sow his seed: and as he sowed,
some fell by the wayside; and it was trodden down, and
the fowls of the air devoured it. 6. And some fell upon
a rock; and as soon as it was sprung up, it withered
away, because it lacked moisture. 7. And some fell
among thorns; and the thorns sprang up with it, and
choked it. 8. And other fell on good ground, and sprang
up, and bare fruit an hundredfold. And when He had said
these things, He cried, He that hath ears to hear, let
him hear. 9. And His disciples asked Him, saying, What
might this parable be? 10. And He said, Unto you it is
given to know the mysteries of the kingdom of God: but
to others in parables; that seeing they might not see,
and hearing they might not understand. 11. Now the
parable is this; The seed is the word of God. 12. Those
by the way–side are they that hear: then cometh the
devil, and taketh away the word out of their hearts,
lest they should believe and be saved. 13. They on the
rock are they which, when they hear, receive the word
with joy; and these have no root, which for a while
believe, and in time of temptation fall away. 14. And
that which fell among thorns are they, which, when they
have heard, go forth, and are choked with cares, and
riches, and pleasures of this life, and bring no fruit
to perfection. 15. But that on the good ground are
they, which in an honest and good heart, having heard
the word, keep it, and bring forth fruit with patience.'
—LUKE viii. 4–16.

Luke is particular in dating this parable as spoken at a time when crowds resorted to Jesus, and the
cities of Galilee seemed emptied out to hear Him. No illusions as to the depth or worth of this
excitement beset Him. Sadly He looked on the eager multitudes, because He looked through them,
and saw how few of them were bringing 'an honest and good heart' for the soil of His word. Just
because He saw the shallowness of the momentary enthusiasm, He spoke this pregnant parable from a
heavy heart, and as He tells us in His explanation of it to the disciples (ver. 10), uses the parabolic
garb as a means of hiding the truth from the unsusceptible, and of bringing it home to those who were
prepared to receive it. Every parable has that double purpose of obscuring and revealing. The
obscuring is punitive, but the punishment is meant to be remedial. God never cheats men by a
revelation that does not reveal, and the very hiding is meant to stimulate to a search which cannot be
vain.

The broad outstanding fact of the parable is tragic. Three failures and one success! It may be
somewhat lightened by observing that the proportion which each 'some' bears to the whole
seed–basketful is not told; but with all alleviation, it is sad enough. What a lesson for all eager
reformers and apostles of any truth, who imagine that they have but to open their mouths and the

world will listen! What a warning for any who are carried off their feet by their apparent 'popularity'! What a solemn appeal to all hearers of God's message!

I. Commentators have pointed out that all four kinds of soil might have been found close together by the lake, and that there may have been a sower at work within sight. But the occasion of the parable lay deeper than the accident of local surroundings. A path through a cornfield is a prosaic enough thing, but one who habitually holds converse with the unseen, and ever sees it shining through the seen, beholds all things 'apparelled in celestial light,' and finds deep truths in commonplace objects. The sower would not intentionally throw seed on the path, but some would find its resting–place there. It would lie bare on the surface of the hard ground, and would not be there long enough to have a chance of germinating, but as soon as the sower's back was turned to go up the next furrow, down would come the flock of thievish birds that fluttered behind him, and bear away the grains. The soil might be good enough, but it was so hard that the seed did not get in, but only lay on it. The path was of the same soil as the rest of the field, only it had been trodden down by the feet of passengers, perhaps for many years.

A heart across which all manner of other thoughts have right of way will remain unaffected by the voice of Jesus, if He spoke His sweetest, divinest tones, still more when He speaks but through some feeble man. The listener hears the words, but they never get farther than the drum of his ear. They lie on the surface of his soul, which is beaten hard, and is non–receptive. How many there are who have been listening to the preaching of the Gospel, which is in a true sense the sowing of the seed, all their lives, and have never really been in contact with it! Tramp, tramp, go the feet across the path, heavy drays of business, light carriages of pleasure, a never–ending stream of traffic and noise like that which pours day and night through the streets of a great city, and the result is complete insensibility to Christ's voice.

If one could uncover the hearts of a congregation, how many of them would be seen to be occupied with business or pleasures, or some favourite pursuit, even while they sit decorously in their pews! How many of them hear the preacher's voice without one answering thought or emotion! How many could not for their lives tell what his last sentence was! No marvel, then, that, as soon as its last sound has ceased, down pounce a whole covey of light–winged fancies and occupations, and carry off the poor fragments of what had been so imperfectly heard. One wonders what percentage of remembrances of a sermon is driven out of the hearers' heads in the first five minutes of their walk home, by the purely secular conversation into which they plunge so eagerly.

II. The next class of hearers is represented by seed which has had somewhat better fate, inasmuch as it has sunk some way in, and begun to sprout. The field, like many a one in hilly country, had places where the hard pan of underlying rock had only a thin skin of earth over it. Its very thinness helped quick germination, for the rock was near enough to the surface to get heated by the sun. So, with undesirable rapidity, growth began, and shoots appeared above ground before there was root enough made below to nourish them. There was only one possible end for such premature growth—namely, withering in the heat. No moisture was to be drawn from the shelf of rock, and the sun was beating fiercely down, so the feeble green stem drooped and was wilted.

It is the type of emotional hearers, who are superficially touched by the Gospel, and too easily receive it, without understanding what is involved. They take it for theirs 'with joy,' but are strangers to the deep exercises of penitence and sorrow which should precede the joy. 'Lightly come, lightly go,' is true in Christian life as elsewhere. Converts swiftly made are quickly lost. True, the most thorough and permanent change may be a matter of a moment; but, if so, into that moment emotions will be compressed like a great river forced through a mountain gorge, which will do the work of years.

Such surface converts fringe all religious revivals. The crowd listening to our Lord was largely made up of them. These were they who, when a ground of offence arose, 'went back, and walked no more with Him.' They have had their successors in all subsequent times of religious movement. Light things are caught up by the wind of a passing train, but they soon drop to the ground again. Emotion is good, if there are roots to it. But 'these have no root.' The Gospel has not really touched the depths of their natures, their wills, their reason, and so they shrivel up when they have to face the toil and self–sacrifice inherent in a Christian life.

III. The third parcel of seed advanced still farther. It rooted and grew. But the soil had other occupants. It was full of seeds of weeds and thorns (not thorn *bushes*). So the two crops ran a race, and as ill weeds grow apace, the worse beat, and stifled the green blades of the springing corn, which, hemmed in and shut out from light and air, came to nothing.

The man represented has not made clean work of his religion. He has received the good seed, but has forgotten that something has to be grubbed up and cast out, as well as something to be taken in, if he would grow the fair fruits of Christian character. He probably has cut down the thorns, but has left their roots or seeds where they were. He has fruit of a sort, but it is scanty, crude, and green. Why? Because he has not turned the world out of his heart. He is trying to unite incompatibles, one of which is sure to kill the other. His 'thorns' are threefold, as Luke carefully distinguishes them into 'cares and riches and pleasures,' but they are one in essence, for they are all 'of this life.' If he is poor, he is absorbed in cares; if rich, he is yet more absorbed in wealth, and his desires go after worldly pleasures, which he has not been taught, by experience of the supreme pleasure of communion with God, to despise.

Mark that this man does not 'fall away.' He keeps up his Christian name to the end. Probably he is a very influential member of the church, universally respected for his wealth and liberality, but his religion has been suffocated by the other growth. He has fruit, but it is not to 'perfection.' If Jesus Christ came to Manchester, one wonders how many such Christians He would discover in the chief seats in the synagogues.

IV. The last class avoids the defects of the three preceding. The soil is soft, deep, and clean. The seed sinks, roots, germinates, has light and air, and brings forth ripened grain. The 'honest and good heart' in which it lodges has been well characterised as one 'whose aim is noble, and who is generously devoted to his aim' (Bruce, *The Parabolic Teaching of Christ*, p. 33). Such a soul Christ recognises as possible, prior to the entrance into it of the word. There are dispositions which prepare for the reception of the truth. But not only the previous disposition, but the subsequent attitude to the word spoken, is emphasised by our Lord. 'They having heard the word, hold it fast.' Docilely received, it is steadily retained, or held with a firm grip, whoever and whatever may seek to pluck it from mind or heart.

Further, not only tenacity of grasp, but patient perseverance of effort after the fruit of Christian character, is needed. There must be perseverance in the face of obstacles within and without, if there is to be fruitfulness. The emblem of growth does not suffice to describe the process of Christian progress. The blade becomes the ear, and the ear the full corn, without effort. But the Christian disciple has to fight and resist, and doggedly to keep on in a course from which many things would withdraw him. The nobler the result, the sorer the process. Corn grows; character is built up as the result, first of worthily receiving the good seed, and then of patient labour and much self–suppression.

These different types of character are capable of being changed. The path may be broken up, the rock blasted and removed, the thorns stubbed up. We make ourselves fit or unfit to receive the seed and bear fruit. Christ would not have spoken the parable if He had not hoped thereby to make some of His hearers who belonged to the three defective classes into members of the fourth. No natural, unalterable incapacity bars any from welcoming the word, housing it in his heart, and bringing forth fruit with patience.

SEED AMONG THORNS

'And that which fell among thorns are they, which, when they have heard, go forth, and are choked with cares, and riches, and pleasures of this life, and bring no fruit to perfection.'—Luke viii. 14.

No sensible sower would cast his seed among growing thorn–bushes, and we must necessarily understand that the description in this verse is not meant to give us the picture of a field in which these were actually growing, but rather of one in which they had been grubbed up, and so preparation been made for the sowing of the seed. They had been grubbed up, but they had not been grubbed out. The roots were there, although the branches and the stems had been cut down, or if the roots were not there, abundant seeds were lying buried, and when the good seed was sown it went into ground full of them—and that was the blunder out of which all the mischief came.

I. These three different instances of failure in this parable represent to us, first, the seed carried off at the very beginning, before it has sunk into the ground and before it has had time to germinate. It lies on the surface and it goes at once. But suppose it is safely piloted past that first danger, then comes another peril. It gets a little deeper into the ground, but there is a shelf of rock an inch or two below the skin of soil, and the poor little rootlets cannot get through that, and so when the hot Syrian sun shines down upon the field, there is an unnatural heat, and a swift vegetation. There is growth, but the same sun that at first stimulated the unnaturally rapid growth, gets a little hotter or continues to pour down during the fervid summer and dries up the premature vegetation which it had called into feeble life. That second seed went further on the road towards fruit.

But suppose a seed is piloted past that second risk, there comes this third one. This seed gets deeper still, and does take root, and does grow, and does bear fruit. That is to say, this is a picture of a real Christian, in whom the seed of the kingdom, which is the word of God, has taken root, and to whom there has been the communication of the divine life that is in the seed; and yet that, too, comes to

119

grief, and our parable tells us how—by three things, the thorns, the growth of the thorns, and the choking of the word.

Luke puts the interpretation of the thorns even more vividly than the other Evangelists, because he represents them as being three different forms of one thing, 'cares and riches and pleasures,' which all come into the one class, 'of this life.' Or, in other words, the present world, with all its various appeals to our animal and sensual nature, with all its possible delights for part of our being, a real and important part of it; and with all the troubles and anxieties which it is cowardly for us to shirk, and impossible for us to escape—this world is ever present to each of us, and if there is anything in us to which it appeals, then certainly the thorns will come up. The cares and the wealth and the pleasures are three classes of one thing. Perhaps the first chiefly besets struggling people; the second mainly threatens well–to–do people; the third, perhaps, is most formidable to leisurely and idle people. But all three appeal to us all, for in every one of us there are the necessary anxieties of life, and every one of us knows that there is real and substantial good to a part of our being, in the possession of a share of this world's wealth, without which no man can live, and all of us carry natures to which the delights of sense do legitimately and necessarily appeal.

So the soil for the growth of the thorns is always in us all. But what then? Are these things so powerful in our hearts as that they become hindrances to our Christian life? That is the question. The cares and the occupation of mind with, and desire for, the wealth and the pleasures are of God's appointment. He did not make them thorns, but you and I make them thorns; and the question for us is, has our Christianity driven out the undue regard to this life, regarded in these three aspects—undue in measure or in any other respect, by which they are converted into hindrances that mar our Christian life? Dear brethren, it is not enough to say, 'I have received the word into my heart.' There is another question besides that—Has the word received into your heart cast out the thorns? Or are they and the seed growing there side by side? The picture of my text is that of a man who, in a real fashion, has accepted the Gospel, but who has accepted it so superficially as that it has not exercised upon him the effect that it ought to produce, of expelling from him the tendencies which may become hindrances to his Christian life. If we have known nothing of 'the expulsive power of a new affection,' and if we thought it was enough to cut down the thickest and tallest thorn–bushes, and to leave all the seeds and the roots of them in our hearts, no wonder if, as we get along in life, they grow up and choke the word. 'Ye cannot serve God and Mammon'; that is just putting into a sentence the lesson of my text.

II. Further, note the growth of the thorns. Luke employs a very significant phrase. He says, 'When they have heard they *go forth*, and are choked with cares and riches and pleasures of this life.' That is to say, the path of daily life upon which we all have to walk, the common duties which necessarily draw us to themselves, will certainly stimulate the growth of the thorns if these are not rooted out. Life is full of appeals to our desires after earthly good or pleasure, to our greed after earthly gain, to our dread of earthly sorrow, of pain, of loss, and of poverty. As surely as we are living, and have to go out into the world day by day, so surely will the thorns grow if they are left in us. And so we come back to the old lesson that because we are set in this world, with all its temptations that appeal so strongly to many needs and desires of our nature, we must make thorough work of our religion if it is to be of any good to us at all, and we are not to go on the Christian pilgrimage with one foot upon the higher level and the other upon the lower, like a man walking with one foot on the kerbstone and the other on the roadway. Let us be one thing or the other, out and out, thorough and consistent. If we have the seed in our hearts, remember that *we* are responsible for its growth.

Let us make certain that we have cast out the thorns. There is an old German proverb, the vulgarity of which may be excused for its point. 'You must not sit near the fire if your head is made of butter.' We should not try to walk through this wicked world without making very certain that we have stubbed the thorns out of our hearts. Oh, dear friends! here is the secret to the miserable inconsistencies of the great bulk of professing Christians. They have got the seed in, but they have not got the thorns out.

III. Lastly, mark the choking of the growth. Of course it is rapid, according to the old saying, 'Ill weeds grow apace.' 'They are choked with the cares and riches and pleasures of this life and bring no fruit to perfection.' The weeds grow faster than the seed. 'Possession is nine–tenths of the law,' and they have got possession of the soil, and their roots go far and strike deep, and so they come up, with their great, strong, coarse, quick–growing stems and leaves, and surround the green, infant, slender shoot, and keep the air and light out from it, and exhaust all the goodness of the soil, which has not nutriment in it enough for the modest seed and for the self–asserting thorn. And so the thorn beats in the race, and grows inches whilst the other grows hairbreadths. Is not that a true statement of our experience? If Christian men and women permit as much of their interest and affection and effort and occupation of mind to go out towards the world and worldly things, as, alas! most of us do, no wonder if the tiny, yellow, rather than green, blade is choked and gets covered with parasitical disease, and perhaps dies at last. You cannot grow two crops on one field. Some of us have tried; it will never do. It must be one thing or another, and we must make up our minds whether we are going to cultivate corn or thorn. May God help us to make the right choice of the crop we desire to bear!

Our text tells us that this man, represented by the seed among thorns, was a Christian, did, and does, bear fruit, but, as Luke says, 'brings no fruit to perfection.' The first seed never grew at all; the second got the length of putting forth a blade; this one has got as far as the ear, but not so far as 'the full corn in the ear.' It has fruited, but the fruit is green and scanty, not ripened, as it ought to be, since it grows under such a sky and was taken out of such a seed–basket as our seed has come from. It brings forth no fruit *to perfection*';—is not that a picture of so many Christian people? One cannot say that they are not Christians. One cannot say that there are no signs of a divine life in them. One cannot say but that they do a good many things that are right and pure, and obviously the result of a Divine Spirit working upon them; but all that they do just falls short of the crowning grace and beauty. There is always something about it that strikes one as being incomplete. They are Christian men and Christian women bringing forth many of the fruits of the Christian life, but the climax somehow or other is always absent. The pyramid goes up many stages, but there is never the gilded summit flashing in the light—'No fruit to perfection.'

Dear brethren, let us take our poor, imperfect services, and lay them down at the Master's feet, and ask Him to help us to make clean work of these hearts of ours, and to turn out of them all our worldly hankerings after the seen and temporal. Then we shall bear fruit that He will gather into His garner. The cares and the pleasures and the wealth that terminate in, and are occupied with, this poor fleeting present are small and insignificant. Let us try to yield ourselves up wholly to the higher influences of that Divine Spirit, and in true consecration receive the engrafted word. And then He will give to us to drink of that river of His pleasures, drinking of which we shall not thirst, nor need to come to any of earth's fountains to draw. If the Saviour comes in in His power, He will cast out the uncleanness that dwells in us and make us fruitful as He would have us to be.

A MIRACLE WITHIN A MIRACLE

'And a woman, having an issue of blood twelve years,
which had spent all her living upon physicians,
neither could be healed of any, 44. Came behind Him,
and touched the border of His garment: and immediately
her issue of blood stanched. 45. And Jesus said, Who
touched Me? When all denied, Peter, and they that were
with Him, said, Master, the multitude throng Thee and
press Thee, and sayest Thou, Who touched Me? 46. And
Jesus said, Somebody hath touched Me: for I perceive
that virtue is gone out of Me. 47. And when the woman
saw that she was not hid, she came trembling, and,
falling down before Him, she declared unto Him before
all the people for what cause she had touched Him, and
how she was healed immediately. 48. And He said unto
her, Daughter, be of good comfort: thy faith hath made
thee whole; go in peace.'—LUKE viii. 43–48.

The story of Jairus's daughter is, as it were, cut in two by that of the poor invalid woman. What an impression of calm consciousness of power and of leisurely dignity is made by Christ's having time to pause, even on His way to a dying sufferer, in order to heal, as if parenthetically, this other afflicted one! How Jairus must have chafed at the delay! He had left his child 'at the point of death' and here was the Healer loitering, as it must have seemed to a father's agony of impatience.

But Jesus, with His infinite calm and as infinite power, can afford to let the one wait and even die, while He tends the other. The child shall receive no harm, and her sister in sorrow has as great a claim on Him as she. He has leisure of heart to feel for each, and power for both. We do not rob one another of His gifts. Attending to one, He does not neglect another.

This miracle illustrates the genuineness and power of feeble and erroneous faith, and Christ's merciful way of strengthening and upholding it. The woman, a poor, shrinking creature, has been made more timid by long illness, disappointed hopes of cure, and by poverty. She does not venture to stop Jesus, as He goes with an important official of the synagogue to heal his daughter, but creeps up in the crowd behind Him, puts out a wasted, trembling hand to touch the tasselled fringe of His robe—and she is whole.

She would fain have glided away with a stolen cure, but Jesus forced her to stand out before the throng, and with all their eyes on her, to conquer diffidence and womanly reticence, and tell all the truth. Strange contrast, this, to His usual avoidance of notoriety and regard for shrinking weakness! But it was true kindness, for it was the discipline by which her imperfect faith was cleared and confirmed.

It is easy to point out the imperfections in this woman's faith. It was very ignorant. She was sure that this Rabbi would heal her, but she expected it to be done by the material contact of her finger with His robe. She had no idea that Christ's will, much less His love, had anything to do with His cures. She thinks that she may carry away the blessing, and He be none the wiser. It is easy to say, What blank ignorance of Christ's way of working! what grossly superstitious notions! Yes, and with them all what a hunger of intense desire to be whole, and what absolute confidence that a finger–tip on His robe was enough!

Her faith was very imperfect, but the main fact is that she had it. Let us be thankful for a living proof of the genuineness of ignorant and even of superstitious faith. There are many now who fall with less excuse into a like error with this woman's, by attaching undue importance to externals, and thinking more of the hem of the garment and its touch by a finger than of the heart of the wearer and the grasp of faith. But while we avoid such errors, let us not forget that many a poor worshipper clasping a crucifix may be clinging to the Saviour, and that Christ does accept faith which is tied to outward forms, as He did this woman's.

There was no real connection between the touch of her finger and her healing, but she thought that there was, and Christ stoops to her childish thought, and lets her make the path for His gift. 'According to thy faith be it unto thee': His mercy, like water, takes the shape of the containing vessel.

The last part of the miracle, when the cured woman is made the bold confessor, is all shaped so as to correct and confirm her imperfect faith. We note this purpose in every part of it. She had thought of the healing energy as independent of His knowledge and will. Therefore she is taught that He was aware of the mute appeal, and of the going out of power in answer to it. The question, 'Who touched me?' has been regarded as a proof that Jesus was ignorant of the person; but if we keep the woman's character and the nature of her disease in view, we can suppose it asked, not to obtain information, but to lead to acknowledgment, and that without ascribing to Him in asking it any feigning of ignorance.

The contrast between the pressure of the crowd and the touch of faith has often been insisted on, and carries a great lesson. The unmannerly crowd hustled each other, trod on His skirts, and elbowed their way to gape at Him, and He took no heed. But His heart detected the touch, unlike all the rest, and went out with healing power towards her who touched. We may be sure that, though a universe waits before Him, and the close–ranked hosts of heaven stand round His throne, we can reach our hands through them all, and get the gifts we need.

She had shrunk from publicity, most naturally. But if she had stolen away, she would have lost the joy of confession and greater blessings than the cure. So He mercifully obliges her to stand forth. In a moment she is changed from a timid invalid to a confessor. A secret faith is like a plant growing in the dark, the stem of which is blanched and weak, and its few blossoms pale and never matured. 'With the mouth confession is made unto salvation.'

Christ's last word to her is tender. He calls her 'Daughter'—the only woman whom He addressed by such a name. He teaches her that her faith, not her finger, had been the medium through which His healing power had reached her. He confirms by His authoritative word the furtive blessing: *Be* whole of thy plague.' And she goes, having found more than she sought, and felt a loving heart where she had only seen a magic–working robe.

CHRIST TO JAIRUS

'When Jesus heard it, He answered, saying, Fear not:
believe only, and she shall be made whole.'
—LUKE viii. 60.

The calm leisureliness of conscious power shines out very brilliantly from this story of the raising of Jairus's daughter. The father had come to Jesus, in an agony of impatience, and besought Him to heal his child, who lay 'at the point of death.' Not a moment was to be lost. Our Lord sets out with him, but on the road pauses to attend to another sufferer, the woman who laid her wasted finger on the hem of Christ's robe. How Jairus must have chafed at the delay, and thought every moment an eternity; and perhaps said hard things In his heart about Christ's apparent indifference! Delay seemed to be fatal, for before Christ had finished speaking to the woman, the messenger comes with a word which appears to me to have in it a touch of bitterness and of blame. 'Trouble not the Master' sounds as if the speaker hinted that the Master was thinking it a trouble, and had not put Himself much about to meet the necessity. But one's gain shall not be another's loss, and Christ does not let any applicant to Him suffer whilst He attends to any other. Each has an equal claim on His heart. So He turns to the father with the words that I have read for my text.

They are the first of three sayings of our Lord round which this whole narrative is remarkably grouped. I have read the first, but I mean to speak about all three. There is a word of encouragement which sustains a feeble faith: there is a word of revelation which smooths the grimness of death; 'She is not dead but sleepeth'; and there is a word of power which goes into the darkness, and brings back the child; 'Maiden, arise!' Now, I think if we take these three, we get the significance of this whole incident.

I. First, then, the word of cheer which sustains a staggering faith.

'When Jesus heard this, He said unto him, Fear not, believe only, and she shall be made whole.' How preposterous this rekindling of hope must have seemed to Jairus when the storm had blown out the last flickering spark! How irrelevant, if it were not cruel, the 'Fear not!' must have sounded when the last possible blow had fallen. And yet, because of the word in the middle, embedded between the obligation to hope and the prohibition to fear, neither the one nor the other is preposterous, 'Only believe.' That is in the centre; and on the one side,' Fear not!'—a command ridiculous without it; and on the other side, 'Hope!' an injunction impossible apart from faith.

Jesus Christ is saying the very same things to us. His fundamental commandment is 'Only believe,' and there effloresce from it the two things, courage that never trembles, and hope that never despairs. 'Only believe'—usually He made the outflow of His miraculous power contingent upon the faith, either of the sufferer himself or of some others. There was no necessity for the connection. We have instances in His life of miracles wrought without faith, without asking, simply at the bidding of His own irrepressible pity. But the rule in regard to His miracles is that faith was the condition that drew

124

out the miraculous energy. The connection between our faith and our experience of His supernatural, sustaining, cleansing, gladdening, enlightening power is closer than that. For without our trust in Him, He can do no mighty works upon us, and there must be confidence, on our part, before there is in our experience the reception into our lives of His highest blessings; just because they are greater and deeper, and belong to a more inward sphere than these outward and inferior miracles of bodily healing. Therefore the connection between our faith and His gifts to us is inevitable, and constant, and the commandment 'Only believe,' assumes a more imperative stringency, in regard to our spiritual experience, than it ever did in regard to those who felt the power of His miracle-working hand. So it stands for us, as the one central appeal and exhortation which Christ, by His life, by the record of His love, by His Cross and Passion, by His dealings and pleadings with us through His Spirit, and His providence to-day, is making to us all. 'Only believe'—the one act that vitally knits the soul to Christ, and makes it capable of receiving unto itself the fullness of His loftiest blessings.

But we must note the two clauses which stand on either side of this central commandment. They deal with two issues of faith. One forbids fear, the other gives fuel for the fire of hope. On the one hand, the exhortation, 'Fear not,' which is the most futile that can be spoken if the speaker does not touch the cause of the fear, comes from His lips with a gracious power. Faith is the one counterpoise of fear. There is none other for the deepest dreads that lie cold and paralysing, though often dormant, in every human spirit; and that ought to lie there. If a man has not faith in God, in Christ, he ought to have fear. For there rise before him, solitary, helpless, inextricably caught into the meshes of this mysterious and awful system of things—a whole host of possible, or probable, or certain calamities, and what is he to do? stand there in the open, with the pelting of the pitiless storm coming down upon him? The man is an idiot if he is not afraid. And what is to calm those rational fears, the fear of wrath, of life, of death, of what lies beyond death? You cannot whistle them away. You cannot ignore them always. You cannot grapple with them in your own strength. 'Only believe,' says the Comforter and the Courage-bringer. The attitude of trust banishes dread, and nothing else will effectually and reasonably do it. 'I will forewarn you whom ye shall fear.' Him who can slay and who judges. You have, and you cannot break, a connection with God. He ought to be one of two things—your ghastliest dread or your absolute trust. 'Only believe then,' 'fear not.' Believe not, *then* be afraid; for you have reason to be.

Men say, 'Oh! keep your courage up'; and they contribute no means to keep it up: Christ says 'Fear not; only believe,' and gives to faith the courage which He enjoins. Like a child that never dreams of any mischief being able to reach it when the mother's breast is beneath its head, and the mother's arms are round its little body, each of us may rest on Christ's breast, and feel His arm round about us. Then we may smile at all that men call evils; and whether they are possible, or probable, or certain, we can look at them all and say, 'Ah! I have circumvented you.' 'All things work together for good to them that' trust Christ. 'Fear not; only believe.'

But on the other hand, from that simple faith will spring up also hope that cannot despair. 'She shall be made whole.' Irreversible disasters have no place in Christian experience. There are no irrevocable losses to him who trusts. There are no wounds that cannot be stanched, when we go to Him who has the balm and the bandage. Although it is true that dead faces do not smile again upon us until we get beyond earth's darkness, it is also true that bonds broken may be knit in a finer fashion, if faith instead of sense weaves them together; and that in the great future we shall find that the true healing of those that went before was not by deliverance from, but by passing through, the death that emancipates from the long disease of earthly life.

Brethren! if we trust Christ we may 'hope perfectly.' If we do not trust Him our firmest hopes are as spiders' webs that are swept away by a besom; and our deepest desires remain unfulfilled. 'Only believe,' then, on the one side, 'Fear not,' and on the other side 'Hope ever.'

II. We have here a word of revelation which softens the grimness of death.

Our Lord reaches the house of affliction, and finds it a house of hubbub and noise. The hired mourners, with their shrill shrieks, were there already, bewailing the child. The tumult jarred upon His calmness, and He says 'Weep not; she is not dead but sleepeth.' One wonders how some people have read those words as if they declared that the apparent physical death was only a swoon or a faint, or some kind of coma, and that so there was no miracle at all in the case. 'They laughed Him to scorn; knowing that she was dead.' You can measure the hollowness of their grief by its change into scornful laughter when a promise of consolation began to open before them. And you can measure their worth as witnesses to the child's resurrection by their absolute certainty of her death.

But notice that our Lord never forbids weeping unless He takes away its cause. 'Weep not,' is another of the futile forms of words with which men try to encourage and comfort one another. There is nothing more cruel than to forbid tears to the sad heart. Jesus Christ never did that except when He was able to bring that which took away occasion for weeping. He lets grief have its way. He means us to run rivers of waters down our cheeks when He sends us sorrows. We shall never get the blessing of these till we have felt the bitterness of them. We shall never profit by them if we stoically choke back the manifestations of our grief, and think that it is submissive to be dumb. Let sorrow have way. Tears purge the heart from which their streams come. But Jesus Christ says to us all, 'Weep not,' because He comes to us all with that which, if I may so say, puts a rainbow into the tear–drops, and makes it possible that the great paradox should be fulfilled in our hearts, 'As sorrowful yet always rejoicing.' Weep not; or if you weep, let the tears have thankfulness as well as grief in them. It is a difficult commandment, but it is possible when His lips tell us not to weep, and we have obeyed the central exhortation, 'Only believe.'

Note, further, in this second of our Lord's words, how He smooths away the grimness of death. I do not claim for Him anything like a monopoly of that most obvious and natural symbolism which regards death as a sleep. It must have occurred to all who ever looked upon a corpse. But I do claim that when He used the metaphor, and by His use of it modified the whole conception of death in the thoughts of His disciples, He put altogether different ideas into it from that which it contained on the lips of others. He meant to suggest the idea of repose—

 'Sleep, full of rest from head to foot.'

The calm immobility of the body so lately racked with pain, or restless in feverish tossings, is but a symbol of the deeper stillness of truer repose which remaineth for the people of God and laps the blessed spirits who 'sleep in Jesus.' He meant to suggest the idea of separation from this material world. He did not mean to suggest the idea of unconsciousness. A man is not unconscious when he is asleep, as dreams testify. He meant, above all, if sleep, then waking.

So the grim fact is smoothed down, not by blinking any of its aspects, but by looking deeper into them. They who, only believing, have lived a life of courage and of hope, and have fronted sorrows, and felt the benediction of tears, pass into the great darkness, and know that they there are rocked to sleep on a loving breast, and, sleeping in Jesus, shall wake with the earliest morning light.

This is a revelation for all His servants. And how deeply these words, and others like them which He spake at the grave of Lazarus and at other times, were dinted into the consciousness of the Christian Church, is manifested by the fact, not only that they are recurrently used by Apostles in their Epistles, but that all through the New Testament you scarcely ever find the physical fact of dissolution designated by the name 'death,' but all sorts of gracious paraphrases, which bring out the attractive and blessed aspects of the thing, are substituted. It is a 'sleep'; it is a 'putting off the tabernacle'; it is a 'departure'; it is a pulling up of the tent-pegs, and a change of place. We do not need the ugly word, and we do not need to dread the thing that men call by it. The Christian idea of death is not the separation of self from its house, of the soul from the body, but the separation of self from God, who is the life.

III. So, lastly, the life-giving word of power.

'Maiden, arise!' All the circumstances of the miracle are marked by the most lovely consideration, on Christ's part, of the timidity of the little girl of twelve years of age. It is because of that that He seeks to raise her in privacy, whereas the son of the widow of Nain and Lazarus were raised amidst a crowd. It is because of that that He selects as His companions in the room only the three chief Apostles as witnesses, and the father and mother of the child. It is because of that that He puts forth His hand and grasps hers, in order that the child's eyes when they open should see only the loving faces of parents, and the not less loving face of the Master; and that her hand, when it began to move again, should clasp, first, His own tender hand. It is for the same reason that the remarkable appendix to the miracle is given—'He commanded that they should give her food.' Surely that is an inimitable note of truth. No legend-manufacturer would have dared to drop down to such a homely word as that, after such a word as 'Maiden, arise!' An economy of miraculous power is shown here, such as was shown when, after Lazarus came forth, other hands had to untie the grave-clothes which tripped him as he stumbled along. Christ will do by miracle what is needful and not one hairs-breadth more. In His calm majesty He bethinks Himself of the hungry child, and entrusts to others the task of giving her food. That homely touch is, to me, indicative of the simple veracity of the historian.

But the life-giving word itself; what can we say about it? Only this one thing: here Jesus Christ exercises a manifest divine prerogative. It was no more the syllables that He spoke than it was the touch of His hand that raised the child. What was it? The forth-putting of His will, which went away straight into the darkness; and if the disembodied spirit was in a locality, went straight there; and somehow or other, laid hold of the spirit, and somehow or other, reinstated it in its home. Christ's will, like the king's writ, runs through all the universe. 'He spake, and it was done';—whose prerogative is that? God's; and God manifest in the flesh exercised it. The words of the Incarnate Word have power over physical things.

127

Here, too, are the prelude and first–fruits of our resurrection. Not that there are not wide differences between the raising of this child, and that future resurrection to which Christian hope looks forward, but that in this one little incident, little, compared with the majestic scale of the latter, there come out these two things—the demonstration that conscious life runs on, irrespective of the accident of its being united with or separated from a bodily organisation; and the other, that Jesus Christ has power over men's spirits, and can fit them at His will to bodies appropriate to their condition. Time is no element in the case. What befalls the particles of the human frame is no element in the case. 'Thou sowest not the body that shall be.' But if that Lord had the power which He showed in that one chamber, with that one child, then, as a little window may show us great matters, so we see through this single incident the time when 'they that are in the graves shall hear His voice, and shall come forth.'

Brethren! there is a higher lesson still; He that gives and gives again, physical life, does so as a symbol of the highest gift which He can bestow upon us all. If we 'only believe,' then, 'you hath He quickened which were dead in trespasses and sins ... and for His great love wherewith He loved us.... He hath raised us up together, and made us sit together, in heavenly places in Christ Jesus.'

BREAD FROM HEAVEN

'And the apostles, when they were returned, told Him all that they had done. And He took them, and went aside privately into a desert place belonging to the city, called Bethsaida. 11. And the people, when they knew it, followed Him; and He received them, and spake unto them of the kingdom of God, and healed them that had need of healing. 12. And when the day began to wear away, then came the twelve, and said unto Him, Send the multitude away, that they may go into the towns and country round about, and lodge, and get victuals; for we are here in a desert place. 13. But He said unto them, Give ye them to eat. And they said, We have no more but five loaves and two fishes; except we should go and buy meat for all this people. 14. (For they were about five thousand men.) And He said to His disciples, Make them sit down by fifties in a company. 15. And they did so, and made them all sit down. 16. Then He took the five loaves, and the two fishes; and, looking up to heaven, He blessed them, and brake, and gave to the disciples to set before the multitude. 17. And they did eat, and were all filled: and there was taken up of fragments that remained to them twelve baskets.'—LUKE ix. 10–17.

The Apostles needed rest after their trial trip as evangelists. John the Baptist's death had just been told to Christ. The Passover was at hand, and many pilgrims were on the march. Prudence and care for His

128

followers as well as Himself suggested a brief retirement, and our Lord sought it at the Eastern Bethsaida, a couple of miles up the Jordan from its point of entrance to the lake. Matthew and Mark tell us that He went by boat, which Luke does not seem to have known. Mark adds that the curious crowd, which followed on foot, reached the place of landing before Him, and so effectually destroyed all hope of retirement. It was a short walk round the north−western part of the head of the lake, and the boat would be in sight all the way, so that there was no escape for its passengers.

Luke records the self−oblivious cordiality of Christ's reception of the intrusive crowd. Without a sigh or sign of impatience, He 'welcomed them'—a difficult thing to do, and one which few of us could have achieved. The motives of most of them can have been nothing higher than what leads vulgar people of all ranks and countries to buzz about distinguished men, utterly regardless of delicacy or considerateness. They want to see the notoriety, no matter what it costs him. But Jesus received them patiently, because, as Mark touchingly tells, He was 'moved with pity,' and saw in their rude crowding round Him the token of their lack of guides and teachers. They seemed to Him, not merely a mob of intrusive sight−seers, but like a huddled mass of unshepherded sheep.

Christ's heart felt more lovingly than ours because His eye saw deeper, and His eye saw deeper because His heart felt more lovingly. If we would live nearer Him, we should see, as He did, enough in every man to draw our pity and help, even though he may jostle and interfere with us.

The short journey to Bethsaida would be in the early morning, and a long day of toil followed instead of the hoped−for quiet. Note that singular expression, 'Them that had need of healing He healed.' Why not simply 'them that were sick'? Probably to bring out the thought that misery made unfailing appeal to Him, and that for Him to see need was to supply it. His swift compassion, His all−sufficient power to heal, and the conditions of receiving His healing, are all wrapped up in the words. Coming to the miracle itself, we may throw the narrative into three parts—the preliminaries, the miracle, and the abundant overplus.

I. Our Lord leads up to the miracle by forcing home on the minds of the disciples the extent of the need and the utter inadequacy of their resources to meet it, and by calling on them and the crowd for an act of obedience which must have seemed to many of them ludicrous. John shows us that He had begun to prepare them, at the moment of meeting the multitude, by His question to Philip. That had been simmering in the disciples' minds all day, while they leisurely watched Him toiling in word and work, and now they come with their solution of the difficulty. Their suggestion was a very sensible one in the circumstances, and they are not to be blamed for not anticipating a miracle as the way out. However many miracles they saw, they never seem to have expected another. That has been thought to be unnatural, but surely it is true to nature. They moved in a confusing mixture of the miraculous and the natural which baffled calculation as to which element would rule at any given moment. Their faith was feeble, and Christ rebuked them for their slowness to learn the lesson of this very miracle and its twin feeding of the four thousand. They were our true brothers in their failure to grasp the full meaning of the past, and to trust His power.

The strange suggestion that the disciples should feed the crowd must have appeared to them absurd, but it was meant to bring out the clear recognition of the smallness of their supply. Therein lie great lessons. Commands are given and apparent duties laid on us, in order that we may find out how impotent we are to do them. It can never be our duty to do what we cannot do, but it is often our duty to attempt tasks to which we are conspicuously inadequate, in the confidence that He who gives them has laid them on us to drive us to Himself, and there to find sufficiency. The best preparation of His servants for their work in the world is the discovery that their own stores are small. Those who have learned that it is their task to feed the multitude, and who have said 'We have no more than such and such scanty resources,' are prepared to be the distributors of His all–sufficient supply.

What a strange scene that must have been as the hundred groups of fifty each arranged themselves on the green grass, in the setting sunlight, waiting for a meal of which there were no signs! It took a good deal of faith to seat the crowd, and some faith for the crowd to sit. How expectant they would be! How they would wonder what was to be done next! How some of them would laugh, and some sneer, and all watch the event! We, too, have to put ourselves in the attitude to receive gifts of which sense sees no sign; and if, in obedience to Christ's word, we sit down expecting Him to find the food, we shall not be disappointed, though the table be spread in the wilderness, and neither storehouse nor kitchen be in sight.

II. The miracle itself has some singular features. Like that of the draught of fishes, it was not called forth by the cry of suffering, nor was the need which it met one beyond the reach of ordinary means. It was certainly one of the miracles most plainly meant to strike the popular mind, and the enthusiasm excited by it, according to John's account, was foreseen by Christ. Why did He evoke enthusiasm which He did not mean to gratify? For the very purpose of bringing the carnal expectations of the crowd to a head, that they might be the more conclusively disappointed. The miracle and its sequel sifted and sent away many 'disciples,' and were meant to do so.

All the accounts tell of Christ's 'blessing.' Matthew and Mark do not say what He blessed, and perhaps the best supplement is 'God,' but Luke says that He blessed the food. What He blesses is blessed; for His words are deeds, and communicate the blessing which they speak. The point at which the miraculous multiplication of the food came in is left undetermined, but perhaps the difference in the tenses of the verbs hints at it. 'Blessed' and 'brake' are in the tense which describes a single act; 'gave' is in that which describes a continuous repeated action. The pieces grew under His touch, and the disciples always found His hands full when they came back with their own empty. But wherever the miraculous element appeared, creative power was exercised by Jesus; and none the less was it creative, because there was the 'substratum' of the loaves and fishes. Too much stress has been laid on their being used, and some commentators have spoken as if without them the miracle could not have been wrought. But surely the distinction between pure creation and multiplication of a thing already existing vanishes when a loaf is 'multiplied' so as to feed a thousand men.

The symbolical aspect of the miracle is set forth in the great discourse which follows it in John's Gospel. Jesus is the 'Bread of God which came down from heaven.' That Bread is broken for us. Not in His Incarnation alone, but in His Death, is He the food of the world; and we have not only to 'eat His flesh,' but to 'drink His blood,' if we would live. Nor can we lose sight of the symbol of His servants' task. They are the distributors of the heaven–sent bread. If they will but take their poor stores to Jesus, with the acknowledgment of their insufficiency, He will turn them into inexhaustible supplies, and they will find that 'there is that scattereth, and yet increaseth.' What Christ blesses is always enough.

III. The abundance left over is significant. Twelve baskets, such as poor travellers carried their belongings in, were filled; that is to say, each Apostle who had helped to feed the hungry had a basketful to bring off for future wants. The 'broken pieces' were not crumbs that littered the grass, but the portions that came from Christ's hands.

His provision is more than enough for a hungry world, and they who share it out among their fellows have their own possession of it increased. There is no surer way to receive the full sweetness and blessing of the Gospel than to carry it to some hungry soul. These full baskets teach us, too, that In Christ's gift of Himself as the Bread of Life there is ever more than at any given moment we can appropriate. The Christian's spiritual experiences have ever an element of infinity in them; and we feel that if we were able to take in more, there would be more for us to take. Other food cloys and does not satisfy, and leaves us starving. Christ satisfies and does not cloy, and we have always remaining, yet to be enjoyed, the boundless stores which neither eternity will age nor a universe feeding on them consume. The Christian's capacity of partaking of Christ grows with what it feeds on, and he alone is safe in believing that 'To—morrow shall be as this day, and much more abundant.'

THE LORD THAT HEALETH THEE'

'He healed them that had need of healing.'—Luke ix. 11.

Jesus was seeking a little quiet and rest for Himself and His followers. For that purpose He took one of the fishermen's boats to cross to the other side of the sea. But the crowd, inconsiderate and selfish, like all crowds, saw the course of the boat, and hurried, as they could easily do, on foot round the head of the lake, to be ready for Him wherever He might land. So when He touched the shore, there they all were, open—mouthed and mostly moved by mere curiosity, and the prospect of a brief breathing—space vanished.

But not a word of rebuke or disappointment came from His lips, and no shade of annoyance crossed His spirit. Perhaps with a sigh, but yet cheerfully, He braced Himself to work where He had hoped for leisure. It was a little thing, but it was the same in kind, though infinitely smaller in magnitude, as that which led Him to lay aside 'the glory that He had with the Father before the world was,' and come to toil and die amongst men.

But what I especially would note are Luke's remarkable words here. Why does he use that periphrasis, 'Them that had need of healing,' instead of contenting himself with straightforwardly saying, 'Them that were sick,' as do the other Evangelists? Well, I suppose he wished to hint to us the Lord's discernment of men's necessities, the swift compassion which moved to supply a need as soon as it was observed, and the inexhaustible power by which, whatsoever the varieties of infirmity, He was able to cure and to bring strength. 'He healed them that had need of healing,' because His love could not look upon a necessity without being moved to supply it, and because that love wielded the resources of an infinite power.

Now, all our Lord's miracles are parables, illustrating upon a lower platform spiritual facts; and that is especially true about the miracles of healing. So I wish to deal with the words before us as having a direct application to ourselves, and to draw from them two or three very old, threadbare, neglected lessons, which I pray God may lead some of us to recognise anew our need of healing, and Christ's infinite power to bestow it. There are three things that I want to say, and I name them here that you may know where I am going. First, we all need healing; second, Christ can heal us all; third, we are not all healed.

I. We all need healing.

The people in that crowd were not all diseased. Some of them He taught; some of them He cured; but that crowd where healthy men mingled with cripples is no type of the condition of humanity. Rather we are to find it in that Pool of Bethesda, with its five porches, wherein lay a multitude of impotent folk, tortured with varieties of sickness, and none of them sound. Blessed be God! we are in *Bethesda*, which means 'house of mercy,' and the fountain that can heal is perpetually springing up beside us all. There is a disease, dear brethren, which affects and infects all mankind, and it is of that that I wish to speak to you two or three plain, earnest words now. Sin is universal.

What does the Bible mean by sin? Everything that goes against, or neglects God's law. And if you will recognise in all the acts of every life the reference, which really is there, to God and His will, you will not need anything more to establish the fact that 'all have sinned, and come short of the glory of God.' Whatever other differences there are between men, there is this fundamental similarity. Neglect—which is a breach—of the law of God pertains to all mankind. Everything that we do ought to have reference to Him. *Does* everything that we do have such reference? If not, there is a quality of evil in it. For the very definition of sin is living to myself and neglecting Him. He is the centre, and if I might use a violent figure, every planet that wrenches itself away from gravitation towards, and revolution round, that centre, and prefers to whirl on its own axis, has broken the law of the celestial spheres, and brought discord into the heavenly harmony. All men stand condemned in this respect.

Now, there is no need to exaggerate. I am not saying that all men are on the same level. I know that there are great differences in the nobleness, purity, and goodness of lives, and Christianity has never been more unfairly represented than when good men have called, as they have done with St. Augustine, the virtues of godless men, 'splendid vices.' But though the differences are not unimportant, the similarity is far more important. The pure, clean–living man, and the loving, gentle woman, though they stand high above the sensuality of the profligate, the criminal, stand in this respect on the same footing that they, too, have to put their hands on their mouths, and their mouths in the dust, and cry 'Unclean!' I do not want to exaggerate, and sure I am that if men will be honest with themselves there is a voice that responds to the indictment when I say sadly, in the solemn language of Scripture, 'we all have sinned and come short of the glory of God.' For there is no difference. If you do not believe in a God, you can laugh at the old wife's notion of 'sin.' If you do believe in a God, you are shut up to believe this other thing, 'Against Thee, Thee only, have I sinned.'

And, brethren, if this universal fact is indeed a fact, it is the gravest element in human nature. It matters very little, in comparison, whether you and I are wise or foolish, educated or illiterate, rich or poor, happy or miserable. All the superficial distinctions which separate men from one another, and are all right in their own places, dwindle away into nothing before this solemn truth that in every frame there is a plague spot, and that the leprosy has smitten us all.

But, brethren, do not let us lose ourselves in generalities. All means each, and each means me. We all know how hard it is to bring general truths to bear, with all their weight, upon ourselves. That is an old commonplace: 'All men think all men mortal but themselves'; and we are quite comfortable when this indictment is kept in the general terms of universality—'All have sinned.' Suppose I sharpen the point a little. God grant that the point may get to some indurated conscience here. Suppose, instead of reading 'All have sinned,' I beseech each one of my hearers to strike out the general word, and put in the individual one, and to say '*I* have sinned.' You have to do with this indictment just as you have to do with the promises and offers of the Gospel—wherever there is a 'whosoever' put your pen through it, and write your own name over it. The blank cheque is given to us in regard to these promises and offers, and we have to fill in our own names. The charge is handed to us, in regard to this indictment, and if we are wise we shall write our own names there, too.

Dear brethren, I leave this on your consciences, and I will venture to ask that, if not here, at any rate when you get quietly home to–night, and lie down on your beds, you would put to yourselves the question, 'Is it I?' And sure I am that, if you do, you will see a finger pointing out of the darkness, and hear a voice sterner than that of Nathan, saying 'Thou art the man.'

II. Christ can heal us all.

I was going to use an inappropriate word, and say, the *superb* ease with which He grappled with, and overcame, all types of disease is a revelation on a lower level of the inexhaustible and all–sufficient fullness of His healing power. He can cope with all sin–the world's sin, and the individual's. And, as I believe, He alone can do it.

Just look at the problem that lies before any one who attempts to stanch these wounds of humanity. What is needed in order to deliver men from the sickness of sin? Well! that evil thing, like the fabled dog that sits at the gate of the infernal regions, is three–headed. And you have to do something with each of these heads if you are to deliver men from that power.

There is first the awful power that evil once done has over us of repeating itself on and on. There is nothing more dreadful to a reflective mind than the damning influence of habit. The man that has done some wrong thing once is a *rara avis* indeed. If once, then twice; if twice, then onward and onward through all the numbers. And the intervals between will grow less, and what were isolated points will coalesce into a line; and impulses wax as motives wane, and the less delight a man has in his habitual form of evil the more is its dominion over him, and he does it at last not because the doing of it is any delight, but because the *not* doing of it is a misery. If you are to get rid of sin, and to eject the disease from a man, you have to deal with that awful degradation of character, and the tremendous chains of custom. That is one of the heads of the monster.

But, as I said, sin has reference to God, and there is another of the heads, for with sin comes guilt. The relation to God is perverted, and the man that has transgressed stands before Him as guilty, with all the dolefulness that that solemn word means; and that is another of the heads.

The third is this—the consequences that follow in the nature of penalty. 'Whatsoever a man soweth, that shall he also reap.' So long as there is a universal rule by God, in which all things are concatenated by cause and effect, it is impossible but that 'Evil shall slay the wicked.' And that is the third head. These three, habit, guilt, and penalty, have all to be dealt with if you are going to make a thorough job of the surgery.

And here, brethren, I want not to argue but to preach. Jesus Christ died on the Cross for you, and your sin was in His heart and mind when He died, and His atoning sacrifice cancels the guilt, and suspends all that is dreadful in the penalty of the sin. Nothing else—nothing else will do that. Who can deal with guilt but the offended Ruler and Judge? Who can trammel up consequences but the Lord of the Universe? The blood of Jesus Christ is the sole and sufficient oblation and satisfaction for the sins of the whole world.

That disposes of two of the monster's heads. What about the third? Who will take the venom out of my nature? What will express the black drop from my heart? How shall the Ethiopian change his skin or the leopard his spots? How can the man that has become habituated to evil 'learn to do well'? Superficially there may be much reformation. God forbid that I should forget that, or seem to minimise it. But for the thorough ejection from your nature of the corruption that you have yourselves brought into it, I believe—and that is why I am here, for I should have nothing to say if I did not believe it—I believe that there is only one remedy, and that is that into the sinful heart there should come, rejoicing and flashing, and bearing on its broad bosom before it all the rubbish and filth of that dunghill, the great stream of the new life that is given by Jesus Christ. He was crucified for our offences, and He lives to bestow upon us the fullness of His own holiness. So the monster's heads are smitten off. Our disease and the tendency to it, and the weakness consequent upon it, are all cast out from us, and He reveals Himself as 'the Lord who healeth thee.'

Now, dear brethren, you may say 'That is all very fine talking.' Yes! but it is something a great deal more than fine talking. For nineteen centuries have established the fact that it is so; and with all their imperfections there have been millions, and there are millions to–day, who are ready to say, 'Behold! it is not a delusion; it is not rhetoric, *I* have trusted in Him and He has made *me* whole.'

Now, if these things that I have been saying do fairly represent the gravity of the problem which has to be dealt with in order to heal the sicknesses of the world, then there is no need to dwell upon the thought of how absolutely confined to Jesus Christ is the power of thus dealing. God forbid that I should not give full weight to all other methods for partial reformation and bettering of humanity. I would wish them all God–speed. But, brethren, there is nothing else that will deal either with my sin in its relation to God, or in its relation to my character, or in its relation to my future, except the message of the Gospel. There are plenty of other things, very helpful and good in their places, but I do want to say, in one word, that there is nothing else that goes deep enough.

Education? Yes! it will do a great deal, but it will do nothing in regard to sin. It will alter the type of the disease, because the cultured man's transgressions will be very different from those of the illiterate boor. But wise or foolish, professor, student, thinker, or savage with narrow forehead and all but dead brain, are alike in this, that they are sinners in God's sight. I would that I could get through the fence that some of you have reared round you, on the ground of your superior enlightenment and education and refinement, and make you feel that there is something deeper than all that, and that you may be a very clever, and a very well educated, a very highly cultured, an extremely thoughtful and philosophical sinner, but you are a sinner all the same.

And again, we hear a great deal at present, and I do not desire that we should hear less, about social and economic and political changes, which some eager enthusiasts suppose will bring the millennium. Well, if the land were nationalised, and all 'the means of production and distribution' were nationalised, and everybody got his share, and we were all brought to the communistic condition, what then? That would not make men better, in the deepest sense of the word. The fact is, these people are beginning at the wrong end. You cannot better humanity merely by altering its environment for the better. Christianity reverses the process. It begins with the inmost man, and it works outwards to the circumference, and that is the thorough way. Why! suppose you took a company of people out of the slums, for instance, and put them into a model lodging–house, how long will it continue a model? They will take their dirty habits with them, and pull down the woodwork for firing, and in a very short time make the place where they are as like as possible to the hovel whence they came. You must change the men, and then you can change their circumstances, or rather they will change them for themselves. Now, all this is not to be taken as casting cold water on any such efforts to improve matters, but only as a protest against its being supposed that these *alone* are sufficient to rectify the ills and cure the sorrows of humanity. 'Ye have healed the hurt of the daughter of my people slightly.' The patient is dying of cancer, and you are treating him for a skin disease. It is Jesus Christ alone who can cure the sins, and therein the sorrows, of humanity.

III. Lastly, we are not all healed.

That is only too plain. All the sick in the crowd round Christ were sent away well, but the gifts He bestowed so broadcast had no relation to their spiritual natures, and gifts that have relation to our spiritual nature cannot be thus given in entire disregard of our actions in the matter.

Christ cannot heal you unless you take His healing power. He did on earth sometimes, though not often, cure physical disease without the requirement of faith on the part of the healed person or his friends, but He cannot (He would if He could) do so in regard to the disease of sin. There, unless a man goes to Him, and trusts Him, and submits his spirit to the operation of Christ's pardoning and hallowing grace, there cannot be any remedy applied, nor any cure effected. That is no limitation of the universal power of the Gospel. It is only saying that if you do not take the medicine you cannot expect that it will do you any good, and surely that is plain common–sense. There are plenty of people who fancy that Christ's healing and saving power will, somehow or other, reach every man, apart from the man's act. It is all a delusion, brethren. If it could it would. But if salvation could be thus given, independent of the man, it would come down to a mere mechanical thing, and would not be worth the having. So I say, first, if you will not take the medicine you cannot get the cure.

I say, second, if you do not feel that you are ill you will not take the medicine. A man crippled with lameness, or tortured with fever, or groping in the daylight and blind, or deaf to all the sounds of this sweet world, could not but know that he was a subject for the healing. But the awful thing about our disease is that the worse you are the less you know it; and that when conscience ought to be speaking loudest it is quieted altogether, and leaves a man often perfectly at peace, so that after he has done evil things he wipes his mouth and says, 'I have done no harm.'

So, dear brethren, let me plead with you not to put away these poor words that I have been saying to you, and not to be contented until you have recognised what is true, that you—*you*, stand a sinful man before God.

There is surely no madness comparable to the madness of the man that prefers to keep his sin and die, rather than go to Christ and live. We all neglect to take up many good things that we might have if we would, but no other neglect is a thousandth part so insane as that of the man who clings to his evil and spurns the Lord. Will you look into your own hearts? Will you recognise that awful solemn law of God which ought to regulate all our doings, and, alas! has been so often neglected, and so often transgressed by each of us? Oh! if once you saw yourselves as you are, you would turn to Him and say, 'Heal me'; and you would be healed, and He would lay His hand upon you. If only you will go, sick and broken, to Him, and trust in His great sacrifice, and open your hearts to the influx of His healing power, He will give you 'perfect soundness'; and your song will be, 'Bless the Lord, O my soul.... Who forgiveth all thine iniquities; who healeth thy diseases.'

May it be so with each of us!

CHRIST'S CROSS AND OURS

'And it came to pass, as He was alone praying, His
disciples were with Him; and He asked them, saying,
Whom say the people that I am I 19. They answering,
said, John the Baptist; but some say, Elias; and
others say, that one of the old prophets is risen
again. 20. He said unto them, But whom say ye that I
am? Peter answering, said, The Christ of God. 21. And
He straitly charged them, and commanded them to tell
no man that thing; 22. Saying, The Son of man must
suffer many things, and be rejected of the elders,
and chief priests, and scribes, and be slain, and be
raised the third day. 23. And He said to them all, If
any man will come after Me. let him deny himself, and
take up his cross daily, and follow Me. 24. For
whosoever will save his life shall lose it; but
whosoever will lose his life for My sake, the same
shall save it. 25. For what is a man advantaged, if he
gain the whole world, and lose himself, or be cast
away? 26. For whosoever shall be ashamed of Me, and of
My words, of him shall the Son of man be ashamed, when
He shall come in His own glory, and in His Father's,
and of the holy angels. 27. But I tell you of a truth,
there be some standing here, which shall not taste of
death, till they see the kingdom of God.'—Luke ix. 18–27.

Expositions Of Holy Scripture

This passage falls into three distinct but closely connected parts: the disciples' confession of Christ by Peters mouth, the revelation to them of Christ's sufferings as necessarily involved in His Messiahship, and His extension to them of the law of suffering as necessarily involved in discipleship. Luke dwells much more lightly than Matthew on the first of these stages, omitting the eulogium and benediction on Simon Bar–Jona, and the great words about the rock on which the Church is built, but he retains the essentials, and emphasises the connection of the three parts by his very brevity in regard to the first.

I. Luke has special interest in recording Christ's prayers, and though he does not tell us where the great confession was made, he tells what Jesus did before it was made. We may well suppose that His solitary thoughts had been busied with the sufferings on which He was soon to enter, and that His resolve to impart the knowledge of these to His followers was felt by Him to be a sharp trial of their loyalty. The moment was a fateful one. How should fateful moments be prepared for but by communion with the Father? No doubt the feebleness of the disciples was remembered in His petitions.

Jesus' double question was intended, first, to make the disciples feel the gulf which separated them from the rest of the nation, and so to make them hold the faster by their unshared faith, and be ready to suffer for it, if needful, as probably it would be. It braces true men to know that they are but a little company in the midst of multitudes who laugh at their belief. That Jesus should have seen that it was safe to accentuate the disciples' isolation indicates the reality which He discerned in their faith, imperfect as it was.

'Whom say ye that I am?' Jesus brings them to articulate utterance of the thought that had been slowly gathering distinctness in their minds. We see our beliefs more clearly, and hold them more firmly, when we put them into definite words. The question acted like a chemical element dropped into a solution, which precipitates its solid matter. Nebulous opinions are gathered up into spheres of light by the process of speaking them. That question is all–important for us. Our conceptions of Christ's nature and office determine our relation to Him and our whole cast of life. True, we may say that He is Lord, and not be His disciples, but we are not His disciples as He would have us unless His Messiahship stands out clear and axiomatic in our thoughts of Him. The conviction must pass into feeling, and thence into life, but it must underlie all real discipleship. Doctrine is not Christianity, but it is the foundation of Christianity. The Apostolic confession here is the 'irreducible minimum' of the Christian creed.

It does not contain more than Nathanael had said at the beginning, but here it is spoken, not as Peter's private belief, but he is the mouthpiece of all. 'Whether it were I or they, so we' believe. This confession summed up the previous development of the disciples, and so marked the end of one stage and the beginning of another. Christ would have them, as it were, take stock of their convictions, as preliminary to opening a new chapter of teaching.

II. That new chapter follows at once. The belief in Him as Messiah is the first story of the building, and the second is next piled on it. The new lesson was a hard one for men whose hopes were coloured by Jewish dreams of a kingdom. They had to see all these vulgar visions melting away, and to face a stern, sad reality. The very fact that He was the Messiah necessarily drew after it the fact of suffering.

137

Whence did the 'must' arise? From the divine purpose, from the necessities of the case, and the aim of His mission. These had shaped prophetic utterances, and hence there was yet another form of the 'must,' namely, the necessity for the Messiah's fulfilling these predictions.

No doubt our Lord led His saddened listeners to many a prophetic saying which current expositions had smoothed over, but which had for many years set before Him His destiny. What a scene that would be—the victim calmly pointing to the tragic words which flashed ominous new meanings to the silent hearers, stricken with awe and grief as the terrible truth entered their minds! What had become of their dreams? Gone, and in their place shame and death. They had fancied a throne; the vision melted into a cross.

We note the minute particularity of Jesus' delineation, and the absolute certainty in His plain declaration of the fact and time of the Resurrection. It is not wonderful that that declaration should have produced little effect. The disciples were too much absorbed and confounded by the dismal thought of His death to have ears for the assurance of His Resurrection. Comfort coming at the end of the announcement of calamities so great finds no entrance into, nor room in, the heart. We all let a black foreground hide from us a brighter distance.

III. The Master's feet mark the disciples' path. If suffering was involved in Messiahship, it is no less involved in discipleship. The cross which is our hope is also our pattern. In a very real sense we have to be partakers of the sufferings of Christ, and no faith in these as substitutionary is vital unless it leads to being conformed to His death. The solemn verses at the close of this lesson draw out the law of Christian self–denial as being inseparable from true discipleship.

Verse 23 lays down the condition of following Jesus as being the daily bearing, by each, of his own cross. Mark that self–denial is not prescribed for its own sake, but simply as the means of 'following.' False asceticism insists on it, as if it were an end; Christ treats it as a means. Mark, too, that it is 'self' which is to be denied—not this or that part of our nature, but the central 'self.' The will is the man, and *it* is to be brought into captivity to Jesus, so that the true Christian says, 'I live; yet not I, but Christ liveth in me.' That is much deeper, harder, wholesomer teaching than separate austerities or forsakings of this or that.

Verse 24 grounds this great requirement on the broad principle that to make self the main object of life is the sure way to ruin oneself, and that to slay self is the road to true life. Note that it is he who *would* save' his life that loses it, because the desire is itself fatal, whether carried out or not; while it is he who *does* 'lose' his life for Christ that preserves it, because even if the extreme evil has been suffered, the possession of our true lives is not imperilled thereby. No doubt the words refer primarily to literal death, and threaten the cowards who sacrifice their convictions for the sake of keeping a whole skin with the failure of their efforts, while they promise the martyr dying in the arena or at the stake a crown of life. But they go far beyond that. They carry the great truth that to hug self and to make its preservation our first aim is ruinous, and the corresponding one, that to slay self for Christ's sake is to receive a better self. Self–preservation is suicide, self–immolation is not only self–preservation, but self–glorification with glory caught from Jesus. Give yourselves to Him, and He gives you back to yourselves, ennobled and transfigured.

Verse 25 urges obedience to the precept, by an appeal to reasonable self—regard and common—sense. The abnegation enjoined does not require that we should be indifferent to our own well—being. It is right to consider what will 'profit,' and to act accordingly. The commercial view of life, if rightly taken, with regard to all a man's nature through all the duration of it, will coincide accurately with the most exalted. It 'pays' to follow Christ. Christian morality has not the hypersensitive fear of appealing to self—interest which superfine moralists profess nowadays. And the question in verse 25 admits of only one answer, for what good is the whole world to a dead man? If our accounts are rightly kept, a world gained shows poorly on the one side, against the entry on the other of a soul lost.

Verse 26 tells in what that losing oneself consists, and enforces the original exhortation by the declaration of a future appearance of the Son of man. He of whom Christ is then ashamed loses his own soul. To live without His smile is to die, to be disowned by Him is to be a wreck. To be ashamed of Jesus is equivalent to that base self—preservation which has been denounced as fatal. If a man disavows all connection with Him, He will disavow all connection with the disavower. A man separated from Jesus is dead while he lives, and hereafter will live a living death, and possess neither the world for which he sacrificed his own soul nor the soul for which he sacrificed it.

We cannot but note the authoritative tone of our Lord in these verses. He claims the obedience and discipleship of all men. He demands that all shall yield themselves unreservedly to Him, and that, even if actual surrender of life is involved, it shall be gladly given. He puts our relation to Him as determining our whole present and future. He assumes to be our Judge, whose smile is life, whose averted face darkens the destiny of a man. Whom say ye that He who dared to speak thus conceived Himself to be? Whom say ye that He is?

Verse 27 recalls us from the contemplation of that far—off appearance to something nearer. Remembering the previous announcement of our Lord's sufferings, these words seem intended to cheer the disciples with the hope that the kingdom would still be revealed within the lifetime of some then present. Remembering the immediately preceding words, this saying seems to assure the disciples that the blessed recompense of the life of self—crucifying discipleship is not to be postponed to that future, but may be enjoyed on earth. Remembering Christ's word, 'Except a man be born again, he cannot see the kingdom of God,' we doubt whether there is any reference here to the destruction of Jerusalem, as is commonly understood. Are not the words rather a declaration that they who are Christ's true disciples shall even here enter into the possession of their true selves, and find the Messianic hopes more than fulfilled? The future indicated will then be no more remote than the completion of His work by His death and Resurrection, or, at the farthest, the descent of the Holy Spirit at Pentecost, by which the fuller life of renewed natures was bestowed on those who were following Jesus in daily self—surrender.

PRAYER AND TRANSFIGURATION

'And as He prayed, the fashion of His countenance was
altered.'—LUKE ix. 29.

This Evangelist is especially careful to record the instances of our Lord's prayers. That is in accordance with the emphasis which he places on Christ's manhood. In this narrative of the

Transfiguration it is to Luke that we owe our knowledge of the connection between our Lord's prayer and the radiance of His face. It may be a question how far such transfiguration was the constant accompaniment of our Lord's devotion. It is to be remembered that this is the only time at which others were present while He prayed, and perhaps it may be that whensoever, on the mountain top or in the solitude of the wilderness, He entered into closer communion with His heavenly Father, that radiance shone from His face, though no eye beheld and no tongue has recorded the glory.

But that is a mere supposition. However that may be, it would seem that the light on Christ's face was not merely a reflection caught from above, but it was also a rising up from within of what always abode there, though it did not always shine through the veil of flesh. And in so far it presents no parallel with anything in our experience, nor any lesson for us. But to regard our Lord's Transfiguration as only the result of the indwelling divinity manifested is to construe only one half of the fact that we have to deal with, and the other half does afford for us a precious lesson. 'As He prayed the fashion of His countenance was altered'; and as we pray, and in the measure in which we truly and habitually do hold communion, shall we, too, partake of His Transfiguration.

The old story of the light that flashed upon the face of the Lawgiver, caught by reflection from the light of God in which He walked, is a partial parallel to Christ's Transfiguration, and both the one and the other incident, amongst their other lessons, do also point to some mysterious and occult relation between the indwelling soul and the envious veil of flesh which, under certain circumstances, might become radiant with the manifestation of that indwelling power.

I. The one great lesson which I seek now to enforce from this incident is, that communion with God transfigures.

Prayer is more than petitions. It is not necessarily cast into words at all. In its widest, which is its truest sense, it is the attitude and exercise of devout contemplation of God and intercourse in heart, mind, and will with Him, a communion which unites aspiration and attainment, longing and fruition, asking and receiving, seeking and finding, a communion which often finds itself beggared for words, and sometimes even seems to transcend thought. How different is such an hour of rapt communion with the living God from the miserable notions which so many professing Christians have of prayer, as if it were but spoken requests, more or less fervent and sincere, for things that they want! The noblest communion of a soul with God can never be free from the consciousness of need and dependence. Petition must ever be an element in it, but supplication is only a corner of prayer. Such conscious converse with God is the very atmosphere in which the Christian soul should always live, and if it be an experience altogether strange to us we had better ask ourselves whether we yet know the realities of the Christian life, or have any claim to the name. 'Truly, our fellowship is with the Father and with His Son, Jesus Christ,' and if we have no share in that fellowship we do not belong to the class of whom it is the mark and possession.

Of course, such communion is not to be attained or maintained without effort. Sense wars against it. Tasks which are duties interrupt the enjoyment of it in its more conscious forms. The hard-working man may well say, 'How can I, with my business cares calling—for my undivided attention all day long, keep up such communion?' The toiling mother may well say, 'How can I, in my little house, with my children round me, and never a quiet minute to myself, get such?' True, it is hard, and the highest and sweetest forms of communion cannot be reached by us while so engaged, and therefore we all need seasons of solitude and repose, in which, being left alone, we may see the Great Vision, and, the clank of the engines being silenced, we may hear the Great Voice saying, 'Come up hither.' Such seasons the busiest have on one day in every week, and such seasons we shall contrive to secure for ourselves daily, if we really want to be intimate with our heavenly Friend.

And for the rest it is not impossible to have real communion with God in the midst of anxious cares and absorbing duties; it is possible to be like the nightingales, that sing loudest in the trees by the dusty roadsides, possible to be in the very midst of anxiety and worldly work, and yet to keep our hearts in heaven and in touch with God. We do not need many words for communion, but we do need to make efforts to keep ourselves near Him in desire and aspiration, and we need jealous and constant watchfulness over our motives for work, and our temper and aim in it, that neither the work nor our way of doing it may draw us away. There will be breaches in the continuity of our conscious communion, but there need not be any in the reality of our touch with God. For He can be with us, 'like some sweet, beguiling melody, so sweet we know not we are listening to it.' There may be a real contact of the spirit with Him, though it would be hard at the moment to put it into words.

'As He prayed, the fashion of His countenance was altered.' Such communion changes and glorifies a man. The very secret of the Gospel way of making men better is—transfiguration by the vision of God. Yes! to be much with God is the true way to mend our characters, and to make them like His. I do not under−value the need of effort in order to correct faults and acquire virtues. We do not receive sanctification as we receive justification, by simple faith. For the latter the condition is 'Only believe,' for the former it is 'Work out your own salvation.' No man is cured of his evil tendencies without a great deal of hard work conscientiously directed to curbing them.

But all the hard work, and all the honest purpose in the world, will not do it without this other thing, the close communion with God, and incomparably the surest way to change what in us is wrong, and to raise what in us is low, and to illumine what in us is dark, is to live in habitual beholding of Him who is righteousness without flaw, and holiness supreme, and light without any darkness at all. That will cure faults. That will pull the poison fangs out of passions. That will do for the evil in us what the snake−charmers do by subtle touches, turn the serpent into a rigid rod that does not move nor sting. That will lift us up high above the trifles of life, and dwarf all here that imposes upon us with the lie that it is great, and precious, and permanent; and that will bring us into loving contact with the living 'Beauty of holiness,' which will change us into its own fair likeness.

We see illustrations of this transforming power of loving communion in daily life. People that love each other, and live beside each other, and are often thinking about one another, get to drop into each other's ways of looking at things; and even sometimes you will catch strange imitations and echoes of the face and voice, in two persons thus knit together. And if you and I are bound to God by a love which lasts, even when it does not speak, and which is with us even when our hands are busy with other things, then be sure of this, we shall get like Him whom we love. We shall be like Him even here, for even here we shall see Him. Partial assimilation is the condition of vision; and the vision is the condition of growing assimilation. The eye would not see the sun unless there were a little sun imaged on the retina. And a man that sees God gets like the God he sees; 'for we all, with unveiled face, beholding as in a glass (or, rather, mirroring as a glass does) the glory of God, are changed into the same image.' The image on the mirror is only on the surface; but if my heart is mirroring God He sinks in, and abides there, and changes me from glory to glory. So it is when we keep near Christ, who is manifest in the flesh, that we get liker Him day by day, and the fashion of our countenances will be altered.

Now there is a test for our Christianity. Does my religion alter me? If it does not, what right or reason have I to believe that it is genuine at all? Is there a process of purifying going on in my inward nature? Am I getting any more like Jesus Christ than I was ten years ago? I say I live with Him and by Him. If I do I shall become like Him. Do not work at the hopeless task of purifying yourselves without His help, but go and stay in the sun if you want to get warm. Lo as the bleachers do, spread the foul cloth on the green grass, below the blazing sunshine, and that will take all the dirt out. Believing and loving, and holding fast by Jesus Christ in true communion, we, too, become like Him we love.

II. Another thought is suggested by these words—namely, that this transfiguring will become very visible in the life if it be really in our inmost selves.

Even in the most literal sense of the words it will be so. Did you never see anybody whose face was changed by holier and nobler purposes coming into their lives? I have seen more than one or two whose features became as the face of an angel as they grew more and more unselfish, and more and more full of that which, in the most literal sense of the words, was in them the beauty of holiness. The devil writes his mark upon people's faces. The world and the flesh do so. Go into the streets and look at the people that you meet. Care, envy, grasping griping avarice, discontent, unrest, blotches of animalism, and many other prints of black fingers are plain enough on many a face. And on the other hand, if a man or a woman get into their hearts the refining influences of God's grace and love by living near the Master, very soon the beauty of expression which is born of consecration and unselfishness, the irradiation of lofty emotions, the tenderness caught from Him, will not be lacking, and some eyes that look upon them will recognise the family likeness.

But that may be said to be mere fancy. Perhaps it is, or perhaps there is truth in it deeper and more far–reaching than we know. Perhaps the life fashions the body, and the 'body of our glory' may be moulded in immortal loveliness by the perfect Christ–derived life within it. But be that as it may, the main point to be observed here is rather this. If we have the real, transforming influence of communion with Jesus Christ in our hearts, it will certainly rise to the surface, and show itself in our lives. As oil poured into water will come to the top, so that inward transforming will not continue hidden within, 'The king's daughter is all–glorious *within*, but also 'her *clothing* is of wrought gold.' The inward life, beautiful because knit to Him, will have corresponding with it and flowing from it an outward life of manifest holy beauty.

'His name shall be in their foreheads,' stamped there, where everybody can see it. Is that where you and I carry Christ's name? It is well that it should be in our hearts, it is hypocrisy that it should be in our foreheads unless it is in our hearts first. But if it be in the latter it will surely be in the former.

Now, dear friends, there is a simple and sure touchstone for us all. Do not talk about communion with Christ being the life of your religion, unless the people that have to do with you, your brothers and sisters, or fathers and mothers, your wives and children, your servants or your masters, would endorse it and say 'Yes! I take knowledge of him, he has been with Jesus.' Do you think that it is easier for anybody to believe in, and to love God, 'whom he hath not seen' because of you, 'his brother whom he hath seen'? The Christ in the heart will be the Christ in the face and in the life.

Alas! why is it that so little of this radiance caught from heaven shines from us? There is but one answer. It is because our communion with God in Christ is so infrequent, hurried, and superficial. We should be like those luminous boxes which we sometimes see, shining in the dark with light absorbed from the day; but, like them, we need to be exposed to the light and to lie in it if we are to be light. 'Now are ye light in the Lord,' and only as we abide in Him by continuous communion shall we resemble Him or reflect Him.

III. The perfection of communion will be the perfection of visible transformation.

Possibly the Transfiguration of Jesus Christ had an element of prophecy in it, and pointed onwards to the order of things when His glorified humanity should be enthroned on the throne of the universe, and have left the limitations of flesh with the folded grave−clothes in the empty sepulchre. As the two majestic forms of the Lawgiver and the Prophet shared His glory on Hermon, and held converse with Him there, so we may see in that mysterious group wrapped in the bright cloud the hint of a hope which was destined to grow to clearness and certainty. Christ's glorified bodily humanity is the type to which all His followers will be conformed. Gazing on Him they shall be like Him, and will grow liker as they gaze. Through eternal ages the double process will go on, and they shall become ever more assimilated, and therefore capable of truer, completer vision, and ever seeing Him more fully as He is, and therefore progressively changed into more perfect resemblance. Nor will that blessed change into advancing glory be shut up in their hearts nor lack beholders. For in that realm of truth and reality all that is within will be visible, our life will no longer fall beneath our aspirations, nor practice be at variance with the longings and convictions of our best selves. Then the Christlike spirit will possess a body which is its glad and perfect servant, and through which its beauty will shine undimmed. 'When Christ, who is our life, shall be manifested, then shall we also be manifested with Him in glory.'

'IN THE HOLY MOUNT'

'And, behold, there talked with Him two men, which
were Moses and Elias: 31. Who appeared in glory, and
spake of His decease which He should accomplish at
Jerusalem.'—LUKE ix. 30, 31.

The mysterious incident which is commonly called the Transfiguration contained three distinct portions, each having its own special significance and lesson. The first was that supernatural change in the face and garments of our Lord from which the whole incident derives its name. The second was the appearance by His side of these two mighty dead participating in the strange lustre in which He walked, and communing with Him of His death. And the last was the descent of the bright cloud, visible as bright even amidst the blazing sunshine on the lone hillside, and the mysterious attesting Voice that spoke from out of its depths.

143

I leave untouched altogether the first and the last of these three portions, and desire briefly to fix our attention on this central one. Now it is to be observed that whilst all the three Synoptic Evangelists tell us of the Transfiguration, of the appearance of Moses and Elias, and of the Cloud and the Voice, only Luke knows, or at least records, and therefore alone probably knows, what it was that they spoke of. Peter and James and John, the only human witnesses, were lying dazed and drunken with sleep, whilst Christ's countenance was changed; and during all the earlier portion at all events of His converse with Moses and Elias. And it was only when these were about to depart that the mortals awoke from their slumber. So they probably neither heard the voices nor knew their theme, and it was reserved for this Evangelist to tell us the precious truth that the thing about which Lawgiver, Prophet, and the Greater than both spake in that mysterious communion was none other than the Cross.

I think, then, that if we look at this incident from the point of view which our Evangelist enables us to take, we shall get large and important lessons as to the significance of the death of Jesus Christ, in many aspects, and in reference to very many different persons. I see at least four of these. This incident teaches us what Christ's death was to Himself; what it was in reference to previous revelation; what it was in reference to past generations; and what it may be in reference to His servants' death. And upon these four points I desire briefly to touch now.

I. First, then, I see here teaching as to what the death of the Lord Jesus Christ was in reference to Himself.

What was it that brought these men—the one who had passed in a whirlwind to heaven, and the other who had been led by a mysterious death to slumber in an unknown grave—what was it that brought these men to stand there upon the side of the slopes of Hermon? It was not to teach Christ of the impending Cross. For, not to touch upon other points, eight days before this mysterious interview He had foretold it in the minutest details to His disciples. It was not for the sake of Peter and James and John, lying coiled in slumber there, that they broke the bands of death, and came back from 'that bourne from which no traveller returns,' but it was for Christ, or for themselves, or perhaps for both, that they stood there.

You remember that in Gethsemane 'there appeared an angel from heaven strengthening Him.' And one of the old devout painters has marvellously embraced the deepest meaning of that vision when he has painted for us the strengthening angel displaying in the heavens the Cross on which He must die, as if the holding of it up before Him as the divine will gave the strength that He needed. And I think in some analogous way we are to regard the mission and message to Jesus of these two men in our text. We know that clear before Him, all His life long, there stood the certainty of the Cross. We know that He came, not merely to teach, to minister, to bless, to guide, but that He came to give His life a ransom for many. But we know, too, that from about this point of time in His life the Cross stood more distinctly, if that may be, before Him; or at all events, that it pressed more upon His vision and upon His spirit. And doubtless after that time when He spoke to the disciples so plainly and clearly of what was coming upon Him, His human nature needed the retirement of the mountain–side and prayer which preceded and occasioned this mysterious incident. Christ shrank from His Cross with sinless, natural, human shrinking of the flesh. That never altered His purpose nor shook His will, but He needed, and He got, strength from the Father, ministered once by an angel from heaven, and ministered, as I suppose, another time by two men who looked at death from the other side, and 'who

144

spoke to Him of His decease which He should accomplish at Jerusalem.'

And now it is to be noticed that the words which our Evangelist employs are remarkable, and one of them, at least, is all but unique. The expression translated in my text 'decease' is the same Greek word which, untranslated, names the second book of the Old Testament— *Exodus*. And it literally means neither more nor less than a departure or 'going out.' It is only employed in this one passage and in another one to which I shall have occasion to refer presently, which is evidently based and moulded upon this one, to signify *death*. And the employment of it, perhaps upon these undying tongues of the sainted dead—or, at all events, in reference to the subject of their colloquy—seems to us to suggest that part of what they had to say to the Master and what they had to hear from Him was that His death was His departure in an altogether unique, solitary, and blessed sense. 'I came forth from the Father, and I am come into the world. Again, I leave the world and go to the Father.' Not dragged by any necessity, but of His own sovereign will, He passes from earth to the state where He was before. And as He stands there on the mountain with His radiant face and His white robes, this thought as to His death brings to Him comfort and strength, even whilst He thinks of the suffering of the Cross.

But, still further, the other word which is here employed helps us to understand what our Lord's death was to Him; 'He should *accomplish*' it as a thing to be fulfilled. And that involves two ideas, the one that Christ in His death was consciously submitting to a gladly accepted divine *must*, and was accomplishing the purpose of Love which dwelt in the heavens and sent Him, as well as His own purpose of love which would redeem and save. The necessity of the death of Christ if sin is to be put away, if we are ever to have a hope of immortality, the necessity of the death of Christ if the mercy of God is to pour out upon a sinful and rebellious world, the necessity of the death of Christ, if the deep purposes of the divine heart are ever to be realised, and the yearning compassion of the Saviour's soul is ever to reach its purpose—all lie in that great word that 'His decease' was by Him to be 'accomplished.' This is the fulfilling of the heart of God, this is the fulfilling of the compassion of the Christ. It is the accomplishment of the divine purpose from eternity.

Still further, the word, as I think, suggests another kind of fulfilment. He was to 'accomplish' His death. That is to say, every drop of that bitter cup, drop by drop, bitterness by bitterness, pang by pang, desolation by desolation, He was to drink; and He drank it. Every step of that road sown with ploughshares and live coals He was to tread, with bleeding, blistered, slow, unshrinking feet. And He trod it. He *accomplished* it; hurrying over none of the sorrow, perfunctorily doing none of the tasks. And after the weary moments had ticked themselves away, and the six hours of agony, when the minutes were as drops of blood falling slowly to the ground, were passed, He inverted the cup, and it was empty, and He said 'It is finished'; and He gave up the ghost, having accomplished His decease in Jerusalem.'

II. Further, note in this incident what that death is in regard to previous revelation.

I need not remind you, I suppose, that we have here the two great representative figures of the past history of Israel—the Lawgiver, who, according to the Old Testament, was not only the medium of declaring the divine will, but the medium of establishing Sacrifice as well as Law, and the Prophet, who, though no written words of his have been preserved, and nothing of a predictive and Messianic character seems to have dropped from His lips, yet stood as the representative and head of the great prophetic order to which so much of the earlier revelation was entrusted. And now here they two stand with Christ on the mountain; and the theme about which they spake with Him there is the theme of which the former revelation had spoken in type and shadow, in stammering words, 'at sundry times and in divers manners,' to the former generations—viz. the coming of the great Sacrifice and the offering of the great Propitiation. All the past of Israel pointed onwards to the Cross, and in that Cross its highest word was transcended, its faintest emblems were explained and expressed, its unsolved problems which it had raised in order that they might be felt to be unsolved, were all answered, and that which had been set forth but in shadow and symbol was given to the world in reality for evermore. In Moses Law and Sacrifice, and in Elijah the prophetic function, met by the side of Christ, 'and spake of His decease.'

Now, dear friends, let me say one word here before I pass on. There is a great deal being said nowadays about the position of the Old Testament, the origin of its ritual, and other critical, and, to some extent, historical, questions. I have no doubt that we have much to learn upon these subjects; but what I would now insist upon is this, that all these subjects, about which people are getting so excited, and some of them so angry, stand, and may be dealt with, altogether apart from this central thought, that the purpose and meaning, the end and object of the whole preliminary and progressive revelation of God from the beginning, are to lead straight up to Jesus Christ and to His Cross. And if we understand that, and feel that 'the testimony of Jesus is the spirit of prophecy,' and that law and sacrifice, commandments and altar, Sinai and Zion, the fiery words that were spoken in the wilderness, and the perpetual burnt-offering that went up in the Temple, had one mission—viz. to 'prepare the way of the Lord'—we have grasped the essential truth as to the Old Revelation; and if we do not understand that, we may be as scholarly and erudite and original as we please, but we miss the one truth which is worth grasping. The relation between the Old revelation and the New is this, that Christ was pointed to by it all, and that in Himself He sums up and surpasses and antiquates, because He fulfils, all the past.

Therefore Moses and Elijah came to witness as well as to encourage. Their presence proclaimed that Christ was the meaning of all the past, and the crown of the divine revelation. And they faded away, and Jesus was found alone standing there, as He stands for ever before all generations and all lands, the sole, the perfect, the eternal Revealer of the heart and will of God. 'God, who at sundry times and in divers manners spake unto the fathers by the prophets, hath in these last days spoken unto us by His Son.'

III. Again, we have here set before us the death of Christ in its relation to past generations.

I need not dwell upon anything that was mysterious or anomalous in the last moments upon earth of either Moses or Elijah. I do not suppose that there is any reference to the undoubted peculiarities which existed in the case of both. But they came from that dim region where the dead were waiting for the coming of the Saviour, and by some means, we know not how, were clothed with something that was like an immortal body, and capable of entering into this material universe. There they stood, witnesses that Christ's death was of interest to all those sleeping generations in the past. We know not anything, or scarcely anything, of the condition of the sainted dead who died before Christ came. But this is clear, that these two came from the land where silent expectancy had ruled, and came perhaps to carry back to their brethren the tidings that the hour was ready to strike, and that soon amongst them there would stand the Eternal Life.

But, be that as it may, does not that group on the mountain–side teach us this, that the Cross of Jesus Christ had a backward as well as a forward power, and that for all the generations who had died, 'not having received the promises, but having seen them and saluted them from afar,' the influence of that Sacrifice had opened the gates of the Kingdom where they were gathered in hope, even as it opens for us, and all subsequent generations, the gates of the paradise of God?

I know not whether there be truth in the ancient idea that when the Master died He passed into that *Hades* where were assembled the disembodied spirits of the righteous dead, and led captivity captive, taking them with Him into a loftier Paradise. But this I am sure of, that Christ's Cross has always been the means and channel whereby forgiveness and hope and heaven have been given to men, and that the old dream of the devout painter which he has breathed upon the walls of the convent in Florence is true in spirit whatever it may be in letter, that the Christ who died went down into the dark regions, burst the bars and broke the gates of iron, and crushed the demon porter beneath the shattered portal, and that out of the dark rock–hewn caverns there came streaming the crowds of the sainted dead, with Adam at their head, and many another who had seen His day afar off and been glad, stretching out eager hands to grasp the life–giving hand of the Redeemer that had come to them too.

Moses and Elias were the 'first–fruits of them that slept,' and there were others, when the bodies of the saints rose from the grave and appeared in the Holy City unto many. And their presence, and the presence of these two there, typified for us the great fact that the Cross of Christ is the redemption of pre–Christian as well as of Christian ages; and that He is the Lord both of the dead and of the living.

IV. And so, lastly, this incident may suggest also what that death of Jesus Christ may be in reference to the deaths of His servants.

I do not find that thought in the words of our text, but in the reference to them which is made in the second epistle attributed to Peter, who was present at the Transfiguration. There is a very remarkable passage in that Epistle, in the context of which there are distinct verbal allusions to the narrative of the Transfiguration, and in it the writer employs the same word to describe his own death which is employed here. It is the only other instance in Scripture of its use in that sense. And so I draw this simple lesson; that mighty death which was accomplished upon Calvary, which is the crown and summit of all Revelation, beyond which God has nothing that He can say or do to make men sure of His heart and recipients of forgiveness, which was the channel of pardon for all past ages, and the hope of the sainted dead—that death may turn for us our departure into its own likeness. For us, too, all the grimness, all the darkness, all the terror, may pass away, and it may become simply a change of place, and a going home to God. If we believe that Jesus died, we believe that He has thereby smoothed and softened and lessened our death into a sleep in Him.

Nor need we forget the special meaning of the word. If we have set our hopes upon Christ, and, as sinful men and women, have cast the burden of our sins, and the weight of our salvation, on His strong arm, then life will be blessed, and death, when it comes, will be a true Exodus, the going out of the slaves from the land of bondage, and passing through the divided sea, not into a weary wilderness, but into the light of the love and the blessedness of the land where our Brother is King, and where we shall share His reign.

I have been speaking to you of what Christ's death is in many regions of the universe, in many eras of time. My brother, what is Christ's death to you? Can you say, 'The life that I live in the flesh I live by the faith of the Son of God, who loved me, and gave Himself for me?'

CHRIST HASTENING TO THE CROSS

'And it came to pass, when the time was come that He
should be received up, He stedfastly set His face to
go to Jerusalem.'—LUKE ix. 51.

There are some difficulties, with which I need not trouble you here, as to bringing the section of this Gospel to which these words are the introduction, into its proper chronological place in relation to the narratives; but, putting these on one side for the present, there seems no doubt that the Evangelist's intention here is to represent the beginning of our Lord's last journey from Galilee to Jerusalem—a journey which was protracted and devious, and the narrative of which in this Gospel, as you will perceive, occupies a very large portion of its whole contents.

The picture that is given in my text is that of a clear knowledge of what waited Him, of a steadfast resolve to accomplish the purpose of the divine love, and that resolve not without such a shrinking of some part of His nature that He had 'to *set* His face to go to Jerusalem.'

The words come into parallelism very strikingly with a great prophecy of the Messiah in the Book of the Prophet Isaiah, where we read, 'The Lord God will help me, therefore shall I not be confounded'—or, as the words have been rendered, 'shall not suffer myself to be overcome by mockery'—'therefore have I set my face like a flint.' In the words both of the Prophet and of the Evangelist there is the same idea of a resolved will, as the result of a conscious effort directed to prevent circumstances which tended to draw Him back, from producing their effect. The graphic narrative of the Evangelist Mark adds one more striking point to that picture of high resolve. He tells us, speaking of what appears to be the final epoch in this long journey to the Cross, 'They were in the way, going up to Jerusalem, and Jesus went before them; and they were amazed: and as they followed, they were afraid.' What a picture that is, Christ striding along the steep mountain path far in advance—impelled by that same longing which sighs so wonderfully in His words, 'How am I straitened till it be accomplished,'—with solemn determination in the gentle face, and His feet making haste to run in the way of the Father's commandments! And lagging behind, the little group, awed into almost stupor, and shrinking in uncomprehending terror from that light of unconquerable resolve and more than mortal heroism that blazed in His eyes!

If we fix, then, on this picture, and as we are warranted in doing, regard it as giving us a glimpse of the very heart of Christ, I think it may well suggest to us considerations that may tend to make more real to us that sacrifice that He made, more deep to us that love by which He was impelled, and may perhaps tend to make our love more true and our resolve more fixed. 'He set His face to go to Jerusalem.'

I. First, then, we may take, I think, from these words, the thought of the perfect clearness with which all through Christ's life He foresaw the inevitable and purposed end.

Here, indeed, the Evangelist leaps over the suffering of the Cross, and thinks only of the time when He shall be lifted up upon the throne; but in that calm and certain prevision which, in His manhood, the Divine Son of God did exercise concerning His own earthly life, between Him and the glory there ever stood the black shadow thrown by Calvary. When He spoke of being 'lifted up,' He ever meant by that pregnant and comprehensive word, at once man's elevation of Him on the accursed tree, and the Father's elevation of Him upon the throne at His right hand! The future was, if I may so say, in His eye so foreshortened that the two things ran into one, and the ambiguous expression did truly connote the one undivided act of prescient consciousness in which He at once recognised the Cross and the throne. And so, when the time was come that He should be received up, He 'steadfastly set His face to go to Jerusalem.'

Now, there is another thing to be noticed. That vision of the certain end which here fills His mind and impels His conduct, was by no means new with Him. Modern unbelieving commentators and critics upon the Gospels have tried their best to represent Christ's life as, at a certain point in it, being modified by His recognition of the fact that His mission was a failure, and that there was nothing left for Him but martyrdom! I believe that that is as untrue to the facts of the Gospel story upon any interpretation of them, as it is repulsive to the instincts of devout hearts; and without troubling you with thoughts about it I need only refer to two words of His. When was it that He said, 'Destroy this temple, and in three days I will build it up'? When was it that He said, 'As Moses lifted up the serpent in the wilderness, even so must the Son of man be lifted up'? The one saying was uttered at the very beginning of His public work, and the other in His conversation with Nicodemus. On the testimony of these two sayings, if there were none else, I think there is no option but to believe that from the first there stood clear before Him the necessity and the certainty of the Cross, and that it was no discovery made at a certain point of His course.

And then, remember that we are not to think of Him as, like many an earthly hero and martyr, regarding a violent and bloody death as being the very probable result of faithful boldness, but to believe that He, looking on from the beginning to that end, regarded it always as being laid upon Him by a certain divine necessity, into which necessity He entered with the full submission and acquiescence of His own will, and from the beginning knew that Calvary was the work for which He had come, and that His love would fail of its expression, and the divine purpose would fail of its realisation, and His whole mission would fail of all its meaning, unless He died for men. The martyr looks to the scaffold and says, 'It stands in my way, and I must either be untrue to conscience or I must go there, and so I will go.' Christ said, 'The Cross is in My path, and on it and from it I shall exercise the influence, to exercise which I have come into the world, and there I shall *do* the thing which I came forth from the Father to do.' He thought of His death not as the end of His work, but as the centre–point of it; not as the termination of His activity, but as its climax, to which all the rest was subordinated, and without which all the rest was nought. He does not die, and so seal a faithful life by an heroic death,—but dies, so bearing and bearing away man's sin. He regarded from the beginning 'the glory that should follow,' and the suffering through which He had to wade to reach it, in one and the same act of prescience, and said, 'Lo, I come, in the volume of the book it is written of Me.'

And I think, dear friends, if we carried with us more distinctly than we do that one simple thought, that in all the human joys, in all the apparently self–forgetting tenderness, of that Lord who had a heart for every sorrow and an ear for every complaint, and a hand open as day and full of melting charity for every need—that in every moment of that life, in the boyhood, in the dawning manhood, in the maturity of His growing human powers—there was always present one black shadow, towards which He ever went straight with the consent of His will and with the clearest eye, we should understand something more of how His life as well as His death was a sacrifice for us sinful men!

We honour and love men who crush down their own sorrows in order to help their fellows. We wonder with almost reverence when we see some martyr, in sight of the faggots, pause to do a kindness to some weeping heart in the crowd, or to speak a cheering word. We admire the leisure and calm of spirit which he displays. But all these pale, and the very comparison may become an insult, before that heart which ever discerned Calvary, and never let the sight hinder one deed of kindness, nor silence one gracious word, nor check one throb of sympathy.

II. Still further, the words before us lead to a second consideration, which I have just suggested in my last sentence—Our Lord's perfect willingness for the sacrifice which He saw before Him.

We have here brought into the narrowest compass, and most clearly set forth, the great standing puzzle of all thought, which can only be solved by action. On the one side there is the distinctest knowledge of a divine purpose that *will* be executed; on the other side there is the distinctest consciousness that at each step towards the execution of it He is constrained by no foreign and imposed necessity, but is going to the Cross by His own will. 'The Son of Man must be lifted up.' 'It *became* Him to make the Captain of salvation perfect through sufferings.' 'It *behoved* Him to be made in all points like His brethren.' The Eternal Will of the Father, the purpose purposed before the foundation of the world, the solemn prophecies from the beginning of time, constituted the necessity, and involved the certainty, of His death on the Cross. But are we, therefore, to think that Jesus Christ was led along the path that ended there, by a force which overbore and paralysed His human will? Was not His life, and especially His death, *obedience*? Was there not, therefore, in Him, as in us all, the human will that could cheerfully submit; and must there not, then, have been, at each step towards the certain end, a fresh act of submission and acceptance of the will of the Father that had sent Him?

'Clear knowledge of the end as divinely appointed and certain'; yes, one might say, and if so, there could have been no voluntariness in treading the path that leads to it. 'Voluntariness in treading the path that leads to it, and if so, there could have been no divine ordination of the end.' Not so! When human thought comes, if I may so say, full butt against a stark, staring contradiction like that, it is no proof that either of the propositions is false. It is only like the sign–boards that the iceman puts upon the thin ice, 'dangerous!' a warning that that is not a place for us to tread. We have to keep a firm hold of what is certified to us, on either side, by its appropriate evidence, and leave the reconciliation, if it can ever be given to finite beings, to a higher wisdom, and, perchance, to another world!

But that is a digression from my more immediate purpose, which is simply to bring before our minds, as clearly as I can, that perfect, continuous, ever–repeated willingness, expressing itself in a chain of constant acts that touch one upon the other, which Christ manifested to embrace the Cross, and to accomplish what was at once the purpose of the Father's will and the purpose of His own.

150

And it may be worth while, just for a moment, to touch lightly upon some of the many points which bring out so clearly in these Gospel narratives the wholly and purely voluntary character of Christ's death.

Take, for instance, the very journey which I am speaking of now. Christ went up to Jerusalem, says my text. What did He go there for? He went, as you will see, if you look at the previous circumstance,—He went in order, if I might use such a word, to precipitate the collision, and to make His Crucifixion certain. He was under the ban of the Sanhedrim; but perfectly safe as long as He had stopped up among the hills of Galilee. He was as unsafe when He went up to Jerusalem as John Huss when he went to the Council of Constance with the Emperor's safe-conduct in his belt; or as a condemned heretic would have been in the old days, if he had gone and stood in that little dingy square outside the palace of the Inquisition at Rome, and there, below the obelisk, preached his heresies! Christ had been condemned in the council of the nation; but there were plenty of hiding-places among the Galilean hills, and the frontier was close at hand, and it needed a long arm to reach from Jerusalem all the way across Samaria to the far north. Knowing that, He steadfastly set His face to go to Jerusalem, and, if I might use the expression, went straight into the lion's mouth. Why? Because He chose to die.

And, then, take another circumstance. If you will look carefully at the Scripture narrative, you will find that from about this point in His life onwards there comes a distinct change in one very important respect. Before this He shunned publicity; after this He courted it. Before this, when He spoke in veiled words of His sufferings, He said to His disciples, 'Tell no man till the Son of man be risen from the dead.' Hereafter though there are frequent prophecies of His sufferings, there is no repetition of that prohibition. He goes up to Jerusalem, and His triumphal entry adds fuel to the fire. His language at the last moment appeals to the publicity of His final visit to that city—'Was I not daily with you in the Temple and ye laid no hands upon Me?' Everything that He could do He does to draw attention to Himself—everything, that is to say, within the limits of the divine decorum, which was ever observed in His life, of whom it was written long, long ago, 'He shall not strive, nor cry, nor cause His voice to be heard in the streets.' There is, then, a most unmistakable change to be felt by any who will carefully read the narratives in their bearing upon this one point—a resolve to draw the eyes of the enemy upon Himself.

And to the same purpose, did you ever notice how calmly, with full self-consciousness, distinctly understanding what He is doing, distinctly knowing to what it will lead, He makes His words ever heavier and heavier, and more and more sharply pointed with denunciations, as the last loving wrestle between Himself and the scribes and Pharisees draws near to its bloody close? Instead of softening He hardens His tones—if I dare use the word, where all is the result of love—at any rate He keeps no terms; but as the danger increases His words become plainer and sterner, and approach as near as ever *His* words could do to bitterness and rebuke. It was then, whilst passionate hate was raging round Him, and eager eyes were gleaming revenge, that He poured out His sevenfold woes upon the 'hypocrites,' the 'blind guides,' the 'fools,' the 'whited sepulchres,' the 'serpents,' the 'generation of vipers,' whom He sees filling up the measure of their fathers in shedding His righteous blood.

And again, the question recurs—Why? And again, besides other reasons, which I have not time to touch upon here, the answer, as it seems to me, must unmistakably be, Because He willed to die, and

He willed to die because He loved us.

The same lesson is taught, too, by that remarkable incident preserved for us by the Gospel of John, of the strange power which accompanied His avowal of Himself to the rude soldiers who had come to seize Him, and which struck them to the ground in terror and impotence. One flash comes forth to tell of the sleeping lightning that He will not use, and then having revealed the might that could have delivered Him from their puny arms, He returns to His attitude of self–surrender for our sakes, with those wonderful words which tell how He gave up Himself that we might be free, 'If ye seek Me, let these go their way.' The scene is a parable of the whole work of Jesus; it reveals His power to have shaken off every hand laid upon Him, His voluntary submission to His else impotent murderers, and the love which moved Him to the surrender.

Other illustrations of the same sort I must leave untouched at present, and only remind you of the remarkable peculiarity of the language in which all the Evangelists describe the supreme moment when Christ passed from His sufferings. 'When He had cried with a loud voice, He yielded up the ghost,'—He sent away the spirit—'He breathed out' (His spirit), 'He gave up the ghost.' In simple truth, He 'committed His spirit' into the Father's hand. And I believe that it is an accurate and fair comment to say, that that is no mere euphemism for death, but carries with it the thought that He was *active* in that moment; that the nails and the spear and the Cross did not kill Christ, but that Christ *willed* to die! And though it is true on the one side, as far as men's hatred and purpose are concerned. 'Whom with wicked hands ye have crucified and slain'; on the other side, as far as the deepest verity of the fact is concerned, it is still more true, 'I have power to lay it down, and I have power to take it again.'

But at all events, whatever you may think of such an exposition as that, the great principle which my text illustrates for us at an earlier stage is, at least, irrefragably established—that our dear Lord, when He died, died, because He *willed* to do so. He was man and therefore He *could* die; but He was not man in such fashion as that He *must* die. In His bodily frame was the possibility, not the necessity, of death. And that being so, the very fact of His death is the most signal proof that He is Lord of death as well as of life. He dies not because He must, He dies not because of faintness and pain and wounds. These and they who inflicted them had no power at all over Him. He chooses to die; and He wills it because He wills to fulfil the eternal purpose of divine love, which is His purpose, and to bring life to the world. His hour of weakness was His hour of strength. They lifted Him on a cross, and it became a throne. In the moment when death seemed to conquer Him, He was really using it that He might abolish it. When He gave tip the ghost, He showed Himself Lord of death as marvellously and as gloriously as when He burst its bands and rose from the grave; for this grisly shadow, too, was His servant, and He says to him, 'Come, and he cometh; do this, and he doeth it.' 'Thou didst overcome the sharpness of death' when Thou didst willingly bow Thy head to it, and didst die not because Thou *must*, but because Thou *wouldest*.

III. Still further, let me remind you how, in the language of this verse, there is also taught us that there was in Christ a natural human shrinking from the Cross.

The steadfast and resolved will held its own, overcoming the natural human reluctance. 'He *set* His face.' People are afraid to talk—and the instinct, the reverent instinct, is right, however we may differ from the application of it—people are afraid to talk, as if there was any shrinking in Christ from the Cross. I believe there was. Was the agony in Gethsemane a reality or a shadow, when He said, 'O My Father, if it be possible, let this cup pass?' What did that prayer mean, if there was not something in His nature that recoiled from the agony and mysterious horror of these awful hours? Let us take heed lest in our reverence we destroy the very notion on which our hope rests—that of Christ as suffering. For that one word involves all that I say—Did Christ *suffer* or did He not? If He suffered, then human nature shrank from it. The two ideas are correlative, you cannot part them—suffering and reluctance, a perfectly innocent, natural, inevitable, human instinct, inseparable from corporeity, that makes men recoil from pain. 'He endured the Cross,' says the Book—if there was not reluctance what was there to 'endure'? 'Despising the shame'—if there was not something from which He shrank, what was there to 'despise'? 'He *set* His face'—if there was not something in Him that hung back, what need was there for the hardening of the countenance? If Christ has suffered, then His flesh and blood quivered beforehand with the pangs and shrank from these, and He would have been spared the cup. Such instinctive recoil is not evil, it is not rebellion, it is not unwillingness to submit to the Father's will. His whole being clave to that, and never swerved from it for one moment. But still, because the path was darkened by mysterious blackness, and led to a Cross, therefore He, even He, who did always the things that pleased the Father, and ever delighted to do His will, needed to ' *set* His face' to go up to the mountain of sacrifice.

And now, if you will take along with that the other thought that I suggested at the beginning of these remarks, and remember that this shrinking must have been as continuous as the vision, and that this overcoming of it must have been as persistent and permanent as the resolve, I think we get a point of view from which to regard that life of Christ's—full of pathos, full of tender appeals to our hearts and to our thankfulness.

All along that consecrated road He walked, and each step represented a separate act of will, and each separate act of will represented a triumph over the reluctance of flesh and blood. As we may say, every time that He planted His foot on the flinty path the blood flowed. Every step was a pain like that of a man enduring the ordeal and walking on burning iron or sharp steel.

The old taunt of His enemies, as they stood beneath His Cross, might have been yielded to—'If Thou be the Son of God, come down and we will believe.' I ask why did not He? I know that, to those who think less loftily of Christ than we who believe Him to be the Son of God, the words sound absurd—but I for one believe that the only thing that kept Him there, the only answer to that question is—Because He loved me with an everlasting love, and died to redeem me. Because of that love, He came to earth; because of that love, He tabernacled among us; because of that love, He gazed all His life long on the Cross of shame; because of that love, He trod unfaltering, with eager haste and solemn resolve, the rough and painful road; because of that love, He listened not to the voice that at the beginning tempted Him to win the world for Himself by an easier path; because of that love, He listened not—though He could have done so—to the voices that at the end taunted Him with their proffered allegiance if He would come down from the Cross; because of that love, He gave up His spirit. And through all the weariness and contumely and pain, that love held His will fixed to its purpose, and bore Him over every hindrance that barred His path. Many waters quench it not. *That* love is stronger than death; mightier than all opposing powers; deep and great beyond all thought or thankfulness. It silences all praise. It beggars all recompense. To believe it is life. To feel it is heaven.

But one more remark I would make on this whole subject. We are far too much accustomed to think of our Saviour as presenting only the gentle graces of human nature. He presents those that belong to the strong side of our nature just as much. In Him are all power, manly energy, resolved consecration; everything which men call heroism is there. 'He steadfastly set His face.' And everything which men call tenderest love, most dewy pity, most marvellous and transcendent patience, is all there too. The type of manhood and the type of womanhood are both and equally in Jesus Christ; and He is *the* Man, whole, entire, perfect, with all power breathed forth in all gentleness, with all gentleness made steadfast and mighty by His strength. 'And he said unto me, Behold the lion of the tribe of Judah. And I beheld, and lo, a lamb!'—the blended symbols of kingly might, and lowly meekness, power in love, and love in power. The supremest act of resolved consecration and heroic self-immolation that ever was done upon earth—an act which we degrade by paralleling it with any other—was done at the bidding of love that pitied us. As we look up at that Cross we know not whether is more wonderfully set forth the pitying love of Christ's most tender heart, or the majestic energy of Christ's resolved will. The blended rays pour out, dear brethren, and reach to each of us. Do not look to that great sacrifice with idle wonder. Bend upon it no eye of mere curiosity. Beware of theorising merely about what it reveals and what it does. Turn not away from it carelessly as a twice-told tale. But look, believing that all that divine and human love pours out its treasure upon you, that all that firmness of resolved consecration and willing surrender to the death of the Cross was for you. Look, believing that you had then, and have now, a place in His heart, and in His sacrifice. Look, remembering that it was because He would save you, that Himself He could not save,

And as, from afar, we look on that great sight, let His love melt our hearts to an answering fervour, and His fixed will give us, too, strength to delight in obedience, to set our faces like a flint. Let the power of His sacrifice, and the influence of His example which that sacrifice commends to our loving copy, and the grace of His Spirit whom He, since that sacrifice, pours upon men, so mould us that we, too, like Him, may 'quit us like men, be strong,' and all our strength and 'all our deeds' be wielded and 'done in charity.'

CHRIST'S MESSENGERS: THEIR EQUIPMENT AND WORK

'After these things, the Lord appointed other seventy also, and sent them two and two before His face into every city and place whither He Himself would come. 2. Therefore said He unto them, The harvest truly is great, but the labourers are few: pray ye therefore the Lord of the harvest, that He would send forth labourers into His harvest. 3. Go your ways: behold, I send you forth as lambs among wolves. 4. Carry neither purse, nor scrip, nor shoes; and salute no man by the way. 5. And into whatsoever house ye enter, first say, Peace be to this house. 6. And if the son of peace be there, your peace shall rest upon it: if not, it shall turn to you again. 7. And in the same house remain, eating and drinking such things as they give: for the labourer is worthy of his hire. Go not from house to

house. 8. And into whatsoever city ye enter, and they
receive you, eat such things as are set before you:
9. And heal the sick that are therein; and say unto
them, The kingdom of God is come nigh unto you. 10. But
into whatsoever city ye enter, and they receive you
not, go your ways out into the streets of the same,
and say, 11. Even the very dust of your city, which
cleaveth on us, we do wipe off against you:
notwithstanding, be ye sure of this, that the kingdom
of God is come nigh unto you.... 17. And the seventy
returned again with joy, saying, Lord, even the devils
are subject unto us through Thy name. 18. And He said
unto them, I beheld Satan as lightning fall from
heaven. 19. Behold, I give unto you power to tread on
serpents and scorpions, and over all the power of the
enemy; and nothing shall by any means hurt you.
20. Notwithstanding in this rejoice not, that the
spirits are subject unto you; but rather rejoice,
because your names are written in heaven.'
—LUKE x. 1–11: 17–20.

The mission of the Seventy is clearly distinguished from and contrasted with that of the Twelve by the word 'others' in verse 1, which points back to Luke ix.1. The Twelve were prohibited from going beyond Jews; the Seventy were under no such restriction, and were probably sent to the half–Gentile districts on the east of Jordan. The number of twelve had reference to the number of the tribes; that of seventy may have referred to the number of the elders, but it has also been suggested that its reference is to the supposed number of the nations. The appointment of the Twelve was to a permanent office; that of the Seventy to a transitory mission. Much of the charge given to either is given to both, as is most natural, since they had the same message, and both were sent to prepare for Christ's personal ministry. But though the Seventy were sent out but for a short time, permanent principles for the guidance, not only of Christian workers, but of all Christian lives, are embodied in the charge which they received.

We note, first, that all personal service should be preceded by intense realisation of the immense field, and of the inadequacy, of Christian effort, which vision will culminate in prayer for more toilers to be 'sent forth.' The word implies a certain measure of compulsion, for an overmastering impulse is always needed to overcome human reluctance and laziness. No man has ever done large service for God who has not felt that, like the prophet, he was laid hold of by the Spirit, and borne away, whether he would or no. 'I must speak,' is felt by every true messenger of God. The prayer was answered by the sending of the pray–ers, as it often is. Note how Jesus implies that He is Lord of the harvest, in that His sending them is the answer to the petition. Note, too, the authority which He claims to exercise supreme sovereignty over the lives of men. He has the right to fling them into deadly peril for no other purpose than to proclaim His name. Lambs, ringed round by wolves with white, gleaming teeth, have little chance of life. Jesus gives His servants full warning of dangers, and on the very warning builds an exhortation to quiet confidence; for, if the sentence ends with 'lambs in the

155

midst of wolves,' it begins with 'I send you forth,' and that is enough, for He will defend them when He seeth the wolf coming. Not only so, but He will also provide for all their needs, so they want no baggage nor money, nor even a staff. A traveller without any of these would be in poor case, but they are not to carry such things, because they carry Jesus. He who sends them forth goes with them whom He sends. Now, this precept, in its literal form, was expressly abolished afterwards (Luke xxii. 36), but the spirit of it is permanent. If Christ sends us, we may trust Him to take care of us as long as we are on His errands.

Energetic pursuit of their work, unimpeded by distractions of social intercourse, is meant by the prohibition of saluting by the way. That does not mean churlish isolation, but any one who has ever seen two Easterns 'saluting' knows what a long–drawn–out affair it is. How far along the road one might have travelled while all that empty ceremony was being got through! The time for salutations is when the journey is over. They mean something then. The great effect of the presence of Christ's servants should be to impart the peace which they themselves possess. We should put reality into conventional courtesies. All Christians are to be peacemakers in the deepest sense, and especially in regard to men's relations with God. The whole scope of our work may be summed up as being to proclaim and bring peace with God, with ourselves, with all others, and with circumstances. The universality of our message is implied in the fact that the salutation is to be given in every house entered, and without any inquiry whether a 'son of peace' is there. The reflex blessedness of Christian effort is taught in the promise that the peace, vainly wished for those who would not receive it, is not wasted like spilt water, but comes back like a dove, to the hand of its sender. If we do no other person good, we bless ourselves by all work for others.

The injunctions as to conduct in the house or city that receives the messengers carry two principles of wide application. First, they demand clear disinterestedness and superiority to vulgar appetites. Christ's servants are not to be fastidious as to their board and lodging. They are not to make demands for more refined diet than their hosts are accustomed to have, and they are not to shift their quarters, though it were from a hovel to a palace. The suspicion that a Christian worker is fond of good living and sensuous delights robs his work of power. But the injunction teaches also that there is no generosity in those who hear the message giving, and no obligation laid on those who deliver it by their receiving, enough to live and work on. The less we obviously look for, the more shall we probably receive. A high–minded man need not scruple to take the 'hire'; a high–minded giver will not suppose that he has hired the receiver to be his servant.

The double substance of the work is next briefly stated. The order in which its two parts stands is remarkable, for the healing of the sick is put first, and the proclamation of the nearness of the kingdom second. Possibly the reason is that the power to heal was a new gift. Its very priority in mention may imply that it was but a means to an end, a part of the equipment for the true and proper work of preaching the coming of the kingdom and its King. At all events, let us learn that Jesus wills the continual combination of regard to the bodily wants and sicknesses, and regard to the spiritual needs of men.

The solemn instructions as to what was to be done in the case of rejection breathe a spirit the reverse of sanguine. Jesus had no illusions as to the acceptance of the message, and He will send no man out to work hiding from him the difficulties and opposition probably to be encountered. Much wisdom lies in deciding when a field of labour or a method of work should be abandoned as hopeless—for the present and for the individual worker, at all events. To do it too soon is cowardice; to delay it too long is not admirable perseverance, but blindness to plain providences. To shake off the dust is equivalent to severing all connection. The messenger will not bring away the least thing belonging to the city. But whatever men's unbelief, it does not affect the fact, but it does affect their relation to the fact. The gracious message was at first that 'the kingdom of God is come nigh *unto you*,' but the last shape of it leaves out 'unto you': for rejection of the word cuts off from beneficial share in the word, and the kingdom, when it comes, has no blessing for the unbelieving soul.

The return of the Seventy soon followed their being sent forth. They came back with a childish, surprised joy, and almost seem to have thought that Jesus would be as much astonished and excited as they were with the proof of the power of His name. They had found that they could not only heal the sick, but cast out demons. Jesus' answer is meant to quiet down their excitement by teaching them that He had known what they were doing whilst they were doing it. When did He behold Satan fall from heaven? The context seems to require that it should be at the time when the Seventy were casting out demons. The contest between the personal Source of evil and Jesus was fought out by the principals, not by their subordinates, and it is already victoriously decided in Christ's sight. Therefore, as the sequel of His victory, He enlarges His gifts to His servants, couching the charter in the words of a psalm (Ps. xci.). Nothing can harm the servant without the leave of the Master, and if any evil befall him in his work, the evil in the evil, the poison on the arrow–head, will be wiped off and taken away. But great as are the gifts to the faithful servant, they are less to be rejoiced in than his personal inclusion among the citizens of heaven. Gifts and powers are good, and may legitimately be rejoiced in; but to possess eternal life, and to belong to the mother–city of us all, the New Jerusalem, is better than all gifts and all powers.

NEIGHBOURS FAR OFF

'And, behold, a certain lawyer stood up, and tempted Him, saying, Master, what shall I do to inherit eternal life? 26. He said unto him, What is written in the law? how readest thou? 27. And he, answering, said, Thou shalt love the Lord thy God with all thy heart, and with all thy soul, and with all thy strength, and with all thy mind; and thy neighbour as thyself. 28. And He said unto him, Thou hast answered right: this do, and thou shalt live. 29. But he, willing to justify himself, said unto Jesus, And who is my neighbour? 30. And Jesus, answering, said, A certain man went down from Jerusalem to Jericho, and fell among thieves, which stripped him of his raiment, and wounded him, and departed, leaving him half dead. 31. And by chance there came down a certain priest that way; and when he saw him, he passed by on the other side. 32. And likewise a Levite, when he was at the place, came and looked on him, and passed by on the other side. 33. But

a certain Samaritan, as he journeyed, came where he
was: and when he saw him, he had compassion on him,
34. And went to him, and bound up his wounds, pouring
in oil and wine, and set him on his own beast, and
brought him to an inn, and took care of him. 35. And on
the morrow, when he departed, he took out two pence,
and gave them to the host, and said unto him, Take care
of him: and whatsoever thou spendest more, when I come
again, I will repay thee. 36. Which now of these three,
thinkest thou, was neighbour unto him that fell among
the thieves! 37. And he said. He that showed mercy on
him. Then said Jesus unto him, Go, and do thou likewise.'
—LUKE x. 25–37.

The lawyer's first question was intended to 'tempt' Jesus, which here seems to mean, rather, 'to test'; that is, to ascertain His orthodoxy or His ability. Christ walks calmly through the snare, as if not seeing it. His answer is unimpeachably orthodox, and withal just hints in the slightest way that the question was needless, since one so learned in the law knew well enough what were the conditions of inheriting life. The lawyer knows the letter too well to be at a loss what to answer. But it is remarkable that he gives the same combination of two passages which Jesus gives in His last duel with the Pharisees (Matt. xxii; Mark xii.). Did Jesus adopt this lawyer's summary? Or is Luke's narrative condensed, omitting stages by which Jesus led the man to so wise an answer?

Our Lord's rejoinder has a marked tone of authority, which puts the lawyer in his right place. His answer is commended, as by one whose estimate has weight; and his practice is implicitly condemned, as by one who knows, and has a right to judge. 'This do' is a sharp sword–thrust. It also unites the two 'loves' as essentially one, by saying 'This'–not 'these'—'do.' The lawyer feels the prick, and it is his defective practice, not his question, which he seeks to 'justify.' He did not think that his love to God needed any justification. He had fully done his duty there, but about the other half he was less sure. So he tried to ride off, lawyer–like, on a question of the meaning of words. 'Who is my neighbour?' is the question answered by the lovely story of the kindly Samaritan.

I. The main purpose, then, is to show how far off men may be, and yet be neighbours. The lawyer's question, 'Who is my neighbour?' is turned round the other way in Christ's form of it at the close. It is better to ask 'Whose neighbour am I?' than 'Who is my neighbour?' The lawyer meant by the word 'a person whom I am bound to love.' He wanted to know how far an obligation extended which he had no mind to recognise an inch farther than he was obliged. Probably he had in his thought the Rabbinical limitations which made it as much duty to 'hate thine enemy' as to 'love thy neighbour.' Probably, too, he accepted the national limitations, which refused to see any neighbours outside the Jewish people.

'Neighbourhood,' in his judgment, implied 'nearness,' and he wished to know how far off the boundaries of the region included in the command lay. There are a great many of us like him, who think that the obligation is a matter of geography, and that love, like force, is inversely as the square of the distance. A good deal of the so–called virtue of 'patriotism' is of this spurious sort. But Christ's way of putting the question sweeps all such limitations aside. 'Who became neighbour to' the wounded man? 'He who showed mercy on him,' said the lawyer, unwilling to name the Samaritan, and by his very reluctance giving the point to his answer which Christ wished to bring out. We are not to love because we are neighbours in any geographical sense, but we become neighbours to the man farthest from us when we love and help him. The relation has nothing to do with proximity. If we prove ourselves neighbours to any man by exercising love to him, then the relation intended by the word is as wide as humanity. We recognise that A. is our neighbour when a throb of pity shoots through our heart, and thereby we become neighbours to him.

The story is not, properly speaking, a parable, or imaginary narrative of something in the physical world intended to be translated into something in the spiritual region, but it is an illustration (by an imaginary narrative) of the actual virtue in question. Every detail is beautifully adapted to bring out the lesson that the obligation of neighbourly affection has nothing to do with nearness either of race or religion, but is as wide as humanity. The wounded man was probably a Jew, but it is significant that his nationality is not mentioned. He is 'a certain man,' that is all. The Samaritan did not ask where he was born before he helped him. So Christ teaches us that sorrow and need and sympathy and help are of no nationality.

That lesson is still more strongly taught by making the helper a Samaritan. Perhaps, if Jesus had been speaking in America, he would have made him a negro; or, if in France, a German; or, if in England, a 'foreigner.' It was a daring stroke to bring the despised name of 'Samaritan' into the story, and one sees what a hard morsel to swallow the lawyer found it, by his unwillingness to name him after all.

The nations have not yet learned the deep, simple truth of this parable. It absolutely forbids all limitations of mercy and help. It makes every man the neighbour of every man. It carries in germ the great truth of the brotherhood of the race. 'Humanity' is a purely Christian word, and a conception that was never dreamed of before Christ had showed us the unity of mankind. We slowly approximate to the realisation of the teaching of this story, which is oftener admired than imitated, and perhaps oftenest on the lips of people who obey it least.

II. Another aspect of the parable is its lesson as to the true manifestations of neighbourliness. The minutely detailed account of the Samaritan's care for the half–dead man is not only graphic, but carries large lessons. Compassionate sentiments are very well. They must come first. The help that is given as a matter of duty, without the outgoing of heart, will be worth little, and soon cease to flow; but the emotion that does not drive the wheels of action, and set to work to stanch the sorrows which cause it to run so easily, is worth still less. It hardens the heart, as all feeling unexpressed in action does. If the priest and Levite had gone up to the man, and said, 'Ah, poor fellow, poor fellow! how sorry we are for you! somebody ought to come and help you,' and so had trudged on their way, they would have been worse than they are painted as being.

The various acts are enumerated as showing the genius of true love. We notice the swift, cool–headed deftness of the man, his having at hand the appliances needed, the business–like way in which he goes about his kindness, his readiness to expend his wine and oil, his willingness to do the surgeon's work, his cheerful giving up of his 'own beast,' while he plodded along on foot, steadying the wounded man on his ass; his care for him at the inn; his generosity, and withal his prudence, in not leaving a great sum in the host's hands, but just enough to tide over a day or two, and his wise hint that he would audit the accounts when he came back. This man's quick compassion was blended with plenty of shrewdness, and was as practical as the hardest, least compassionate man could have been. There is need for organisation, 'faculty,' and the like, in the work of loving our neighbour. A thousand pities that sometimes Christian charity and Christian common–sense dissolve partnership. The Samaritan was a man of business, and he did his compassion in a business–like fashion, as we should try to do.

III. Another lesson inwrought into the parable is the divorce between religion and neighbourliness, as shown in the conduct of the priest and Levite. Jericho was one of the priestly cities, so that there would be frequent travellers on ecclesiastical errands. The priest was 'going down' (that is from Jerusalem), so he could not plead a 'pressing public engagement' at the Temple. The verbal repetition of the description of the conduct of both him and the Levite serves to suggest its commonness. They two did exactly the same thing, and so would twenty or two hundred ordinary passers by. They saw the man lying in a pool of blood, and they made a wide circuit, and, even in the face of such a sight, went on their way. Probably they said to themselves, 'Robbers again; the sooner we get past this dangerous bit, the better.' We see that they were heartless, but they did not see it. We do the same thing ourselves, and do not see that we do; for who of us has not known of many miseries which we could have done something to stanch, and have left untouched because our hearts were unaffected? The world would be a changed place if every Christian attended to the sorrows that are plain before him.

Let professing Christians especially lay to heart the solemn lesson that there does lie in their very religion the possibility of their being culpably unconcerned about some of the world's wounds, and that, if their love to God does not find a field for its manifestation in active love to man, worship in the Temple will be mockery. Philanthropy is, in our days, often substituted for religion. The service of man has been put forward as the only real service of God. But philanthropic unbelievers and unphilanthropic believers are equally monstrosities. What God hath joined let not man put asunder. That simple 'and,' which couples the two great commandments, expresses their indissoluble connection. Well for us if in our practice they are blended in one!

It is not spiritualising this narrative when we say that Jesus is Himself the great pattern of the swift compassion and effectual helpfulness which it sets forth. Many unwise attempts have been made to tack on spiritual meanings to the story. These are as irreverent as destructive of its beauty and significance. But to say that Christ is the perfect example of that love to every man which the narrative portrays, has nothing in common with these fancies. It is only when we have found in Him the pity and the healing which we need, that we shall go forth into the world with love as wide as His.

HOW TO PRAY

'And it came to pass, that, as He was praying in a
certain place, when He ceased, one of His disciples
said unto Him, Lord, teach us to pray, as John also
taught His disciples. 2. And He said unto them, When
ye pray, say, Our Father which art in heaven, Hallowed

be Thy name. Thy kingdom come. Thy will be done, as in
heaven, so in earth. 3. Give us day by day our daily
bread. 4. And forgive us our sins; for we also forgive
every one that is indebted to us. And lead us not into
temptation; but deliver us from evil. 5. And He said
unto them, Which of you shall have a friend, and shall
go unto him at midnight, and say unto him, Friend, lend
me three loaves; 6. For a friend of mine in his journey
is come to me, and I have nothing to set before him?
7. And he from within shall answer and say, Trouble me
not: the door is now shut, and my children are with me
in bed; I cannot rise and give thee. 8. I say unto you,
Though he will not rise and give him, because he is his
friend, yet because of his importunity he will rise and
give him as many as he needeth. 9. And I say unto you,
Ask, and it shall be given to you; seek, and ye shall
find; knock, and it shall be opened unto you. 10. For
every one that asketh receiveth; and he that seeketh
findeth; and to him that knocketh it shall be opened.
11. If a son shall ask bread of any of you that is a
father, will he give him a stone? or if he ask a fish,
will he for a fish give him a serpent? 12. Or if he
shall ask an egg, will he offer him a scorpion? 13. If
ye then, being evil, know how to give good gifts unto
your children: how much more shall your heavenly Father
give the Holy Spirit to them that ask Him!—LUKE xi. 1–13.

Christ's praying fired the disciples with desire to pray like Him. There must have been something of absorption and blessedness in His communion with the Father which struck them with awe and longing, and which they would fain repeat. Do our prayers move any to taste the devotion and joy which breathe through them? But low conceptions mingled with high desires in their request. They think that if He will give them a form, that will be enough; and they wish to be as well off as John's disciples, whose relation to their master seems to them parallel with theirs to Jesus.

Our Lord's answer meets and transcends their wish. He does give them a model prayer, and He adds encouragements to pray which inculcate confidence and persistence. The passage, then, falls into two parts—the pattern prayer (vs. 2–4), and the spirit of prayer as enforced by some encouragements (vs. 5–13). The material is so rich that we can but gather the surface wealth. Deep mines must lie unexplored here.

I. The pattern of prayer. We call it the Lord's Prayer, but it is so only in the sense that He gives it. It is our prayer for our use. His own prayers remain unrecorded, except those in the upper room and at Gethsemane. This is the type to which His servants' prayers are to be conformed. 'After this manner pray ye,' whether in these words or not. And the repetition of the words is often far enough away from catching their spirit. To suppose that our Lord simply met the disciples' wish by giving them a form

161

misconceives the genius of His work. He gave something much better; namely, a pattern, the spirit of which we are to diffuse through all our petitions,

Two salient features of the prayer bring out the two great characteristics of all true Christian prayer. First, we note the invocation. It is addressed to the Father. Our prayers are, then, after the pattern only when they are the free, unembarrassed, confident, and utterly frank whispers of a child to its father. Confidence and love should wing the darts which are to reach heaven. That name, thoroughly realised, banishes fear and self-will, and inspires submission and aspiration. To cry,' Abba, Father,' is the essence of all prayer. Nothing more is needed.

The broad lesson drawn from the order of requests is the second point to be noticed. If we have the child's spirit, we shall put the Father's honour first, and absolutely subordinate our own interests to it. So the first half of the prayer, like the first half of the Decalogue, deals with God's name and its glory. Alas! it is hard even for His child to keep this order. Natural self-regard must be cast out by love, if we are thus to pray. How few of us have reached that height, not in mere words, but in unspoken desires!

The order of the several petitions in the first half of the prayer is significant. God's name (that is, His revealed character) being hallowed (that is, recognised as what it is), separate from all limitation and creatural imperfection, and yet near in love as a Father is, the coming of His kingdom will follow; for where He is known and honoured for what He is He will reign, and men, if they rightly knew Him, would fall before Him and serve Him. The hallowing of His name is the only foundation for His kingdom among us, and all knowledge of Him which does not lead to submission to His rule is false or incomplete.

The outward, visible establishment of God's kingdom in human society follows individual acquaintance with His name. The doing of God's will is the sign of His kingdom having come. The ocean is blue, like the sky which it mirrors. Earth will be like heaven.

The second half of the prayer returns to personal interests; but God's child has many brethren, and so His prayer is, not for 'me' and 'my,' but for 'us' and 'ours.' Our first need, if we start from the surface and go inwards, is for the maintenance of bodily life. So the petition for bread has precedence, not as being most, but least, important. We are to recognise God's hand in blessing our daily toil. We are to limit our desires to necessaries, and to leave the future in His hands. Is this 'the manner' after which Christians pray for perishable good? Where would anxious care or eager rushing after wealth be, if it were?

A deeper need, the chief in regard to the inner man, is deliverance from sin, in its two aspects of guilt and power. So the next petition is for pardon. Sin incurs debt. Forgiveness is the remission of penalty, but the penalty is not merely external punishment. The true penalty is separation from God, and His forgiveness is His loving on, undisturbed by sin. If we truly call God Father, the image of His mercifulness will be formed in us, and unless we are forgiving, we shall certainly lose the consciousness of being forgiven, and bind our sins on our backs in all their weight. God's children need always to pray 'after this manner, 'for sin is not entirely conquered.

Pardon is meant to lead on to holiness. Hence the next clause in effect prays for sanctification. Knowing our own weakness, we may well ask not to be placed in circumstances where the inducements to sin would be strong, even while we know that we may grow thereby, if we resist. The shortened form of the prayer in Luke, according to the Revised Version, omits 'deliver us from evil'; but that clause is necessary to complete the idea. Whether we read 'evil' or 'the evil one,' the clause refers to us as tempted, and, as it were, in the grip of an enemy too strong for us. God alone can extricate us from the mouth of the lion. He will, if we ask Him. The only evil is to sin away our consciousness of sonship and to cling to the sin which separates us from God.

II. A type of prayer is not all that we need. The spirit in which we pray is still more important. So Jesus goes on to enjoin two things chiefly; namely, persistence and filial confidence. He presents to us a parable with its application (vs. 5–10), and the germ of a parable with its (vs. 11–13). Observe that these two parts deal with encouragements to confidence drawn, first, from our own experience in asking, and, second, with encouragements drawn from our own experience in giving. In the former we learn from the man who will not take 'no,' and so at last gets 'yes'; in the latter, from the Father who will certainly give His child what he asks.

In the parable two points are to be specially noted—the persistent suppliant pleads not for himself so much as for the hungry traveller, and the man addressed gives without any kindliness, from the mere wish to be left at peace. As to both points, an *a fortiori* argument is implied. If a man can so persevere when pleading for another, how much more should we do so when asking for ourselves! And if persistence has such power with selfish men, how much more shall it avail with Him who slumbers not nor sleeps, and to whom we can never come at an inopportune moment, and who will give us because we are His friends, and He ours! The very ugliness of character ascribed to the owner of the loaves, selfish in his enjoyment of his bed, in his refusal to turn out on an errand of neighbourliness, and in his final giving, thus serves as a foil to the character of Him to whom our prayers are addressed.

The application of the parable lies in verses 9 and 10. The efforts enjoined are in an ascending scale, and 'ask' and 'knock' allude to the parable. To 'seek' is more than to ask, for it includes active exertion; and for want of seeking by conduct appropriate to our prayers, we often ask in vain. If we pray for temporal blessings, and then fold our hands, and sit with our mouths open for them to drop into, we shall not get them. If we ask for higher goods, and rise from our knees to live worldly lives, we shall get them as little. Knocking is more than either, for it implies a continuous hammering on the door, like Peter's when he stood in the morning twilight at Mary's gate. Asking and seeking must be continuous if they are to be rewarded.

Verse 10 grounds the promise of verse 9 on experience. It is he who asks that gets. In men's giving it is not universally true that petitions are answered, nor that gifts are not given unasked. Nor is it true about God's lower gifts, which are often bestowed on the unthankful, and not seldom refused to His children. But it is universally true in regard to His highest gifts, which are never withheld from the earnest asker who adds to his prayers fitting conduct, and prays always without fainting, and which are not and cannot be given unless desire for them opens the heart for their reception, and faith in God assures him who prays that he cannot ask in vain.

163

The germ of a parable with its application (vs. 11–13) draws encouragement from our own experience in giving. It guards against misconceptions of God which might arise from the former parable, and comes back to the first word of the Lord's Prayer as itself the guarantee of every true desire of His child being heard and met. Bread, eggs, and fish are staple articles of food. In each case something similar in appearance, but useless or hurtful, is contrasted with the thing asked by the child. The round loaves of the East are not unlike rounded, wave–washed stones, water–serpents are fishlike, and the oval body of a quiescent scorpion is similar to an egg. Fathers do not play tricks with their hungry children. Though we are all sinful, parental love survives, and makes a father wise enough to know what will nourish and what would poison his child.

Alas! that is only partially true, for many a parent has not a father's heart, and is neither impelled by love to give good things to, nor to withhold evil ones from, his child. But it is true with sufficient frequency to warrant the great *a fortiori* argument which Jesus bases on it. Our heavenly Father's love, the archetype of all parental affection, is tainted by no evil and darkened by no ignorance. He loves perfectly and wisely, therefore He cannot but give what His child needs.

But the child often mistakes, and thinks that stones are bread, serpents fish, and scorpions eggs. So God often has to deny the letter of our petitions, in order not to give us poison. Luke's version of the closing promise, in which 'the Holy Spirit' stands instead of Matthew's 'good things,' sets the whole matter in the true light; for that Spirit brings with Him all real good, and, while many of our desires have, for our own sakes, to be denied, we shall never hold up empty hands and have to let them fall still empty, if we desire that great encyclopediacal gift which our loving Father waits to bestow. It cannot be given without our petition, it will never be withheld from our petition.

THE PRAYING CHRIST

'... As He was praying in a certain place, when He ceased, one of His disclples said unto Him, Lord, teach us to pray.'—LUKE xi. 1.

It is noteworthy that we owe our knowledge of the prayers of Jesus principally to the Evangelist Luke. There is, indeed, one solemn hour of supplication under the quivering shadows of the olive–trees in Gethsemane which is recorded by Matthew and Mark as well; and though the fourth Gospel passes over that agony of prayer, it gives us, in accordance with its ruling purpose, the great chapter that records His priestly intercession. But in addition to these instances the first Gospel furnishes but one, and the second but two, references to the subject. All the others are found in Luke.

I need not stay to point out how this fact tallies with the many other characteristics of the third Gospel, which mark it as eminently the story of the Son of Man. The record which traces our Lord's descent to Adam rather than to Abraham; which tells the story of His birth, and gives us all we know of the 'child Jesus'; which records His growth in wisdom and stature, and has preserved a multitude of minute points bearing on His true manhood, as well as on the tenderness of His sympathy and the universality of His work, most naturally emphasises that most precious indication of His humanity—His habitual prayerfulness. The Gospel of the King, which is the first Gospel, or of the Servant, which is the second, or of the Son of God, which is the fourth, had less occasion to dwell on this. Royalty, practical Obedience, Divinity, are their respective themes. Manhood is Luke's, and he is ever pointing us to the kneeling Christ.

Consider, then, for a moment, how precious the prayers of Jesus are, as bringing Him very near to us in His true manhood. There are deep and mysterious truths involved with which we do not meddle now. But there are also plain and surface truths which are very helpful and blessed. We thank God for the story of His weariness when He sat on the well, and of His slumber when, worn out with a hard day's work, He slept on the hard wooden pillow in the stern of the fishing–boat among the nets and the litter. It brings Him near to us when we read that He thirsted, and nearer still when the immortal words fall on our wondering ears, 'Jesus wept.' But even more precious than these indications of His true participation in physical needs and human emotion, is the great evidence of His prayers, that He too lived a life of dependence, of communion, and of submission; that in our religious life, as in all our life, He is our pattern and forerunner. As the Epistle to the Hebrews puts it, He shows that He is not ashamed to call us brethren by this, that He too avows that He lives by faith; and by His life—and surely pre–eminently by His prayers—declares, I will put my trust in Him.' We cannot think of Christ too often or too absolutely as the object of faith; and as the hearer of our cries; but we may, and some of us do, think of Him too seldom as the pattern of faith, and as the example for our devotion. We should feel Him a great deal nearer us; and the fact of His manhood would not only be grasped more clearly by orthodox believers, but would be felt in more of its true tenderness, if we gave more prominence in our thoughts to that picture of the praying Christ.

Another point that may be suggested is, that the highest, holiest life needs specific acts and times of prayer. A certain fantastical and overstrained spirituality is not rare, which professes to have got beyond the need of such beggarly elements. Some tinge of this colours the habits of many people who are scarcely conscious of its presence, and makes them somewhat careless as to forms and times of public or of that of private worship. I do not think that I am wrong in saying that there is a growing laxity in that matter among people who are really trying to live Christian lives. We may well take the lesson which Christ's prayers teach us, for we all need it, that no life is so high, so holy, so full of habitual communion with God, that it can afford to do without the hour of prayer, the secret place, the uttered word. If we are to 'pray without ceasing,' by the constant attitude of communion and the constant conversion of work into worship, we must certainly have, and we shall undoubtedly desire, special moments when the daily sacrifice of doing good passes into the sacrifice of our lips. The devotion which is to be diffused through our lives must be first concentrated and evolved in our prayers. These are the gathering–grounds which feed the river. The life that was all one long prayer needed the mountain–top and the nightly converse with God. He who could say, 'The Father hath not left Me alone, for I do always the things that please Him,' felt that He must also have the special communion of spoken prayer. What Christ needed we cannot afford to neglect.

Thus Christ's own prayers do, in a very real sense, 'teach us to pray.' But it strikes me that, if we will take the instances in which we find Him praying, and try to classify them in a rough way, we may gain some hints worth laying to heart. Let me attempt this briefly now.

First, then, the praying Christ teaches us to pray as a rest after service.

The Evangelist Mark gives us, in his brief, vivid way, a wonderful picture in his first chapter of

Christ's first Sabbath–day of ministry in Capernaum. It was crowded with work. The narrative goes hurrying on through the busy hours, marking the press of rapidly succeeding calls by its constant reiteration—'straightway,' 'immediately,' 'forthwith,' 'anon,' 'immediately.' He teaches in the synagogue; without breath or pause He heals a man with an unclean spirit; then at once passes to Simon's house, and as soon as He enters has to listen to the story of how the wife's mother lay sick of a fever. They might have let Him rest for a moment, but they are too eager, and He is too pitying, for delay. As soon as He hears, He helps. As soon as He bids it, the fever departs. As soon as she is healed, the woman is serving them. There can have been but a short snatch of such rest as such a house could afford. Then when the shadows of the western hills began to fall upon the blue waters of the lake, and the sunset ended the restrictions of the Sabbath, He is besieged by a crowd full of sorrow and sickness, and all about the door they lie, waiting for its opening. He could not keep it shut any more than His heart or His hand, and so all through the short twilight, and deep into the night, He toils amongst the dim, prostrate forms. What a day it had been of hard toil, as well as of exhausting sympathy! And what was His refreshment? An hour or two of slumber; and then, 'in the morning, rising up a great while before day, He went out, and departed into a solitary place, and there prayed' (Mark i. 35).

In the same way we find Him seeking the same repose after another period of much exertion and strain on body and mind. He had withdrawn Himself and His disciples from the bustle which Mark describes so graphically. 'There were many coming and going, and they had no leisure, so much as to eat.' So, seeking quiet, He takes them across the lake into the solitudes on the other side. But the crowds from all the villages near its head catch sight of the boat in crossing, and hurry round; and there they all are at the landing–place, eager and exacting as ever. He throws aside the purpose of rest, and all day long, wearied as He was, 'taught them many things.' The closing day brings no respite. He thinks of their hunger, before His own fatigue, and will not send them away fasting. So He ends that day of labour by the miracle of feeding the five thousand. The crowds gone to their homes, He can at last think of Himself; and what is His rest? He loses not a moment in 'constraining' His disciples to go away to the other side, as if in haste to remove the last hindrance to something that He had been longing to get to. 'And when He had sent them away, He departed into a mountain to pray' (Mark vi. 46; Matt. xiv. 23).

That was Christ's refreshment after His toil. So He blended contemplation and service, the life of inward communion and the life of practical obedience. How much more do we need to interpose the soothing and invigorating influences of quiet communion between the acts of external work, since our work may harm us, as His never did Him. It may disturb and dissipate our communion with God; it may weaken the very motive from which it should arise; it may withdraw our gaze from God and fix it upon ourselves. It may puff us up with the conceit of our own powers; it may fret us with the annoyances of resistance; it may depress us with the consciousness of failure; and in a hundred other ways may waste and wear away our personal religion. The more we work the more we need to pray. In this day of activity there is great danger, not of doing too much, but of praying too little for so much work. These two—work and prayer, action and contemplation—are twin–sisters. Each pines without the other. We are ever tempted to cultivate one or the other disproportionately. Let us imitate Him who sought the mountain–top as His refreshment after toil, but never left duties undone or sufferers unrelieved in pain. Let us imitate Him who turned from the joys of contemplation to the joys of service without a murmur, when His disciples broke in on His solitude with, 'all men seek Thee,' but never suffered the outward work to blunt His desire for, nor to encroach on the hour of, still communion with His Father. Lord, teach us to work; Lord, teach us to pray.

The praying Christ teaches us to pray as a preparation for important steps.

Whilst more than one Gospel tells us of the calling of the Apostolic Twelve, the Gospel of the manhood alone narrates (Luke vi. 12) that on the eve of that great epoch in the development of Christ's kingdom, 'He went out into a mountain to pray, and continued all night in prayer to God.' Then, 'when it was day,' He calls to Him His disciples, and chooses the Twelve.

A similar instance occurs, at a later period, before another great epoch in His course. The great confession made by Peter, 'Thou art the Christ, the Son of the living God,' was drawn forth by our Lord to serve as basis for His bestowment on the Apostles of large spiritual powers, and for the teaching, with much increased detail and clearness, of His approaching sufferings. In both aspects it distinctly marks a new stage. Concerning it, too, we read, and again in Luke alone (ix. 18), that it was preceded by solitary prayer.

Thus He teaches us where and how we may get the clear insight into circumstances and men that may guide us aright. Bring your plans, your purposes to God's throne. Test them by praying about them. Do nothing large or new—nothing small or old either, for that matter—till you have asked there, in the silence of the secret place, 'Lord, what wouldest Thou have me to do?' There is nothing bitterer to parents than when children begin to take their own way without consulting them. Do you take counsel of your Father, and have no secrets from Him. It will save you from many a blunder and many a heartache; it will make your judgment clear, and your step assured, even in new and difficult ways, if you will learn from the praying Christ to pray before you plan, and take counsel of God before you act.

Again, the praying Christ teaches us to pray as the condition of receiving the Spirit and the brightness of God.

There were two occasions in the life of Christ when visible signs showed His full possession of the Divine Spirit, and the lustre of His glorious nature. There are large and perplexing questions connected with both, on which I have no need to enter. At His baptism the Spirit of God descended visibly and abode on Jesus. At His transfiguration His face shone as the light, and His garments were radiant as sunlit snow. Now on both these occasions our Gospel, and our Gospel alone, tells us that it was whilst Christ was in the act of prayer that the sign was given: 'Jesus being baptized, and praying, the heaven was opened, and the Holy Ghost descended' (iii. 21, 22). 'As He prayed, the fashion of His countenance was altered, and His raiment was white and glistening' (ix. 29).

Whatever difficulty may surround the first of these narratives especially, one thing is clear, that in both of them there was a true communication from the Father to the man Jesus. And another thing is, I think, clear too, that our Evangelist meant to lay stress on the preceding act as the human condition of such communication. So if we would have the heavens opened over our heads, and the dove of God descending to fold its white wings, and brood over the chaos of our hearts till order and light come there, we must do what the Son of Man did—pray. And if we would have the fashion of our countenances altered, the wrinkles of care wiped out, the traces of tears dried up, the blotches of unclean living healed, and all the brands of worldliness and evil exchanged for the name of God written on our foreheads, and the reflected glory irradiating our faces, we must do as Christ did—pray. So, and only so, will God's Spirit fill our hearts, God's brightness flash in our faces, and the vesture of heaven clothe our nakedness.

Again, the praying Christ teaches us to pray as the preparation for sorrow. Here all the three Evangelists tell us the same sweet and solemn story. It is not for us to penetrate further than they carry us into the sanctities of Gethsemane. Jesus, though hungering for companionship in that awful hour, would take no man with Him there; and He still says, 'Tarry ye here, while I go and pray yonder.' But as we stand afar off, we catch the voice of pleading rising through the stillness of the night, and the solemn words tell us of a Son's confidence, of a man's shrinking, of a Saviour's submission. The very spirit of all prayer is in these broken words. That was truly 'The Lord's Prayer' which He poured out beneath the olives in the moonlight. It was heard when strength came from heaven, which He used in 'praying more earnestly.' It was heard when, the agony past and all the conflict ended in victory, He came forth, with that strange calm and dignity, to give Himself first to His captors and then to His executioners, the ransom for the many.

As we look upon that agony and these tearful prayers, let us not only look with thankfulness, but let that kneeling Saviour teach us that in prayer alone can we be forearmed against our lesser sorrows; that strength to bear flows into the heart that is opened in supplication; and that a sorrow which we are made able to endure is more truly conquered than a sorrow which we avoid. We have all a cross to carry and a wreath of thorns to wear. If we want to be fit for our Calvary—may we use that solemn name?—we must go to our Gethsemane first.

So the Christ who prayed on earth teaches us to pray; and the Christ who intercedes in heaven helps us to pray, and presents our poor cries, acceptable through His sacrifice, and fragrant with the incense from His own golden censer.

'O Thou by whom we come to God,
The Life, the Truth, the Way;
The path of prayer Thyself hast trod;
Lord! teach us how to pray.'

THE RICH FOOL

'And one of the company said unto Him, Master, speak
to my brother, that he divide the inheritance with me.
14. And He said unto him, Man, who made Me a judge or
a divider over you? 15. And He said unto them, Take
heed, and beware of covetousness: for a man's life
consisteth not in the abundance of the things which he
possesseth. 16. And He spake a parable unto them,
saying, The ground of a certain rich man brought forth
plentifully: 17. And he thought within himself, saying,

168

What shall I do, because I have no room where to bestow
my fruits! 18. And he said, This will I do: I will pull
down my barns, and build greater; and there will I
bestow all my fruits and my goods. 19. And I will say
to my soul, Soul, thou hast much goods laid up for many
years; take thine ease, eat, drink, and be merry.
20. But God said unto him, Thou fool, this night thy
soul shall be required of thee: then whose shall those
things be, which thou hast provided! 21. So is he that
layeth up treasure for himself, and is not rich toward
God. 22. And He said unto his disciples, Therefore I
say unto you, Take no thought for your life, what ye
shall eat; neither for the body, what ye shall put on.
23. The life is more than meat, and the body is more
than raiment'—LUKE xii. 13–23.

What a gulf between the thoughts of Jesus and those of this unmannerly interrupter! Our Lord had been speaking solemnly as to confessing Him before men, the divine help to be given, and the blessed reward to follow, and this hearer had all the while been thinking only of the share in his father's inheritance, out of which he considered that his brother had cheated him. Such indifference must have struck a chill into Christ's heart, and how keenly he felt it is traceable in the curt and stern brushing aside of the man's request. The very form of addressing him puts him at a distance. 'Man' is about as frigid as can be. Our Lord knew the discouragement of seeing that His words never came near some of His hearers, and had no power to turn their thoughts even for a minute from low objects. 'What do I care about being confessed before the angels, or about the Holy Spirit to teach me? What I want is my share of the paternal acres. A rabbi who will help me to these is the rabbi for me.' John Bunyan's 'man with the muck-rake' had his eyes so glued to the ground and the muck that he did not see the crown hanging above him. How many of us find the sermon time a good opportunity for thinking about investments and business!

Christ's answer is intentionally abrupt and short. It deals with part only of the man's error, the rest of which, being an error to which we are all exposed, and which was the root of the part special to him, is dealt with in the parable that follows. Because the man was covetous, he could see in Jesus nothing more than a rabbi who might influence his brother. Our sense of want largely shapes our conception of Christ. Many to-day see in Him mainly a social (and economical) reformer, because our notion of what we and the world need most is something to set social conditions right, and so to secure earthly well-being. They who take Jesus to be first and foremost 'a judge or a divider' fail to see His deepest work or their own deepest need. He will be all that they wish Him to be, if they will take Him for something else first. He will 'bid' men 'divide the inheritance' with their brethren after men have gone to Him for salvation.

But covetousness, or the greedy clutching at more and more of earthly good, has its roots in us all, and unless there is the most assiduous weeding, it will overrun our whole nature. So Jesus puts great emphasis into the command, 'Take heed, and keep yourselves,' which implies that without much 'heed' and diligent inspection of ourselves (for the original word is 'see'), there will be no guarding against the subtle entrance and swift growth of the vice. We may be enslaved by it, and never suspect that we are. Further, the correct reading is 'from *all* covetousness,' for it has many shapes, besides the grossest one of greed for money. The reason for the exhortation is somewhat obscure in construction, but plain in its general meaning, and sufficiently represented by the Authorised and Revised Versions. The Revised Version margin gives the literal translation, 'Not in a man's abundance consisteth his life, from the things which he possesseth,' on which we may note that the second clause is obviously to be completed from the first, and that the difference between the two seems to lie mainly in the difference of prepositions, 'from' or 'out of' in the second clause standing instead of 'in' in the first, while there may be also a distinction between 'abundance' and 'possessions' the former being a superfluous amount of the latter. The whole will then mean that life does not *consist in* possessions, however abundant, nor does it *come out of* anything that simply belongs to us in outward fashion. Not what we possess, but what we are, is the important matter.

But what does 'life' mean? The parable shows that we cannot leave out the notion of physical life. No possessions keep a man alive. Death knocks at palaces and poor men's hovels. Millionaires and paupers are huddled together in his net. But we must not leave out the higher meaning of life, for it is eminently true that the real life of a man has little relation to what he possesses. Neither nobleness nor peace nor satisfaction, nor anything in which man lives a nobler life than a dog, has much dependence on property of any sort. Wealth often chokes the channels by which true life would flow into us. 'We live by admiration, hope, and love,' and these may be ours abundantly, whatever our portion of earth's riches. Covetousness is folly, because it grasps at worldly good, under the false belief that thereby it will secure the true good of life, but when it has made its pile, it finds that it is no nearer peace of heart, rest, nobleness, or joy than before, and has probably lost much of both in the process of making it. The mad race after wealth, which is the sin of this luxurious, greedy, commercial age, is the consequence of a lie—that life does consist in the abundance of possessions. It consists in knowing 'Thee the only true God, and Jesus Christ, whom Thou hast sent.' Is there any saying of Jesus Christ's more revolutionary, or less believed by His professed followers, than this?

The story of the rich fool is not a parable in the narrower meaning of that word—that is, a description of some event or thing in the natural sphere, transferred by analogy to the spiritual—but an imaginary narrative exemplifying in a concrete instance the characteristics of the class of covetous men. The first point noted is that accumulated wealth breeds anxiety rather than satisfaction. The man is embarrassed by his abundance. The trouble of knowing how to keep it is as great as the labour of acquiring it, and the enjoyment of it is still in the future. Many a rich man is more worried about his securities than he was in making his money. There are so many 'bags with holes' that he is at his wits' end for investments, and the first thing he looks at in his morning's paper is the share list, the sight of which often spoils his breakfast.

The next point is the selfish and arrogant sense of possession, as betrayed by the repetition of 'my'—my fruits, my barns, my corn, and my goods. He has no thought of God, nor of his own stewardship. He recognises no claim on his wealth. If he had looked a little beyond himself, he would have seen many places where he could have bestowed his fruits. Were there no poor at his gates? He had better have poured some riches into the laps of these than have built a new barn. Corn laid up would breed weevils; dispersed, it would bring blessings.

Again, this type of covetous men is a fool because he reckons on 'many years.' The goods may last, but will he? He can make sure that they will suffice for a long time, but he cannot make sure of the long time. Again, he blunders tragically in his estimate of the power of worldly goods to satisfy. 'Eat, drink,' might be said to his body, but to say it to his soul, and to fancy that these pleasures of sense would put it at ease, is the fatal error which gnaws like a worm at the root of every worldly life. The word here rendered 'take thine ease' is cognate with Christ's in His great promise, 'Ye shall find rest unto your souls.' Not in abundance of worldly goods, but in union with Him, is that rest to be found which the covetous man vainly promises himself in filled barns and luxurious idleness.

There is a grim contrast between what the rich man said and what God said. The man's words were empty breath; God's are powers, and what He says is a deed. The divine decree comes crashing into the abortive human plans like a thunder–clap into a wood full of singing birds, and they are all stricken silent. So little does life consist in possessions that all the abundance cannot keep the breath in a man for one moment. His life is 'required of him,' not only in the sense that he has to give it up, but also inasmuch as he has to answer for it. In that requirement the selfishly used wealth will be 'a swift witness against' him, and instead of ministering to life or ease, will 'eat his flesh as fire.' Molten gold dropping on flesh burns badly. Wealth, trusted in and selfishly clutched, without recognition of God the giver or of others' claims to share it, will burn still worse.

The 'parable' is declared to be of universal application. Examples of it are found wherever there are men who selfishly lay up treasures for their own delectation, and 'are not rich toward God.' That expression is best understood in this connection to mean, not rich in spiritual wealth, but in worldly goods used with reference to God, or for His glory and service. So understood, the two phrases, laying up treasure for oneself and being rich towards God, are in full antithesis.

ANXIOUS ABOUT EARTH, OR EARNEST ABOUT THE KINGDOM

'And He said unto His disciples, Therefore I say unto you, Take no thought for your life, what ye shall eat; neither for the body, what ye shall put on. 23. The life is more than meat, and the body is more than raiment. 24. Consider the ravens: for they neither sow nor reap; which neither have storehouse nor barn; and God feedeth them: how much more are ye better than the fowls? 25. And which of you with taking thought can add to his stature one cubit? 26. If ye then be not able to do that thing which is least, why take ye thought for the rest? 27. Consider the lilies how they grow: they toil not, they spin not; and yet I say unto you, that Solomon in all his glory was not arrayed like one of these. 28. If then God so clothe the grass, which is to–day in the field, and to–morrow is cast into the oven; how much more will He clothe you, O ye of little faith! 29. And seek not ye what ye shall eat, or what ye shall drink, neither be ye of doubtful mind.

171

30. For all these things do the nations of the world
seek after: and your Father knoweth that ye have need
of these things. 31. But rather seek ye the kingdom of
God; and all these things shall he added unto you.'
—LUKE xii. 22–31.

The parable of the rich fool was spoken to the multitude, but our Lord now addresses the disciples. 'Therefore' connects the following with the foregoing teachings. The warnings against anxiety are another application of the prohibition of laying up treasure for self. Torturing care is the poor man's form of worldliness, as luxurious self–indulgence is the rich man's. There are two kinds of gout, as doctors tell us—one from high living, and one from poverty of blood. This passage falls into two parts—the prohibition against anxious care (vs. 22–31), and the exhortation to set the affections on the true treasure (vs. 31–34).

I. The first part gives the condemnation of anxiety about earthly necessities. The precept is first stated generally, and then followed by a series of reasons enforcing it. As to the precept, we may remark that the disciples were mostly poor men, who might think that they were in no danger of the folly branded in the parable. They had no barns bursting with plenty, and their concern was how to find food and clothing, not what to do with superfluities. Christ would have them see that the same temper may be in them, though it takes a different shape. Dives and Lazarus may be precisely alike.

The temper condemned here is 'self–consuming care,' the opposite of trust. Its misery is forcibly expressed by the original meaning of the Greek word, which implies being torn in pieces, and thus paints the distraction and self–inflicted harrassment which are the lot of the anxious mind. Prudent foresight and strenuous work are equally outside this prohibition. Anxiety is so little akin to foresight that it disables from exercising it, and both hinders from seeing what to do to provide daily bread, and from doing it.

The disciples' danger of being thus anxious may be measured by the number and variety of reasons against it given by Jesus. The first of these is that such anxiety does not go deep enough, and forgets how we come to have lives to be fed and bodies to be clothed. We have received the greater, life and body, without our anxiety. The rich fool could keep his goods, but not his 'soul' or 'life.' How superficial, then, after all, our anxieties are, when God may end life at any moment! Further, since the greater is given, the less which it needs will also be given. The thought of God as 'a faithful creator' is implied. We must trust Him for the 'more'; we may trust Him for the less.

The second reason bids us look with attention at examples of unanxious lives abundantly fed. Perhaps Elijah's feathered providers, or the words of the Psalmist (Ps. cxlvii. 9), were in Christ's mind. The raven was one of the 'unclean' birds, and of ill omen, from Noah's days, and yet had its meat in due season, though that meat was corpses. Notice the allusions to the preceding parable in 'sow not, neither reap,' and in 'neither have storehouse nor barn.' In these particulars the birds are inferior to us, and, so to speak, the harder to care for. If they who neither work nor store still get their living, shall not we, who can do both? Our superior value is in part expressed by the capacity to sow and reap; and these are more wholesome occupations for a man than worrying.

How lovingly Jesus looked on all creatures, and how clearly He saw everywhere God's hand at work! As Luther said, 'God spends every year in feeding sparrows more than the revenues of the King of France.'

The third reason is the impotence of anxiety (ver. 25). It is difficult to decide between the two possible renderings here. That of 'a cubit' to the 'stature' corresponds best with the growth of the lilies, while 'age' preserves an allusion to the rich fool, and avoids treating the addition of a foot and a half to an ordinary man's height as a small thing. But age is not measured by cubits, and it is best to keep to 'stature.'

At first sight, the argument of verse 23 seems to be now inverted, and what was 'more' to be now 'least.' But the supposed addition, if possible, would be of the smallest importance as regards ensuring food or clothing, and measured by the divine power required to effect it, is less than the continual providing which God does. That smaller work of His, no anxiety will enable us to do. How much less can we effect the complicated and wide–reaching arrangements needed to feed and clothe ourselves! Anxiety is impotent. It only works on our own minds, racking them in vain, but has no effect on the material world, not even on our own bodies, still less on the universe.

The fourth reason bids us look with attention at examples of unanxious existence clothed with beauty. Christ here teaches the highest use of nature, and the noblest way of looking at it. The scientific botanist considers how the lilies grow, and can tell all about cells and chlorophyll and the like. The poet is in raptures with their beauty. Both teach us much, but the religious way of looking at nature includes and transcends both the others. Nature is a parable. It is a visible manifestation of God, and His ways there shadow His ways with us, and are lessons in trust.

The glorious colours of the lily come from no dyer's vats, nor the marvellous texture of their petals from any loom. They are inferior to us in that they do not toil or spin, and in their short blossoming time. Man's 'days are as grass; as a flower of the field so he flourisheth'; but his date is longer, and therefore he has a larger claim on God. 'God clothes the grass of the field' is a truth quite independent of scientific truths or hypotheses about how He does it. If the colours of flowers depend on the visits of insects, God established the dependence, and is the real cause of the resulting loveliness.

The most modern theories of the evolutionist do not in the least diminish the force of Christ's appeal to creation's witness to a loving Care in the heavens. But that appeal teaches us that we miss the best and plainest lesson of nature, unless we see God present and working in it all, and are thereby heartened to trust quietly in His care for us, who are better than the ravens because we have to sow and reap, or than the lilies because we must toil and spin.

Verse 29 adds to the reference to clothing a repeated prohibition as to the other half of our anxieties, and thus rounds off the whole with the same double warning as in verse 22. But it gives a striking metaphor in the new command against 'being of doubtful mind.' The word so rendered means to be lifted on high, and thence to be tossed from height to depth, as a ship in a storm. So it paints the wretchedness of anxiety as ever shuttlecocked about between hopes and fears, sometimes up on the crest of a vain dream of good, sometimes down in the trough of an imaginary evil. We are sure to be thus the sport of our own fancies, unless we have our minds fixed on God in quiet trust, and therefore stable and restful.

Verse 30 gives yet another reason against not only anxiety, but against that eager desire after outward things which is the parent of anxiety. If we 'seek after' them, we shall not be able to avoid being anxious and of doubtful mind. Such seeking, says Christ, is pure heathenism. The nations of the world who know not God make these their chief good, and securing them the aim of their lives. If we do the like, we drop to their level. What is the difference between a heathen and a Christian, if the Christian has the same objects and treasures as the heathen? That is a question which a good many so–called Christians at present would find it hard to answer.

But the crowning reason of all is kept for the last. Much of what precedes might be spoken by a man who had but the coldest belief in Providence. But the great and blessed faith in our Father, God, scatters all anxious care. How should we be anxious if we know that we have a Father in heaven, and that He knows our needs? He recognises our claims on Him. He made the needs, and will send the supply. That is a wide truth, stretching far beyond the mere earthly wants of food and raiment. My wants, so far as God has made me to feel them, are prophecies of God's gifts. He has made them as doors by which He will come in and bless me. How, then, can anxious care fret the heart which feels the Father's presence, and knows that its emptiness is the occasion for the gift of a divine fullness? Trust is the only reasonable temper for a child of such a father. Anxious care is a denial of His love or knowledge or power.

II. Verses 31–34 point out the true direction of effort and affection, and the true way of using outward good so as to secure the higher riches. It is useless to tell men not to set their longings or efforts on worldly things unless you tell them of something better. Life must have some aim, and the mind must turn to something as supremely good. The only way to drive out heathenish seeking after perishable good is to fill the heart with the love and longing for eternal and spiritual good. The ejected demon comes back with a troop at his heels unless his house be filled. To seek 'the kingdom,' to count it our highest good to have our wills and whole being bowed in submission to the loving will of God, to labour after entire conformity to it, to postpone all earthly delights to that, and to count them all but loss if we may win it—this is the true way to conquer worldly anxieties, and is the only course of life which will not at last earn the stern judgment, 'Thou fool.'

That direction of all our desires and energies to the attainment of the kingdom which is the state of being ruled by the will of God, is to be accompanied with joyous, brave confidence. How should they fear whose desires and efforts run parallel with the 'Father's good pleasure'? They are seeking as their chief good what He desires, as His chief delight, to give them. Then they may be sure that, if He gives that, He will not withhold less gifts than may be needed. He will not 'spoil the ship for a ha'p'orth of tar,' nor allow His children, whom He has made heirs of a kingdom, to starve on their road to their crown. If they can trust Him to give them the kingdom, they may surely trust Him for bread and clothes.

Mark, too, the tenderness of that 'little flock.' They might fear when they contrasted their numbers with the crowds of worldly men; but, being a flock, they have a shepherd, and that is enough to quiet anxiety.

Seeking and courage are to be crowned by surrender of outward good and the use of earthly wealth in such manner as that it will secure an unfailing treasure in heaven. The manner of obeying this command varies with circumstances. For some the literal fulfilment is best; and there are more Christian men to-day whose souls would be delivered from the snares if they would part with their possessions than we are willing to believe.

Sometimes the surrender is rather to be effected by the conscientious consecration and prayerful use of wealth. That is for each man to settle for himself. But what is not variable is the obligation to set the kingdom high above all else, and to use all outward wealth, as Christ's servants, not for luxury and self-gratification, but as in His sight and for His glory. Let us not be afraid of believing what Jesus and His Apostles plainly teach, that wealth so spent here is treasured in heaven, and that a Christian's place in the future life depends upon this among other conditions—how he used his money here.

STILLNESS IN STORM

'... Neither be ye of doubtful mind.'—LUKE xii. 29.

I think that these words convey no very definite idea to most readers. The thing forbidden is not very sharply defined by the expression which our translators have employed, but the original term is very picturesque and precise.

The word originally means 'to be elevated, to be raised as a meteor,' and comes by degrees to mean to be raised in one special way—namely, as a boat is tossed by a tough sea. So there is a picture in this prohibition which the fishermen and folk dwelling by the Sea of Galilee with its sudden squalls would understand: 'Be not pitched about'; now on the crest, now in the trough of the wave.

The meaning, then, is substantially identical with that of the previous words, 'Take no thought for your life,' with this difference, that the figures by which the thing prohibited is expressed are different, and that the latter saying is wider than the former.

The former prohibits 'taking thought,' by which our Lord of course means not reasonable foresight, but anxious foreboding. And the word which He uses, meaning at bottom as it does, 'to be distracted or rent asunder,' conveys a striking picture of the wretched state to which such anxiety brings a man. Nothing tears us to pieces like foreboding care. Then our text forbids the same anxiety, as well as other fluctuations of feeling that come from setting our hopes and hearts on aught which can change; and its figurative representation of the misery that follows on fastening ourselves to the perishable, is that of the poor little skiff, at one moment high on the crest of the billow, at the next down in the trough of the sea.

So both images point to the unrest of worldliness, and while the unrest of care is uppermost in the one, the other includes more than simply care, and warns us that all occupation with simply creatural things, all eager seeking after 'what ye shall eat or what ye shall drink' or after more refined forms of earthly good, brings with it the penalty and misery of 'for ever tossing on the tossing wave.' Whosoever launches out on to that sea is sure to be buffeted about. Whoso sets his heart on the uncertainty of anything below the changeless God will without doubt be driven from hope to fear, from joy to sorrow, and his soul will be agitated as his idols change, and his heart will be desolate when his idols perish.

Our Lord, we say, forbids our being thus tossed about. He seems to believe that it is in our own power to settle whether we shall be or no. That sounds strange; one can fancy the answer: 'What is the use of telling a man not to be buffeted about by storm? Why, he cannot help it. If the sea is running high the little boat cannot lie quiet as if in smooth water. Do not talk to me about not being moved, unless you can say to the tumbling sea of life, "Peace, be still!" and make it

"quite forget to rave,
  While birds of peace sit brooding on the charmed wave."'

The objection is sound after a fashion. Change there must be, and fluctuation of feeling. But there is such a thing as 'peace subsisting at the heart of endless agitation.' You may remember the attempt that was made some years ago to build a steamer in which the central saloon was to hang perfectly still while the outer hull of the ship pitched and rolled with the moving sea. It was a failure, but the theory was sound and looked practicable. At any rate, it is a parable of what may be in our lives. If I might venture, without seeming irreverence, to modernise and so to illustrate this command of our Lord's, I would say, that He here bids us do for our life's voyage across a stormy sea, exactly what the 'Bessemer' ship was an attempt to do in its region—so to poise and control the oscillations of the central soul that however the outward life may be buffeted about, there may be moveless rest within. He knows full well that we must have rough weather, but He would have us counteract the motion of the sea, and keep our hearts in stillness. 'In the world ye shall have tribulation,' but in Him ye may have peace.

He does not wish us to be blind to the facts of life, but to take *all* the facts into our vision. A partial view of the so–called facts certainly will lead to tumultuous alternations of hope and fear, of joy and sorrow. But if you will take them all into account, you can be quiet and at rest. For here is a fact as real as the troubles and changes of life: 'Your Father knoweth that ye have need of these things.' Ah! the recognition of that will keep our inmost hearts full of sweet peace, whatever may befall the outward life. Only take all the facts of your condition, and accept Christ's word for that greatest and surest of all—the loving Father's knowledge of your needs, and it will not be hard to obey Christ's command, and keep yourself still, because fixed on Him.

But now consider the teachings here as to the true source of the agitation which our Lord forbids. The precept itself affords no light on that subject, but the context shows us the true origin of the evil.

The first point to observe is how remarkably our Lord identifies this anxiety and restlessness which He forbids with what at first sight seems its exact opposite, namely a calmness and peace which he also condemns as wholly bad. The whole series of warnings of which our text is part begins with the story of the rich man whose ground brought forth plentifully. His fault was not that he was tossed about with care and a doubtful mind, but the very opposite. His sin was in saying, 'Soul, thou hast much goods laid up for many years; take thine ease, eat, drink, and be merry.'

Notice, then, that our Lord begins by pointing out the great madness and the great sin of being thus at rest, and trusting in earthly possessions: and then with a 'Therefore, I say unto you,' He turns to the opposite pole of worldly feeling, and shows us how, although opposite, it is yet related. The warning, 'Take no thought for your life' follows as an inference from the picture of the folly of the man that lays up treasure for himself and is not rich towards God.

That is to say, the two faults are kindred and in some sense the same. The rich fool stretching himself out to rest on the pile of his possessions, and the poor fool tossing about on the billows of unquiet thought, are at bottom under the influence of the same folly, though their circumstances are opposite, and their moods seem to be so too.

The one man is just the other turned inside out. When he is rich and has got plenty of outward goods, he has no anxiety, because he thinks that they are supreme and all-sufficient. When he is poor and has not got enough of them, he has no rest, because he thinks that they are supreme and all-sufficient. Anxious care and satisfied possession are at bottom the very same thing. The man who says, 'My mountain stands strong,' because he has got a quantity of money or the like; and the man who says, 'Oh, dear me, what is going to become of me?' because he thinks he has not got enough, only need to exchange circumstances and they will exchange cries.

The same figure is concave or convex according to the side from which you look at it. From one it swells out into rounded fullness; from the other it gapes as in empty hungriness. So the rich fool of the preceding parable and the anxious, troubled man of my text are the same man looked at from opposite sides or set in opposite circumstances. The root of both the rest of the one and of the anxiety of the other is the over-estimate of outward good.

Then, still further, notice how our Lord here brands this forbidden fluctuation of feeling as being at bottom pure heathenism. Most significant double reasons for our text follow it, introduced by a double 'for.' The first reason is, 'For all these things do the nations of the world seek after'; the second is, 'For your Father knoweth that ye have need of these things.' The former points the lesson of the contradiction between such trouble of mind and the position of disciples. For pure heathens it is all natural; for men who do not know that they have a Father in heaven, there is nothing strange or anomalous in care and anxiety, nor in the race after riches. But for you, it is in diametrical contradiction to all your professions, in flagrant inconsistency with all your belief, in flat denial of that mighty truth that you have a Father who cares for you, and that His love is enough. Every time you yield to such cares or thoughts you are going down to the level of pure heathenism. That is a sharp saying. Our Lord's steady hand wields the keen dissecting-knife here, and lays bare with unsparing cuts the ugly growth. We give the thing condemned a great many honourable names, such as 'laying up for a rainy day,' or 'taking care for the future of my children,' or 'providing things honest in the sight of all men,' and a host of others, with which we gloss and gild over unchristian worldly-mindedness.

There are actions and feelings which are rightly described by such phrases, that are perfectly right, and against them Jesus Christ never said a word.

But much of what we deceive ourselves by calling reasonable foresight is rooted distrust of God, and much practical heathenism creeps into our lives under the guise of 'proper prudence.' The ordinary maxims of the world christen many things by names of virtues and yet they remain vices notwithstanding.

I do not know that there is any region in which Christian men have more to be on their guard, lest they be betrayed into deadening inconsistencies, than this of the true limits of care for material wealth, and of provision for the future outward life.

Those of us, especially, who are engaged in business, and who live in our great commercial cities, have hard work to keep from dropping down to the heathen level which is adopted on all sides. It is not easy for such a man to resist the practical belief that money is the one thing needful, and he the happy man who has made a fortune. The false estimate of worldly good is in the air about us, and we have to be on our guard, or else, before we know where we are, we shall have breathed the stupefying poison and feel its narcotic influence slackening the pulses and dimming the eye of our spirits. We need special watchfulness and prayer, or we shall not escape this subtle danger, which is truly for many of us 'the pestilence that walketh in darkness.'

So be not tossed about by these secularities, for the root of them all is heathenish distrust of your Father in heaven.

Then, finally, we have the cure for all agitation. Christ here puts in our own hands, in that thought, 'Your Father knoweth that ye have need of these things,' the one weapon with which we can conquer. There is the true anchorage for tempest-tossed spirits, the land-locked haven where they can ride, whatever winds blow and waves break outside the bar.

I remarked that our Lord here seemed to give an injunction which the facts of life would prevent our obeying, and so it would be, had He not pointed us to that firm truth, which, if we believe it, will keep us unmoved. There is no more profitless expenditure of breath than the ordinary moralist's exhortations to, or warnings against, states of feeling and modes of mind. Our emotions are very partially under our direct control. Life cannot be calm by willing to be so. But what we can do is to think of a truth which will sway our moods. If you can substitute some other thought for the one which breeds the emotion you condemn, it will fall silent of itself, just as the spindles will stop if you shut off steam, or the mill-wheel if you turn the stream in another direction. So Christ gives us a great thought to cherish, knowing that if we let it have fair play in our minds, we shall be at rest: 'Your Father knoweth that ye have need of these things.' Surely that is enough for calmness. Why should, or how can we be, troubled if we believe that?

'He knows.' What a wonderful confidence in His heart and resources is silently implied in that word! If He knows that you need, you may be quite sure that you will not want. 'He knows'; and His fatherly heart is our guarantee that to know and to supply our need, are one and the same thing with Him; and His deep treasure of exhaustless good is our guarantee that our need can never go beyond His fullness, nor He ever, like us, see a sorrow He cannot comfort, a want that He cannot meet.

Enough that He knows; 'the rest goes without saying.' The whole burden of solicitude is shifted off our shoulders, if once we get into the light of that great truth. A man is made restful in the midst of all the changes and storms of life, not by trying to work himself into tranquillity, not by mere dint of coercing his feelings through sheer force of will, not by ignoring any facts, but simply by letting this truth stand before his mind. It scatters cares, as the silent moon has power, by her mild white light, to clear away a whole skyful of piled blacknesses.

One other word of practical advice, as to how to carry out this injunction, is suggested by the context, which goes on, 'Seek ye first the kingdom of God.'

A boat will roll most when, from lack of a strong hand at the helm, she has got broadside to the run of the sea. There she lies rocking about just as the blow of the wave may fall, and drifting wherever the wind may take her. There are two directions in which she will be comparatively steady; one, when her head is kept as near the wind as may be, and the other when she runs before it. Either will be quieter than washing about anyhow. May we make a parable out of that? If you want to have as little pitching and tossing as possible on your voyage, keep a good strong hand on the tiller. Do not let the boat lie in the trough of the sea, but drive her right against the wind, or as near it as she will sail. That is to say, have a definite aim to which you steer, and keep a straight course for that. So Christ says to us here. Be not filled with agitations, but seek the Kingdom. The definite pursuit of the higher good will deaden the lower anxieties. The active energies called out in the daily efforts to bring my whole being under the dominion of the sovereign will of God, will deliver me from a crowd of tumultuous desires and forebodings. I shall have neither leisure nor inclination to be anxious about outward things, when I am engaged and absorbed in seeking the kingdom. So 'bear up and steer right onward,' and it will be smooth sailing.

Sometimes, too, we shall have to try the other tack, and run *before* the storm, which again will give us the minimum of commotion. That, being translated, is, 'Let the winds and the waves sometimes have their way.' Yield to them in the sweetness of submission and the strength of resignation. Even when all the stormy winds strive on the surface sea, recognise them as God's messengers 'fulfilling His word.' Submission is not rudderless yielding to the gale, that tosses us on high and sinks us again, as the waves list. This frees us from their power, even while they roll mountains high.

Then keep firm trust in your Father's knowledge; strenuously seek the kingdom. In quietness accept the changeful methods of his unchanging providence. Thus shall your hearts be kept in peace amidst the storm of life, with the happy thought, '*So* He bringeth them unto their desired haven.'

THE EQUIPMENT OF THE SERVANTS

'Let your loins be girded about, and your lights
burning; 36. And ye yourselves like unto men that wait
for their Lord.'—Luke xii. 35, 36.

These words ought to stir us like the sound of a trumpet. But, by long familiarity, they drop upon dull ears, and scarcely produce any effect. The picture that they suggest, as an emblem of the Christian state, is a striking one. It is midnight, a great house is without its master, the lord of the palace is absent, but expected back, the servants are busy in preparation, each man with his robe tucked about his middle, in order that it may not interfere with his work, his lamp in his hand that he may see to go about his business and his eye ever turned to the entrance to catch the first sign of the coming of his

179

master. Is that like your Christian life? If we are His servants that is what we ought to be, having three things—girded loins, lighted lamps, waiting hearts. These are sharp tests, solemn commandments, but great privileges, for blessedness as well as strength, and calm peace whatever happens, belong to those who obey these injunctions and have these things.

I. The girded loins.

Every child knows the long Eastern dress; and that the first sign that a man is in earnest about any work would be that he should gather his skirts around him and brace himself together.

The Christian service demands concentration. It needs the fixing of all a man's powers upon the one thing, the gathering together of all the strength of one's nature, and binding it with cords until its softest and loosest particles are knit together, and become strong. Why! you can take a handful of cotton–down, and if you will squeeze it tight enough, it will be as hard and as heavy as a bullet and will go as far, and have as much penetrating power and force of impact. The reason why some men hit and make no dint is because they are not gathered together and braced up by a vigorous concentration.

The difference between men that succeed and men that fail in ordinary pursuits is by no means so much intellectual as moral; and there is nothing which more certainly commands any kind of success than giving yourselves with your whole concentrated power to the task in hand. If we succeed in anything we must focus all our power on it. Only by so doing, as a burning–glass does the sun's rays, shall we set anything on fire.

And can a vigorous Christian life be grown upon other conditions than those which a vigorous life of an ordinary sort demands? Why should it be easier to be a prosperous Christian than to be a prosperous tradesman? Why should there not be the very same law in operation in the realm of the higher riches and possessions that rules in the realm of the lower? 'Gird up the loins *of your mind*,' says the Apostle, echoing the Master's word here. The first condition of true service is that you shall do it with concentrated power.

There is another requirement, or perhaps rather another side of the same, expressed in the figure. One reason why a man tucked up his robe around his waist, when he had anything to do that needed all his might, was that it might not catch upon the things that protruded, and so keep him back. Concentration, and what I may call detachment, go together. In order that there shall be the one, there must be the other. They require each other, and are, in effect, but the two sides of the same thing contemplated in regard to hindrances without, or contemplated in regard to the relation of the several parts of a man's nature to each other.

Observe that Luke immediately precedes the text with:—'Sell that ye have, and give alms; provide yourselves bags which wax not old, a treasure in the heavens that faileth not, where no thief approacheth, neither moth corrupteth. For where your treasure is, there will your heart be also. Let your loins be girded about.' That is to say, do not let your affections go straggling anywhere and everywhere, but gather them together, and that you may gather them together tear away the robe from the briars and thorns which catch you as you pass, and gird the long flowing skirts close to yourselves in order that they may not be caught by these hindrances. There is no Christian life worth living except upon condition of wrenching oneself away from dependence upon idolatry of, or longing for, perishable things. The lesson of my text is the same as the solemn lesson which the beloved Apostle sharpened his gentle lips to pronounce when he said, 'If any man love the world, the love of the Father is not in him.' 'Gird up your loins,' detach heart, desire, effort from perishable things, and lift them above the fleeting treasures and hollow delusive sparkles of earth's preciousness, and set them on the realities and eternities at God's right hand. 'For where the treasure is, there will the heart be also,' and only that heart can never be stabbed by disappointment, nor bled to death by losses, whose treasure is as sure as God and eternal as Himself. 'Let your loins be girded about.'

And then there is another thing suggested, which is the consequence of these two. The girding up of the loins is not only the symbol of concentration and detachment, but of that for which the concentration and the detachment are needful—viz. alert readiness for service. The servant who stands before his lord with his belt buckled tight indicates thereby that he is ready to run whenever and wherever he is bid. Our girded loins are not merely in order to give strength to our frame, but in order that, having strength given to our frame, we may be ready for all work. That which is needful for any faithful discharge of any servant's duty is most of all needful for the discharge of the highest duty and the noblest service to the Master who has the right to command all our service.

There are three emblems in Scripture to all of which this metaphor applies. The soldier, before he flings himself into the fight, takes in another hole in his leather belt in order that there may be strength given to his spine, and he may feel himself all gathered together for the deadly struggle, and the Christian soldier has to do the same thing. 'Stand therefore, having your loins girt about with truth.'

The traveller, before he starts upon his long road, girds himself, and gathers his robes round him; and we have to 'run with perseverance the race set before us'; and shall never do it if our garments, however delicately embroidered, are flapping about our feet and getting in our way when we try to run.

The servant has to be *succinct*, girded together for his work, even as the Master, when He took upon Him the form of a servant, 'took a towel and girded Himself.' His servants have to follow His example, to put aside the needless vesture and brace themselves with the symbol of service. So as soldiers, pilgrims, servants, the condition of doing our work is, girding up the loins.

II. Further, there are to be the burning lamps.

If we follow the analogy of Scripture symbolism, significance belongs to that emblem, making it quite worthy to stand by the side of the former one. You remember Christ's first exhortation in the Sermon on the Mount immediately following the Beatitudes: 'Ye are the salt of the earth, ye are the light of the world. Men do not light a candle, and put it under a bushel. *Let your light so shine before men*, that they may see your good deeds.' If we apply that key to decipher the hieroglyphics, the burning lamps which the girded servants are to bear in the darkness are the whole sum of the visible acts of Christian people, from which there may flash the radiance of purity and kindness, 'So shines a good deed in a naughty world.' The lamp which the Christian servant is to bear is a character illuminated from above (for it is a kindled lamp, and the light is derived), and streaming out a brilliance into the encircling murky midnight which speaks of hospitable welcome and of good cheer in the lighted hall within.

Now, what is the connection between that exhibition of a lustrous and pure Christian character and the former exhortation? Why this, if you do not gird your loins your lamp will go out. Without the concentrated effort and the continually repeated detachment and the daily renewed 'Lord! here am I, send me,' of the alert and ready servant, there will be no shining of the life, no beauty of the character, but dimness will steal over the exhibition of Christian graces. Just as, often, in the wintry nights, a star becomes suddenly obscured, and we know not why, but some thin vaporous cloud has come between us and it, invisible in itself but enough to blur its brightness, so obscuration will befall the Christian character unless there be continual concentration and detachment. Do you want your lights to blaze? You trim them—though it is a strange mixture of metaphor—you trim them when you gird your loins.

III. Lastly, the waiting hearts.

An attitude of expectancy does not depend upon theories about the chronology of prophecy. It is Christ's will that, till He comes, we know 'neither the day nor the hour.' We may, as I suppose most of us do, believe that we shall die before He comes. Be it so. That need not affect the attitude of expectance, for it comes to substantially the same thing whether Christ comes to us or we go to Him. And the certain uncertainty of the end of our individual connection with this fleeting world stands in the same relation to our hopes as the coming of the Master does, and should have an analogous effect on our lives. Whatever may be our expectation as to the literal coming of the Lord, that future should be very solid, very real, very near us in our thoughts, a habitual subject of contemplation, and ever operative upon our hearts and conduct.

Ah! if we never, or seldom, and then sorrowfully, look forward to the future, and contemplate our meeting with our Master, I do not think there is much chance of our having either our loins girt, or our lamps burning.

One great motive for concentration, detachment, and alertness of service, as well as for exhibiting the bright graces of the Christian character, is to be found in the contemplation of the two comings of the Lord. We should be ever looking back to the Cross, forward to the Throne, and upwards to the Christ, the same on them both. If we have our gathering together with Him ever in view, then we shall be willing to yield all for Him, to withdraw ourselves from everything besides for the excellency of His knowledge; and whatsoever He commands, joyfully and cheerfully to do.

The reason why such an immense and miserable proportion of professing Christians are all unbraced and loose-girt, and their lamps giving such smoky and foul-smelling and coarse radiance, is because they look little back to the Cross, and less forward to the Great White Throne. But these two solemn and sister sights are far more real than the vulgar and intrusive illusions of what we call the present. That is a shadow, they are the realities; that is but a transitory scenic display, like the flashing of the Aurora Borealis for a night in the wintry sky, these are the fixed, unsetting stars that guide our course. Therefore let us turn away from the lying present, with its smallnesses and its falsities, and look backwards to Him that died, forward to Him that is coming. And, as we nourish our faith on the twofold fact, a history and a hope, that Christ has come, and that Christ shall come, we shall find that all devotion will be quickened, and all earnestness stirred to zeal, and the dim light will flame into radiance and glory.

He comes in one of two characters which lie side by side here, as they do in fact. To the waiting servants He comes as the Master who shall gird Himself and go forth and serve them; to those who wait not, He comes as a thief, not only in the suddenness nor the unwelcomeness of His coming, but as robbing them of what they would fain keep, and dragging from them much that they ought never to have had. And it depends upon ourselves whether, we waiting and watching and serving and witnessing for Him, He shall come to us as our Joy, or as our Terror and our Judge.

THE SERVANT–LORD

Verily I say unto you, that He shall gird Himself, and
make them to sit down to meat, and will come forth,
and serve them.—LUKE xii. 37.

No one would have dared to say that except Jesus Christ. For surely, manifold and wonderful as are the glimpses that we get in the New Testament of the relation of perfect souls in heaven to Him, none of them pierces deeper, rises higher, and speaks more boundless blessing, than such words as these. Well might Christ think it necessary to preface them with the solemn affirmation which always, upon His lips, points, as it were, an emphatic finger to, or underlines that which He is about to proclaim. 'Verily I say unto you,' if we had not His own word for it, we might hesitate to believe. And while we have His own word for it, and do not hesitate to believe, it is not for us to fathom or exhaust, but lovingly and reverently and humbly, because we know it but partially, to try to plumb the unfathomable depth of such words. 'He shall gird Himself, and cause them to sit down to meat; and come forth and serve them.'

I. Then we have, first of all, the wonderful revelation of the Servant–Lord.

For the name of dignity is employed over and over again in the immediate context, and so makes more wonderful the assumption here of the promise of service.

And the words are not only remarkable because they couple so closely together the two antagonistic ideas, as we fancy them, of rule and service, authority and subordination, but because they dwell with such singular particularity of detail upon all the stages of the menial office which the Monarch takes upon Himself. First, the girding, assuming the servant's attire; then the leading of the guests, wondering and silent, to the couches where they can recline; then the coming to them as they thus repose at the table, and the waiting upon their wants and supplying all their need. It reminds us of the wonderful scene, in John's Gospel, where we have coupled together in the same intimate and interdependent fashion the two thoughts of dignity and of service—'Jesus, knowing that the Father had given all things into His hand, and that He came from God and went to God,' made this use of His consciousness and of His unlimited and universal dominion, that 'He laid aside His garments, and took a towel, and girded Himself, and washed the disciples' feet'; thus teaching what our text teaches

183

in still another form, that the highest authority means the lowliest service, that the purpose of power is blessing, that the very sign and mark of dignity is to stoop, and that the crown of the Universe is worn by Him who is the Servant of all.

But beyond that general idea which applies to the whole of the divine dealings and especially to the earthly life of Him who came, not to be ministered unto, but to minister, the text sets forth special manifestations of Christ's ministering love and power, which are reserved for heaven, and are a contrast with earth. The Lord who is the Servant girds Himself. That corresponds with the commandment that went before, 'Let your loins be girded,' and to some extent covers the same ground and suggests the same idea. With all reverence, and following humbly in the thoughts that Christ has given us by the words, one may venture to say that He gathers all His powers together in strenuous work for the blessing of His glorified servants, and that not only does the metaphor express for us His taking upon Himself the lowly office, but also the employment of all that He is and has there in the heavens for the blessing of the blessed ones that sit at His table.

Here upon earth, when He assumed the form of a Servant in His entrance into humanity, it was accompanied with the emptying Himself of His glory. In the symbolical incident in John's Gospel, to which I have already referred, He laid aside His garments before He wrapped around Him the badge of service. But in that wondrous service by the glorified Lord there is no need for divesting ere He serves, but the divine glories that irradiate His humanity, and by which He, our Brother, is the King of kings and the Lord of the Universe, are all used by Him for this great, blessed purpose of gladdening and filling up the needs of the perfected spirits that wait, expectant of their food, upon Him. His girding Himself for service expresses not only the lowliness of His majesty and the beneficence of His power, but His use of all which He has and is for the blessing of those whom He keeps and blesses.

I need not remind you, I suppose, how in this same wonderful picture of the Servant–Lord there is taught the perpetual—if we may so say, the increased—lowliness of the crowned Christ. When He was here on earth, He was meek and holy; exalted in the heavens, He is, were it possible, meeker and more lowly still, because He stoops from a loftier elevation. The same loving, gentle, gracious heart, holding all its treasures for its brethren, is the heart that now is girded with the golden girdle of sovereignty, and which once was girt with the coarse towel of the slave. Christ is for ever the Servant, because He is for ever the Lord of them that trust in Him. Let us learn that service is dominion; that 'he that is chiefest among us' is thereby bound to be 'the servant' and the helper 'of all.'

II. Notice, the servants who are served and serve.

There are two or three very plain ideas, suggested by the great words of my text, in regard to the condition of those whom the Lord thus ministers to, and waits upon. I need not expand them, because they are familiar to us all, but let me just touch them. 'He shall make them to sit down to meat.' The word, as many of you know, really implies a more restful attitude—'He shall make them recline at meat.' What a contrast to the picture of toil and effort, which has just been drawn, in the command,' Let your loins be girded about, and your lamps burning, and ye yourselves as men that wait for their Lord!' Here, there must be the bracing up of every power, and the careful tending of the light amid the darkness and the gusts that threaten to blow it out, and every ear is to be listening and every eye strained, for the coming of the Lord, that there may be no unpreparedness or delay in flinging open the gates. But then the tension is taken off and the loins ungirded, for there is no need for painful effort, and the lamps that burn dimly and require tending in the mephitic air are laid aside, and 'they need no candle, for the Lord is the light thereof'; and there is no more intense listening for the first foot-fall of One who is coming, for He has come, and expectation is turned into fellowship and fruition. The strained muscles can relax, and instead of effort and weariness, there is repose upon the restful couches prepared by Him. Threadbare and old as the hills as the thought is, it comes to us toilers with ever new refreshment, like a whiff of fresh air or the gleam of the far-off daylight at the top of the shaft to the miner, cramped at his work in the dark. What a witness the preciousness of that representation of future blessedness as rest to us all bears to the pressure of toil and the aching, weary hearts which we all carry! The robes may flow loose then, for there is neither pollution to be feared from the golden pavement, nor detention from briars or thorns, nor work that is so hard as to be toil or so unwelcome as to be pain. There is rest from labour, care, change, and fear of loss, from travel and travail, from tired limbs and hearts more tired still, from struggle and sin, from all which makes the unrest of life.

Further, this great promise assures us of the supply of all wants that are only permitted to last long enough to make a capacity for receiving the eternal and all-satisfying food which Christ gives the restful servants. Though 'they hunger no more,' they shall always have appetite. Though they 'thirst no more,' they shall ever desire deeper draughts of the fountain of life. Desire is one thing, longing is another. Longing is pain, desire is blessedness; and that we shall want and know ourselves to want, with a want which lives but for a moment ere the supply pours in upon it and drowns it, is one of the blessednesses to which we dare to look forward. Here we live, tortured by wishes, longings, needs, a whole menagerie of hungry mouths yelping within us for their food. There we wait upon the Lord, and He gives a portion in due season.

The picture in the text brings with it all festal ideas of light, society, gladness, and the like, on which I need not dwell. But let me just remind you of one contrast. The ministry of Christ, when He was a servant here upon earth, was symbolised by His washing His disciples' feet, an act which was part of the preparation of the guests for a feast. The ministry of Christ in heaven consists, not in washing, for 'he that is washed is clean every whit' there, and for ever more—but in ministering to His guests that abundant feast for which the service and the lustration of earth were but the preparation. The servant Christ serves us here by washing us from our sins in His own blood, both in the one initial act of forgiveness and by the continual application of that blood to the stains contracted in the miry ways of life. The Lord and Servant serves His servants in the heavens by leading them, cleansed to His table, and filling up every soul with love and with Himself.

But all that, remember, is only half the story. Our Lord here is not giving us a complete view of the retributions of the heavens, He is only telling us one aspect of them. Repose, society, gladness, satisfaction, these things are all true. But heaven is not lying upon couches and eating of a feast. There is another use of this metaphor in this same Gospel, which, at first sight, strikes one as being contradictory to this. Our Lord said: 'Which of you, having a servant ploughing or feeding cattle, will say unto him by and by, when he is come from the field, go and sit down to meat, and will not rather say unto him, make ready wherewith I may sup, and gird thyself, and serve me, till I have eaten and drunken; and afterward thou shalt eat and drink.' These two representations are not contradictory. Put the two halves together like the two pictures in a stereoscope and, as you look, they will go together into one solid image, of which the one part is the resting at the table of the feast, and the other part is that entrance into heaven is not cessation, but variation, of service. It was dirty, cold, muddy work out there in the field ploughing, and when the man comes back with his soiled, wet raiment and his weary limbs a change of occupation is rest. It is better for him to be set to 'make ready wherewith I may eat and drink,' than to be told to sit down and do nothing.

So the servants are served, and the servants serve. And these two representations are not contradictory, but they fill up the conception of perfect blessedness. For remember, if we may venture to say so, that the very same reason which makes Christ the Lord serve His servants makes the servants serve Christ the Lord. For love, which underlies their relationship, has for its very life–breath doing kindnesses and good to its objects, and we know not whether it is more blessed to the loving heart to minister to, or to be ministered to by, the heart which it loves. So the Servant–Lord and the servants, serving and served, are swayed in both by the same motive and rejoice in the interchange of offices and tokens of love.

III. Mark the earthly service which leads to the heavenly rest.

I have already spoken about Christ's earthly service, and reminded you that there is needed, first of all, that we should partake in His purifying work through His blood and His Spirit that dwells in us, ere we can share in His highest ministrations to His servants in the heavens. But there is also service of ours here on earth, which must precede our receiving our share in the wonderful things promised here. And the nature of that service is clearly stated in the preceding words, 'Blessed are those servants whom the Lord when He cometh shall find'—doing what? Trying to make themselves better? Seeking after conformity to His commandments? No! 'Whom the Lord when He cometh shall find *watching*.' It is character rather than conduct, and conduct only as an index of character—disposition rather than deeds—that makes it possible for Christ to be hereafter our Servant–Lord. And the character is more definitely described in the former words. Loins girded, lights burning, and a waiting which is born of love. The concentration and detachment from earth, which are expressed by the girded loins, the purity and holiness of character and life, which are symbolised by the burning lights, and the expectation which desires, and does not shrink from, His coming in His Kingdom to be the Judge of all the earth—these things, being built upon the acceptance of Christ's ministry of washing, fit us for participation in Christ's ministry of the feast, and make it possible that even we shall be of those to whom the Lord, in that day, will come with gladness and with gifts. 'Blessed are the servants whom the Lord shall find so watching.'

SERVANTS AND STEWARDS HERE AND HEREAFTER

'Blessed are those servants, whom the Lord, when He
cometh, shall find watching: Verily I shall say unto
you, that He shall gird Himself, and make them to sit
down to meat, and will come forth and serve them.

Blessed is that servant whom his Lord, when He cometh,
shall find so doing. 44. Of a truth I say unto you,

186

that He will make him ruler over all that he hath.
—LUKE xii. 37, 43, and 44.

You will, of course, observe that these two passages are strictly parallel in form. Our Lord evidently intends them to run side by side, and to be taken together. The divergences are as significant and instructive as the similarities, and the force of these will be best brought out by just recalling, in a sentence or two, the occasion for the utterance of the second of the two passages which I have taken for my text. When our Lord had finished His previous address and exhortations, Peter characteristically pushed his oar in with the question, 'Do these commandments refer to us, the Apostles, or to all,' the whole body of disciples? Our Lord admits the distinction, recognises in His answer that the 'us,' the Twelve, were nearer Christ than the general mass of His followers, and answers Peter's question by reiterating what He has been saying in a slightly different form. He had spoken before about servants. Now He speaks about 'stewards,' because the Apostles did stand in that relation to the other disciples, as being slaves indeed, like the rest of the household, but slaves in a certain position of authority, by the Master's appointment, and charged with providing the nourishment which, of course, means the religious instruction, of their fellow-servants.

So, notice that the first benediction is upon the 'servants,' the second is upon the servants who are 'stewards.' The first exhortation requires that when the Master comes He shall find the servants watching; the second demands that when He comes He shall find the stewards doing their work. The first promise of reward gives the assurance that the watching servants shall be welcomed into the house, and be waited on by the Master himself; the second gives the assurance that the faithful steward shall be promoted to higher work. We are all servants, and we are all, if we are Christian men, stewards of the manifold grace of God.

So, then, out of these two passages thus brought together, as our Lord intended that they should be, we gather two things: the twofold aspect of life on earth—watchfulness and work; and the twofold hope of life in heaven—rest and rule. 'Blessed is that servant whom his Lord, when He cometh, shall find watching.' 'Blessed is that steward whom his Lord, when He cometh, shall find'—not merely watching, but—'so doing.'

I. The twofold attitude here enjoined.

The first idea in watchfulness is keeping awake; and the second is looking out for something that is coming. Both these conceptions are intertwined in both our Lord's use of the metaphor of the watching servant, and in the echoes of it which we find abundantly in the Apostolic letters. The first thing is to keep ourselves awake all through the soporific night, when everything tempts to slumber. Even the wise virgins, with trimmed lamps and girt loins, do in some degree succumb to the drowsy influences around them, and like the foolish ones, slumber, though the slumbers of the two classes be unlike. Christian people live in the midst of an order of things which tempts them to close the eyes of their hearts and minds to all the real and unseen glories above and around them, and that might be within them, and to live for the comparatively contemptible and trivial things of this present. Just as when a man sleeps, he loses his consciousness of solid external realities, and passes into a fantastic world of his own imaginations, which have no correspondence in external facts, and will vanish like

'The baseless fabric of a dream,
If but a cock shall crow,'

so the men who are conscious only of this present life and of the things that are seen, though they pride themselves on being wide awake, are, in the deepest of their being, fast asleep, and are dealing with illusions which will pass and leave nought behind, as really as are men who lie dreaming upon couches, and fancy themselves hard at work. Keep awake; that is the first thing; which, being translated into plain English, points just to this, that unless we make a dead lift of continuous effort to keep firm grasp of God and Christ, and of all the unseen magnificences that are included in these two names, as surely as we live we shall lose our hold upon them, and fall into the drugged and diseased sleep in which so many men around us are plunged. It sometimes seems to one as if the sky above us were raining down narcotics upon us, so profoundly are the bulk of men unconscious of realities, and befooled by the illusions of a dream.

Keep yourselves awake first, and then let the waking, wide–opened eye, be looking forward. It is the very *differentia*, so to speak, the characteristic mark and distinction of the Christian notion of life, that it shifts the centre of gravity from the present into the future, and makes that which is to come of far more importance than that which is, or which has been. No man is living up to the height of his Christian responsibilities or privileges unless there stands out before him, as the very goal and aim of his whole life, what can never be realised until he has passed within the veil, and is at rest in the 'secret place of the Most High.' To live for the future is, in one aspect, the very definition of a Christian.

But the text reminds us of the specific form which that future anticipation is to take. It is not for us, as it is for men in the world, to fix our hopes for the future on abstract laws of the progress of humanity, or the evolution of the species, or the gradual betterment of the world, and the like. All these may be true: I say nothing about them. But what we have to fill our future with is that 'that same Jesus shall so come in like manner as ye have seen Him go.' It is much to be lamented that curious chronological speculations have so often discredited that great central hope of the Church, which is properly altogether independent of them; and that, because people have got befogged in interpreting such symbols as beasts, and horses, and trumpets, and seals, and the like, the Christian Church as a whole should so feebly be holding by that great truth, without which, as it seems to me, the truth which many of us are tempted to make the exclusive one, loses half its significance. No man can rightly understand the whole contents of the blessed proclamation, 'Christ has come,' unless he ends the sentence with 'and Christ will come.' Blessed is 'that servant whom the Lord, when He cometh, shall find watching.'

Of course I need not remind you that much for which that second coming of the Lord is precious, and an object of hope to the world and the Church, is realised by the individual in the article of death. Whether Christ comes to the world or I go to Christ, the important thing is that there result union and communion, the reign of righteousness and peace, the felicities of the heavenly state. And so, dear brethren, just because of the uncertainty that drapes the future, and which we are often tempted to make a reason for dismissing the anticipation of it from our minds, we ought the more earnestly to give heed that we keep that end ever before us, and whether it is reached by His coming to us, or our going to Him, anticipate, by the power of realising faith grasping the firm words of Revelation, the unimaginable, and—until it is experienced—the incommunicable blessedness revealed in these great, simple words, 'So shall we ever be with the Lord.'

But, then, look at the second of the aspects of Christian duty which is presented here, that watchfulness is to lead on to diligent work.

The temptation for any one who is much occupied with the hope of some great change and betterment in the near future is to be restless and unable to settle down to his work, and to yield to distaste of the humdrum duties of every day. If some man that kept a little chandler's shop in a back street was expecting to be made a king to-morrow, he would not be likely to look after his poor trade with great diligence. So we find in the Apostle Paul's second letter—that to the Thessalonians—that he had to encounter, as well as he could, the tendency of hope to make men restless, and to insist upon the thought—which is the same lesson as is taught us by the second of our texts—that if a man hoped, then he had with quietness to work and eat his own bread, and not be shaken in mind.

'Blessed is that servant whom his Lord, when He cometh, shall find so doing.' It may seem humble work to serve out hunches of bread and pots of black broth to the family of slaves, when the steward is expecting the coming of the master of the house, and his every nerve is tingling with anticipation. But it is steadying work, and it is blessed work. It is better that a man should be found doing the homeliest duty as the outcome of his great expectations of the coming of his Master, than that he should be fidgeting and restless and looking only at that thought till it unfits him for his common tasks. Who was it who, sitting playing a game of chess, and being addressed by some scandalised disciple with the question, 'What would you do if Jesus Christ came, and you were playing your game?' answered, 'I would finish it'? The best way for a steward to be ready for the Master, and to show that he is watching, is that he should be 'found so doing' the humble task of his stewardship. The two women that were squatting on either side of the millstone, and helping each other to whirl the handle round in that night were in the right place, and the one that was taken had no cause to regret that she was not more religiously employed. The watchful servant should be a working servant.

II. And now I have spent too much time on this first part of my discourse; so I must condense the second. Here are two aspects of the heavenly state, rest and rule.

'Verily I say unto you, He shall gird Himself, and make them to sit down to meat, and will come forth and serve them.' I do not know that there is a more wonderful promise, with more light lying in its darkness, in all Scripture than that. Jesus Christ continues in the heavens to be found in 'the form of a servant.' As here He girded Himself with the towel of humiliation in the upper room, so there He girds Himself with the robes of His imperial majesty, and uses all His powers for the nourishment and blessedness of His servants. His everlasting motto is, 'I am among you as one that serveth.' On earth His service was to wash His disciples' feet; in heaven the pure foot contracts no stain, and needs no basin: but in heaven He still serves, and serves by spreading a table, and, as a King might do at some ceremonial feasts, waiting on the astonished guests.

I say nothing about all the wonderful ideas that gather round that familiar but never-to-be-worn-into-commonplace emblem of the feast. Repose, in contrast with the girded loins and the weary waiting of the midnight watch; nourishment, and the satisfaction of all desires; joy,

189

society—all these things, and who knows how much more, that we shall have to get there to understand, lie in that metaphor, 'Blessed is that servant' who is served by the Master, and nourished by His presence?

But modern popular presentations of the future life have far too predominantly dwelt upon that side of it. It is a wonderful confession of 'the weariness, the fever, and the fret,' the hunger and loneliness of earthly experience, that the thought of heaven as the opposite of all these things should have almost swallowed up the other thought with which our Lord associates it here. He would not have us think only of repose. He unites with that representation, so fascinating to us weary and heavy-laden, the other of administrative authority. He will set him 'over all that he hath.'

The steward gets promotion. 'On twelve thrones judging the twelve tribes of Israel'—these are to be the seats, and that is to be the occupation of the Twelve. 'Thou hast been faithful over a few things; I will make thee ruler over many things.' The relation between earthly faithfulness and heavenly service is the same in essence as that between the various stages of our work here. The reward for work here is more work; a wider field, greater capacities. And what depths of authority, of new dignity, of royal supremacy, lie in those solemn and mysterious words, I know not—'He will set him over all that he hath.' My union with Christ is to be so close as that all His is mine and I am master of it. But at all events this we can say, that faithfulness here leads to larger service yonder; and that none of the aptitudes and capacities which have been developed in us here on earth will want a sphere when we pass yonder.

So let watchfulness lead to faithfulness, and watchful faithfulness and faithful watchfulness will lead to repose which is activity, and rule which is rest.

FIRE ON EARTH

'I am come to send fire on the earth; and what will I,
if it be already kindled!'—LUKE xii. 49.

We have here one of the rare glimpses which our Lord gives us into His inmost heart, His thought of His mission, and His feelings about it. If familiarity had not weakened the impression, and dulled the edge, of these words, how startling they would seem to us! 'I am come'—then, He was, before He came, and He came by His own voluntary act. A Jewish peasant says that He is going to set the world on fire—and He did it. But the triumphant certitude and consciousness of a large world-wide mission is all shadowed in the next clause. I need not trouble you with questions as to the precise translation of the words that follow. There may be differences of opinion about that, but I content myself with simply suggesting that a fair representation of the meaning would be, 'How I wish that it was already kindled!' There is a longing to fulfil the purpose of His coming and a sense that something has to be done first, and what that something if, our Lord goes on to say in the next verse. This desirable end can only be reached through a preliminary painful ordeal, 'but I have a baptism to be baptized with, and how am I straitened till it be accomplished.' If I might use such an incongruous figure, the fire that is to flash and flame through the world emerges from the dark waters of that baptism. Our Lord goes on still further to dwell upon the consequence of His mission and of His sufferings. And that, too, shadows the first triumphant thought of the fire that He was to send on earth. For, the baptism being accomplished, and the fire therefore being set at liberty to flame through the world, what follows? Glad reception? Yes, and angry rejection. Suppose ye that I am come to give peace on earth? I tell you, nay! but rather division.' The fire, the baptism, and the sword; these three may sum up our Lord's vision of the purpose, means, and mingled result of His mission. But it is only with regard to the first of these that I wish to speak now.

I. The fire which Christ longed to cast upon the earth.

Now, opinions differ as to what is meant by this fire Some would have, it to mean the glow of love kindled in believing hearts, and others explain it by other human emotions or by the transformation effected in the world by Christ's coming. But while these things are the results of the fire kindled on earth, that fire itself means not these effects, but the cause of them. It is *brought* before it kindles a flame on earth.

He does not kindle it simply in humanity, but He launches it into the midst of humanity. It is something from above that He flings down upon the earth. So it is not merely a quickened intelligence, a higher moral life, or any other of the spiritual and religious transformations which are effected in the world by the mission of Christ that is primarily to be kept in view here, but it is the Heaven–sent cause of these transformations and that flame. If we catch the celestial fire, we shall flash and blaze, but the fire which we catch is not originated on earth. In a word it is God's Divine Spirit which Christ came to communicate to the world.

I need not remind you, I suppose, how such an interpretation of the words before us is in entire correspondence with the symbolism both of the Old and New Testament. I do not dwell upon the former at all, and with regard to the latter I need only remind you of the great words by which the Forerunner of the Lord set forth His mighty work, in contrast with the superficial cleansing which John himself had to proclaim. 'I indeed baptize you with water, but He shall baptize you with the Holy Ghost and with fire.' I need only point to the Pentecost, and the symbol there, of which the central point was the cloven tongues, which symbolised not only the speech which follows from all deep conviction, but the descent from above of the Spirit of God, who is the Spirit of burning, on each bowed and willing head. With these analogies to guide us, I think we shall not go far wrong if we see in the words of my text our Lord's great symbolical promise that the issue of His mission shall be to bring into the heart of the world, so to speak, and to lodge in the midst of humanity which is one great whole, a new divine influence that shall flame and burn through the world.

So, then, my text opens out into thoughts of the many–sided applications of this symbol. What hopes for the world and ourselves are suggested by that fire? Let us stick to the symbol closely, and we shall then best understand the many–sided blessings that flash and coruscate in the gift of the Spirit.

It is the gift of life. No doubt, here and there in Scripture, fire stands for a symbol of destroying power. But that is a less frequent use than that in which it stands as a symbol of life. In a very real sense life is warmth and death is cold. Is not respiration a kind of combustion? Do not physiologists tell us that? Is not the centre of the system and the father of all physical life that great blazing sun which radiates heat? And is not this promise, 'I will send fire on the earth,' the assurance that into the midst of our death there shall come the quick energy of a living Spirit which shall give us to possess

191

some shadow of the immortal Being from which itself flows?

But, beyond that, there is another great promise here, of a quickening energy. I use the word 'quickening,' not in the sense of life–giving, but in the sense of stimulating. We talk about 'the flame of genius,' the 'fervour of conviction,' about 'fiery zeal,' about 'burning earnestness,' and the like; and, conversely, we speak of 'cold caution,' and 'chill indifference,' and so on. Fire means love, zeal, swift energy. This, then, is another side of this great promise, that into the torpor of our sluggish lives He is waiting to infuse a swift Spirit that shall make us glow and flame with earnestness, burn with love, aspire with desire, cleave to Him with the fervour of conviction, and be, in some measure, like those mighty spirits that stand before the Throne, the seraphim that burn with adoration and glow with rapture. A fire that shall destroy all our sluggishness, and change it into swift energy of glad obedience, may be kindled in our spirits by the Holy Spirit whom Christ gives.

Still farther, the promise of my text sets forth, not only life–giving and stimulating energy, but purifying power. Fire cleanses, as many an ancient ritual recognised. For instance, the thought that underlay even that savage 'passing the children through the fire to Moloch' was, that thus passed, humanity was cleansed from its stains. And that is true. Every man must be cleansed, if he is cleansed at all, by the touch of fire. If you take a piece of foul clay, and push it into a furnace, as it warms it whitens, and you can see the stains melting off it as the fire exercises its beneficent and purifying mastery. So the promise to us is of a great Spirit that will come, and by communicating His warmth will dissipate our foulness, and the sins that are enwrought into the substance of our natures will exhale from the heated surface, and disappear. The ore is flung into the blast furnace, and the scum rises to the surface, and may be ladled off, and the pure stream, cleansed because it is heated, flows out without scoriae or ash. All that was 'fuel for the fire' is burned; and what remains is more truly itself and more precious. And so, brother, you and I have, for our hope of cleansing, that we shall be passed through the fire, and dwell in the everlasting burnings of a Divine Spirit and a changeless love.

The last thought suggested by the metaphor is that it promises not only life–giving, stimulating, purifying, but also transforming and assimilating energy. For every lump of coal in your scuttles may be a parable; black and heavy, it is cast into the fire, and there it is turned into the likeness of the flame which it catches and itself begins to glow, and redden, and crackle, and break into a blaze. That is like what you and I may experience if we will. The incense rises in smoke to the heavens when it is heated: and our souls aspire and ascend, an odour of a sweet smell, acceptable to God, when the fire of that Divine Spirit has loosed them from the bonds that bind them to earth, and changed them into His own likeness, We all are 'changed from glory to glory even as by the Spirit of the Lord.'

So I think if you take these plain teachings of this symbol you learn something of the operations of that Divine Spirit to which our Lord pointed in the great words of my text.

II. And now I have a second thought to suggest—viz., what Christ had to do before His longing could be satisfied.

He longed, but the longing wish was not able to bring that on which it was fixed. He had come to send this divine fire upon the earth; but there was something that stood in the way; and something needed to be done as a preliminary before the ultimate purpose of His coming could be accomplished.

What that was, as I have already tried to point out, the subsequent verse tells us. I do not need, nor would it be congruous with my present purpose, to comment upon it at any length. We all know what He meant by the 'baptism,' that He had to be baptized with, and what were the dark waters into which He had to pass, and beneath which His sacred head had to be plunged. We all know that by the 'baptism' He meant His passion and His Cross. I do not dwell, either, upon the words of pathetic human shrinking with which His vision of the Cross is here accompanied, but I simply wish to signalise one thing, that in the estimation of Jesus Christ Himself it was not in His power to kindle this holy fire in humanity until He had died for men's sins. That must come first; the Cross must precede Pentecost. There can be no Divine Spirit in His full and loftiest powers poured out upon humanity until the Sacrifice has been offered on the Cross for the sins of the world. We cannot read all the deep reasons in the divine nature, and in human receptivity, which make that sequence absolutely necessary, and that preliminary indispensable. But this, at least, we know, that the Divine Spirit whom Christ gives uses as His instrument and sword the completed revelation which Christ completed in His Cross, Resurrection, and Ascension, and that, until His weapon was fashioned, He could not come.

That thought is distinctly laid down in many places in Scripture, to which I need not refer in more than a word. For instance, the Apostle John tells us that, when our Lord spoke in a cognate figure about the rivers of water which should flow from them who believed on Him, He spake of that Holy Spirit who 'was not given because that Jesus was not yet glorified.' We remember the words in the upper chamber, 'If I go not away, the Comforter will not come unto you, but if I depart I will send Him unto you.' But enough for us that He recognised the necessity, and that here His baptism of suffering comes into view, not so much for what it was itself, the sacrifice for the world's sin, as for that to which it was the necessary preliminary and introduction, the bestowment on humanity of the gift of the Divine Spirit. The old Greek legend of the Titan that stole fire from heaven tells us that he brought it to earth in a reed. Our Christ brings the heavenly fire in the fragile, hollow reed of His humanity, and the reed has to be broken in order that the fire may blaze out. 'How I wish that it were kindled! but I have a baptism to be baptized with.'

III. Lastly, what the world has to do to receive the fire.

Take these triumphant words of our Lord about what He was to do after His Cross, and contrast with them the world as it is to–day, ay! and the Church as it is to–day. What has become of the fire? Has it died down into grey ashes, choked with the cold results of its own former flaming power? Was Jesus Christ deceiving Himself? was He cherishing an illusion as to the significance and permanence of the results of His work in the world? No! There is a difference between B.C. and A.D. which can only be accounted for by the fulfilment of the promise in my text, that He did bring fire and set the world aflame. But the condition on which that fire will burn either through communities, society, humanity, or in an individual life, is trust in Him that gives it, and cleaving to Him, and the appropriate discipline. 'This spake He of the Holy Spirit which they that believe on Him should receive.'

And they that do *not* believe upon Him—what of them? The fire is of no advantage to them. Some of you do as people in Swiss villages do where there is a conflagration—you cover over your houses with incombustible felts or other materials, and deluge them with water, in the hope that no spark may light on you. There is no way by which the fire can do its work on us except our opening our hearts for the Firebringer. When He comes He brings the vital spark with Him, and He plants it on the hearth of our hearts. Trust in Him, believe far more intensely than the most of Christian people of this day do in the reality of the gift of supernatural divine life from Jesus Christ. I do believe that hosts of professing Christians have no firm grip of this truth, and, alas! very little verification of it in their lives. Your heavenly Father gives the Holy Spirit to them that ask Him. 'Covet earnestly the best gifts'; and take care that you do not put the fire out—'quench not the Holy Spirit,' as you will do if you 'fulfil the lusts of the flesh.' I remember once being down in the engine–room of an ocean–going steamer. There were the furnaces, large enough to drive an engine of five or six thousand horsepower. A few yards off there were the refrigerators, with ice hanging round the spigots that were put in to test the temperature. Ah! that is like many a Christian community, and many an individual Christian. Here is the fire; there is the frost. Brethren, let us seek to be baptized with fire, lest we should be cast into it, and be consumed by it.

END OP VOL. I.

VOLUME II: ST. LUKE *Chaps. XIII to XXIV*

CONTENTS

TRUE SABBATH OBSERVANCE

'And He was teaching in one of the synagogues on the Sabbath. 11. And, behold, there was a woman which had a spirit of infirmity eighteen years, and was bowed together, and could in no wise lift up herself. 12. And when Jesus saw her, He called her to Him, and said unto her, Woman, thou art loosed from thine infirmity. 13. And He laid His hands on her: and immediately she was made straight, and glorified God. 14. And the ruler of the synagogue answered with indignation, because that Jesus had healed on the Sabbath day, and said unto the people, There are six days in which men ought to work: in them therefore come and be healed, and not on the Sabbath day. 15. The Lord then answered him, and said, Thou hypocrite, doth not each one of you on the Sabbath loose his ox or his ass from the stall and lead him away to watering! 16. And ought not this woman, being

a daughter of Abraham, whom Satan hath bound, lo,
these eighteen years, be loosed from this bond on the
Sabbath day? 17. And when He had said these things, all
His adversaries were ashamed: and all the people
rejoiced for all the glorious things that were done by
Him.'—LUKE xiii. 10-17.

This miracle was wrought, unasked, on a woman, in a synagogue, and by all these characteristics was specially interesting to Luke. He alone records it. The narrative falls into two parts—the miracle, and the covert attack of the ruler of the synagogue, with our Lord's defence.

What better place than the synagogue could there be for a miracle of mercy? The service of man is best built on the service of God, and the service of God is as truly accomplished in deeds of human kindness done for His sake as in oral worship. The religious basis of beneficence and the beneficent manifestation of religion are commonplaces of Christian practice and thought from the beginning, and are both set forth in our Lord's life. He did not substitute doing good to men for worshipping God, as a once much–belauded but now all–but–forgotten anti–Christian writer has done; but He showed us both in their true relations. We have Christ's authority for regarding the woman's infirmity as the result of demoniacal possession, but the case presents some singular features. There seems to have been no other consequence than her incapacity to stand straight. Apparently the evil power had not touched her moral nature, for she had somehow managed to drag herself to the synagogue to pray; she 'glorified God' for her cure, and Christ called her 'a daughter of Abraham,' which surely means more than simply that she was a Jewess. It would seem to have been a case of physical infirmity only, and perhaps rather of evil inflicted eighteen years before than of continuous demoniacal possession.

But be that as it may, there is surely no getting over our Lord's express testimony here, that purely physical ills, not distinguishable from natural infirmity, were then, in some instances, the work of a malignant, personal power. Jesus knew the duration of the woman's 'bond' and the cause of it, by the same supernatural knowledge. That sad, bowed figure, with eyes fixed on the ground, and unable to look into His face, which yet had crawled to the synagogue, may teach us lessons of patience and of devout submission. She might have found good excuses for staying at home, but she, no doubt, found solace in worship; and she would not have so swiftly 'glorified God' for her cure, if she had not often sought Him in her infirmity. They who wait on Him often find more than they expect in His house.

Note the flow of Christ's unasked sympathy and help. We have already seen several instances of the same thing in this Gospel. The sight of misery ever set the chords of that gentle, unselfish heart vibrating, as surely as the wind draws music from the Aeolian harp strings. So it should be with us, and so would it be, if we had in us 'the law of the Spirit of life in Christ' making us 'free from the law of' self. But His spontaneous sympathy is not merely the perfection of manhood; it is the revelation of God. Unasked, the divine love pours itself on men, and gives all that it can give to those who do not seek, that they may be drawn to seek the better gifts which cannot be given unasked. God 'tarrieth not for man, nor waiteth for the sons of men,' in giving His greatest gift. No prayers besought Heaven for a Saviour. God's love is its own motive, and wells up by its inherent diffusiveness. Before we call, He answers.

Note the manner of the cure. It is twofold—a word and a touch. The former is remarkable, as not being, like most of the cures of demoniacs, a command to the evil spirit to go forth, but an assurance to the sufferer, fitted to inspire her with hope, and to encourage her to throw off the alien tyranny. The touch was the symbol to her of communicated power—not that Jesus needed a vehicle for His delivering strength, but that the poor victim, crushed in spirit, needed the outward sign to help her in realising the new energy that ran in her veins, and strengthened her muscles. Unquestionably the cure was miraculous, and its cause was Christ's will.

But apparently the manner of cure gave more place to the faith of the sufferer, and to the effort which her faith in Christ's word and touch heartened her to put forth, than we find in other miracles. She 'could in no wise lift herself up,' not because of any malformation or deficiency in physical power, but because that malign influence laid a heavy hand on her will and body, and crushed her down. Only supernatural power could deliver from supernatural evil, but that power wrought through as well us OB her; and when she believed that she was loosed from her infirmity, and had received strength from Jesus, she was loosed.

This makes the miracle no less, but it makes it a mirror in which the manner of our deliverance from a worse dominion of Satan is shadowed. Christ is come to loose us all from the yoke of bondage, which bows our faces to the ground, and makes us unfit to look up. He only can loose us, and His way of doing it is to assure us that we are free, and to give us power to fling off the oppression in the strength of faith in Him.

Note the immediate cure and its immediate result. The 'back bowed down always' for eighteen weary years is not too stiff to be made straight at once. The Christ–given power obliterates all traces of the past evil. Where He is the physician, there is no period of gradual convalescence, but 'the thing is done suddenly'; and, though in the spiritual realm, there still hang about pardoned men remains of forgiven sin, they are 'sanctified' in their inward selves, and have but to see to it that they work out in character and conduct that 'righteousness and holiness of truth' which they have received in the new nature given them through faith.

How rapturous was the gratitude from the woman's lips, which broke in upon the formal, proper, and heartless worship of the synagogue! The immediate hallowing of her joy into praise surely augurs a previously devout heart. Thanksgiving generally comes thus swiftly after mercies, when prayer has habitually preceded them. The sweetest sweetness of all our blessings is only enjoyed when we glorify God for them. Incense must be kindled, to be fragrant, and our joys must be fired by devotion, to give their rarest perfume.

The cavils of the ruler and Christ's defence are the second part of this incident. Note the blindness and cold–heartedness born of religious formalism. This synagogue official has no eye for the beauty of Christ's pity, no heart to rejoice in the woman's deliverance, no ear for the music of her praise. All that he sees is a violation of ecclesiastical order. That is the sin of sins in his eyes. He admits the reality of Christ's healing power, but that does not lead him to recognition of His mission. What a strange state of mind it was that acknowledged the miracle, and then took offence at its being done on the Sabbath!

Note, too, his disingenuous cowardice in attacking the people when he meant Christ. He blunders, too, in his scolding; for nobody had come to be healed. They had come to worship; and even if they had come for healing, the coming was no breach of Sabbath regulations, whatever the healing might be. There are plenty of people like this stickler for propriety and form, and if you want to find men blind as bats to the manifest tokens of a divine hand, and hard as millstones towards misery, and utterly incapable of glowing with enthusiasm or of recognising it, you will find them among ecclesiastical martinets, who are all for having 'things done decently and in order,' and would rather that a hundred poor sufferers should continue bowed down than that one of their regulations should be broken in lifting them up. The more men are filled with the spirit of worship, the less importance will they attach to the pedantic adherence to its forms, which is the most part of some people's religion.

Mark the severity, which is loving severity, of Christ's answer. He speaks to all who shared the ruler's thoughts, of whom there were several present (v. 17, 'adversaries'). Piercing words which disclose hidden and probably unconscious sins, are quite in place on the lips into which grace was poured. Well for those who let Him tell them their faults now, and do not wait for the light of judgment to show themselves to themselves for the first time.

Wherein lay these men's hypocrisy? They were pretending zeal for the Sabbath, while they were really moved by anger at the miracle, which would have been equally unwelcome on any day of the week. They were pretending that their zeal for the Sabbath was the result of their zeal for God, while it was only zeal for their Rabbinical niceties, and had no religious element in it at all. They wished to make the Sabbath law tight enough to restrain Jesus from miracles, while they made it loose enough to allow them to look after their own interests.

Men may be unconscious hypocrites, and these are the most hopeless. We are all in danger of fancying that we are displaying our zeal for the Lord, when we are only contending for our own additions to, or interpretations of, His will. There is no religion necessarily implied in enforcing forms of belief or conduct.

Our Lord's defence is, first of all, a conclusive *argumentum ad hominem*, which shuts the mouths of the objectors; but it is much more. The Talmud has minute rules for leading out animals on the Sabbath: An ass may go out with his pack saddle if it was tied on before the Sabbath, but not with a bell or a yoke; a camel may go out with a halter, but not with a rag tied to his tail; a string of camels may be led if the driver takes all the halters in his hand, and does not twist them, but they must not be tied to one another—and so on for pages. If, then, these sticklers for rigid observance of the Sabbath admitted that a beast's thirst was reason enough for work to relieve it, it did not lie in their mouths to find fault with the relief of a far greater human need.

But the words hold a wider truth, applicable to our conduct. The relief of human sorrow is always in season. It is a sacred duty which hallows any hour. 'Is not this the fast [and the feast too] that I have chosen ... to let the oppressed go free, and that ye break every yoke?' The spirit of the words is to put the exercise of beneficence high above the formalities of worship.

Note, too, the implied assertion of the dignity of humanity, the pitying tone of the 'lo, these eighteen years,' the sympathy of the Lord with the poor woman, and the implication of the terrible tragedy of Satan's bondage. If we have His Spirit in us, and look at the solemn facts of life as He did, all these pathetic considerations will be present to our minds as we behold the misery of men, and, moved by the thoughts of their lofty place in God's scheme of things, of their long and dreary bondage, of the evil power that holds them fast, and of what they may become, even sons and daughters of the Highest, we shall be fired with the same longing to help which filled Christ's heart, and shall count that hour consecrated, and not profaned, in which we are able to bring liberty to the captives, and an upward gaze of hope to them that have been bowed down.

THE STRAIT GATE

'And He went through the cities and villages, teaching, and journeying toward Jerusalem. 23. Then said one unto Him, Lord, are there few that be saved? And He said unto them, 24. Strive to enter in at the strait gate: for many, I say unto you, will seek to enter in, and shall not he able. 25. When once the Master of the house is risen up, and hath shut to the door, and ye begin to stand without, and to knock at the door, saying, Lord, Lord, open unto us; and He shall answer and say unto you, I know you not whence ye are: 26. Then shall ye begin to say, We have eaten and drunk in Thy presence, and Thou hast taught in our streets. 27. But He shall say, I tell you, I know you not whence ye are; depart from Me, all ye workers of iniquity. 28. There shall be weeping and gnashing of teeth, when ye shall see Abraham, and Isaac, and Jacob, and all the prophets, in the kingdom of God, and you yourselves thrust out. 29. And they shall come from the east, and from the west, and from the north, and from the south, and shall sit down in the kingdom of God. 30. And, behold, there are last which shall be first and there are first which shall be last.'—LUKE xiii. 22–30

'Are there few that be saved?' The questioner's temper and motives may be inferred from the tone of Christ's answer, which turns attention from a mere piece of speculative curiosity to the grave personal aspect of the condition of 'salvation,' and the possibility of missing it. Whether few or many went in, there would be many left out, and among these some of the listeners. Jesus speaks to 'them,' the multitude, not to the questioner. The men who approach solemn subjects lightly, and use them as material for raising profitless questions for the sake of getting religious teachers in a corner, exist still, and are best answered after Christ's manner.

Of course, the speaker meant by being 'saved' participation in Messiah's kingdom, regarded in the carnal Jewish fashion; and our Lord's reply is primarily directed to setting forth the condition of entrance into that kingdom, as the Jew expected it to be manifested on earth. But behind that immediate reference lies a solemn unveiling of the conditions of salvation in its deepest meaning, and of the danger of exclusion from it.

I. We note, first, the all–important exhortation with which Christ seeks to sober a frivolous curiosity. In its primary application, the 'strait gate' may be taken to be the lowliness of the Messiah, and the consequent sharp contrast of His kingdom with Jewish high–flown and fleshly hopes. The passage to the promised royalty was not through a great portal worthy of a palace, but by a narrow, low–browed wicket, through which it took a man trouble to squeeze. For us, the narrow gate is the self–abandonment and self–accusation which are indispensable for entrance into salvation.

'The door of faith' is a narrow one; for it lets no self–righteousness, no worldly glories, no dignities, through. Like the Emperor at Canossa, we are kept outside till we strip ourselves of crowns and royal robes, and stand clothed only in the hair–shirt of penitence. Like Milton's rebel angels entering their council chamber, we must make ourselves small to get in. We must creep on our knees, so low is the vault; we must leave everything outside, so narrow is it. We must go in one by one, as in the turnstiles at a place of entertainment. The door opens into a palace, but it is too strait for any one who trusts to himself.

There must be effort in order to enter by it. For everything in our old self–confident, self–centred nature is up in arms against the conditions of entrance. We are not saved by effort, but we shall not believe without effort. The main struggle of our whole lives should be to cultivate self–humbling trust in Jesus Christ, and to 'fight the good fight of faith.'

II. We note the reason for the exhortation. It is briefly given in verse 24 (last clause), and both parts of the reason there are expanded in the following verses. Effort is needed for entrance, because many are shut out. The questioner would be no better for knowing whether few would enter, but he and all need to burn in on their minds that many will *not*.

Very solemnly significant is the difference between *striving* and *seeking*. It is like the difference between wishing and willing. There may be a seeking which has no real earnestness in it, and is not sufficiently determined, to do what is needful in order to find. Plenty of people would like to possess earthly good, but cannot brace themselves to needful work and sacrifice. Plenty would like to 'go to heaven,' as they understand the phrase, but cannot screw themselves to the surrender of self and the world. Vagrant, halfhearted seeking, such as one sees many examples of, will never win anything, either in this world or in the other. We must strive, and not only seek.

That is true, even if we do not look beyond time; but Jesus carries our awed vision onwards to the end of the days, in the expansion of his warning, which follows in verses 25–27. No doubt, the words had a meaning for His hearers in reference to the Messianic kingdom, and a fulfilment in the rejection of the nation. But we have to discern in them a further and future significance.

Observe that the scene suggested differs from the similar parable of the virgins waiting for their Lord, in that it does not describe a wedding feast. Here it is a householder already in his house, and, at the close of the day, locking up for the night. Some of his servants have not returned in time, have not come in through the narrow gate, which is now not only narrow, but closed by the master's own hand.

The translation of that is that, by a decisive act of Christ's in the future, the time for entrance will he ended. As in reference to each stage of life, specific opportunities are given in it for securing specific results, and these can never be recovered if the stage is past; so mortal life, as a whole, is the time for entrance, and if it is not used for that purpose, entrance is impossible. If the youth will not learn, the man will be ignorant. If the sluggard will not plough because the weather is cold, he will 'beg in harvest.' If we do not strive to enter at the gate, it is vain to seek entrance when the Master's own hand has barred it.

The language of our Lord here seems to shut us up to the conclusion that life is the time in which we can gain our entrance. It is no kindness to suggest that perhaps He does not shut the door quite fast. We know, at all events, that it is wide open now.

The words put into the mouths of the excluded sufficiently define their characters, and the reasons why they sought in vain. Why did they want to be in? Because they wished to get out of the cold darkness into the warm light of the bountiful house. But they neither knew the conditions of entrance nor had they any desire after the true blessings within. Their deficiencies are plainly marked in their pleas for admission. At first, they simply ask for entrance, as if thinking that to wish was to have. Then, when the Householder says that He knows nothing about them, and cannot let strangers in, they plead as their qualification that they had eaten and drunk in His presence, and that He had taught in their streets. In these words, the relations of Christ's contemporaries are described, and their immediate application to them is plain.

Outward connection with Jesus gave no claim to share in His kingdom. We have to learn the lesson which we who live amidst a widely diffused, professing Christianity sadly need. No outward connection with Christ, in Christian ordinances or profession, will avail to establish a claim to have the door opened for us. A man may be a most respectable and respected church–member, and have listened to Christian teaching all his days, and have in life a vague wish to be 'saved,' and yet be hopelessly unfit to enter, and therefore irremediably shut out.

The Householder's answer, in its severity and calmness, indicates the inflexible impossibility of opening to such seekers. It puts stress on two things—the absence of any vital relationship between Him and them, and their moral character. He knows nothing about them, and not to be known by the Master of the house is necessarily to be shut out from His household. They are known of the Shepherd who know Him and hear His voice. They who are not must stay in the desert. Such mutual knowledge is the basis of all righteousness, and righteousness is the essential condition of entrance.

These seekers are represented as still working iniquity. They had not changed their moral nature. They wished to enter heaven, but they still loved evil. How could they come in, even if the door had been open? Let us learn that, while faith is the door, without holiness no man shall see the Lord. The worker of iniquity has only an outward relation to Jesus. Inwardly he is separated from Him, and, at last, the outward relation will be adjusted to the inward, and departure from Him will be inevitable, and that is ruin.

III. Boldly and searchingly personal as the preceding words had been, the final turn of Christ's answer must have had a still sharper and more distasteful edge. He had struck a blow at Jewish trust in outward connection with Messiah as ensuring participation in His kingdom. He now says that the Gentiles shall fill the vacant places. Many Jews will be unable to enter, for all their seeking, but still there will be many saved; for troops of hated Gentiles shall come from every corner of the earth, and the sight of them sitting beside the fathers of the nation, while Israel after the flesh is shut out, will move the excluded to weeping—the token of sorrow, which yet has in it no softening nor entrance–securing effect, because it passes into 'gnashing of teeth,' the sign of anger. Such sorrow worketh death.

Such fierce hatred, joined with stiff–necked obstinacy, has characterised the Jew ever since Jerusalem fell. 'If God spared not the natural branches, take heed lest He also spare not thee.' Israel was first, and has become last. The same causes which sent it from the van to the rear have worked like effects in 'Christendom,' as witness Asia Minor and the mosques into which Christian churches have been turned.

These causes will produce like effects wherever they become dominant. Any church and any individual Christian who trusts in outward connection with Christ, and works iniquity, will sooner or later fall into the rear, and if repentance and faith do not lead it or him through the strait gate, will be among those 'last' who are so far behind that they are shut out altogether. Let us 'be not high–minded, but fear.'

CHRIST'S MESSAGE TO HEROD

'And he said unto them, Go ye, and tell that fox,
Behold, I cast out devils, and I do cures to–day and
to–morrow, and the third day I shall be perfected.
33. Nevertheless I must walk to–day, and to–morrow,
and the day following: for it cannot be that a prophet
perish out of Jerusalem.'—LUKE xiii. 32, 33.

Even a lamb might be suspicious if wolves were to show themselves tenderly careful of its safety. Pharisees taking Christ's life under their protection were enough to suggest a trick. These men came to Christ desirous of posing as counterworking Herod's intention to slay Him. Our Lord's answer, bidding them go and tell Herod what He immediately communicates to them, shows that He regarded them as in a plot with that crafty, capricious kinglet. And evidently there was an understanding between them. For some reason or other, best known to his own changeable and whimsical nature, the man who at one moment was eagerly desirous to see Jesus, was at the next as eagerly desirous to get Him out of his territories; just as he admired and murdered John the Baptist. The Pharisees, on the other hand, desired to draw Him to Jerusalem, where they would have Him in their power more completely than in the northern district. If they had spoken all their minds they would have said, 'Go hence, or else we cannot kill Thee.' So Christ answers the hidden schemes, and not the apparent solicitude, in the words that I have taken for my text. They unmask the plot, they calmly put aside the threats of danger. They declare that His course was influenced by far other considerations. They show that He clearly saw what it was towards which He was journeying. And then, with sad irony, they declare that it, as it were, contrary to prophetic decorum and established usage that a prophet should be slain anywhere but in the streets of the bloody and sacred city.

There are many deep things in the words, which I cannot touch in the course of a single sermon; but I wish now, at all events, to skim their surface, and try to gather some of their obvious lessons.

I. First, then, note Christ's clear vision of His death.

There is some difficulty about the chronology of this period with which I need not trouble you. It is enough to note that the incident with which we are concerned occurred during that last journey of our Lord's towards Jerusalem and Calvary, which occupies so much of this Gospel of Luke. At what point in that fateful journey it occurred may be left undetermined. Nor need I enter upon the question as to whether the specification of time in our text, 'to–day, and to–morrow, and the third day,' is intended to be taken literally, as some commentators suppose, in which case it would be brought extremely near the goal of the journey; or whether, as seems more probable from the context, it is to be taken as a kind of proverbial expression for a definite but short period. That the latter is the proper interpretation seems to be largely confirmed by the fact that there is a slight variation in the application of the designation of time in the two verses of our text, 'the third day' in the former verse being regarded as the period of the perfecting, whilst in the latter verse it is regarded as part of the period of the progress towards the perfecting. Such variation in the application is more congruous with the idea that we have here to deal with a kind of proverbial expression for a limited and short period. Our Lord is saying in effect, 'My time is not to be settled by Herod. It is definite, and it is short. It is needless for him to trouble himself; for in three days it will be all over. It is useless for him to trouble himself, or for you Pharisees to plot, for until the appointed days are past it will not be over, whatever you and he may do.' The course He had yet to run was plain before Him in this last journey, every step of which was taken with the Cross full in view.

Now the worst part of death is the anticipation of death; and it became Him who bore death for every man to drink to its dregs that cup of trembling which the fear of it puts to all human lips. We rightly regard it as a cruel aggravation of a criminal's doom if he is carried along a level, straight road with his gibbet in view at the end of the march. But so it was that Jesus Christ travelled through life.

My text comes at a comparatively late period of His history. A few months or weeks at the most intervened between Him and the end. But the consciousness which is here so calmly expressed was not of recent origin. We know that from the period of His transfiguration He began to give His death a very prominent place in His teaching, but it had been present with Him long before He thus laid emphasis upon it in His communications with His disciples. For, if we accept John's Gospel as historical, we shall have to throw back His first public references to the end to the very beginning of His career. The cleansing of the Temple, at the very outset of His course, was vindicated by Him by the profound words, 'Destroy this Temple, and in three days I will raise it up.' During the same early visit to the capital city He said to Nicodemus, 'As Moses lifted up the serpent in the wilderness, even so must the Son of Man be lifted up.' So Christ's career was not like that of many a man who has begun, full of sanguine hope as a possible reformer and benefactor of his fellows, and by slow degrees has awakened to the consciousness that reformers and benefactors need to be martyrs ere their ideals can be realised. There was no disillusioning in Christ's experience. From the commencement He knew that He came, not only to minister, but also 'to give His life a ransom for the many.' And it was *not* a mother's eye, as a reverent modern painter has profoundly, and yet erroneously, shown us in his great work in our own city gallery—it was not a mother's eye that first saw the shadow of the Cross fall on her unconscious Son, but it was Himself that all through His earthly pilgrimage knew Himself to be the Lamb appointed for the sacrifice. This Isaac toiled up the hill, bearing the wood and the knife, and knew where and who was the Offering.

Brethren, I do not think that we sufficiently realise the importance of that element in our conceptions of the life of Jesus Christ. What a pathos it gives to it all! What a beauty it gives to His gentleness, to His ready interest in others, to His sympathy for all sorrow, and tenderness with all sin! How wonderfully it deepens the significance, the loveliness, and the pathos of the fact that 'the Son of Man came eating and drinking,' remembering everybody but Himself, and ready to enter into all the cares and the sorrows of other hearts, if we think that all the while there stood, grim and certain, before Him that Calvary with its Cross! Thus, through all His path, He knew to what He was journeying.

II. Then again, secondly, let me ask you to note here our Lord's own estimate of the place which His death holds in relation to His whole work.

Notice that remarkable variation in the expression in our text. 'The third day I shall be *perfected*.... It cannot be that a prophet *perish* out of Jerusalem.' Then, somehow or other, the 'perishing' is 'perfecting.' There may be a doubt as to the precise rendering of the word translated by 'perfecting'; but it seems to me that the only meaning congruous with the context is that which is suggested by the translation of our Authorised Version, and that our Lord does not mean to say 'on the third day I shall complete My work of casting out devils and curing diseases,' but that He masses the whole of His work into two great portions—the one of which includes all His works and ministrations of miracles and of mercy; and the other of which contains one unique and transcendent fact, which outweighs and towers above all these others, and is the perfecting of His work, and the culmination of His obedience, service, and sacrifice.

Now, of course, I need not remind you that the 'perfecting' thus spoken of is not a perfecting of moral character or of individual nature, but that it is the same perfecting which the Epistle to the Hebrews speaks about when it says, 'Being made perfect, He became the Author of eternal salvation to all them which obey Him.' That is to say, it is His perfecting in regard to office, function, work for the world, and not the completion or elevation of His individual character. And this 'perfecting' is effected in His 'perishing.'

Now I want to know in what conceivable sense the death of Jesus Christ can be the culmination and crown of His work, without which it would be a torso, an incomplete fragment, a partial fulfilment of the Father's design, and of His own mission, unless it be that that death was, as I take it the New Testament with one voice in all its parts declares it to be, a sacrifice for the sins of the world. I know of no construing of the fact of the death on the Cross which can do justice to the plain words of my text, except the old-fashioned belief that therein He made atonement for sin, and thereby, as the Lamb of God, bore away the sins of the world.

Other great lives may be crowned by fair deaths, which henceforward become seals of faithful witness, and appeals to the sentiments of the heart, but there is no sense that I know of in which from Christ's death there can flow a mightier energy than from such a life, unless in the sense that the death is a sacrifice.

Now I know there has been harm done by the very desire to exalt Christ's great sacrifice on the Cross; when it has been so separated from His life as that the life has not been regarded as a sacrifice, nor the death as obedience. Rather the sacrificial element runs through His whole career, and began when He became flesh and tabernacled amongst us; but yet as being the apex of it all, without which it were all—imperfect, and in a special sense redeeming men from the power of death, that Cross is set forth by His own word. For Him to 'perish' was to 'be perfected.' As the ancient prophet long before had said, 'When His soul shall make an offering for sin,' then, paradoxical as it may seem, the dead Man shall 'see,' and 'shall see His seed.' Or, as He Himself said, 'If a corn of wheat fall into the ground it abideth alone, but if it die it bringeth forth much fruit.'

I do not want to insist upon any theories of Atonement. I do want to insist that Christ's own estimate of the significance and purpose and issue of His death shall not be slurred over, but that, recognising that He Himself regarded it as the perfecting of His work, we ask ourselves very earnestly how such a conception can be explained if we strike out of our Christianity the thought of the sacrifice for the sins of the world. Unless we take Paul's gospel, 'How that He died for our sins according to the Scriptures,' I for one do not believe that we shall ever get Paul's results, 'Old things are passed away; all things are become new.' If you strike the Cross off the dome of the temple, the fires on its altars will soon go out. A Christianity which has to say much about the life of Jesus, and knows not what to say about the death of Christ, will be a Christianity that will neither have much constraining power in our lives, nor be able to breathe a benediction of peace over our deaths. If we desire to be perfected in character, we must have faith in that sacrificial death which was the perfecting of Christ's work.

III. And so, lastly, notice our Lord's resolved surrender to the discerned Cross.

There is much in this aspect in the words of my text which I cannot touch upon now; but two or three points I may briefly notice.

Note then, I was going to say, the superb heroism of His calm indifference to threats and dangers. He will go hence, and relieve the tyrant's dominions of His presence; but He is careful to make it plain that His going has no connection with the futile threatenings by which they have sought to terrify Him. 'Nevertheless'—although I do not care at all for them or for him—'nevertheless I must journey to—day and tomorrow! But that is not because I fear death, but because I am going to My death; for the prophet must die in Jerusalem.' We are so accustomed to think of the 'gentle Jesus, meek and mild' that we forget the 'strong Son of God.' If we were talking about a man merely, we should point to this calm, dignified answer as being an instance of heroism, but we do not feel that that word fits Him. There are too many vulgar associations connected with it, to be adapted to the gentleness of His fixed purpose that blenched not, nor faltered, whatsoever came in the way.

Light is far more powerful than lightning. Meekness may be, and in Him was, wedded to a will like a bar of iron, and a heart that knew not how to fear. If ever there was an iron hand in a velvet glove it was the hand of Christ. And although the perspective of virtues which Christianity has introduced, and which Christ exhibited in His life, gives prominence to the meek and the gentle, let us not forget that it also enjoins the cultivation of the 'wrestling thews that throw the world.' 'Quit you like men; be strong; let all your deeds be done in charity.'

Then note, too, the solemn law that ruled His life. 'I *must* walk.' That is a very familiar expression upon His lips. From that early day when He said, 'Wist ye not that I *must* be about My Father's business,' to that last when He said, 'The Son of Man *must* be lifted up,' there crops out, ever and anon, in the occasional glimpses that He allows us to have of His inmost spirit, this reference of all His actions to a necessity that was laid upon Him, and to which He ever consciously conformed. That necessity determined what He calls so frequently 'My time; My hour'; and influenced the trifles, as they are called, as well as the great crises, of His career. It was the Father's will which made the Son's *must*. Hence His unbroken communion and untroubled calm.

If we want to live near God, and if we want to have lives of peace amidst convulsions, we, too, must yield ourselves to that all encompassing sovereign necessity, which, like the great laws of the universe, shapes the planets and the suns in their courses and their stations; and holds together two grains of dust, or two motes that dance in the sunshine. To gravitation there is nothing great and nothing small. God's *must* covers all the ground of our lives, and should ever be responded to by our 'I will.'

And that brings me to the last point, and that is, our Lord's glad acceptance of the necessity and surrender of the Cross. What was it that made Him willing to take that 'must' as the law of His life? First, a Son's obedience; second, a Brother's love. There was no point in Christ's career, from the moment when in the desert He put away the temptation to win the kingdoms of the world by other than the God–appointed means, down to the last moment when on His dying ears there fell another form of the same temptation in the taunt, 'Let Him come down from the cross, and we will believe on Him'; when He could not, if He had chosen to abandon His mission, have saved Himself. No compulsion, no outward hand impelling Him, drove Him along that course which ended on Calvary; but only that He would save others, and therefore 'Himself He cannot save.'

True, there were natural human shrinkings, just as the weight and impetus of some tremendous billow buffeting the bows of the ship makes it quiver; but this never affected the firm hand on the rudder, and never deflected the vessel from its course. Christ's 'soul was troubled,' but His will was fixed, and it was fixed by His love to us. Like one of the men who in after ages died for His dear sake, He may be conceived as refusing to be bound to the stake by any bands, willing to stand there and be destroyed because He wills. Nothing fastened Him to the Cross but His resolve to save the world, in which world was included each of us sitting listening and standing speaking, now. Oh, brethren! shall not we, moved by such love, with like cheerfulness of surrender, give ourselves to Him who gave Himself for us?

THE LESSONS OF A FEAST

'And it came to pass, as He went into the house of one
of the chief Pharisees to eat bread on the Sabbath day,
that they watched Him. 2. And, behold, there was a
certain man before Him which had the dropsy. 3. And
Jesus answering spake unto the lawyers and Pharisees,
saying, Is it lawful to heal on the Sabbath day? 4. And
they held their peace. And He took him, and healed him,

and let him go; 5. And answered them, saying, Which of
you shall have an ass or an ox fallen into a pit, and
will not straightway pull him out on the Sabbath day?
6. And they could not answer Him again to these things.
7. And He put forth a parable to those which were
bidden, when He marked how they chose out the chief
rooms; saying unto them, 8. When thou art bidden of any
man to a wedding, sit not down in the highest room,
lest a more honourable man than thou be bidden of him;
9. And he that bade thee and him come and say to thee,
Give this man place; and thou begin with shame to take
the lowest room. 10. But when thou art bidden, go and
sit down in the lowest room; that when he that bade
thee cometh, he may say unto thee, Friend, go up
higher: then shalt thou have worship in the presence
of them that sit at meat with thee. 11. For whosoever
exalteth himself shall be abased; and he that humbleth
himself shall be exalted. 12. Then said He also to him
that bade Him, When thou makest a dinner or a supper,
call not thy friends, nor thy brethren, neither thy
kinsmen, nor thy rich neighbours; lest they also bid
thee again, and a recompense be made thee. 13. But when
thou makest a feast, call the poor, the maimed, the
lame, the blind: 14. And thou shalt be blessed; for
they cannot recompense thee: for thou shalt be
recompensed at the resurrection of the just.'
—LUKE xiv. 1–14.

Jesus never refused an invitation, whether the inviter were a Pharisee or a publican, a friend or a foe. He never mistook the disposition of His host. He accepted 'greetings where no kindness is,' and on this occasion there was none. The entertainer was a spy, and the feast was a trap. What a contrast between the malicious watchers at the table, ready to note and to interpret in the worst sense every action of His, and Him loving and wishing to bless even them! The chill atmosphere of suspicion did not freeze the flow of His gentle beneficence and wise teaching. His meek goodness remained itself in the face of hostile observers. The miracle and the two parables are aimed straight at their errors.

I. How came the dropsical man there? Possibly he had simply strayed in to look on at the feast, as the freedom of manners then would permit him to do. The absence of any hint that he came hoping for a cure, and of any trace of faith on his part, or of speech to him on Christ's, joined with his immediate dismissal after his cure, rather favours the supposition that he had been put as the bait of the trap, on the calculation that the sight of him would move Jesus to heal him. The setters of the snare were 'watching' whether it would work, and Jesus 'answered' their thoughts, which were, doubtless, visible in their eyes. His answer has three stages—a question which is an assertion, the cure, and another affirming question. All three are met with sulky silence, which speaks more than words would have done. The first question takes the 'lawyers' on their own ground, and in effect asserts that to heal did not break the Sabbath. Jesus challenges denial of the lawfulness of it, and the silence of the Pharisees confesses that they dare not deny. 'The bare fact of healing is not prohibited,' they might have said, 'but the acts necessary for healing are.' But no acts were necessary for this Healer's power to operate. The outgoing of His will had power. Their finespun distinctions of deeds lawful and unlawful were spiders' webs, and His act of mercy flew high above the webs, like some fair winged creature glancing in the sunshine, while the spider sits in his crevice balked. The broad principle involved in Jesus' first question is that no Sabbath law, no so—called religious restriction, can ever forbid helping the miserable. The repose of the Sabbath is deepened, not disturbed, by activity for man's good.

The cure is told without detail, probably because there were no details to tell. There is no sign of request or of faith on the sufferer's part; there seems to have been no outward act on Christ's beyond 'taking' him, which appears simply to mean that He called him nearer, and then, by a simple exercise of His will, healed him. There is no trace of thanks or of wonder in the heart of the sufferer, who probably never had anything more to do with his benefactor. Silently he comes on the stage, silently he gets his blessing, silently he disappears. A strange, sad instance of how possible it is to have a momentary connection with Jesus, and even to receive gifts from His hand, and yet to have no real, permanent relation to Him!

The second question turns from the legal to a broader consideration. The spontaneous workings of the heart are not to be dammed back by ceremonial laws. Need calls for immediate succour. You do not wait for the Sabbath's sun to set when your ox or your ass is in a pit. (The reading 'son' instead of 'ox,' as in the Revised Version margin, is incongruous.) Jesus is appealing to the instinctive wish to give immediate help even to a beast in trouble, and implies that much more should the same instinct be allowed immediate play when its object is a man. The listeners were self—condemned, and their obstinate silence proves that the arrow had struck deep.

II. The cure seems to have taken place before the guests seated themselves. Then came a scramble for the most honourable places, on which He looked with perhaps a sad smile. Again the silence of the guests is noticeable, as well as the calm assumption of authority by Jesus, even among such hostile company. Where He comes a guest, He becomes teacher, and by divine right He rebukes. The lesson is given, says Luke, as 'a parable,' by which we are to understand that our Lord is not here giving, as might appear if His words are superficially interpreted, a mere lesson of proper behaviour at a feast, but is taking that behaviour as an illustration of a far deeper thing. Possibly some too ambitious guest had contrived to seat himself in the place of honour, and had had to turn out, and, with an embarrassed mien, had to go down to the very lowest place, as all the intermediate ones were full. His eagerness to be at the top had ended in his being at the bottom. That is a 'parable,' says Jesus, an illustration in the region of daily life, of large truths in morals and religion. It is a poor motive for outward humility and self—abasement that it may end in higher honour. And if Jesus was here only giving directions for conduct in regard to men, He was inculcating a doubtful kind of morality. The devil's

darling sin
Is the pride that apes humility.'

Jesus was not recommending that, but what is crafty ambition, veiling itself in lowliness for its own purposes, when exercised in outward life, becomes a noble, pure, and altogether worthy, thing in the spiritual sphere. For to desire to be exalted in the kingdom is wholly right, and to humble one's self with a direct view to that exaltation is to tread the path which He has hallowed by His own footsteps. The true aim for ambition is the honour that cometh from God only, and the true path to it is through the valley; for 'God resisteth the proud, but giveth grace to the humble.'

III. Unbroken silence still prevailed among the guests, but again Jesus speaks as teacher, and now to the host. A guest does not usually make remarks on the composition of the company, Jesus could make no 'recompense' to His entertainer, but to give him this counsel. Again, He inculcated a wide general lesson under the guise of a particular exhortation appropriate to the occasion. Probably the bulk of the guests were well–to–do people of the host's own social rank, and, as probably, there were onlookers of a lower degree, like the dropsical man. The prohibition is not directed against the natural custom of inviting one's associates and equals, but against inviting them only, and against doing so with a sharp eye to the advantages to be derived from it. That weary round of giving a self–regarding hospitality, and then getting a return dinner or evening entertainment from each guest, which makes up so much of the social life among us, is a pitiful affair, hollow and selfish. What would Jesus say—what does Jesus say—about it all? The sacred name of hospitality is profaned, and the very springs of it dried up by much of our social customs, and the most literal application of our Lord's teaching here is sorely needed.

But the words are meant as a 'parable,' and are to be widened out to include all sorts of kindnesses and helps given in the sacred name of charity to those whose only claim is their need. 'They cannot recompense thee'—so much the better, for, if an eye to their doing so could have influenced thee, thy beneficence would have lost its grace and savour, and would have been simple selfishness, and, as such, incapable of future reward. It is only love that is lavished on those who can make no return which is so free from the taint of secret regard to self that it is fit to be recognised as love in the revealing light of that great day, and therefore is fit to be 'recompensed in the resurrection of the just.'

EXCUSES NOT REASONS

'They all with one consent began to make excuse.
—LUKE xiv. 18.

Jesus Christ was at a feast in a Pharisee's house. It was a strange place for Him—and His words at the table were also strange. For He first rebuked the guests, and then the host; telling the former to take the lower rooms, and bidding the latter widen his hospitality to those that could not recompense him. It was a sharp saying; and one of the other guests turned the edge of it by laying hold of our Lord's final words: 'Thou shalt be recompensed at the resurrection of the just,' and saying, no doubt in a pious tone and with a devout shake of the head, 'Blessed is he that shall eat bread in the Kingdom of God.' It was a very proper thing to say, but there was a ring of conventional, commonplace piety about it, which struck unpleasantly on Christ's ear. He answers the speaker with that strange story of the great feast that nobody would come to, as if He had said, 'You pretend to think that it is a blessed thing to eat bread in the Kingdom of God, Why! You will not eat bread when it is offered to you.'

I dare say you all know enough of the parable to make it unnecessary for me to go over it. A great feast is prepared; invitations, more or less general, are sent out at first, everything is ready; and, behold, there is a table, and nobody to sit at it. A strange experience for a hospitable man! And so he sends his servants to beat up the unwilling guests, and, one after another, with more or less politeness, refuses to come.

I need not follow the story further. In the latter part of the parable our Lord shadows the transference of the blessings of the Kingdom to the Gentiles, outcasts as the Jews thought them, skulking in the hedges and tramping on the highways. In the first part He foreshadows the failure of His own preaching amongst His own people. But Jews and Englishmen are very much alike. The way in which these invited guests treated the invitation to this feast is being repeated, day by day, by thousands of men round us; and by some of ourselves. 'They all, with one consent, began to make excuse.'

I. The first thing that I would desire you to notice is the strangely unanimous refusal.

The guests' conduct in the story is such as life and reality would afford no example of. No set of people, asked to a great banquet, would behave as these people in the parable do. Then, is the introduction of such an unnatural trait as this a fault in the construction of narrative? No! Rather it is a beauty, for the very point of the story is the utter unnaturalness of the conduct described, and the contrast that is presented between the way in which men regard the lower blessings from which these people are represented as turning, and in which they regard the loftier blessings that are offered. Nobody would turn his back upon such a banquet if he had the chance of going to it. What, then, shall we say of those who, by platoons and regiments, turn their backs upon this higher offer? The very preposterous unnaturalness of the conduct, if the parable were a true story, points to the deep meaning that lies behind it: that in that higher region the unnatural is the universal, or all but universal.

And, indeed, it is so. One would almost venture to say that there is a kind of law according to which the more valuable a thing is the less men care to have it; or, if you like to put it into more scientific language, the attraction of an object is in the inverse ratio to its worth. Small things, transitory things, material things, everybody grasps at; and the number of graspers steadily decreases as you go up the scale in preciousness, until, when you reach the highest of all, there are the fewest that want them. Is there anything lower than good that merely gratifies the body? Is there anything that the most of men want more? Are there many things lower in the scale than money? Are there many things that pull more strongly? Is not truth better than wealth? Are there more pursuers of it than there are of the former? For one man who is eager to know, and counts his life well spent, in following knowledge

'Like a sinking star,
Beyond the furthest bounds of human thought,'

there are a hundred who think it rightly expended in the pursuit after the wealth that perishes. Is not goodness higher than truth, and are not the men that are content to devote themselves to becoming wise more numerous than those that are content to devote themselves to becoming pure? And, topmost of all, is there anything to be compared with the gifts that are held out to us in that great Saviour and in His message? And is there anything that the mass of men pass by with more unanimous refusal than the offered feast which the great King of humanity has provided for His

211

subjects? What is offered for each of us, pressed upon us, in the gift of Jesus Christ? Help, guidance, companionship, restfulness of heart, power of obedience, victory over self, control of passions, supremacy over circumstances, tranquillity deep and genuine, death abolished, Heaven opened, measureless hopes following upon perfect fruition, here and hereafter. These things are all gathered into, and their various sparkles absorbed in, the one steady light of that one great encyclopaediacal word—Salvation. These gifts are going begging, lying at our doors, offered to every one of us, pressed upon all on the simple condition of taking Christ for Saviour and King. And what do we do with them? 'They all, with one consent, began to make excuse.'

One hears of barbarous people that have no use for the gold that abounds in their country, and do not think it half as valuable as glass beads. That is how men estimate the true and the trumpery treasures which Christ and the world offer. I declare it seems to me that, calmly looking at men's nature, and their duration, and then thinking of the aims of the most of them, we should not be very far wrong if we said an epidemic of insanity sits upon the world. For surely to turn away from the gold and to hug the glass beads is very little short of madness. 'This their way is their folly, and their posterity approve their sayings.'

And now notice that this refusal may be, and often in fact is, accompanied with lip recognition of the preciousness of the neglected things. That Pharisee who put up the pillow of his pious sentiment—a piece of cant, because he did not feel what he was saying—to deaden the cannon–ball of Christ's word, is only a pattern of a good many of us who think that to say, 'Blessed is he that eateth bread in the Kingdom of God,' with the proper unctuous roll of the voice, is pretty nearly as good as to take the bread that is offered to us. There are no more difficult people to get at than the people, of whom I am sure I have some specimens before me now, who bow their heads in assent to the word of the Gospel, and by bowing them escape its impact, and let it whistle harmlessly over. You that believe every word that I or my brethren preach, and never dream of letting it affect your conduct—if there be degrees in that lunatic asylum of the world, surely you are candidates for the highest place.

II. Now, secondly, notice the flimsy excuses.

'They all, with one consent, began.' I do not suppose that they had laid their heads together, or that our Lord intends us to suppose that there was a conspiracy and concert of refusal, but only that without any previous consultation, all had the same sentiments, and offered substantially the same answer. All the reasons that are given come to one and the same thing—viz. occupation with present interests, duties, possessions, or affections. There are differences in the excuses which are not only helps to the vividness of the narrative, but also express differences in the speakers. One man is a shade politer than the others. He puts his refusal on the ground of necessity. He 'must,' and so he courteously prays that he may be held excused. The second one is not quite so polite; but still there is a touch of courtesy about him too. He does not pretend necessity as his friend had done, but he simply says, 'I *am* going'; and that is not quite so courteous as the former answer, but still he begs to be excused. The last man thinks that he has such an undeniable reason that he may be as brusque as he likes, and so he says, 'I have married a wife, and therefore I cannot come' and I do not make any apologies. So with varying degrees of apparent recognition of the claims of host and feast, the ground of refusal is set forth as possessions in two cases, and as affections in the third; and these so fill the men's hearts and minds that they have no time to attend to the call that summons them to the feast.

Now it is obvious to note that the alleged necessity in one of these excuses was no necessity at all. Who made the 'must'? The man himself. The field would not run away though he waited till to–morrow. The bargain was finished, for he had bought it. There was no necessity for his going, and the next day would have done quite as well as to–day; so the 'must' was entirely in his own mind. That is to say, a great many of us mask inclinations under the garb of imperative duties and say, 'We are so pressed by necessary obligations and engagements that we really have not got any time to attend to these higher questions which you are trying to press upon us.' You remember the old story. 'I must live,' said the thief. 'I do not see the necessity,' said the judge. A man says, 'I *must* be at business to–morrow morning at half–past eight. How can I think about religion?' Well, if you really *must*, you *can* think about it. But if you are only juggling and deceiving yourself with inclinations that pose as necessities, the sooner the veil is off the better, and you understand whereabouts you are, and what is your true position in reference to the Gospel of Jesus Christ.

But then let me, only in a word, remind you that the other side of the excuse is a very operative one. 'I have married a wife, and therefore I cannot come.' There are some of us around whom the strong grasp of earthly affections is flung so embracingly and sweetly that we cannot, as we think, turn our loves upward and fix them upon God. Fathers and mothers, husbands and wives, parents and children, remember Christ's deep words, 'A man's foes shall be they of his own household'; and be sure that the prediction is fulfilled many a time by the hindrances of their love even more than by the opposition of their hatred.

All these excuses refer to legitimate things. It is perfectly right that the man should go and see after his field, perfectly right that the ten bullocks should be harnessed and tried, perfectly right that the sweetness of wedded love should be tasted and drunk, perfectly wrong that any of them should be put as a reason for not accepting Christ's offer. Let us take the lesson that legitimate business and lawful and pure affections may ruin a soul, and may constitute the hindrance that blocks its road to God.

Brethren, I said that these were flimsy excuses. I shall have to explain what I mean by that in a moment. As excuses they are flimsy; but as reasons which actually operate with hundreds of people, preventing them from being Christians, they are not flimsy; they are most solid and real. Our Lord does not mean them as exhaustive. There are a great many other grounds upon which different types of character turn away from the offered blessings of the Gospel, which do not come within view of the parable. But although not exhaustive they are widely operative. I wonder how many men and women there are listening to me now of whom it is true that they are so busy with their daily occupations that they have not time to be religious, and of how many men, and perhaps more especially women, among us at this moment it is true that their hearts are so ensnared with loves that belong to earth—beautiful and potentially sacred and elevating as these are—that they have not time to turn themselves to the one eternal Lover of their souls. Let me beseech you, dear friends—and you especially who are strangers to this place and to my voice—to do what I cannot, and would not if I could, lay these thoughts on your own hearts, and ask yourselves, 'Is it I?'

And then before I pass from this point of my discourse, remember that the contrariety between these duties and the acceptance of the offered feast existed only in the imagination of the men that made them. There is no reason why you should not go to the feast and see after your field. There is no reason why you should not love your wife and go to the feast. God's summons comes into collision with many wishes, but with no duties or legitimate occupations. The more a man accepts and lives upon the good that Jesus Christ spreads before him, the more fit will he be for all his work, and for all his enjoyments. The field will be better tilled, the bullocks will be better driven, the wife will be more wisely, tenderly, and sacredly loved if in your hearts Christ is enthroned, and whatsoever you do you do as for Him. It is only the excessive and abusive possession of His gifts and absorption in our duties and relations that turns them into impediments in the path of our Christian life. And the flimsiness of the excuse is manifest by the fact that the contrarity is self–created.

III. Lastly, note the real reason.

I have said that as pretexts the three explanations were unsatisfactory. When a man pleads a previous engagement as a reason for not accepting an invitation, nine times out of ten it is a polite way of saying, 'I do not want to go.' It was so in this case. How all these absolute impossibilities, which made it perfectly out of the question that the three recreants should sit down at the table, would have melted into thin air if, by any chance, there had come into their minds a wish to be there! They would have found means to look after the field and the cattle and the home, and to be in their places notwithstanding, if they had wanted. The real reason that underlies men's turning away from Christ's offer is, as I said in the beginning of my remarks, that they do not care to have it. They have no inclinations and no tastes for the higher and purer blessings.

Brother, do not let us lose ourselves in generalities. I am talking about you, and about the set of your inclinations and tastes. And I want you to ask yourself whether it is not a fact that some of you like oxen better than God; whether it is not a fact that if the two were there before you, you would rather have a good big field made over to you than have the food that is spread upon that table.

Well then what is the cause of the perverted inclination? Why is it that when Christ says, 'Child, come to Me, and I will give thee pardon, peace, purity, power, hope, Heaven, Myself,' there is no responsive desire kindled in the heart? Why do I not want God? Why do I not care for Jesus Christ? Why do the blessings about which preachers are perpetually talking seem to me so shadowy, so remote from anything that I need, so ill–fitting to anything that I desire? There must be something very deeply wrong. This is what is wrong, your heart has shaken itself loose from dependence upon God; and you have no love as you ought to have for Him. You prefer to stand alone. The prodigal son, having gone away into the far country, likes the swine's husks better than the bread in his father's house, and it is only when the supply of the latter coarse dainty gives out that the purer taste becomes strong. Strange, is it not? but yet it is true.

Now there are one or two things that I want to say about this indifference, resulting from preoccupation and from alienation, and which hides its ugliness behind all manner of flimsy excuses. One is that the reason itself is utterly unreasonable. I have said the true reason is indifference. Can anybody put into words which do not betray the absurdity of the position, the conduct of the man who says, 'I do not want God; give me five yoke of oxen. That is the real good, and I will stick by that.' There is one mystery in the world, and if it were solved everything would be solved; and that mystery is that men turn away from God and cleave to earth. No account can be given of sin. No account can be given of man's preference for the lesser and the lower; and neglect of the greater and the higher, except to say it is utterly inexplicable and unreasonable.

I need not say such indifference is shameful ingratitude to the yearning love which provides, and the infinite sacrifice by which was provided, this great feast to which we are asked. It cost Christ pains, and tears, and blood, to prepare that feast, and He looks to us, and says to us, 'Come and drink of the wine which I have mingled, and eat of the bread which I have provided at such a cost.' There are monsters of ingratitude, but there are none more miraculously monstrous than the men who look, as some of us are doing, untouched on Christ's sacrifice, and listen unmoved to Christ's pleadings.

The excuses will disappear one day. We can trick our consciences; we can put off the messengers; we cannot deceive the Host. All the thin curtains that we weave to veil the naked ugliness of our unwillingness to accept Christ will be burnt up one day. And I pray you to ask yourselves, 'What shall I say when He comes and asks me, "Why was thy place empty at My table"?' 'And he was speechless.' Do not, dear brethren, refuse that gift, lest you bring upon yourselves the terrible and righteous wrath of the Host whose invitation you are slighting, and at whose table you are refusing to sit.

THE RASH BUILDER

'Which of you, intending to build a tower, sitteth not
down first, and counteth the cost, whether he have
sufficient to finish it?'—LUKE xiv. 28.

Christ sought for no recruits under false pretences, but rather discouraged than stimulated light–hearted adhesion. His constant effort was to sift the crowds that gathered round Him. So here great multitudes are following Him, and how does He welcome them? Does He lay Himself out to attract them? Luke tells us that He *turned* and faced the following multitude; and then, with a steady hand, drenched with cold water the too easily kindled flame. Was that because He did not wish them to follow Him? He desired every soul in that crowd for His own, and He knew that the best way to attract is sometimes to repel; and that a plain statement of the painful consequences of a course will quench no genuine enthusiasm, but may turn a mere flash in the pan into a purpose that will flame through a life.

So our Lord lays down in stringent words the law of discipleship as being self–sacrifice; the abandonment of the dearest, and the acceptance of the most painful. And then He illustrates the law by these two expanded similes or condensed parables, of the rash builder and the rash soldier. Each contains a side of the Christian life, and represents one phase of what a true disciple ought to be. I wish to look with you now at the first of these two comparisons.

I. Consider then, first, the building, or the true aim of discipleship.

The building of the tower represents what every human life ought to aim at, the rearing up of a strong, solid structure in which the builder may dwell and be at rest.

But then remember we are always building, consciously or unconsciously. By our transitory actions we are all rearing up a house for our souls in which we have to dwell; building character from out of the fleeting acts of conduct, which character we have to carry with us for ever. Soft invertebrate animals secrete their own shells. That is what we are doing—making character, which is the shield of self, as it were; and in which we have to abide.

My friend, what are you building? A prison; a mere garden–house of lustful delights; or a temple fortress in which God may dwell reverenced, and you may abide restful? Observe that whilst all men are thus unconsciously and habitually rearing up a permanent abode by their transient actions, every life that is better than a brute's ought to have for its aim the building up of ourselves into firm strength. The development of character is what we ought to ask from, and to secure by, this fleeting life of ours. Not enjoyment; that is a miserable aim. Not the satisfaction of earthly desires; not the prosperity of our business or other ordinary avocations. The demand that we should make upon life, and the aim which we should have clearly before us in all that we do, is that it may contribute to the formation of a pure and noble self, to the development of character into that likeness to Jesus Christ, which is perfection and peace and blessedness.

And while that is true about all life, it is eminently true in regard to the highest form of life, which is the Christian life. There are dreadful mistakes and imperfections in the ordinary vulgar conception of what a Christian is, and what he is a Christian for. What do you think men and women are meant to be Christians for? That they may get away from some material and outward hell? Possibly. That they may get celestial happiness? Certainly. But are these the main things? By no means. What people are meant to be Christians for is that they may be shaped into the likeness of Jesus Christ; or to go back to the metaphor of my text, the meaning and aim of Christian discipleship is not happiness, but the building up of the tower in which the man may dwell.

Ah, friend; is that your notion of what a Christian is; and of what he is a Christian for, to be like the Master? Alas! alas! how few of us, honestly and continually and practically, lay to heart the stringent and grand conception which underlies this metaphor of our Lord's, who identifies the man that was thinking of being His disciple with the man that sits down intending to build a tower.

II. So, secondly, note the cost of the building, or the conditions of discipleship.

Building is an expensive amusement, as many a man who has gone rashly in for bricks and mortar has found out to his cost. And the most expensive of all sorts of building is the building up of Christian character. That costs more than anything else, but there are a number of other things less noble and desirable, which share with it, to some extent, in the expenditure which it involves.

Discipleship demands constant reference to the plan. A man that lives as he likes, by impulse, by inclination, or ignobly yielding to the pressure of circumstances and saying, 'I could not help myself, I was carried away by the flood,' or 'Everybody round about me is doing it, and I could not be singular'—will never build anything worth living in. It will be a born ruin—if I may so say. There must be continual reference to the plan. That is to say, if a man is to do anything worth doing, there must be a very clear marking out to himself of what he means to secure by life, and a keeping of the aim continually before him as his guide and his pole–star. Did you ever see the pretty architect's plans, that were all so white and neat when they came out of his office, after the masons have done with them—all thumb–marked and dirty? I wonder if your Bibles are like that? Do we refer to the standard of conduct with anything like the continual checking of our work by the architect's intention, which every man who builds anything that will stand is obliged to practise? Consult your plan, the pattern of your Master, the words of your Redeemer, the gospel of your God, the voice of judgment and conscience, and get into the habit of living, not like a vegetable, upon what happens to be nearest its roots, nor like a brute, by the impulses of the unreasoning nature, but clear above these put the understanding, and high above that put the conscience, and above them all put the will of the Lord. Consult your plan if you want to build your tower.

Then, further, another condition is continuous effort. You cannot 'rush' the building of a great edifice. You have to wait till the foundations get consolidated, and then by a separate effort every stone has to be laid in its bed and out of the builder's hands. So by slow degrees, with continuity of effort, the building rises.

Now there has been a great deal of what I humbly venture to call one−sidedness talked about the way by which Christian character is to be developed and perfected. And one set of the New Testament metaphors upon that subject has been pressed to the exclusion of the others, and the effortless growth of the plant has been presented as if it were the complete example of Christian progress. I know that Jesus Christ has said: 'First the blade, then the ear; after that the full corn in the ear.' But I know that He has also said, 'Which of you, intending to build a tower'—and that involves the idea of effort; and that He has further said, 'Or what king, going to make war against another king'—and that involves the idea of antagonism and conflict. And so, on the whole, I lay it down that this is one of the conditions of building the tower, that the energy of the builder should never slacken, but, with continual renewal of effort, he should rear his life's building.

And then, still further, there is the fundamental condition of all; and that is, self−surrender. Our Lord lays this down in the most stringent terms in the words before my text, where He points to two directions in which that spirit is required to manifest itself. One is detachment from persons that are dearest, and even from one's own selfish life; the other is the acceptance of things that are most contrary to one's inclinations, against the grain, painful and hard to bear. And so we may combine these two in this statement: If any man is going to build a Christlike life he will have to detach himself from surrounding things and dear ones, and to crucify self by suppression of the lower nature and the endurance of evils. The preceding parable which is connected in subject with the text, the story of the great supper, and the excuses made for not coming to it, represents two−thirds of the refusals as arising from the undue love for, and regard to, earthly possessions, and the remaining third as arising from the undue love to, and regard for, the legitimate objects of affection. And these are the two chords that hold most of us most tightly. It is not Christianity alone, dear brethren, that says that if you want to do anything worth doing, you must detach yourself from outward wealth. It is not Christianity alone that says that, if you want to build up a noble life, you must not let earthly love dominate and absorb your energy; but it is Christianity that says so most emphatically, and that has best reason to say so.

Concentration is the secret of all excellence. If the river is to have any scour in it that will sweep away pollution and corruption, it must not go winding and lingering in many curves, howsoever flowery may be the banks, nor spreading over a broad bed, but you must straighten it up and make it deep that it may run strong. And if you will diffuse yourself all over these poor, wretched worldly goods, or even let the rush of your heart's outflow go in the direction of father and mother, wife and children, brethren and sisters, forgetting Him, then you will never come to any good nor be of use in this world. But if you want to be Christians after Christ's pattern, remember that the price of the building is rigidly to sacrifice self, 'to scorn delights and live laborious days,' and to keep all vagrant desires and purposes within rigid limits, and absolutely subordinated to Himself.

On the other hand, there is to be the acceptance of what is painful to the lower nature. Unpleasant consequences of duty have to be borne, and the lower self, with its appetites and desires, has to be crucified. The vine must be mercilessly pruned in tendrils, leaves, and branches even, though the rich sap may seem to bleed away to waste, if we are to grow precious grapes out of which may be expressed the wine of the Kingdom. We must be dead to much if we are to be alive to anything worth living for.

Now remember that Christ's demand of self–surrender, self–sacrifice, continuous effort, rigid limitation, does not come from any mere false asceticism, but is inevitable in the very nature of the case, and is made also by all worthy work. How much every one of us has had to shear off our lives, how many tastes we have had to allow to go ungratified, how many capacities undeveloped, in how many directions we have had to hedge up our way, and not do, or be this, that, or the other; if we have ever done anything in any direction worthy the doing! Concentration and voluntary limitation, in order to fix all powers on the supreme aim which judgment and conscience have enjoined is the condition of all excellence, of all sanity of living, and eminently of all Christian discipleship.

III. Further, note the failures.

The tower of the rash builder stands a gaunt, staring ruin.

Whosoever throws himself upon great undertakings or high aims, without a deliberate forecast of the difficulties and sacrifices they involve, is sure to stop almost before he has begun. Many a man and woman leaves the starting–point with a rush, as if they were going to be at the goal presently, and before they have run fifty yards turn aside and quietly walk out of the course. I wonder how many of you began, when you were lads or girls, to study some language, and stuck before you had got through twenty pages of the grammar, or to learn some art, and have still got the tools lying unused in a dusty corner. And how many of you who call yourselves Christians began in the same fashion long ago to run the race? 'Ye did run well.' What did hinder you? What hindered Atalanta? The golden apples that were flung down on the path. Oh, the Church is full of these abortive Christians; ruins from their beginning, standing gaunt and windowless, the ground–plan a great palace, the reality a hovel that has not risen a foot for the last ten years. I wonder if there are any stunted Christians of that sort in this congregation before me, who began under the influence of some impulse or emotion, genuine enough, no doubt, but who had taken no account of how much it would cost to finish the building. And so the building is not finished, and never will be.

But I should remark here that what I am speaking about as failure is not incomplete attainment of the aim. For all our lives have to confess that they incompletely attain their aim; and lofty aims, imperfectly realised, and still maintained, are the very salt of life, and beautiful 'as the new moon with a ragged edge, e'en in its imperfection beautiful.' Paul was an old man and an advanced Christian when he said, 'Not as though I had already attained, either were already perfect, but I follow after.'

218

And the highest completeness to which the Christian builder can reach in this life is the partial accomplishment of his aim and the persistent adherence to and aspiration after the unaccomplished aim. It is not these incomplete but progressive and aspiring lives that are failures, but it is the lives of men who have abandoned high aims, and have almost forgotten that they ever cherished them.

And what does our Lord say about such? That everybody laughs at them. It is not more than they deserve. An out–and–out Christian will often be disliked, but if he is made a mock of there will be a *soupcon* of awe and respect even in the mockery. Half–and–half Christians get, and richly deserve, the curled lip and sarcasm of a world that knows when a man is in earnest, and knows when he is an incarnate sham.

IV. Lastly, I would have you observe the inviting encouragement hidden in the apparent repelling warning.

If we read my text isolated, it may seem as if the only lesson that our Lord meant to be drawn from it was a counsel of despair. 'Unless you feel quite sure that you can finish, you had better not begin.' Is that what He meant to say? I think not. He did mean to say, 'Do not begin without opening your eyes to what is involved in the beginning.' But suppose a man had taken His advice, had listened to the terms, and had said, 'I cannot keep them, and I am going to fling all up, and not try any more'—is that what Jesus Christ wanted to bring him to? Surely not. And that it is not so arises plainly enough from the observation that this parable and the succeeding one are both sealed up, as it were, with 'So likewise, whosoever he be of you that forsaketh not all that he hath, he cannot be My disciple.'

Now, if I may so say, there are two kinds of 'forsaking all that we have.' One is the forsaking by which we become disciples; and the other the forsaking by which we continue true disciples. The conviction that they had not sufficient to finish is the very conviction that Christ wished to root in the minds of the crowds. He exhibits the difficulties in order that they may feel they cannot cope with them. What then? That they may 'forsake' all their own power to cope with them.

That is the first kind of 'forsaking all that we have.' That makes a disciple. The recognition of my own utter impotence to do the things which yet I see must be done, is the underside of trust in Him. And that trust in Him brings the power that makes it possible for us to do the things which we cannot of ourselves do, and the consciousness of the impotence to do which is the first step toward doing them. It is the self–sufficient man who is sure to be bankrupt before he has finished his building; but he who has no confidence in himself, and recognises the fact that he cannot build, will go to Jesus Christ and say, 'Lord, I am poor and needy. Come Thou Thyself and be my strength.' Such a forsaking of all that we have in the recognition of our own poverty and powerlessness brings into the field an Ally for our reinforcement that has more than the twenty thousand that are coming against us, and will make us strong.

And then, if, knowing our weakness, our misery, our poverty, and cleaving to Jesus Christ in simple confidence in His divine power breathed into our weakness, and His abundant riches lavished upon our poverty, we cast ourselves into the work to which He calls us by His grace, then we shall find that the sweet and certain assurance that we have Him for the possession and the treasure of our lives will make parting with everything else, not painful, but natural and necessary and a joy, as the expression of our supreme love to Him. It should not, and would not be difficult to fling away paste gems and false riches if our hands were filled with the jewels that Christ bestows. And it will not be difficult to slay the old man when the new Christ lives in us, by our faith and submission.

So, dear brethren, it all comes to this. We are all builders; what kind of a work is your life's work going to turn out? Are you building on the foundation, taking Jesus Christ for the anchor of your hope, for the basis of your belief, for the crown of your aims, for your all and in all? Are you building upon Him? If so, then the building will stand when the storm comes and the 'hail sweeps away the refuges' that other men have built elsewhere. But are you building on that foundation the gold of self–denial, the silver of white purity, the precious stones of variously–coloured and Christlike virtues? Then your work will indeed be incomplete, but its very incompleteness will be a prophecy of the time when 'the headstone shall be brought forth with shoutings'; and you may humbly trust that the day which 'declares every man's work of what sort it is' will not destroy yours, but that it will gleam and flash in the light of the revealing and reflecting fires. See to it that you are building *for* eternity, *on* the foundation, *with* the fair stones which Jesus Christ gives to all those who let Him shape their lives. He is at once, Architect, Material, Foundation; and in Him 'every several building fitly framed together groweth into a holy temple in the Lord.'

'THAT WHICH WAS LOST'

'An hundred sheep ... ten pieces of silver,... two
sons.'—LUKE XV. 4,8,11.

The immediate occasion of these three inimitable parables, which have found their way to the heart of the world, needs to be remembered in order to grasp their import and importance. They are intended to vindicate Christ's conduct in associating with outcasts and disreputable persons whom His Pharisaical critics thought a great deal too foul to be touched by clean hands. They were not meant to set forth with anything like completeness either what wanderers had to do to go back to God, or what God had done to bring wanderers back to Himself. If this had been remembered, many misconceptions, widespread and mischievous, especially affecting the meaning of the last of the three parables—that of the Prodigal Son—would have been avoided. The purpose of the parables accounts for Christ's accepting the division which His antagonists made of men, into 'righteous,' like themselves, and 'unclean,' like the publicans and sinners. There was a far deeper truth to be spoken about the condition of humanity than that. But for the purposes of His argument Christ passes it by. The remembrance of the intention of the parables explains their incompleteness as a statement of what people call 'the way of salvation.' They were not meant to teach us that, but they were meant to show us that a human instinct which prizes lost things because they are lost has something corresponding to it in the divine nature, and so to vindicate the conduct of Christ.

I venture to isolate these three statements of the subjects of the parables, because I think that looking at the threefold aspect in which the one general thought is presented may help us to some useful considerations.

I. I ask you, then, to look with me, first, at the varying causes of loss.

The sheep was lost, the *drachma* was lost, the son was lost. But in each case the reason for the loss was different. Whilst I would avoid all fanciful inserting into our Lord's words of more than they can fairly bear, I would also avoid superficial evacuating them of any of their depth of significance. So I think it is not unintentional nor unimportant that in these three metaphors there are set forth three obviously distinct operative causes for man's departure from God.

The sheep did not intend to go anywhere, either to keep with or to leave the shepherd. It simply knew that grass was sweet, and that there, ahead of it, was another tuft, and it went after that. So it nibbled itself away out of the path, out of the shepherd's care, out of the flock's companionship. It was heedless; and therefore it was lost.

Now that is a fair statement of facts in regard to thousands of men, of whom I have no doubt there are some listening to me now. They do not intend any mischief, they have no purpose of rebellion or transgression, but they live what we call animal lives. The sheep knows only where the herbage is abundant and fresh: and it goes there. An animal has no foresight, and is the happier because it cannot look before and after. It has only a rudimentary conscience, if it has that. Its inclinations are restrained by no sense of obligation. Many men live just so, without restraint upon appetite, without checking of inclination, without foresight except of the material good which a certain course of conduct may get. So, all unwitting, meaning no mischief, they wander further and further from the right road, and find themselves at last in a waterless desert.

Dear friends, am I speaking to any now who have too much yielded to inclinations, who have been unwilling to look forward to the end, and ask themselves what all will come to at the last, and who scarcely know what it is to take heed unto their ways, except in so far as worldly prudence may dictate certain courses of conduct for the purpose of securing certain worldly and perishable ends? I would plead, especially with the younger portion of my congregation, to take the touching picture of this first parable as a solemn prophecy of what certainly befalls every man who sets out upon his path without careful consideration of whither it leads to at the last; and who lives for the present, in any of its forms, and who lets himself be led by inclinations or appetites. The animal does so, and, as a rule, its instincts are its sufficient guide. But you and I are blessed or cursed, as the case may be, with higher powers, which, if we do not use, we shall certainly land in the desert. If a man who is meant to guide himself by intelligence, reason, will, foresight, conscience, chooses to go down to the level of the beast, the faculties that serve the beast will not serve the man. And even the sheep is lost from the flock if it yields only to these.

But how it speaks of the Lord's tender sympathy for the wanderers that He should put in the forefront of the parables this explanation of the condition of men, and should not at first charge it upon them as sin, but only as heedlessness and folly! There is much that in itself is wrong and undesirable, the criminality of which is diminished by the fact that it was heedlessly done, though the heedlessness itself is a crime.

Now turn to the second parable. The coin was heavy, so it fell; it was round, so it rolled; it was dead, so it lay. And there are people who are things rather than persons, so entirely have they given up their wills, and so absolutely do they let themselves be determined by circumstances. It was not the *drachma* that lost itself, but it was the law of gravitation that lost it, and it had no power of resistance.

Expositions Of Holy Scripture

This also is an explanation—partial, as I shall have to show you in a moment, but still real,—of a great deal of human wandering. There are masses of men who have no more power to resist the pressure of circumstances and temptations than the piece of silver had when it dropped from the woman's open palm and trundled away into some dark corner. That lightens the darkness of much of the world's sin.

But for you to abnegate the right and power of resisting circumstances is to abdicate the sovereignty with which God has crowned you. All men are shaped by externals, but the shape which the externals impose upon us is settled by ourselves. Here are two men, for instance, exposed to precisely the same conditions: but one of them yields, and is ruined; the other resists, and is raised and strengthened. As Jesus Christ, so all things have a double operation. They are 'either a savour of life unto life or a savour of death unto death.' There is the stone. You may build upon it, or you may stumble over it: you take your choice. Here is the adverse circumstance. You may rule it, or you may let it rule you. Circumstances and outward temptations are the fool's masters, and the wise man's servants. It all depends on the set of the sail and the firmness of the hand that grasps the tiller, which way the wind shall carry the ship. The same breeze speeds vessels on directly opposite courses, and so the same circumstances may drive men in two contrary directions, sending the one further and further away from, and drawing the other nearer and nearer to, the haven of their hearts.

Dear friends, as we have to guard against the animal life of yielding to inclinations and inward impulse, of forgetting the future, and of taking no heed to our paths, so, unless we wish to ruin ourselves altogether, we have to fight against the mechanical life which, with a minimum of volition, lets the world do with us what it will. And sure I am that there are men and women in this audience at this time who have let their lives be determined by forces that have swept them away from God.

In the third parable the foolish boy had no love to his father to keep him from emigrating. He wanted to be his own master, and to get away into a place where he thought he could sow his wild oats and no news of it ever reach the father's house. He wanted to have the fingering of the money, and to enjoy the sense of possession. And so he went off on his unblessed road to the harlots and the swine's trough.

And *that* is no parable; that is a picture. The other two were parabolical representations; this is the thing itself. For carelessness of the bonds that knit a heart to God; hardness of an unresponsive heart unmelted by benefits; indifference to the blessedness of living by a Father's side and beneath His eye; the uprising of a desire of independence and the impatience of control; the exercise of self will—these are causes of loss that underlie the others of which I have been speaking, and which make for every one of us the essential sinfulness of our sin. It is rebellion, and it is rebellion against a Father's love.

Now, notice, that whilst the other two that we have been speaking about do partially explain the terrible fact that we go away from God, their explanation is only partial, and this grimmer truth underlies them. There are modern theories, as there were ancient ones, that say: 'Oh! sin is a theological bugbear. There is not any such thing. It is only indifference, ignorance, error.' And then there are other theorists that say: 'Sin! There is no sin in following natural laws and impulses. Circumstances shape men; heredity shapes them. The notion that their actions are criminal is a mere figment of an exploded superstition.'

Yes! and down below the ignorance, and inadvertence, and error, and heredity, and domination of externals, there lies the individual choice in each case. The man knows—however he sophisticates himself, or uses other people to provide him with sophistries—that he need not have done that thing unless he had chosen to do it. You cannot get beyond or argue away that consciousness. And so I say that all these immoral teachings, which are very common to–day, omit from the thing that they profess to analyse the very characteristic element of it, which is, as our Lord taught us, not the following inclination like a silly sheep; not the rolling away, in obedience to natural law, like the drachma; but the rising up of a rebellious will that desires a separation, and kicks against control, as in the case of the son.

So, dear friends, whilst I thankfully admit that much of the darkness of human conduct may be lightened by the representations of our two first parables, I cannot but feel that we have to leave to God the determination in each case of how far these have diminished individual criminality; and that we have to remember for ourselves that our departure from God is not explicable unless we recognise the fact that we have chosen rather to be away from Him than to be with Him; and that we like better to have our goods at our own disposal, and to live as it pleases ourselves.

II. So note, secondly, the varying proportions of loss and possession.

A hundred sheep; ten drachmas; two sons. The loss in one case is 1 per cent., a trifle; in the other case 10 per cent., more serious; in the last case 50 per cent., heartbreaking. Now, I do not suppose that our Lord intended any special significance to be attached to these varying numbers. Rather they were simply suggested by the cast of the parable in which they respectively occurred. A hundred sheep is a fair average flock; ten pieces of silver are the modest hoard of a poor woman; two sons are a family large enough to represent the contrast which is necessary to the parable. But still we may permissibly look at this varying proportion in order to see whether it, too, cannot teach us something.

It throws light upon the owner's care and pains in seeking. In one aspect, these are set forth most strikingly by the parable in which the thing lost bears the smallest proportion to the thing still retained. The shepherd might well have said: 'One in a hundred does not matter much. I have got the ninety and nine.' But he went to look for it. But, in another aspect, the woman, of course, has a more serious loss to face, and possibly seeks with more anxiety. And when you come up to the last case, where half the household is blotted out, as it were, then we can see the depth of anxiety and pains and care which must necessarily follow.

But beyond the consideration that the ascending proportion suggests increasing pains and anxiety, there is another lesson, which seems to me even more precious, and it is this, that it matters very little to the loser how much he keeps, or what the worth of the lost thing is. There is something in human nature which makes anything that is lost precious by reason of its loss. Nobody can tell how large a space a tree fills until it is felled. If you lose one tiny stone out of a ring, or a bracelet, it makes a gap, and causes annoyance altogether disproportionate to the lustre that it had when it was there. A man loses a small portion of his fortune in some unlucky speculation, and the loss annoys him a great deal more than the possession solaced him, and he thinks more about the hundreds that have vanished than about the thousands that remain. Men are made so. It is a human instinct, that apart altogether from the consideration of its intrinsic worth, and the proportion it bears to that which is still possessed, the lost thing draws, and the loser will take any pains to find it.

So Christ says, When a woman will light a candle and sweep the house and search diligently till she finds her lost sixpence (for the drachma was worth little more), and will bring in all her neighbours to rejoice with her, that is like God; and the human instinct which prizes lost things, not because of their value, but because they are lost, has something corresponding to it in the heart of the Majesty of the heavens. It is Christ's vindication, of course, as I need not remind you, of His own conduct. He says in effect, to these Pharisees, 'You are finding fault with Me for doing what we all do. I am only acting in accordance with a natural human instinct; and when I thus act God Himself is acting in and through Me.'

If I had time, I think I could show that this principle, brought out in my texts, really sweeps away one of the difficulties which modern science has to suggest against Evangelical Christianity. We hear it said, 'How can you suppose that a speck of a world like this, amidst all these flaming orbs that stud the infinite depths of the heavens, is of so much importance in God's sight that His Son came down to die for it?' The magnitude of the world, as compared with others, has nothing to do with the question. God's action is determined by its moral condition. If it be true that here is sin, which rends men away from Him, and that so they are lost, then it is supremely natural that all the miracles of the Christian revelation should follow. The *rationale* of the Incarnation lies in this, 'A certain man had a hundred sheep.... One of them went astray ... and He went into the wilderness and found it.'

III. Now I meant to have said a word about the varying glimpses that we have here, into God's claims upon us, and His heart.

Ownership is the word that describes His relation to us in the first two parables; love is the word that describes it in the third. But the ownership melts into love, because God does not reckon that He possesses men by natural right of creation or the like, unless they yield their hearts to Him, and give themselves, by their own joyful self—surrender, into His hands. But I must not be tempted to speak upon that matter; only, before I close, let me point you to that most blessed and heart—melting thought, that God accounts Himself to have lost something when a man goes away from Him.

That word 'the lost' has another, and in some senses a more tragical, significance in Scripture. The lost are lost to themselves and to blessedness. The word implies destruction; but it also carries with it this, that God prizes us, is glad to have us, and, I was going to say, feels an incompleteness in His possessions when men depart from Him.

Oh, brethren, surely such a thought as that should melt us; and if, as is certainly the case, we have strayed away from Him into green pastures, which have ended in a wilderness, without a blade of grass; or if we have rolled away from Him in passive submission to circumstances; or if we have risen up in rebellion against Him, and claimed our separate right of possession and use of the goods that fall to us, if we would only think that He considers that He has lost us, and prizes us because we are lost to Him, and wants to get us back again, surely, surely it would draw us to Himself. Think of the greatness of the love into which the ownership is merged, as measured by the infinite price which He has paid to bring us back, and let us all say, 'I will arise and go to my Father.'

THE PRODIGAL AND HIS FATHER

'And He said, A certain man had two sons: 12. And the
younger of them said to his father, Father, give me
the portion of goods that falleth to me. And he
divided unto them his living. 13. And not many days
after the younger son gathered all together, and took
his journey into a far country, and there wasted his
substance with riotous living. 14. And when he had
spent all, there arose a mighty famine in that land;
and he began to be in want. 15. And he went and joined
himself to a citizen of that country; and he sent him
into his fields to feed swine. 16. And he would fain
have filled his belly with the husks that the swine
did eat: and no man gave unto him. 17. And when he
came to himself, he said, How many hired servants of
my father's have bread enough, and to spare, and I
perish with hunger! 18. I will arise and go to my
father, and will say unto him, Father, I have sinned
against Heaven, and before thee, 19. And am no more
worthy to be called thy son: make me as one of thy
hired servants. 20. And he arose, and came to his
father. But when he was yet a great way off, his
father saw him, and had compassion, and ran, and fell
on his neck, and kissed him. 21. And the son said unto
him, Father, I have sinned against Heaven, and in thy
sight, and am no more worthy to be called thy son.
22. But the father said to his servants, Bring forth
the best robe, and put it on him; and put a ring on
his hand, and shoes on his feet: 23. And bring hither
the fatted calf, and kill it; and let us eat, and be
merry: 24. For this my son was dead, and is alive
again; he was lost, and is found. And they began to
be merry.'—LUKE xv. 11–24.

The purpose of the three parables in this chapter has to be kept in mind. Christ is vindicating His action in receiving sinners, which had evoked the murmurings of the Pharisees. The first two parables, those of the lost sheep and the lost drachma, appeal to the common feeling which attaches more importance to lost property just because it is lost than to that which is possessed safely. This parable rises to a higher level. It appeals to the universal emotion of fatherhood, which yearns over a wandering child just because he has wandered.

We note a further advance, in the proportion of one stray sheep to the ninety–nine, and of one lost coin to the nine, contrasted with the sad equality of obedience and disobedience in the two sons. One per cent., ten per cent., are bearable losses, but fifty per cent. is tragic.

I. The first part (vs. 11–16) tells of the son's wish to be his own master, and what came of it. The desire to be independent is good, but when it can only be attained by being dependent on him whose authority is irksome, it takes another colour. This foolish boy wished to be able to use his father's property as his own, but he had to get the father's consent first. It is a poor beginning of independence when it has to be set up in business by a gift.

That is the essential absurdity in our attempts to do without God and to shake off His control. We can only get power to seem to do it by misusing His gifts. When we say, 'Who is Lord over us?' the tongues which say it were given us by Him. The next step soon followed. 'Not many days after,' of course, for the sense of ownership could not be kept up while near the father. A man who wishes to enjoy worldly good without reference to God is obliged, in self–defence, to hustle God out of his thoughts as soon and as completely as possible.

The 'far country' is easily reached; and it is far, though a step can land us in it. A narrow bay may compel a long journey round its head before those on its opposite shores can meet. Sin takes us far away from God, and the root of all sin is that desire of living to one's self which began the prodigal's evil course.

The third step in his downward career, wasting his substance in riotous living, comes naturally after the two others; for all self–centred life is in deepest truth waste, and the special forms of gross dissipation to which youth is tempted are only too apt to follow the first sense of being their own masters, and removed from the safeguards of their earthly father's home. Many a lad in our great cities goes through the very stages of the parable, and, when a mother's eye is no longer on him, plunges into filthy debauchery. But living which does not outrage the proprieties may be riotous all the same; for all conduct which ignores God and asserts self as supreme is flagrantly against the very nature of man, and is reckless waste.

Such a 'merry' life is sure to be 'short.' There is always famine in the land of forgetfulness of God, and when the first gloss is off its enjoyments, and one's substance is spent, its pinch is felt. The unsatisfied hunger of heart, which dogs godless living, too often leads but to deeper degradation and closer entanglement with low satisfactions. Men madly plunge deeper into the mud in hope of finding the pearl which has thus far eluded their search.

A miserable thing this young fool had made of his venture, having spent his capital, and now being forced to become a slave, and being set to nothing better than to feed swine. The godless world is a hard master, and has very odious tasks for its bondsmen. The unclean animals are fit companions for one who made himself lower than they, since filth is natural to them and shameful for him. They are better off than he is, for husks do nourish them, and they get their fill, but he who has sunk to longing for swine's food cannot get even that. The dark picture is only too often verified in the experience of godless men.

II. The wastrel's returning sanity is described in verses 17–20_a. 'He came to himself.' Then he had been beside himself before. It is insanity to try to shake off God, to aim at independence, to wander from Him, to fling away our 'substance,' that is, our true selves, and to starve among the swine–troughs. He remembers the bountiful housekeeping at home, as starving men dream of feasts, and he thinks of himself with a kind of pity and amazement.

There is no sign that his conscience smote him, or that his heart woke in love to his father. His stomach, and it only, urged him to go home. He did, indeed, feel that he had been wrong, and had forfeited the right to be called a son, but he did not care much for losing that name, or even for losing the love to which it had the right, if only he could get as much to eat as one of the hired servants, whose relation to the master was less close, and, in patriarchal times, less happy, than that of slaves born in the house.

One good thing about the lad was that he did not let the grass grow under his feet, but, as soon as he had made the resolution, began to carry it into effect. The bane of many a resolve to go back to God is that it is 'sicklied o'er' by procrastination. The ragged prodigal has not much to leave which need hold him, but many such a one says, 'I will arise and go to my father to-morrow,' and lets all the to-morrows become yesterdays, and is sitting among the swine still.

Low as the prodigal's motive for return was, the fact of his return was enough. So is it in regard to our attitude to the gospel. Men may be drawn to give heed to its invitations from the instinct of self-preservation, or from their sense of hungry need, and the belief that in it they will find the food they crave for, while there may be little consciousness of longing for more from the Father than the satisfaction of felt wants. The longing for a place in the Father's heart will spring up later, but the beginning of most men's taking refuge in God as revealed in Christ is the gnawing of a hungry heart. The call to all is, 'Ho, every one that thirsteth, come ye to the waters, and he that hath no money; come ye, buy, and eat.'

III. The climax of the parable, for which all the rest is but as scaffolding, is the father's welcome (vs. 20_b–24). Filial love may die in the son's heart, but paternal yearning lives in the father's. The wanderer's heart would be likely to sink as he came nearer the father's tent. It had seemed easy to go back when he acted the scene in imagination, but every step homewards made the reality more difficult.

No doubt he hesitated when the old home came in sight, and perhaps his resolution would have oozed out at his finger ends if he had had to march up alone in his rags, and run the gauntlet of servants before he came to speech with his father. So his father's seeing him far off and running to meet him is exquisitely in keeping, as well as movingly setting forth how God's love goes out to meet His returning prodigals. That divine insight which discerns the first motions towards return, that divine pity which we dare venture to associate with His infinite love, that eager meeting the shamefaced and slow-stepping boy half-way, and that kiss of welcome before one word of penitence or request had been spoken, are all revelations of the heart of God, and its outgoings to every wanderer who sets his face to return.

Beautifully does the father's welcome make the son's completion of his rehearsed speech impossible. It does not prevent his expression of penitence, for the more God's love is poured over us, the more we feel our sin. But he had already been treated as a son, and could not ask to be taken as a servant. Beautifully, too, the father gives no verbal answer to the lad's confession, for his kiss had answered it already; but he issues instructions to the servants which show that the pair have now reached the home and entered it together.

The gifts to the prodigal are probably significant. They not only express in general the cordiality of the welcome, but seem to be capable of specific interpretations, as representing various aspects of the blessed results of return to God. The robe is the familiar emblem of character. The prodigal son is treated like the high–priest in Zechariah's vision; his rags are stripped off, and he is clothed anew in a dress of honour. 'Them he also justified: and whom he justified, them he also sanctified.' The ring is a token of wealth, position, and honour. It is also a sign of delegated authority, and is an ornament to the hand. So God gives His prodigals, when they come back, an elevation which unforgiven beings do not reach, and sets them to represent Him, and arrays them in strange beauty. No doubt the lad had come back footsore and bleeding, and the shoes may simply serve to keep up the naturalness of the story. But probably they suggest equipment for the journey of life. That is one of the gifts that accompany forgiveness. Our feet are shod with the preparedness of the gospel of peace.

Last of all comes the feast. Heaven keeps holiday when some poor waif comes shrinking back to the Father. The prodigal had been content to sink his sonship for the sake of a loaf, but he could not get bread on such terms. He had to be forgiven and bathed in the outflow of his father's love before he could be fed; and, being thus received, he could not but be fed. The feast is for those who come back penitently, and are received forgivingly, and endowed richly by the Father in heaven.

GIFTS TO THE PRODIGAL

'... Bring forth the best robe, and put it on him; and
put a ring on his hand, and shoes on his feet: 23. And
bring hither the fatted calf, and kill it....'
—LUKE XV. 22, 23.

God's giving always follows His forgiving. It is not so with us. We think ourselves very magnanimous when we pardon; and we seldom go on to lavish favours where we have overlooked faults. Perhaps it is right that men who have offended against men should earn restoration by acts, and should have to ride quarantine, as it were, for a time. But I question whether forgiveness is ever true which is not, like God's, attended by large–hearted gifts. If pardon is only the non–infliction of penalty, then it is natural enough that it should be considered sufficient by itself, and that the evildoer should not be rewarded for having been bad. But if pardon is the outflow of the love of the offended to the offender, then it can scarcely be content with simply giving the debtor his discharge, and turning him into the world penniless.

However that may be with regard to men, God's forgiveness is essentially the communication of God's love to us sinners, as if we had never sinned at all. And, that being so, that love cannot stay its working until it has given all that it can bestow or we can receive. God does not do things by halves; and He always gives when He forgives.

Now that is the great truth of the last part of this immortal parable. And it is one of the points in which it differs from, and towers high above, the two preceding ones. The lost sheep was carried back to the pastures, turned loose there, needed no further special care, and began to nibble as if nothing

228

had happened. The lost drachma was simply put back in the woman's purse. But the lost son was pardoned, and, being pardoned, was capable of receiving, and received, greater gifts than he had before. These gifts are very remarkably detailed in the words of our text.

Now, of course, it is always risky to seek for a spiritual interpretation of every point in a parable, many of which points are mere drapery. But, on the other hand, we may very easily fall into the error of treating as insignificant details which really are meant to be full of instruction. And I cannot help thinking—although many would differ from me,—that this detailed enumeration of the gifts to the prodigal is meant to be translated into the terms of spiritual experience. So I desire to look at them as suggesting for us the gifts of God which accompany forgiveness. I take the catalogue as it stands—the Robe, the Ring, the Shoes, the Feast.

I. First, the Robe.

'Bring forth the best robe, and put it on him.' That was the command. This detail, of course, like all the others, refers back to, and casts light upon, the supposed condition of the spendthrift when he came back. There he stood, ragged, with the stain of travel and the stench of the pig–sty upon his garments, some of them, no doubt, remains of the tawdry finery that he had worn in the world; wine–spots, and stains, and filth of all sorts on the rags. The father says, 'Take them all off him, and put the best robe upon him.' What does that mean?

Well, we all know the very familiar metaphor by which qualities of mind, traits of character, and the like are described as being the dress of the spirit. We talk about being 'arrayed in purity,' 'clad in zeal,' 'clothed with humility,' 'vested with power,' and so on. If we turn to Scripture, we find running through it a whole series of instances of this metaphor, which guide us at once to its true meaning. Zechariah saw in vision the high priest standing at the heavenly tribunal, clad in filthy garments. A voice said, 'Take away the filthy garments from him,' and the interpretation is added: 'Behold! I have caused thine iniquity to pass from thee, and I will clothe thee with a change of raiment.' You remember our Lord's parable of the man with a wedding garment. You remember the Apostle Paul's frequent use of the metaphor of 'putting off the old man, putting on the new.' You remember, finally, the visions of the last days, in which the Seer in Patmos saw the armies in heaven that followed their victorious Commander, 'clothed in fine linen, white and pure, which is the righteousness of the saints.' If we put all these together, surely I am not forcing a meaning on a non–significant detail, when I say that here we have shadowed for us the great thought, that the result of the divine forgiveness coming upon a man is that he is clothed with a character which fits him to sit down at his Father's table. They tell us that forgiveness is impossible, because things done must have their consequences, and that character is the slow formation of actions, precipitated, as it were, from our deeds. That is all true. But it does not conflict with this other truth that there may and does come into men's hearts, when they set their faith on Jesus Christ, a new power which transforms the nature and causes old things to pass away.

God's forgiveness revolutionises a life. Similar effects follow even human pardons for small offences. Brute natures are held in by penalties, and to them pardon means impunity, and impunity means licence, and licence means lust. But wherever there is a heart with love to the offended in it, there is nothing that will so fill it with loathing of its past self as the assurance that the offended, though loved, One loves, and is not offended, and that free forgiveness has come. Whether is it the rod or the mother's kiss that makes a child hate its sin most? And if we lift our thoughts to Him, and think how He, up there in the heavens,

'Who mightest vengeance best have took,'

bends over us in frank, free forgiveness, then surely that, more than all punishments or threatenings or terrors, will cause us to turn away from our evil, and to loathe the sins which are thus forgiven. The prophet went very deep when he said, 'Thou shalt be ashamed and confounded, and never open thy mouth any more because of thine iniquity, when I am pacified towards thee for all that thou hast done, saith the Lord.'

But not only so, there is given along with forgiveness, and wrapped up in it, a new power, which makes all things new, and changes a man. It would be a poor Gospel for me to stand up and preach if I had only to proclaim to men the divine forgiveness; and if that only meant that hell's door was barred and some outward heaven was flung open. But the true Gospel offers forgiveness as preliminary to the bestowal of the highest gifts of God. The pardoned man is stripped of his rags and clothed with a new nature which God Himself bestows.

That is what we all need. We have not all been in the pig-sty; we have not all fallen into gross sin. We *have* all turned our backs on our Father; we *have* all wanted to be independent; we *have* all preferred the far-off land to being near home. And, dear brethren, the character that you have made for yourselves clings to you like the poisoned Nessus' shirt to Hercules. You cannot strip it off. You may get part of it away, but you cannot entirely cast it from your limbs, nor free yourselves from the entanglements of its tatters. Go to God, and He will smile away your sin, and His forgiving love will melt the stains and the evil, as the sun this morning drank up the mists; and they who come knowing themselves to be foul, and needing forgiveness, will surely receive from Him 'the fine linen white and pure, the righteousness of saints.'

II. The Ring.

This prodigal lad only wanted to be placed in the position of a slave, but his father said, 'Put a ring on his finger.' The ring is an emblem of wealth, position, honour; that is one signification of this gift to the penitent. Still further, it is an ornament to the hand on which it glistens; that is another. It is a sign of delegated authority and of representative character; as when Joseph was exalted to be the second man in Egypt, and Pharaoh's signet ring was plucked off and placed upon his finger. All these thoughts are, as it seems to me, clustered in, and fairly deducible from, this one detail.

Freedom, exaltation, dignity of position are expressed. And that opens up a thought which needs to be set forth with many reservations, and much guarding, but still is true—viz., that, by the mercy and miraculous loving-kindness and quickening power of God in the Gospel, it is possible that the lower a man falls the higher he may rise. I know, of course, that it is better to be innocent than to be cleansed. I know, and every man that looks into his own heart knows, that forgiven sins may leave scars; that the memory may be loaded with many a foul and many a painful remembrance; that the fetters may be stricken off the limbs, but the marks of them, and the way of walking that they compelled, may persist long after deliverance. But I know, too, that redeemed men are higher in final position than angels that never fell; and that, though it is too much to say that the greater the sinner the greater the saint, it still remains true that sin repented and forgiven may be, as it were, an elevation upon which a man may stand to reach higher than, apparently, he otherwise would in the divine life.

And so, though I do not say to any man, Make the experiment; for, indeed, the poorest of us has sins enough to get all the benefit out of repentance and forgiveness which is included in them, yet, if there is any man here—and I hope there is—saying to himself, 'I have got too low down ever to master this, that, or the other evil; I have stained myself so foully that I cannot hope to have the black marks erased,' I say to such; 'Remember that the man who ended with a ring on his finger, honoured and dignified, was the man that had herded with pigs, and stank, and all but rotted, with his fleshly crimes.' And so nobody need doubt but that for him, however low he has gone, and however far he has gone, there is restoration possible to a higher dignity than the pure spirits that never transgressed at any time God's commandment will ever attain; for he who has within himself the experience of repentance, of pardon, and who has come into living contact with Jesus Christ as Redeemer, can teach angels how blessed it is to be a child of God.

Nor less distinctly are the other two things which I have referred to brought out in this metaphor. Not only is the ring the sign of dignity, but it is also the sign of delegated authority and representative character. God sets poor penitents to be His witnesses in His world, and to do His work here. And a ring is an ornament to the hand that wears it; which being translated is this: where God gives pardon, He gives a strange beauty of character, to which, if a man is true to himself, and to his Redeemer, he will assuredly attain. There should be no lives so lovely, none that flash with so many jewelled colours, as the lives of the men and women who have learned what it is to be miserable, what it is to repent, what it is to be forgiven. So, though our 'hands have been full of blood,' as the prophet says, though they have dabbled in all manner of pollution, though they have been the ready instruments of many evil things, we may all hope that, cleansed and whitened, even our hands will not want the lustre of that adornment which the loving father clasped upon the fingers of his penitent boy.

III. Further, 'Shoes on his feet.'

No doubt he had come back barefooted and filthy and bleeding, and it was needful for the 'keeping' of the narrative that this detail should appear. But I think it is something more than drapery.

Does it not speak to us of equipment for the walk of life? God *does* prepare men for future service, and for every step that they have to take, by giving to them His forgiveness for all that is past. The sense of the divine pardon will in itself fit a man, as nothing else will, for running with patience the race that is set before him. God does communicate, along with His forgiveness, to every one who seeks it, actual power to 'travel on life's common way in cheerful godliness'; and his feet are 'shod with the preparedness of the gospel of peace.'

Ah, brethren, life is a rough road for us all, and for those whose faces are set towards duty, and God, and self-denial, it is especially so, though there are many compensating circumstances. There are places where sharp flints stick up in the path and cut the feet. There are places where rocks jut out for us to stumble over. There are all the trials and sorrows that necessarily attend upon our daily lives, and which sometimes make us feel as if our path were across heated ploughshares, and every step was a separate agony. God will give us, if we go to Him for pardon, that which will defend us against the pains and the sorrows of life. The bare foot is cut by that which the shod foot tramples upon unconscious.

There are foul places on all our paths, over which, when we pass, if we have not something else than our own naked selves, we shall certainly contract defilement. God will give to the penitent man, if he will have it, that which will keep his feet from soil, even when they walk amidst filth. And if, at any time, notwithstanding the defence, some mud should stain the foot, and he that is washed needs again to wash his feet, the Master, with the towel and the basin, will not be far away.

There are enemies and dangers in life. A very important part of the equipment of the soldier in antiquity was the heavy boot, which enabled him to stand fast, and resist the rush of the enemy. God will give to the penitent man, if he will have it, that which will set his foot upon a rock, 'and establish his goings,' and which 'will make him able to withstand in the evil day, and having done all, to stand.'

Brethren, defence, stability, shielding from pains, and protection against evil are all included in this great promise, which each of us may realise, if we will, for ourselves.

IV. Lastly, the Feast.

Now that comes into view in the parable, mainly as teaching us the great truth that Heaven keeps holiday, when some poor waif comes shrinking back to his Father. But I do not touch upon that truth now, though it is the main significance of this last part of the story.

The prodigal was half starving, and the fatted calf was killed 'for him,' as his ill−conditioned brother grumbled. Remember what it was that drove him back—not his heart, nor his conscience, but his stomach. He did not bethink himself to go back, because dormant filial affection woke up, or because a sense that he had been wrong stirred in him, but because he was hungry; and well he might be, when 'the husks that the swine did eat' were luxuries beyond his reach. Thank God for the teaching that even so low a motive as that is accepted by God; and that, if a man goes back, even for no better reason—as long as he does go back, he will be welcomed by the Father. This poor boy was quite content to sink his sonship for the sake of a loaf; and all that he wanted was to stay his hunger. So he had to learn that he could not get bread on the terms that he desired, and that what he wished most was not what he needed first. He had to be forgiven and bathed in the outflow of his father's love before he could be fed. And, being thus received, he could not fail to be fed. So the message for us is, first, forgiveness, and then every hunger of the heart satisfied; all desires met; every needful nourishment communicated, and the true bread ours for ever, if we choose to eat. 'The meek shall eat and be satisfied.'

I need not draw the picture—that picture of which there are many originals sitting in these pews before me—of the men that go for ever roaming with a hungry heart, through all the regions of life separate from God; and whether they seek their nourishment in the garbage of the sty, or whether fastidiously they look for it in the higher nutriment of mind and intellect and heart, still are condemned to be unfilled.

Brethren, 'Why do you spend your money for that ... which satisfies not?' Here is the true way for all desires to be appeased. Go to God in Jesus Christ for forgiveness, and then everything that you need shall be yours. 'I counsel thee to buy of Me ... white raiment that thou mayest be clothed.' 'He that eateth of this bread shall live for ever.'

THE FOLLIES OF THE WISE

'The children of this world are in their generation wiser than the children of light.'—LUKE xvi. 8.

The parable of which these words are the close is remarkable in that it proposes a piece of deliberate roguery as, in some sort, a pattern for Christian people. The steward's conduct was neither more nor less than rascality, and yet, says Christ, 'Do like that!'

The explanation is to be found mainly in the consideration that what was faithless sacrifice of his master's interests, on the part of the steward, is, in regard to the Christian man's use of earthly gifts, the right employment of the possessions which have been entrusted to him. But there is another vindication of the singular selection of such conduct as an example, in the consideration that what is praised is not the dishonesty, but the foresight, realisation of the facts of the case, promptitude, wisdom of various kinds exhibited by the steward. And so says our Lord—shutting out the consideration of ends, and looking only for a moment at means,—the world can teach the Church a great many lessons; and it would be well for the Church if its members lived in the fashion in which the men of the world do. There is eulogium here, a recognition of splendid qualities, prostituted to low purposes; a recognition of wisdom in the adaptation of means to an end; and a limitation of the recognition, because it is only *in their generation* that 'the children of this world are wiser than the children of light.'

I. So we may look, first, at these two classes, which our Lord opposes here to one another.

'The children of this world' would have, for their natural antithesis, the children of another world. The 'children of light' would have, for their natural antithesis, 'the children of darkness.' But our Lord so orders His words as to suggest a double antithesis, one member of which has to be supplied in each case, and He would teach us that whoever the children of this world may be, they are 'children of darkness'; and that the 'children of light' are so, just because they are the children of another world than this. Thus He limits His praise, because it is the sons of darkness that, in a certain sense, are wiser than the enlightened ones. And that is what makes the wonder and the inconsistency to which our Lord is pointing. We can understand a man being a consistent, thorough-paced fool all through. But men whose folly is so dashed and streaked with wisdom, and others whose wisdom is so spotted and blurred with folly, are the extraordinary paradoxes which experience of life presents to us.

The children of this world are of darkness; the children of light are the children of another world. Now I need not spend more than a sentence or two in further explaining these two antitheses. I do not intend to vindicate them, or to vindicate our Lord's distinct classification of men into these two halves. What does He mean by the children of this world? The old Hebrew idiom, the children of so–and–so, simply suggests persons who are so fully possessed and saturated with a given quality, or who belong so entirely to a given person, as that they are spoken of as if they stood to it, or to him, in the relation of children to their parents. And a child of this world is a man whose whole thoughts, aims, and objects of life are limited and conditioned by this material present. But the word which is employed here, translated rightly enough 'world,' is not the same as that which is often used, especially in John's writings, for the same idea. Although it conveys a similar idea, still it is different. The characteristic quality of the visible and material world which is set forth by the expression here employed is its transiency. 'The children of this epoch' rather than 'of this world' is the meaning of the phrase. And it suggests, not so much the inadequacy of the material to satisfy the spiritual, as the absurdity of a man fixing his hopes and limiting his aims and life–purpose within the bounds of what is destined to fade and perish. Fleeting wealth, fleeting honours, mortal loves, wisdom, and studies that pass away with the passing away of the material; these, however elevating some of them may be, however sweet some of them may be, however needful all of them are in their places, are not the things to which a man can safely lash his being, or entrust his happiness, or wisely devote his life. And therefore the men who, ignoring the fact that they live and the world passes, make themselves its slaves, and itself their object, are convicted by the very fact of the disproportion between the duration of themselves and of that which is their aim, of being children of the darkness.

Then we come to the other antithesis. The children of light are so in the measure in which their lives are not dependent exclusively upon, nor directed solely towards, the present order and condition of things. If there be a *this,* then there is a *that.* If there be an age which is qualified as being present, then that implies that there is an age or epoch which is yet to come. And that coming 'age' should regulate the whole of our relations to that age which at present is. For life is continuous, and the coming epoch is the outcome of the present. As truly as 'the child is father of the man,' so truly is Eternity the offspring of Time, and that which we are to–day determines that which we shall be through the ages. He that recognises the relations of the present and the future, who sees the small, limited things of the moment running out into the dim eternity beyond, and the track unbroken across the gulfs of death and the broad expanse of countless years, and who therefore orders the little things here so as to secure the great things yonder, he, and only he, who has made time the 'lackey to eternity,' and in his pursuit of the things seen and temporal, regards them always in the light of things unseen and eternal, is a child of light.

II. The second consideration suggested here is the limited and relative wisdom of the fools.

The children of this world, who are the children of darkness, and who at bottom are thoroughly unwise, considered relatively, 'are wiser than the children of light.' The steward is the example. 'A rogue is always'—as one of our thinkers puts it—'a roundabout fool.' He would have been a much wiser man if he had been an honester one; and, instead of tampering with his lord's goods, had faithfully administered them.

But, shutting out the consideration of the moral quality of his action, look how much there was in it that was wise, prudent, and worthy of praise. There were courage, fertility of resource, a clear insight into what was the right thing to do. There was a wise adaptation of means to an end. There was promptitude in carrying out the wise means that suggested themselves to him. The design was bad.

Granted. We are not talking about goodness, but about cleverness. So, very significantly, in the parable the person cheated cannot help saying that the cheat was a clever one. The 'lord,' although he had suffered by it, 'commended the unjust steward, because he had done wisely.'

Did you never know in Manchester some piece of sharp practice, about which people said, 'Ah, well, he is a clever fellow,' and all but condoned the immorality for the sake of the smartness? The lord and the steward belong to the same level of character; and vulpine sagacity, astuteness, and qualities which ensure success in material things seem to both of them to be of the highest value. 'The children of this world, *in their generation'—but only in it—are wiser than the children of light.'*

Now I draw a very simple, practical lesson, and it is just this, that if Christian men, in their Christian lives, would practise the virtues that the world practises, in pursuit of its shabby aims and ends, their whole Christian character would be revolutionised. Why, a boy will spend more pains in learning to whistle than half of you do in trying to cultivate your Christian character. The secret of success religiously is precisely the same as the secret of success in ordinary things. Look at the splendid qualities that go to the making of a successful housebreaker. Audacity, resource, secrecy, promptitude, persistence, skill of hand, and a hundred others, are put into play before a man can break into your back kitchen and steal your goods. Look at the qualities that go to the making of a successful amuser of people. Men will spend endless time and pains, and devote concentration, persistence, self–denial, diligence, to learning how to play upon some instrument, how to swing upon a trapeze, how to twist themselves into abnormal contortions. Jugglers and fiddlers, and circus–riders and dancers, and people of that sort spend far more time upon efforts to perfect themselves in their profession, than ninety–nine out of every hundred professing Christians do to make themselves true followers of Jesus Christ. They know that nothing is to be got without working for it, and there is nothing to be got in the Christian life without working for it any more than in any other.

Shut out the end for a moment, and look at the means. From the ranks of criminals, of amusers, and of the purely worldly men of business that we come in contact with every day, we may get lessons that ought to bring a blush to all our cheeks, when we think to ourselves how a wealth of intellectual and moral qualities and virtues, such as we do not bring to bear on our Christian lives, are by these men employed in regard of their infinitely smaller pursuits.

Oh, brethren! we ought to be our own rebukes, for it is not only other people who show forth in other fields of life the virtues that would make so much better Christians of us, if we used them in ours, but that we ourselves carry within ourselves the condemning contrast. Look at your daily life! Do you give anything like the effort to grow in the knowledge of your Lord and Saviour, Jesus Christ, that you do to make or maintain your position in the world? When you are working side by side with the children of this world for the same objects, you keep step with them, and are known to be diligent in business as they are. When you pass into the church, what do you do there? Are we not ice in one half of our lives, and fire in the other? We may well lay to heart these solemn words of our Lord, and take shame when we think that not only do the unwise, who choose the world as their portion, put us to shame in their self–denial, their earnestness, their absorption, their clear insight into facts, their swiftness in availing themselves of every opportunity, their persistence and their perseverance, but that we rebuke ourselves because of the difference between the earnestness with which we follow the things that are of this world, and the languor of our pursuit after the things that are unseen and eternal.

Of course the reasons for the contrast are easy enough to apprehend, and I do not need to spend time upon them. The objects that so have power to stimulate and to lash men into energy, continuously through their lives, lie at hand, and a candle near will dim the sunshine beyond. These objects appeal to sense, and such make a deeper impression than things that are shown to the mind, as every picture–book may prove to us. And we, in regard to the aims of our Christian life, have to make a continual effort to bring and keep them before us, or they are crowded out by the intrusive vulgarities and dazzling brilliances of the present. And so it comes to pass that the men who hunt after trifles that are to perish set examples to the men who say that they are pursuing eternal realities. 'Go to the ant, thou sluggard, consider her ways and be wise.' Go to the men of the world, thou Christian, and do not let it be said that the devil's scholars are more studious and earnest than Christ's disciples.

III. Lastly, note the conclusive folly of the partially wise.

'In their generation,' says Christ; and that is all that can be said, The circle runs round its 360 degrees, and these people take a segment of it, say forty–five degrees, and all the rest is as non–existent. If I am to call a man a wise man out and out, there are two things that I shall have to be satisfied about concerning him. The one is, what is he aiming at? and the other, how does he aim at it? In regard to the means, the men of the world bear the bell, and carry away the supremacy. Let in the thought of the end, and things change. Two questions reduce all the world's wisdom to stark, staring insanity. The first question is, 'What are you doing it for?' And the second question is, 'And suppose you get it, what then?' Nothing that cannot pass the barrier of these two questions satisfactorily is other than madness, if taken to be the aim of a man's life. You have to look at the end, and the whole circumference of the circle of the human being, before you serve out the epithets of 'wise' and 'foolish.'

I need not dwell on the manifest folly of men who give their lives to aims and ends of which I have already said that they are disproportioned to the capacity of the pursuer. Look at yourselves, brothers; these hearts of yours that need an infinite love for their satisfaction, these active spirits of yours that can never be at rest in creatural perfection; these troubled consciences of yours that stir and moan inarticulately over unperceived wounds until they are healed by Christ. How can any man with a heart and a will, and a progressive spirit and intellect, find what he needs in anything beneath the stars? 'Whose image and superscription hath it? They say unto Him, Caesar's'; we say 'God's.' 'Render unto God the things that are God's.' The man who makes anything but God his end and aim is relatively wise and absolutely foolish.

Let me remind you too, that the same sentence of folly passes, if we consider the disproportion between the duration of the objects and of him who makes them his aim. You live, and if you are a wise man, your treasures will be of the kind that last as long as you. 'They call their lands after their own name; they think that their houses shall continue for ever. They go down into the dust. Their glory shall not descend after them,' and, therefore, 'this, their way, is their folly.'

Brethren, all that I would say may be gathered into two words. Let there be a proportion between your aims and your capacity. That signifies, let God be your end. And let there be a correspondence between your end and your means. That signifies, 'Thou shalt love the Lord thy God with all thy heart, and with all thy soul, and with all thy strength, and with all thy mind.' Or else, when everything comes to be squared up and settled, the epitaph on your gravestone will deservedly be; 'Thou fool !'

TWO KINDS OF RICHES

'He that is faithful in that which is least is faithful
also in much: and he that is unjust in the least is
unjust also in much. 11. If therefore ye have not been
faithful in the unrighteous mammon, who will commit to
your trust the true riches? 12. And if ye have not been
faithful in that which is another man's, who shall give
you that which is your own?'—LUKE xvi. 10–12.

That is a very strange parable which precedes my text, in which our Lord takes a piece of crafty dishonesty on the part of a steward who had been embezzling his lord's money as in some sense an example for us Christian people, There are other instances in which He does the same thing, finding a soul of goodness in things evil, as, for instance, in the parable of the Unjust Judge. Similar is the New Testament treatment of war or slavery, both of which diabolical things are taken as illustrations of what in the highest sphere are noble and heavenly things.

But having delivered the parable, our Lord seems, in the verses that I have read, to anticipate the objection that the unfaithfulness of the steward can never be an example for God's stewards; and in the words before us, amongst other things, He says substantially this, that whilst the steward's using his lord's wealth in order to help his lord's debtors was a piece of knavery and unfaithfulness, in us it is not unfaithfulness, but the very acme of faithfulness. In the text we have the thought that there are two kinds of valuable things in the world, a lower and a higher; that men may be very rich in regard to the one, and very poor in regard to the other. In respect to these, 'There is that maketh himself rich, and yet hath nothing; there is that maketh himself poor, and yet hath great riches.' More than that, the noblest use of the lower kind of possessions is to secure the possession of the highest. And so He teaches us the meaning of life, and of all that we have.

Now, there are three things in these words to which I would turn your attention—the two classes of treasure, the contrast of qualities between these two, and the noblest use of the lower.

I. The Two Classes of Treasure.

Now, we shall make a great mistake if we narrow down the interpretation of that word 'mammon' in the context (which is 'that which is least,' etc., here) to be merely money. It covers the whole ground of all possible external and material possessions, whatsoever things a man can only have in outward seeming, whatsoever things belong only to the region of sense and the present. All that is in the world, in fact, is included in the one name. And you must widen out your thoughts of what is referred to here in this prolonged contrast which our Lord runs between the two sets of treasures, so as to include, not only money, but all sorts of things that belong to this sensuous and temporal scene. And, on the other hand, there stands opposite to it, as included in, and meant by, that which is 'most,' 'that which is the true riches,' 'that which is your own'; everything that holds of the unseen and spiritual, whether it be treasures of intellect and lofty thought, or whether it be pure and noble aims, or whether it be ideals of any kind, the ideals of art, the aspirations of science, the lofty aims of the scholar and the student—all these are included. And the very same standard of excellence which declares that the treasures of a cultivated intellect, of a pure mind, of a lofty purpose, are higher than the utmost of material good, and that 'wisdom is better than rubies,' the very same standard, when applied in another direction, declares that above the treasures of the intellect and the taste are to be ranked all the mystical and great blessings which are summoned up in that mighty word salvation. And we must take a step further, for neither the treasures of the intellect, the mind, and the heart, nor the treasures of the spiritual life which salvation implies, can be realised and reached unless a man possesses God. So in the deepest analysis, and in the truest understanding of these two contrasted classes of wealth you have but the old antithesis: the world—and God. He that has God is rich, however poor he may be in reference to the other category; and he that has Him not is poor, however rich he may be. 'The lines are fallen to me in pleasant places,' says the Psalmist; and 'I have a goodly heritage,' because he could also say, 'God is the strength of my heart and my portion for ever.' So there is the antithesis, the things of time and sense, the whole mass of them knit together on the one hand; the single God alone by Himself on the other. Of these two classes of valuable things our Lord goes on next to tell us the relative worth. For we have here

II. The Contrast between the Two.

That contrast is threefold, as you observe, 'that which is least.' or, perhaps better, 'that which is very little.' and 'that which is much.' That is a contrast in reference to degree. But degree is a shallow word, which does not cover the whole ground, nor go down to the depths. So our Lord comes next to a contrast in regard to essential nature, 'the unrighteous mammon' and 'the true riches.' But even these contrasts in degree and in kind do not exhaust all the contrasts possible, for there is another, the contrast in reference to the reality of our possession: 'that which is another's'; 'that which is your own.' Let us, then, take these three things, the contrast in degree, the contrast in kind, the contrast in regard to real possession.

First, then, and briefly, mental and spiritual and inward blessings, salvation, God, are more than all externals. Our Lord gathers all the conceivable treasures of earth, jewels and gold and dignities, and scenes of sensuous delights, and everything that holds to the visible and the temporal, and piles them into one scale, and then He puts into the other the one name, God; and the pompous nothings fly up and are nought, and have no weight at all. Is that not true? Does it need any demonstration, any more talk about it? No!

But then comes in sense and appeals to us, and says, 'You cannot get beyond my judgment. These things are good.' Jesus Christ does not say that they are not, but sense regards them as far better than they are. They are near us, and a very small object near us, by the laws of perspective, shuts out a mightier one beyond us. We in Manchester live in a community which is largely based on, and actuated and motived in its diligence by the lie that material good is better than spiritual good, that it is better to be a rich man and a successful merchant than to be a poor and humble and honest student; that it is better to have a balance at your bankers than to have great and pure and virginal thoughts in a clean heart; that a man has done better for himself when he has made a fortune than when he has God in his heart. And so we need, and God knows it was never more needed in Manchester than to-day, that we should preach and preach and preach, over and over again, this old-fashioned threadbare truth, which is so threadbare and certain that it has lost its power over the lives of many of us, that all that, at its mightiest, is very little, and that this, at its least, is very much. Dear brethren, you and I know how hard it is always, especially how hard it is in business lives, to keep this as our practical working faith. We say we believe, and then we go away and live as if we believed the opposite. I beseech you listen to the scale laid down by Him who knew all things in their measure and degree, and let us settle it in our souls, and live as if we had settled it, that it is better to be wise and good than to be rich and prosperous, and that God is more than a universe of worlds, if we have Him for our own.

But to talk about a contrast in degree degrades the reality, for it is no matter of difference of measurement, but it is a matter of difference of kind. And so our Lord goes on to a deeper phase of the contrast, when He pits against one another 'the unrighteous mammon' and 'the true riches.' Now, there is some difficulty in that contrast. The two significant terms do not seem to be precise opposites, and possibly they are not intended to be logically accurate counterparts of each other. But what is meant by 'the unrighteous mammon'? I do not suppose that the ordinary explanation of that verse is quite adequate. We usually suppose that by so stigmatising the material good, He means to suggest how hard it is to get it—and you all know that—and how hard it is to keep it, and how hard it is to administer it, without in some measure falling into the sin of unrighteousness. But whilst I dare say that may be the signification intended, if we were to require that the word here should be a full and correct antithesis to the other phrase, 'the true riches,' we should need to suppose that 'unrighteous' here meant that which falsely pretended to be what it was not. And so we come to the contrast between the deceitfulness of earthly good and the substantial reality of the heavenly. Will any fortune, even though it goes into seven figures, save a man from the miseries, the sorrows, the ills that flesh is heir to? Does a great estate make a man feel less desolate when he stands by his wife's coffin? Will any wealth 'minister to a mind diseased'? Will a mountain of material good calm and satisfy a man's soul? You see faces just as discontented, looking out of carriage windows, as you meet in the street. 'Uneasy lies the head that wears a crown.' There is no proportion between abundance of external good of any kind and happy hearts. We all know that the man who is rich is not happier than the poor man. And I, for my part, believe that the raw material of happiness is very equally distributed through the world, and that it is altogether a hallucination by which a poor man thinks, 'If I were wealthy like that other man, how different my life would be.' No, it would not; you would be the same man. The rich man that fancies that because he is rich he is 'better off,' as they say, than his poor brother, and the poor man who thinks that he would be 'better off' if he were richer than he is now, are the same man turned inside out, so to speak; and common to both of them is that fallacy, that wealth and material good contribute much to the real blessedness and nobleness of the man who happens to own it.

But then, perhaps, we have rather to regard this unrighteous mammon as so designated from another point of view. You will remember that all through the context our Lord has been insisting on the notion of stewardship. And I take it that what He means here is to remind us that whenever we claim any of our possessions, especially our external ones, as our own, we thereby are guilty of defrauding both God and man, and are unrighteous, and it is unrighteous thereby. Stewardship is a word which describes our relation to all that we have. Forget that, and then whatever you have becomes 'the unrighteous mammon.' There is the point in which Christ's teaching joins hands with a great deal of unchristian teaching in this present day which is called Socialism and Communism. Christianity is not communistic. It asserts as against other men your right of property, but it limits that right by this, that if you interpret your right of property to mean the right to 'do what you like with your own,' ignoring your stewardship to God, and the right of your fellows to share in what you have, then you are an unfaithful steward, and your mammon is unrighteous. And that principle, the true communism of Christianity, has to be worked into modern society in a way that some of us do not dream of, before modern society will be organised on Christian principles. These words of my text are no toothless words which are merely intended to urge Christian people on to a sentimental charity, and to a niggardly distribution of part of their possessions: but they underlie the whole conception of ownership, as the New Testament sets it forth. Wherever the stewardship that we owe to God, and the participation that we owe to men, are neglected in regard to anything that we have, there God's good gifts are perverted and have become 'unrighteous mammon.'

And, then, on the other hand, our Lord sets forth here the contrast in regard to 'the true riches', which are such, inasmuch as they really correspond to the idea of wealth being a true good to a man, and making him rich to all the intents of bliss. He that has the treasures of a pure mind, of a lofty aim, of a quiet conscience, of a filled and satisfied and therefore calmed heart; he that has the treasure of salvation; he that has the boundless wealth of God——he has the bullion, while the poor rich people that have the material good have the scrip of an insolvent company, which is worth no more than the paper on which it is written. There are two currencies—one solid metal, the other worthless paper. The one is 'true riches,' and the other the 'unrighteous mammon.'

Then there is a last contrast, and that is with regard to the reality of our possession. On the one hand, that which I fondly call my own is by our Lord stamped with the proprietor's mark, of somebody else, 'that which is Another's.' It was His before He gave it, it was His when He gave it, it is His after He has given it. My name is never to be written on my property so as to erase the name of the Owner. I am a steward; I am a trustee; it all belongs to Him. That is one rendering of this word. But the phrase may perhaps point in another direction. It may suggest how shadowy and unreal, as being merely external, and how transitory is our ownership of wealth and outward possessions. A man says, 'It is mine.' What does he mean by that? It is not his own in any real sense. I get more good out of a rich man's pictures, or estate, if I look at them with an eye that loves them, than he does. The world belongs to the man that can enjoy it and rightly use it. And the man that enjoys it and uses it aright is the man who lives in God. Nothing is really yours except that which has entered into the substance of your soul, and become incorporated with your very being, so that, as in wool dyed in the grain, the colour will never come out. What I am, that I have; what I only have, that, in the deepest sense, I have not. 'Shrouds have no pockets,' says the Spanish proverb. 'His glory will not descend after him,' says the psalm. That is a poor possession which only is outward whilst it lasts, and which ends so soon. But there is wealth that comes into me. There are riches that cannot be parted from me. I can make my own a great inheritance, which is wrought into the very substance of my being, and will continue so inwrought, into whatsoever worlds or states of existence any future may carry me. So, and only so, is anything my own. Let these contrasts dominate our lives.

I see our space is gone; I must make this sermon a fragment, and leave what I intended to have made the last part of it for possible future consideration. Only let me press upon you in one closing word this, that the durable riches are only found in God, and the riches that can be found in God are brought to every one of us by Him 'in whom are hid all the treasures of wisdom and knowledge,' of goodness and grace. If we will make ourselves poor, by consciousness of our need, and turn with faith to Jesus, then we shall receive from Him those riches which are greatest, which are true, which are our own in that they pass into our very being, in that they were destined for us from all eternity by the love of God; and in having them we shall be rich indeed, and for ever.

THE GAINS OF THE FAITHFUL STEWARD

'If ye have not been faithful in that which is another
man's, who shall give you that which is your own?'
—LUKE xvi. 12.

In a recent sermon on this context I dealt mainly with the threefold comparison which our Lord runs between the higher and the lower kind of riches. The one is stigmatised as 'that which is least,' the unrighteous mammon,' 'that which is another's'; whilst the higher is magnified as being 'that which is most,' 'the true riches,' 'your own.' What are these two classes? On the one hand stand all possessions which, in and after possession, remain outside of a man, which may survive whilst he perishes, or perish while he survives. On the other hand are the riches which pass into him, and become inseparable from him. Noble aims, high aspirations, pure thoughts, treasures of wisdom, treasures of goodness—these are the real wealth corresponding to man's nature, destined for his enrichment, and to last with him for ever. But we may gather the whole contrast into two words: the small, the 'unrighteous,' the wealth which being mine is not mine but remains another's, and foreign to me, is the world. The great riches, the 'true riches,' the good destined for me, and for which I am destined, is God. In these two words you have the antithesis, the real antithesis, God *versus* the world.

Now let us turn rather to the principle which our Lord here lays down, in reference to these two classes of good, or of possessions. He tells us that the faithful use of the world helps us to the possession of God; or, to put it into other words, that how we handle money and what money can buy, has a great deal to do with our religious enjoyment and our religious life, and that that is true, both in regard to our partial possession of God here and now, and to our perfect possession of Him in the world to come.

Now I wish to say one or two very plain things about this matter, and I hope that you will not turn away from them because they are familiar and trite. Considering how much of your lives, especially as regards men of business, is taken up with money, its acquisition, its retention, its distribution, there are few things that have more to do with the vigour or feebleness of your Christian life than the way in which you handle these perishable things.

I wish to say a word or two, first, about

I. What our Lord means by this faithfulness to which He attaches such tremendous issues.

Now, you will remember, that the starting point of my text is that parable of the unjust steward, whose conduct, knavish as it was, is in some sense presented by our Lord to His disciples, and to us, as a pattern. But my text, and the other two verses which are parallel with it, seem to have amongst their other purposes this: to put in a caveat against supposing that it is the unfaithfulness of the steward which is recommended for our imitation. And so the first point that is suggested in regard to this matter of faithfulness about the handling of outward good is that we have to take care that it is rightly acquired, for though the unjust steward was commended for the prudent use that he made of dishonestly acquired gain, it is the prudent use, and not the manner of the acquisition which we are to take as our examples. Initial unfaithfulness in acquisition is not condoned or covered over by any pious and benevolent use hereafter. Mediaeval barons left money for masses. Plenty of Protestants do exactly the same thing. Brewers will build cathedrals, and found picture galleries, and men that have made their money foully will fancy that they atone for that by leaving it for some charitable purpose. The caustic but true wit of a Scottish judge said about a great bequest which was supposed to be—whether rightly or wrongly, I know not—of that sort, that it was 'the heaviest fire insurance premium that had been paid in the memory of man.' 'The money does not stink,' said the Roman Emperor, about the proceeds of an unsavoury tax. But the money unfaithfully won does stink when it is thrown into God's treasury. 'The price of a dog shall not come into the sanctuary of the Lord.' Do not think that money doubtfully won is consecrated by being piously spent.

But there are more things than that here, for our Lord sums up the whole of a Christian man's duties in regard to the use of this external world and all its good, in that one word 'faithful,' which implies discharge of responsibility, recognition of obligation, the continual consciousness that we are not proprietors but stewards. Unless we carry that consciousness with us into all the phases of our connection with perishable goods they become—as I shall have to show you in a moment,—hindrances instead of helps to our possession of God.

I am not going to talk revolutionary socialism, or anything of that sort, but I am bound to reiterate my own solemn conviction that until, practically as well as theoretically, the Christian Church in all its branches brings into its creed, and brings out in its practice, the great thought of stewardship, especially in regard to material and external good, but also in regard to the durable riches of salvation, the nations will be full of unrest, and thunder-clouds heavily boding storm and destruction will lower on the horizon. What we have, we have that we may impart; what we have in all forms of having, we have because we have received. We are distributing centres, that is all—I was going to say like a nozzle, perforated with many holes, at the end of the spout of a watering-can. That is a Christian man's relation to his possessions. We are stewards. 'It is required in stewards that a man be found faithful'

Now let me ask you to notice—

II. The bearing of this faithfulness in regard to the lower wealth on our possession of the higher.

Jesus says in this context, twice over, that faithfulness with regard to the former is the condition of our being entrusted with the latter. Now, remember, by way of illustration of this thought, what all this outward world of goodness and beauty is mainly meant for. What? It is all but scaffolding by which, and within the area of which, the building may arise. The meaning of the world is to make character. All that we have, aye! and all that we do, and the whole of the events and circumstances with which we come in contact here on earth, are then lifted to their noblest function, and are then understood in their deepest meaning when we look upon them as we do upon the leaping-poles and bars and swings of a gymnasium,—as meant to develop thews and muscles, and make men of us. That is what they are here for, and that is what we are here for. Not enjoyment, and not sorrow, except in so far as these two are powers in developing character, not plunging ourselves in the enjoyments of sense. Wealth and poverty, gain and loss, love gratified and love marred, possessions sweet, when preserved, and possessions that become sweeter by being removed; all these are simply meant as whetstones on which the keen blade may be sharpened, as forces against which, trying ourselves, our deftness and strength may be increased. They are all meant to make us men, and if we faithfully use these externals with a recognition of their source, with a wise estimate of their subordination so as that our desires shall not cleave to them solely, and with a fixed determination to use them as ministers to make ourselves nobler, wiser, stronger, liker to God and His Christ, then the world will minister to our possession of God, and being 'faithful in that which is least,' we shall thereby be more capable of receiving that which is greatest. But if, on the other hand, we so forget our true wealth, and become so besotted and absorbed in our adhesion to, and our desires after, fleeting good, then the capacities that were noble will fade and shrivel, being unused; aims and purposes that were elevated and pure will die out unsatisfied; windows in our souls which commanded a wide, glorious prospect will gradually be bricked up; burdens which hinder our running will be piled upon our backs, and the world will have conquered us, whilst we are dreaming that we have conquered the world. You look at a sea anemone in a pool on the rocks when the tide is out, all its tendrils outstretched, and its cavity wide open. Some little bit of seaweed, or some morsel of half–putrefying matter, comes in contact with it, and instantly every tentacle is retracted, and the lips are tightly closed, so that you could not push a bristle in. And when your tentacles draw themselves in to clutch the little portion of worldly good, of whatever sort it is, that has come into your hold, there is no room to get God in there, and being 'unfaithful in that which is least' you have made it impossible that you should possess 'that which is most.' Ah! there are some of us that were far better Christians long ago, when we were poorer men, than we are to–day, and there are some of us that know what it is to have the heart so filled with baser liquors that there is no room for the ethereal nectar. If the world has filled my soul, where is God to dwell?

There is another way in which we may look at this matter. I have said that the main use of these perishable and fragmentary good things around us is to develop character, by our administration of them. Another way of putting the same thought is that their main use is to show us God. If we faithfully use the lesser good it will become transparent, and reveal to us the greater. We hear a great deal about deepening the spiritual life by prayers, and conventions, and Bible readings and the like. I have no word to say except in full sympathy with all such. But I do believe that the best means, the most powerful means, by which the great bulk of Christian men could deepen their spiritual lives would be a more honest and thoroughgoing attempt to 'be faithful in that which is least.' We have so much to do with it necessarily, that few, if any, things have more power in shaping our whole characters than our manner of administering the wealth, the material good, that comes to our hands.

And so, dear brethren, I beseech you remember that the laws of perspective are such as that a minute thing near at hand shuts out the vision of a mighty thing far off, and a hillock by my side will hide the Himalayas at a distance, and a sovereign may block out God; and 'that which is least' has the diabolical power of seeming greater to us than, and of obscuring our vision of, 'that which is most.'

May I remind you that all these thoughts about the bearing of faithfulness in administering the lower of our possessions, on the attainment of higher, apply to us whatever be the amount of these outward goods that we have? I suppose there were not twelve poorer men in all Palestine that day than the twelve to whom my text was originally addressed. Three of them had left their nets and their fishing–boats, one of them we know had left his counting–house, as a publican, and all his receipts and taxes behind him. What they had we know not, but at all events they were the poor of this world. Do not any of you that happen to be modestly or poorly off think that my sermon is a sermon for rich men. It is not what we have, but how we handle it, that is in question. 'The cares of this world, and the deceitfulness of riches,' were bracketed together by Jesus Christ as the things that 'choke the word,' and make it unfruitful. The poor man who wants, and the rich man who uses unfaithfully, are alike hit by the words of my text.

Now, further, let me ask you to look at

III. The bearing of faithfulness in this life on the fuller possession of our true riches in the life hereafter.

There lies under this whole context a striking conception of life here in its relation to the life hereafter, A father sets his son, or a master sets his apprentice, to some small task, an experiment made upon a comparatively worthless body, supplies him with material which it does not much matter whether he spoils or not, and then if by practice the hand becomes deft, he is set to better work. God sets us to try our 'prentice hands here in the world, and if we administer that rightly, not necessarily perfectly, but so as to show that there are the makings of a good workman in us by His gracious help, then the next life comes, with its ampler margin, with its wider possibilities, with its nobler powers, and there we are set to use in loftier fashion the powers which we made our own being here. 'Thou hast been faithful over a few things, I will make thee ruler over many things.'

I have said that the great use of the world and all its wealth is to make character. I have said that that character determines our capacity for the possession of God. I have said that our administration of worldly wealth is one chief factor in determining our character. Now I say that that character persists. There are great changes, changes the significance and the scope and the consequences of which we can never know here. But the man remains, in the main direction of his being, in the character which he has made for himself by his use of God's world and of Christ's Spirit. And so the way in which we handle the trivialities and temporalities here has eternal consequences. We sit in a low room with the telegraph instrument in front of us, and we click off our messages, and they are recorded away yonder, and we shall have to read them one day. Transient causes produce permanent effects. The seas which laid down the great sandstone deposits that make so large a portion of the framework of this world have long since evaporated. But the footprints of the seabird that stalked across the moist sand, and the little pits made by the raindrops that fell countless millenniums ago on the red ooze, are there yet, and you may see them in our museums. And so our faithfulness, or our unfaithfulness, here has made the character which is eternal, and on which will depend whether we shall, in the joys of that future life, possess God in fullness, or whether we shall lose Him, as our portion and our Friend.

Now, dear brethren, do not forget that all this that I have been saying is the second page in Christ's teaching; and the first page is an entirely different one. I have been saying that we make character, and that character determines our possession of God and His grace. But there is another thing to be said. The central thought of Christ's gospel is that God, in His sweetness, in His pardoning mercy, in His cleansing Spirit, is given to the very men whose characters do not deserve it. And the same Lord who said, 'If ye have not been faithful in that which is least, who shall give you that which is greatest?' says also from the heavens,' I counsel thee to buy of Me gold tried in the fire, that thou mayest be rich.' My text, and the principle that is involved in it, do not contradict the great truth that we are saved by simple faith, however unworthy we are. That is the message to begin with. And unless you have received it you are not standing in the place where the message that I have been insisting upon has a personal bearing on you. But if you have taken Christ for your salvation, remember, Christian brother and sister, that it is not the same thing in regard either to your Christian life on earth, or to your heavenly glory, whether you have been living faithfully as stewards in your handling of earth's perishable good, or whether you have clung to it as your real portion, have used it selfishly, and by it have hidden God from your hearts. To Christian men is addressed the charge that we trust not in the uncertainty of riches, but in the living God, and that we be 'rich in good works, ready to distribute, willing to communicate, that we lay up in store for ourselves a good foundation against the time to come'; and so 'lay hold on the life that is life indeed.'

DIVES AND LAZARUS

'There was a certain rich man, which was clothed in purple and fine linen, and fared sumptuously every day: 20. And there was a certain beggar named Lazarus, which was laid at his gate, full of sores, 21. And desiring to be fed with the crumbs which fell from the rich man's table: moreover the dogs came and licked his sores. 22. And it came to pass, that the beggar died, and was carried by the angels into Abraham's bosom: the rich man also died, and was buried; 23. And in hell he lifted up his eyes, being in torments, and seeth Abraham afar off, and Lazarus in his bosom. 24. And he cried, and said, Father Abraham, have mercy on me, and send Lazarus, that he may dip the tip of his finger in water, and cool my tongue; for I am tormented in this flame. 25, But Abraham said, Son, remember that thou in thy lifetime receivedst thy good things, and likewise Lazarus evil things: but now he is comforted, and thou art tormented. 26. And besides all this, between us and you there is a great gulf fixed: so that they which would pass from hence to you cannot; neither can they pass to us, that would come from thence. 27. Then he said, I pray thee therefore, father, that thou wouldest send him to my father's house: 28. For I have five brethren; that he may testify unto them lest they also come into this place of torment. 29. Abraham saith unto him, They have Moses and the prophets; let them hear them. 30. And he said, Nay, father Abraham: but if one went unto them from the dead, they will repent. 31. And he said unto him, If

they hear not Moses and the prophets, neither will they
be persuaded, though one rose from the dead.'
—Luke xvi. 19–31.

This, the sternest of Christ's parables, must be closely connected with verses 13 and 14. Keeping them in view, its true purpose is plain. It is meant to rebuke, not the possession of wealth, but its heartless, selfish use. Christ never treats outward conditions as having the power of determining either character or destiny. What a man does with his conditions settles what he is and what becomes of him. Nor does the parable teach that the use of wealth is the only determining factor, but, as every parable must do, it has to isolate the lesson it teaches in order to burn it into the hearers.

There are three parts in the story—the conduct of the rich man, his fate, and the sufficiency of existing warnings to keep us from his sin and his end.

I. Properly speaking, we have here, not a parable—that is, a representation of physical facts which have to be translated into moral or religious truths—but an imaginary narrative, embodying a normal fact in a single case. The rich man does not stand for something else, but is one of the class of which Jesus wishes to set forth the sin and fate. It is very striking that neither he nor the beggar is represented as acting, but each is simply described. The juxtaposition of the two figures carries the whole lesson.

It has sometimes been felt as a difficulty that the one is not said to have done anything bad, nor the other to have been devout or good; and some hasty readers have thought that Jesus was here teaching the communistic doctrine that wealth is sin, and that poverty is virtue. No such crude trash came from His lips. But He does teach that heartless wallowing in luxury, with naked, starving beggars at the gate, is sin which brings bitter retribution. The fact that the rich man does nothing is His condemnation. He was not damned because he had a purple robe and fine linen undergarments, nor because he had lived in abundance, and every meal had been a festival, but because, while so living, he utterly ignored Lazarus, and used his wealth only for his own gratification. Nothing more needs to be said about his character; the facts sufficiently show it.

Still less needs to be said about that of Lazarus. In this part of the narrative he comes into view simply as the means of bringing out the rich man's heartlessness and self–indulgence. For the purposes of the narrative his disposition was immaterial; for it is not our duty to help only deserving or good people. Manhood and misery are enough to establish the right to sympathy and succour. There may be a hint of character in the name 'Lazarus,' which probably means 'God is help.' Since this is the only name in the parables, it is natural to give it significance, and it most likely suggests that the beggar clung to God as his stay. It may glance, too, at the riddle of life, which often seems to mock trust by continued trouble. Little outward sign had Lazarus of divine help, yet he did not cast away his confidence. No doubt, he sometimes got some crumbs from Dives' table, but not from Dives. That the dogs licked his sores does not seem meant as either alleviation or aggravation, but simply as vividly describing his passive helplessness and utterly neglected condition. Neither he nor any one drove them off.

But the main point about him is that he was at Dives' gate, and therefore thrust before Dives' notice, and that he got no help. The rich man was not bound to go and hunt for poor people, but here was one pushed under his nose, as it were. Translate that into general expressions, and it means that we all have opportunities of beneficence laid in our paths, and that our guilt is heavy if we neglect these. 'The poor ye have always with you.' The guilt of selfish use of worldly possessions is equally great whatever is the amount of possessions. Doing nothing when Lazarus lies at our gate is doing great wickedness. These truths have a sharp edge for us as well as for the 'Pharisees who were covetous'; and they are wofully forgotten by professing Christians.

II. In the second part of the narrative, our Lord follows the two, who had been so near each other and yet so separated, into the land beyond the grave. It is to be especially noticed that, in doing so, He adopts the familiar Rabbinical teaching as to Hades. He does not thereby stamp these conceptions of the state of the dead with His assent; for the purpose of the narrative is not to reveal the secrets of that land, but to impress the truth of retribution for the sin in question. It would not be to a group of Pharisaic listeners that He would have unveiled that world.

He takes their own notions of it—angel bearers, Abraham's bosom, the two divisions in Hades, the separation, and yet communication, between them. These are Rabbis' fancies, not Christ's revelations. The truths which He wished to force home lie in the highly imaginative conversation between the rich man and Abraham, which also has its likeness in many a Rabbinical legend.

The difference between the ends of the two men has been often noticed, and lessons, perhaps not altogether warranted, drawn from it. But it seems right to suppose that the omission of any notice of the beggar's burial is meant to bring out that the neglect and pitilessness, which had let him die, left his corpse unburied. Perhaps the dogs that had licked his sores tore his flesh. A fine sight that would be from the rich man's door! The latter had to die too, for all his purple, and to be swathed in less gorgeous robes. His funeral is mentioned, not only because pomp and ostentation went as far as they could with him, but to suggest that he had to leave them all behind. 'His glory shall not descend after him.'

The terrible picture of the rich man's torments solemnly warns us of the necessary end of a selfish life such as his. The soul that lives to itself does not find satisfaction even here; but, when all externals are left behind, it cannot but be in torture. That is not drapery. Character makes destiny, and to live to self is death. Observe, too, that the relative positions of Dives and Lazarus are reversed—the beggar being now the possessor of abundance and delights, while the rich man is the sufferer and the needy.

Further note that the latter now desires to have from the former the very help which in life he had not given him, and that the retribution for refusing succour here is its denial hereafter. There had been no sharing of 'good things' in the past life, but the rich man had asserted his exclusive rights to them. They had been 'thy good things' in a very sinful sense, and Lazarus had bean left to carry his evil things alone. There shall be no communication of good now. Earth was the place for mutual help and impartation. That world affords no scope for it; for there men reap what they have sown, and each character has to bear its own burden.

Finally, the ineffaceableness of distinctions of character, and therefore of destiny, is set forth by the solemn image of the great gulf which cannot be crossed. It is indeed to be remembered that our Lord is speaking of 'the intermediate state,' before resurrection and final judgment, and that, as already remarked, the intention of the narrative is not to reveal the mysteries of the final state. But still the impression left by the whole is that life here determines life hereafter, and that character, once set and hardened here, cannot be cast into the melting–pot and remoulded there.

III. The last part of the narrative teaches that the fatal sin of heartless selfishness is inexcusable. The rich man's thought for his brethren was quite as much an excuse for himself. He thought that, if he had only known, things would have been different. He shifts blame from himself on to the insufficiency of the warnings given him. And the two answers put into Abraham's mouth teach the sufficiency of 'Moses and the prophets,' little as these say about the future, and the impossibility of compelling men to listen to a divine message to which they do not wish to listen.

The fault lies, not in the deficiency of the warnings, but in the aversion of the will. No matter whether it is Moses or a spirit from Hades who speaks, if men do not wish to hear, they will not hear. They will not be persuaded—for persuasion has as much, or more, to do with the heart and inclination than with the head. We have as much witness from heaven as we need. The worst man knows more of duty than the best man does. Dives is in torments because he lived for self; and he lived for self, not because he did not know that it was wrong, but because he did not choose to do what he knew to be right.

MEMORY IN ANOTHER WORLD

'Abraham said, Son, remember!'—LUKE xvi. 25.

It is a very striking thought that Christ, if He be what we suppose Him to be, knew all about the unseen present which we call the future, and yet was all but silent in reference to it. Seldom is it on His lips at all. Of arguments drawn from another world He has very few. Sometimes He speaks about it, but rather by allusion than in anything like an explicit revelation. This parable out of which my text is taken, is perhaps the most definite and continuous of His words about the invisible world; and yet all the while it lay there before Him; and standing on the very verge of it, with it spread out clear before His gaze, He reads off but a word or two of what He sees, and then shuts it in in darkness, and says to us, in the spirit of a part of this parable, 'You have Moses and the prophets—hear them: if these are not enough, it will not be enough for you if all the glories of heaven and all the ghastliness of hell are flashed and flamed before you.' We, too, if we are to 'prophesy according to the proportion of faith,' must not leave out altogether references to a future life in its two departments, and such motives as may be based upon them; only, I think, we ought always to keep them in the same relative amount to the whole of our teaching in which Christ kept them.

This parable, seeing that it *is* a parable, of course cannot be trusted as if it were a piece of simple dogmatic revelation, to give us information, facts, so as to construct out of it a theory of the other world. We are always in the double danger in parables, of taking that for drapery which was meant to be essence, and taking that for essence which was meant to be drapery. And so I do not profess to read from this narrative any very definite and clear knowledge of the future; but I think that in the two words which I have ventured to take as a text, we get the basis of very impressive thoughts with regard to the functions of memory in another world.

'Son, remember!' It is the voice, the first voice, the perpetual voice, which meets every man when he steps across the threshold of earth into the presence chamber of eternity. All the future is so built upon and interwoven with the past, that for the saved and for the lost alike this word might almost be taken as the motto of their whole situation, as the explanation of their whole condition. Memory in another world is indispensable to the gladness of the glad, and strikes the deepest note in the sadness of the lost. There can be no need to dwell at any length on the simple introductory thought, that there must be memory in a future state. Unless there were remembrance, there could be no sense of individuality. A man cannot have any conviction that he is himself, but by constant, though often unconscious, operation of this subtle act of remembrance. There can be no sense of personal identity except in proportion as there is clearness of recollection. Then again, if that future state be a state of retribution, there must be memory. Otherwise, there might be joy, and there might be sorrow, but the why and the wherefore of either would be entirely struck out of a man's consciousness, and the one could not be felt as reward, nor the other as punishment. If, then, we are to rise from the grave the same men that we are laid in it, and if the future life has this for its characteristic, that it is a state either of recompense and reward, or of retribution and suffering, then, for both, the clearness and constant action, of memory are certainly needed. But it is not to the simple fact of its existence that I desire to direct your attention now. I wish, rather, to suggest to you one or two modifications under which it must apparently work in another world. When men remember *there*, they will remember very differently from the way in which they remember *here*. Let us look at these changes–constituting it, on the one hand, an instrument of torture; and, on the other, a foundation of all our gladness.

I. First, in another state, memory will be so widened as to take in the whole life.

We believe that what a man is in this life, he is more in another, that tendencies here become results yonder, that his sin, that his falsehood, that his whole moral nature, be it good or bad, becomes there what it is only striving to be here. We believe that in this present life our capacities of all sorts are hedged in, thwarted, damped down, diluted, by the necessity which there is for their working through this material body of ours. We believe that death is the heightening of a man's stature—if he be bad, the intensifying of his badness; if he be good, the strengthening of his goodness. We believe that the contents of the intellectual nature, the capacities of that nature also, are all increased by the fact of having done with earth and having left the body behind. It is, I think, the teaching of common–sense, and it is the teaching of the Bible. True, that for some, that growth will only be a growth into greater power of feeling greater sorrow. Such an one grows up into a Hercules; but it is only that the Nessus shirt may wrap round him more tightly, and may gnaw him with a fiercer agony. But whether saved or lost—he that dies is greater than when yet living; and all his powers are intensified and strengthened by that awful experience of death and by what it brings with it.

Memory partakes in the common quickening. There are not wanting analogies and experiences in our present life to let us see that, in fact, when we talk about forgetting we ought to mean nothing more than the temporary cessation of conscious remembrance. Everything which you do leaves its effect with you for ever, just as long–forgotten meals are in your blood and bones to-day. Every act that a man performs is there. It has printed itself upon his soul, it has become a part of himself: and though, like a newly painted picture, after a little while the colours sink in, why is that? Only because they have entered into the very fibre of the canvas, and have left the surface because they are incorporated with the substance, and they want but a touch of varnish to flash out again! We forget *nothing*, in the sense of not being able, some time or another, to recall it; we forget much in the sense of ceasing for a time to have it in our thoughts.

For we know, in our own case, how strangely there come swimming up before us, out of the depths of the dim waters of oblivion—as one has seen some bright shell drawn from the sunless sea–caves, and gleaming white and shapeless far down before we had it on the surface—past thoughts, we know not whence or how. Some one of the million of hooks, with which all our life is furnished, has laid hold of some subtle suggestion which has been enough to bring them up into consciousness. We said we had forgotten them. What does it mean? Only that they had sunk into the deep, beneath our consciousness, and lay there to be brought up when needful. There is nothing more strange than the way in which some period of my life, that I supposed to be an entire blank—if I will think about it for a little while, begins to glimmer into form. As the developing solution brings out the image on the photographic plate, so the mind has the strange power, by fixing the attention, as we say (a short word which means a long, mysterious thing) upon that past that is half–remembered and half–forgotten, of bringing it into clear consciousness and perfect recollection. And, there are instances, too, of a still more striking kind, familiar to some of us how in what people call morbid states, men remember their childhood, which they had forgotten for long years. You may remember that old story of the dying woman beginning to speak in a tongue unknown to all that stood around her bed. When a child she had learned some northern language, in a far–off land. Long before she had learned to shape any definite remembrances of the place, she had been taken away, and not having used, had forgotten the speech. But at last there rushed up again all the old memories, and the tongue of the dumb was loosed, and she spake! People would say, 'the action of disease.' It may be, but that explains nothing. Perhaps in such states the spirit is working in a manner less limited by the body than in health, and so showing some slight prelude of its powers when it has shuffled off this mortal coil. But be that as it may, these morbid phenomena, and the other more familiar facts already referred to, unite to show us that the sphere of recollection is much wider than that occupied at any given moment by memory. Recollection is the servant of Memory, as our great poet tells us in his wise allegory, and

'does on him still attend,
To reach whenever he for ought does send.'

We cannot lay aside anything that we have ever done or been so utterly but that that servant can find it and bring it to his lord. We forget nothing so completely but that we shall be able to recall it. Of that awful power we may say, without irreverence, 'Thou hast set our iniquities before thee, our secret sins in the light of thy countenance.'

The fragmentary remembrances which we have now, lift themselves above the ocean of forgetfulness like islands in some Archipelago, the summits of sister hills, though separated by the estranging sea that covers their converging sides and the valleys where their roots unite. The solid land is there, though hidden. Drain off the sea, and there will be no more isolated peaks, but continuous land. In this life we have but the island memories heaving themselves into sight, but in the next the Lord shall 'cause the sea to go back by the breath of His mouth,' and the channels of the great deep of a human heart's experiences and actions shall be laid bare. 'There shall be no more sea'; but the solid land of a whole life will appear when God says, 'Son, remember!'

So much, then, for my first consideration—namely, that memory in a future state will comprehend the whole of life. Another thing is, that memory in a future state will probably be so rapid as to embrace all the past life at once. We do not know, we have no conception of, the extent to which our thinking, and feeling, and remembrance, are made tardy by the slow vehicle of this bodily organisation in which the soul rides. But we have in our own lives instances enough to make us feel that there lie in us dormant, mysterious powers by which the rapidity of all our operations of thought and feeling will be enhanced marvellously, like the difference between a broad-wheeled waggon and an express train! At some turning point of your life, when some great joy flashed, or some great shadow darkened upon you all at once; when some crisis that wanted an instantaneous decision appeared—why, what regions of thought, purpose, plan, resolution; what wilderness of desolate sorrow, and what paradises of blooming gladness, your soul has gone through in a moment. Well, then, take another illustration: A sleeper, feeling a light finger laid upon his shoulder, does not know what it is; in an instant he awakes and says, 'Is it you?' but between that touch and that word there may be a whole life run through, a whole series of long events dreamt and felt. As on the little retina of an eye there can be painted on a scale inconceivably minute, every tree and mountain-top in the whole wide panorama—so, in an instant, one may run through almost a whole lifetime of mental acts. Then, again, you remember that illustration, often used on this subject, about the experience of those who have been brought face to face with sudden death, and escaped it. The drowning man, when he comes to himself, tells us, that in the interval betwixt the instant when he felt he was going and the passing away of consciousness, all his life stood before him; as if some flash in a dark midnight had lighted up a whole mountain country—there it all was! Ah, brethren! we know nothing yet about the rapidity with which we may gather before us a whole series of events; so that although we have to pass from one to another, the succession may be so swift, as to produce in our own minds the effect of all being co-existent and simultaneous. As the child flashing about him a bit of burning stick, may seem to make a circle of flame, because the flame-point moves so quickly—so memory, though it does go from point to point, and dwells for some inconceivably minute instant on each part of the remembrance, may yet be gifted with such lightning speed, with such rapidity and awful quickness of glance, as that to the man himself the effect shall be that his whole life is spread out there before him in one instant, and that he, Godlike, sees the end and the beginning side by side. Yes; from the mountain of eternity we shall look down, and behold the whole plain spread before us. Down here we get lost and confused in the devious valleys that run off from the roots of the hills everywhere, and we cannot make out which way the streams are going, and what there is behind that low shoulder of hill yonder: but when we get to the summit peak, and look down, it will all shape itself into one consistent whole, and we shall see it all at once. The memory shall be perfect—perfect in the range of its grasp, and perfect in the rapidity with which it brings up all its objects before us at every instant.

Once more: it seems as if, in another world, memory would not only contain the whole life, and the whole life simultaneously; but would perpetually attend or haunt us. A constant remembrance! It does not lie in our power even in this world, to decide very much whether we shall remember or forget. It does not come within a man's will to forget or to remember. He cannot say, 'I will remember'; for if he could, he would have remembered already. He cannot say, 'I will forget'; for the very effort fixes his attention on the obnoxious thing. All that we can do, when we seek to remember, is to wander back to somewhere about that point in our life where the shy thing lurks, and hope to catch some sight of it in the leafy coverts: and all we can do, when we want to forget, is to try and fill our mind with other subjects, and in the distractions of them to lose the oppressive and burdensome thoughts. But we know that that is but a partial remedy, that we cannot succeed in doing it. There are presences that will not be put by. There are memories that *will* start up before us, whether we are willing or not. Like the leprosy in the Israelite's house, the foul spot works its way out through all the plaster and the paint; and the house is foul because it is there. Oh, my friend! you are a happy and a singular man if there is nothing in your life that you have tried to bury, and the obstinate thing *will* not be buried, but meets you again when you come away from its fancied grave. I remember an old castle where they tell us of a foul murder committed in a vaulted chamber with a narrow window, by torchlight one night; and there, they say, there are the streaks and stains of blood on the black oak floor; and they have planed, and scrubbed, and planed again, and thought they were gone—but there they always are, and continually up comes the dull reddish–black stain, as if oozing itself out through the boards to witness to the bloody crime again! The superstitious fable is a type of the way in which a foul thing, a sinful and bitter memory—gets ingrained into a man's heart. He tries to banish it, and gets rid of it for a while. He goes back again, and the spots are there, and will be there for ever; and the only way to get rid of them is to destroy the soul in which they are.

Memory is not all within the power of the will on earth: and probably, memory in another world is still more involuntary and still more constant. Why? Because I read in the Bible that there is work in another world for God's servants to do; but I do not read that there is work for anybody else but God's servants to do. The work of an unforgiven sinner is done when he dies, and that not only because he is going into the state of retribution, but because no rebel's work is going to be suffered in that world. The time for that is past. And so, if you will look, all the teachings of the Bible about the future state of those who are not in blessedness, give us this idea—a monotonous continuance of idleness, shutting them up to their own contemplations, the memories of the past and the agonies of the future. There are no distractions for such a man in another world. He has thought, he has conscience, he has remembrance. He has a sense of pain, of sin, of wrong, of loss. He has one 'passive fixed endurance, all eternal and the same'; but I do not read that his pain is anodyned and his sorrow soothed by any activity that his hand finds to do. And, in a most tragic sense, we may say, 'there is neither work, nor labour, nor device,' in that dark world where the fruits of sin are reaped in monotonous suffering and ever–present pain. A memory, brethren, that i>will have its own way—what a field for sorrow and lamentation that is, when God says at last, 'Now go—go apart; take thy life with thee; read it over; see what thou hast done with it!' One old Roman tyrant had a punishment in which he bound the dead body of the murdered to the living body of the murderer, and left them there scaffolded. And when that voice comes, 'Son, remember!' to the living soul of the godless, unbelieving, impenitent man, there is bound to him the murdered past, the dead past, his own life; and, in Milton's awful and profound words,

'Which way I fly is hell—myself am hell!'

There is only one other modification of this awful faculty that I would remind you of; and that is, that in a future life memory will be associated with a perfectly accurate knowledge of the consequences and a perfectly sensitive conscience as to the criminality of the past. You will have cause and consequence put down before you, meeting each other at last. There will be no room then to say, 'I wonder how such and such a thing will work out,' 'I wonder how such a thing can have come upon me'; but every one will have his whole life to look back upon, and will see the childish sin that was the parent of the full–grown vice, and the everlasting sorrow that came out of that little and apparently transitory root. The conscience, which here becomes hardened by contact with sin, and enfeebled because unheeded, will then be restored to its early sensitiveness and power, as if the labourer's horny palm were to be endowed again with the softness of the infant's little hand. If you will take and think about that, brother, *there* is enough—without any more talk, without any more ghastly, sensual external figures—*there* is enough to make the boldest tremble; a memory embracing all the past, a memory rapidly grasping and constantly bringing its burden, a judgment which admits of no mistakes, and a conscience which has done with palliations and excuses!

It is not difficult to see how that is an instrument of torture. It is more difficult to see how such a memory can be a source of gladness; and yet it can. The old Greeks were pressed with that difficulty: they said to themselves, If a man remembers, there can be no Elysium for him. And so they put the river of forgetfulness, the waters of Lethe, betwixt life and the happy plains. Ah, *we* do not want any river of oblivion betwixt us and everlasting blessedness. Calvary is on this side, and that is enough! Certainly it is one of the most blessed things about 'the faith that is in Christ Jesus,' that it makes a man remember his own sinfulness with penitence, not with pain—that it makes the memory of past transgressions full of solemn joy, because the memory of *past* transgressions but brings to mind the depth and rushing fullness of that river of love which has swept them all away as far as the east is from the west. Oh, brother, brother! you cannot forget your sins; but it lies within your own decision whether the remembrance shall be thankfulness and blessedness, or whether it shall be pain and loss for ever. Like some black rock that heaves itself above the surface of a sunlit sea, and the wave runs dashing over it, and the spray, as it falls down its sides, is all rainbowed and lightened, and there comes beauty into the mighty grimness of the black thing;—so a man's transgressions rear themselves up, and God's great love, coming sweeping itself against them and over them, makes out of the sin an occasion for the flashing more brightly of the beauty of His mercy, and turns the life of the pardoned penitent into a life of which even the sin is not pain to remember. So, then, lay your hand upon Christ Jesus. Put your heart into His keeping. Go to Him with your transgressions, He will forget them, and make it possible for you to remember them in such a way that the memory will become to you the very foundation of all your joy, and will make heaven's anthem deeper and more harmonious when you say, 'Now unto Him that hath washed us from our sins in His own blood, and hath made us kings and priests unto God, unto Him be glory for ever and ever!' And, on the other hand, *if not*, then, 'Son, remember!' will be the word that begins the future retribution, and shuts you up with a wasted past, with a gnawing conscience, and an upbraiding heart: to say,

'I backward cast my ee
On prospects drear!
And forward, though I canna see,
I guess and fear!'

GOD'S SLAVES

'Doth He thank that servant because he did the things that were commanded him! I trow not. 10. So likewise ye, when ye shall have done all those things which are commanded you, say, We are unprofitable servants: we have done that which was our duty to do.'

Expositions Of Holy Scripture

—LUKE xvii. 9–10.

There are two difficulties about these words. One is their apparent entire want of connection with what precedes—viz., the disciples' prayer, 'Lord, increase our faith,' and the other is the harshness and severity of tone which marks them, and the view of the less attractive side of man's relation to God which is thrown into prominence in them. He must be a very churlish master who never says 'Thank you,' however faithful his servant's obedience may be. And he must be a very inconsiderate master, who has only another kind of duty to lay upon the shoulders of the servant that has come in after a long day's ploughing and feeding of cattle. Perhaps, however, the one difficulty clears away the other, and if we keep firm hold of the thought that the words of my text, and those which are associated with them, are an answer to the prayer, 'Lord, increase our faith,' the stern and somewhat repelling characteristics of the words may somewhat change.

I. So I look, first, at the husk of apparent harshness and severity. The relation between master and hired servant is not the one that is in view, but the relation between a master and the slave who is his property, who has no rights, who has no possessions, whose life and death and everything connected with him are at the absolute disposal of his master. It is a foul and wicked relation when existing between men, and it has been full of cruelty and atrocities. But Jesus Christ lays His hand upon it, and says, 'That is the relation between men and God; that is the relation between men and Me.'

And what is involved therein? Absolute authority; so that the slave is but, as it were, an animated instrument in the hand of the master, with no will of his own, and no rights and no possessions. That is not all of our relation to God, blessed be His Name! But that is *in* our relation to Him, and the highest title that a man can have is the title which the Apostles in after days bound upon their foreheads as a crown of honour—'A slave of Jesus Christ.'

Then, if that relation is laid as being the basis of all our connection with God, whatever else there may be also involved, these two things which in the human relation are ugly and inconsiderate, and argue a very churlish and selfish nature on the part of the human master, belong essentially to our relation to God. 'Which of you, having a servant, ploughing or feeding cattle, will say unto him ... when he has come from the field, Go (immediately) and sit down to meat, and will not rather say unto him, Make ready wherewith I may sup, and gird thyself and serve me, till I have eaten and drunken: and afterward thou shalt eat and drink?' You will get your supper by–and–by, but you are here to work, says the master, and when you have finished one task, that does not involve that you are to rest; it involves only that you are to take up another. And however wearisome has been the ploughing amongst the heavy clods all day long, and tramping up and down the furrows, when you come in you are to clean yourself up, and get my supper ready, 'and afterward thou shalt eat and drink.'

As I have said, such a speech would argue a harsh human master, but is there not a truth which is not harsh in it in reference to us and God? Duty never ends. The eternal persistence through life of the obligation to service is what is taught us here, as being inherent in the very relation between the Lord and Owner of us all and us His slaves. Moralists and irreligious teachers say grand things about the eternal sweep of the great law of duty. The Christian thought is the higher one, 'Thou hast beset me behind and before, and laid Thine hand upon me,' and wherever I am I am under obligation to serve Thee, and no past record of work absolves me from the work of the present. From the cradle to the grave I walk beneath an all—encompassing, overarching firmament of duty. As long as we draw breath we are bound to the service of Him whose slaves we are, and whose service is perfect freedom.

Such is the bearing of this apparently repulsive representation of our text, which is not so repulsive if you come to think about it. It does not in the least set aside the natural craving for recreation and relaxation and repose. It does not overlook God's obligation to keep His slave alive, and in good condition for doing His work, by bestowing upon him the things that are needful for him, but it does meet that temptation which comes to us all to take that rest which circumstances may make manifestly not God's will, and it says to us, 'Forget the things that are behind, and reach forth unto the things that are before.' You have done a long day's work with plough or sheep—crook. The reward for work is more work. Come away indoors now, and nearer the Master, prepare His table. 'Which of you, having a servant, will not do so with him?' And that is how He does with us.

Then, the next thought here, which, as I say, has a harsh exterior, and a bitter rind, is that one of the slave doing his work, and never getting so much as 'thank you' for it. But if you lift this interpretation too, into the higher region of the relation between God and His slaves down here, a great deal of the harshness drops away. For what does it come to? Just to this, that no man among us, by any amount or completeness of obedience to the will of God establishes claims on God for a reward. You have done your duty—so much the better for you, but is that any reason why you should be decorated and honoured for doing it? You have done no more than your duty. 'So, likewise, ye, when ye have done all things that are commanded you'—even if that impossible condition were to be realised—'say we are unprofitable servants'; not in the bad sense in which the word is sometimes used, but in the accurate sense of not having brought any profit or advantage, more than was His before, to the Master whom we have thus served. It is a blessed thing for a man to call *himself* an unprofitable servant; it is an awful thing for the Master to call him one. If *we* say 'we are unprofitable servants,' we shall be likely to escape the solemn words from the Lord's lips: 'Take ye away the unprofitable servant, and cast him into outer darkness.' There are two that may use the word, Christ the Judge, and man the judged, and if the man will use it, Christ will not. 'If we judge ourselves we shall not be judged.'

Now, although, as I have said about the other part of this text, it is not meant to exhaust our relations to God, or to say the all—comprehensive word about the relation of obedience to blessedness; it is meant to say

'Merit lives from man to man,
And not from man, O Lord! to Thee.'

No one can reasonably build upon his own obedience, or his own work, nor claim as by right, for reward, heaven or other good. So my text is the anticipation of Paul's teaching about the impossibility of a man's being saved by his works, and it cuts up by the root, not only the teaching as to a treasure of 'merits of the saints,' and 'works of supererogation,' and the like; but it tells us, too, that we must beware of the germs of that self—complacent way of looking at ourselves and our own obedience, as if they had anything at all to do with our buying either the favour of God, or the rewards of the faithful servant.

II. Now, all that I have been saying may sound very harsh. Let us take a second step, and try if we can find out the kernel of grace in the harsh husk.

I hold fast by the one clue that Jesus Christ is here replying to the Apostle's prayer, 'Lord, increase our faith.' He had been laying down some very hard regulations for their conduct, and, naturally, when they felt how difficult it would be to come within a thousand miles of what He had been bidding them, they turned to Him with that prayer. It suggests that faith is there, in living operation, or they would not have prayed to Him for its increase. And how does He go about the work of increasing it? In two ways, one of which does not enter into my present subject. First, by showing the disciples the power of faith, in order to stimulate them to greater effort for its possession. He promised that they might say to the fig tree, 'Be thou plucked up and planted in the sea,' and it should obey them. The second way was by this context of which I am speaking now. How does it bear upon the Apostles' prayer? What is there in this teaching about the slave and his master, and the slave's work, and the incompatibility of the notion of reward with the slave's service, to help to strengthen faith? There is this that this teaching beats down every trace of self−confidence, and if we take it in and live by it, makes us all feel that we stand before God, whatever have been our deeds of service, with no claims arising from any virtue or righteousness of our own. We come empty−handed. If the servant who has done all that is commanded has yet to say, 'I can ask nothing from Thee, because I have done it, for it was all in the line of my duty,' what are we to say, who have done so little that was commanded, and so much that was forbidden?

So, you see, the way to increased faith is not by any magical communication from Christ, as the Apostles thought, but by taking into our hearts, and making operative in our lives, the great truth that in us there is nothing that can make a claim upon God, and that we must cast ourselves, as deserving nothing, wholly into His merciful hands, and find ourselves held up by His great unmerited love. Get the bitter poison root of self−trust out of you, and then there is some chance of getting the wholesome emotion of absolute reliance on Him into you. Jesus Christ, if I might use a homely metaphor, in these words pricks the bladder of self−confidence which we are apt to use to keep our heads above water. And it is only when it is pricked, and we, like the Apostle, feel ourselves beginning to sink, that we fling out a hand to Him, and clutch at His outstretched hand, and cry, 'Lord, save me, I perish!' One way to increase our faith is to be rooted and grounded in the assurance that duty is perennial, and that our own righteousness establishes no claim whatever upon God.

III. Finally, we note the higher view into which, by faith, we come.

I have been saying, with perhaps vain repetition, that the words of our text and context do not exhaust the whole truth of man's relation to God. They do exhaust the truth of the relation of God to any man that has not faith in his heart, because such a man is a slave in the worst sense, and any obedience that he renders to God's will externally is the obedience of a reluctant will, and is hard and harsh, and there is no end *to* it, and no good *from* it. But if we accept the position, and recognise our own impotence, and non−desert, and humbly say, 'Not by works of righteousness which we have done, but by His mercy He saves us,' then we come into a large place. The relation of master and slave does not cover all the ground *then*. 'Henceforth, I call you not slaves, but friends,' And when the wearied slave comes into the house, the new task is not a new burden, for he is a son as well as a slave; but the work is a delight, and it is a joy to have something more to do for his Father. If our service is the service of sons, sweetened by love, then there will be abundant thanks from the Father, who is not only our owner, but our lover.

For Christian service—that is to say, service based upon faith and rendered in love—*does* minister delight to our Father in heaven, and He Himself has called it an 'odour of a sweet smell, acceptable unto God.' And if our service on earth has been thus elevated and transformed from the compulsory obedience of a slave to the joyful service of a son, then our reception when at sundown the plough is left in the furrow and we come into the house will be all changed too. 'Which of you, having a servant, will say to him, Go and sit down to meat, and will not rather say to him, Make ready whilst I eat and drink?' That is the law for earth, but for heaven it is this, 'Blessed are those servants whom the Lord, when He cometh, shall find watching. Verily, I say unto you, that He shall gird Himself, and make them to sit down to meat, and will come forth and serve them.' The husk is gone now, I think, and the kernel is left. Loving service is beloved by God, and rewarded by the ministering, as a servant of servants, to us by Him who is King of kings and Lord of lords.

'Lord, increase our faith,' that we may so serve Thee on earth, and so be served by Thee in heaven.

WHERE ARE THE NINE?

'And it came to pass, as He went to Jerusalem, that He passed through the midst of Samaria and Galilee. 12. And as He entered into a certain village, there met Him ten men that were lepers, which stood afar off: 13. And they lifted up their voices, and said, Jesus, Master, have mercy on us. 14. And when He saw them, He said unto them, Go show yourselves unto the priests. And it came to pass, that, as they went, they were cleansed. 15. And one of them, when he saw that he was healed, turned back, and with a loud voice glorified God. 16. And fell down on his face at His feet, giving Him thanks: and he was a Samaritan. 17. And Jesus answering said, Were there not ten cleansed? but where are the nine? 18. There are not found that returned to give glory to God, save this stranger. 19. And He said unto him, Arise, go thy way, thy faith hath made thee whole.'—LUKE xvii. 11–19.

The melancholy group of lepers, met with in one of the villages on the borders of Samaria and Galilee, was made up of Samaritans and Jews, in what proportion we do not know. The common misery drove them together, in spite of racial hatred, as, in a flood, wolves and sheep will huddle close on a bit of high ground. Perhaps they had met in order to appeal to Jesus, thinking to move Him by their aggregated wretchedness; or possibly they were permanently segregated from others, and united in a hideous fellowship.

I. We note the lepers' cry and the Lord's strange reply. Of course they had to stand afar off, and the distance prescribed by law obliged them to cry aloud, though it must have been an effort, for one symptom of leprosy is a hoarse whisper. Sore need can momentarily give strange physical power. Their cry indicates some knowledge. They knew the Lord's name, and had dim notions of His authority, for He is addressed as Jesus and as Master. They knew that He had power to heal, and they hoped that He had 'mercy,' which they might win for themselves by entreaty. There was the germ of trust in the cry forced from them by desperate need. But their conceptions of Him, and their consciousness of their own necessities, did not rise above the purely physical region, and He was nothing to them but a healer.

Still, low and rude as their notions were, they did present a point of contact for Christ's 'mercy,' which is ever ready to flow into every heart that is lowly, as water will into all low levels. Jesus seems to have gone near to the lepers, for it was 'when He saw,' not when He heard, them that He spoke. It did not become Him to 'cry, nor cause His voice to be heard in the street,' nor would He cure as from afar, but He approaches those whom He heals, that they may see His face, and learn by it His compassion and love. His command recognised and honoured the law, but its main purpose, no doubt, was to test, and thereby to strengthen, the leper's trust. To set out to the priest while they felt themselves full of leprosy would seem absurd, unless they believed that Jesus could and would heal them. He gives no promise to heal, but asks for reliance on an implied promise. He has not a syllable of sympathy; His tender compassion is carefully covered up. He shuts down, as it were, the lantern-slide, and not a ray gets through. But the light was behind the screen all the while. We, too, have sometimes to act on the assumption that Jesus has granted our desires, even while we are not conscious that it is so. We, too, have sometimes to set out, as it were, for the priests, while we still feel the leprosy.

II. We note the healing granted to obedient faith. The whole ten set off at once. They had got all they wanted from the Lord, and had no more thought about Him. So they turned their backs on Him. How strange it must have been to feel, as they went along, the gradual creeping of soundness into their bones! How much more confidently they must have stepped out, as the glow of returning health asserted itself more and more! The cure is a transcendent, though veiled, manifestation of Christ's power; for it is wrought at a distance, without even a word, and with no vehicle. It is simply the silent forth-putting of His power. 'He spake, and it was done' is much, for only a word which is divine can affect matter. But 'He willed, and it was done,' is even more.

III. We note the solitary instance of thankfulness. The nine might have said, 'We are doing what the Healer bade us do; to go back to Him would be disobedience.' But a grateful heart knows that to express its gratitude is the highest duty, and is necessary for its own relief. How like us all it is to hurry away clutching our blessings, and never cast back a thought to the giver! This leper's voice had returned to Him, and his 'loud' acknowledgments were very different from the strained croak of his petition for healing. He knew that he had two to thank—God and Jesus; he did not know that these two were one. His healing has brought him much nearer Jesus than before, and now he can fall at His feet. Thankfulness knits us to Jesus with a blessed bond. Nothing is so sweet to a loving heart as to pour itself out in thanks to Him.

'And he was a Samaritan.' That may be Luke's main reason for telling the story, for it corresponds to the universalistic tendency of his Gospel. But may we not learn the lesson that the common human virtues are often found abundantly in nations and individuals against whom we are apt to be deeply prejudiced? And may we not learn another lesson—that heretics and heathen may often teach orthodox believers lessons, not only of courtesy and gratitude, but of higher things? A heathen is not seldom more sensitive to the beauty of Christ, and more touched by the story of His sacrifice, than we who have heard of Him all our days.

IV. We note Christ's sad wonder at man's ingratitude and joyful recognition of 'this stranger's' thankfulness. A tone of surprise as well as of sadness can be detected in the pathetic double questions. 'Were not *the* ten'—all of them, the ten who stood there but a minute since—'cleansed? but where are the nine?' Gone off with their gift, and with no spark of thankfulness in their selfish hearts. 'Were there none found that returned to give glory to God, save this stranger?' The numbers of the thankless far surpass those of the thankful. The fewness of the latter surprises and saddens Jesus still. Even a dog knows and will lick the hand that feeds it, but 'Israel doth not know, My people doth not consider.' We increase the sweetness of our gifts by thankfulness for them. We taste them twice when we ruminate on them in gratitude. They live after their death when we bless God and thank Jesus for them all. We impoverish ourselves still more than we dishonour Him by the ingratitude which is so crying a fault. One sorrow hides many joys. A single crumpled rose–leaf made the fairy princess's bed uncomfortable. Some of us can see no blue in our sky if one small cloud is there. Both in regard to earthly and spiritual blessings we are all sinners by unthankfulness, and we all lose much thereby.

Jesus rejoiced over 'this stranger,' and gave him a greater gift at last than he had received when the leprosy was cleared from his flesh. Christ's raising of him up, and sending him on his way to resume his interrupted journey to the priest, was but a prelude to 'Thy faith hath made thee whole,' or, as the Revised Version margin reads, 'saved thee.' Surely we may take that word in its deepest meaning, and believe that a more fatal leprosy melted out of this man's spirit, and that the faith which had begun in a confidence that Jesus could heal, and had been increased by obedience to the command which tried it, and had become more awed and enlightened by experience of bodily healing, and been deepened by finding a tongue to express itself in thankfulness, rose at last to such apprehension of Jesus, and such clinging to Him in grateful love, as availed to save 'this stranger' with a salvation that healed his spirit, and was perfected when the once leprous body was left behind, to crumble into dust.

THREE KINDS OP PRAYING

'And He spake a parable unto them to this end, that men ought always to pray, and not to faint; 2. Saying, There was in a city a judge, which feared not God, neither regarded man: 3. And there was a widow in that city; and she came unto him, saying, Avenge me of mine adversary. 4. And he would not for a while: but afterward he said within himself, Though I fear not God, nor regard man; 5. Yet because this widow troubleth me, I will avenge her, lest by her continual coming she weary me. 6. And the Lord said, Hear what the unjust judge saith. 7. And shall not God avenge His own elect, which cry day and night unto Him, though He bear long with them! 8. I tell you that He will avenge them speedily. Nevertheless when the Son

of man cometh, shall He find faith on the earth?
9. And He spake this parable unto certain which
trusted in themselves that they were righteous, and
despised others: 10. Two men went up into the temple
to pray; the one a Pharisee, and the other a publican.
11. The Pharisee stood and prayed thus with himself,
God, I thank thee, that I am not as Other men are,
extortioners, unjust, adulterers, or even as this
publican. 11. I fast twice in the week, I give tithes
of all that I possess. 13. And the publican, standing
afar off, would not lift up so much as his eyes unto
heaven, but smote upon his breast, saying, God be
merciful to me a sinner. 14. I tell you, this man went
down to his house justified rather than the other: for
every one that exalteth himself shall be abased; and
he that humbleth himself shall be exalted.'
—LUKE xviii. 1–14.

The two parables in this passage are each prefaced by Luke's explanation of their purpose. They are also connected by being both concerned with aspects of prayer. But the second was apparently not spoken at the same time as the first, but is put here by Luke as in an appropriate place.

I. The wearisome widow and the unrighteous judge. The similarities and dissimilarities between this parable and that in chapter xi. 5–8 are equally instructive. Both take a very unlovely character as open to the influence of persistent entreaty; both strongly underscore the unworthiness and selfishness of the motive for yielding. Both expect the hearers to use common–sense enough to take the sleepy friend and the worried judge as contrasts to, not parables, of Him to whom Christians pray. But the judge is a much worse man than the owner of the loaves, and his denial of the justice which it was his office to dispense is a crime; the widow's need is greater than the man's, and the judge's cynical soliloquy, in its unabashed avowal of caring for neither God nor man, and being guided only by regard to comfort, touches a deep depth of selfishness. The worse he was, the more emphatic is the exhortation to persistence. If the continual dropping of the widow's plea could wear away such a stone as that, its like could wear away anything. Yes, and suppose that the judge were as righteous and as full of love and wish to help as this judge was of their opposites; suppose that instead of the cry being a weariness it was a delight; suppose, in short, that, to go back to chapter xi., we 'call on Him as Father who, without respect of persons, judgeth': then our 'continual coming' will surely not be less effectual than hers was.

But we must note the spiritual experience supposed by the parable to belong to the Christian life. That forlorn figure of the widow, with all its suggestions of helplessness and oppression, is Christ's picture of His Church left on earth without Him. And though of course it is a very incomplete representation, it is a true presentation of one side and aspect of the devout life on earth. 'In the world ye shall have tribulation,' and the truer His servants are to Him, and the more their hearts are with Christ in God, the more they will feel out of touch with the world, and the more it will instinctively be their 'adversary.' If the widow does not feel the world's enmity, it will generally be because she is not a 'widow indeed.'

And another notable fact of Christian experience underlies the parable; namely that the Church's cry for protection from the adversary is often apparently unheard. In chapter xi. the prayer was for supply of necessities, here it is for the specific blessing of protection from the adversary. Whether that is referred to the needs of the Church or of the individual, it is true that usually the help sought is long delayed. It is not only 'souls under the altar' that have to cry 'How long, O Lord, dost Thou not avenge?' One thinks of years of persecution for whole communities, or of long, weary days of harassment and suffering for individuals, of multitudes of prayers and groans sent up into a heaven that, for all the answers sent down, might as well be empty, and one feels it hard to hold by the faith that 'verily, there is a God that' heareth.

We have all had times when our faith has staggered, and we have found no answer to our heart's question: 'Why tarry the wheels of His chariot?' Many of us have felt what Mary and Martha felt when 'Jesus abode still two days in the place where He was' after He had received their message, in which they had been so sure of His coming at once when He heard that 'he whom Thou lovest is sick,' that they did not ask Him to come. The delays of God's help are a constant feature in His providence, and, as Jesus says here, they are but too likely to take the life out of faith.

But over against these we have to place Jesus' triumphant assurance here: 'He will avenge them speedily.' Yes, the longest delay may yet be 'right early,' for heaven's clock does not beat at the same rate as our little chronometers. God is 'the God of patience,' and He has waited for millenniums for the establishment of His kingdom on earth; His 'own elect' may learn long–suffering from Him, and need to take to heart the old exhortation, 'If the vision tarry, wait for it, for it will surely come, and will not tarry.' Yes, God's delays are not delays, but are for our profit that we may always pray and not faint, and may keep alight the flame of the sure hope that the Son of man cometh, and that in His coming all adversaries shall be destroyed, and the widow, no longer a widow, but the bride, go in to the feast and forget her foes, and 'the days of her mourning be ended.'

II. The Pharisee and the publican.

Luke's label on this parable tells us that it was spoken to a group of the very people who were personated in it by the Pharisee. One can fancy their faces as they listened, and how they would love the speaker! Their two characteristics are self–righteousness and depreciation of every one else, which is the natural result of such trust in self. The self–adulation was absolute, the contempt was all–embracing, for the Revised Version rightly renders 'set *all* others at nought.' That may sound exaggerated, but the way to judge of moral characteristics is to take them in their fullest development and to see what they lead to then. The two pictures heighten each other. The one needs many strokes to bring out the features, the other needs but one. Self–righteousness takes many shapes, penitence has but one emotion to express, one cry to utter.

Every word in the Pharisee's prayer is reeking with self–complacency. Even the expression 'prayed with himself' is significant, for it suggests that the prayer was less addressed to God than to himself, and also that his words could scarcely be spoken in the hearing of others, both because of their arrogant self–praise and of their insolent calumnies of 'all the rest.' It was not prayer to God, but soliloquy in his own praise, and it was in equal parts adulation of himself and slander of other men. So it never went higher than the inner roof of the temple court, and was, in a very fatal sense, 'to himself.'

God is complimented with being named formally at first, and in the first two words, 'I thank thee,' but that is only formal introduction, and in all the rest of his prayer there is not a trace of praying. Such a self–satisfied gentleman had no need to ask for anything, so he brought no petitions. He uses the conventional language of thanksgiving, but his real meaning is to praise himself to God, not to thank God for himself. God is named once. All the rest is I, I, I. He had no longing for communion, no aspiration, no emotion.

His conception of righteousness was mean and shallow. And as St. Bernard notes, he was not so much thankful for being righteous as for being alone in his goodness. No doubt he was warranted in disclaiming gross sins, but he was glad to be free from them, not because they were sins, but because they were vulgar. He had no right to fling mud either on 'all the rest' or on 'this publican,' and if he had been really praying or giving thanks he would have had enough to think of in God and himself without casting sidelong and depreciatory glances at his neighbours. He who truly prays 'sees no man any more,' or if he does, sees men only as subjects for intercession, not for contempt. The Pharisee's notion of righteousness was primarily negative, as consisting in abstinence from flagrant sins, and, in so far as it was positive, it dealt entirely with ceremonial acts. Such a starved and surface conception of righteousness is essential to self–righteousness, for no man who sees the law of duty in its depth and inwardness can flatter himself that he has kept it. To fast twice a week and to give tithes of all that one acquired were acts of supererogation, and are proudly recounted as if God should feel much indebted to the doer for paying Him more than was required. The Pharisee makes no petitions. He states his claims, and tacitly expects that God will meet them.

Few words are needed to paint the publican; for his estimate of himself is simple and one, and what he wants from God is one thing, and one only. His attitude expresses his emotions, for he does not venture to go near the shining example of all respectability and righteousness, nor to lift his eyes to heaven. Like the penitent psalmist, his iniquities have taken hold on him, so that he is 'not able to look up.' Keen consciousness of sin, true sorrow for sin, earnest desire to shake off the burden of sin, lowly trust in God's pardoning mercy, are all crowded into his brief petition. The arrow thus feathered goes straight up to the throne; the Pharisee's prayer cannot rise above his own lips.

Jesus does not leave His hearers to apply the 'parable,' but drives its application home to them, since He knew how keen a thrust was needed to pierce the triple breastplate of self–righteousness. The publican was 'justified'; that is, accounted as righteous. In the judgment of heaven, which is the judgment of truth, sin forsaken is sin passed away. The Pharisee condensed his contempt into '*this* publican'; Jesus takes up the 'this' and turns it into a distinction, when He says, '*this man* went down to his house justified.' God's condemnation of the Pharisee and acceptance of the publican are no anomalous aberration of divine justice, for it is a universal law, which has abundant exemplifications, that he that exalteth himself is likely to be humbled, and he that humbles himself to be exalted. Daily life does not always yield examples thereof, but in the inner life and as concerns our relations to God, that law is absolutely and always true.

ENTERING THE KINGDOM

'And they brought unto Him also infants, that He would touch them: but when His disciples saw it, they rebuked them. 16. But Jesus called them unto Him, and said, Suffer little children to come unto Me, and forbid them not: for of such is the kingdom of God. 17. Verily I say unto you, Whosoever shall not receive the kingdom of God as a little child shall in no wise enter therein. 18. And a certain ruler asked Him, saying, Good Master, what shall I do to inherit eternal life? 19. And Jesus said unto him, Why callest thou Me good? none is good, save one, that is, God. 20. Thou knowest the commandments, Do not commit adultery, Do not kill, Do not steal, Do not bear false witness, Honour thy father and thy mother. 21. And he said, All these have I kept from my youth up. 22. Now when Jesus heard these things, He said unto him, Yet lackest thou one thing: sell all that thou hast, and distribute unto the poor, and thou shalt have treasure in heaven: and come, follow Me. 23. And when he heard this, he was very sorrowful: for he was very rich. 24. And when Jesus saw that he was very sorrowful He said, How hardly shall they that have riches enter into the kingdom of God? 25. For it is easier for a camel to go through a needle's eye, than for a rich man to enter into the kingdom of God. 26. And they that heard it said, Who then can be saved? 27. And He said, The things which are impossible with men are possible with God. 28. Then Peter said, Lo, we have left all, and followed Thee. 29. And He said unto them, Verily I say unto you, There is no man that hath left house, or parents, or brethren, or wife, or children, for the kingdom of God's sake, 30. Who shall not receive manifold more in this present time, and in world to come life everlasting.'—LUKE xviii. 15–30.

In this section Luke rejoins the other two Evangelists, from whom his narrative has diverged since Luke ix. 51. All three bring together these two incidents of the children in Christ's arms and the young ruler. Probably they were connected in time as well as in subject. Both set forth the conditions of entering the kingdom, which the one declares to be lowliness and trust, and the other to be self–renunciation.

I. We have the child–likeness of the subjects of the kingdom. No doubt there was a dash of superstition in the impulse that moved the parents to bring their children to Jesus, but it was an eminently natural desire to win a good man's blessing, and one to which every parent's heart will respond. It was not the superstition, but the intrusive familiarity, that provoked the disciples' rebuke. A great man's hangers—on are always more careful of his dignity than he is, for it increases their own importance.

The tender age of the children is to be noted. They were 'babes,' and had to be brought, being too young to walk, and so having scarcely yet arrived at conscious, voluntary life. It is 'of such' that the subjects of the kingdom are composed. What, then, are the qualities which, by this comparison, Jesus requires? Certainly not innocence, which would be to contradict all his teaching and to shut out the prodigals and publicans, and clean contrary to the whole spirit of Luke's Gospel. Besides, these scarcely conscious infants were not 'innocent,' for they had not come to the age of which either innocence or guilt can be predicated. What, then, had they which the children of the kingdom must have?

Perhaps the sweet and meek little 131st Psalm puts us best on the track of the answer. It may have been in our Lord's mind; it certainly corresponds to His thought. 'My heart is not haughty, nor mine eyes lofty.... I have stilled and quieted my soul; like a weaned child with his mother.' The infant's lowliness is not yet humility; for it is instinct rather than virtue. It makes no claims, thinks no lofty thoughts of self; in fact, has scarcely begun to know that there is a self at all. On the other hand, clinging trust is the infant's life. It, too, is rudimentary and instinctive, but the impulse which makes the babe nestle in its mother's bosom may well stand for a picture of the conscious trust which the children of the kingdom must have. The child's instinct is the man's virtue. We have

'To travel back
And tread again that ancient track,'

regaining as the conscious temper of our spirits those excellences of humility and trust of which the first faint types may be seen in the infant in arms. The entrance gate is very low, and, if we hold our heads high, we shall not get through it. It must be on our hands and knees that we go in. There is no place in the kingdom for those who trust in themselves. We must rely wholly on God manifest in His Son.

So intent is Luke in pointing the lesson that he passes by in silence the infinitely beautiful and touching incident which the world perhaps knows better than any other in our Lord's life—that of His taking the infants in His arms and blessing them. In many ways that incident would have been peculiarly suitable for this Gospel, which delights to bring out the manhood and universal beneficence of Jesus. But if Luke knew of it, he did not care to bring in anything which would weaken the lesson of the conditions of entering the kingdom.

II. We have self—renunciation as the condition of entering the kingdom. The conversation with the ruler (vs. 18–23) sets forth its necessity; the sad exclamation to the bystanders (vs. 24–27) teaches its difficulty; and the dialogue with Peter as representing the twelve (vs. 28–30), its reward.

(1) The necessity of self—renunciation. The ruler's question has much blended good and evil. It expresses a true earnestness, a dissatisfaction with self, a consciousness of unattained bliss and a

longing for it, a felt readiness to take any pains to secure it, a confidence in Christ's guidance—in short, much of the child spirit. But it has also a too light estimate of what good is, a mistaken notion that 'eternal life' can be won by external deeds, which implies fatal error as to its nature and his own power to do these. This superficial estimate of goodness, and this over confidence in his ability to do good acts, are the twin mistakes against which Christ's treatment of him is directed.

Adopting Luke's version of our Lord's answer, the counter–question, which begins it, lays hold of the polite address, which had slipped from the ruler's lips as mere form, and bids him widen out his conceptions of 'good.' Jesus does not deny that He has a right to the title, but questions this man's right to give it Him. The ruler thought of Jesus only as a man, and, so thinking, was too ready with his adjective. Conventional phrases of compliment may indicate much of the low notions from which they spring. He who is so liberal with his ascriptions of goodness needs to have his notions of what it is elevated. Jesus lays down the great truth which this man, in his confidence that he by his own power could do any good needed for eternal life, was perilously forgetting. God is the only good, and therefore all human goodness must come from Him; and if the ruler is to do 'good,' he must first be good, by receiving goodness from God.

But the saying has an important bearing on Christ's character. The world calls Him good. Why? There is none good but God. So we are face to face with this dilemma—Either Jesus Christ is God manifest in the flesh, or He is not good.

Having thus tried to deepen his conceptions, and awaken his consciousness of imperfection, our Lord meets the man on his own ground by referring him to the Law, which abundantly answered his inquiry. The second half of the commandments are alone quoted by Him; for they have especially to do with conduct, and the infractions of them are more easily recognised than those of the first. The ruler expected that some exceptional and brilliant deeds would be pointed out and he is relegated to the old homely duties, which it is gross crime not to do.

A shade of disappointment and impatience is in his protestation that he had done all these ever since he was a lad. No doubt he had, and his coming to Jesus confessed that though he had, the doing had not brought him 'eternal life.' Are there not many youthful hearts which would have to say the same, if they would be frank with themselves? They have some longings after a bliss and calm which they feel is not theirs. They have kept within the lines of that second half of the Decalogue, but that amount and sort of 'good thing' has not brought peace. Jesus looks on all such as He did on this young man, 'loves' them, and speaks further to them as He did to him. What was lacking? The soul of goodness, without which these other things were 'dead works.' And what is that soul? Absolute self–renunciation and following Christ. For this man the former took the shape of parting with his wealth, but that external renunciation in itself was as 'dead' and impotent to bring eternal life as all his other good acts had been. It was precious as a means to an end—the entrance into the number of Christ's disciples; and as an expression of that inward self–surrender which is essential for discipleship.

The real stress of the condition is in its second half, 'Follow me.' He who enters the company of Christ's followers enters the kingdom, and has eternal life. If he does not do that, he may give his goods to feed the poor, and it profiteth him nothing. Eternal life is not the external wages for external acts, but the outcome and consequence of yielding self to Jesus, through whom goodness, which keeps the law, flows into the soul.

The requirement pierced to the quick. The man loved the world more than eternal life, after all. But though he went away, he went sorrowful; and that was perhaps the presage that he would come back.

(2) Jesus follows him with sad yearning, and, we may be sure, still sought to draw him back. His exclamation is full of the charity which makes allowance for temptation. It speaks a universal truth, never more needed than in our days, when wealth has flung its golden chains round so many professing Christians. How few of us believe that it gets harder for us to be disciples as we grow richer! There are multitudes in our churches who would be far nearer Christ than they are ever likely to be, if they would literally obey the injunction to get rid of their wealth.

We are too apt to take such commands as applicable only to the individuals who received them, whereas, though, no doubt, the spirit, and not the letter, is the universal element in them, there are far more of us than we are willing to confess, who need to obey the letter in order to keep the spirit. What a depth of vulgar adoration of the power of money is in the disciples' exclamation, 'If rich men cannot get into the kingdom, who can get in!' Or perhaps it rather means, If self−renunciation is the condition, who can fulfil it? The answer points us all to the only power by which we can do good, and overcome self; namely by God's help. God is 'good,' and we can be good too, if we look to Him. God will fill our souls with such sweetness that earth will not be hard to part with.

(3) The last paragraph of this passage teaches the reward of self−renunciation. Peter shoves his oar in, after his fashion. It would have been better if he had not boasted of their surrender, but yet it was true that they had given up all. Only a fishing−boat and a parcel of old nets, indeed, but these were all they had to give; and God's store, which holds His children's surrendered valuables, has many things of small value in it—cups of cold water and widows' mites lying side by side with crowns and jewels.

So Jesus does not rebuke the almost innocent self−congratulation, but recognises in it an appeal to his faithfulness. It was really a prayer, though it sounded like a vaunt, and it is answered by renewed assurances. To part with outward things for Christ's sake or for the kingdom's sake—which is the same thing—is to win them again with all their sweetness a hundred−fold sweeter. Gifts given to Him come back to the giver mended by His touch and hallowed by lying on His altar. The present world yields its full riches only to the man who surrenders all to Jesus. And the 'eternal life,' which the ruler thought was to be found by outward deeds, flows necessarily into the heart which is emptied of self, that it may be filled with Him who is the life, and will be perfected yonder.

THE MAN THAT STOPPED JESUS

'And Jesus stood, and commanded him to be brought
unto Him: and when he was come near, He asked him,
41. Saying, What wilt thou that I shall do unto
thee?'—LUKE xviii. 40–41.

This story of the man that stopped Christ is told by the three 'Synoptic' Evangelists, and it derives a special value from having occurred within a week of the Crucifixion. You remember how graphically Mark tells how the blind man hears who is passing and immediately begins to cry with a loud voice to Christ to have mercy upon him; how the officious disciples—a great deal more concerned for the Master's dignity than He was Himself—tried to silence him; and how, with a sturdy persistence and independence of externals which often goes along with blindness, 'he cried the more a great deal' because they did try, and then how he won the distinction of being the man that stopped Christ. When Jesus stood still, and commanded him to be called, the crowd wheeled right round at once, and instead of hindering, encumbered him with help, and bade him to 'rise, and be of good cheer.' Then he flings away some poor rag that he had had to cover himself sitting there, and wearing his under–garment only, comes to Christ, and Jesus asks, 'What do you want?' A promise in the shape of a question. Bartimaeus knows what he wants, and answers without hesitation, and so he gets his request.

Now, I think in all this incident, and especially in its centre part, which I have read, there are great lessons for us. And the first of them is, I see here a wonderful revelation of Christ's quick sympathy at a moment when He was most absorbed.

I said that all this occurred within a week of our Lord's Crucifixion. If you will recall the way in which that last journey to Jerusalem is described in the Evangelists, you will see that there was something very extraordinary about the determination and tension of spirit which impelled Jesus along the road, all the way from Galilee. Mark says that the disciples followed and were amazed. There was something quite unlike what they had been accustomed to, in His face and bearing, and it was so strange to them that they were puzzled and frightened. We read, too, that their amazement and fright prevented them from going very near Him on the road; 'as they *followed* they were afraid.' Then the story goes on to tell how James and John, with their arrogant wish, did draw closer to Him, the rest of them lagging behind, conscious of a certain unaccustomed distance between Him and them, which only the ambitious two dared to diminish. Further, one of the Evangelists speaks of His face being 'set' to go to Jerusalem, the gentle lineaments fixed in a new expression of resolution and absorption. The Cross was flinging its shadow over Him. He was bracing Himself up for the last struggle. If ever there was a moment of His life when we might have supposed that He would be oblivious of externals, and especially of the individual sorrows of one poor blind beggar sitting by the roadside, it was that moment. But however plunged in great thoughts about the agonising suffering that He was going to front, and the grand work that He was going to do, and the great victory that He was going to win so soon, He had

'A heart at leisure from itself
To soothe and sympathise.'

Even at that supreme hour He stood still and commanded him to be called. I wonder if it is saying too much to say that in the exercise of that power of healing and helping Bartimaeus, Jesus found some relief from the pressure of impending sorrow.

Brethren, is not that a lesson for us all? It is not spiritualising, allegorising, cramming meanings into an incident that are not in it, when we say—Think of Jesus Christ as one of ourselves, knowing that

He was going to His death within a week, and then think of Him turning to this poor man. Is not that a pattern for us? We are often more selfish in our sorrows than in our joys. Many of us are inclined, when we are weighed down by personal sorrows, to say, 'As long as I have this heavy weight lying on my heart, how can you expect me to take an interest in the affairs of others, or to do Christian work, or to rise to the calls of benevolence and the cries of need?' We do not expect *you* to do it; but Jesus Christ did it, 'leaving us an example that we should follow in His steps.' Next to the blessed influences of God's own Spirit, and the peace–bringing act of submission, there is no such comfort for sorrow, as to fling ourselves into others' griefs, and to bear others' burdens. Our Lord, with His face set like a flint, on the road to the Cross, but yet sufficiently free of heart to turn to Bartimaeus, reads a lesson that rebukes us all, and should teach us all.

Further, do we not see here a beautiful concrete instance, on the lower plane, of the power of earnest desire.

No enemy could have stopped Christ on that road; no opposition could have stopped Him, no beseeching on the part of loving and ignorant friends, repeating the temptation in the wilderness—or the foolish words of Peter, 'This shall not be unto Thee,' could have stopped Him. He would have trodden down all such flimsy obstacles, as a lion 'from the thickets of Jordan' crashes through the bulrushes, but this cry stopped Him, 'Jesus, thou Son of David, have mercy on me, and the Cross and all else that He was hastening to, great as it was for the world, had to wait its turn, for something else had to be done first. There was noise enough on the road, the tramp of many feet, the clatter of many eager tongues, but the voice of one poor man sitting in the dust there by the roadside, found its way through all the noise to Christ's ears. 'Which things are an allegory.' There is an ocean of praise always, as I might so say breaking upon Christ's Throne, but the little stream of my petitions flows distinguishable through all that sea. As one of our poets says, we may even think of Him as 'missing my little human praise' when the voice of one poor boy was not heard. Surely amidst all the encouragements that we have to believe that our cry is not sent up into an empty heaven, nor into deaf ears, and that all the multitude of creatures that wait before that Throne do not prevent the individualising knowledge and the individualising love of Jesus Christ from coming straight to every one of us, this little incident is not the least instructive and precious. He that heard Bartimaeus will hear us.

In like manner, may I not say that here we have an illustration of how Christ, who has so much besides to do, would suspend other work, if it were needful, in order to do what we need? As I have said, the rest had to wait. Bartimaeus stopped Christ. And our hand, if it be the hand of faith, put out to the hem of the garment as Jesus of Nazareth passeth by, will so far stop Him as that He will do what we wish, if what we wish is in accordance with our highest good. There was another man in Jericho who stopped Christ, on that same journey; for not only the petition of Bartimaeus, but the curiosity—which was more than curiosity—of Zacchaeus, stopped Him, and He who stood still, though He had His face set like a flint to go to Jerusalem, because Bartimaeus cried, stood still and looked up into the sycamore tree where the publican was—the best fruit that ever it bore—and said, 'Zacchaeus; come down, I must abide at thy house.' Why *must* He abide? Because He discerned there a soul that He could help and save, and that arrested Him on His road to the Cross.

So, dear friends, amidst all the work of administering the universe which He does, and of guiding and governing and inspiring His Church, which He does, if you ask for the supply of your need He would put that work aside for a moment, if necessary, to attend to you. That is no exaggeration; it is only a strong way of putting the plain truth that Christ's love individualises each of its objects; and lavishes itself upon each one of us; as if there were no other beings in the universe but only our two selves.

And then, remember too, that what Bartimaeus got was not taken from anyone else. Nobody suffered because Jesus paused to help him. They sat down in ranks, five thousand of them, and as they began to eat, those that were first served would be looked upon with envious eye by the last 'ranks,' who would be wondering if the bits of bread and the two small fishes were enough to go round. But the first group was fed full and the last group had as much, and they took up 'of the fragments that remained, twelve baskets full.'

'Enough for all, enough for each,
Enough for evermore.'

There is one more thought rising out of this story. It teaches a wonderful lesson as to the power which Christ puts into the hand of believing prayer.

'What wilt thou that I shall do unto thee?' He had asked the same question a little while before, under very different circumstances. When James and John came and tried to beguile Him into a blind promise, because they knew that It was not likely that they would get what they asked if they said it out at first. He avoided the snare with that same question, To them the question was a refusal; they had said: 'Master, we will that Thou wouldst do whatever we should desire'; and He said: 'What is it that ye desire? Let Me know that first.' But when blind Bartimaeus cried, Jesus smiled down upon him—though his sightless eyeballs could not see the smile, there would be a smile in the cadence of His words—and He said: 'What wouldst thou that I should do for thee?' To this suppliant that question was a promise—'I will do what you want.' He puts the key of the royal treasure–house into the hand of faith, and says, 'Go in and help yourself. Take what you will.'

Only, of course, we must remember that there are limitations in the very nature of the case, imposed not arbitrarily, but because the very nature of the truest gifts creates them, and these limitations to some of us sound as if they took all the blessedness out of the act of prayer. 'We know,' says one of the Apostles, 'that if we ask anything according to His will He heareth us.' Some of us think that that is a very poor kind of charter, but it sets the necessary limit to the omnipotence of faith. 'What wouldst thou that I should do for thee?' Unless our answer always, and at bottom, is, 'Not my will, but Thine,' we have not yet learnt the highest blessing, nor the truest meaning, of prayer. For to pray does not mean to insist, to press our wishes on God, but it means, first, to desire that our wills may be brought into harmony with His. The old Rabbis hit upon great truths now and then, and one of them said, 'Make God's will thy will, that He may make thy will His will.' If any poor, blind Bartimaeus remembers that, and asks accordingly, he has the key to the royal treasury in his possession, and he may go in and plunge his hand up to the wrist in jewels and diamonds, and carry away bars of gold, and it will all be his.

When this man, who had no sight in his eyeballs, knew that whatever he wanted he should have, he did not need to pause long to consider what it was that he wanted most. If you and I had that

269

Aladdin's lamp given to us, and had only to rub it for a mighty spirit to come that would fulfil our wishes, I wonder if we should be as sure of what we wanted. If we were as conscious of our need as the blind man was of his, we should pause as little in our response to the question: 'What wouldst thou that I should do for thee?' 'Lord! Dost Thou not see that mine eyes are dark? What else but sight can I want?' Jesus still comes to us with the same question. God grant that we may all say; 'Lord, how canst Thou ask us? Dost Thou not see that my soul is stained, my love wandering, my eyeballs dim? Give me Thyself!' If we thus ask, then the answer will come as quickly to us as it did to this blind man: 'Go thy way! Thy faith hath saved thee,' and that 'Go thy way' will not be dismissal from the Presence of our Benefactor, but our 'way' will be the same as Bartimaeus' was, when he received his sight, and 'followed Jesus in the way.'

MELTED BY KINDNESS

'And when Jesus came to the place, He looked up, and saw
him, and said unto him, Zacchaeus, make haste, and come
down; for to-day I must abide at thy house.'
—LUKE xix. 5.

It is characteristic of Luke that only he tells the story of Zacchaeus. He always dwells with special interest on incidents bringing out the character of Christ as the Friend of outcasts. His is eminently the Gospel of forgiveness. For example, we owe to Him the three supreme parables of the lost sheep, the lost coin, and the prodigal son, as well as those of the Pharisee and the publican praying in the Temple; and of the good Samaritan. It is he that tells us that all the publicans and sinners came near to Jesus to hear Him; and he loses no opportunity of enforcing the lesson with which this incident closes, 'The Son of Man is come to seek and to save that which was lost.' It is because of the light that it throws upon that great thought that he tells this fascinating story of Zacchaeus. I need not repeat it. We all remember it, and the quaintness and grotesqueness of part of it fix it in people's memories. We know how the rich tax gatherer, pocketing his dignity, and unable to see over the heads of the crowd, scrambled up into the branches of the sycamore tree that overhung the road; and there was found by the eye of love, and surprised by the words of kindness, which melted him down, and made a new man of him on the spot. The story seems to me to be full of teaching, to which I desire to turn your attention at this time.

I. First, note the outcast, drawn by imperfect motives to Jesus Christ.

It has been supposed that this man was a Gentile, but his Jewish name establishes his origin. And, if so, the fact that he was a publican and a Jew says a good deal about his character. There are some trades which condemn, to a certain extent, the men who engage in them. You would not expect to find a man of sensitive honour acting as a professional spy; or one of earnest religious character keeping a public-house. You would not expect to find a very good Jew condescending to be the tool of the Roman Government. Zacchaeus was at the head of the revenue office in Jericho, a position of considerable importance, inasmuch as there was a large volume of trade through that city from its situation near the fords of the Jordan, and from the fertility of the plain in which it stood. He had made some money, and probably made it by very questionable means. He was the object, not undeservedly, of the execration and suspicion of his countrymen. Italians did not love Italians who took service under Austria. Irishmen did not love Irishmen who in the bad old days used to collect church cess. And so Jews had no very kind feeling towards Jews who became Caesar's servants. That a man should be in such a position indicated that he cared more for money than for patriotism, religion, or popular approval. His motto was the motto of that Roman Emperor who said, 'Money has no smell,' out of whatever cesspool it may have been fished up. But the consciousness of being encompassed by universal hatred would induce the object of it to put on an extra turn of the screw, and avenge upon individuals the general hostility. So we may take it for granted that Zacchaeus, the head of the Jericho custom–house, and rich to boot, was by no means a desirable character.

What made him want to see Jesus Christ? He said to himself, curiosity; but probably he was doing himself injustice, and there was something else working below than merely the wish to see what sort of man was this Rabbi Joshua from Galilee that everybody was talking about. Had he heard that Jesus had a soft place in His heart for his class? Or was he, perhaps, beginning to get tired of being the butt of universal hatred, and finding that money scarcely compensated for that? Or was there some reaching out towards some undefined good, and a dissatisfaction with a very defined present, though unnamed, evil? Probably so. Like some of us, he put the trivial motive uppermost because he was half ashamed of the half–conscious better one.

I wonder if there are any here now who said to themselves that they would come out of curiosity to hear the preacher, or from some such ordinary motive, and who all the while have, lying deep below that, another reason altogether, a dim feeling that it is not all right between them and God, and that here may be the place to have it put right? At all events, from whatsoever imperfect motives little Zacchaeus was perched up in the sycamore there, he went to see Christ, and he got more than he went for. Unconsciously we may be drawn, and imperfect motives may lead us to a perfect Saviour.

He sets us an example in another way. Do not be too punctilious about dignity in pursuing aims that you know to be good. It would be a sight to bring jeers and grins on the faces of the crowd to see the rich man of the custom–house sitting up amongst the leaves. But he did not mind about that if he got a good look at the Rabbi when He passed. People care nothing for ridicule if their hearts are set upon a thing. I wish there were more of us who did not mind being laughed at if only what we did helped us to see Jesus Christ. Do not be afraid of ridicule. It is not a test of truth; in nine cases out of ten it is the grimace of fools.

II. Then, further, notice the self–invited Guest.

When the little procession stopped under the sycamore tree, Zacchaeus would begin to feel uncomfortable. He may have had experience in past times of the way in which the great doctors of orthodoxy were in the habit of treating a publican, and may have begun to be afraid that this new one was going to be like all the rest, and elicit some kind of mob demonstration against him. The crowd would be waiting with intense curiosity to see what would pass between the Rabbi and the revenue collector. They would all be very much astonished. 'Zacchaeus! make haste and come down. To–day I must abide at thy house.' Perhaps it was the first time since he had been a child at his mother's knee that he had heard his name pronounced in tones of kindness. There was not a ragged beggar in Jericho who would not have thought himself degraded by putting his foot across the threshold that Jesus now says He will cross.

It is the only time in which we read that Jesus volunteered to go into any house. He never offers to go where He is not wanted, any more than He ever stays away where He is. And so the very fact of His saying 'I will abide at thy house,' is to me an indication that, deep down below Zacchaeus' superficial and vulgar curiosity, there was something far more noble which our Lord fosters into life and consciousness by this offer.

Many large truths are suggested by it on which we may touch. We have in Christ's words an illustration of His individualising knowledge. 'Zacchaeus, come down.' There is no sign that anybody had told Christ the name, or that He knew anything about Zacchaeus before by human knowledge. But the same eye that saw Nathanael under the fig–tree saw Zacchaeus in the sycamore; and, seeing in secret, knew without being told the names of both. Christ does not name men in vain. He generally, when He uses an individual's name in addressing him, means either to assert His knowledge of his character, or His authority over him, or in some way or other to bespeak personal adhesion and to promise personal affection. So He named some of His disciples, weaving a bond that united each single soul to Himself by the act. This individualising knowledge and drawing love and authority are all expressed, as I think, in that one word 'Zacchaeus.' And these are as true about us as about him. The promises of the New Testament, the words of Jesus Christ, the great, broad, universal 'whosoevers' of His assurance and of His commandments are as directly meant for each of us as if they were in an envelope with our names upon them and put into our hands. We, too, are spoken to by Him by our names, and for us, too, there may be a personal bond of answering love that knits us individually to the Master, as there certainly is a bond of personal regard, compassion, affection, and purpose of salvation in His heart in regard of each single soul of all the masses of humanity. I should have done something if I should have been able to gather into a point, that blessedly pierced some heart to let the life in, the broad truths of the Gospel. 'Whosoever will, let him come.' Say to yourself, 'That is me.' 'Whosoever cometh I will in no wise cast out.' Say to yourself, 'That is me.' And in like manner with all the general declarations, and especially with that chiefest of them all, 'God so loved the world that He gave His only begotten Son, that whosoever believeth in Him should not perish.' Read it as you may—and you will never read it right until you do—'God so loved *me*'—John, Mary, or whatever be your name—'Jesus so loved *me* that if *I* believe upon Him *I* shall not perish, but have everlasting life.'

Then, note, further, how here we get the revelation, in a concrete form, of Christ's perfect willingness and desire to make common cause, and dwell with the most degraded and outcast. I have said that this is the only instance in which He volunteered to be a guest. Pharisees asked Him, and He did not refuse. The publican's dwelling, which was tabooed, He opened the door of by His own hand. And that is what He always does.

This little incident may be taken to be, not merely a symbol of His whole dealings, but an illustration, in small, of the same principle which has its largest embodiment and illustration in the fact of His Incarnation and Manhood. Why did Jesus Christ take flesh and dwell among us? Because He desired to seek and to save that which is lost. Why did He go into the publican's house, and brave the sneers of the crowd, and associate Himself with the polluted? For the same reason. Microscopic crystals and gigantic ones are due to the same forces working in the same fashion. This incident is more than a symbol; it is a little instance of the operation of the law which finds its supreme and transcendent instance in the fact that the Eternal Son of God bowed the heavens and came down 'and dwelt among us, and we beheld His glory.'

His example is our pattern. A Christian church which does not imitate its Master in its frank and continual willingness to associate itself with the degraded and the outcast has lost one of the truest signs of its being vitalised with the life of Christ. There is much in this day in the condition of Christian communities to make men dissatisfied and fearful. But there is one thing which, though in all its developments one cannot sympathise with it, is in its essence wholly good, and that is the new and quickened consciousness that a church which does not address itself to the outcasts has no business to live; and that Christian people who are too proud of their righteousness to go amongst the unclean and the degraded are a great deal more of Pharisees than Christians, and have need to learn which be the first principles of the religion which they profess. Self–righteousness gathers up its skirts in holy horror; perfect righteousness goes cheerily and without fear amongst the outcasts, for where should the physician go but to the sick, and where should Christ be found but in the house of the publican?

Further, the saying of our Lord suggests His recognition of the great law that ruled His life. Chronology here is of much importance. We do not generally remember that the scene with Zacchaeus was within about a week of the Crucifixion. Our Lord was on that last journey to Jerusalem to die, during the whole of which there was over His demeanour a tension of holy impatience, altogether unlike His usual manner, which astonished and amazed the disciples as they followed Him. He set His face like a flint to go to Jerusalem; and strode before them on the way as if He were eager to reach the culmination of His sufferings and of His work. Thus borne on the wings of the strong desire to be perfected on the Cross, He is arrested on His path. Nothing else was able to stop Him, but 'To–day I *must* abide in thy house.' There was a soul to be saved; and the world's sacrifice had to wait till the single soul was secured. Christ hurrying, if I may use the word, at all events steadfastly and without wavering, pressing towards the Cross, let His course be stopped by this need. The highest 'must' was obedience to the Father's will, and parallel with that need there was the other, of rescuing the Father's prodigal sons. So this elder Brother owned the obligation, and paused on the road to Calvary, to lodge in the house of Zacchaeus. Let us learn the sweet lesson, and take the large consolations that lie in such a thought.

Again, the utterance of this self–invited Guest suggests His over–abundant fulfilment of timid, half–conscious desires. I said at the beginning of my remarks that only curiosity was on the surface; but that the very fact that our Lord addressed Himself to the man seemed to imply that He descried in him something more than mere vulgar curiosity. And the glad leap with which Zacchaeus came down from his tree might have revealed to Zacchaeus himself, as no doubt it did to some of the bystanders, what it was that he had been dimly wishing. So with us all there are needs, longings, half–emerging wishes, that have scarcely come into the field of consciousness, but yet have power enough to modify our actions. Jesus Christ understands all about us, and reads us better than we do ourselves; and is ready to meet, and by meeting to bring into full relief, these vague feelings after an undefined good. Brethren, He is to us, if we will let Him be, all that we want; and He is to us all that we need, although we only half know that we need it, and never say to ourselves that we wish it.

There is a last thought deducible from these words of our Lord's; and that is, His leaving a man to decide whether he will have Him or no. 'Make haste and come down, for to–day I *must* abide at thy

273

house. Yes! but if Zacchaeus had stuck in his tree, Christ's 'must' would not have been fulfilled. He would have gone on to Jerusalem if the publican had not scrambled down in haste. He forces Himself on no man; He withholds Himself from no man. He respects that awful prerogative of being the architects of our own evil and our own good, by our own free and unconstrained choice.

Did you ever think that it was now or never with this publican; that Jesus Christ was never to go through the streets of Jericho any more; that it was Zacchaeus' last chance; and that, if he had not made haste, he would have lost Christ for ever? And so it is yet. There may be some in this place at this moment to whom Jesus Christ is now making His last appeal. I know not; no man knows. A Rabbi said, when they asked him when a man should repent, 'Repent on the last day of your lives.' And they said, 'But we do not know when that will be.' And he said, 'Then repent *now*.' So I say, because some of you may never hear Christ's Gospel again, and because none of us know whether we shall or not; make sure work of it *now*, and do not let Jesus Christ go out of the city and up the road between the hills yonder; for if once the folds of the ravine shut Him from sight He will never be back in Jericho, or seen by Zacchaeus any more for ever.

III. And so, lastly, notice the outcast melted by kindness.

We do not know at what stage in our Lord's intercourse with the publican he 'stood and said, Half of my goods I give to the poor,' and so on. But whensoever it was, it was the sign of the entire revolution that had been wrought upon him by the touch of that loving hand, and by the new fountain of sympathy and love that he had found in Jesus Christ.

Some people have supposed, indeed, that his words do not mark a vow for the future, but express his practice in the past. But it seems to me to be altogether incongruous that Zacchaeus should advertise his past good in order to make himself out to be not quite so bad as people thought him, and, therefore, not so unworthy of being Christ's host. Christ's love kindles sense of our sin, not complacent recounting of our goodness. So Zacchaeus said, 'Lord! Thou hast loved me, and I wonder. I yield, and fling away my black past; and, so far as I can, make restitution for it.'

The one transforming agency is the love of Christ received into the heart. I do not suppose that Zacchaeus knew as much about Jesus Christ even after the conversation as we do; nor did he see His love in that supreme death on the Cross as we do. But the love of the Lord made a deep dint in his heart, and revolutionised his whole nature. The thing that will alter the whole current and set of a man's affections, that will upset his estimate of the relative value of material and spiritual, and that will turn him inside out and upside down, and make a new man of him, is the revelation of the supreme love that in Jesus Christ has come into the world, with an individualising regard to each of us, and has died on the Cross for the salvation of us all. Nothing else will do it. People had frowned on Zacchaeus, and it made him bitter. They had execrated and persecuted him; and his only response was setting his teeth more firmly and turning the screw a little tighter when he had the chance. You can drive a man into devilry by contempt. If you want to melt him into goodness, try love. The Ethiopian cannot change his skin, but Jesus Christ can change his heart, and that will change his skin by degrees. The one transforming power is faith in the love of Jesus Christ.

Further, the one test of a true reception of Him is the abandonment of past evil and restitution for it as far as possible. People say that our Gospel is unreal and sentimental, and a number of other ugly adjectives. Well! If it ever is so, it is the fault of the speakers, and not of the Gospel. For its demands from every man that accepts it are intensely practical, and nothing short of a complete turning of his back upon his old self, shown in the conclusive forsaking of former evil, however profitable or pleasant, and reparation for harm done to men, satisfies them.

It is useless to talk about loving Jesus Christ and trusting Him, and having the sweet assurance of forgiveness, and a glorious hope of heaven, unless these have made you break off your bad habits of whatsoever sort they may be, and cast them behind your backs. Strong emotion, sweet deep feeling, assured confidence in the sense of forgiveness and the hope of heaven, are all very well. Let us see your faith by your works; and of these works the chief is—Behold the evil that I did, I do it no more: 'Behold! Lord! the half of my goods I give to the poor.' There was a young ruler, a chapter before this, who could not make up his mind to part with wealth in order to follow Christ. This man has so completely made up his mind to follow Christ that he does not need to be bidden to give up his worldly goods. The half given to the poor, and fourfold restoration to those whom he had wronged, would not leave much. How astonished Zacchaeus would have been if anybody had said to him that morning, 'Zacchaeus! before this night falls you will be next door to a pauper, and you will be a happier man than you are now!'

So, dear friends, like him, all of us may, if we will, and if we need, make a sudden right–about–face that shall alter the complexion of our whole future. People tell us that sudden conversions are suspicious. So they may be in certain cases. But the moment when a man makes up his mind to change the direction in which his face is set will always be a moment, however long may be the hesitation, and the meditation, and the preparation that led up to it.

Jesus Christ is standing before each of us as truly as He did before that publican, and is saying to us as truly as He said to him, 'Let Me in.' 'Behold! I stand at the door and knock. If any man open ... I will enter.' If He comes in He will teach you what needs to be turned out if He is to stop; and will make the sacrifice blessed and not painful; and you will be a happier and a richer man with Christ and nothing than with all beside and no Christ.

THE TRADING SERVANTS

'Then came the first, saying, Lord, thy pound hath
gained ten pounds.... And the second came, saying,
Lord, thy pound hath gained five pounds.'
—LUKE xix.16, 18.

The Evangelist, contrary to his usual practice, tells us what was the occasion of this parable. It was spoken at Jericho, on our Lord's last journey to Jerusalem, Bethany was but a day's march distant; Calvary but a week ahead. An unusual tension of spirit marked our Lord's demeanour, and was noticed by the disciples with awe. It infected them, and the excitable crowd, which was more than usually excitable because on its way to the passover festival. The air was electric, and everybody felt that something was impending. They 'thought that the kingdom of God should *immediately* appear.' So Christ spoke this parable to damp down that expectation which might easily flash up into the flame of rebellion. He tells them His real programme. He was to go a long way off to receive the kingdom. That was a familiar experience amongst the nations tributary to Rome, and more than one of the Herodian family had passed through it. In the meantime there was to be a period of expectancy. It was to be a long time, for he had to go to a 'far country,' and it was to be extended enough for the servants to turn their money over many times during His absence. When He did return it was not to do what they expected. They thought that the kingdom meant Jewish lordship over subject nations. He teaches them that it meant the destruction of the rebellious citizens, and a rigid scrutiny of the servants' faithfulness.

Now, the words of my two texts bring out in connection with this outline of the future some large lessons which I desire to draw.

I. Notice the small capital that the servants receive to trade with.

It was a pound apiece, which, numismatic authorities tell us, is somewhat about the same value as some L6 odd of English money; though, of course, the purchasing power would be considerably greater. A small amount, and an equal amount to every servant—these are the two salient points of this parable. They make the broad distinction between it and the other parable, which is often mixed up with it, the parable of the talents. There, instead of the amount being excessively small, it is exceedingly great; for a talent was worth some L400, and ten talents would be L4000, a fair capital for a man to start with. The other point of difference between the two parables, which belongs to the essence of each, is that while the gift in the one case is identical, in the other case it is graduated and different.

Now, to suppose that these are but two varying versions of the same parable, which the Evangelists have manipulated is, in my judgment, to be blind to the plainest of the lessons to be drawn from them.

There are two sorts of gifts. In one, all Christian men, the Master's servants, are alike; in another, they differ. Now, what is the thing in which all Christians are alike? What gift do they all possess equally; rich and poor, largely endowed or slenderly equipped; 'talented'—as we use the word from the parable—or not? The rich man and the poor, the wise man and the foolish, the cultured man and the ignorant, the Fijian and the Englishman, have one thing alike—the message of salvation which we call the Gospel of the blessed Lord. That is the 'pound.' We all stand upon an equal platform there, however differently we are endowed in respect of capacities and other matters. All have it; and all have the same.

Now if that is the interpretation of this parable, there are considerations that flow from that thought, and on which I would dwell for a moment.

The first of them is the apparent smallness of the gift. You may feel a difficulty in accepting that explanation, and may have been saying to yourselves that it cannot be correct, because Jesus Christ would never compare the unspeakable gift of His message of salvation through Him, to that paltry sum. But throw yourselves back to the moment of utterance, and I think you will feel the pathos and power of the metaphor. Here was that handful of disciples set in the midst of a hostile world, dead against them, with its banded superstitions, venerable idolatries, systematised philosophies, the force of the mightiest instruments of material power that the world had ever seen, in the organisation and military power of Rome. And there stood twelve Galilean men, with their simple, unlettered message; one poor 'pound,' and that was all. 'The foolishness of preaching,' the message which to 'the Jews was a stumbling–block, and to the Greeks was folly,' was all that they were equipped with. Their Master, who left them to seek a Kingdom, had so little to bestow, before He received His crown, that all that He could spare them was that small sum. They had to go into business in a very poor way. They had to be content to do a very insignificant retail trade. 'The foolishness of God is wiser than men; and the weakness of God is stronger than men.' The old experience of the leather sling and the five stones out of the brook, in the hand of the stripling, that made short work of the brazen armour of the giant, and penetrated with a whizz into his thick skull, and laid him prostrate, was to be repeated. 'He called his servants, and gave them'—a pound apiece! If you and I, Christian men and women, were true to the Master's legacy, and believed that we have in it more wealth than the treasures of wisdom and knowledge or force which the world has laid up, we should find that our mite was more than they all have in their possession.

Further, the texts suggest the purpose for which the pound is given. The servants had to live on it themselves, no doubt. So have we. They had to trade with it. So have we. Now that means two things. We get the Gospel, not as some of us lazily suppose, in order to secure that we shall not be punished for our past sins whilst we live, and go to heaven when we die. We get it, not only to enjoy its consolations and its sweetness, but to do business with.

And there are two ways in which this trading is to be done by us. The main one is the honest application of the principles and powers of the Gospel to the moulding of our own characters, and the making us better, purer, gentler, more heavenly–minded, and more Christlike. That is the first trading that we have to carry on with the Word. We get it not for an indolent assent, as so many of us misuse it. We receive it not merely to say, 'Oh I believe it,' and there an end, but that we may bring it to bear upon all our conduct, and that it may be the chief formative influence in our characters. Christian people! is that what you do with your Christianity? Is the Gospel moulding you, hour by hour, moment by moment? Have you brought all its great truths to bear upon your daily lives? Have you inwrought its substance into, not merely your understandings or your emotions, but your daily conduct? Is it indeed the life of your lives, and the leaven that is leavening your whole character? You have it to trade with; see that you do not wrap it in a napkin, and stow it idly away in some corner.

Then there is the other way of trading and that is, telling it to others. That is an obligation incumbent on all Christians. There may be differences in regard to other gifts, which determine the manner in which each shall use the equal gift which we all possess alike. But these are of subordinate importance. The main thing is to feel that the possession of Christian faith, which is our way of receiving the pound, carries with it indissolubly the obligation of Christian evangelism. However it may be discharged, discharged it is to be, by every true servant. I am sometimes half disposed to think that it would have been better for the Church if there had never been any men in my position, on whom the mass of unspiritual, idle because busy, and silent because little–loving, Christian professors contentedly roll the whole obligation to preach God's Gospel. My brethren, the world is not going to be evangelised by officials. Until all Christian people wake up to the sense that they have the 'pound' to trade with, there will be nothing adequate done to bring the world to the obedience and the love of Jesus Christ. You say you have the Gospel; if you have it what are you doing with it?

Self—centred Christianity, if such a thing were possible, is a mistake. It is generally a sham; it is always a crime. A man that puts away his pound, and never goes out and says, 'Come, share with me in the wealth that I have found in Jesus Christ' will be like a miser that puts his hoardings into an old stocking, and hides it in the ground somewhere. When he goes to dig it up, he is only too likely to find that all the coins have slipped out. If you want to keep your Christianity, let the air into it. If you want it to increase, sow it. There are hosts of you who would be far happier Christian people, if you came out of your shells and traded with your pound.

II. Observe the varying profits of the trading.

The one man says, 'Thy pound hath gained ten pounds.' The other says, 'Thy pound hath gained five pounds.' And the others who are not mentioned, no doubt, had also varying results to present. Now that inequality of profits from an equal capital to start with, is but a picturesque way of saying what is, alas! too obviously true, that Christian people do not all stand on the same level in regard to the use they have made of, and the benefits they have derived from, the one equal gift which was bestowed upon them. It is the same to every one at the beginning, but differences develop as they go on. One man makes twice as much out of it as another does.

Now, let us distinctly understand what sort of differences these are which our Lord signalises here. Let me clear away a mistake which may interfere with the true lessons of this parable, that the differences in question are the superficial ones in apparent results which follow from difference of endowments, or from difference of influential position. That is the kind of meaning that is often attached to the 'ten pounds' or the 'five pounds' in the text. We think that the ten pounder is the man who has been able to do some large spiritual work for Jesus Christ, that fills the world with its greatness, the man who has been set in some most conspicuous place, and by reason of intellectual ability or other talent has been able to gather in many souls into the kingdom; but that is not Christ's way of estimating. We should be going dead in the teeth of everything that He teaches if we thought that such as these were the differences intended. No, no! Every man that co—operates in a great work with equal diligence and devotion has an equal place in his eyes. The soldier that clapped Luther on the back as he was going into the Diet of Worms, and said, 'You have a bigger fight to fight than we ever had; cheer up, little monk!' stands on the same level as the great reformer, if what he did was done from the game motive and with as full consecration of himself. The old law of Israel states the true principle of Christian recompense: they that 'abide by the stuff' have the same share in the spoil as they 'that go down into the battle.' All servants who have exercised equal faithfulness and equal diligence stand on the same level and have the same success; no matter how different may be their estimation in the eyes of men; no matter how different may be the conspicuousness of the places that they fill in the eyes of the world whilst they live, or in the records of the Church when they are dead. Equal diligence will issue in equal results in the development of character, and the only reason for the diversity of results is the diversity of faithfulness and of zeal in trading with the pound.

Notice, too, before I go further, how all who trade make profits. There are no bad debts in that business. There are no investments that result in a loss. Everybody that goes into it makes something by it; which is just to say that any man who is honest and earnest in the attempt to utilise the powers of Christ's Gospel for his own culture, or for the world's good, will succeed in reality, however he may seem to fail in appearance. There are no commercial failures in this trading. The man with his ten pounds of profit made them because he worked hardest. The man that made the five made all that his work entitled him to. There was no one who came and said, 'Lord! I put thy pound into my little shop, and I did my best with it, and it is all gone!' Every Christian effort is crowned with success.

III. Lastly, we have here the final declaration of profits.

The master has come back. He is a king now, but he is the master still, and he wants to know what has become of the money that was left in the servants' hands. Now, that is but a metaphorical way of bringing to our minds that which we cannot conceive of without metaphor—viz., the retribution that lies beyond the grave for us all. Although we cannot conceive it without metaphor, we may reach, through the metaphor to some apprehension, at any rate, of the facts that lie behind it. There are two points in reference to this final declaration of profits suggested here.

The first is this, that all the profit is ascribed to the capital. Neither of the two men say: 'I, with thy pound, have gained,' but 'Thy pound hath gained.' That is accurately true. For if I accept, and live by, any great moral truth or principle, it is the principle or the truth that is the real productive cause of the change in my life and character. I, by my acceptance of it, simply put the belt on the drum that connects my loom with the engine, but it is the engine that drives the looms and the shuttle, and brings out the web at last. And so, Christian people who, with God's grace in their hearts, have utilised the 'pound,' and thereby made themselves Christlike, have to say, 'It was not I, but Christ in me. It was the Gospel, and not my faith in the Gospel, that wrought this change.' Is it your teeth or your dinner that nourishes you? Is it the Gospel or your trust in the Gospel that is the true cause of your sanctifying?

With regard to the other aspect of this trading, the same thing is true. Is it my word or Christ's Word ministered by me that helps any of my hearers who are helped? Surely! surely! there is no question about that. It is the 'pound' that gains the 'pounds.' 'Paul planted, Apollos watered, but God gave the increase. So, then, neither is he that planteth anything nor he that watereth, but God that giveth the increase.'

The other consideration suggested by these words is the exact knowledge of the precise results of a life, which is possessed at last. Each servant knew precisely what was the net outcome of his whole activity. That is exactly what we do not know here, and never shall, and never can know. But yonder all illusions will have vanished; and there will be two sorts of disillusionising then. Men, for instance, of my profession, whose names are familiar, and who hold high places in the esteem of the Church, and may be tempted to suppose that they have done a great deal—I am afraid that many of us will find, when we get yonder, that we have not done nearly so much as our admirers in this world, and we ourselves, were sometimes tempted to think that we had done. The searching light that comes in will show a great many seamy places in the cloth that looks very sound when it is inspected in the twilight. And there will be another kind of disillusionising. Many a man has said, 'Lord! I have laboured in vain, and spent my strength for nought,' who will find out that he was mistaken, and that where he saw failure there were solid results; that where he thought the grain had perished in the furrows, it had sprung up and borne fruit unto life everlasting. 'Lord! when saw we Thee in prison, and visited Thee?' We never knew that we had done anything of the sort. 'Behold! I was left alone,' said the widowed Jerusalem when she was restored to her husband, 'these'—children that have gathered round me—'where had they been?' We shall know, for good or bad, exactly the results of our lives.

We shall have to tell them. The slothful servant, too, was under this compulsion of absolute honesty. If he had not been so, do you think he would have ventured to stand up before his master, a king now, and insult him to his face? But he had to turn himself inside out, and tell then what he had thought in his inmost heart. So 'every one of us shall give an account of himself to God'; and like a man in the bankruptcy court, we shall have to explain our books, and go into all our transactions. We are working in the dark today. Our work will be seen as it is, in the light. The coral reef rises in the ocean, and the creatures that made it do not see it. The ocean will be drained away, and the reef will stand up sheer and distinct.

My brother! 'I counsel thee to buy of me gold tried in the fire'—and when you have bought your pound, see that you use it; for 'it is required in stewards that a man be found faithful.'

THE REWARDS OF THE TRADING SERVANTS

'Because thou hast been faithful in a very little,
have thou authority over ten cities... Be thou also
over five cities.'—LUKE xix. 17, 19.

The relation between this parable of the pounds and the other of the talents has often been misunderstood, and is very noteworthy. They are not two editions of one parable variously manipulated by the Evangelists, but they are two parables presenting two kindred and yet diverse aspects of one truth. They are neither identical, as some have supposed, nor contradictory, as others have imagined; but they are complementary. The parable of the talents represents the servants as receiving different endowments; one gets five; another two; another one. They make the same rate of profit with their different endowments. The man that turned his two talents into four did just as well as he that turned his five into ten. In either case the capital is doubled. Since the diligence is the same, the rewards are the same, and to each is given the identical same eulogium and the same entrance into the joy of his Lord. So the lesson of that parable is that, however unequal are our endowments, there may be as much diligence shown in the use of the smallest as in the greatest, and where that is the case, the man with the small endowments will stand on the same level of recompense as the man with the large.

But that is not all. This parable comes in to complete the thoughts. Here all the servants get the same gift, the one pound, but they make different profits out of it, one securing twice as much as the other. And, inasmuch as the diligence has been different, the rewards are different. So the lesson of this parable is that unequal faithfulness in the use of the same opportunities results in unequal retribution and reward. Unequal faithfulness, I say, because, of course, in both parables it is presupposed that the factor in producing the profit is not any accidental circumstance, but the earnestness and faithfulness of the servant. Christ does not pay for results; He pays for motives. And it is not because the man has made a certain number of pounds, but because in making them he has shown a certain amount of faithfulness, that he is rewarded. Christ does not say, 'Well done! good and *successful* servant,' but 'Well done! good and *faithful* servant.'

So, keeping these two sides of the one truth in view, I desire now to draw out two or three of the lessons which seem to me to lie in the principle laid down in my texts, of the unequal results of the unequal diligence of these servants.

I. I would note the solemn view of this present life that underlies the whole.

'Thou hast been faithful in a very little; have thou authority over five cities.' Well, that rests upon the thought that all our present life here is a stewardship, which in its nature is preparatory to larger work yonder. And that is the point of view from which alone it is right to look at, and possible to understand, this else unintelligible and bewildering life on earth. Clearly enough, to anybody that has eyes in his head, moral ends are supreme in man's relation to nature, and in man's life. We are here for the sake of making character, and of acquiring aptitudes and capacities which shall be exercised hereafter. The whole of our earthly career is the exercise of stewardship in regard to all the gifts with which we have been entrusted, in order that by the right exercise of that stewardship we may develop ourselves and acquire powers.

Now if it is clear that the whole meaning and end of the present life are to make character, and that we have to do with the material and the transient only, in order that, like the creatures that build up the coral reefs, we may draw from the ever–varying waves of the ocean that welters around us solid substance which we can pile up into an enduring monument—is this process of making character, and developing ourselves, to be cut short by such a contemptible thing as the death of the body? One very distinguished evolutionist, who has been forced onwards from his position to a kind of theism, declares that he is driven to a belief in immortality because he must believe in the reasonableness of God's work. And it seems to me that if indeed—as is plainly the case—moral ends are supreme in our life's history, it brings utter intellectual bewilderment and confusion to suppose that these ends are kept in view up till the moment of death, and that then down comes the guillotine and cuts off all. God does not take the rough ore out of the mine, and deal with it, and change it to polished steel, and shape His weapons, and then take them when they are at their highest temper and their sharpest edge, and break them across His knee. No! if here we are shaped, it is because yonder there is work for the tool.

So all here is apprenticeship, and the issues of to–day are recorded in eternity. We are like men perched up in a signal–box by the side of the line; we pull over a lever here, and it lifts an arm half a mile off. The smallest wheel upon one end of a shaft may cause another ten times its diameter to revolve, at the other end of the shaft through the wall there. Here we prepare, yonder we achieve.

II. Note the consequent littleness and greatness of this present.

'Thou hast been faithful in a very little.' Some of you may remember a recent sermon on the previous part of this parable, in which I tried to bring out an explanation of the small sum with which these servants were entrusted—the pound apiece for their little retail businesses—and found reason to believe that the interpretation of that gift was the Gospel of Jesus Christ which, in comparison with the world's wisdom and philosophies and material forces, seemed such a very insignificant thing. If we keep that interpretation in view in treating my present text, then there is hinted to us the contrast between the necessary limitations and incompletenesses even of the revelation of God in Jesus Christ which we have here, and the flood of glory and of light, which shall pour upon our eyes when the veil of flesh and sense has dropped away. Here we know in part; here, even with the intervention of the Eternal and Incarnate Word of God, the Revealer of the Father, we see as in a glass darkly; there face to face. The magnificences and the harmonies of that great revelation of God in Jesus Christ, which transcends all human thought and all worldly wisdom, are but a point, in comparison with the continent of illumination which shall come to us hereafter. 'The moon that rules the night' is the revelation that we have to−day, the reflection and echo of the sun that will rule the unsetting day of the heavens.

But I pass from that aspect of the words before us to the other, which, I suppose, is rather to be kept in view, in which the faithfulness in a very little points to the smallness of this present, as measured against that infinite future to which it conducts. Much has been said upon that subject, which is very antagonistic to the real ideas of Christianity. Life here, and this present, have been depreciated unduly, untruly, and unthankfully. And harm has been done, not only to the men who accept that estimate, but to the world that scoffs at it. There is nothing in the Bible, which is at all in sympathy with the so−called religious depreciation of the present, but there is this—'the things that are seen are temporal; the things that are unseen are eternal.' The lower hills look high when beheld from the flat plain that stretches on this side of them; but, if the mist lifts, the great white peaks come out beyond them, glittering in the sunshine, and with the untrodden snows on their inaccessible pinnacles; and nobody thinks about the green foothills, with the flowers upon them, any more. Brethren, think away the mist, for you can, and open your eyes, and see the snow−clad hills of eternity, and then you will understand how low is the elevation of the heights in the foreground. The greatness of the future makes the present little, but the little present is great, because its littleness is the parent of the great future. 'The child is father of the man'; and earth's narrow range widens out into the infinitude of eternity and of heaven. The only thing that gives real greatness and sublimity to our mortal life is its being the vestibule to another. Historically you will find that, wherever faith in a future life has become dim, as it has become dim in large sections of the educated classes to−day, there the general tone of strenuous endeavour has dropped, and the fatal feeling of 'It is not worth while' begins to creep over society. 'Is life worth living?' is the question that is asked on all sides of us to−day. And the modern recrudescence of pessimism has along with it, as one of the main thoughts which cut the nerves of effort, doubt of, and disbelief in, a future. It is because the very little opens out into the immeasurably great, and the passing moments tick us onwards into an unpassing eternity, that the moments are worth living through, and the fleeting insignificances of earth's existence become solemn and majestic as the portals of heaven.

III. Notice the future form of activity prepared for by faithful trading.

'Thou hast been faithful in a very little; have thou authority over ten cities.' Now I do not need to spend a word in dwelling on the contrast between the two pictures of the huckster with his little shop and the pound of capital to begin with, and the vizier that has control of ten of the cities of his master. That is too plain to need any enforcement. We are all here, all us Christian people especially, like men that keep a small shop, in a back street, with a few trivial things in the window, but we are heirs of a kingdom. That is what Christ wants us to lay to heart, so that the little shop shall not seem so very small, and its smoky obscurity shall be irradiated by true visions of what it will lead to.

Nor do I wish to risk any kind of fanciful and precarious speculations as to the manner and the sphere of the authority that is here set forth; only I would keep to one or two plain things. Faithfulness here prepares for participation in Christ's authority hereafter. For we are not to forget that whilst the master, the nobleman, was away seeking the kingdom, all that he could give his servants was the little stock–in–trade with which he started them, and that it is because he has won his kingdom that he is able to dispense to them the larger gifts of dominion over the ten and the five cities. The authority is delegated, but it is more than that— it is shared. For it is participation in, and not merely delegation from, the King and His rule, that is set forth in this and in other places of Scripture, for 'they shall sit down with Me on My throne, even as I also overcame and am set down with My Father on His throne.'

If, then, the rule set forth, in whatever sphere and in whatever fashion it may be exercised, is participation in Christ's authority, let us not forget that therefore it is a rule of which the manifestation is service. In heaven as on earth, and for the Lord in heaven as for the Lord on earth, and for the servants in heaven as for the servants on earth, the law stands irrefragable and eternal—'If any man will be chief among you, let him be your minister.' The authority over the ten cities is the capacity and opportunity of serving and helping every citizen in them all. What that help may be let us leave. It is better to be ignorant than to speculate about matters where there is no possibility of certainty. Ignorance is more impressive than knowledge, only be sure that no dignity can live amidst the pure light of the heavens, except after the fashion of the dignity of the Lord of all, who there, as here, is the servant of all.

But there is a thought in connection with this great though dim revelation of the future, which may well be laid to heart by us. And that is, that however close and direct the dependence on, and the communion with, Jesus Christ, the King of all His servants, in that future state is, it shall not be so close and direct as to exclude room for the exercise of brotherly sympathy and brotherly aid. We shall have Christ for our life and our light and our glory. But there, as here, we shall help one another to have Him more fully, and to understand Him more perfectly. What further lies in these great words, I do not venture to guess. Enough to know that Christ will be all in all, and that Christ in each will help the others to know Christ more fully.

Only remember, we have to take this great conception of the future as being one that implies largely increased and ennobled activity. A great deal of very cheap ridicule has been cast upon the Christian conception of the future life as if it was an eternity of idleness and of repose. Of repose, yes; of idleness, no! For it is no sinecure to be the governor of ten cities. There will be a good deal of work to be done, in order to discharge that office properly. Only it will be work that does not disturb repose, and at one and the same moment His servants will serve in constant activity, and gaze upon His face in calm contemplation. Christ's session at the right hand of God does not interfere with Christ's continual activity here. And, in like manner, His servants shall rest from their labours, but not from their work; they shall serve Him undisturbed, and shall repose, but not idly.

IV. Lastly, our texts remind us of the variety in recompense which corresponds to diversity in faithfulness.

I need but say a word about that. The one man gets his ten cities because his faithfulness has brought in ten pounds. The other gets five, corresponding to his faithfulness. As I said, our Lord pays, not for results, except in so far as these are conditioned and secured by the diligence of His servants. And so we come to the old familiar, and yet too often forgotten, conception of degrees in dignity, degrees in nearness to Him. That thought runs all through the New Testament representations of a future life, sometimes more clearly, sometimes more obscurely, but generally present. It is in entire accordance with the whole conception of that future, because the Christian notion of it is not that it is an arbitrary reward, but that it is the natural outcome of the present; and, of course, therefore, varying according to the present, of which it is the outcome. We get what we have wrought for. We get what we are capable of receiving, and what we are capable of receiving depends upon what has been our faithfulness here.

Now, that is perfectly consistent with the other side of the truth which the twin parable sets forth—viz., that the recompenses of the future are essentially one. All the servants, who were entrusted with the Talents, received the same eulogium, and entered into the same joy of their Lord. That is one side of the truth. And the other is, that the degree in which Christian people, when they depart hence, possess the one gift of eternal life, and Christ–shared joy is conditioned by their faithfulness and diligence here. Do not let the Gospel that says 'The gift of God is eternal life' make you forget the completing truths, that the measure in which a man possesses that eternal life depends on his fitness for it, and that fitness depends on his faithfulness of service and his union with his Lord.

We obscure this great truth often by reason of the way in which we preach the deeper truth on which it rests—forgiveness and acceptance all unmerited, through faith in Jesus Christ. But the two things are not contradictory; they are complementary. No man will be faithful as a steward who is not full of faith as a penitent sinner. No man will enter into the joy of his Lord, who does not enter in through the gate of penitence and trust, but, having entered, we are ranked according to the faithfulness of our service and diligence of stewardship. 'Wherefore, giving all diligence, make your calling and election sure, for so an entrance shall be ministered unto you *abundantly* into the everlasting kingdom of our Lord and Saviour Jesus Christ.'

A NEW KIND OF KING

'And when He was come nigh, even now at the descent of
the mount of Olives, the whole multitude of the
disciples began to rejoice and praise God with a loud
voice for all the mighty works that they had seen;
38. Saying, Blessed be the King that cometh in the
name of the Lord: peace in heaven, and glory in the
highest. 38. And some of the Pharisees from among the
multitude said unto Him, Master, rebuke Thy disciples.
40. And He answered and said unto them, I tell you
that, if these should hold their peace, the stones
would immediately cry out. 41. And when He was come
near, He beheld the city, and wept over it, 42. Saying,
If thou hadst known, even thou, at least in this thy
day, the things which belong unto thy peace! but now

they are hid from thine eyes. 43. For the days shall
come upon thee, that thine enemies shall cast a trench
about thee, and compass thee round, and keep thee in
on every side, 44. And shall lay thee even with the
ground, and thy children within thee; and they shall
not leave in thee one stone upon another; because thou
knewest not the time of thy visitation. 45. And he
went into the temple, and began to cast out them that
sold therein, and them that bought; 46. Saying unto
them, It is written, My house is the house of prayer:
but ye have made it a den of thieves. 47. And He
taught daily in the temple. But the chief priests and
the scribes and the chief of the people sought to
destroy Him, 48. And could not find what they might
do: for all the people were very attentive to hear
Him.'—LUKE xix. 37–48.

'He went on before.' What concentrated determination, and almost eagerness, impelled His firm and
swift steps up the steep, weary road! Mark tells that the disciples followed, 'amazed'—as they well
might be—at the unusual haste, and strange preoccupation on the face, set as a flint.

Luke takes no notice of the stay at Bethany and the sweet seclusion which soothed Jesus there. He
dwells only on the assertion of royalty, which stamped an altogether unique character on the
remaining hours of Christ's life.

I. The narrative brings into prominence Christ's part in originating the triumphal entry (vs. 30–34). He
sent for the colt with the obvious intention of stimulating the people to just such a demonstration as
followed.

As to the particulars, we need only note that the most obvious explanation of His knowledge of the
circumstances that the messengers would encounter, is that it was supernatural. Only one other
explanation is possible; namely, that the owners of the animal were secret disciples, with whom our
Lord had arranged to send for it, and had settled a sign and countersign, by which they would know
His messengers. But that is a less natural explanation.

Note the remarkable blending of dignity and poverty in 'The Lord hath need of him.' It asserts
sovereign authority and absolute rights, and it confesses need and penury. He is a King, but He has to
borrow even a colt to make His triumphal entry on. Though He was rich, for our sakes He became
poor.

Jesus then deliberately brought about His public entry. He thereby acts in a way perfectly unlike His
whole previous course. And He stirs up popular feelings at a time when they were specially excitable
by reason of the approaching Passover and its crowds. Formerly He had avoided the danger which He
now seems to court, and had gone up to the feast 'as it were in secret.' But it was fitting that once, for
the last time, He should assert before the gathered Israel that He was their King, and should make a

last appeal. Formerly He had sought to avoid attracting the attention of the rulers; now He knows that the end is near, and deliberately makes Himself conspicuous, though—or we might say because—He knew that thereby He precipitated His death.

The nature of His dominion is as plainly taught by the humble pomp as is its reality. A pauper King, who makes His public entrance into His city mounted on a borrowed ass, with His followers' clothes for a saddle, attended by a shouting crowd of poor peasants, for weapons or banners had but the branches plucked from other people's trees, was a new kind of king.

We do not need Matthew's quotation of the prophet's vision of the meek King coming to Zion on an ass, to understand the contrast of this kingdom with such a dominion as that of Rome, or of such princes as the Herods. Gentleness and peace, a sway that rests not on force nor wealth, are shadowed in that rustic procession and the pathetic poverty of its leader, throned on a borrowed colt, and attended, not by warriors or dignitaries, but by poor men unarmed, and saluted, not with the blare of trumpets, but with the shouts of joyful, though, alas! fickle hearts.

II. We have the humble procession with the shouting disciples and the background of hostile spies. The disciples eagerly caught at the meaning of bringing the colt, and threw themselves with alacrity into what seemed to them preparation for the public assertion of royalty, for which they had long been impatient. Luke tells us that they lifted Jesus on to the seat which they hurriedly prepared, while some spread their garments in the way—the usual homage to a king:

'Ride on triumphantly; behold, we lay
Our lusts and proud wills in Thy way.'

How different the vision of the future in their minds and His! They dreamed of a throne; He knew it was a Cross. Round the southern shoulder of Olivet they came, and, as the long line of the Temple walls, glittering in the sunshine across the valley, burst on the view, and their approach could be seen from the city, they broke into loud acclamations, summoning, as it were, Jerusalem to welcome its King.

Luke's version of their chant omits the Jewish colouring which it has in the other Gospels, as was natural, in view of his Gentile readers. Christ's royalty and divine commission are proclaimed from a thousand throats, and then up swells the shout of praise, which echoes the angels' song at Bethlehem, and ascribes to His coming, power to make peace in heaven with an else alienated world, and thus to make the divine glory blaze with new splendour even in the highest heavens.

Their song was wiser than they knew, and touched the deepest, sweetest mysteries of the unity of the Son with the Father, of reconciliation by the blood of His Cross, and of the new lustre accruing to God's name thereby, even in the sight of principalities and powers in heavenly places. They meant none of these things, but they were unconscious prophets. Their shouts died away, and their faith was almost as short-lived. With many of them, it withered before the branches which they waved.

High-wrought emotion is a poor substitute for steady conviction. But cool, unemotional recognition of Christ as King is as unnatural. If our hearts do not glow with loyal love, nor leap up to welcome

Him; if the contemplation of His work and its issues on earth and in heaven does not make our dumb tongues sing—we have need to ask ourselves if we believe at all that He is the King and Saviour of all and of us. There were cool observers there, and they make the foil to the glad enthusiasm. Note that these Pharisees, mingling in the crowd, have no title for Jesus but 'Teacher.' He is no king to them. To those who regard Jesus but as a human teacher, the acclamations of those to whom He is King and Lord always sound exaggerated.

People with no depth of religious life hate religious emotion, and are always seeking to repress it. A very tepid worship is warm enough for them. Formalists detest genuine feeling. Propriety is their ideal. No doubt, too, these croakers feared that this tumult might come to formidable size, and bring down Pilate's heavy hand on them.

Christ's answer is probably a quoted proverb. It implies His entire acceptance of the character which the crowd ascribed to Him, His pleasure in their praises, and, in a wider aspect, His vindication of outbursts of devout feeling, which shock ecclesiastical martinets and formalists.

III. We see the sorrowing King plunged in bitter grief in the very hour of His triumph. Who can venture to speak of that infinitely pathetic scene? The fair city, smiling across the glen, brings before His vision the awful contrast of its lying compassed by armies and in ruins. He hears not the acclamation of the crowd. 'He wept,' or, rather, 'wailed,'—for the word does not imply tears so much as cries. That sorrow is a sign of His real manhood, but it is also a part of His revelation of the very heart of God. The form is human, the substance divine. The man weeps because God pities. Christ's sorrow does not hinder His judgments. The woes which wring His heart will nevertheless be inflicted by Him. Judgment is His 'strange work,' alien from His desires; but it is His work. The eyes which are as a flame of fire are filled with tears, but their glance burns up the evil.

Note the yearning in the unfinished sentence, 'If thou hadst known.' Note the decisive closing of the time of repentance. Note the minute prophetic details of the siege, which, if ever they were spoken, are a distinct proof of His all-seeing eye. And from all let us fix in our hearts the conviction of the pity of the judge, and of the judgment by the pitying Christ.

IV. We have Christ's exercise of sovereign authority in His Father's house. Luke gives but a summary in verses 45–48, dwelling mainly on two points. First he tells of casting out the traders. Two things are brought out in the compressed narrative—the fact, and the Lord's vindication of it. As to the former, it was fitting that at the end of His career, as at the beginning, He should cleanse the Temple. The two events are significant as His first and last acts. The second one, as we gather from the other Evangelists, had a greater severity about it than the first.

The need for a second purifying indicated how sadly transient had been the effect of the first, and was thus evidence of the depth of corruption and formalism to which the religion of priests and people had sunk. Christ had come to cleanse the Temple of the world's religion, to banish from it mercenaries and self-interested attendants at the altar, and, in a higher application of the incident, to clear away all the degradations and uncleannesses which are associated with worship everywhere but in His Church, and which are ever seeking, like poisonous air, to find their way in thither also, through any unguarded chink.

The vindication of the act is in right royal style. The first cleansing was defended by Him by pointing to the sanctity of 'My Father's house'; the second, by claiming it as 'My house.' The rebuke of the hucksters is sterner the second time. The profanation, once driven out and returning, is deeper; for whereas, in the first instance, it had made the Temple 'a house of merchandise,' in the second it turned it into a 'den of robbers.' Thus evil assumes a darker tint, like old oak, by lapse of time, and swiftly becomes worse, if rebuked and chastised in vain.

The second part of this summary puts in sharp contrast three things—Christ's calm courage in continuous teaching in the Temple, the growing bitter hatred of the authorities, who drew in their train the men of influence holding no office, and the eager hanging of the people on His words, which baffled the murderous designs of the rulers. The same intentional publicity as in the entrance is obvious. Jesus knew that His hour was come, and willingly presents Himself a sacrifice. Meekly and boldly He goes on the appointed way. He sees all the hate working round Him, and lets it work. The day's task of winning some from impending ruin shall still be done. So should His servants live, in patient discharge of daily duty, in the face of death, if need be.

The enemies, who heard His words and found in them only food for deeper hatred, may warn us of the possibilities of antagonism to Him that lie in the heart, and of the terrible judgment which they drag down on their own heads, who hear, unmoved, His daily teaching, and see, unrepentant, His dying love. The crowd that listened, and, in less than a week yelled 'Crucify Him,' may teach us to take heed how we hear, and to beware of evanescent regard for His teaching, which, if it do not consolidate into resolved and thoroughgoing acceptance of His work and submission to His rule, will certainly cool into disregard, and may harden into hate.

TENANTS WHO WANTED TO BE OWNERS

'Then began He to speak to the people this parable; A certain man planted a vineyard, and let it forth to husbandmen, and went into a far country for a long time. 10. And at the season he sent a servant to the husbandmen, that they should give him of the fruit of the vineyard: but the husbandmen beat him, and sent him away empty. 11. And again he sent another servant: and they beat him also, and entreated him shamefully, and sent him away empty. 12. And again he sent a third: and they wounded him also, and cast him out. 13. Then said the lord of the vineyard, What shall I do? I will send my beloved son: it may be they will reverence him when they see him. 14. But when the husbandmen saw him, they reasoned among themselves, saying, This is the heir: come, let us kill him, that the inheritance may be ours. 15. So they cast him out of the vineyard, and killed him. What therefore shall the lord of the vineyard do unto them? 16. He shall come and destroy these husbandmen, and shall give the vineyard to

others. And when they heard it, they said, God forbid.
17. And he beheld them, and said, what is this then that
is written, The stone which the builders rejected, the
same is become the head of the corner? 18. Whosoever
shall fall upon that stone shall be broken; but on
whomsoever it shall fall, it will grind him to powder.
19. And the chief priests and the scribes the same hour
sought to lay hands on Him; and they feared the people:
for they perceived that He had spoken this parable
against them.'—LUKE xx. 9–19.

As the crisis came near, Jesus increased His severity and plainness of speech. This parable, which was spoken very near the end of the protracted duel with the officials in the Temple, is transparent in its application, and hit its mark immediately. The rulers at once perceived that it was directed against them. The cap fitted too well not to be put on. But it contains prophecy as well as history, and the reference to Jesus' impending fate is almost as transparent as the indictment of the rulers, while the prediction of the transference of the vineyard to others is as easy of translation as either of the other points.

Such plain speaking was fitting for last words. The urgency of Christ's pleading love, as much as the intensity of His moral indignation, made them plain.

I. We note, first, the vineyard, its lord and its tenants. The metaphor was familiar, for Isaiah had 'sung a song touching' Israel as God's vineyard, and other prophets had caught up the emblem, so that it had become a commonplace, known by all. The parable distinctly alludes to Isaiah's words, and almost reproduces them. Matthew's version enlarges on details of the appliances provided by the owner, which makes the parallel with Isaiah still more noticeable. But Luke summarises these into the simple 'planted.' That covers the whole ground.

God had given Israel a system of revelation, law, and worship, which was competent to produce in those who received it, the fruit of obedience and thankfulness. The husbandmen are primarily the rulers, as the scribes and chief priests perceived; but the nation which endorsed, by permitting their action, is included. The picture drawn applies to us as truly as to the Jews. The transference of the vineyard to another set of tenants, which Christ threatened at the close of the parable, has been accomplished, and so we, by our possession of the Gospel, are entrusted with the vineyard, and are responsible for rendering the fruits of holy living and love.

The owner 'let it out, and went into another country for a long time.' That is a picturesque way of saying that we have apparent possession, and are left free to act, God not being manifestly close to us. He stands off, as it were, from the creatures whom He has made, and gives them room to do as they will. But all our possessions, as well as the revelation of Himself in Christ, are only let to us, and we have rent to pay.

The collectors sent for the fruit are, of course, the series of prophets. Luke specifies three—a round number, indicating completeness. He says nothing about the times between their missions, but implies that the three covered the whole period till the sending of the son. Their treatment was uniform, as the history of Israel proved. The habit of rejecting the prophets was hereditary.

There is such a thing as national solidarity stretching through ages. The bold charge made by Stephen was only an echo of this parable, when he cried, 'As your fathers did, so do ye. Which of the prophets did not your fathers persecute?' Each generation made the ancestral sin its own, and staggered under a heavier burden of guilt, till, at last, came a generation which had to bear the penalty of all the blood of prophets shed from the beginning. Nations live, though their component atoms die, and only national repudiation of bequeathed sins can avert the crash which, sooner or later, avenges them.

The husbandmen treated the messengers with increasing contumely and cruelty. Content with beating the first, they added shameful treatment in the second case, and proceeded to wounding in the third. If God's repeated appeals do not melt, they harden, the heart. The persistence of His messengers leads to fiercer hatred, if it does not produce yielding love. There is no bitterness equal to that of the man who has often stiffened conscience against the truth.

II. So far, no doubt could be entertained of the meaning of the scathing parable. There was probably as little about that of the next part. We cannot but notice the broad distinction which Jesus draws between Himself and the mightiest of the prophets. They were the owner's 'slaves'; He was His 'beloved Son.' The writer of the Epistle to the Hebrews begins his letter with the same contrast, which he may have learned from the parable. It is a commonplace for us, but let us ponder how it must have sounded to that hostile, eager crowd, and ask ourselves how such assumptions can be reconciled with the 'sweet reasonableness' of Jesus if he belonged to the same category as an Isaiah or a Micah.

The yearning of divine love for the fruit of reverence and obedience is wonderfully expressed by the bold putting of an uncertain hope into the owner's mouth. He must have known that he was running a risk in sending his son, but he so much desires to bring the dishonest workmen back to their duty that he is willing to run it. The highly figurative expression is meant to emphasise God's longing for men's hearts, and His patient love which 'hopeth all things' and will not cease from effort to win us so long as an arrow remains in His quiver.

III. Our Lord now passes to prophecy. Deep sadness is in His tone as He tells how the only effect of His coming had been to stir up opposition. They 'saw Him' and were they touched? No, they only gripped their privileges the tighter, and determined more fiercely to assert their ownership.

Nothing is more remarkable in the parable than the calmness of Jesus in announcing His impending fate. He knows it all, and His voice has no tremor, as He tells it as though He were speaking of another. The very announcement that He penetrated the murderous designs hidden in many of the hearers' hearts would tend to precipitate their execution of these; but He is ready for the Cross, and its nearness has no terror, not because He was impassive, or free from the shrinking proper to flesh, but because He was resolved to save. Therefore He was resolved to suffer.

The husbandmen's reasonings with one another bring into plain words thoughts which probably were not consciously held by any even of the rulers. They open the question as to how far the rulers knew the truth of Christ's claims. They at least knew what these were, and they had fought down dawning convictions which, fairly dealt with, would have broadened into daylight. They would not have been so fiercely antagonistic if they had not been pricked by an uneasy doubt whether, after all, perhaps there was something in these claims.

Nothing steels men against admitting a truth so surely as the suspicion that, if they were to inquire a little farther, they might find themselves believing it. Knowledge and ignorance blended in these rulers as in us all. If they had not known at all, they would not have needed the Saviour's dying prayer for their forgiveness; if they had known fully, its very ground would have been taken away.

The motive put into their mouths is the wish to seize the vineyard for their own; and was not the very soul of the rulers' hostility the determination to keep hold of the prerogatives of their offices, while priests and people alike were deaf to Jesus, because they wished to be no more troubled by being reminded of their obligations to render obedience to God? The root of all rejection of Christ is the desire of self–will to reign supreme. Men resent being reminded that they are tenants, and are determined to assert ownership.

Jesus carries the hearers beyond the final crime which filled the measure of sin, and exhausted the resources of God. The sharp turn from narrative to question, in verse 15, not only is like the sudden thrust of a spear, but marks the transition from the present and immediate future to a more distant day. The slaying of the heir was the last act of the vine–dressers. The owner would act next. Luke, like Mark, puts the threatening of retribution into Christ's lips, while Matthew makes it the answer of the rulers to his question. Luke alone gives the exclamation, 'God forbid!' The ready answer in Matthew, and the pious interjection in Luke, have the same purpose,—to blunt the application of the parable to themselves by appearing to be unconcerned.

Their levity and reluctance to take home the lesson moved our Lord to sternness, which burned in His steadfast eyes as He looked on them, and must have been remembered by some disciple whose memory has preserved that look for us. It was the prelude to a still less veiled prophecy of the fall of Israel. Jesus lays His hand on the ancient prophecy of the stone rejected by the builders, and applies it to Himself. He is the sure foundation of which Isaiah had spoken. He is the stone rejected by Israel, but elevated to the summit of the building, and there joining two diverging walls.

The solemn warning closing the parable had its special meaning in regard to Israel, but its dread force extends to us. To fall on the stone while it lies lowly on the earth is to lame one's self, but to have it fall on a man when it rushes down from its elevation is ruin utter and irremediable. 'If they escaped not who refused Him that spake on earth, much more shall not we escape, if we turn away from Him that speaketh from heaven.'

WHOSE IMAGE AND SUPERSCRIPTION?

'Whose image and superscription hath it?'—Luke xx. 24.

It is no unusual thing for antagonists to join forces in order to crush a third person obnoxious to both. So in this incident we have an unnatural alliance of the two parties in Jewish politics who were at daggers drawn. The representatives of the narrow conservative Judaism, which loathed a foreign yoke, in the person of the Pharisees and Scribes, and the Herodians, the partisans of a foreigner and a usurper, lay their heads together to propose a question to Christ which they think will discredit or destroy Him. They would have answered their own question in opposite ways. One would have said, 'It *is* lawful to give tribute to Caesar'; the other would have said, 'It is not.' But that is a small matter when malice prompts. They calculate, 'If He says, No! we will denounce Him to Pilate as a rebel. If He says, Yes! we will go to the people and say, Here is a pretty Messiah for you, that has no objection to the foreign yoke. Either way we shall end Him.'

Jesus Christ serenely walks through the cobwebs, and lays His hand upon the fact. 'Let Me see a silver penny!'—which, by the bye, was the amount of the tribute—'Whose head is that?' The currency of the country proclaims the monarch of the country. To stamp his image on the coin is an act of sovereignty. 'Caesar's head declares that you are Caesar's subjects, whether you like it or not, and it is too late to ask questions about tribute when you pay your bills in his money.' 'Render to Caesar the things that are Caesar's.'

Does not the other side of Christ's answer—'to God the things that are God's'—rest upon a similar fact? Does not the parallelism require that we should suppose that the destiny of things to be devoted to God is stamped upon them, whatever they are, at least as plainly as the right of Caesar to exact tribute was inferred from the fact that his money was the currency of the country? The thought widens out in a great many directions, but I want to confine it to one special line of contemplation, and to take it as suggesting to each of us this great truth, that the very make of men shows that they belong to God, and are bound to yield themselves to Him. If the answer to the question be plain, and the conclusion irresistible, about the penny with the image of Tiberius, the answer is no less plain, nor the conclusion less irresistible, when we turn the interrogation within, and, looking at our own being, say to ourselves, 'Whose image and superscription hath *it*?'

I. First, then, note the image stamped upon man, and the consequent obligation.

We can very often tell what a thing is for by noticing its make. The instructed eye of an anatomist will, from a bone, divine the sphere in which the creature to whom it belonged was intended to live. Just as plainly as gills or lungs, fins or wings, or legs and arms, declare the element in which the creature that possesses them is intended to move, so plainly stamped upon all our natures is this, that God is our Lord since we are made in a true sense in His image, and that only in Him can we find rest.

I need not remind you, I suppose, of the old word, 'Let us make man in our own image.' Nor need I, I suppose, insist at any length upon the truth that though, by the fact of man's sin, the whole glory and splendour of the divine image in which he was made is marred and defaced, there still remain such solemn, blessed, and awful resemblances between man and God that there can be no mistake as to which beings in the universe are the most kindred; nor any misunderstanding as to who it is after whose likeness we are formed, and in whose love and life alone we can be blessed.

I am not going to weary you with thoughts for which, perhaps, the pulpit is not the proper place; but let me just remind you of one or two points. Is there any other being on this earth that can say of itself 'I am'? God says *I am that I am*. *You and I cannot say that, but we alone, in this order of things, possess that solemn and awful gift, the consciousness of our personal being. And, brethren, whoever is able to say to himself 'I am' will never know rest until he can turn to God and say 'Thou art,' and then, laying his hand in the Great Father's hand, venture to say 'We are.' We are made in His image, in that profoundest of all senses.*

But to come to something less recondite. We are like God in that we can love; we are like Him in that we can perceive the right, and that the right is supreme; we are like Him in that we have the power to say 'I will.' And these great capacities demand that the creature who thus knows himself to be, who thus knows the right, who thus can love, who thus can purpose, resolve, and act, should find his home and his refuge in fellowship with God.

But if you take a coin, and compare it with the die from which it has been struck, you will find that wherever in the die there is a relief, in the coin there is a sunken place; and conversely. So there are not only resemblances in man to the divine nature, which bear upon them the manifest marks of his destiny, but there are correspondences, wants, on our side, being met by gifts upon His; hollow emptinesses in us being filled, when we are brought into contact with Him, by the abundance of His outstanding supplies and gifts. So the poorest, narrowest, meanest life has in it a depth of desire, an ardour, and sometimes a pain and a madness of yearning and longing which nothing but God can fill. Though we often misunderstand the voice, and so make ourselves miserable by vain efforts, our 'heart and our flesh,' in every fibre of our being, 'cry out for the living God.' And what we all want is some one Pearl of great price into which all the dispersed preciousness and fragmentary brilliances that dazzle the eye shall be gathered. We want a Person, a living Person, a present Person, a sufficient Person, who shall satisfy our hearts, our whole hearts, and that at one and the same time, or else we shall never be at rest.

Because, then, we are made dependent, because we possess these wild desires, because immortal thirst attaches to our nature, because we have consciences that need illuminating, wills that are only free when they are absolutely submissive, hearts that are dissatisfied, and left yearning, after all the sweetnesses of limited, transient, and creatural affections, we bear on our very fronts the image of God; and any man that wisely looks at himself can answer the question, 'Whose image and superscription hath it?' in but one way. 'In the image of God created He him.'

Therefore by loving fellowship, by lowly trust, by ardour of love, by submissiveness of obedience, by continuity of contemplation, by the sacrifice of self, we must yield ourselves to God if we would pay the tribute manifestly owing to the Emperor by the fact that His image and superscription are upon the coin.

II. And so let me ask you to look, in the next place, at the defacement of the image and the wrong expenditure of the coin.

You sometimes get into your hands money on which there has been stamped, by mischief, or for some selfish purpose, the name of some one else than the king's or queen's which surrounds the head upon it. And in like manner our nature has gone through the stamping–press again, and another likeness has been deeply imprinted upon it. The image of God, which every man has, is in some senses and aspects ineffaceable by any course of conduct of theirs. But in another aspect it is not like the permanent similitude stamped upon the solid metal of the penny, but like the reflection, rather, that falls upon some polished plate, or that is cast upon the white sheet from a lantern. If the polished plate be rusty and stained, the image is faint and indistinct; if it be turned away from the light the image passes. And that is what some of you are doing. By living to yourselves, by living day in and day out without ever remembering God, by yielding to passions, lusts, ambitions, low desires, and the like, you are doing your very best to erase the likeness which still lingers in your nature. Is there any one here that has yielded to some lust of the flesh, some appetite, drunkenness, gluttony, impurity, or the like, and has so sold himself to it, as that that part of the divine image, the power of saying 'I will,' has pretty nearly gone? I am afraid there must be some who, by long submission to passion, have lost the control that reason and conscience and a firm steady purpose ought to give. Is there any man here who, by long course of utter neglect of the divine love, has ceased to feel that there is a heart at the centre of the universe, or that He has anything to do with it? Brethren, the awful power that is given to men of degrading themselves till, lineament by lineament, the likeness in which they are made vanishes, is the saddest and most tragical thing in the world. 'Like the beasts that perish,' says one of the psalms, the men become who, by the acids and the files of worldliness and sensuality and passion, have so rubbed away the likeness of God that it is scarcely perceptible in them. Do I speak to some such now? If there is nothing else left there is this, a hunger for absolute good and for the satisfaction of your desires. That is part of the proof that you are made for God, and that only in Him can you find rest.

All occupations of heart and mind and will and active life with other things to the exclusion of supreme devotion to God are, then, sacrilege and rebellion. The emperor's head was the token of sovereignty and carried with it the obligation to pay tribute. Every fibre in your nature protests against the prostitution of itself to anything short of God. You remember the story in the Old Testament about that saturnalia of debauchery, the night when Babylon fell, when Bel-shazzar, in the very wantonness of godless insolence, could not be satisfied with drinking his wine out of anything less sacred than the vessels that had been brought from the Temple at Jerusalem. That is what many of us are doing, taking the sacred cup which is meant to be filled with the wine of the kingdom and pouring into it the foaming but poisonous beverages which steal away our brains and make us drunk, the moment before our empire totters to its fall and we to our ruin. 'All the consecrated things of the house of the Lord they dedicated to Baal,' says one of the narratives in the Book of Chronicles. That is what some of us are doing, taking the soul that is meant to be consecrated to God and find its blessedness there, and offering it to false gods in whose service there is no blessedness.

For, dear friends, I beseech you, lay this to heart that you cannot thus use the Godlike being that you possess without bringing down upon your heads miseries and unrest. The raven, that black bird of evil omen, went out from the ark, and flew homeless over the weltering ocean. The souls that seek not God fly thus, strangers and restless, through a drowned and lifeless world. The dove came back with an olive branch in its beak. Souls that are wise and have made their nests in the sanctuary can there fold their wings and be at peace. As the ancient saint said, 'We are made for God, and only in God have we rest.' 'Oh, that thou hadst hearkened to me, then had thy peace been as a river, and thy righteousness as the waves of the sea.' Cannot you see the blessed, gentle gliding of the full stream through the meadows with the sunshine upon its ripples? Such is the heart that has yielded itself to God. In solemn contrast to that lovely image, the same prophet has for a repeated refrain in his book, 'The wicked is like the troubled sea which cannot rest,' but goes moaning round the world, and breaking in idle foam upon every shore, and still is unquiet for evermore. Brethren, only when we render to God the thing that is God's—our hearts and ourselves–have we repose.

III. Now, lastly, notice the restoration and perfecting of the defaced image.

Because man is like God, it is possible for God to become like man. The possibility of Revelation and of Redemption by an incarnate Saviour depend upon the reality of the fact that man is made in the image of God. Thus there comes to us that divine Christ, who lays 'His hands upon both' and being on the one hand the express image of His person, so that He can say, 'He that hath seen Me hath seen the Father,' on the other hand 'was in all points made like unto His brethren,' with only the exception that the defacement which had obliterated the divine image in them left it clear, untarnished, and sharply cut in Him.

Therefore, because Jesus Christ has come, our Brother, 'bone of our bone, and flesh of our flesh,' made like unto us, and in our likeness presenting to us the very image of God and eradiation of His light, therefore no defacement that it is possible for men or devils to make on this poor humanity of ours need be irrevocable and final. All the stains may be blotted out, all the usurping superscriptions may be removed and the original imprint restored. The dints may be elevated, the too lofty points may be lowered, the tarnish and the rust may be rubbed off, and, fairer than before, the likeness of God may be stamped on every one of us, 'after the image of Him that created us,' if only we will turn ourselves to that dear Lord, and cast our souls upon Him. Christ hath become like us that we might become like Him, and therein be partakers of the divine nature. 'We all, reflecting as a glass does the glory of the Lord, may be changed into the same image from glory to glory.'

Nor do the possibilities stop there, for we look forward to a time when, if I might pursue the metaphor of my text, the coinage shall be called in and reminted, in new forms of nobleness and of likeness. We have before us this great prospect, that 'we shall be like Him, for we shall see Him as He is'; and in all the glories of that heaven we shall partake, for all that is Christ's is ours, and 'we that have borne the image of the earthly shall also bear the image of the heavenly.'

I come to you, then, with this old question: 'Whose image and superscription hath it?' and the old exhortation founded thereupon: 'Render therefore to God the thing that is God's'; and yield yourselves to Him. Another question I would ask, and pray that you may lay it to heart, 'To what purpose is this waste?' What are you doing with the silver penny of your own soul? Wherefore do ye 'spend it for that which is not bread?' Give yourselves to God; trust yourselves to the Christ who is like you, and like Him. And, resting upon His great love you will be saved from the prostitution of capacities, and the vain attempts to satisfy your souls with the husks of earth; and whilst you remain here will be made partakers of Christ's life, and growingly of His likeness, and when you remove yonder, your body, soul, and spirit will be conformed to His image, and transformed into the likeness of His glory, 'according to the mighty working whereby He is able even to subdue all things unto Himself.'

WHEN SHALL THESE THINGS BE?

'And when ye shall see Jerusalem compassed with armies,
then know that the desolation thereof is nigh. 21. Then

let them which are in Judea flee to the mountains; and
let them which are in the midst of it depart out; and
let not them that are in the countries enter thereinto.
22. For these be the days of vengeance, that all things
which are written may he fulfilled. 23. But woe unto
them that are with child, and to them that give suck,
in those days! for there shall be great distress in the
land, and wrath upon this people. 24. And they shall
fall by the edge of the sword, and shall be led away
captive into all nations; and Jerusalem shall be
trodden down of the Gentiles, until the times of the
Gentiles be fulfilled. 25. And there shall be signs in
the sun, and in the moon, and in the stars; and upon
the earth distress of nations, with perplexity; the sea
and the waves roaring; 26. Men's hearts failing them
for fear, and for looking after those things which are
coming on the earth; for the powers of heaven shall be
shaken. 27. And then shall they see the Son of man
coming in a cloud, with power and great glory. 28. And
when these things begin to come to pass, then look up,
and lift up your heads; for your redemption draweth
nigh. 29. And He spake to them a parable; Behold the
fig–tree, and all the trees; 30. When they now shoot
forth, ye see and know of your own selves that summer
is now nigh at hand. 31. So likewise ye, when ye see
these things come to pass, know ye that the kingdom of
God is nigh at hand. 32. Verily I say unto you, This
generation shall not pass away till all be fulfilled.
33. Heaven and earth shall pass away; but My words
shall not pass away. 34. And take heed to yourselves,
lest at any time your hearts be overcharged with
surfeiting, and drunkenness, and cares of this life,
and so that day come upon you unawares. 35. For as a
snare shall it come on all them that dwell on the face
of the whole earth. 36. Watch ye therefore, and pray
always, that ye may be accounted worthy to escape all
these things that shall come to pass, and to stand
before the Son of Man.'—LUKE xxi. 20–36.

This discourse of our Lord's is in answer to the disciples' double question as to the time of the overthrow of the Temple and the premonitory signs of its approach. The former is answered with the indefiniteness which characterises prophetic chronology; the latter is plainly answered in verse 20.

The whole passage divides itself in four well–marked sections.

I. There is the prediction of the fall of Jerusalem (vs. 20–24). The 'sign' of her 'desolation' was to be the advance of the enemy to her walls. Armies had been many times encamped round her, and many times been scattered; but this siege was to end in capture, and no angel of the Lord would stalk by night through the sleeping host, to stiffen sleep into death, nor would any valour of the besieged avail. Their cause was to be hopeless from the first. Flight was enjoined. Usually the inhabitants of the open country took refuge in the fortified capital when invasion harrowed their fields; but this time, for 'them that are in the country' to 'enter therein' was to throw away their last chance of safety. The Christians obeyed, and fled, as we all know, across Jordan to Pella. The rest despised Jesus' warning—if they knew it,——and perished.

Mark the reason for the exhortation not to resist, but to flee: These are days of vengeance, that all things which are written may be fulfilled.' That is to say, the besiegers are sent by God to execute His righteous and long–ago–pronounced judgments. Therefore it is vain to struggle against them. Behind the Roman army is the God of Israel. To dash against their cohorts is to throw one's self on the thick bosses of the Almighty's buckler, and none who dare do that can 'prosper.' Submission to His retributive hand is the only way to escape being crushed by it. Chastisement accepted is salutary, but kicking against it drives the goad deeper into the rebellious limb.

So great is the agony to be, that what should be a joy, the birth of children, will be a woe, and the sweet duties of motherhood a curse, while the childless will be happier than the fugitives burdened with helpless infancy. We should note, too, that the 'distress' which comes upon the land is presented in darker colours, and traced to its origin, in (God's)'wrath' dealt out 'unto this people.' Happier they who 'fall by the edge of the sword' than they who are led 'captive into all the nations.'

A gleam of hope shoots through the stormy prospect, for the treading down of Jerusalem by the Gentiles has a term set to it. It is to continue 'till the times of the Gentiles are fulfilled.' That expression is important, for it clearly implies that these 'times' are of considerable duration, and it thus places a period of undefined extent between the fall of Jerusalem and the subsequent prophecy. The word used for 'times' generally carries with it the notion of opportunity, and here seems to indicate that the break–up of the Jewish national existence would usher in a period in which the 'Gentiles' would have the kingdom of God offered to them. The history of the world since the city fell is the best comment on this saying.

II. Since the 'times of the Gentiles' are thus of indefinite duration, they make a broad line of demarcation between what precedes and what follows them. Clearly the prophecy in verses 25–27 is separated in time from the fall of Jerusalem, and it is no objection to that view that the separation is not more emphatically pointed out by our Lord. These verses distinctly refer to His last coming to judgment. Verse 27 is too grand and too distinctly cast in the mould of the other predictions of that coming to be interpreted of His ideal coming in the judgments on the city.

The 'signs in sun and moon and stars' may refer in accordance with a familiar symbolism, to the overthrow of royalties and dominions; the sea roaring may, in like manner, symbolise agitations among the people; but the 'cloud' and the 'power and great glory' with which the Son of man comes, can mean nothing else than what they mean in other prophetic passages; namely, His visible appearance, invested with the shekinah light, and wielding divine authority before the gaze of a world.

The city's fall, then, was the initial stage of a process, the duration of which is undefined here, but implied to be considerable, and of which the closing stage is the personal coming of Jesus. The same conclusion is supported by verse 28, which treats that fall as the beginning of the fulfilment of the prophecy.

III. That verse forms a transition to the section containing the illustrative parable and the reiteration of the assurance that Christ's words would certainly be fulfilled. The disciples might naturally quake at the prospect, and wonder how they could face the reality. Jesus gives them strong words of cheer, which apply to all dreaded contingencies and to all social convulsions. What is a messenger of destruction to Christless men and institutions is a harbinger of full 'redemption' to His servants. Earthquakes but open their prison doors and loose their bands, they should not shake their hearts.

Historically the fall of Jerusalem was a powerful factor in the deliverance of the Church from Jewish swaddling–bands which hampered its growing limbs. For all Christians the destruction of what can perish brings fuller vision and possession of what cannot be shaken. To Christ's friends, all things work for good. So the parable which at first sight seems strangely incongruous becomes blessedly significant and fitting. The gladsome blossoming of the trees, the herald of the glories of summer, is a strange emblem of such a tragedy, and summer itself is a still stranger one of that solemn last judgment. But the might of humble trust in Him who comes to judge makes His coming summer–like in the light and warmth with which it floods the soul, and the rich fruitage which it produces there.

Observe, too, that the parable confirms the idea of a process having stages, for the lesson of the blossoming fig–tree is not that summer has come, but that it is nigh.

The solemn assurance in verse 32, made more weighty by the 'Verily I say,' seems at first sight to bring the final judgment within the lifetime of the generation of the hearers. But it is noteworthy that the expression 'till all things are fulfilled' is almost verbally identical with that in verse 22, which refers only to the destruction of Jerusalem, and is therefore most naturally interpreted as having the same restricted application here. The difference between the two phrases is significant, since in the former the certainty of fulfilment is deduced from the fact of 'the things' being written—that is, they must be accomplished because they have been foretold in Scripture,—whereas in the latter Christ rests the certainty of fulfilment on His own word. That majestic assurance in verse 33 comes well from His lips, and makes claim that His word shall outlast the whole present material order, and be fulfilled in every detail. Think of a mere man saying that!

IV. Exhortations corresponding to the predictions follow. Christ's revelation of the future was neither meant to gratify idle curiosity nor to supply a timetable in advance, but to minister encouragement and to lead to watchfulness. Whether 'that day' (ver. 34) is understood of the fall of Jerusalem or of the final coming of the Lord, it will come 'as a snare' upon men who are absorbed with the earth which they inhabit. They will be captured by it, as a covey of birds in a field busily picking up grain, are netted by one sudden fling of the fowler's net. A wary eye would have saved them.

The exhortation is as applicable to us, for, whatever are our views about unfulfilled prophecy, death comes to us all at a time which we know not, as the Book of Ecclesiastes, using the same figure, says; 'Man knoweth not his time ... as the birds that are caught in the snare.' Hearts must be kept above the grosser satisfactions of sense and the less gross cares of life, being neither stupefied with gorging earth's good, nor preoccupied with its gnawing anxieties, both of which are destructive of the clear realisation of the certain future. We are to preserve an attitude of wakefulness and of expectancy, and, as the sure way to it, and to clearing our hearts of perishable delights and shortsighted, self–consuming cares, we are to keep them in a continual posture of supplication. If our study of unfulfilled prophecy does that for us, it will have done what Jesus means it to do; if it does not it matters little what theories about its chronology we may adopt.

The two stages which we have tried to point out in this passage are clearly marked at the close, where escaping 'all these things that shall come to pass' and standing 'before the Son of man' are distinguished. True, both stages were to be included in the experience of Christ's hearers, but they are none the less separate stages.

Luke's version of this great discourse gives less prominence to the final coming than does Matthew's, and does not blend the two stages so inextricably together; but it gives no hint of the duration of the 'times of the Gentiles,' and might well leave the impression that these were brief. Now in this close setting together of a nearer and a much more remote future, with little prominence given to the interval between, our Lord is but bringing His prophecy into line with the constant manner of the older prophets. They and He paint the future in perspective, and the distance, seen behind the foreground, seems nearer than it really is. The spectator does not know how many weary miles have to be traversed before the distant blue hills are to be reached, nor what deep gorges lie between.

Such bringing together of events far apart in time of fulfilment rests in part on the fact that there have been many 'days of the Lord,' many 'comings of Christ,' each of which is a result on a small scale of the same retributive action of the Judge of all, as shall be manifested on the largest scale in the last and greatest day of the Lord. Therefore the true use of all these predictions is that which Christ enforces here; namely, that they should lead us to prayerful watchfulness and to living above earth, its goods and cares.

THE LORD'S SUPPER

'Then came the day of unleavened bread, when the passover must be killed. 8. And He sent Peter and John, saying, Go and prepare us the passover, that we may eat. 9. And they said unto Him, Where wilt thou that we prepare? 10. And He said unto them, Behold, when ye are entered into the city, there shall a man meet you, bearing a pitcher of water; follow him into the house where he entereth in. 11. And ye shall say unto the goodman of the house, The Master saith unto thee, Where is the guestchamber, where I shall eat the passover with My disciples? 12. And he shall shew you a large upper room furnished: there make ready.

13. And they went, and found as He had said unto them: and they made ready the passover. 14. And when the hour was come, He sat down, and the twelve apostles with Him. 15. And He said unto them, With desire I have desired to eat this passover with you before I suffer: 16. For I say unto you, I will not any more eat thereof, until it be fulfilled in the kingdom of God. 17. And He took the cup, and gave thanks, and said, Take this, and divide it among yourselves: 18. For I say unto you, I will not drink of the fruit of the vine, until the kingdom of God shall come. 19. And He took bread, and gave thanks, and brake it, and gave unto them, saying, This is My body which is given for you: this do in remembrance of Me. 20. Likewise also the cup after supper, saying, This cup is the new testament in My blood, which is shed for you.'—LUKE xxii. 7–20.

Paul had his account of the Last Supper direct from Christ. Luke apparently had his from Paul, so that the variations from Matthew and Mark are invested with singular interest, as probably traceable to the Lord of the feast Himself. Our passage has three sections—the preparation, the revelation of Christ's heart, and the institution of the rite.

I. The Preparation.—Peculiar to Luke are the names of the disciples entrusted with it, and the representation of the command, as preceding the disciples' question 'Where?' The selection of Peter and John indicates the confidential nature of the task, which comes out still more plainly in the singular directions given to them. Luke's order of command and question seems more precise than that of the other Gospels, as making our Lord the originator instead of merely responsive to the disciples' suggestion.

How is the designation of the place which Christ gives to be understood? Was it supernatural knowledge, or was it the result of previous arrangement with the 'goodman of the house'? Most probably the latter; for he was in so far a disciple that he recognised Jesus as 'the Master,' and was glad to have Him in his house, and the chamber on the roof was ready 'furnished' when they came. Why this mystery about the place? The verses before our passage tell the reason.

Judas was listening, too, for the answer to 'Where?' thinking that it would give him the 'opportunity' which he sought 'to betray Him in the absence of the multitude.' Jesus had much to say to His disciples, and needed the quiet hours in the upper room, and therefore sent away the two with directions which revealed nothing to the others. If He had told the group where the house was, the last supper might never have been instituted, nor the precious farewell words, the holy of holies of John's Gospel, ever been spoken. Jesus takes precautions to delay the Cross. He takes none to escape it, but rather sets Himself in these last days to bring it near. The variety in His action means no change in His mind, but both modes are equally the result of His self–forgetting love to us all. So He sends away Peter and John with sealed orders, as it were, and the greedy ears of the traitor are balked, and none know the appointed place till Jesus leads them to it. The two did not come back, but Christ guided the others to the house, when the hour was come.

II. Verses 14–18 give a glimpse into Christ's heart as He partook, for the last time, of the Passover. He discloses His earnest desire for that last hour of calm before He went out to face the storm, and reveals His vision of the future feast in the perfect kingdom. That desire touchingly shows His brotherhood in all our shrinking from parting with dear ones, and in our treasuring of the last sweet, sad moments of being together. That was a true human heart, 'fashioned alike' with ours, which longed and planned for one quiet hour before the end, and found some bracing for Gethsemane and Calvary in the sanctities of the Upper Room. But the desire was not for Himself only. He wished to partake of that Passover, and then to transform it for ever, and to leave the new rite to His servants.

Our Lord evidently ate of the Passover; for we cannot suppose that His words in verse 15 relate to an ungratified wish, but, as evidently, that eating was finished before He spoke. We shall best conceive the course of events if we suppose that the earlier stages of the paschal ceremonial were duly attended to, and that the Lord's Supper was instituted in connection with its later parts. We need not discuss what was the exact stage at which our Lord spoke and acted as in verses 15–17. It is sufficient to note that in them He gives what He does not taste, and that, in giving, His thoughts travel beyond all the sorrow and death to reunion and perfected festal joys. These anticipations solaced His heart in that supreme hour. 'For the joy that was set before Him' He 'endured the Cross,' and this was the crown of His joy, that all His friends should share it with Him, and sit at His table in His kingdom.

The prophetic aspect of the Lord's Supper should never be left out of view. It is at once a feast of memory and of hope, and is also a symbol for the present, inasmuch as it represents the conditions of spiritual life as being participation in the body and blood of Christ. This is where Paul learned his 'till He come'; and that hope which filled the Saviour's heart should ever fill ours when we remember His death.

III. Verses 19 and 20 record the actual institution of the Lord's Supper. Note its connection with the rite which it transforms. The Passover was the memorial of deliverance, the very centre of Jewish ritual. It was a family feast, and our Lord took the place of the head of the household. That solemnly appointed and long–observed memorial of the deliverance which made a mob of slaves into a nation is transfigured by Jesus, who calls upon Jew and Gentile to forget the venerable meaning of the rite, and remember rather His work for all men. It is strange presumption thus to brush aside the Passover, and in effect to say, 'I abrogate a divinely enjoined ceremony, and breathe a new meaning into so much of it as I retain.' Who is He who thus tampers with God's commandments? Surely He is either One having a co–ordinate authority, or——? But perhaps the alternative is best left unspoken.

The separation of the symbols of the body and blood plainly indicates that it is the death of Jesus, and that a violent one, which is commemorated. The double symbol carries in both its parts the same truth, but with differences. Both teach that all our hopes are rooted in the death of Jesus, and that the only true life of our spirits comes from participation in His death, and thereby in His life. But in addition to this truth common to both, the wine, which represents His blood, is the seal of the 'new covenant.' Again we mark the extraordinary freedom with which Christ handles the most sacred parts of the former revelation, putting them aside as He wills, to set Himself in their place. He declares, by this rite, that through His death a new 'covenant' comes into force as between God and man, in which all the anticipations of prophets are more than realised, and sins are remembered no more, and the knowledge of God becomes the blessing of all, and a close relationship of mutual possession is established between God and us, and His laws are written on loving hearts and softened wills.

Nor is even this all the meaning of that cup of blessing; for blood is the vehicle of life, and whoso receives Christ's blood on his conscience, to sprinkle it from dead works, therein receives, not only cleansing for the past, but a real communication of 'the Spirit of life' which was 'in Christ' to be the life of his life, so as that he can say, 'I live; yet not I, but Christ liveth in me.' Nor is even this all; for, as wine is, all the world over, the emblem of festivity, so this cup declares that to partake of Christ is to have a fountain of joy in ourselves, which yet has a better source than ourselves. Nor is this all; for 'this cup' is prophecy as well as memorial and symbol, and shadows the new wine of the kingdom and the marriage supper of the Lamb.

'This is My body' could not have meant to the hearers, who saw Him sitting there in bodily form, anything but 'this is a symbol of My body.' It is but the common use of the word in explaining a figurative speech or act. 'The field is the world; the tares are the children of the wicked one; the reapers are the angels,'—and so in a hundred cases.

Luke alone preserves for us the command to 'do this,' which at once establishes the rite as meant to be perpetual, and defines the true nature of it. It is a memorial, and, if we are to take our Lord's own explanation, only a memorial. There is nothing here of sacramental efficacy, but simply the loving desire to be remembered and the condescending entrusting of some power to recall him to these outward symbols. Strange that, if the communion were so much more, as the sacramentarian theory makes it, the feast's own Founder should not have said a word to hint that it was.

And how deep and yet lowly an insight into His hold on our hearts the institution of this ordinance shows Him to have had! The Greek is, literally, 'In order to My remembrance.' He knew that—strange and sad as it may seem, and impossible as, no doubt, it did seem to the disciples—we should be in constant danger of forgetting Him; and therefore, in this one case, He enlists sense on the side of faith, and trusts to these homely memorials the recalling, to our treacherous memories, of His dying love. He wished to live in our hearts, and that for the satisfaction of His own love and for the deepening of ours.

The Lord's Supper is a standing evidence of Christ's own estimate of where the centre of His work lies. We are to remember His death. Why should it be selected as the chief treasure for memory, unless it was something altogether different from the death of other wise teachers and benefactors? If it were in His case what it is in all others, the end of His activity for blessing, and no part of His message to the world, what need is there for the Lord's Supper, and what meaning is there in it, if Christ's death were not the sacrifice for the world's sin? Surely no view of the significance and purpose of the Cross but that which sees in it the propitiation for the world's sins accounts for this rite. A Christianity which strikes the atoning death of Jesus out of its theology is surely embarrassed to find a worthy meaning for His dying command, 'This do in remembrance of Me.'

But if the breaking of the precious alabaster box of His body was needed in order that 'the house' might be 'filled with the odour of the ointment,' and if His death was the indispensable condition of pardon and impartation of His life, then 'wheresoever this gospel shall be preached in the whole world, there,' as its vital centre, shall His death be proclaimed, and this rite shall speak of it for a memorial of Him, and 'show the Lord's death till He come.'

PARTING PROMISES AND WARNINGS

'And there was also a strife among them, which of them should be accounted the greatest. 25. And He said unto them, The kings of the Gentiles exercise lordship over them; and they that exercise authority upon them are called benefactors. 26. But ye shall not be so: but he that is greatest among you, let him be as the younger; and he that is chief, as he that doth serve. 27. For whether is greater, he that sitteth at meat, or he that serveth? is not he that sitteth at meat? but I am among you as He that serveth. 28. Ye are they which have continued with Me in My temptations. 29. And I appoint unto you a kingdom, as My Father hath appointed unto Me; 30. That ye may eat and drink at My table in My kingdom and sit on thrones judging the twelve tribes of Israel. 31. And the Lord said, Simon, Simon, behold, Satan hath desired to have you, that he may sift you as wheat: 32. But I have prayed for thee, that thy faith fail not: and when thou art converted, strengthen thy brethren. 33. And he said unto Him, Lord, I am ready to go with Thee, both into prison, and to death. 34. And He said, I tell thee, Peter, the cock shall not crow this day, before that thou shalt thrice deny that thou knowest Me. 35. And He said unto them, When I sent you without purse, and scrip, and shoes, lacked ye any thing? And they said, Nothing. 36. Then said He unto them, But now, he that hath a purse, let him take it, and likewise his scrip: and he that hath no sword, let him sell his garment, and buy one. 37. For I say unto you, that this that is written must yet be accomplished in Me, And He was reckoned among the transgressors: for the things concerning Me have an end.'—LUKE xxii. 24–37.

It was blameworthy, but only too natural, that, while Christ's heart was full of His approaching sufferings, the Apostles should be squabbling about their respective dignity. They thought that the half—understood predictions pointed to a brief struggle immediately preceding the establishment of the kingdom, and they wished to have their rank settled in advance. Possibly, too, they had been disputing as to whose office was the menial task of presenting the basin for foot—washing. So little did the first partakers of the Lord's Supper 'discern the Lord's body,' and so little did His most loving friends share His sorrows.

I. Our Lord was not so absorbed in His anticipations of the near Cross as to be unobservant of the wrangling among the Apostles. Even then His heart was enough at leisure from itself to observe, to pity, and to help. So He at once turns to deal with the false ideas of greatness betrayed by the dispute. The world's notion is that the true use and exercise of superiority is to lord it over others. Tyrants are flattered by the title of benefactor, which they do not deserve, but the giving of which shows that, even in the world, some trace of the true conception lingers. It was sadly true, at that time, that power was used for selfish ends, and generally meant oppression. One Egyptian king, who bore the title Benefactor, was popularly known as Malefactor, and many another old–world monarch deserved a like name.

Jesus lays down the law for His followers as being the exact opposite of the world's notion. Dignity and pre–eminence carry obligations to serve. In His kingdom power is to be used to help others, not to glorify oneself. In other sayings of Christ's, service is declared to be the way to *become* great in the kingdom, but here the matter is taken up at another point, and greatness, already attained on whatever grounds, is commanded to be turned to its proper use. The way to become great is to become small, and to serve. The right use of greatness is to become a servant. That has become a familiar commonplace now, but its recognition as the law for civic and other dignity is all but entirely owing to Christianity. What conception of such a use of power has the Sultan of Turkey, or the petty tyrants of heathen lands? The worst of European rulers have to make pretence to be guided by this law; and even the Pope calls himself 'the servant of servants.'

It is a commonplace, but like many another axiom, universal acceptance and almost as universal neglect are its fate. Ingrained selfishness fights against it. Men admire it as a beautiful saying, and how many of us take it as our life's guide? We condemn the rulers of old who wrung wealth out of their people and neglected every duty; but what of our own use of the fraction of power we possess, or our own demeanour to our inferiors in world or church? Have all the occupants of royal thrones or presidential chairs, all peers, members of Parliament, senators, and congressmen, used their position for the public weal? Do we regard ours as a trust to be administered for others? Do we feel the weight of our crown, or are we taken up with its jewels, and proud of ourselves for it? Christ's pathetic words, giving Himself as the example of greatness that serves, are best understood as referring to His wonderful act of washing the disciples' feet. Luke does not record it, and probably did not know it, but how the words are lighted up if we bring them into connection with it!

II. Verses 28 to 30 naturally flow from the preceding. They lift a corner of the veil, and show the rewards, when the heavenly form of the kingdom has come, of the right use of eminence in its earthly form. How pathetic a glimpse into Christ's heart is given in that warm utterance of gratitude for the imperfect companionship of the Twelve! It reveals His loneliness, His yearning for a loving hand to grasp, His continual conflict with temptations to choose an easier way than that of the Cross. He has known all the pain of being alone, and feeling in vain for a sympathetic heart to lean on. He has had to resist temptation, not only in the desert at the beginning, or in Gethsemane at the end, but throughout His life. He treasures in His heart, and richly repays, even a little love dashed with much selfishness, and faithfulness broken by desertion. We do not often speak of the tempted Christ, or of the lonely Christ, or of the grateful Christ, but in these great words we see Him as being all these.

The rewards promised point onwards to the perfecting of the kingdom in the future life. We notice the profound thought that the kingdom which His servants are to inherit is conferred on them, 'as My Father hath appointed unto Me,'—that is, that it is a kingdom won by suffering and service, and wielded by gentleness and for others. 'If we suffer, we shall also reign with Him.' The characteristics of the future royalty of Christ's servants are given in highly figurative language. A state of which we have no experience can only be revealed under forms drawn from experience; but these are only far-off approximations, and cannot be pressed.

The sacred Last Supper suggested one metaphor. It was the last on earth, but its sanctity would be renewed in heaven, and sadness and separation and the following grief would not mar the perfect, perpetual, joyful feast. What dim visions of rule and delegated authority may lie in the other promise of judging the twelve tribes of Israel, we must wait till we go to that world to understand. But this is clear, that continuing with Jesus here leads to everlasting companionship hereafter, in which all desires shall be satisfied, and we shall share in His authority and be representatives of His glory.

III. But Jesus abruptly recalls Himself and the Twelve from these remoter prospects of bliss to the nearer future of trial and separation. The solemn warning to Peter follows with startling suddenness. Why should they be fighting about precedence when they were on the verge of the sorest trial of their constancy? And as for Peter, who had, no doubt, not been the least loud-voiced in the strife, he needed most of all to be sobered. Our narrow limits forbid our doing even partial justice to the scene with him; but we note the significant use of the old name 'Simon,' reminding the Apostle of his human weakness, and its repetition, giving emphasis to the address.

We note, too, the partial withdrawal of the veil which hides the spirit world from us, in the distinct declaration of the agency of a personal tempter, whose power is limited, though his malice is boundless, and who had to obtain God's permission ere he could tempt. His sieve is made to let the wheat through, and to retain the chaff. It will be hard to empty this saying of its force. Christ taught the existence and operation of Satan; but He taught, too, that He Himself was Satan's victorious antagonist and our prevailing intercessor. He is so still. He does not seek to avert conflict from us, but prays that our faith fail not, and Himself, too, fulfils the prayer by strengthening us.

Faith, then, conquers, and withstands Satan's sifting. If it holds out, we shall not fall, though all the winds howl round us. We are not passive between the two antagonists, but have to take our share in the struggle. Partial failures may be followed by recovery, and even tend to increase our power to strengthen other tempted ones, by the experience gained of our own weakness, which deepens humility and forbearance with others' faults, and by the experience of Christ's strength, which makes us able to direct them to the source of all safety.

Peter's passionate avowal of readiness to bear anything, if only he was with Christ, is the genuine utterance of a warm impulsive heart, which took too little heed of Christ's solemn warning, and fancied that the tide of present feeling would always run as strong as now. Emotion fluctuates. Steadfast devotion is chary of mortgaging the future by promises. He who knows himself is slow to say, 'I will,' for he knows that 'Oh that I may!' is fitter for his weakness. Very likely, if Peter had been offered fetters or the scaffold then and there, he would have accepted them bravely; but it was a different thing in the raw, cold morning, after an agitating night, and the Master away at the far end of the great hall. A flippant maid's tongue was enough to finish him then.

It is sometimes easier to bear a great load for Christ than a small one. Some of us could be martyrs at the stake more easily than confessors among sneering neighbours. Jesus had spared the Apostle in the former warning of his fall, but He spoke plainly at last, since the former had been ineffectual; and He addressed him by his new name of Peter, as if to heighten the sin of denial by recalling the privileges bestowed.

IV. The last part of the passage deals with the new conditions consequent on Christ's departure. The Twelve had been exempt from the care of providing for themselves while He was with them, but now they are to be launched into the world alone, like fledglings from the nest. Not that His presence is not with them or with us, but that His absence throws the task of providing for wants and guarding against dangers on themselves, as had not been the case during the blessed years of companionship. Hence the injunctions in verse 36 lay down the permanent law for the Church, while verse 37 assigns as its reason the speedy fulfilment of the prophecies of Messiah's sufferings.

Substantially the meaning of the whole is: 'I am on the point of leaving you, and, when I am gone, you must use common-sense means for provision and protection. I provided for you while I was here, without your co-operation. Remember how I did so, and trust Me to provide in future, through your co-operation.'

The life of faith does not exclude ordinary prudence and the use of appropriate means. It is more in accord with Christ's mind to have a purse to keep money in, and a wallet for food-stores, than to go out, as some good people do, saying, 'The Lord will provide.' Yes, He will; but it will be by blessing your common-sense and effort. As to the difficulty felt in the injunction to buy a sword, our Lord would be contradicting His whole teaching if He was here commanding the use of arms for the defence of His servants or the promotion of His kingdom. That He did not mean literal swords is plain from His answer to the Apostles, who produced the formidable armament of two.

'It is enough.' A couple are plenty to fight the Roman Empire with. Yes, two too many, as was soon seen. The expression is plainly an intensely energetic metaphor, taking line with purse and scrip. The plain meaning of the whole is that we are called on to provide necessary means of provision and defence, which He will bless. The only sword permitted to His followers is the sword of the Spirit.

CHRIST'S IDEAL OF A MONARCH [Footnote: Preached on the occasion of the death of Queen Victoria.]

'And He said unto them, The kings of the Gentiles exercise lordship over them; and they that exercise authority upon them are called benefactors. 26. But ye shall not be so: but he that is greatest among you, let him be as the younger; and he that is chief, as he that doth serve.'—LUKE xxii. 25-26.

There have been sovereigns of England whose death was a relief. There have been others who were mourned with a certain tepid and decorous regret. But there has never been one on whose bier have been heaped such fragrant wreaths of universal love and sorrow as have been laid upon hers whom we have not yet learned to call by another name than that which has been musical for all these years—the Queen. Why has her people's love thus compassed her? Surely, chiefly because they felt and saw that Christ's ideal of rule, as stated in these words of our text, was her ideal, which she had gone far to realise. Here is the secret of her hold upon her people. Here is the reason why, from almost all the world, tributes have come, and as has been well said, 'They that loved not England loved her.'

Now it would be impossible for me to speak words remote from the thought that has been filling the nation's mind in these days. I can add nothing to the many eloquent and just appreciations to which we have listened in this past week, but I can draw your attention to the underlying secret which moulded and shaped that life. And it becomes the pulpit to do so. We Christians ought to infuse a Christian element into everything. We should 'not sorrow as others,' nor should we admire as others. We all unite in praising her, but eulogiums which ignore the ground of the virtues which they extol are superficial and misleading. I ask you to turn to the revelation of the secret of the nation's love and sorrow suggested by the words of my text.

Christ sets forth, in two sharply contrasted pictures, the world's ideal of a king and His ideal. The upper room was a strange place, and the eve of Calvary was a still stranger time, for disciples to squabble about pre-eminence. The Master was absorbed in the thought of His Cross, the servants were quarrelling about their places in His Kingdom. Perhaps it was the foot-washing that brought about the unseemly strife that arose among them, each desiring to hand on the menial office to another. Jesus Christ did it Himself; and to that, perhaps, refer the touching words which Luke gives as following the text; 'I am among you as he that serveth,' with the towel round His loins, and the basin in His hand.

The world's ideal of a King.

Now, the one picture which He draws for us here, the world's ideal of a king, is the portrait familiar enough to all who know anything about that ancient order of society, of tyrants and despots, in Assyria, Babylonia. Pharaohs and all the little kings round about Judaea; the vile old Herod and his equally vile brood, were recent or living examples of what the Master said when He sketched 'the kings of the Gentiles,' They 'lord it over them.' Arrogant superiority, imperious masterfulness, irresponsible wills, caprices ungoverned, an absolute oblivion of duties, no thought of responsibilities—these were the features of that ancient type of monarch: and which, in spite of all constitutional hedges and limitations, there is abundant room for the repetition of, even in so-called Christian countries.

And then, side by side with that, comes another characteristic: 'They that exercise authority upon them are called "benefactors."' They demand titles which shall credit them with virtues that they never try to possess, and live in a region filled with the fumes from a thousand venal censers of a flattery which intoxicates and makes giddy. A king in Egypt, very near our Lord's time, had borne the title 'benefactor,' the very word that is employed here; even as many a most ungracious sovereign has been called 'Your Most Gracious Majesty.'

The position tempts to such a type. And although the world has outgrown it, yet, as I have said, there is ample room for the recurrence to the old and obsolete form, unless a mightier hindrance than human nature knows, come in to prevent it. An ancient prophet lamented over the shepherds of Israel 'that do feed themselves,' and indignantly asked, 'should not the shepherds feed the sheep?' He meant precisely the same contrast which is drawn out at length in these two pictures that we have before us now.

The Christian conception.

'Ye shall not be so.' The Christian conception is in sharp contrast to, and the Christian realisation of the conception, should be the absolute opposite of that type to which I have already referred. 'He that is greatest among you, let him be as the younger'; that suggests modesty and meekness of demeanour in bearing the loftiest office. 'And he that is chief as he that doth serve'; that expresses an activity, not self–regarding and self–centred, but ever used for others. The simple words of Jesus Christ are the noblest expression of, and, as I believe, have been the mightiest impulse in producing, the modern recognition which, thank God! is becoming more and more pronounced every day amongst us, that power means duty, that elevation means the obligation to stoop, that true authority expresses itself in service. We see that conviction growing in all classes in England. Those who are lifted high are learning to–day, as they never learned before, the responsibilities and obligations of their position. And those who are low are beginning to apply the principle as they never did before, and to test the worthiness of the lofty, highly–endowed, wealthy, and noble, by their discharge of the obligations of their position. And although it anticipates what I have to say subsequently, I cannot but ask here, who shall say how the Queen's example of authority becoming service has steadied the Empire, and made a peaceful transition from the old type of authority to the new, a possibility? Although not directly stated in my text, there is implied in it another thought, namely, that whilst power obliges to service, service brings power. He that uses his influence, his authority, his capacities, his possessions, not for himself, but for his brothers, will find that by the service he has garnered in a harvest of authority, and power of command which nothing else can ever give.

Christ's ideal of a monarch.

And now I may turn, without passing beyond the bounds of the pulpit on such an occasion as the present, to look at the great illustration of the Christian ideal which the royal life now closed has given. I venture to say that, without exaggeration, and without irreverence, our Queen might have taken for her own the declaration of our Lord Himself on this occasion, 'I am among you as one that serveth.' She served her people by the diligent discharge of the duties that were laid upon her. During a strenuous reign of sixty–three years, she left no arrears, nothing neglected, nothing postponed, nothing undone. In sorrow as in joy, when life was young, and the love of husband and family joys were new, as when husband and children were taken away, and she was an old woman, lonelier because of her throne, she laboured as 'ever in the great Taskmaster's eye.' That was serving her nation by the will of God. She served her people by that swift, sincere sympathy which claimed a share alike in great national and in small private sorrows. Was there some shipwreck or some storm, that widowed humble fisherfolk in their villages? The Queen's sympathy was the first to reach them.

Were the blinds drawn down in some colliery village because of an explosion? The Queen's message was there to bring a gleam of light into darkened homes. Did some great name in literature or science pass away? Who but she was first to recognise the loss, to speak gracious words of appreciation? Did some poor shepherd die, in the strath where she made her Highland home? The widowed Queen was beside the widowed peasant, to share and to solace. Knowing sorrow herself only too well, she had learned to run to the help of the wretched. Dowered doubly with a woman's gift of sympathy, she had not let the altitude of a throne freeze its flow.

She served her people yet more by letting them feel that she took them into her confidence, spreading before them in the days of her widowhood the cherished records that her happy pen had written in the vanished days of her wifehood, opening her heart to us in mute petition that we might give our hearts to her. She served her people by the simplicity of her tastes and habits in these days of senseless luxury, and fierce, sensuous excitement of living. She served her people by the purity of her life, and so far as she could by putting a barrier around her Court, across which nothing that was foul could pass. 'He that worketh iniquity shall not tarry in my house,' said an ancient king on taking his throne. And our Queen, to the utmost of her power, said the same; and frowned down—stern for once in a righteous cause—impurity in high places. Una had her lion, and this protest of a woman's delicacy against the vices of modern society is not the least of the services for which we have to thank her.

Let me remind you that all this patient self–surrender had its root in Christian faith. She had taken her Lord for her example because her faith had knit her to Him as her Saviour.

Therefore she, as no other English sovereign, conquered the heart of the nation, and was best loved by the best men and women. Never was there a more striking confirmation of the truth that whoever in any region reigns to serve will serve to reign.

And now, before I close, let me remind you that the principles which I have been trying to express grip us in our several spheres, quite as tightly as they do those who may be more largely endowed, or more loftily placed than ourselves. There is no ideal for a Christian monarch which is not the ideal also for a Christian peasant. That which is the duty of the highest is no less the duty of the lowest. For us all it remains true that what we have we are bound to use, not for ourselves, but as recognising both our stewardship to God and the solidarity of humanity; to use for Him, that is to say, for men. This is the secret of all high, noble, blessed life for evermore.

And, brethren, whilst I for one heartily rejoice in the growing consciousness of responsibility which is being diffused through all ranks of society today, and, bless God, for one impulse to that recognition which, as I believe, came from the life now peacefully closed, I shall be no doubt charged by some of you with old–fashioned narrowness if I reiterate my own earnest conviction that we can rely on nothing to bring about a thoroughgoing, a widely–diffused, and a permanent altruism—to use the modern word—except the force that comes from the motive which Jesus Christ Himself adduced, in this very conversation, when He said, 'I am among you as he that serveth.' There is our example, aye! and more than our example, lodged in Him, and available for us, by our simple faith in Him. In love that seeks to copy, lies the only power that will cast out self, that 'anarch old,' from his usurped seat in our hearts, and will throne Jesus Christ there. It needs a mighty lever to heave a planet from its orbit, and to set it circling round another sun; and there is nothing that will deliver any man, in any rank of life, from the dominion of self, except submission to the dominion of Him who, because He died to serve, deserves, and has won, the supreme right of authority and dominion over human life.

To use anything for self is to miss its highest goodness, and to mar ourselves. To use anything for Christ and our brethren is to find its sweetest sweetness, and to bless ourselves to the very uttermost. Self–absorption is self–destruction; self–surrender is self–acquisition.

If we can truly say, 'I am among you as he that serveth,' if all our possessions suggest to us obligations and all our powers impose on us duties: then be we prince or peasant, rich or poor, entrusted with many talents or with but one, we shall make the best of life here, and pass to higher authority, which is nobler service hereafter. Be the servant of all, and all are yours; serve Christ, and possess yourselves—these are the lessons from that royal life of service. May we learn them! May the King walk in his mother's steps and hearken to 'the oracle which his mother taught him!

THE LONELY CHRIST

'Ye are they which have continued with Me in My
temptations'—LUKE xxii 28.

We wonder at the disciples when we read of the unseemly strife for precedence which jars on the tender solemnities of the Last Supper. We think them strangely unsympathetic and selfish; and so they were. But do not let us be too hard on them, nor forget that there was a very natural reason for the close connection which is found in the gospels between our Lord's announcements of His sufferings and this eager dispute as to who should be the greatest in the kingdom. They dimly understood what He meant, but they did understand this much, that His 'sufferings' were immediately to precede His 'glory'—and so it is not, after all, to be so much wondered at if the apparent approach of these made the settlement of their places in the impending kingdom seem to them a very pressing question. We should probably have thought so too, if we had been among them.

Perhaps, too, the immediate occasion of this strife who should be accounted the greatest, which drew from Christ the words of our text, may have been the unwillingness of each to injure his possible claim to pre–eminence by doing the servant's tasks at the modest meal. May we not suppose that the basin and the towel were refused by one after another, with muttered words growing louder and angrier: 'It is not my place,' says Peter; 'you, Andrew, take it—and so from hand to hand it goes, till the Master ends the strife and takes it Himself to wash their feet. Then, when He had sat down again, He may have spoken the words of which our text is part—in which He tells the wrangling disciples what is the true law of honour in His kingdom, namely, *service*, and points to Himself as the great example. With what emphasis the pathetic incident of the foot–washing invests the clause before our text: 'I am among you as he that serveth.' On that disclosure of the true law of pre–eminence in His kingdom there follows in this and following verses the assurance, that, unseemly as their strife, there was reward for them, and places of dignity there, because in all their selfishness and infirmity, they had still clung to their Master.

This being the original purpose of these words, I venture to use them for another. They give us, if I mistake not, a wonderful glimpse into the heart of Christ, and a most pathetic revelation of His thoughts and experiences, all the more precious because it is quite incidental and, we may say, unconscious.

I. See then, here, the tempted Christ.

In one sense, our Lord is His own perpetual theme. He is ever speaking of Himself, inasmuch as He is ever presenting what He is to us, and what He claims of us. In another sense, He scarcely ever speaks of Himself, inasmuch as deep silence, for the most part, lies over His own inward experiences. How precious, therefore, and how profoundly significant is that word here—'in My temptations'! So He summed up all His life. To feel the full force of the expression, it should be remembered that the temptation in the wilderness was past before His first disciple attached himself to Him, and that the conflict in Gethsemane had not yet come when these words were spoken. The period to which they refer, therefore, lies altogether within these limits, including neither. After the former, 'Satan,' we read, 'departed from Him for a season.' Before the latter, we read, 'the prince of this world cometh.' The space between, of which people are so apt to think as free from temptation, is the time of which our Lord is speaking now. The time when His followers 'companied with Him' is to His consciousness the time of His 'temptations.'

That is not the point of view from which the Gospel narratives present it, for the plain reason that they are not autobiographies, and that Jesus said little about the continuous assaults to which He was exposed. It is not the point of view from which we often think of it. We are too apt to conceive of Christ's temptations as all gathered together—curdled and clotted, as it were, at the two ends of His life, leaving the space between free. But we cannot understand the meaning of that life, nor feel aright the love and help that breathe from it, unless we think of it as a field of continual and diversified temptations.

How remarkable is the choice of the expression! To Christ, His life, looking back on it, does not so much present itself in the aspect of sorrow, difficulty or pain, as in that of temptation. He looked upon all outward things mainly with regard to their power to help or to hinder His life's work. So for us, sorrow or joy should matter comparatively little. The evil in the evil should be felt to be sin, and the true cross and burden of life should be to us, as to our Master, the appeals it makes to us to abandon our tasks, and fling away our filial dependence and submission.

This is not the place to plunge into the thorny questions which surround the thought of the tempted Christ. However these may be solved, the great fact remains, that His temptations were most real and unceasing. It was no sham fight which He fought. The story of the wilderness is the story of a most real conflict; and that conflict is waged all through His life. True, the traces of it are few. The battle was fought on both sides in grim silence, as sometimes men wage a mortal struggle without a sound. But if there were no other witness of the sore conflict, the Victor's shout at the close would be enough. His last words, 'I have overcome the world,' sound the note of triumph, and tell how sharp had been the strife. So long and hard had it been that He cannot forget it even in heaven, and from the throne holds forth to all the churches the hope of overcoming, 'even as I also overcame.' As on some battlefield whence all traces of the agony and fury have passed away, and harvests wave, and larks sing where blood ran and men groaned their lives out, some grey stone raised by the victors remains, and only the trophy tells of the forgotten fight, so that monumental word, 'I have overcome' stands to all ages as the record of the silent, life–long conflict.

It is not for us to know how the sinless Christ was tempted. There are depths beyond our reach. This we can understand, that a sinless manhood is not above the reach of temptation; and this besides, that, to such a nature, the temptations must be suggested from without, not presented from within. The desire for food is simply a physical craving, but another personality than His own uses it to incite the Son to abandon dependence for His physical life on God. The trust in God's protection is holy and good, and it may be truest wisdom and piety to incur danger in dependence on it, when God's service calls, but a mocking voice without suggests, under the cloak of it, a needless rushing into peril at no call of conscience, and for no end of mercy, which is not religion but self–will. The desire to have the world for His own lay in Christ's deepest heart, but the enemy of Christ and man, who thought the world his already, used it as giving occasion to suggest a smoother and shorter road to win all men unto Him than the 'Via Dolorosa' of the Cross. So the sinless Christ was tempted at the beginning, and so the sinless Christ was tempted, in various forms of these first temptations, throughout His life. The path which He had to tread was ever before Him, the shadow of the Cross was flung along His road from the first. The pain and sorrow, the shame and spitting, the contradiction of sinners against Himself, the easier path which needed but a wish to become His, the shrinking of flesh—all these made their appeal to Him, and every step of the path which He trod for us was trodden by the power of a fresh consecration of Himself to His task and a fresh victory over temptation.

Let us not seek to analyse. Let us be content to worship, as we look, Let us think of the tempted Christ, that our conceptions of His sinlessness may be increased. His was no untried and cloistered virtue, pure because never brought into contact with seducing evil, but a militant and victorious goodness, that was able to withstand in the evil day. Let us think of the tempted Christ that our thankful thoughts of what He bore for us may be warmer and more adequate, as we stand afar off and look on at the mystery of His battle with our enemies and His. Let us think of the tempted Christ to make the lighter burden of our cross, and our less terrible conflict easier to bear and to wage. So will He 'continue with *us* in *our* temptations,' and patience and victory flow to us from Him.

II. See here the lonely Christ.

There is no aspect of our Lord's life more pathetic than that of His profound loneliness. I suppose the most utterly solitary man that ever lived was Jesus Christ. If we think of the facts of His life, we see how His nearest kindred stood aloof from Him, how 'there were none to praise, and very few to love'; and how, even in the small company of His friends, there was absolutely none who either understood Him or sympathised with Him. We hear a great deal about the solitude in which men of genius live, and how all great souls are necessarily lonely. That is true, and that solitude of great men is one of the compensations which run through all life, and make the lot of the many little, more enviable than that of the few great. 'The little hills rejoice together on every side,' but far above their smiling companionships, the Alpine peak lifts itself into the cold air, and though it be 'visited all night by troops of stars,' it is lonely amid the silence and the snow. Talk of the solitude of pure character amid evil, like Lot in Sodom, or of the loneliness of uncomprehended aims and unshared thoughts—who ever experienced that as keenly as Christ did? That perfect purity must needs have been hurt by the sin of men as none else have ever been. That loving heart yearning for the solace of an answering heart must needs have felt a sharper pang of unrequited love than ever pained another. That spirit to which the things that are seen were shadows, and the Father and the Father's house the ever–present, only realities must have felt itself parted from the men whose portion was in this life, by a gulf broader than ever opened between any other two souls that shared together human life.

The more pure and lofty a nature, the more keen its sensitiveness, the more exquisite its delights, and the sharper its pains. The more loving and unselfish a heart, the more its longing for companionship: and the more its aching in loneliness.

Very significant and pathetic are many points in the Gospel story bearing on this matter. The very choice of the Twelve had for its first purpose, 'that they should be with Him,' as one of the Evangelists tells us. We know how constantly He took the three who were nearest to Him along with Him, and that surely not merely that they might be 'eyewitnesses of His majesty' on the holy mount, or of His agony in Gethsemane, but as having a real gladness and strength even in their companionship amid the mystery of glory as amid the power of darkness. We read of His being alone but twice in all the gospels, and both times for prayer. And surely the dullest ear can hear a note of pain in that prophetic word: 'The hour cometh that ye shall be scattered, every man to his own, and shall leave Me alone'; while every heart must feel the pitiful pathos of the plea, 'Tarry ye here, and watch with Me.' Even in that supreme hour, He longs for human companionship, however uncomprehending, and stretches out His hands in the great darkness, to feel the touch of a hand of flesh and blood—and, alas, for poor feeble love!—He gropes for it in vain. Surely that horror of utter solitude is one of the elements of His passion grave and sorrowful enough to be named by the side of the other bitterness poured into that cup, even as it was pain enough to form a substantive feature of the great prophetic picture: 'I looked for some to take pity, but there was none; and for comforters, but I found none.'

So here, a deep pain in His loneliness is implied in these words of our text which put the disciples' participation in the glories of His throne as the issue of their loyal continuance with Him in the conflict of earth. These, and these only, had been by His side, and so much does He care for their companionship, that therefore they shall share His dominion.

That lonely Christ sympathises with all solitary hearts. If ever we feel ourselves misunderstood and thrown back upon ourselves; if ever our hearts' burden of love is rejected; if our outward lives be lonely and earth yields nothing to stay our longing for companionship; if our hearts have been filled with dear ones and are now empty or filled only with tears, let us think of Him and say, 'Yet I am not alone.' He lived alone, alone He died, that no heart might ever be solitary any more. 'Could ye not watch with Me?' was His gentle rebuke in Gethsemane. 'Lo, *I* am with *you* always,' is His mighty promise from the throne. In every step of life we may have Him for a companion, a friend closer than all others, nearer us than our very selves, if we may so say—and in the valley of the shadow of death we need fear no evil, for He will be with us.

III. See here the grateful Christ.

I almost hesitate to use the word, but there seems a distinct ring of thanks in the expression, and in the connection. And we need not wonder at that, if we rightly understand it. There is nothing in it inconsistent with our Lord's character and relations to His disciples. Do you remember another instance in which one seems to hear the same tone, namely, in the marked warmth with which He acknowledges the beautiful service of Mary in breaking the fragrant casket of nard upon His head?

All true love is glad when it is met, glad to give, and glad to receive. Was it not a joy to Jesus to be waited on by the ministering women? Would He not thank them because they served Him for love? I trow, yes. And if any one stumbles at the word 'grateful' as applied to Him, we do not care about the word so long as it is seen that His heart was gladdened by loving friends, and that He recognised in their society a ministry of love.

Notice, too, the loving estimate of what these disciples had done. Their companionship had been imperfect enough at the best. They had given Him but blind affection, dashed with much selfishness. In an hour or two they would all have forsaken Him and fled. He knew all that was lacking in them, and the cowardly abandonment which was so near. But He has not a word to say of all this. He does not count jealously the flaws in our work, or reject it because it is incomplete. So here is the great truth clearly set forth, that where there is a loving heart, there is acceptable service. It is possible that our poor, imperfect deeds shall be an odour of a sweet smell, acceptable, well–pleasing to Him. Which of us that is a father is not glad at his children's gifts, even though they be purchased with his own money, and be of little use? They mean love, so they are precious. And Christ, in like manner, gladly accepts what we bring, even though it be love chilled by selfishness, and faith broken by doubt,—submission crossed by self–will. The living heart of the disciples' acceptable service was their love, far less intelligent and entire than ours may be. They were joined to their Lord, though with but partial sympathy and knowledge, in His temptations. It is possible for us to be joined to Jesus Christ more closely and more truly than they were during His earthly life. Union with Him here is union with Him hereafter. If we abide in Him amid the shows and shadows of earth, He will continue with us in our temptations, and so the fellowships begun on earth will be perfected in heaven, 'if so be that we suffer with Him, that we may also be glorified together.'

A GREAT FALL AND A GREAT RECOVERY

'But I have prayed for thee, that thy faith fail not;
and when thou art converted, strengthen thy brethren.'
—Luke xxii. 32.

Our Lord has just been speaking words of large and cordial praise of the steadfastness with which His friends had continued with Him in His temptations, and it is the very contrast between that continuance and the prevision of the cowardly desertion of the Apostle which occasioned the abrupt transition to this solemn appeal to him, which indicates how the forecast pained Christ's heart. He does not let the foresight of Peter's desertion chill His praise of Peter's past faithfulness as one of the Twelve. He does not let the remembrance of Peter's faithfulness modify His rebuke for Peter's intended and future desertion. He speaks to him, with significant and emphatic reiteration of the old name of Simon that suggests weakness, unsanctified and unhelped: 'Simon, Simon, Satan hath desired to have you, that he may sift you as wheat.' *There* is a glimpse given, a corner of the curtain being lifted, into a dim region in which faith should not refuse to discern so much light as Christ has given, because superstition has so often fancied that it saw what it only dreamed. But passing from that, the words before us seem to me to suggest a threefold thought of the Intercessor for tempted souls; of the consequent re–illumination of eclipsed faith; and of the larger service for which the discipline of fall and recovery fits him who falls. Let me say a word or two about each of these thoughts.

I. We have the Intercessor for tempted souls.

Notice that majestic 'but' with which my text begins, 'Satan hath desired to have you, that he may sift you as wheat, *but* I have prayed for thee.' He presents Himself, then, as the Antagonist, the confident and victorious Antagonist, of whatsoever mysterious, malignant might may lie beyond the confines of sense, and He says, 'My prayer puts the hook in leviathan's nose, and the malevolent desire to sift, in order that not the chaff but the wheat may disappear, comes all to nothing by the side of My prayer.'

Note the discrimination of the intercession. He 'hath desired to have you'—that is plural; 'I have prayed for thee'—that is singular. The man that was in the greatest danger was the man nearest to Christ's heart, and chiefly the object of Christ's intercession. So it is always—the tenderest of His words, the sweetest of His consolations, the strongest of His succours, the most pleading and urgent of His petitions, the mightiest gifts of His grace, are given to the weakest, the neediest, the men and women in most sorrow and stress and peril, and they who want Him most always have Him nearest. The thicker the darkness, the brighter His light; the drearier our lives, the richer His presence; the more solitary we are, the larger the gifts of His companionship. Our need is the measure of His prayer. 'Satan hath desired to have you, but thou, Peter, dost stand in the very focus of the danger, and so on *thee* are focussed, too, the rays of My love and care.' Be sure, dear friends, that it is always so for us, and that when you want Christ most, Christ is most to you.

Then, I need not touch at any length upon that great subject on which none of us can speak adequately or with full comprehension—viz. our Lord as the Intercessor for us in all our weakness and need. We believe in His continual manhood, we believe that He prayed upon earth, we believe that He prays in heaven. His prayer is no mere utterance of words: it is the presentation of a fact, the bringing ever before the Infinite Divine Mind, as it were, of His great work of sacrifice, as the condition which determines, and the channel through which flows, the gift of sustaining grace from God Himself. And so we may be sure that whensoever there come to any of us trials, difficulties, conflicts, temptations, they are known to our Brother in the skies, and the stormier the gales that threaten us, the closer He wraps His protection round us. We have an Advocate and an Intercessor before the Throne; His prayer is always heard. Oh, brethren! how different our endurance would be, if we vividly believed that Christ was praying for us! How it would take the sting out of sorrow, and blunt the edge of temptation, if we realised that! O for a faith that shall rend the heavens, and rise above the things seen and temporal, and behold the eternal order of the universe, the central Throne, and at the right hand of God, the Intercessor for all who love and trust Him!

II. Notice again the consequent re–illumination of eclipsed faith.

'I have prayed for thee, that thy faith fail not.' Did it fail? If we look only at Peter's denial, we must answer, Yes. If we look at the whole of the future life of the Apostle, we answer, No. Eclipse is not extinction; the momentary untruthfulness to one's deepest convictions is not the annihilation of these convictions. Christ's prayer is never vain, and Christ's prayer was answered just because Peter, though he fell, did not lie in the mud, but staggered to his feet again, and with sore weeping and many an agony of shame, struggled onward, with unconquerable hope, in the path from which, for a moment, he strayed. Better one great outburst like his, the nature of which there is no possibility of mistaking, than the going on, as so many professing Christians do, from year to year, walking in a vain show of godliness, and fancying themselves to be disciples, when all the while they are recreants and apostates. There is more chance of the recovery of a good man that has fallen into some sin, 'gross as a mountain, open, palpable,' than there is of the recovery of those who let their religion trickle out of them in drops, and never know that their veins are empty until the heart ceases to beat at all.

Here, then, we have two large lessons from which we may take strength, taught us by this darkening and re–illumination of an eclipsed faith. One is that the sincerest love, the truest desire to follow Jesus, the firmest faith, may be overborne, and the whole set of a life contradicted for a time. Thank God, there is a vast difference between conduct which is inconsistent with being a Christian and conduct which is incompatible with being a Christian. It is dangerous, perhaps, to apply the difference too liberally in judging ourselves; it is imperative to apply it always in judging our fellows. But if it be true that Peter meant, down to the very bottom of his heart, all that he said when he said, 'I will lay down my life for Thee,' while yet within a few hours afterwards the sad prophecy of our Lord was fulfilled—'Thou shalt deny Me thrice!'—let us take the lesson, not, indeed, to abate our horror of the sin, but on the one hand to cut the comb of our own self–confidence, and on the other hand to judge with all charity and tenderness the faults of our brethren. 'Be not high–minded, but fear,' and when we look into the black gulf into which Peter fell bodily, let us cry, 'Hold Thou me up and I shall be safe.'

The other lesson is that the deepest fall may be recovered. Our Lord in the words of our text does not definitely prophesy what He subsequently declares in plain terms, the fall of Peter, but He implies it when He says, 'when thou art converted'—or, as the Revised Version reads it much more accurately, 'when once thou hast turned again strengthen thy brethren.' Then, the Apostle's face had been turned the wrong way for a time, and he needed to turn right–about–face in order to renew the old direction of his life. He came back for two reasons—one because Christ prayed for him, and the other because he 'turned himself.' For the only way back is through the valley of weeping and the dark lane of penitence; and whosoever has denied with Peter, or at least grovelled with Peter, or perhaps grovelled much more than Peter, 'denying the Lord that bought him' by living as if He was not his Lord, will never come back to the place that Peter again won for himself, but by the road by which Peter went. 'The Lord turned and looked upon him,' and Christ's face, with love and sorrow and reproach in it, taught him his sin, and bowed his heart, 'and he went out and wept bitterly.'

Peter and Judas both 'went out'; the one 'went out and hanged himself,' because his conviction of his sin was unaccompanied with a faith in his Master's love, and his repentance was only remorse; and the other 'went out and wept bitterly,' and so came back with a clean heart. And on the Resurrection morning he was ready for the message: 'Go, tell His disciples, *and Peter*, He goeth before you into Galilee.' And the Lord appeared to him, in that conversation, the existence of which was known, though the particulars were unknown, to the rest; and when 'He appeared unto Cephas,' spoke his full forgiveness. There is the road back for all wanderers.

III. The last thought is, the larger service for which such an experience will fit him who falls.

'Strengthen thy brethren when once thou hast turned again.' I need not remind you how nobly the

Apostle fulfilled this commandment. Satan desired to have him, that he might sift him as wheat; but Satan's sifting was in order that he might get rid of the wheat and harvest the chaff. His malice worked indirectly the effect opposite to his purpose, and achieved the same result as Christ's winnowing seeks to accomplish—namely, it got rid of the chaff and kept the wheat. Peter's vanity was sifted out of him, his self–confidence was sifted out of him, his rash presumption was sifted out of him, his impulsive readiness to blurt out the first thought that came into his head was sifted out of him, and so his unreliableness and changeableness were largely sifted out of him, and he became what Christ said he had in him the makings of being—'Cephas, a rock,' or, as the Apostle Paul, who was never unwilling to praise the others, said, a man 'who looked like a pillar.' He 'strengthened his brethren,' and to many generations the story of the Apostle who denied the Lord he loved has ministered comfort. To how many tempted souls, and souls that have yielded to temptation, and souls that, having yielded, are beginning to grope their way back again out of its vulgar delights and surfeiting sweetnesses, and find that there is a desert to be traversed before they can again reach the place where they stood before, has that story ministered hope, as it will minister to the very end! The bone that is broken is stronger, they tell us, at the point of junction, when it heals and grows again, than it ever was before. And it may well be that a faith that has made experience of falling and restoration has learned a depth of self–distrust, a firmness of confidence in Christ, a warmth of grateful love which it would never otherwise have experienced.

The Apostle about whom we have been speaking seems to have carried in his mind and memory an abiding impression from that bitter experience, and in his letter when he was an old man, and all that past was far away, he writes many words which sound like echoes and reminiscences of it. In the last chapter of his epistle, in which he speaks of himself as a witness of the sufferings of Christ, there are numbers of verses which seem to point to what had happened in the Upper Room. 'Ye younger, submit yourselves unto the elder.' Jesus Christ had then said, 'He that is the greater among you, let him be as the younger.' Peter says, 'Be clothed with humility'; he remembers Christ wrapping a towel around Him, girding Himself, and taking the basin. He says, 'God resisteth the proud,' and he remembers how proud he had been, with his boast: 'Though all should ... yet will not I,' and how low he fell because he was 'fool' enough to 'trust in his own heart.' 'Be sober, be vigilant; because your adversary, the devil, as a roaring lion, walketh about, seeking whom he may devour: whom resist, steadfast in the faith.' 'The God of all grace stablish, strengthen, settle you.' He thus strengthened his brethren when he reminded them of the temptation to which he himself had so shamefully succumbed, and when he referred them for all their strength to the source of it all, even God in Christ.

GETHSEMANE

'And He came out, and went, as He was wont, to the
mount of Olives; and His disciples also followed Him.
40. And when He was at the place, He said unto them,
Pray that ye enter not into temptation. 41. And He
was withdrawn from them about a stone's cast, and
kneeled down, and prayed, 42. Saying, Father, If Thou
be willing, remove this cup from Me; nevertheless, not
My will, but Thine, be done. 43. And there appeared an
angel unto Him from heaven, strengthening Him. 44. And,

being in an agony, He prayed more earnestly: and His
sweat was as it were great drops of blood falling down
to the ground. 45. And when He rose up from prayer,
and was come to His disciples, He found them sleeping
for sorrow. 46. And said unto them, Why sleep ye? rise
and pray, lest ye enter into temptation. 47. And while
He yet spake, beheld a multitude, and he that was
called Judas, one of the twelve, went before them, and
drew near unto Jesus to kiss Him. 48. But Jesus said
unto him, Judas, betrayest thou the Son of man with a
kiss? 49. When they which were about Him saw what would
follow, they said unto Him, Lord, shall we smite with
the sword? 50. And one of them smote a servant of the
high priest, and cut off his right ear. 51. And Jesus
answered and said, Suffer ye thus far. And He touched
his ear, and healed him. 52. Then Jesus said unto the
chief priests, and captains of the temple, and the
elders, which were come to Him, Be ye come out, as
against a thief, with swords and staves? 53. When I
was daily with you in the temple, ye stretched forth
no hands against Me; but this is your hour, and the
power of darkness.'—Luke xxii. 39–53.

'Put off thy shoes from off thy feet.' Cold analysis is out of place here, where the deepest depth of a Saviour's sorrows is partly disclosed, and we see Him bowing His head to the waves and billows that went over Him, for our sakes. Luke's account is much condensed, but contains some points peculiar to itself. It falls into two parts—the solemn scene of the agony, and the circumstances of the arrest.

I. We look with reverent awe and thankfulness at that soul–subduing picture of the agonising and submissive Christ which Luke briefly draws. Think of the contrast between the joyous revelry of the festival–keeping city and the sadness of the little company which crossed the Kedron and passed beneath the shadow of the olive–trees into the moonlit garden. Jesus needed companions there; but He needed solitude still more. So He is 'parted from them'; but Luke alone tells us how short the distance was—'as it were a stone's throw,' and near enough for the disciples to see and hear something before they slept.

That clinging to and separation from His humble friends gives a wonderful glimpse into Christ's desolation then. And how beautiful is His care for them, even at that supreme hour, which leads to the injunction twice spoken, at the beginning and end of His own prayers, that they should pray, not for Him, but for themselves. He never asks for men's prayers, but He does for their love. He thinks of His sufferings as temptation for the disciples, and for the moment forgets His own burden, in pointing them the way to bear theirs. Did self–oblivious love ever shine more gloriously in the darkness of sorrow?

Luke omits the threefold withdrawal and return, but notes three things—the prayer, the angel appearance, and the physical effects of the agony. The essentials are all preserved in his account. The prayer is truly 'the Lord's prayer,' and the perfect pattern for ours. Mark the grasp of God's fatherhood, which is at once appeal and submission. So should all prayer begin, with the thought, at all events, whether with the word 'Father' or no. Mark the desire that 'this cup' should pass. The expression shows how vividly the impending sufferings were pictured before Christ's eye. The keenest pains of anticipation, which make so large a part of so many sorrows, were felt by Him. He shrank from His sufferings. Did He therefore falter in His desire and resolve to endure the Cross? A thousand times, no! His will never wavered, but maintained itself supreme over the natural recoil of His human nature from pain and death. If He had not felt the Cross to be a dread, it had been no sacrifice. If He had allowed the dread to penetrate to His will, He had been no Saviour. But now He goes before us in the path which all have, in their degree, to travel, and accepts pain that He may do His work.

That acceptance of the divine will is no mere 'If it must be so, let it be so,' much as that would have been. But He receives in His prayer the true answer—for His will completely coincides with the Father's, and 'mine' is 'thine.' Such conformity of our wills with God's is the highest blessing of prayer and the true deliverance. The cup accepted is sweet; and though flesh may shrink, the inner self consents, and in consenting to the pain, conquers it.

Luke alone tells of the ministering angel; and, according to some authorities, the forty–third and forty–fourth verses are spurious. But, accepting them as genuine, what does the angelic appearance teach us? It suggests pathetically the utter physical prostration of Jesus. Sensuous religion has dwelt on that offensively, but let us not rush to the opposite extreme, and ignore it. It teaches us that the manhood of Jesus needed the communication of divine help as truly as we do. The difficulty of harmonising that truth with His divine nature was probably the reason for the omission of this verse in some manuscripts. It teaches the true answer to His prayer, as so often to ours; namely, the strength to bear the load, not the removal of it. It is remarkable that the renewal of the solemn 'agony' and the intenser earnestness of prayer follow the strengthening by the angel.

Increased strength increased the conflict of feeling, and the renewed and intensified conflict increased the earnestness of the prayer. The calmness won was again disturbed, and a new recourse to the source of it was needed. We stand reverently afar off, and ask, not too curiously, what it is that falls so heavily to the ground, and shines red and wet in the moonlight. But the question irresistibly rises, Why all this agony of apprehension? If Jesus Christ was but facing death as it presents itself to all men, His shrinking is far beneath the temper in which many a man has fronted the scaffold and the fire. We can scarcely save His character for admiration, unless we see in the agony of Gethsemane something much more than the shrinking from a violent death, and understand how there the Lord made to meet on Him the iniquity of us all. If the burden that crushed Him thus was but the common load laid on all men's shoulders, He shows unmanly terror. If it were the black mass of the world's sins, we can understand the agony, and rejoice to think that our sins were there.

II. The arrest. Three points are made prominent—the betrayer's token, the disciples' resistance, the reproof of the foes, and in each the centre of interest is our Lord's words. The sudden bursting in of the multitude is graphically represented. The tumult broke the stillness of the garden, but it brought deeper peace to Christ's heart; for while the anticipation agitated, the reality was met with calmness. Blessed they who can unmoved front evil, the foresight of which shook their souls! Only they who pray as Jesus did beneath the olives, can go out from their shadow, as He did, to meet the foe.

The first of the three incidents of the arrest brings into strong prominence Christ's meek patience, dignity, calmness, and effort, even at that supreme moment, to rouse dormant conscience, and save the traitor from himself. Judas probably had no intention by his kiss of anything but showing the mob their prisoner; but he must have been far gone in insensibility before he could fix on such a sign. It was the token of friendship and discipleship, and no doubt was customary among the disciples, though we never hear of any lips touching Jesus but the penitent woman's, which were laid on His feet, and the traitor's. The worst hypocrisy is that which is unconscious of its own baseness.

Every word of Christ's answer to the shameful kiss is a sharp spear, struck with a calm and not resentful hand right into the hardened conscience. There is wistful tenderness and a remembrance of former confidences in calling Him by name. The order of words in the original emphasises the kiss, as if Jesus had said, 'Is that the sign you have chosen? Could nothing else serve you? Are you so dead to all feeling that you can kiss and betray?' The Son of man flashes on Judas, for the last time, the majesty and sacredness against which he was lifting his hand. 'Betrayest thou?' which comes last in the Greek, seeks to startle by putting into plain words the guilt, and so to rend the veil of sophistications in which the traitor was hiding his deed from himself. Thus to the end Christ seeks to keep him from ruin, and with meek patience resents not indignity, but with majestic calmness sets before the miserable man the hideousness of his act. The patient Christ is the same now as then, and meets all our treason with pleading, which would fain teach us how black it is, not because He is angry, but because He would win us to turn from it. Alas that so often His remonstrances fall on hearts as wedded to their sin as was Judas's!

The rash resistance of the disciple is recorded chiefly for the sake of Christ's words and acts. The anonymous swordsman was Peter, and the anonymous victim was Malchus, as John tells us. No doubt he had brought one of the two swords from the upper room, and, in a sudden burst of anger and rashness, struck at the man nearest him, not considering the fatal consequences for them all that might follow. Peter could manage nets better than swords, and missed the head, in his flurry and in the darkness, only managing to shear off a poor slave's ear. When the Church takes sword in hand, it usually shows that it does not know how to wield it, and as often as not has struck the wrong man. Christ tells Peter and us, in His word here, what His servants' true weapons are, and rebukes all armed resistance of evil. 'Suffer ye thus far' is a command to oppose violence only by meek endurance, which wins in the long run, as surely as the patient sunshine melts the thick ice, which is ice still, when pounded with a hammer.

If 'thus far' as to His own seizure and crucifying was to be 'suffered,' where can the breaking–point of patience and non–resistance be fixed? Surely every other instance of violence and wrong lies far on this side of that one. The prisoner heals the wound. Wonderful testimony that not inability to deliver Himself, but willingness to be taken, gave Him into the hands of His captors! Blessed proof that He lavishes benefits on His foes, and that His delight is to heal all wounds and stanch every bleeding heart!

The last incident here is Christ's piercing rebuke, addressed, not to the poor, ignorant tools, but to the prime movers of the conspiracy, who had come to gloat over its success. He asserts His own innocence, and hints at the preposterous inadequacy of 'swords and staves' to take Him. He is no 'robber,' and their weapons are powerless, unless He wills. He recalls His uninterrupted teaching in the Temple, as if to convict them of cowardice, and perchance to bring to remembrance His words there. And then, with that same sublime and strange majesty of calm submission which marks all His last hours, He unveils to these furious persecutors the true character of their deed. The sufferings of Jesus were the meeting–point of three worlds—earth, hell, and heaven. 'This is your hour.' But it was also Satan's hour, and it was Christ's 'hour,' and God's. Man's passions, inflamed from beneath, were used to work out God's purpose; and the Cross is at once the product of human unbelief, of devilish hate, and of divine mercy. His sufferings were 'the power of darkness.'

Mark in that expression Christ's consciousness that He is the light, and enmity to Him darkness. Mark, too, His meek submission, as bowing His head to let the black flood flow over Him. Note that Christ brands enmity to Him as the high–water mark of sin, the crucial instance of man's darkness, the worst thing ever done. Mark the assurance that animated Him, that the eclipse was but for an 'hour.' The victory of the darkness was brief, and it led to the eternal triumph of the Light. By dying He is the death of death. This Jonah inflicts deadly wounds on the monster in whose maw He lay for three days. The power of darkness was shivered to atoms in the moment of its proudest triumph, like a wave which is beaten into spray as it rises in a towering crest and flings itself against the rock.

THE CROSS THE VICTORY AND DEFEAT OF DARKNESS

'This is your hour, and the power of darkness.'
—Luke xxii. 53.

The darkness was the right time for so dark a deed. The surface meaning of these pathetic and far–reaching words of our Lord's in the garden to His captors is to point the correspondence between the season and the act. As He has just said, 'He had been daily with them in the Temple,' but in the blaze of the noontide they laid no hands upon Him. They found a congenial hour in the midnight. But the words go a great deal deeper than allusive symbolism of that sort. Looking at them as giving us a little glimpse into the thoughts and feelings of Christ, we can scarcely help tracing in them the very clear consciousness that He was the Light, and that all antagonism to Him was the work of darkness in an eminent and especial sense. But whilst this unobscured consciousness, which no mere man could venture so unqualifiedly to assert, is manifest in the words, there is also in them, to my ear, a tone of majestic resignation, as if He said, 'There! do your worst!' and bowed His head, as a man might do, standing breast high in the sea, that the wave might roll over Him. And there is in them, too, a shrinking as of horror from the surging upon Him of the black tide to which He bows His head.

But whilst thus pathetic and significant in their indication of the feelings of our Lord, they have a wider and a deeper meaning still, I think, if we ponder them; inasmuch as they open before us some aspects of His sufferings and eminently of His Cross, which it becomes us all to lay to heart. And it is to these that I desire to turn your attention for a few moments.

I. I see in them, then, first, this great thought, that the Cross of Jesus Christ is the centre and the meeting–point for the energies of three worlds.

'This is your hour.' Now our Lord habitually speaks of His sufferings, and of other points in His life, as being 'My hour,' by which, of course, He means the time appointed to Him by God for the doing of an appointed work. And that idea is distinctly to be attached to the use of the word here. But, on the other hand, there is emphasis laid on '*your*,' and that hour is thereby designated as a time in which they could do as they would. It was their opportunity, or, as we say in our colloquialism, now was their time when, unhindered, they might carry into effect their purposes.

So there is given us the thought of His passion and death as being the most eminent and awful instance of men being left unchecked to work out whatsoever was in their evil hearts, and to carry into effect their blackest purposes.

But, on the other hand, there goes with the phrase the idea to which I have already referred; and 'this is their hour,' not merely in the sense that it was their opportunity, but also that it was the hour appointed by God and allotted them for their doing the thing which their unhindered evil passions impelled them to do. And so we are brought face to face with the most eminent instance of that great puzzle that runs through all life—how God works out His lofty designs by means of responsible agents, 'making the wrath of men to praise Him,' and girding Himself with the remainder.

Nor is that all. For the next words of my text bring in a third set of powers as in operation. 'This is your hour' lets us see man overarched by the abyss of the heavens, 'and the power of darkness' lets us see the deep and awful forces that are working beneath and surging upwards into humanity, and opens the subterranean volcanoes. I do not say that there is any reference here to a personal Antagonist of good, in whom these dark tendencies are focussed, but there is a distinct reference to 'the darkness' as a whole, a kind of organic whole, which operates upon men. Even when they think themselves to be freest, and are carrying out their own wicked designs, they are but the slaves of impulses that come straight from the dark kingdom. If I may turn from the immediate purpose of my sermon for a moment, I pray you to consider that solemn aspect of our life, a film between two firmaments, like the earth with the waters above and the waters beneath. On the one side it is open and pervious to heavenly influences, and moulded by the overarching and sovereign will, and on the other side it is all honeycombed beneath with, and open to, the uprisings of evil, straight from the bottomless pit.

But if we turn to the more immediate purpose of the words, think for a moment of the solemn and wonderful aspect which the Cross of Christ assumes, thus contemplated. Three worlds focus their energies upon it—heaven, earth, hell. Looked at from one side it is all radiant and glorious, as the transcendent exhibition of the divine love and sweetness and sacrifice and righteousness and tenderness. But the sunshine that plays upon it shifts and passes, and looked at from another point of view it is swathed in blackness, as the most awful display of man's unbridled antagonism to the good. And looked at from yet another, it assumes a still more lurid aspect as the last stroke which the kingdom of darkness attempted to strike in defence of its ancient and solitary reign. So earth, heaven, hell, the God that works through man's evil passions, and yet does not acquit them though He utilises them to a lofty issue; man that is evil and thinks himself free; and the kingdom of darkness that uses him as its slave—all have part in that cross, which is thus the result of such diametrically opposite forces.

The divine government which reached its most beneficent ends through the unbridled antagonism of sinful men, and made even the dark counsels of the kingdom of darkness tributary to the diffusion of the light, works ever in the same fashion. Antagonism and obedience both work out its purposes. Let us learn to bow before that all—encompassing Providence in whose great scheme both are included. Let us not confuse ourselves by the attempt to make plain to our reason the harmony of the two certain facts—man's freedom and God's sovereignty. Enough for us to remember that the sin is none the less though the issue may coincide with the divine purpose, for sin lies in the motive, which is ours, not in the unintended result, which is God's. Enough for us to realise the tremendous solemnity of the lives we live, with all sweet heavenly influences falling on them from above, and all sulphurous suggestions rising into them from the fires beneath, and to see to it that we keep our hearts open to the one, and fast closed against the other.

'This is your hour'—a time in which you feel yourselves free, and yet are instruments in the hands of God, and also are tools in the claws of evil.

II. Still further, my text brings before us the thought that the Cross is the high—water mark of man's sin.

'This is the power of darkness'—the specimen instance of what it would and can do. Strange to think that, amidst all the black catalogue of evil deeds that have been done in this world from the beginning, there is one deed which is the worst, and that it is this one! Not that the doers were 'sinners above all men': for that is a question of knowledge and of motives, but that the deed in itself was the worst thing that ever man did. Of course I take for granted the belief that Jesus Christ is the Son of God; that He came from heaven, that He lived a life of perfect purity and beauty, and that He died on the Cross as the Gospel tells us. And taking these things for granted, is it not true that His rejection, His condemnation, and His death do throw the most awful and solemn light upon what poor humanity left to itself, and yielding to the suggestions and the impulses of the kingdom of darkness, does when it comes in contact with the Light?

It is the great crucial instance of the incapacity of the average man to behold spiritual beauty and lofty elevation of character. People lament over the blindness of embruted souls to natural beauty, to art, to high thinking, and so on; but all these, tragic as they are, are nothing as compared with this stunning fact, that perfect righteousness and perfect tenderness and ideal beauty of character walked about the world for thirty and three years, and that all the wise and religious men who came across Him thought that the best thing they could do was to crucify Him. So it has ever been from the days of Cain and Abel. As the Apostle John asks, 'Wherefore slew be him?' For a very good reason, 'Because his own works were evil, and his brother's righteous.' That is reason enough for killing any prophets and righteous men. It was so in the past, and in modified forms it is so today. The plain fact is that humanity has in it a depth of incapacity to behold, and of angry indisposition to admire, lofty and noble lives. The power of the darkness to blind men is set forth once in the superlative degree that we may all beware of it in the lower instances, by that fact, the most tragical in the history of the world, 'the Light shineth in the darkness, and the darkness apprehendeth it not.'

And not only does that Cross mark the high—water mark of man's blindness, and of man's hatred to the lofty and the true and the good, but it marks, too, the awful power that seems, by the very make of the world, to be lodged on the side of evil and against good. The dice seem to be so terribly loaded.

Virtue and beauty and truth and tenderness, and all that is noble and lofty and heart–appealing, have no chance against a mere piece of savage brutality. And that fact, which has been repeated over and over again from the beginning, and so largely makes the misery of mankind, reaches its very climax, and most solemn and awful illustration, in the fact that a handful of ruffians and a detachment of Roman soldiers were able to put an end to the life of God manifest in the flesh. If we have nothing more to say about Jesus than that He lived upon earth and did works of goodness and of beauty for a few short years, and then died, and there an end, it seems to me that the story of the Death of Christ is the most despairing page in the whole history of humanity, and that it accentuates and makes still more dreadful the dreadful old puzzle of how it comes that, in a world with a God in it, evil seems to be so riotously preponderant and good seems to be ever trodden under foot. Either the Death of Christ, if He died and did not rise again, is the strongest argument in the history of mankind for rank atheism, or else it is true that He rose, the King of humanity, glorified and exalted by the vain attempts of His foes.

And now notice that this high–water mark, as I have called it, or climax of human sin, was reached through very common and ordinary transgressions. Judas betrayed Christ because he had always felt uncomfortable with his earthly tendencies beside that pure spirit, and also because he wanted to jingle the thirty pieces of silver in his pocket. The priests did Him to death because He claimed the Messiahship and to be the Son of God, and their formalism rose against Him, and their blindness to all spiritual elevation made them hate Him. Pilate sent Him to the Cross because he was a coward, and thought that the life of a Jewish peasant was a small thing to give in order to secure his position. And the mob howled at His heels, and wagged their heads as they passed by, oblivious of His miracles and His benevolence, simply because of the vulgar hatred of anything that is lofty, and because they were so absorbed in material things that they had no eyes for that radiant beauty. In the whole list of these motives there is not a sin that you and I do not commit, nor is there any one of them which may not be reproduced, and as a matter of fact, is reproduced, by hundreds and thousands in this professedly Christian land.

Oh, brethren! the actual murderers are not the worst criminals, though their deed be the worst, considered in itself. Those Roman soldiers who nailed His hands to the Cross, and went back to their barracks that night, quite comfortable and unconscious that they had been doing anything beyond their routine military duty, were innocent and white–handed compared with the men and women among us, who, with the additional evidence of the Cross, and the empty grave, and the throne in the heavens, and the Christian Church, still stand aloof and say, 'We see no beauty in Him that we should desire Him.' Take care lest your attitude to Jesus Christ bring the level of your criminality close up to that high–water mark, or carry it even beyond it, for it is possible to 'crucify the Son of God afresh,' and they who do so have the greater guilt.

III. Now, lastly, my text suggests that the temporary triumph of the darkness is the eternal victory of the light.

'*This* is your hour'—not the next. 'This is your *hour*.' Sixty minutes tick, and it will be gone. When Christ was beaten He was Conqueror, and as He looked upon His Cross He said, 'I have overcome the world.' The eclipse which hung over the little hill and the land of Palestine, during the long hours of that slowly passing day, ended before He died. And His death was but the passing for a brief moment of the shadow of death across the bright luminary which, when the shadow has passed, shines out and 'with new spangled beams, flames in the forehead of the morning sky.' The darkness triumphed, and in its triumph it was overcome.

He, by dying, is the death of death. This Jonah inflicted a mortal wound on the loathly monster in whose maw He lay for three days. He, by bearing the penalty of sin, takes away the penalty of it for us all. He, in the quenching of the light of His life in the night of death, reveals God more than even He did in His life, and is never more truly the Illuminator of mankind than when He lies in the darkness of the grave and brings immortality to light. He, by His death, delivers men from the kingdom of darkness, and translates them into His own kingdom; giving them new powers for holiness, new hopes, inspiriting them to rebellion against the tyrants that have dominion over them; and thus conquering when He falls. The power of the darkness is broken like a crested wave, toppling over at its highest and dissolving in ineffectual spray.

So we have encouragement for all momentary checks and defeats, if there be such in our experience, when we are doing Christ's work. The history of the Church repeats in all ages, generation after generation, the same law to which the Master submitted: 'Except a corn of wheat fall into the ground and die it abideth alone; but if it die it bringeth forth much fruit.' We conquer when we are overcome; Christ conquered so, and His servants after Him.

And now apply all these principles which I have so imperfectly stated to your own personal lives. Men and the kingdom of darkness over-reached and outwitted themselves when they slew Jesus Christ. And so all antagonism to Him, whether it be theoretical or whether it be practical, and alienation of heart only, is suicidal folly. When it most succeeds it is nearest the breaking point of utter failure, like a man sawing off the branch on which he sits. Every man that sets himself against God in Christ, either to argue Him down and talk Him out of existence, or to 'break His bands asunder and cast away His cords,' has begun a Sisyphean task which will never come to any good. All sin is essentially irrational and opposed to the whole motion of the universe, and must necessarily be annihilated and come to nothing. The coarse title of one of our old English plays carries a great truth in it; 'The Devil is an Ass,' and for the man that obeys the kingdom of darkness the right epitaph is 'Thou fool! Oh, brothers! do not fling yourselves into that hopeless struggle. Put yourselves on the right side in this age-long conflict, of which the issue was determined before evil was, and was accomplished when Christ died. For be sure of this, that as certainly as 'The darkness is past, and the true Light now shineth,' so certainly all they that fight against the light—and all men fight against it who shut their eyes to it—are engaged in a conflict of which only one issue is possible, and that is defeat, bitter, complete, absolute. Rather let us all, though we be evil, and though there be a bad self in us that knows itself to be evil and hates the Light—let us all go to it. It may pain the eye, but it is the only cure for the ophthalmia. Let us go to it, spread ourselves out before it, and say, 'Search me, O Christ, and try me, and see if there be any wicked way in me. Lead me, a blind man, into the light.' And His answer will come: 'I am the Light of the world; he that followeth Me shall not walk in darkness, but shall have the Light of life.'

IN THE HIGH PRIEST'S PALACE

'Then took they Him, and led Him, and brought Him into
the high priest's house. And Peter followed afar off.
55. And when they had kindled a fire in the midst of
the hall, and were set down together, Peter sat down
among them. 56. But a certain maid beheld him as he
sat by the fire, and earnestly looked upon him, and
said, This man was also with Him. 57. And he denied
Him, saying, Woman, I know Him not. 58. And, after a
little while, another saw him, and said, Thou art also
of them. And Peter said, Man, I am not. 59. And about
the space of one hour after another confidently
affirmed, saying, Of a truth this fellow also was with
Him; for he is a Galilean. 60. And Peter said, Man, I
know not what thou sayest. And immediately, while he
yet spake, the cock crew. 61. And the Lord turned, and
looked upon Peter: and Peter remembered the word of
the Lord, how He had said unto him, Before the cock
crow, thou shalt deny Me thrice. 62. And Peter went
out, and wept bitterly. 63. And the men that held
Jesus mocked Him and smote Him. 64. And when they had
blindfolded Him, they struck Him on the face, and
asked Him, saying, Prophesy, who is it that smote
Thee? 65. And many other things blasphemously spake
they against Him. 66. And as soon as it was day, the
elders of the people, and the chief priests, and the
scribes, came together, and led Him into their
council, 67. Saying, Art Thou the Christ? tell us. And
He said unto them, If I tell you, ye will not believe:
68. And If I also ask you, ye will not answer Me, nor
let Me go. 69. Hereafter shall the Son of man sit on
the right hand of the power of God. 70. Then said they
all, Art Thou then the Son of God? And He said unto
them, Ye say that I am. 71. And they said, What need
we any further witness? for we ourselves have heard of
His own mouth.'—LUKE xxii. 54–71.

The present passage deals with three incidents, each of which may be regarded either as an element in
our Lord's sufferings or as a revelation of man's sin. He is denied, mocked, and formally rejected and
condemned. A trusted friend proves faithless, the underlings of the rulers brutally ridicule His
prophetic claims, and their masters vote Him a blasphemer for assenting His divinity and
Messiahship.

I. We have the failure of loyalty and love in Peter's denials. I may observe that Luke puts all Peter's denials before the hearing by the council, from which it is clear that the latter was later than the hearing recorded by Matthew and John. The first denial probably took place in the great hall of the high priest's official residence, at the upper end of which the prisoner was being examined, while the hangers—on huddled round the fire, idly waiting the event.

The morning air bit sharply, and Peter, exhausted, sleepy, sad, and shivering, was glad to creep near the blaze. Its glinting on his face betrayed him to a woman's sharp eye, and her gossiping tongue could not help blurting out her discovery. Curiosity, not malice, moved her; and there is no reason to suppose that any harm would have come to Peter, if he had said, as he should have done, 'Yes, I am His disciple.' The day for persecuting the servants was not yet come, but for the present it was Jesus only who was aimed at.

No doubt, cowardice had a share in the denials, but there was more than that in them. Peter was worn out with fatigue, excitement, and sorrow. His susceptible nature would be strongly affected by the trying scenes of the last day, and all the springs of life would be low. He was always easily influenced by surroundings, and just as, at a later date, he was 'carried away' by the presence at Antioch of the Judaisers, and turned his back on the liberal principles which he had professed, so now he could not resist the current of opinion, and dreaded being unlike even the pack of menials among whom he sat. He was ashamed of his Master and hid his colours, not so much for fear of bodily harm as of ridicule. Was there not a deeper depth still in his denials, even the beginnings of doubt whether, after all, Jesus was what he had thought Him? Christ prayed that Peter's 'faith' should not 'fail' or be totally eclipsed, and that may indicate that the assault was made on his 'faith' and that it wavered, though it recovered steadfastness.

If he had been as sure of Christ's work and nature as when he made his great confession, he could not have denied Him. But the sight of Jesus bound, unresisting, and evidently at the mercy of the rulers, might well make a firmer faith stagger. We have not to steel ourselves to bear bodily harm if we confess Christ; but many of us have to run counter to a strong current flowing around us, and to be alone in the midst of unsympathising companions ready to laugh and gibe, and some of us are tempted to waver in our convictions of Christ's divinity and redeeming power, because He still seems to stand at the bar of the wise men and leaders of opinion, and to be treated by them as a pretender. It is a wretched thing to be persecuted out of one's Christianity in the old—fashioned fire and sword style; but it is worse to be laughed out of it or to lose it, because we breathe an atmosphere of unbelief. Let the doctors at the top of the hall and the lackeys round the fire who take their opinions from them say what they like, but let them not make us ashamed of Jesus.

Peter slipped away to the gateway, and there, apparently, was again attacked, first by the porteress and then by others, which occasioned the second denial, while the third took place in the same place, about an hour afterwards. One sin makes many. The devil's hounds hunt in packs. Consistency requires the denier to stick to his lie. Once the tiniest wing tip is in the spider's web, before long the whole body will be wrapped round by its filthy, sticky threads.

If Peter had been less confident, he would have been more safe. If he had said less about going to prison and death, he would have had more reserve fidelity for the time of trial. What business had he thrusting himself into the palace? Over–reliance on self leads us to put ourselves in the way of temptations which it were wiser to avoid. Had he forgotten Christ's warnings? Apparently so. Christ predicts the fall that it may not happen, and if we listen to Him, we shall not fall.

The moment of recovery seems to have been while our Lord was passing from the earlier to the later examination before the rulers. In the very floodtide of Peter's oaths, the shrill cock–crow is heard, and at the sound the half–finished denial sticks in his throat. At the same moment he sees Jesus led past him, and that look, so full of love, reproof, and pardon, brought him back to loyalty, and saved him from despair. The assurance of Christ's knowledge of our sins against Him melts the heart, when the assurance of His forgiveness and tender love comes with it. Then tears, which are wholly humble but not wholly grief, flow. They do not wash away the sin, but they come from the assurance that Christ's love, like a flood, has swept it away. They save from remorse, which has no healing in it.

II. We have the rude taunts of the servants. The mockery here comes from Jews, and is directed against Christ's prophetic character, while the later jeers of the Roman soldiers make a jest of His kingship. Each set lays hold of what seems to it most ludicrous in His pretensions, and these servants ape their masters on the judgment seat, in laughing to scorn this Galilean peasant who claimed to be the Teacher of them all. Rude natures have to take rude ways of expression, and the vulgar mockery meant precisely the same as more polite and covert scorn means from more polished people; namely, rooted disbelief in Him. These mockers were contented to take their opinions on trust from priests and rabbis. How often, since then, have Christ's servants been objects of popular odium at the suggestion of the same classes, and how often have the ignorant people been misled by their trust in their teachers to hate and persecute their true Master!

Jesus is silent under all the mockery, but then, as now, He knows who strikes Him. His eyes are open behind the bandage, and see the lifted hands and mocking lips. He will speak one day, and His speech will be detection and condemnation. Then He was silent, as patiently enduring shame and spitting for our sakes. Now He is silent, as long–suffering and wooing us to repentance; but He keeps count and record of men's revilings, and the day comes when He whose eyes are as a flame of fire will say to every foe, 'I know thy works.'

III. We have the formal rejection and condemnation by the council. The hearing recorded in verses 66 to 71 took place 'as soon as it was day,' and was apparently a more formal official ratification of the proceedings of the earlier examination described by Matthew and John. The ruler's question was put simply in order to obtain material for the condemnation already resolved on. Our Lord's answer falls into two parts, in the first of which He in effect declines to recognise the *bona fides* of His judges and the competency of the tribunal, and in the second goes beyond their question, and claims participation in divine glory and power. 'If I tell you, ye will not believe'; therefore He will not tell them.

Jesus will not unfold His claims to those who only seek to hear them in order to reject, not to examine, them. Silence is His answer to ingrained prejudice masquerading as honest inquiry. It is ever so. There is small chance of truth at the goal if there be foregone conclusions or biased questions at the starting–point. 'If I ask you, ye will not answer.' They had taken refuge in judicious but self–condemning silence when He had asked them the origin of John's mission and the meaning of the One Hundred and Tenth Psalm, and thereby showed that they were not seeking light. Jesus will gladly speak with any who will be frank with Him, and let Him search their hearts; but He will not unfold His mission to such as refuse to answer His questions. But while thus He declines to submit Himself to that tribunal, and in effect accuses them of obstinate blindness and a fixed conclusion to reject the claims which they were pretending to examine, He will not leave them without once more asserting an even higher dignity than that of Messiah. As a prisoner at their bar, He has nothing to say to them; but as their King and future Judge, He has something. They desire to find materials for sentence of death, and though He will not give these in the character of a criminal before His judges, He also desires that the sentence should pass, and He will declare His divine prerogatives and fall possession of divine power in the hearing of the highest court of the nation.

It was fitting that the representatives of Israel, however prejudiced, should hear at that supreme moment the full assertion of full deity. It was fitting that Israel should condemn itself, by treating that claim as blasphemy. It was fitting that Jesus should bring about His death by His twofold claim—that made to the Sanhedrim, of being the Son of God, and that before Pilate, of being the King of the Jews.

The whole scene teaches us the voluntary character of Christ's Death, which is the direct result of this tremendous assertion. It carries our thoughts forward to the time when the criminal of that morning shall be the Judge, and the judges and we shall stand at His bar. It raises the solemn question, Did Jesus claim truly when He claimed divine power? If truly, do we worship Him? If falsely, what was He? It mirrors the principles on which He deals with men universally, answering 'him that cometh, according to the multitude of his idols,' and meeting hypocritical pretences of seeking the truth about Him with silence, but ever ready to open His heart and the witness to His claims to the honest and docile spirits who are ready to accept His words, and glad to open their inmost secrets to Him.

CHRIST'S LOOK

'And the Lord turned and looked upon Peter.'
—Luke xxii. 61.

All four Evangelists tell the story of Peter's threefold denial and swift repentance, but we owe the knowledge of this look of Christ's to Luke only. The other Evangelists connect the sudden change in the denier with his hearing the cock crow only, but according to Luke there were two causes co-operating to bring about that sudden repentance, for, he says, 'Immediately, while he yet spake, the cock crew. And the Lord turned and looked upon Peter.' And we cannot doubt that it was the Lord's look enforcing the fulfilment of His prediction of the cock-crow that broke down the denier.

Now, it is very difficult, if not impossible, to weave a consecutive whole out of the four versions of the story of Peter's triple denial. But this at least is clear from them all, that Jesus was away at the upper, probably the raised, end of the great hall, and that if any of the three instances of denial took place within that building, it was at such a distance that neither could the words be heard, nor could a look from one end of it to the other have been caught. I think that if we try to localise, and picture the whole scene ourselves, we are obliged to suppose that that look, which smote Peter into swift collapse of penitence, came as the Lord Jesus was being led bound down the hall out through the porch, past the fire, and into the gloomy archway, on His road to further suffering. As He was thus brought for a moment close to him, 'the Lord turned and looked upon Peter,' and then He passed from his sight for ever, as he would fear.

I wish, then, to deal—although it must be very imperfectly and inadequately—with that look that changed this man. And I desire to consider two things about it: what it said, and what it did.

I. What it said.—It spoke of Christ's knowledge, of Christ's pain, of Christ's love.

Of Christ's knowledge—I have already suggested that we cannot suppose that the Prisoner at one end of the hall, intensely occupied with the questionings and argumentation of the priests, and with the false witnesses, could have heard the denial, given in tones subdued by the place, at the other end. Still less could He have heard the denials in louder tones, and accompanied with execrations, which seemed to have been repeated in the porch without. But as He passed the Apostle that look said: 'I heard them all—denials and oaths and passion; I heard them all.' No wonder that after the Resurrection, Peter, with that remembrance in his mind, fell at the Master's feet and said, 'Lord! Thou knowest all things. Thou didst know what Thou didst not hear, my muttered recreancy and treason, and my blurted out oaths of denial. Thou knowest all things.' No wonder that when he stood up amongst the Apostles after the Resurrection and the Ascension, and was the mouthpiece of their prayers, remembering this scene as well as other incidents, he began his prayer with 'Thou, Lord, which knowest the hearts of all men.' But let us remember that this—call it, if you like, supernatural—knowledge which Jesus Christ had of the denial, is only one of a great body of facts in His life, if we accept these Gospels, which show that, as one of the Evangelists says, at almost the beginning of his history, 'He needed not that any man should testify of man, for He knew what was in man.' It is precisely on the same line, as His first words to Peter, whom He greeted as he came to Him with 'Thou art Simon; thou shalt be Cephas.' It is entirely on the same line as the words with which He greeted another of this little group, 'When thou wast under the fig-tree I saw thee.' It is on the same line as the words with which He penetrated to the unspoken thoughts of His churlish entertainer when He said, 'Simon! I have somewhat to say unto thee.' It is on the lines on which we have to think of that Lord now as knowing us all. He looks still from the judgment-seat, where He does not stand as a criminal, but sits as the supreme and omniscient Arbiter of our fates, and Judge of our actions. And He beholds us, each of us, moment by moment, as we go about our work, and often, by our cowardice, by our faithlessness, by our inconsistencies, 'deny the Lord that bought' us. It is an awful thought, and therefore do men put it away from them: 'Thou God seest me.' But it is stripped of all its awfulness, while it retains all its purifying and quickening power, when we think, as our old hymn has it:

'Though now ascended up on high,
He bends on earth a Brother's eye.'

And we have not only to feel that the eye that looks upon us is cognisant of our denials, but that it is an eye that pities our infirmities, and knowing us altogether, loves us better than we know. Oh! if we believed in Christ's look, and that it was the look of infinite love, life would be less solitary, less sad, and we should feel that wherever His glance fell there His help was sure, and there were illumination and blessedness. The look spoke of Christ's knowledge.

Again, it spoke of Christ's pain. Peter had not thought that he was hurting his Master by his denials; he only thought of saving himself. And, perhaps, if it had come into his loving and impulsive nature, which yielded to the temptation the more readily because of the same impulsiveness which also led it to yield swiftly to good influences, if he had thought that he was adding another pang to the pains of his Lord whom he had loved through all his denial, even his cowardice would have plucked up courage to 'confess, and deny not but confess,' that he belonged to the Christ. But he did not remember all that. And now there came into his mind—from that look, the bitter thought, 'I have wrung His heart with yet another pang, and at this supreme moment, when there is so much to rack and pain; I have joined the tormentors.'

And so, do we not pain Jesus Christ? Mysterious as it is, yet it seems as if, since it is true that we please Him when we are obeying Him, it must be somehow true that we pain Him when we deny Him, and some kind of shadow of grief may pass even over that glorified nature when we sin against Him, and forget Him, and repay His love with indifference, and reject His counsel. We know that in His earthly life there was no bitterer pang inflicted upon Him than the one which the Psalmist prophesied, 'He that ate bread with Me hath lifted up his heel against Me.' And we know that in the measure in which human nature is purified and perfected, in that measure does it become more susceptible and sensitive to the pain of faithless friends. Chilled love, rejected endeavours to help—which are, perhaps, the deepest and the most spiritual of sorrows which men can inflict upon one another, Jesus Christ experienced in full measure, heaped up and running over. And we, even we today, may be 'grieving the Holy Spirit of God, whereby we are sealed unto the day of redemption.' Christ's knowledge of the Apostle's denials brought pain to His heart.

Again, the look spoke of Christ's love. There was in it saddened disapprobation, but there was not in it any spark of anger; nor what, perhaps, would be worse, any ice of withdrawal or indifference. But there even at that supreme moment, lied against by false witnesses, insulted and spit upon by rude soldiers, rejected by the priests as an impostor and a blasphemer, and on His road to the Cross, when, if ever, He might have been absorbed in Himself, was His heart at leisure from itself, and in divine and calm self-oblivion could think of helping the poor denier that stood trembling there beneath His glance. That is of a piece with the majestic, yet not repelling calm, which marks the Lord in all His life, and which reaches its very climax in the Passion and on the Cross. Just as, whilst nailed there, He had leisure to think of the penitent thief, and of the weeping mother, and of the disciple whose loss of his Lord would be compensated by the gaining of her to take care of, so as He was being borne to Pilate's judgment, He turned with a love that forgot itself, and poured itself into the denier's heart. Is not that a divine and eternal revelation for us? We speak of the love of a brother who, sinned against seventy times seven, yet forgives. We bow in reverence before the love of a mother who cannot forget, but must have compassion on the son of her womb. We wonder at the love of a father who goes out to seek the prodigal. But all these are less than that love which beamed lambent from the eye of Christ, as it fell on the denier, and which therein, in that one transitory glance, revealed for the faith and thankfulness of all ages an eternal fact. That love is steadfast as the heavens, firm as the foundations of the earth. 'Yea! the mountains may depart and the hills be removed, but My loving kindness shall not depart, neither shall the covenant of My peace be removed.' It cannot be frozen, into indifference. It cannot be stirred into heat of anger. It cannot be provoked to withdrawal. Repelled, it returns; sinned against, it forgives; denied, it meekly beams on in self-revelation; it hopeth all things, it beareth all things. And He who, as He passed out to Pilate's bar, cast His look of love on the denier, is looking upon each of us, if we would believe it, with the same look, pitiful and patient, reproachful, and yet forgiving, which unveils all His love, and would fain draw us in answering love, to cast ourselves at His feet, and tell Him all our sin.

And now, let us turn to the second point that I suggested.

II. What the look did.

First, it tore away the veil that hid Peter's sin from himself. He had not thought that he was doing anything wrong when he denied. He had not thought about anything but saving his own skin. If he had reflected for a moment no doubt he would have found excuses, as we all can do. But when Christ stood there, what had become of the excuses? As by a flash he saw the ugliness of the deed that he himself had done. And there came, no doubt, into his mind in aggravation of the denial, all that had passed from that very first day when he had come to Christ's presence, all the confidences that had been given to him, how his wife's mother had been healed, how he himself had been cared for and educated, how he had been honoured and distinguished, how he had boasted and vowed and hectored the day before. And so he 'went out and wept bitterly.'

Now *our* sin captures us by lying to us, by blinding our consciences. You cannot hear the shouts of the men on the bank warning you of your danger when you are in the midst of the rapids, and so our sin deafens us to the still small voice of conscience. But nothing so surely reveals to us the true moral character of any of our actions, be they right or wrong, as bringing them under Christ's eye, and thinking to ourselves. 'Durst I do that if He stood there beside me and saw it?' Peter could deny Him when He was at the far end of the hall. He could not have denied Him if he had had Him by his side. And if we will take our actions, especially any of them about which we are in doubt, into His presence, then it will be wonderful how conscience will be enlightened and quickened, how the fiend will start up in his own shape, and how poor and small the motives which tempted so strongly to do wrong will come to look, when we think of adducing them to Jesus. What did a maid—servant's flippant tongue matter to Peter then? And how wretchedly inadequate the reason for his denial looked when Christ's eye fell upon him. The most recent surgical method of treating skin diseases is to bring an electric light, ten times as strong as the brightest street lights, to bear upon the diseased patch, and fifty minutes of that search—light clears away the disease. Bring the beam from Christ's eye to bear on your lives, and you will see a great deal of leprosy, and scurf, and lupus, and all that you see will be cleared away. The look tore down the veil.

What more did it do? It melted the denier's heart into sorrow. I can quite understand a conscience being so enlightened as to be convinced of the evil of a certain course, and yet there being none of that melting into sorrow, which, as I believe, is absolutely necessary for any permanent victory over sins. No man will ever conquer his evil as long as he only shudderingly recoils from it. He has to be broken down into the penitential mood before he will secure the victory over his sin. You remember the profound words in our Lord's pregnant parable of the seeds, how one class which transitorily was Christian, had for its characteristic that immediately with joy they received the word. Yes; a Christianity that puts repentance into a parenthesis, and talks about faith only, will never underlie a permanent and thorough moral reformation. There is nothing that brings 'godly sorrow,' so surely as a glimpse of Christ's love; and nothing that reveals the love so certainly as the 'look.' You may hammer at a man's heart with law, principle, and moral duty, and all the rest of it, and you may get him to feel that he is a very poor creature, but unless the sunshine of Christ's love shines down upon him, there will be no melting, and if there is no melting there will be no permanent bettering.

And there was another thing that the look did. It tore away the veil from the sin; it made rivers of water flow from the melted heart in sorrow of true repentance; and it kept the sorrow from turning into despair. Judas 'went out and hanged himself.' Peter 'went out and wept bitterly.' What made the one the victim of remorse, and the other the glad child of repentance? How was it that the one was stiffened into despair that had no tears, and the other was saved because he could weep? Because the one saw his sin in the lurid light of an awakened conscience, and the other saw his sin in the loving look of a pardoning Lord. And that is how you and I ought to see our sins. Be sure, dear friend, that the same long-suffering, patient love is looking down upon each of us, and that if we will, like Peter, let the look melt us into penitent self-distrust and heart-sorrow for our clinging sins, then Jesus will do for us, as He did for that penitent denier on the Resurrection morning. He will take us apart by ourselves and speak healing words of forgiveness and reconciliation, so that we, like him, will dare in spite of our faithlessness, to fall at His feet and say, 'Lord, Thou knowest all things; Thou knowest that I, erst faithless and treacherous, love Thee; and all the more because Thou hast forgiven the denial and restored the denier.'

'THE RULERS TAKE COUNSEL TOGETHER'

'And the whole multitude of them arose, and led Him unto Pilate. 2. And they began to accuse Him, saying, We found this fellow perverting the nation, and forbidding to give tribute to Caesar, saying that He Himself is Christ a King. 3. And Pilate asked Him, saying, Art thou the King of the Jews? And He answered him and said, Thou sayest it. 4. Then said Pilate to the chief priests and to the people, I find no fault in this man. 5. And they were the more fierce, saying, He stirreth up the people teaching throughout all Jewry, beginning from Galilee to this place. 6. When Pilate heard of Galilee, he asked whether the man were a Galilean. 7. And as soon as he knew that He belonged unto Herod's jurisdiction, he sent Him to Herod, who himself also was at Jerusalem at that time. 8. And when Herod saw Jesus, he was exceeding glad: for he was desirous to see Him of a long season, because he had heard many things of Him; and he hoped to have seen some miracle done by Him. 9. Then he questioned with Him in many words; but He answered him nothing. 10. And the chief priests and scribes stood and vehemently accused Him. 11. And Herod with his men of war set Him at nought, and mocked Him, and arrayed Him in a gorgeous robe, and sent Him again to Pilate.

12. And the same day Pilate and Herod were made
friends together: for before they were at enmity
between themselves.'—LUKE xxiii. 1–12.

Luke's canvas is all but filled by the persecutors, and gives only glimpses of the silent Sufferer. But the silence of Jesus is eloquent, and the prominence of the accusers and judges heightens the impression of His passive endurance. We have in this passage the Jewish rulers with their murderous hate; Pilate contemptuously indifferent, but perplexed and wishing to shirk responsibility; and Herod with his frivolous curiosity. They present three types of unworthy relations to Jesus Christ.

I. We see first the haters of Jesus. So fierce is their hatred that they swallow the bitter pill of going to Pilate for the execution of their sentence. John tells us that they began by trying to get Pilate to decree the crucifixion without knowing Jesus' crime; but that was too flagrant injustice, and too blind confidence in them, for Pilate to grant. So they have to manufacture a capital charge on the spot, and they are equal to the occasion. By the help of two lies, and one truth so twisted as to be a lie, they get up an indictment, which they think will be grave enough to compel the procurator to do as they wish.

Their accusation, if it had been ever so true, would have been ludicrous on their lips; and we may be sure that, if it had been true, they would have been Jesus' partisans, not His denouncers.' The Gracchi complaining of sedition' are nothing to the Sanhedrim accusing a Jew of rebellion against Rome. Every man in that crowd was a rebel at heart, and would have liked nothing better than to see the standard of revolt lifted in a strong hand. Pilate was not so simple as to be taken in by such an accusation from such accusers, and it fails. They return to the charge, and the 'more urgent' character of the second attempt is found in its statement of the widespread extent of Christ's teaching, but chiefly in the cunning introduction of Galilee, notoriously a disaffected and troublesome district.

What a hideous and tragic picture we have here of the ferocity of the hatred, which turned the very fountains of justice and guardians of a nation into lying plotters against innocence, and sent these Jewish rulers cringing before Pilate, pretending loyalty and acknowledging his authority! They were ready for any falsehood and any humiliation, if only they could get Jesus crucified. And what had excited their hatred? Chiefly His teachings, which brushed aside the rubbish both of ceremonial observance and of Rabbinical casuistry, and placed religion in love to God and consequent love to man; then His attitude of opposition to them as an order; and finally His claim, which they never deigned to examine, to be the Son of God. That, they said, was blasphemy, as it was, unless it were true,—an alternative which they did not look at. So blinded may men be by prejudice, and so mastered by causeless hatred of Him who loves them all!

These Jewish rulers were men like ourselves. Instead of shuddering at their crime, as if it were something far outside of anything possible for us, we do better if we learn from it the terrible depths of hostility to Jesus, the tragic blindness to His character and love, and the degradation of submission to usurpers, which must accompany denial of His right to rule over us. 'They hated Me without a cause,' said Christ; but He pointed to that hatred as sure to be continued towards Him and His servants as long as 'the world' continues the world.

II. We have Pilate, indifferent and perplexed. Luke's very brief account should be supplemented by

John's, which shows us how important the conversation, so much abbreviated by Luke, was. Of course Pilate knew the priests and rulers too well to believe for a moment that the reason they gave for bringing Jesus to him was the real one, and his taking Jesus apart to speak with Him shows a wish to get at the bottom of the case. So far he was doing his duty, but then come the faults. These may easily be exaggerated, and we should remember that Pilate was the most ignorant, and therefore the least guilty, of all the persons mentioned in this passage. He had probably never heard the name of Jesus till that day, and saw nothing but an ordinary Jewish peasant, whom his countrymen, like the incomprehensible and troublesome people they were, wished, for some fantastic reason, to get killed.

But that dialogue with his Prisoner should have sunk deeper into his mind and heart. He was in long and close enough contact with Jesus to have seen glimpses of the light, which, if followed, would have led to clear recognition. His first sin was indifference, not unmingled with scorn, and it blinded him. Christ's lofty and wonderful explanation of the nature of His kingdom and His mission to bear witness to the truth fell on entirely preoccupied ears, which were quick enough to catch the faintest whispers of treason, but dull towards 'truth.' When Jesus tried to reach his conscience by telling him that every lover of truth would listen to His voice, he only answered by the question, to which he waited not for an answer, 'What is truth?'

That was not the question of a theoretical sceptic, but simply of a man who prided himself on being 'practical,' and left all talk about such abstractions to dreamers. The limitations of the Roman intellect and its characteristic over–estimate of deeds and contempt for pure thought, as well as the spirit of the governor, who would let men think what they chose, as long as they did not rebel, spoke in the question. Pilate is an instance of a man blinded to all lofty truth and to the beauty and solemn significance of Christ's words, by his absorption in outward life. He thinks of Jesus as a harmless fanatic. Little did he know that the truth, which he thought moonshine, would shatter the Empire, which he thought the one solid reality. So called practical men commit the same mistake in every generation. 'All flesh is as grass;... the word of the Lord endureth for ever.'

Further, Pilate sinned in prostituting his office by not setting free the prisoner when he was convinced of His innocence. 'I find no fault in this man,' should have been followed by immediate release. Every moment afterwards, in which He was kept captive, was the condemnation of the unjust judge. He was clearly anxious to keep his troublesome subjects in good humour, and thought that the judicial murder of one Jew was a small price to pay for popularity. Still he would have been glad to have escaped from what his official training had taught him to recoil from, and what some faint impression, made by his patient prisoner, gave him a strange dread of. So he grasps at the mention of Galilee, and tries to gain two good ends at once by handing Jesus over to Herod.

The relations between Antipas and him were necessarily delicate, like those between the English officials and the rajahs of native states in India; and there had been some friction, perhaps about 'the Galileans, whose blood' he 'had mingled with their sacrifices.' If there had been difficulties in connection with such a question of jurisdiction, the despatch of Jesus to Herod would be a graceful way of making the *amende honorable*, and would also shift an unpleasant decision on to Herod's shoulders. Pilate would not be displeased to get rid of embarrassment, and to let Herod be the tool of the priests' hate.

How awful the thought is of the contrast between Pilate's conceptions of what he was doing and the reality! How blind to Christ's beauty it is possible to be, when engrossed with selfish aims and outward things! How near a soul may be to the light, and yet turn away from it and plunge into darkness! How patient that silent prisoner, who lets Himself be bandied about from one tyrant to another, not because they had power, but because He loved the world, and would bear the sins of every one of us! How terrible the change when these unjust judges and He will change places, and Pilate and Herod stand at His judgment–seat!

III. We have the wretched, frivolous Herod. This is the murderer of John Baptist—'that fox,' a debauchee, a coward, and as cruel as sensuous. He had all the vices of his worthless race, and none of the energy of its founder. He is by far the most contemptible of the figures in this passage. Note his notion of, and his feeling to, Jesus. He thought of our Lord as of a magician or juggler, who might do some wonders to amuse the vacuous *ennui* of his sated nature. Time was when he had felt some twinge of conscience in listening to the Baptist, and had almost been lifted to nobleness by that strong arm. Time was, too, when he had trembled at hearing of Jesus, and taken Him for his victim risen from a bloody grave. But all that is past now. The sure way to stifle conscience is to neglect it. Do that long and resolutely enough, and it will cease to utter unheeded warnings. There will be a silence which may look like peace, but is really death. Herod's gladness was more awful and really sad than Herod's fear. Better to tremble at God's word than to treat it as an occasion for mirth. He who hates a prophet because he knows him to be a prophet and himself to be a sinner, is not so hopeless as he who only expects to get sport out of the messenger of God.

Then note the Lord's silence. Herod plies Jesus with a battery of questions, and gets no answer. If there had been a grain of earnestness in them all, Christ would have spoken. He never is silent to a true seeker after truth. But it is fitting that frivolous curiosity should be unanswered, and there is small likelihood of truth being found at the goal when there is nothing more noble than that temper at the starting–point. Christ's silence is the penalty of previous neglect of Christ's and His forerunner's words. Jesus guides His conduct by His own precept, 'Give not that which is holy unto the dogs'; and He knows, as we never can, who come into that terrible list of men to whom it would only add condemnation to speak of even His love. The eager hatred of the priests followed Jesus to Herod's palace, but no judicial action is recorded as taking place there. Their fierce earnestness of hate seems out of place in the frivolous atmosphere. The mockery, in which Herod is not too dignified to join his soldiers, is more in keeping. But how ghastly it sounds to us, knowing whom they ignorantly mocked! Cruelty, inane laughter, hideous pleasure in an innocent man's pain, disregard of law and justice—all these they were guilty of; and Herod, at any rate, knew enough of Jesus to give a yet darker colouring to his share in the coarse jest.

But how the loud laugh would have fallen silent if some flash had told who Jesus was! Is there any of our mirth, perhaps at some of His servants, or at some phase of His gospel, which would in like manner stick in our throats if His judgment throne blazed above us? Ridicule is a dangerous weapon. It does more harm to those who use it than to those against whom it is directed. Herod thought it an exquisite jest to dress up his prisoner as a king; but Herod has found out, by this time, whether he or the Nazarene was the sham monarch, and who is the real one. Christ was as silent under mockery as to His questioner. He bears all, and He takes account of all. He bears it because He is the world's Sacrifice and Saviour. He takes account of it, and will one day recompense it, because He is the world's King, and will be its Judge. Where shall we stand then—among the silenced mockers, or among the happy trusters in His Passion and subjects of His dominion?

A SOUL'S TRAGEDY

'Then Herod questioned with Him in many words; but He answered him nothing.'—LUKE xxiii. 9.

Four Herods play their parts in the New Testament story. The first of them is the grim old tiger who slew the infants at Bethlehem, and soon after died. This Herod is the second—a cub of the litter, with his father's ferocity and lust, but without his force. The third is the Herod of the earlier part of the Acts of the Apostles, a grandson of the old man, who dipped his hands in the blood of one Apostle, and would fain have slain another. And the last is Herod Agrippa, a son of the third, who is only remembered because he once came across Paul's path, and thought it such a good jest that anything should be supposed capable of making a Christian out of *him*.

There is a singular family likeness in the whole of them, and a very ugly likeness it is. This one was sensual, cruel, cunning, infirm of purpose, capricious like a child or a savage. Roman policy amused him with letting him play at being a ruler, but kept him well in hand. And I suppose he was made a worse man by the difficulties of his position as a subject–prince.

Now I wish to put together the various incidents in this man's life recorded in the Gospels, and try to gather some lessons from them for you.

I. First, I take him as an example of half–and–half convictions, and of the inner discord that comes from these.

I do not need to remind you of the shameful story of his repudiation of his own wife, and of his disgusting alliance with the wife of his half–brother, who was herself his niece. She was the stronger spirit, a Biblical Lady Macbeth, the Jezebel to this Ahab; and, to complete the parallel, Elijah was not far away. John the Baptist's outspoken remonstrances of course made an implacable enemy of Herodias, who did all she could to compass his death, but was unable to manage that, though she secured his imprisonment. The reason for her inability is given by the Evangelist Mark, in words which are very inadequately rendered by our Authorised Version, but may be found more correctly translated in the Revised Version. It is there said that King 'Herod feared John'—the gaoler afraid of his prisoner!—'knowing that he was a just man and a holy'—goodness is awful. The worst men know it, and it extorts respect. 'And kept him safe'—from Herodias, that is. 'And when he heard him he was perplexed'—drawn this way and that way by these two magnets, alternately veering to lust and to purity, hesitating between the kisses of the beautiful temptress at his side and the words of the prophet. And yet, with strange inconsistency, in all his vacillations 'he heard him gladly'; for his better part approved the nobler voice. And so he staggered on, having religion enough to spoil some of his sinful delights, but not enough to shake them off.

That is a picture for which in its essence many a man and woman among us might have sat. For I suppose that there is nothing more common than these half–and–half convictions which, like

337

inefficient bullets, get part way through the armoured shell of a ship, and there stick harmless. Many of us have the clearest convictions in our understandings, which have never penetrated to that innermost chamber of all, where the will sits sovereign. It is so about little things, it is so about great ones. Nothing is more common than that a man shall know perfectly well that some possibly trivial habit stands in the way of something that it is his interest or his duty to pursue; but the knowledge lies inoperative in the outermost part of him. It is so in regard to graver things. The majority of the slaves of any vice whatsoever know perfectly well that they ought to give it up, and yet nothing comes of the conviction.

'He was much perplexed.' What a picture that is of the state of unrest and conflict into which such half–and–half impressions of duty cast a man. Such a one is like a vessel with its head now East, now West, because there is some weak or ignorant steersman at the helm. I know nothing more sure to produce inward unrest and disturbance and desolation than that a man's knowledge of duty should be clear, and his obedience to that knowledge partial. If we have John down in the dungeon, if conscience is not allowed to be master, there may be feasting and revelry going on above, but the stern voice will come up through the grating now and then, and that will spoil all the laughter. 'When he heard him, he was much perplexed.'

The reason for these imperfect convictions is generally found, as Herod shows us, in the unwillingness to get rid of something which has fastened its claws around us, and which we love too well, although we know it is a serpent, to shake off. If Herod had once been man enough to screw himself up, and say to Herodias, 'Now you pack, and go about your business!' everything else would have come right in time. But he could not make up his mind to sacrifice the honeyed poison, and so everything went wrong in time. My friend, how many of us are prevented from following out our clearest convictions because they demand a sacrifice? 'If thine eye cause thee to stumble, pluck it out, and cast it from thee. It is better for thee.'

And then, further, note that these irresolute convictions and shirking of plain duty are not atoned for by, though they are often accompanied with, a strange acquiescence in, and approval of, God's truth. Herod fancied, inconsistently enough, that he was making some kind of compensation for disobedience to the message, by liking to listen to the messenger. And there are a great many of us, all whose Christianity consists in giving ear to the words which we never think of obeying. I wonder how many of you there are who fancy that you have no more concern with this sermon of mine than approving or disapproving of it, as the case may be; and how many of us there are who, all our lives long, have substituted criticism of the Gospel as ministered by us poor preachers—be it approving or disapproving criticism—for obedience to the Christ and acceptance of His salvation.

II. We see in Herod an example of the utter powerlessness of such partial convictions and reformation.

I am not going to tell over again the ghastly story of John's death, which no other words than the Evangelist's can tell half so powerfully. I need only remind you of the degradation of the poor child Salome to the position of a dancing girl, the half–tipsy generosity of the excited monarch, the grim request from lips so young and still reddened by the excitement of the dance, Herod's unavailing sorrow, his fantastic sense of honour which scrupled to break a wicked promise, but did not scruple to kill a righteous man, and the ghastly picture of the girl carrying a bleeding head—such a gift!—to her mother.

But out of that jumble of lust and blood I desire to gather one lesson. There you have—in an extreme form, it is true—a tremendous illustration of what half–and–half convictions may come to. Whether or no we ever get anything like as far on the road as this man did matters very little. The process which brought him there is the thing that I seek to point to. It was because he had so long tampered with the voice of his conscience that it was lulled into silence at that last critical moment. And this is always the case, that if a man is false to the feeblest conviction that he has in regard to the smallest duty, he is a worse man all over ever after. We cannot neglect any conviction of what we ought to do, without lowering the whole tone of our characters and laying ourselves open to assaults of evil from which we would once have turned shuddering and disgusted. A partial thaw is generally followed by intenser frost. An abortive insurrection is sure to issue in a more grinding tyranny. A soul half melted and then cooled off is less easy to melt than it was before. And so, dear brethren, remember this, that if you do not swiftly and fully carry out in life and conduct whatsoever you know you ought to be or do, you cannot set a limit to what, some time or other, if a strong and sudden temptation is sprung upon you, you may become. 'Is thy servant a dog that he should do this thing?' Yes! But he did it. No mortal reaches the extreme of evil all at once, says the wise old proverb; and the path by which a man is let down into depths that he never thought it was possible that he should traverse is by the continual neglect of the small admonitions of conscience. Neglected convictions mean, sooner or later, an outburst of evil.

John's murder may illustrate another thing too—viz. how simple, facile weakness of character may be the parent of all enormities. Herod did not want to kill John. He very much wanted to keep him alive. But he was not man enough to put his foot down, and say, 'There! I have said it; and there is to be no more talk about slaying this prophet of God.' So the continual drop, drop, drop, of Herodias' suggestions and wishes wore a hole, in the loose–textured stone at last; and he did the thing that he hated to do and had long fought against. Why? Because he was a poor weak creature.

The lesson from this is one that I would urge upon all you young people especially, that in a world like this, where there are so many more voices soliciting us to evil than inviting us to good, to be weak is, in the long run, to be wicked. So do you cultivate the wholesome habit of saying 'No,' and do not be afraid of anything but of hurting your conscience and sinning against God.

III. Once more, we have in Herod an example of the awakening of conscience.

When Jesus began to be talked about beyond the narrow limits of the shores of the Sea of Galilee, and especially when He began to organise the Apostolate, and His name was spread abroad, some rumours reached even the court, and there were divergent opinions about Him. One man said, It is Elias; and another said, It is a prophet, 'and Herod said, It is John, whom I beheaded. He has risen from the dead, and therefore mighty works do show forth themselves in him.'

Ah, brethren! when a man has, away back in the chambers of his memory, some wrong thing, be it great or be it little, he is at the mercy of any chance or accident to have it revived in all its vividness. It is an awful thing to walk this world with a whole magazine of combustibles in our memories, on which any spark may fall and light lurid and sulphurous flames. A chance thing may do it, a scent, a look upon a face, a sound, or any trifle may bring all at once before the wrongdoer that ancient evil. And no lapse of time makes it less dreadful when it is unveiled. The chance thrust of a boat–hook that gets tangled in the grey hairs of a corpse, brings it up grim to the surface. Press a button, by accident, upon a wall in some old castle, and a door flies open that leads away down into black depths. You and I have depths of that sort in our hearts. Then there are no more illusions about whose fault the deed was. When Herod killed John, he said, 'Oh! It is not I! It is Herodias. It is Salome. It is my oath. It is the respect I bear to the people who heard me swear. I must do it, but I am not responsible.' But when, in 'the sessions of silent thought,' the deed came back to him, Salome and Herodias, the oath, and the company were all out of sight, and he said, 'I! *I* did it.'

That is what we all shall have to do some day, in this world possibly, in the next certainly. Men sophisticate themselves with talk about palliations, and excuses, and temptations, and companions and the like. And philosophers sophisticate themselves nowadays with a great many learned explanations, which tend to show that a man is not to blame for the wrong things he does. But all that rubbish gets burned up when conscience wakes, and the doer says, 'Whom *I* beheaded.'

Brethren, unless we take refuge in the great sacrifice for the sins of the world which Jesus Christ has made, we shall, possibly in this life, and certainly hereafter, be surrounded by a company of our own evil deeds risen from the dead, and every one of them will shake its gory locks at us, and say, '*Thou didst it.*'

IV. The last lesson that I gather from this man's life is the final insensibility which these half–and–half convictions tend to produce.

Jesus Christ was sent by Pilate to Herod as a kind of peace–offering. The two had been squabbling about some question of jurisdiction; and so, partly to escape from the embarrassment of having to deal with this enigmatical Prisoner, and partly out of a piece of politic politeness, Pilate sends Jesus to Herod, because He was in his jurisdiction. Think of the Lord of men and angels being handed about from one to the other of these two scoundrels, as a piece of politeness!

When Christ stands before Herod, note that all its former convictions, partial or entire, and all its terrors superficial or deep, have faded clean away from this frivolous soul. All that he feels now is a childish delight in having this well–known Man before him, and a hope that, for his delectation, Jesus will work a miracle; much as he might expect a conjurer to do one of his tricks! That is what killing John came to—an incapacity to see anything in Jesus.

'And he asked Him many questions, and Jesus answered him nothing.' He locked His lips. Why? He was doing what He Himself enjoined: 'Give not that which is holy to the dogs. Cast not your pearls before swine.' He said nothing, because He knew it was useless to say anything. So the Incarnate Word, whose very nature and property it is to speak, was silent before the frivolous curiosity of the man that had been false to his deepest convictions.

It is a parable, brother, of what is being repeated over and over again amongst us. I dare not say that Jesus Christ is ever absolutely dumb to any man on this side of the grave; but I dare not refrain from saying that this condition of insensibility to His words is one that we may indefinitely approach, and that the surest way to approach it and to reach it is to fight down, or to neglect, the convictions that lead up to Him. John was the forerunner of Christ, and if Herod had listened to John, to him John would have said: 'Behold the Lamb of God!' To you I say it, and beseech you to take that Lamb of God as the Sacrifice for your sins, for the Healer and Cleanser of your memories and your consciences, for the Helper who will enable you joyfully to make all sacrifices to duty, and to carry into effect every conviction which His own merciful hand writes upon your hearts. And oh, dear friends, many of you strangers to me, to whom my voice seldom comes, let me plead with you not to be content with 'hearing' any of us 'gladly,' but to do what our words point to, and to follow Christ the Saviour. If you hear the Gospel, however imperfectly, as you are hearing it proclaimed now, and if you neglect it as—must I say?—you are doing now, you will bring another film over your eyes which may grow thick enough to shut out all the light; you will wind another fold about your hearts which may prove impenetrable to the sword of the Spirit; you will put another plug in your ears which may make them deaf to the music of Christ's voice. Do what you know you ought to do, yield yourselves to Jesus Christ. And do it now, whilst impressions are being made, lest, if you let them sleep, they may never return. Felix trembled when Paul reasoned; but he waved away the messenger and the message, and though he sent for Paul often, and communed with him, he never trembled any more.

'There is a tide in the affairs of men
Which, taken at the flood,'

would lead us into the haven of rest in Christ; and, if allowed to pass, may leave us, stranded and shipwrecked, among the rocks.

JESUS AND PILATE

'And Pilate, when he had called together the chief priests and the rulers and the people, 14. Said unto them, Ye have brought this man unto me, as one that perverteth the people: and, behold, I having examined Him before you, have found no fault in this man touching those things whereof ye accuse Him: 15. No, nor yet Herod; for I sent you to him: and lo, nothing worthy of death is done unto Him. 16. I will therefore chastise Him, and release Him. 17. (For of necessity he must release one unto them at the feast.) 18. And they cried out all at once, saying, Away with this man, and release unto us Barabbas: 19. (Who for a certain sedition made in the city, and for murder, was cast into prison.) 20. Pilate therefore, willing to release Jesus, spake again to them. 21. But they cried, saying, Crucify Him, crucify Him. 22. And he said unto them the third time, Why, what evil hath He done? I have found no cause of death in Him: I will therefore chastise Him, and let Him go. 23. And they were

instant with loud voices, requiring that He might he
crucified. And the voices of them and of the chief
priests prevailed. 24. And Pilate gave sentence that
it should be as they required. 25. And he released
unto them him that for sedition and murder was cast
into prison, whom they had desired; but he delivered
Jesus to their will. 26. And as they led Him away,
they laid hold upon one Simon, a Cyrenian, coming out
of the country, and on him they laid the cross, that
he might bear it after Jesus.'—LUKE xxiii. 13–26.

Luke here marks out three stages of the struggle between Pilate and the Jews. Thrice did he try to release Jesus; thrice did they yell their hatred and their demand for His blood. Then came the shameful surrender by Pilate, in which, from motives of policy, he prostituted Roman justice. Knowingly he sacrificed one poor Jew to please his turbulent subjects; unknowingly he slew the Christ of God.

I. The first weak attempt to be just.

Pilate invested it with a certain formality by convoking a representative gathering of all classes, 'chief priests and the rulers and the people.' The nation was summoned to decide solemnly whether they would or would not put their Messiah to death, and a Roman governor was their summoner. Surely the irony of fate (or, rather, of Providence) could go no further than that. Pilate's *resume* of the proceedings up to the moment of his speaking is not without a touch of sarcasm, in the contrast between 'ye' and 'I' and 'Herod.' It is almost as if he had said, 'Why, herein is a marvellous thing, that you should have a quicker scent for rebellion than I or Herod!' He was evidently suspicious of the motives which induced the 'rulers' to take the new role of eager defenders of Roman authority, and ready to suspect something below such an extraordinary transformation. Jews delivering up a Jew because he was an insurgent against Caesar,—there must be something under that! He lays stress on their having heard his examination of the accused, as showing that he had gone into the matter thoroughly, that the charges had broken down to their knowledge. He represents his sending Jesus to Herod as done from the high motive of securing the completest possible investigation, instead of its being a despicable attempt to shirk responsibility and to pay an empty compliment to an enemy. He reiterates his conviction of Jesus' innocence, and then, after all this flourish about his own carefulness to bring judicial impartiality to bear on the case, he makes the lame and impotent conclusion of offering to 'chastise Him.'

What for? The only course for a judge convinced of a prisoner's innocence is to set him free. But this was a bribe to the accusers, offered in hope that the smaller punishment would content them. Pilate knew that he was perpetrating flagrant injustice in such a suggestion, and he tried to hide it by using a gentle word. 'Chastise' sounds almost beneficent, but it would not make the scourging less cruel, nor its infliction less lawless. Compromises are always ticklish to engineer, but a compromise between justice and injustice is least likely of all to answer. This one signally failed. The fierce accusers of Jesus were quick to see the sign of weakness, both in the proposal itself and in their being asked if it would be acceptable to them. Not so should a Roman governor have spoken. If pressure had made the iron wall yield so far, a little more and it would fall flat, and let them at their victim.

Pilate was weak, vacillating, did not know what he wished. He wished to do right, but he wished more to conciliate, for he knew that he was detested, and feared to be accused to Rome. The other side knew what they wanted, and were resolute. Encouraged by the hesitation of Pilate, they 'cried out all together.' One hears the strident yells from a thousand throats shrieking out the self–revealing and self–destroying choice of Barabbas. He was a popular hero for the very reason that he was a rebel. He had done what his admirers had accused Jesus of doing, and for which they pretended that they had submitted Him to Pilate's judgment. The choice of Barabbas convicts the charges against Jesus of falsehood and unreality. The choice of Barabbas reveals the national ideal. They did not want a Messiah like Jesus, and had no eyes for the beauty of His character, nor ears for the words of grace poured into His lips. They had no horror of 'a murderer,' and great admiration for a rebel. Barabbas was the man after their own heart. A nation that can reject Jesus and choose Barabbas is only fit for destruction. A nation judges itself by its choice of heroes. The national ideal is potent to shape the national character. We to–day are sinking into an abyss because of our admiration for the military type of hero; and there is not such an immense difference between the mob that rejected Jesus and applauded Barabbas and the mobs that shout round a successful soldier, and scoff at the law of Christ if applied to politics.

II. The second, weaker attempt.

Pilate repeated his proposal of release, but it was all but lost in the roar of hatred. Note the contrast between 'Pilate spoke' (v. 20) and 'they shouted.' It suggests his feeble effort swept away by the rush of ferocity. And they have gathered boldness from his hesitation, and are now prescribing the mode of Christ's punishment. Now first the terrible word 'Crucify' is heard. Both Matthew and Mark tell us that the priests and rulers had 'stirred up' the people to choose Barabbas, but apparently the mob, once roused, needed no further stimulant.

Crowds are always cruel, and they are as fickle as cruel. The very throats now hoarse with fiercely roaring 'Crucify Him' had been strained by shouting 'Hosanna' less than a week since. The branches strewed in His path had not had time to wither. 'The voice of the people is the voice of God,'—sometimes. But sometimes it sounds very like the voice of the enemy of God, and one would have more confidence in it if it did not so often and so quickly speak, not only 'in divers,' but in diverse, 'manners.' To make it the arbiter of men's merit, still more to trim one's course so as to catch the breeze of the popular breath, is folly, or worse. Men admire what they resemble, or try to resemble, and Barabbas has more of his sort than has Jesus.

III. The final yielding.

It is to Pilate's credit that he kept up his efforts so long. Luke wishes to impress us with his persistency, as well as with the fixed determination of the Jews, by his note of 'the third time.' Thrice was the choice offered to them, and thrice did they put away the possibility of averting their doom. But Pilate's persistency had a weak place, for he was afraid of his subjects, and, while willing to save Jesus, was not willing to imperil himself in doing it. Self–interest takes the strength out of resolution to do right, like a crumbling stone in a sea wall, which lets in the wave that ruins the whole structure.

Pilate had come to the end of his shifts to escape pronouncing sentence. The rulers had refused to judge Jesus according to their law. Herod had sent Him back with thanks, but unsentenced. The Jews would not have Him, but Barabbas, released, nor would they accept scourging in lieu of crucifying. So he has to decide at last whether to be just and fear not, or basely to give way, and draw down on his head momentary applause at the price of everlasting horror. Luke notices in all three stages the loud cries of the Jews, and in this last one he gives special emphasis to them. 'Their voices prevailed.' What a condemnation for a judge! He 'gave sentence that what they asked for should be done.' Baseness in a judge could go no farther. The repetition of the characterisation of Barabbas brings up once more the hideousness of the people's choice, and the tragic words 'to their will' sets in a ghastly light the flagrant injustice of the judge, and yet greater crime of the Jews. To deliver Jesus to their will was base; to entertain such a 'will' towards Jesus was more than base,—it was 'the ruin of them, and of all Israel.' Our whole lives here and hereafter turn on what is our 'will' to Him.

WORDS FROM THE CROSS

'And when they were come to the place which is called Calvary, there they crucified Him, and the malefactors, one on the right hand, and the other on the left. 34. Then said Jesus, Father, forgive them; for they know not what they do. And they parted His raiment, and cast lots. 35. And the people stood beholding. And the rulers also with them derided Him, saying, He saved others; let Him save Himself, if He be Christ, the chosen of God. 36. And the soldiers also mocked Him, coming to Him and offering Him vinegar. 37. And saying, if Thou be the king of the Jews, save Thyself. 38. And a superscription also was written over Him in letters of Greek, and Latin, and Hebrew, THIS IS THE KING OF THE JEWS. 39. And one of the malefactors which were hanged railed on Him, saying, If Thou be Christ, save Thyself and us. 40. But the other answering rebuked him, saying, Dost not thou fear God, seeing thou art in the same condemnation? 41. And we indeed justly; for we receive the due reward of our deeds: but this Man hath done nothing amiss. 42. And he said unto Jesus, Lord, remember me when Thou comest into Thy kingdom. 43. And Jesus said unto him, Verily I say unto thee, To-day shalt thou be with Me in paradise. 44. And it was about the sixth hour, and there was darkness over all the earth until the ninth hour. 45. And the sun was darkened, and the vail of the temple was rent in the midst. 46. And when Jesus had cried with a loud voice, He said, Father, into Thy hands I commend My spirit: and having said thus, He gave up the ghost.'—LUKE xxiii. 33–46.

344

The calm tone of all the narratives of the Crucifixion is very remarkable. Each Evangelist limits himself to the bare recording of facts, without a trace of emotion. They felt too deeply to show feeling. It was fitting that the story which, till the end of time, was to move hearts to a passion of love and devotion, should be told without any colouring. Let us beware of reading it coldly! This passage is more adapted to be pondered in solitude, with the thought, 'All this was borne for me,' than to be commented on. But a reverent word or two is permissible.

Luke's account is noticeably independent of the other three. The three sayings of Christ's, round which his narrative is grouped, are preserved by him alone. We shall best grasp the dominant impression which the Evangelist unconsciously had himself received, and sought to convey, by gathering the whole round these three words from the Cross.

I. The first word sets Jesus forth as the all–merciful Intercessor and patient friend of sinners. It is very significantly set in the centre of the paragraph (vs. 33–38) which recounts the heartless cruelty and mockery of soldiers and rulers. Surrounded by that whirlwind of abuse, contempt and ferocious glee at His sufferings, He gave back no taunt, nor uttered any cry of pain, nor was moved to the faintest anger, but let His heart go out in pity for all who took part in that wicked tragedy; and, while 'He opened not His mouth' in complaint or reviling, He did open it in intercession. But the wonderful prayer smote no heart with compunction, and, after it, the storm of mocking and savage triumph hurtled on as before.

Luke gathers all the details together in summary fashion, and piles them on one another without enlarging on any. The effect produced is like that of a succession of breakers beating on some lonely rock, or of blows struck by a battering–ram on a fortress.

'They crucified Him,'—there is no need to say who 'they' were. Others than the soldiers, who did the work, did the deed. Contempt gave Him two malefactors for companions and hung the King of the Jews in the place of honour in the midst. Did John remember what his brother and he had asked? Matter–of–fact indifference as to a piece of military duty, and shameless greed, impelled the legionaries to cast lots for the clothes stripped from a living man. What did the crucifying of another Jew or two matter to them? Gaping curiosity, and the strange love of the horrible, so strong in the vulgar mind, led the people, who had been shouting Hosanna! less than a week ago, to stand gazing on the sight without pity but in a few hearts.

The bitter hatred of the rulers, and their inhuman glee at getting rid of a heretic, gave them bad preeminence in sin. Their scoff acknowledged that He had 'saved others,' and their hate had so blinded their eyes that they could not see how manifestly His refusal to use His power to save Himself proved Him the Son of God. He could not save Himself, just because He would save these scoffing Rabbis and all the world. The rough soldiers knew little about Him, but they followed suit, and thought it an excellent jest to bring the 'vinegar,' provided in kindness, to Jesus with a mockery of reverence as to a king. The gibe was double–barrelled, like the inscription over the Cross; for it was meant to hit both this Pretender to royalty and His alleged subjects.

And to all this Christ's sole answer was the ever–memorable prayer. One of the women who bravely stood at the Cross must have caught the perhaps low–voiced supplication, and it breathed so much of the aspect of Christ's character in which Luke especially delights that he could not leave it out. It opens many large questions which cannot be dealt with here. All sin has in it an element of ignorance, but it is not wholly ignorance as some modern teachers affirm. If the ignorance were complete, the sin would be nonexistent. The persons covered by the ample folds of this prayer were ignorant in very different degrees, and had had very different opportunities of changing ignorance for knowledge. The soldiers and the rulers were in different positions in that respect. But none were so entirely blind that they had no sin, and none were so entirely seeing that they were beyond the reach of Christ's pity or the power of His intercession. In that prayer we learn, not only His infinite forgivingness for insults and unbelief levelled at Himself, but His exaltation as the Intercessor, whom the Father heareth always. The dying Christ prayed for His enemies; the glorified Christ lives to make intercession for us.

II. In the second saying Christ is revealed as having the keys of Hades, the invisible world of the dead. How differently the same circumstances work on different natures! In the one malefactor, physical agony and despair found momentary relief in taunts, flung from lips dry with torture, at the fellow-sufferer whose very innocence provoked hatred from the guilty heart. The other had been led by his punishment to recognise in it the due reward of his deeds, and thus softened, had been moved by Christ's prayer, and by his knowledge of Christ's innocence, to hope that the same mercy which had been lavished on the inflicters of His sufferings, might stretch to enfold the partakers in it.

At that moment the dying thief had clearer faith in Christ's coming in His kingdom than any of the disciples had. Their hopes were crumbling as they watched Him hanging unresisting and gradually dying. But this man looked beyond the death so near for both Jesus and himself, and believed that, after it, He would come to reign. We may call him the only disciple that Christ then had.

How pathetic is that petition, 'Remember me'! It builds the hope of sharing in Christ's royalty on the fact of having shared in His Cross. 'Thou wilt not forget Thy companion in that black hour, which will then lie behind us.' Such trust and clinging, joined with such penitence and submission, could not go unrewarded.

From His Cross Jesus speaks in royal style, as monarch of that dim world. His promise is sealed with His own sign-manual, 'Verily, I say.' It claims to have not only the clear vision of, but the authority to determine, the future. It declares the unbroken continuance of personal existence, and the reality of a state of conscious blessedness, in which men are aware of their union with Him, the Lord of the realm and the Life of its inhabitants. It graciously accepts the penitent's petition, and assures him that the companionship, begun on the Cross, will be continued there. 'With Me' makes 'Paradise' wherever a soul is.

III. The third word from the Cross, as recorded by Luke, reveals Jesus as, in the act of dying, the Master of death, and its Transformer for all who trust Him into a peaceful surrender of themselves into the Father's hands. The circumstances grouped round the act of His death bring out various aspects of its significance. The darkness preceding had passed before He died, and it bore rather on His sense of desertion, expressed in the unfathomably profound and awful cry, 'Why hast Thou forsaken Me?' The rent veil is generally taken to symbolise the unrestricted access into the presence of God, which we have through Christ's death; but it is worth considering whether it does not rather indicate the divine leaving of the desecrated shrine, and so is the beginning of the fulfilment of the deep word, 'Destroy this Temple.'

But the centre–point of the section is the last cry which, in its loudness, indicated physical strength quite incompatible with the exhaustion to which death by crucifixion was generally due. It thus confirms the view which sees, both in the words of Jesus and in the Evangelist's expression for His death, clear indications that He died, not because His physical powers were unable to live longer, but by the exercise of His own volition. He died because He chose, and He chose because He loved and would save. As St. Bernard says, 'Who is He who thus easily falls asleep when He wills? To die is indeed great weakness, but to die thus is immeasurable power. Truly the weakness of God is stronger than men.'

Nor let us forget that, in thus dying, Jesus gave us an imitable example, as well as revealed inimitable power. For, if we trust ourselves, living and dying, to Him, we shall not be dragged reluctantly, by an overmastering grasp against which we vainly struggle, out of a world where we would fain stay, but we may yield ourselves willingly, as to a Father's hand, which draws His children gently to His own side, and blesses them, when there, with His fuller presence.

THE DYING THIEF

'And he said unto Jesus, Lord, remember me when Thou comest into Thy kingdom.'—LUKE xxiii, 42.

There is an old and true division of the work of Christ into three parts—prophet, priest, and king. Such a distinction manifestly exists, though it may be overestimated, or rather, the statement of it may be exaggerated, if it be supposed that separate acts of His discharge these separate functions, and that He ceases to be the one before He becomes the other. Rather it is true that all His work is prophetic, that all His work is priestly, and that His prophetic and priestly work is the exercise of His kingly authority. But still the division is a true one, and helps to set before us, clearly and definitely, the wide range of the benefits of Christ's mission and death. It is noteworthy that these three groups round the Cross, the third of which we have to speak of now—that of the 'daughters of Jerusalem,' that of the deriding scribes and the indifferent soldiers, and this one of the two thieves—each presents us Christ in one of the three characters. The words that He spoke upon the Cross, with reference to others than Himself, may be gathered around, and arranged under, that threefold aspect of Christ's work. The *prophet* said, 'Daughters of Jerusalem, weep not for Me, but weep for yourselves, for the days are coming.' The *priest* said, 'Father, forgive them, for they know not what they do. 'The *king*, in His sovereignty, ruled the heart of that penitent man from His Cross, and while the crown shone athwart the smoke and the agony of the death, the king 'opened the gates of the kingdom of heaven unto all believers' when He said, 'This day shalt thou be with Me in Paradise!'

We shall not attempt, in dealing with this incident, to paint pictures. I have a far more important thing to do than even to try to bring vividly before your minds the scene on that little hill of Calvary. It is the meaning that we are concerned with, and not the mere externals. I take it for granted, then, that we know the details:—the dying man in his agony, beginning to see dimly, as his soul closed upon earthly things, who this was—patient, loving, mighty there in His sufferings; and using his last breath to cry, 'Lord, remember me!'—and the sufferer throned in the majesty of His meekness, and divinity of His endurance; calm, conscious, full of felt but silent power, accepting homage, bending to the penitence, loving the sinner, and flinging open the gates of the pale kingdoms into which He was to pass, with these His last words.

First, then, we see here an illustration of the Cross in its power of drawing men to itself. It is strange to think that, perhaps, at that moment the only human being who thoroughly believed in Christ was that dying robber. The disciples are all gone. The most faithful of them are recreant, denying, fleeing. A handful of women are standing there, not knowing what to think about it, stunned but loving; and alone (as I suppose), alone of all the sons of men, the crucified malefactor was in the sunshine of faith, and could say 'I believe!' As everything of the future history of the world and of the Gospel is typified in the events of the Crucifixion, it was fitting that here again and at the last there should be a prophetic fulfilment of His own saying, 'I, if I be lifted up, will draw all men unto Me.'

But mark, here we have a striking instance of the universal law of the progress of the Gospel, in the two-fold effort of the contemplation of the Cross. By its foot was to be seen the derision of the scribes and the stupor of the soldiery; and now here are the two thieves—the one chiming in with the universal reproaches; and the other beholding the same event, having the same circumstances displayed before him, and they influence him *thus*. Brethren, it is just the history of the Gospel wherever it goes. It is its history now, and among us. The Gospel is preached equally to every man. The same message comes to us all, offering us the same terms. Christ stands before each of us in the same attitude. And what is the consequence? A parting of the whole mass of us, some to one side and some to the other. So, when you take a magnet, and hold it to an indiscriminate heap of metal filings, it will gather out all the iron, and leave behind all the rest. 'I, if I be lifted up,' said He, 'will draw all men unto Me.' The attractive power will go out over the whole race of His brethren; but from some there will be no response. In some hearts there will be no yielding to the attraction. Some will remain rooted, obstinate, steadfast in their place; and to some the lightest word will be mighty enough to stir all the slumbering pulses of their sin-ridden hearts, and to bring them, broken and penitent, for mercy to His feet. To the one He is 'a savour of life unto life, and to the other a savour of death unto death.' The broadest doctrine of the universal adaptation, and the universal intention too, of the Gospel, as the 'power of God unto salvation,' contains hidden in its depths this undeniable fact, that, be the cause what it may (and as I believe, the cause lies with us, and is our fault) this separating, judging effect follows from all faithful preaching of Christ's words. He came to judge the world, 'that they which see not' (as He Himself said) 'might see, and they which see might be made blind,' And on the Cross that process went on in two men, alike in necessity, alike in criminality, alike in this, that Death's icy finger was just being laid upon their heart, to stop all the flow of its wild blood and passion, but different in this, that the one of them turned himself, by God's grace, and laid hold on the Gospel that was offered to him, and the other turned himself away, and derided, and died.

And now, there is another consideration. If we look at this man, this penitent thief, and contrast him, his previous history, and his present feelings, with the people that stood around, and rejected and scoffed, we get some light as to the sort of thing that unfits men for perceiving and accepting the Gospel when it is offered to them. Remember the other classes of persons who were there. There were Roman soldiers, with very partial knowledge of what they were doing, and whose only feeling was that of entire indifference; and there were Jewish Rabbis, Pharisees, Priests, and people, who knew a little more of what they were doing, and whose feeling was derision and scorn. Now, if we mark the ordinary scriptural representation, especially as to the last class, we cannot help seeing that there comes out this principle:—The thing of all others that unfits men for the reception of Christ as a Saviour, and for the simple reliance on His atoning blood and divine mercy, is not gross, long profligacy, and outward, vehement transgression; but it is self-complacency, clean, fatal self-righteousness and self-sufficiency.

Why was it that Scribes and Pharisees turned away from Him? For three reasons. Because of their pride of wisdom. 'We are the men who know all about Moses and the traditions of the elders; we judge this new phenomenon not by the question, How does it come to our consciences, and how does it appeal to our hearts? but we judge it by the question, How does it fit our Rabbinical learning and subtle casuistical laws? *We* are the Priests and the Scribes; and the people that know not the law, *they* may accept a thing that only appeals to the common human heart, but for us, in our intellectual superiority, living remote from the common wants of the lower class, not needing a rough outward Gospel of that sort, we can do without such a thing, and we reject it.' They turned away from the Cross, and their hatred darkened into derision, and their menaces ended in a crucifixion, not merely because of a pride of wisdom, but because of a complacent self-righteousness that knew nothing of the fact of sin, that never had learned to believe itself to be full of evil, that had got so wrapped up in ceremonies as to have lost the life; that had degraded the divine law of God, with all its lightning splendours, and awful power, into a matter of 'mint and anise and cummin.' They turned away for a third reason. Religion had become to them a mere set of traditional dogmas, to think accurately or to reason clearly about which was all that was needful. Worship having become ceremonial, and morality having become casuistry, and religion having become theology, the men were as hard as a nether millstone, and there was nothing to be done with them until these three crusts were peeled off the heart, and, close and burning, the naked heart and the naked truth of God came into contact.

Brethren, change the name, and the story is true about *us*. God forbid that I should deny that every form of gross, sensual immorality, 'hardens all within' (as one poor victim of it said), 'and petrifies the feeling.' God forbid that I should seem to be speaking slightingly of the exceeding sinfulness of such sin, or to be pouring contempt upon the laws of common morality. Do not misapprehend me so. Still it is not sin in its outward forms that makes the worst impediment between a man and the Cross, but it is sin plus self-righteousness which makes the insurmountable obstacle to all faith and repentance. And oh! in our days, when passion is tamed down by so many bonds and chains; when the power of society lies upon all of us, prescribing our path, and keeping most of us from vice, partly because we are not tempted, and partly because we have been brought up like some young trees behind a wall, within the fence of decent customs and respectable manners,—we have far more need to tell orderly, respectable moral men—'My brother, that thing that you have is worth nothing, as settling your position before God'; than to stand up and thunder about crimes which half of us never heard of, and perhaps only an infinitesimal percentage of us have ever committed. All sin separates from God, but the thing that makes the separation permanent is not the sin, but the ignorance of the sin. Self-righteousness, aye, and pride of wisdom, they—they have perverted many a nature, many a young man's glowing spirit, and have turned him away from the Gospel. If there be a man here who is looking at the simple message of peace and pardon and purity through Christ, and is saying to himself, Yes; it may fit the common class of minds that require outward signs and symbols, and must pin their faith to forms; but for me with my culture, for me with my spiritual tendencies, for me with my new lights, *I* do not want any objective redemption; *I* do not want anything to convince *me* of a divine love, and I do not need any crucified Saviour to preach to *me* that God is merciful!—this incident before us has a very solemn lesson in it for him. And if there be a man here who is living a life of surface blamelessness, it has as solemn a lesson for him. Look at the Scribe, and look at the Pharisee—religious men in their way, wise men in their way, decent and respectable men in their way; and look at that poor thief that had been caught in the wilderness amongst the caves and dens, and had been brought red–handed with blood upon his sword, and guilt in his heart, and nailed up there in the short and summary process of a Roman jurisprudence;—and think that Scribe, and Pharisee, and Priest, saw nothing in Christ; and that the poor profligate wretch saw this in Him,—innocence that showed heavenly against his diabolical blackness; and his heart stirred, and he laid hold of Him in the stress of his mighty agony—as a drowning man catches at anything that protrudes from the bank; and he held and shook it, and the thing was fast, and he was safe! Not transgression shuts a man out from mercy. Transgression, which belongs to us all, makes us subjects for the mercy; but it is pride, self–righteousness, trust in ourselves, which 'bars the gates of mercy on mankind'; and the men that *are* condemned are condemned not only because they have transgressed the commandments of God, but '*this* is the condemnation, that light came into the world, and men loved darkness rather than light, because their deeds were evil.'

And then (and but a word) we see here, too, the elements of which acceptable faith consists. One does not exactly know by what steps or through what process this poor dying thief passed, which issued in faith—whether it was an impression from Christ's presence, whether it was that he had ever heard anything about Him before, or whether it was only that the wisdom which dwells with death was beginning to clear his eyes as life ebbed away. But however he *came* to the conviction, mark what it was that he believed and expressed,—I am a sinful man; all punishment that comes down upon me is richly deserved: This man is pure and righteous; 'Lord, remember me when Thou comest into Thy kingdom!' That is all—that is all. That is the thing that saves a man. How much he *did* know—whether he knew all the depth of what he was saying, when he said 'Lord!' is a question that we cannot answer; whether he understood what the 'kingdom' was that he was expecting, is a question that we cannot solve; but this is clear—the intellectual part of faith may be dark and doubtful, but the moral and emotional part of it is manifest and plain. There was, '*I* am nothing— *Thou* art everything: I bring myself and my emptiness unto Thy great fullness: fill it and make me blessed!' Faith has that. Faith has in it repentance—repentance has in it faith too. Faith has in it the recognition of the certainty and the justice of a judgment that is coming down crashing upon every human head; and then from the midst of these fears, and sorrows, and the tempest of that great darkness, there rises up in the night of terrors, the shining of one perhaps pale, quivering, distant, but divinely given hope, 'My Saviour! My Saviour! He is righteous: He has died—He lives! I will stay no longer; I will cast myself upon Him!'

Once more—this incident reminds us not only of the attractive power of the Cross, but of the prophetic power of the Cross. We have here the Cross as pointing to and foretelling the Kingdom. Pointing out, and foretelling: that is to say, of course, and only, if we accept the scriptural statement of what these sufferings were, the Person that endured them, and the meaning of their being endured. But the only thing I would dwell upon here, is, that when we think of Christ as dying for us, we are never to separate it from that other solemn and future coming of which this poor robber catches a glimpse. They crowned Him with thorns, and they gave Him a reed for His sceptre. That mockery, so natural to the strong practical Romans in dealing with one whom they thought a harmless enthusiast, was a symbol which they who did it little dreamed of. The crown of thorns proclaims a sovereignty founded on sufferings. The sceptre of feeble reed speaks of power wielded in gentleness. The Cross leads to the crown. The brow that was pierced by the sharp acanthus wreath, therefore wears the diadem of the universe. The hand that passively held the mockery of the worthless, pithless reed, therefore rules the princes of the earth with the rod of iron. He who was lifted up to the Cross, was, by that very act, lifted up to be a Ruler and Commander to the peoples. For the death of the Cross God hath highly exalted Him to be a Prince and a Saviour. The way to glory for Him, the power by which He wields the kingdom of the world, is precisely through the suffering. And therefore, whensoever there arises before us the image of the one, oh! let there rise before us likewise the image of the other. The Cross links on to the kingdom—the kingdom lights up the Cross. My brother, the Saviour comes—the Saviour comes a King. The Saviour that comes a King is the Saviour that has been here and was crucified. The kingdom that He establishes is all full of blessing, and love, and gentleness; and to us (if we will unite the thoughts of Cross and Crown) there is opened up not only the possibility of having boldness before Him in the day of judgment, but there is opened up this likewise—the certainty that He 'shall receive of the travail of His soul and be satisfied.' Oh, remember that as certain as the historical fact—He died on Calvary; so certain is the prophetic fact—He shall reign, and you and I will stand there! I durst not touch that subject. Take it into your own hearts; and think about it—a kingdom, a judgment–seat, a crown, a gathered universe; separation, decision, execution of the sentence. And oh! ask yourselves, 'When that gentle eye, with lightning in its depths, falls upon *me*, individualises *me*, summons out *me* to its bar—how shall I stand?' 'Herein is our love made perfect, that we may have boldness before Him in the day of judgment,' 'Lord, remember me when Thou comest into Thy kingdom.'

Finally. Here is the Cross as revealing and opening the true Paradise.—'This day shalt thou be with Me in Paradise.' We have no concern at present with the many subtle inferences as to the state of the dead, and as to the condition of our Lord's human spirit before the Resurrection, which have been drawn from these words. To me they do seem fairly to bear the broad and single conclusion that the spirits of the saved do enter at death into a state of conscious presence with their Saviour, and therefore of joy and felicity. But beyond this we have no firm ground for going. It is of more practical worth to note that the penitent's vague prayer is answered, and over–answered. He asks, 'When Thou comest'—whensoever that may be—'remember me.' 'I shall stand afar off; do not let me be utterly forgotten.' Christ answers—'Remember thee! thou shalt be *with Me*, close to My side. Remember thee *when* I come!—*this day* shalt thou be with Me.'

And what a contrast that is—the conscious blessedness rushing in close upon the heels of the momentary darkness of death. At the one moment there hangs the thief writhing in mortal agony; the wild shouts of the fierce mob at his feet are growing faint upon his ear; the city spread out at his feet, and all the familiar sights of earth are growing dim to his filmy eye. The soldier's spear comes, the legs are broken, and in an instant there hangs a relaxed corpse; and the spirit, the spirit—is where? Ah! how far away; released from all its sin and its sore agony, struggling up at once into such strange divine enlargement, a new star swimming into the firmament of heaven, a new face before the throne of God, another sinner redeemed from earth! The conscious immediate blessedness of the departed—be he what he may, be his life whatsoever it may have been—who at last, dark, sinful, standing with one foot on the verge of eternity, and poising himself for the flight, flings himself into the arms of Christ—the everlasting blessedness, the Christ–presence and the Christ–gladness, that is the message that the robber leaves to us from his cross. Paradise is opened to us again. The Cross is the true 'tree of life.' The flaming cherubim, and the sword that turneth every way, are gone, and the broad road into the city, the Paradise of God, with all its beauties and all its peaceful joy—a better Paradise, 'a statelier Eden,' than that which we have lost, is flung open to us for ever.

Do not trust a death–bed repentance, my brother. I have stood by many a death–bed, and few indeed have they been where I could have believed that the man was in a condition physically (to say nothing of anything else) clearly to see and grasp the message of the Gospel. There is no limit to the mercy. I know that God's mercy is boundless. I know that 'whilst there is life there is hope.' I know that a man, going—swept down that great Niagara—if, before his little skiff tilts over into the awful rapids, he can make one great bound with all his strength, and reach the solid ground—I know he may be saved. It is an awful risk to run. A moment's miscalculation, and skiff and voyager alike are whelming in the green chaos below, and come up mangled into nothing, far away down yonder upon the white turbulent foam. '*One* was saved upon the Cross,' as the old divines used to tell us, 'that none might despair; and only one, that none might presume.' 'Now is the accepted time, and *now* is the day of salvation!'

THE FIRST EASTER SUNRISE

'Now, upon the first day of the week, very early in the morning, they came onto the sepulchre, bringing the spices which they had prepared, and certain others with them. 2. And they found the stone rolled away from the sepulchre. 3. And they entered in, and found not the body of the Lord Jesus. 4. And it came to pass, as they were much perplexed thereabout, behold, two men stood by them in shining garments: 5. And as they were afraid, and bowed down their faces to the earth, they said unto them, Why seek ye the living among the dead? 6. He is not here, but is risen: remember how He spake unto you when He was yet in Galilee, 7. Saying, The Son of man must be delivered into the hands of sinful men, and be crucified, and the third day rise again. 8. And they remembered His words, 9. And returned from the sepulchre, and told all these things unto the eleven, and to all the rest. 10. It was Mary Magdalene, and Joanna, and Mary the mother of James, and other women that were with them, which told these things unto the apostles. 11. And their words seemed to them as idle tales, and they believed them not. 12. Then arose Peter, and ran unto the sepulchre; and stooping down, he beheld the linen clothes laid by themselves, and departed, wondering in himself at that which was come to pass.'—LUKE xxiv. 1–12.

No Evangelist narrates the act of Resurrection. Apocryphal Gospels cannot resist the temptation of describing it. Why did the Four preserve such singular reticence about what would have been irresistible to 'myth' makers? Because they were not myth–makers, but witnesses, and had nothing to say as to an act that no man had seen. No doubt, the Resurrection took place in the earliest hours of the first day of the week. The Sun of Righteousness rose before the Easter Day sun. It was midsummer day for Him, while it was but spring for earth's calendar. That early rising has no setting to follow.

The divergences of the Evangelists reach their maximum in the accounts of the Resurrection, as is natural if we realise the fragmentary character of all the versions, the severely condensed style of Matthew's, the incompleteness of the genuine Mark's, the evidently selective purpose in Luke's, and the supplementary design of John's. If we add the perturbed state of the disciples, their separation from each other, and the number of distinct incidents embraced in the records, we shall not wonder at the differences, but see in them confirmation of the good faith of the witnesses, and a reflection of the hurry and wonderfulness of that momentous day. Differences there are; contradictions there are not, except between the doubtful verses added to Mark and the other accounts. We cannot put all the pieces together, when we have only them to guide us. If we had a complete and independent narrative to go by, we could, no doubt, arrange our fragments. But the great certainties are unaffected by the small divergences, and the points of agreement are vital. They are, for example, that none saw the Resurrection, that the first to know of it were the women, that angels appeared to them at the tomb, that Jesus showed Himself first to Mary Magdalene, that the reports of the Resurrection were not believed. Whether the group with whom this passage has to do were the same as that whose experience Matthew records we leave undetermined. If so, they must have made two visits to the tomb, and two returns to the Apostles,—one, with only the tidings of the empty sepulchre, which Luke tells; one, with the tidings of Christ's appearance, as in Matthew. But harmonistic considerations do not need to detain us at present.

Sorrow and love are light sleepers, and early dawn found the brave women on their way. Nicodemus had bound spices in with the body, and these women's love–gift was as 'useless' and as fragrant as Mary's box of ointment. Whatever love offers, love welcomes, though Judas may ask 'To what purpose is this waste?' Angel hands had rolled away the stone, not to allow of Jesus' exit, for He had risen while it was in its place, but to permit the entrance of the 'witnesses of the Resurrection.' So little did these women dream of such a thing that the empty tomb brought no flash of joy, but only perplexity to their wistful gaze. 'What does it mean?' was their thought. They and all the disciples expected nothing less than they did a Resurrection, therefore their testimony to it is the more reliable.

Luke marks the appearance of the angels as sudden by that 'behold.' They were not seen approaching, but at one moment the bewildered women were alone, looking at each other with faces of dreary wonder, and the next, 'two men' were standing beside them, and the tomb was lighted by the sheen of their dazzling robes. Much foolish fuss has been made about the varying reports of the angels, and 'contradictions' have been found in the facts that some saw them and some did not, that some saw one and some saw two, that some saw them seated and some saw them standing, and so on. We know so little of the laws that govern angelic appearances that our opinion as to the probability or veracity of the accounts is mere guess–work. Where should a flight of angels have gathered and hovered if not there? And should they not 'sit in order serviceable' about the tomb, as around the 'stable' at

Bethlehem? Their function was to prepare a way in the hearts of the women for the Lord Himself, to lessen the shock,—for sudden joy shocks and may hurt,—as well as to witness that these 'things angels desire to look into.'

Their message flooded the women's hearts with better light than their garments had spread through the tomb. Luke's version of it agrees with Mark and Matthew in the all–important central part, 'He is not here, but is risen' (though these words in Luke are not beyond doubt), but diverges from them otherwise. Surely the message was not the mere curt announcement preserved by any one of the Evangelists. We may well believe that much more was said than any or all of them have recorded. The angels' question is half a rebuke, wholly a revelation, of the essential nature of 'the Living One,' who was so from all eternity, but is declared to be so by His rising, of the incongruity of supposing that He could be gathered to, and remain with, the dim company of the dead, and a blessed word, which turns sorrow into hope, and diverts sad eyes from the grave to the skies, for all the ages since and to come. The angels recall Christ's prophecies of death and resurrection, which, like so many of His words to the disciples and to us, had been heard, and not heard, being neglected or misinterpreted. They had questioned 'what the rising from the dead should mean,' never supposing that it meant exactly what it said. That way of dealing with Christ's words did not end on the Easter morning, but is still too often practised.

If we are to follow Luke's account, we must recognise that the women in a company, as well as Mary Magdalene separately, came back first with the announcement of the empty tomb and the angels' message, and later with the full announcement of having seen the Lord. But apart from the complexities of attempted combination of the narratives, the main point in all the Evangelists is the disbelief of the disciples, 'Idle tales,' said they, using a very strong word which appears only here in the New Testament, and likens the eager story of the excited women to a sick man's senseless ramblings. That was the mood of the whole company, apostles and all. Is that mood likely to breed hallucinations? The evidential value of the disciples' slowness to believe cannot be overrated.

Peter's race to the sepulchre, in verse 12 of Luke xxiv., is omitted by several good authorities, and is, perhaps, spurious here. If allowed to stand as Luke's, it seems to show that the Evangelist had a less complete knowledge of the facts than John. Mark, Peter's 'interpreter,' has told us of the special message to him from the risen, but as yet unseen, Lord, and we may well believe that that quickened his speed. The assurance of forgiveness and the hope of a possible future that might cover over the cowardly past, with the yearning to sob his heart out on the Lord's breast, sent him swiftly to the tomb. Luke does not say that he went in, as John, with one of his fine touches, which bring out character in a word, tells us that he did; but he agrees with John in describing the effect of what Peter saw as being only 'wonder,' and the result as being only that he went away pondering over it all, and not yet able to grasp the joy of the transcendent fact. Perhaps, if he had not had a troubled conscience, he would have had a quicker faith. He was not given to hesitation, but his sin darkened his mind. He needed that secret interview, of which many knew the fact but none the details, ere he could feel the full glow of the Risen Sun thawing his heart and scattering his doubts like morning mists on the hills.

THE LIVING DEAD

'Why seek ye the living among the dead! 6. He is not
here, but is risen.'—LUKE xxiv. 5,6.

We can never understand the utter desolation of the days that lay betwixt Christ's Death and His Resurrection. Our faith rests on centuries. We know that that grave was not even an interruption to the progress of His work, but was the straight road to His triumph and His glory. We know that it was the completion of the work of which the raising of the widow's son and of Lazarus were but the beginnings. But these disciples did not know that. To them the inferior miracles by which He had redeemed others from the power of the grave, must have made His own captivity to it all the more stunning; and the thought which such miracles ending so must have left upon them, must have been something like, 'He saved others; Himself He cannot save.' And therefore we can never think ourselves fully back to that burst of strange sudden thankfulness with which these weeping Marys found those two calm angel forms sitting with folded wings, like the Cherubim over the Mercy–seat, but overshadowing a better propitiation, and heard the words of my text, 'Why seek ye the living among the dead? He is not here, but is risen.'

But yet, although the words before us, in the full depth and preciousness of their meaning, of course could only be once fulfilled, we may not only gather from them thoughts concerning that one death and resurrection, but we may likewise apply them, in a very permissible modification of meaning, to the present condition of all who have departed in His faith and fear; since for us, too, it is true that, whenever we go to an open grave, sorrowing for those whom we love, or oppressed with the burden of mortality in any shape, if our eyes are anointed, we can see there sitting the quiet angel forms; and if our ears be purged from the noise of earth, we can hear them saying to us, in regard to all that have gone away, 'Why seek ye the living in these graves? They are not here; they are risen, as He said.' The thoughts are very old, brethren. God be thanked that they *are* old! Perhaps to some of you they may come now with new power, because they come with new application to your own present condition. Perhaps to some of you they may sound very weak, and 'words weaker than your grief will make grief more';—but such as they are, let us look at them for a moment or two together now.

The first thought, then, that these words of the angel messengers, and the scene in which we find them, suggest, is this—The dead are the living.

Language, which is more accustomed and adapted to express the appearances than the realities of things, leads us astray very much when we use the phrase 'the dead' as if it expressed the continuance of the condition into which men pass in the act of dissolution. It misleads us no less, when we use it as if it expressed in itself the whole truth even as to that act of dissolution. 'The dead' and 'the living' are not names of two classes which exclude each other. Much rather, there are *none* who are *dead*. The dead are the living who have died. Whilst they were dying they lived, and after they were dead they lived more fully. All live unto God. 'God is not the God of the dead, but of the living.' Oh, how solemnly sometimes that thought comes up before us, that all those past generations which have stormed across this earth of ours, and then have fallen into still forgetfulness, live yet. Somewhere at this very instant, they now verily *are*! We say, 'They *were*, they *have been*'. There are no have beens! Life is life for ever. *To be* is eternal being. Every man that has died is at this instant in the full possession of all his faculties, in the intensest exercise of all his capacities, standing somewhere in God's great universe, ringed with the sense of God's presence, and feeling in every fibre of his being that life, which comes after death, is not less real, but more real, not less great, but more great, not less full or intense, but more full and intense, than the mingled life which, lived here on earth, was a centre of life surrounded with a crust and circumference of mortality. The dead are the living. They lived whilst they died; and after they die, they live on for ever.

Such a conviction has as a matter of fact been firmly grasped as an unquestionable truth and a familiar operative belief only within the sphere of the Christian revelation. From the natural point of view the whole region of the dead is 'a land of darkness, without any order, where the light is as darkness.' The usual sources of human certainty fail us here. Reason is only able to stammer a peradventure. Experience and consciousness are silent. 'The simple senses' can only say that it looks as if Death were an end, the final Omega. Testimony there is none from any pale lips that have come back to unfold the secrets of the prison–house.

The history of Christ's Death and Resurrection, His dying words ' *This day* thou shalt be with Me in Paradise,' the full identity of being with which He rose from the grave, the manhood changed and yet the same, the intercourse of the forty days before His ascension, which showed the continuance of all the old love 'stronger than death,' and was in all essential points like His former intercourse with His disciples, though changed in form and introductory to the times when they should see Him no more in the flesh–these teach us, not as a peradventure, nor as a dim hope, nor as a strong foreboding which may be in its nature prophetic, but as a certainty based upon a historical fact, that Death's empire is partial in its range and transitory in its duration. But, after we are convinced of that, we can look again with new eyes even on the external accompaniments of death, and see that sense is too hasty in its conclusion that death is the final end. There is no reason from what we see passing before our eyes then to believe, that it, with all its pitifulness and all its pain, has any power at all upon the soul. True, the spirit gathers itself into itself, and, poising itself for its flight, becomes oblivious of what is passing round about it. True, the tenant that is about to depart from the house in which he has dwelt so long, closes the windows before he goes. But what is there in the cessation of the power of communication with an outer world—what is there in the fact that you clasp the nerveless hand, and it returns no pressure; that you whisper gentle words that you think might kindle a soul under the dull, cold ribs of death itself, and get no answer—that you look with weeping gaze to catch the response of affection from out of the poor filmy, closing, tearless eyes there, and look in vain—what is there in all that to lead to the conviction that *the spirit* is participant of that impotence and silence? Is not the soul only self–centring itself, retiring from, the outposts, but not touched in the citadel? Is it not only that as the long sleep of life begins to end, and the waking eye of the soul begins to open itself on realities, the sights and sounds of the dream begin to pass away? Is it not but that the man, in dying, begins to be what he fully is when he is dead, 'dead unto sin,' dead unto the world, that he may 'live unto God' that he may live with God, that he may live really? And so we can look upon that ending of life, and say, 'It is a very small thing; it only cuts off the fringes of my life, it does not touch *me* at all' It only plays round about the husk, and does not get at the core. It only strips off the circumferential mortality, but the soul rises up untouched by it, and shakes the bands of death from off its immortal arms, and flutters the stain of death from off its budding wings, and rises fuller of life *because of death*, and mightier in its vitality in the very act of submitting the body to the law, 'Dust thou art, and unto dust shalt thou return.'

Touching but a part of the being, and touching that but for a moment, death is no state, it is an act. It is not a condition, it is a transition. Men speak about life as 'a narrow neck of land, betwixt two unbounded seas': they had better speak about death as that. It is an isthmus, narrow and almost impalpable, on which, for one brief instant, the soul poises itself; whilst behind it there lies the inland lake of past being, and before it the shoreless ocean of future life, all lighted with the glory of God, and making music as it breaks even upon these dark, rough rocks. Death is but a passage. It is not a house, it is only a vestibule. The grave has a door on its inner side. We roll the stone to its mouth and come away, thinking that we have left them there till the Resurrection. But when the outer access to earth is fast closed, the inner portal that opens on heaven is set wide, and God says to His child, 'Come, enter into thy chambers and shut thy doors about thee ... until the indignation be overpast!' Death is a superficial thing, and a transitory thing—a darkness that is caused by the light, and a darkness that ends in the light—a trifle, if you measure it by duration; a trifle if you measure it by depth. The death of the mortal is the emancipation and the life of the immortal. Then, brethren, we may go with the words of my text, and look upon every green hillock below which any that are dear to us are lying, and say to ourselves, 'Not *here*—God be thanked, no—not here: living, and not dead; *yonder*, with the Master!' Oh, we think far too much of the grave, and far too little of the throne and the glory! We are far too much the creatures of sense; and the accompaniments of dissolution and departure fill up our hearts and our eyes. Think them all away, believe them all away, love them all away. Stand in the light of Christ's life, and Christ's death, and Christ's rising, till you feel, 'Thou art a shadow, not a substance—no real thing at all.' Yes, a shadow; and where a shadow falls there must be sunlight above to cast it. Look up, then, above the shadow Death, above the sin and separation from God, of which it is the shadow! Look up to the unsetting light of the Eternal life on the throne of the universe, and see bathed in it the living dead in Christ!

God has taken them to Himself, and we ought not to think (if we would think as the Bible speaks) of death as being anything else than the transitory thing which breaks down the brazen walls and lets us into liberty. For, indeed, if you will examine the New Testament on this subject, I think you will be surprised to find how very seldom—scarcely ever—the word 'death' is employed to express the mere fact of the dissolution of the connection between soul and body. It is strange, but significant, that the Apostles, and Christ Himself, so rarely use the word to express that which we exclusively mean by it. They use all manner of other expressions as if they felt that the *fact* remains, but that all that made it death has gone away. In a real sense, and all the more real because the external fact continues, Christ 'hath abolished death.' Two men may go down to the grave together: of one this may be the epitaph, 'He that believeth in Christ shall never die'; and of the other—passing through precisely the same physical experience and appearance, the dissolution of soul and body, we may say,—'There, that is death—death as God sent it, to be the punishment of man's sin.' The outward fact remains the same, the whole inner character of it is altered. As to them that believe, though they have passed through the experience of painful separation—slow, languishing departure, or suddenly being caught up in some chariot of fire; not only are they living now, but they never died at all! Have you understood 'death' in the full, pregnant sense of the expression, which means not only that *shadow*, the separation of the body from the soul; but that *reality*, the separation of the soul from life, because of the separation of the soul from God?

Then, secondly, this text, indeed the whole incident, may set before us the other consideration that since they have died, they live a better life than ours.

357

I am not going to enter here, at any length, or very particularly, into what seem to me to be the irrefragable scriptural grounds for holding the complete, uninterrupted, and even intensified consciousness of the soul of man, in the interval between death and the Resurrection. 'Absent from the body, present with the Lord.' 'This day shalt thou be with Me in Paradise.' These words, if there were none other, are surely enough; seeing that of all that dark region we know only what it pleases God to tell us in the Bible, and seeing that it does not please Him to give us more than hints and glimpses of any part of it. But putting aside all attempts to elaborate a full doctrine of the intermediate state from the few Scripture expressions that bear on it, I merely allege, in general terms, that the present life of departed saints is fuller and nobler than that which they possessed on earth. They are even now, whatever be the details of their condition, 'the spirits of just men made perfect.' As yet the body is not glorified—but the spirits of the perfected righteous are now parts of that lofty society whose head is Christ, whose members are the angels of God, the saints on earth and the equally conscious redeemed who 'sleep in Jesus.'

In what particulars is their life now higher than it was? First, they have close fellowship with Christ; then, they are separated from this present body of weakness, of dishonour, of corruption; then, they are withdrawn from all the trouble, and toil, and care of this present life; and then, and not least surely, they have death behind them, not having that awful figure standing on their horizon waiting for them to come up with it. These are some of the elements of the life of the sainted dead. What a wondrous advance on the life of earth they reveal if we think of them! They are closer to Christ; they are delivered from the body, as a source of weakness; as a hinderer of knowledge; as a dragger–down of all the aspiring tendencies of the soul; as a source of sin; as a source of pain. They are delivered from all the necessity of labour which is agony, of labour which is disproportionate to strength, of labour which often ends in disappointment, of labour which is wasted so often in mere keeping life in, of labour which at the best is a curse, though it be a merciful curse too. They are delivered from that 'fear of death' which, though it be stripped of its sting, is never extinguished in any soul of man that lives; and they can smile at the way in which that narrow and inevitable passage bulked so large before them all their days, and after all, when they came to it, was so slight and small! If these are parts of the life of them that 'sleep in Jesus,' if they are fuller of knowledge, fuller of wisdom, fuller of love and capacity of love, and object of love; fuller of holiness, fuller of energy, and yet full of rest from head to foot; if all the hot tumult of earthly experience is stilled and quieted, all the fever beating of this blood of ours for ever at an end; all the 'slings and arrows of outrageous fortune' done with for ever, and if the calm face which we looked last upon, and out of which the lines of sorrow, and pain, and sickness melted away, giving it a nobler nobleness than we had ever seen upon it in life, is only an image of the restful and more blessed being into which they have passed,—if the dead are thus, then 'Blessed are the dead!'

No wonder that one aspect of that blessedness—the '*sleeping* in Jesus'—has been the one that the weary have laid hold of at all times; but do not let us forget what lies even in that figure of sleep, or distort it as if it meant to express a less vivid life than that here below. I think we sometimes misunderstand what the Bible means when it speaks about death as a sleep, by taking it to express the idea that that intermediate state is one of a kind of depressed consciousness, and of a less full vitality than the present. Not so. Sleep is rest, that is one reason for the scriptural application of the word to death. Sleep is the cessation of all connection with the external world, that is another reason. As we play with the names of those that are familiar to us, so a loving faith can venture to play, as it were, with the awful name of Him who is King of Terrors, and to minimise it down to that shadow and reflection of itself which we find in the nightly act of going to rest. That may be another reason. But sleep is not unconsciousness; sleep does not touch the spirit. Sleep sets us free from relations to the outer world but the soul works as hard, though in a different way, when we slumber as when we wake. People who know what it is to dream, ought never to fancy that when the Bible talks about death as sleep, it means to say to us that death is unconsciousness. By no means. Strip the man of the disturbance that comes from a fevered body, and he will have a calmer soul. Strip him of the hindrances that come from a body which is like an opaque tower around his spirit, with only a narrow slit here and a narrow door there—five poor senses, with which he can come into connection with an outer universe; and, then surely, the spirit will have wider avenues out to God, and larger powers of reception, because it has lost the earthly tabernacle which, just in proportion as it brought the spirit into connection with the earth to which the tabernacle belongs, severed its connection with the heavens that are above. They who have died in Christ live a fuller and a nobler life, by the very dropping away of the body; a fuller and a nobler life, by the very cessation of care, change, strife and struggle; and, above all, a fuller and nobler life, because they 'sleep *in Jesus,*' and are gathered into His bosom, and wake with Him yonder beneath the altar, clothed in white robes, and with palms in their hands, 'waiting the adoption—to wit, the redemption of the body.' For though death be a progress—a progress to the spiritual existence; though death be a birth to a higher and nobler state; though it be the gate of life, fuller and better than any which we possess; though the present state of the departed in Christ is a state of calm blessedness, a state of perfect communion, a state of rest and satisfaction;—yet it is not the final and perfect state, either.

And, therefore, in the last place, the better life, which the dead in Christ are living now, leads on to a still fuller life when they get back their glorified bodies.

The perfection of man is body, soul, and spirit. That is man, as God made him. The spirit perfected, the soul perfected, without the bodily life, is but part of the whole. For the future world, in all its glory, we have the firm basis laid that it, too, is to be in a real sense a material world, where men once more are to possess bodies as they did before, only bodies through which the spirit shall work conscious of no disproportion, bodies which shall be fit servants and adequate organs of the immortal souls within, bodies which shall never break down, bodies which shall never hem in nor refuse to obey the spirits that dwell in them, but which shall add to their power, and deepen their blessedness, and draw them closer to the God whom they serve and the Christ after the likeness of whose glorious body they are fashioned and conformed. 'Body, soul, and spirit,' the old combination which was on earth, is to be the perfect humanity of heaven. The spirits that are perfected, that are living in blessedness, that are dwelling in God, that are sleeping in Christ, at this moment are waiting, stretching out (I say, not longing, but) expectant hands of faith and hope; for that they would not be unclothed, but clothed upon with their house which is from heaven, that mortality might be swallowed up of life.

We have nothing to say, now and here, about what that bodily condition may be—about the differences and the identities between it and our present earthly house of this tabernacle. Only *this* we know—reverse all the weakness of flesh, and you get some faint notion of the glorious body. It is sown in corruption, dishonour, and weakness. It is raised in incorruption, glory, and power. Nay, more, it is sown a natural body, fit organ for the animal life or nature, which stands connected with this material universe; 'it is raised a spiritual body,' fit servant for the spirit that dwells in it, that works through it, that is perfected in its redemption.

Why, then, seek the living among the dead? 'God giveth His beloved sleep'; and in that peaceful sleep, realities, not dreams, come round their quiet rest, and fill their conscious spirits and their happy hearts with blessedness and fellowship. And when thus lulled to sleep in the arms of Christ they have rested till it please Him to accomplish the number of His elect, then, in His own time, He will make the eternal morning to dawn, and the hand that kept them in their slumber shall touch them into waking, and shall clothe them when they arise according to the body of His own glory; and they looking into His face, and flashing back its love, its light, its beauty, shall each break forth into singing as the rising light of that unsetting day touches their transfigured and immortal heads, in the triumphant thanksgiving 'I am satisfied, for I awake in Thy likeness.'

'Therefore, comfort one another with these words,' and remember that *we* are of the day, not of the night; let us not, then, sleep as do others; but let us reckon that Christ hath died for us, that whether we wake on earth or sleep in the grave, or wake in heaven, we may live together with Him!

THE RISEN LORD'S SELF–REVELATION TO WAVERING DISCIPLES

'And, behold, two of them went that same day to a village called Emmaus, which was from Jerusalem about threescore furlongs. 14. And they talked together of all these things which had happened. 15. And it came to pass, that, while they communed together and reasoned, Jesus Himself drew near, and went with them. 16. But their eyes were holden that they should not know Him. 17. And He said unto them, What manner of communications are these that ye have one to another, as ye walk, and are sad? 18. And the one of them, whose name was Cleopas, answering said unto Him, Art Thou only a stranger in Jerusalem, and hast not known the things which are come to pass there in these days? 19. And He said unto them, What things? And they said unto Him, Concerning Jesus of Nazareth, which was a prophet mighty in deed and word before God and all the people: 20. And how the chief priests and our rulers delivered Him to be condemned to death, and have crucified Him. 21. But we trusted that it had been He which should have redeemed Israel: and besides all this, to–day is the third day since these things were done. 22. Yea, and certain women also of our company made us astonished, which were early at the sepulchre; 23. And when they found not His body, they came, saying, that they had also seen a vision of angels,

which said that He was alive. 24. And certain of them which were with us went to the sepulchre, and found it even so as the women had said: but Him they saw not. 26. Then He said unto them, O fools, and slow of heart to believe all that the prophets have spoken: 26. Ought not Christ to have suffered these things, and to enter into His glory? 27. And beginning at Moses and all the prophets, He expounded unto them in all the scriptures the things concerning Himself. 28. And they drew nigh unto the village, whither they went: and He made as though He would have gone further. 29. But they constrained Him, saying, Abide with us: for it is toward evening, and the day is far spent. And He went in to tarry with them. 30. And it came to pass, as He sat at meat with them, He took bread, and blessed it, and brake, and gave to them. 31. And their eyes were opened, and they knew Him; and He vanished out of their sight. 32 And they said one to another, Did not our heart burn within us, while He talked with us by the way and while He opened to us the scriptures?'
—LUKE xxiv. 13–32.

These two disciples had left their companions after Peter's return from the sepulchre and before Mary Magdalene hurried in with her tidings that she had seen Jesus. Their coming away at such a crisis, like Thomas's absence that day, shows that the scattering of the sheep was beginning to follow the smiting of the shepherd. The magnet withdrawn, the attracted particles fall apart. What arrested that process? Why did not the spokes fall asunder when the centre was removed? John's disciples crumbled away after his death. When Theudas fell, all his followers 'were dispersed' and came to nought. The Church was knit more closely together after the death that, according to all analogy, should have scattered it. Only the fact of the Resurrection explains the anomaly. No reasonable men would have held together unless they had known that their Messianic hopes had not been buried in Christ's grave. We see the beginnings of the Resurrection of these hopes in this sweet story.

I. We have first the two sad travellers and the third who joins them. Probably the former had left the group of disciples on purpose to relieve the tension of anxiety and sorrow by walking, and to get a quiet time to bring their thoughts into some order. They were like men who had lived through an earthquake; they were stunned, and physical exertion, the morning quiet of the country, and the absence of other people, would help to calm their nerves, and enable them to realise their position. Their tone of mind will come out more distinctly presently. Here it is enough to note that the 'things which had come to pass' filled their minds and conversation. That being so, they were not left to grope in the dark. 'Jesus Himself drew near, and went with them.' Honest occupation of mind with the truth concerning Him, and a real desire to know it, are not left unhelped. We draw Him to our sides when we wish and try to grasp the real facts concerning Him, whether they coincide with our prepossessions or not.

It is profoundly interesting and instructive to note the characteristics of the favoured ones who first saw the risen Lord. They were Mary, whose heart was an altar of flaming and fragrant love; Peter, the penitent denier; and these two, absorbed in meditation on the facts of the death and burial. What attracts Jesus? Love, penitence, study of His truth. He comes to these with the appropriate gifts for them, as truly—yea, more closely—as of old. Perhaps the very doubting that troubled them brought Him to their help. He saw that they especially needed Him, for their faith was sorely wounded. Necessity is as potent a spell to bring Jesus as desert. He comes to reward fixed and fervent love, and He comes, too, to revive it when tremulous and cold.

'Their eyes were holden,' says Luke; and similarly 'their eyes were opened' (ver. 31). He makes the reason for His not being recognised a subjective one, and his narrative affords no support to the theory of a change in our Lord's resurrection body. How often does Jesus still come to us, and we discern Him not! Our paths would be less lonely, and our thoughts less sad, if we realised more fully and constantly our individual share in the promise,' I am with you always.'

II. We have next the conversation (vs. 17–28). The unknown new–comer strikes into the dialogue with a question which, on some lips, would have been intrusive curiosity, and would have provoked rude retorts. But there was something in His voice and manner which unlocked hearts. Does He not still come close to burdened souls, and with a smile of love on His face and a promise of help in His tones, ask us to tell Him all that is in our hearts? 'Communications' told to Him cease to sadden. Those that we cannot tell to Him we should not speak to ourselves.

Cleopas naively wonders that there should be found a single man in Jerusalem ignorant of the things which had come to pass. He forgot that the stranger might know these, and not know that they were talking about them. Like the rest of us, he fancied that what was great to him was as great to everybody. What *could* be the subject of their talk but the one theme? The stranger assumes ignorance, in order to win to a full outpouring. Jesus wishes us to put all fears and doubts and shattered hopes into plain words to Him. Speech to Christ cleanses our bosoms of much perilous stuff. Before He speaks in answer we are lightened.

Very true to nature is the eager answer of the two. The silence once broken, out flows a torrent of speech, in which love and grief, disciples' pride in their Master, and shattered hopes, incredulous bewilderment and questioning wonder, are blended.

That long speech (vs. 19–24) gives a lively conception of the two disciples' state of mind. Probably it fairly represented the thought of all. We note in it the limited conception of Jesus as but a prophet, the witness to His miracles and teaching (the former being set first, as having more impressed their minds), the assertion of His universal appreciation by the 'people,' the charging of the guilt of Christ's death on 'our rulers,' the sad contrast between the officials' condemnation of Him and their own fond Messianic hopes, and the despairing acknowledgment that these were shattered.

The reference to 'the third day' seems to imply that the two had been discussing the meaning of our Lord's frequent prophecy about it. The connection in which they introduce it looks as if they were beginning to understand the prophecy, and to cherish a germ of hope in His Resurrection, or, at all events, were tossed about with uncertainty as to whether they dared to cherish it. They are chary of allowing that the women's story was true; naively they attach more importance to its confirmation by men. 'But Him they saw not,' and, so long as He did not appear, they could not believe even angels saying 'that He was alive.'

The whole speech shows how complete was the collapse of the disciples' Messianic hopes, how slowly their minds opened to admit the possibility of Resurrection, and how exacting they were in the matter of evidence for it, even to the point of hesitating to accept angelic announcements. Such a state of mind is not the soil in which hallucinations spring up. Nothing but the actual appearance of the risen Lord could have changed these sad, cautious unbelievers to lifelong confessors. What else could have set light to these rolling smoke-clouds of doubt, and made them flame heaven-high and world-wide?

'The ingenuous disclosure of their bewilderment appealed to their Companion's heart, as it ever does. Jesus is not repelled by doubts and perplexities, if they are freely spoken to Him. To put our confused thoughts into plain words tends to clear them, and to bring Him as our Teacher. His reproach has no anger in it, and inflicts no pain, but puts us on the right track for arriving at the truth. If these two had listened to the 'prophets,' they would have understood their Master, and known that a divine 'must' wrought itself out in His Death and Resurrection. How often, like them, do we torture ourselves with problems of belief and conduct of which the solution lies close beside us, if we would use it?

Jesus claimed 'all the prophets' as His witnesses. He teaches us to find the highest purpose of the Old Testament in its preparation for Himself, and to look for foreshadowings of His Death and Resurrection there. What gigantic delusion of self-importance that was, if it was not the self-attestation of the Incarnate Word, to whom all the written word pointed! He will still, to docile souls, be the Interpreter of Scripture. They who see Him in it all are nearer its true appreciation than those who see in the Old Testament everything but Him.

III. We have finally the disclosure and disappearance of the Lord. The little group must have travelled slowly, with many a pause on the road, while Jesus opened the Scriptures; for they left the city in the morning, and evening was near before they had finished their 'threescore furlongs' (between seven and eight miles). His presence makes the day's march seem short.

'He made as though He would have gone further,' not therein assuming the appearance of a design which He did not really entertain, but beginning a movement which He would have carried out if the disciples' urgency had not detained Him. Jesus forces His company on no man. He 'would have gone further' if they had not said 'Abide with us.' He will leave us if we do not keep Him. But He delights to be held by beseeching hands, and our wishes 'constrain' Him. Happy are they who, having felt the sweetness of walking with Him on the weary road, seek Him to bless their leisure and to add a more blissful depth of repose to their rest!

The humble table where Christ is invited to sit, becomes a sacred place of revelation. He hallows common life, and turns the meals over which He presides into holy things. His disciples' tables should be such that they dare ask their Lord to sit at them. But how often He would be driven away by luxury, gross appetite, trivial or malicious talk! We shall all be the better for asking ourselves whether we should like to invite Jesus to our tables. He is there, spectator and judge, whether invited or not.

Where Jesus is welcomed as guest He becomes host. Perhaps something in gesture or tone, as He blessed and brake the bread, recalled the loved Master to the disciples' minds, and, with a flash, the glad 'It is He!' illuminated their souls. That was enough. His bodily presence was no longer necessary when the conviction of His risen life was firmly fixed in them. Therefore He disappeared. The old unbroken companionship was not to be resumed. Occasional appearances, separated by intervals of absence, prepared the disciples gradually for doing without His visible presence.

If we are sure that He has risen and lives for ever, we have a better presence than that. He is gone from our sight that He may be seen by our faith. That 'now we see Him not' is advance on the position of His first disciples, not retrogression. Let us strive to possess the blessing of 'those who have not seen, and yet have believed.'

DETAINING CHRIST

'And they drew nigh unto the village, whither they
went: and He made as though He would have gone further.
29. But they constrained Him, saying, Abide with us:
for it is toward evening, and the day is far spent.
And He went in to tarry with them.'—LUKE xxiv. 28, 29.

Of course, a chance companion, picked up on the road, is dropped when the journey's end is reached. When these two disciples had come to Emmaus, perhaps arriving at some humble inn or caravanserai, or perhaps at the home of one of them, it would have been an unmannerly intrusion for the Stranger who had met them on the road, and could accompany them there without rudely forcing Himself on them, to have inflicted His company further on them unless they had wished it. And so 'He made as though He would have gone further,' not pretending what He did not mean, but doing what was but natural and proper in the circumstances. But Jesus had a further motive for showing His intention of parting company at the door of t he house in Emmaus. He desired to evoke the expression of the desire of His two fellow–walkers that He should tarry with them. Having evoked it, then with infinite willingness omnipotence lets itself be controlled by feebleness, and Jesus suffers Himself to be constrained by those whom, unknown to themselves, He was gently and mightily constraining. 'He *made as though,' unfortunately suggests to an English reader the idea of acting a part, and of seeming to intend what was not really intended. But there is no such thought in Luke's mind.*

The first suggestion that strikes one from this incident is just this: Jesus Christ will certainly leave us if we do not detain Him.

It is no more certain that that walk to Emmaus had its end, and that that first day of the week, day of Resurrection though it was, was destined to close in sunset and evening darkness, than that all seasons of quickened intercourse with Jesus Christ, all times when duty and grace and privilege seem to be very great and real, all times when we awake more than ordinarily to the recognition of the Presence of the Lord with us and of the glories that lie beyond, tend to end and to leave us bare and deprived of the vision, unless there be on our parts a distinct and resolute effort to make perpetual that which in its nature is transient and comes to a close, unless we avert its cessation. All motion tends to rest, and Christian feeling falls under the same law. Nay, the more thrilling the moment's experience the more exhausting is it, and the more certain to be followed by depression and collapse. 'Action and reaction are equal and contrary.' The height of the wave determines the depth of the trough. Therefore Christian people have to be specially careful towards the end of a time of special vitality and earnestness; because, unless they by desire and by discipline of their minds interpose, the natural result will be deadness in proportion to the previous excitement. 'He made as though He would have gone further,' and He certainly will unless His retreating skirts be grasped at by the outstretched hands of faith and desire, and the prayer go after Him, 'Abide with us for it is toward evening.'

That is quite true, too, in another application of the incident. Convictions, spiritual experiences of a rudimentary sort, certainly die away and leave people harder and worse than they were before, unless they be fostered and cherished and brought to maturity and invested with permanence by the honest efforts of the subjects of the same. The grace of God, in the preaching of His Gospel, is like a flying summer shower. It falls upon one land and then passes on with its treasures and pours them out somewhere else. The religious history of many countries and of long centuries is a commentary written out in great and tragic characters on the profound truth that lies in the simple incident of my text. Look at Palestine, look at Asia Minor, at the places where the Gospel first won its triumphs; look at Eastern Europe. What is the present condition of these once fair lands but an illustration of this principle, that Christ who comes to men in His grace is kept only by the earnestness and faithfulness and desire of the men to whom He comes?

And you and I, dear brethren, both as members of a Christian community and in our individual capacity, have our religious blessings on the same conditions as Ephesus and Constantinople had theirs, and may fling them away by the same negligence as has ruined large tracts of the world through long ages of time. Christ will certainly go unless you keep Him.

Then further, notice from my text this other thought, that Christ seeks by His action to stimulate our desires for Him.

'He made as though He would have gone further.' But while His feet were directed to the road His heart remained with His two fellow–travellers whom He was apparently leaving, and His wish was that the sight of His retiring figure might kindle in their hearts great outgoings of desire to which He would so gladly yield. It is the same action on His part, only under a slightly different form, but actuated by the same motive and the same in substance, as we find over and over again in the gospels. You remember the instances. I need only refer to them in a word.

Here is one: the dark lake, the rising moon behind the Eastern hills, a figure coming out of the gloom across the stormy sea, and when He reached the tossing fishing cobble it seemed as if He would have passed by; and He would, but that the cry flung out over the dark water stopped Him.

Here are two blind men sitting by the roadside crying 'Thou Son of David, have mercy upon us.' Not a word, not even a glance over His shoulder, no stopping of His resolved stride; onwards towards Jerusalem, Pilate, and Calvary. Because He did not heed their cry? Because He did not infinitely long to help them? No. The purpose of His apparent indifference was attained when 'they cried the more earnestly, Thou Son of David, have mercy upon us.'

Here is another. A woman half mad with anguish for her demon-ridden daughter, calling after Him with the shrill shriek of Eastern sorrow and disturbing the fine nerves of the disciples, but causing no movements nor any sign that He even heard, or if He heard, heeded, the ear-piercing and heart-moving cries. Why was that ear which was always open to the call of misery closed now? Because He wished to bring her to such an agony of desire as might open her heart very wide for an amplitude of blessing; and so He let her cry, knowing that the longer she called the more she would wish, and that the more she wished the more He would bestow.

And that is what He does with us all sometimes: seeming to leave our wishes and our yearnings all unnoticed. Then the devil says to us, 'What's the use of crying to Him? He does not hear you.' But faith hears the promise: 'Open thy mouth wide and I will fill it,' though to sense there seems to be 'no voice nor any that answered.'

Christ has no other reason in any of the delays and trying prolongations of His answers than to make us capable of larger blessing, because delay deepens our longing. He is infinitely wishful to-day, as He was on that Resurrection evening, to draw near to every heart and pour upon it the whole sunlit cataract of the mighty fact that He lives to bless. But He cannot come to us unless we desire Him, and He cannot give to us more of Himself than we wish; and therefore He is obliged, as the first thing, to make our desires larger and fuller, and then He will answer them. 'He could there do no mighty works because of their unbelief.'

Our faithlessness limits His power; our faith is the measure of our capacity.

Lastly, the text reminds us that Jesus Christ is glad to be forced.

'They *constrained*': a very strong word, kindred to the other one which our Lord Himself employs when He speaks about the 'kingdom of heaven suffering violence, and the violent taking it by force.' That bold expression gives emphatic utterance to the truth that there is a real power lodged in the desires of humble hearts that desire Him, so as that they can prescribe to Him what He shall do for them and how much of Himself He shall give them. Our feebleness can in a measure set in motion and regulate the energy of Omnipotence. 'They constrained Him.'

Do you remember who it was that was called 'a prince with God' and how he won the title and was able to prevail? We, too, have the charter given to us that we can—I speak it reverently—guide God's hand and compel Omnipotence to bless us. We master Nature by yielding to it and utilising its energies. We have power with God by yielding to Him and conforming our desires to the longings of His heart and asking the things that are according to His will. 'Concerning the work of My hands *command* ye Me.' And what we, leaning on His promise and in unison with His mighty purpose of love, desire, *that* will as certainly come down to us as every stream must pour into the lowest levels and fill the depressions in its course.

You can make sure of Christ if two things are yours. He will always remain with us if, on the one hand, we wish for Him honestly and really to be with us all the day long, which would be extremely inconvenient for some of us; and if, on the other hand, we take care not to do the acts nor cultivate the tempers which drive Him away. For 'How can two walk together except they be agreed?' And how can we ask Him to come in and sit down in a house which is all full of filth and worldliness? Turn the demons out and open the door, and anything is more likely than that the door will stand gaping and the doorway be unfilled by the meek presence of the Christ that enters in.

The old prayer is susceptible of application to our community and to our individual hearts. When Israel prayed, 'Arise, O Lord, into Thy rest; Thou and the Ark of Thy strength,' the answer was prompt and certain. 'This is My rest for ever; here will I dwell, for I have desired it.' But the divine desire was not accomplished till the human desire opened the Temple gates for the entrance of the Ark.

'He made as though He would have gone further'; but they constrained Him, and then He entered in.

THE MEAL AT EMMAUS

'And it came to pass, as He sat at meat with them, He
took bread, and blessed it, and brake, and gave to
them. 31. And their eyes were opened, and they knew Him;
and He vanished out of their sight.'—LUKE xxiv. 30, 31.

Perhaps the most striking characteristic of the Gospel accounts of our Lord's intercourse with His disciples, in the interval between the Resurrection and His Ascension, is the singular union of mystery and simplicity which they present. There is a certain air of remoteness and depth over all the intercourse, as if it meant more, and was intended to teach more, than appears on the surface, as I believe it was intended. And yet, at the same time, there is, along with that, in most singular combination, the very utmost simplicity, amounting almost sometimes to baseness and rudeness, as for instance, here. Some poor house of entertainment, possibly, at any rate, some poor man's house, in a little country village; the company these two talkative, and yet despondent disciples; the fare and the means of manifestation a bit of barley–bread; and out of these materials are woven lessons that will live in the Church in all ages. 'He took bread and blessed it, and brake.' These are the words, almost verbatim, of the institution of the Lord's Supper. They are the words, almost verbatim, with which more than one of the Evangelists describes the miraculous feeding of the four and the five thousand; and it was the old familiar act, expressed by the Evangelist by the old familiar words, that opened the disciples' eyes, and they knew Him. How simply the process of discovery is told! It was quite natural that a casual stranger upon the road should not say who He was; it was quite as natural that when He entered into the closer relationship of sitting with the disciples at the table, and sharing their hospitality, they should expect, as indeed they did expect, that as they had been frank with Him, He would be frank with them, and they would find out now who this unknown teacher and apparent Rabbi was. And so, as it would seem, in silence, or at least with nothing of any moment, the meal went on, but all at once, at some point in the meal, the guest assumes the position of the master of the house, takes upon Himself the function and office of host, interrupts the progress of the meal by the solemn prayer of blessing; and whilst the singularity of the action drew their attention, perhaps some little peculiarity in His way of doing it, or something else, opened the door for a whole stream of associations and half–dormant remembrances to rush in, and they remembered what they had heard of the last supper,—for these two were not at it,—and they remembered what they had seen,—miraculous feedings; and they remembered no doubt how He had always done with them in the happy old days when He communed with them. At all events, by the natural action of breaking the bread and sharing it amongst them, the subjective hindrances which had stood in the way of their recognising Him dropped away like scales from their eyes, and they beheld Him, and then, without a word, He vanished out of their sight, and the wearied, hungry men girded up their loins and rushed back to Jerusalem to tell the brethren the story.

Now, I think that, taking the event as it stands before us, and especially marking the obviously intended parallelism in expression, and I hare no doubt in action, between former miracles, the institution of the Lord's Supper, and this neither sacramental nor religious meal in the little village—I think we may get some lessons worth pondering.

I confine myself quite simply to the three points of the narrative:—

  The distribution of the bread;
  The discovery;
  And the disappearance.

'He took bread and blessed it, and brake and gave to them, and their eyes were opened, and they knew Him; and He vanished out of their sight.'

I. Look, then, for a moment or two at the thoughts which I think are intended to be conveyed to us by that first point—the action of breaking and distributing the bread.

I have said, incidentally, in my previous remarks, that there is a singular air of remoteness, removedness, mystery, reticence, about our Lord's relations to His disciples in the interval of these forty days; and I suppose that that change from the frankness of His former relations and the close contact in which the Apostles and disciples had been brought during all the previous three years—I suppose that that was intended to be the beginning of the preparation of weaning and preparing them to do without Him altogether. And along with that removedness, there is also, as I take it, and as I have already said, a great depth of significance about the whole of these events which lead people to deal with them as being symbols, types, exhibitions on a material platform of great spiritual truths; and although the habit of finding symbolical meaning in historical events, especially as applied to the Gospels, has been full of all manner of mischief, yet that there is that element is not to be denied; and whilst we have to keep it down and be very careful in our application of it, lest in finding ingenious fanciful meanings, we lose the plain prose, which is always the best and the most important, yet that element is there, and we have to take heed that we do not push the denial of it to excess, as the recognition of it has often been pushed. And so, from these two points of view. I think the thing should be looked at. The plain prose, then, of the matter is this—that at a given point in this humble road–side meal, our Lord having been guest, having been constrained to enter in by the loving importunity of these people, becomes the host, takes upon Himself the position of the head of the household, and in that position so acts as to bring to the disciples' remembrance former deeds of miracles, and the institution of the ordinance of the Lord's Supper, and that was the means of their recognition.

Well, then, if so, I think that we may say fairly that in this breaking and distribution of the bread, there is first of all this lesson—the old familiar blessed intercourse between Him and them had not been put an end to then by all that had passed during these three mysterious days; but they were as they used to be in regard to the closeness of their relationship and the reality of their intercourse. No doubt, in the former years, Christ had been in the habit of always acting as the Head of the little family. When they gathered for their frugal meals, He was the master, they the disciples; He the elder brother, and they gathered about Him. And He assumes the old position; and if we will try for a moment to throw ourselves into their position and to see with their eyes, we shall understand the pathetic beauty—I was going to say the poetic beauty, but perhaps you would not like that word to be applied to the history of our Redeemer—the pathetic beauty of the deed. They had been thinking of themselves as forsaken of Him; the grave had broken off all their sweet and blessed intercourse; they were alone now. 'We trusted that it had been He which should have redeemed Israel.' He is gone! Even the poor consolation of looking upon the place where He lies is denied us; for whatever may be doubtful this is certain, that the grave is open and the body is not there. And so they felt lost and scattered; and there comes to them this gleam of consolation—I take my place amongst you just as I used to do; 'I am He that liveth and was dead, and behold, I am alive for evermore.' We used to sit together at the table; let that be repeated here once more that you may learn, and all the world through you may learn, that the accident of death, which affects only the externals of society, has no power over the reality of the bond that knits even two human hearts with love together, still less a power over the reality of the bond that binds us to our Master. Death vanishes as a nothing in their intercourse; they stand where they were; the fellowship is unbroken; the society is the same; all that there used to be of love and friendship, of peaceful concord, of true association; it abides for ever!

Thus, heavy with meaning and full of immortal hope may be the simplest act wrought with the simplest materials, when the dead Christ who lives takes His old place in the midst of His disciples, and once again as He used to do, parts the bread between them. And, dear brethren, though it has nothing to do with my present purpose, may this thought not add a wider application to our text; may it not be a comfort and hope to many of us to remember that the grim shadow that stretches athwart our path, and gathers into its blackness so many of our sunny sparkling joys, and takes the light and the movement and the colour out of them, is only a shadow, and that the substance lives in the shadow as it used to live in the sunshine, and passes through the shadow and comes out on the other side, blazing in more than its former lustre, and rich with more than its former preciousness? For all whom we have loved and lost, the death which was a nothing in regard to Christ's intercourse with His disciples, is a nothing, too, in regard to our real intercourse and sense of society and unity with them. They live in Him, and they are more worthy to be loved than ever they were before. He who has conquered Death for Himself has conquered it for us all; and every true and pure human affection rooted in Him is as immortal as the love that binds souls to Himself. Therefore, let us remember that they sit at His table, and that we shall sit there some day too.

II. Well, then, still further, another idea that I think belongs to this first part of our thoughts as to the profound significance of our Lord's here assuming the office and function of host, is this—we are thereby taught the same lesson that we are taught by His institution of the Communion, and taught by the whole details of His relation to His disciples upon earth—that the true idea of the relation which results from Him and His Presence is that of the Family.

He takes His place at the head of the table; He is the Lord of the household, though it be but a

369

household of two men, and they belong to the family and the society which He founds. Now it seems to me that next to the great lesson which the Lord's Supper teaches us in reference to our individual dependence upon Him, His death as being all our hope and all our life, this is the most important lesson that it teaches—the simplicity of the rite, the fact that it was based upon the Jewish rite, which was a purely domestic one; the fact that our Lord steps into the place of the head of the household by His very presiding at the Passover service amongst His disciples; the fact that He parts the common materials of the common meal and uses them and it as the symbols of His death, and of our life thereby—all that teaches us the same thing which the whole strain of His teaching and the whole strain of the New Testament sets forth—that the Church of Christ is then understood when we think of it as being one family in Him, bound together by the bands of a close brotherhood, relying upon Him as the fountain of its life; having fellowship with one Father through that elder Brother; pledged, therefore, to all fraternal kindness and frankness of communion and of mutual help, and gladdened by the hope of journeying onwards to Him. We cannot, of course, apply the analogy round and round; but of all the forms of human association which Christ has honoured and glorified by laying His hand upon them, and showing that they are symbols of the society that He founds, and of which He is the centre, it is not the kingdom, but the family that is the nearest approach to the Church of the living God.

And you and I, Christian men and women, if we come and sit at that table of our Lord, let us remember that we thereby declare, not only for ourselves that we enter into individual relations of reliance upon Him, and draw our life from Him, but that we pledge ourselves to the family bond, to be true to the brotherhood, that we declare ourselves the sons of God and the brethren of all that are partakers of the like precious faith. The thing has become a word, a name amongst us. I wonder if any of you remember the bitter saying of one of our modern teachers; he says that he found out somehow or other how much less 'brethren' in the Church meant than 'brothers' out of it. Let us learn the lesson and take the rebuke, and remember that if the Lord's Supper means anything, it means that we belong to the household of faith, and are members of the great family in heaven and in earth.

III. Well, then, still further connected with this first idea of the lesson and significance of the distribution of the bread, I think we may take another consideration, which is, in fact, only another application of the one I have already been suggesting—Where Christ is invited as a guest, He becomes the host.

They constrained Him to abide with them; they made Him welcome to their rude hospitality. It was little—a hut where poor men lay, a bit of barley–bread. But it was theirs, and they gave it Him; and He entered in and supped with them, and then, in the middle of it, the relations were inverted, and they that had been showing the hospitality became the guests, and the table that had been theirs became His. 'And He took the bread and gave it to them.' You have the same inversion of relation in that first miracle that He wrought at Cana of Galilee, where invited as a guest, at a point in the entertainment He provides the supplies for the further conduct of it. You remember the words which contain the spiritual application of the same thought—'Behold, I stand at the door and knock. If any man open the door, I will enter in and sup with him and he with Me.' To put away the metaphor, it amounts to this—our Master never comes empty–handed. Where He is invited, He comes to bestow; where He is welcomed, He comes with His gifts; where we say, 'Do Thou take what I offer,' He says, 'Do thou take Myself.' All His requirements are veiled promises; all His commandments are assurances of His gifts. He bestows that He may receive; He seems to take that He may enrich. They that give to Christ receive back again more than all that they gave, according to the profound words, 'There is no man that hath left father or mother, or wife or children, or houses or lands, for My sake and the Gospel's, but shall receive a hundredfold more in this life, and in the world to come life everlasting.' The Christ that is asked to come in order to receive, abides in order to bestow.

And then there is a second point, going on with the flow of this little narrative before us, about which a word or two may be said. The consequence of this assumption of the position of master, host, bestower is—'Their eyes were opened, and they knew Him.' The discovery of His person follows on the distribution of His gifts.

Now, there is one point to be remarked before I deal with the lessons which I think are capable of being gathered from this part of our subject, and that is, that this narrative gives no sort of support, as it seems to me, to the ordinary notion that, subsequent to the Resurrection, there had passed upon our Lord's corporeal frame any change whatsoever as the commencement of the glorification of His earthly body. If you observe, the course of the narrative takes pains to point out to us distinctly, that whatever may have been the reason why they did not recognise Him at first, that reason was entirely in them, and not at all in Him. It is not that He was changed; it is that 'their eyes were holden'; and when they did recognise Him, it is not that any change whatsoever is recorded as having passed upon Him, but 'their eyes were opened, and they knew Him.' And the same thing may be said, as I believe, about the whole of the appearances, mysterious as they were, of our Lord, in the interval between the Resurrection and the Ascension. I do not think, for my part, (although I would by no means speak with confidence about a matter that is so fragmentarily dealt with in Scripture), but I do not think, for my part, that the narrative gives any support whatsoever to the idea of any change analogous to that which takes place upon us at our resurrection, having begun to take place upon our Lord so long as He remained upon earth. The Ascension and the Resurrection of Jesus Christ, in His case, are parts of one process. He was raised with the body with which He was crucified; He ascended up on high, and there the glorification, as far as Scripture teaches, is, I conceive, commenced. At all events, there is nothing in our narrative to support the idea of an incipient transformation having begun with the Resurrection.

But, passing by that, which has nothing to do with my main present purpose, I may notice just one or two considerations in reference to this discovery of our Lord. And the first and main one that I would suggest is this—Where Christ is loved and desired, the veriest trifles of common life may be the means of His discovery. We know not what was the special point which brought dormant remembrance to life again, and quickened the associations of the two, so that they knew Jesus; even as we do not know what was the hindrance, whether supernatural or whether by reason of their own fault, which prevented the earlier recognition; but this at least we see, that in all probability something in the manner of taking the bread and breaking it, the well–remembered action of the Master, brought back to mind the whole of the former relation, and a rush of associations and memories pulled away the veil and scaled off the mists from their eyes. And so, dear brethren, if we have loving, and waiting, and Christ–desiring spirits, everything in this world—the common meal, the events of every day, the most veritable trifles of our earthly relationships—they will all have hooks and barbs, as it were, which will draw after them thoughts of Him. There is nothing so small but that to it there may be attached some filament which will bring after it the whole majesty and grace of Christ and His love. Whether ye eat or drink, or whatsoever ye do, do all in remembrance of Him, and do all to His glory. Oh, if we had in our inmost spirits a closer fellowship with Him, and a truer relation to Him, we should be more quick of apprehension. And, as in regard to those that we love, when they are away from us, the fold of a garment, some bit of cloth lying about the room, something upon the table, some common incident of the day that used to be done in company with them, may bring a flood of memories that sometimes is too strong for a weak heart, so with the Lord, if we loved Him—everything would be (as it is to those whose ears are purged) vocal with His name, and everything would be flushed with the light that falls from His face, and everything would suffice to remind us of our love, our hope, our joy. Especially let us remember that He has entrusted—with strange humility and with wonderful knowledge of us, and with the truest sympathy and tenderness for our weakness—He has entrusted a large portion of our most spiritual remembrance and recognition of Him to material things. Did it ever strike you what a depth of what I may call Christ's condescension there lay in this? 'Take this bread and this wine, and if you will not remember Me because I loved you so well, if you will not remember Me because I died for you, if earthly things and material realities will drive Me out of your thoughts, at least remember Me because and when earthly things and material realities become My agents and My memorials. If you forget the Cross, perhaps a bit of bread will remind you of Me; and I am not too proud to spurn the remembrance that roots itself even in the material things of earth and by such means as that.' 'He took the bread and brake it.' They had listened to all His words upon the road, and it never occurred to them who He was; they had walked beside Him all day long, and even their burning hearts did not make them suspect that it was the Master. It must needs be so—they whom wisdom and truth and His spiritual Presence cannot teach to recognise, may be led to recognise Him by the movement of His hands with the barley loaf, and some intonation of His voice in blessing it. 'This do in remembrance of Me' is the word of that deep pity that knows our frame and remembers that we are dust, and is a word of the most marvellous condescension that ever was uttered in human ears.

IV. And then there is the final consideration here upon which I touch but for a moment. The distribution and the discovery are followed by the disappearance of the Lord, 'They knew Him, and'—and what? And He let their hearts run over in thankful words? No. 'They knew Him,' and so they all went back to Jerusalem happy together? No. 'They knew Him, and—He vanished out of their sight.' Yes, for two reasons. First, because when Christ's Presence is recognised sense may be put aside. 'It is expedient for you that I go away.' You and I, dear brethren, need no visible manifestation; we have lost nothing though we have lost the bodily Presence of our Master. It is more than made up to us, as He Himself assures us, and as we shall see ourselves if we think for a moment, by the clearer knowledge of His spiritual verity and stature, by the deeper experience of the profounder aspects of His mission and message, by the indwelling Spirit, and by the knowledge of Him working evermore for us all. His going is a step in advance. 'If I go not away the Comforter will not come to you; but if I depart, I will send Him unto you.' The earthly manifestation was only the basis and the platform for that which is purer and deeper in kind, and more precious and powerful; and when the platform has been laid, then there is no need for the continuance thereof. And so, when He was manifested to the heart He disappeared from the eyes; and we, who have not beheld Him, stand upon no lower level than they who did, for the voice of our experience is, 'Whom having not seen we love; in whom, though now we see Him not, yet believing, we rejoice with joy that is unspeakable and full of glory.'

And for another reason.—When Christ is discerned there is work to be done. 'Their eyes were opened, and they knew Him, and He vanished out of their sight; and ... they rose up that same hour; and returned to Jerusalem' and said, He was known to us in breaking of bread, and He talked with us by the way. Yes, the vision of Christ binds us to work, and while the more close and intimate and silent communion has its rights and its place in life, it is never to be made a substitute for the active exercise of our Christian vocation to bear witness of Him, and to tell His name to those who need the consolation of His Resurrection, and the joyful news that He lives to bless. So then that meal by the wayside may stand as type and symbol of the way in which we, like the two pedestrians on the road and at the table, may have heart intercourse with Jesus, and may be impelled thereby to labour for Him.

There was another time, after the Resurrection, when in like manner we read that our Lord took bread, and blessed and brake and gave it to them; and that was in that mysterious meal upon the shores of the Galilean Lake, which has always been recognised as having a symbolical meaning—though the exposition and detail have often been exaggerated and made absurd. In the one case it was two travellers who met their Lord; it was in an inn that the recognition took place; it was a brief moment of vision, followed by disappearance, and the disappearance led on to work; but in the other story it was when the morning broke that the Lord was manifest; it was after the night of toil that His form appeared; His words to them were, 'Bring of the fruits of your labours and lay them upon the beach at My feet.' And in the light of the eternal morning, after the weary night of toil, they who on earth in their journey and pilgrimage have had Him walking with them as third in their sweet society, and sitting with them in the tents and changeful residences of earth, may expect to find Him waiting for them upon the shore; and, as one says, 'It is the Lord!' and another dashes through the water to reach Christ, the invitation to all of them will be, 'Come and sit with Me at My table in My kingdom; I provide the meal, and you add to it by that which you have caught.' 'They rest from their labours and their works do follow them.' And so 'they go no more out, but are ever with the Lord.'

PETER ALONE WITH JESUS

'The Lord is risen indeed, and hath appeared to Simon.'
—LUKE xxiv. 34.

The other appearances of the risen Lord to individuals on the day of Resurrection are narrated with much particularity, and at considerable length. John gives us the lovely account of our Lord's conversation with Mary Magdalene, Luke gives us in full detail the story of the interview with the two travellers on the road to Emmaus. Here is another appearance, known to 'the eleven, and them that were with them' on the Resurrection evening, and enumerated by Paul in his list of the appearances of the Lord, the account of which was the common gospel of himself and all the others, and yet deep silence is preserved in regard to it. No word escaped Peter's lips as to what passed in the conversation between the denier and his Lord. That is very significant.

The other appearances of the risen Lord to individuals on the day of Resurrection suggest their own reasons. He appeared first to Mary Magdalene because she loved much. The love that made a timid woman brave, and the sorrow that filled her heart, to the exclusion of everything else, drew Jesus to her. The two on the road to Emmaus were puzzled, honest, painful seekers after truth. It was worth Christ's while to spend hours of that day of Resurrection in clearing, questioning, and confirming sincere minds. Does not this other appearance explain itself? The brief spasm of cowardice and denial had changed into penitence when the Lord looked, and the bitter tears that fell were not only because of the denial, but because of the wound of that sharp arrow, the poisoned barb of which we are happy if we have not felt the thought—'He will never know how ashamed and miserable I am; and His last look was reproach, and I shall never see His face any more.' To respond to, and to satisfy, love, to clear and to steady thought, to soothe the agony of a penitent, were worthy works for the risen Lord. I venture to think that such a record of the use of such a day bears historical truth on its very face, because it is so absolutely unlike what myth−making or hallucination, or the excited imagination of enthusiasts would have produced, if these had been the sources of the story of the Resurrection. But apart from that, I wish in this sermon to try to gather the suggestions that come to us from this interview, and from the silence which is observed concerning them.

With regard to—

I. The fact of the appearance itself.

We can only come into the position rightly to understand its precious significance, if we try to represent to ourselves the state of mind of the man to whom it was granted. I have already touched upon that; let me, in the briefest possible way, recapitulate. As I have said, the momentary impulse to the cowardly crime passed, and left a melted heart, true penitence, and profound sorrow. One sad day slowly wore away. Early on the next came the message which produced an effect on Peter so great, that the gospel, which in some sense is his gospel (I mean that 'according to Mark') alone contains the record of it—the message from the open grave: 'Tell my disciples *and Peter* that I go before you into Galilee.' There followed the sudden rush to the grave, when the feet made heavy by a heavy conscience were distanced by the light step of happy love, and 'the other disciple did outrun Peter.' The more impulsive of the two dashed into the sepulchre, just as he afterwards threw himself over the side of the boat, and floundered through the water to get to his Lord's feet, whilst John was content with looking, just as he afterwards was content to sit in the boat and say, 'It is the Lord.' But John's faith, too, outran Peter's, and he departed 'believing,' whilst Peter only attained to go away 'wondering.' And so another day wore away, and at some unknown hour in it, Jesus stood before Peter alone.

What did that appearance say to the penitent man? Of course, it said to him what it said to all the rest, that death was conquered. It lifted his thoughts of his Master. It changed his whole atmosphere from gloom to sunshine, but it had a special message for him. It said that no fault, no denial, bars or diverts Christ's love. Peter, no doubt, as soon as the hope of the Resurrection began to dawn upon him, felt fear contending with his hope, and asked himself, 'If He is risen, will He ever speak to me again?' And now here He is with a quiet look on His face that says, 'Notwithstanding thy denial, see, I have come to thee.'

Ah, brethren! the impulsive fault of a moment, so soon repented of, so largely excusable, is far more venial than many of our denials. For a continuous life in contradiction to our profession is a blacker crime than a momentary fall, and they who, year in and year out, call themselves Christians, and deny their profession by the whole tenor of their lives, are more deeply guilty than was the Apostle, But Jesus Christ comes to us, and no sin of ours, no denial of ours, can bar out His lingering, His reproachful, and yet His restoring, love and grace. All sin is inconsistent with the Christian profession. Blessed be God; we can venture to say that no sin is incompatible with it, and none bars off wholly the love that pours upon us all. True; we may shut it out. True; so long as the smallest or the greatest transgression is unacknowledged and unrepented, it forms a non–conducting medium around us, and isolates us from the electric touch of that gracious love. But also true; it is there hovering around us, seeking an entrance. If the door be shut, still the knocking finger is upon it, and the great heart of the Knocker is waiting to enter. Though Peter had been a denier, because he was a penitent the Master came to him. No fault, no sin, cuts us off from the love of our Lord.

And then the other great lesson, closely connected with this, but yet capable of being treated separately for a moment, which we gather from the fact of the interview, is that Jesus Christ is always near the sorrowing heart that confesses its evil. He knew of Peter's penitence, if I might so say, in the grave; and, therefore, risen, His feet hasted to comfort and to soothe him. As surely as the shepherd hears the bleat of the lost sheep in the snowdrift, as surely as the mother hears the cry of her child, so surely is a penitent heart a magnet which draws Christ, in all His potent fullness and tenderness, to itself. He that heard and knew the tears of the denier, and his repentance, when in the dim regions of the dead, no less hears and knows the first faint beginnings of sorrow for sin, and bends down from His seat on the right hand of God, saying, 'I dwell in the high and holy place, with him also that is of a humble and contrite spirit, to revive the spirit of the humble, and to revive the heart of the contrite ones.' No fault bars Christ's love. Christ is ever near the penitent spirit; and whilst he is yet a great way off, He has compassion, and runs and falls on his neck and kisses him.

Now let us look at—

II. The interview of which we know nothing.

We know nothing of what did pass; we know what must have passed. There is only one way by which a burdened soul can get rid of its burden. There is only one thing that a conscience–stricken denier can say to his Saviour. And—blessed be God!—there is only one thing that a Saviour can say to a conscience–stricken denier. There must have been penitence with tears; there must have been full absolution and remission. And so we are not indulging in baseless fancies when we say that we know what passed in that conversation, of which no word ever escaped the lips of either party concerned. So then, with that knowledge, just let me dwell upon one or two considerations suggested.

One is that the consciousness of Christ's love, uninterrupted by our transgression, is the mightiest power to deepen penitence and the consciousness of unworthiness. Do you not think that when the Apostle saw in Christ's face, and heard from His lips, the full assurance of forgiveness, he was far more ashamed of himself than he had ever been in the hours of bitterest remorse? So long as there blends with the sense of my unworthiness any doubt about the free, full, unbroken flow of the divine love to me, my sense of my own unworthiness is disturbed. So long as with the consciousness of demerit there blends that thought—which often is used to produce the consciousness, viz., the dread of consequences, the fear of punishment—my consciousness of sin is disturbed. But sweep away fear of penalty, sweep away hesitation as to the divine love, then I am left face to face with the unmingled vision of my own evil, and ten thousand times more than ever before do I recognise how black my transgression has been; as the prophet puts it with profound truth, 'Thou shalt be ashamed and confounded, and never open thy mouth any more, because of thy sins, when I am pacified towards thee for all that thou hast done.' If you would bring a man to know how bad he is, do not brandish a whip before his face, or talk to him about an angry God. You may bray a fool in a mortar, and his foolishness will not depart from him. You may break a man down with these violent pestles, and you will do little more. But get him, if I may continue the metaphor, not into the mortar, but set him in the sunshine of the divine love, and that will do more than break, it will melt the hardest heart that no pestle would do anything but triturate. The great evangelical doctrine of full and free forgiveness through Jesus Christ produces a far more vital, vigorous, transforming recoil from transgression than anything besides. 'Do we make void the law through faith? God forbid! Yea, we establish the law.'

Then, further, another consideration may be suggested, and that is that the acknowledgment of sin is followed by immediate forgiveness. Do you think that when Peter turned to his Lord, who had come from the grave to soothe him, and said, 'I have sinned,' there was any pause before He said, 'and thou art forgiven'? The only thing that keeps the divine love from flowing into a man's heart is the barrier of unforgiven, because unrepented, sin. So soon as the acknowledgment of sin takes away the barrier—of course, by a force as natural as gravitation—the river of God's love flows into the heart. The consciousness of forgiveness may be gradual; the fact of forgiveness is instantaneous. And the consciousness may be as instantaneous as the fact, though it often is not. 'I believe in the forgiveness of sins'; and I believe that a man, that you, may at one moment be held and bound by the chains of sin, and that at the next moment, as when the angel touched the limbs of this very Apostle in prison, the chains may drop from off ankles and wrists, and the prisoner may be free to follow the angel into light and liberty. Sometimes the change is instantaneous, and there is no reason why it should not be an instantaneous change, experienced at this moment, by any man or woman among us. Sometimes it is gradual. The Arctic spring comes with a leap, and one day there is thick-ribbed ice, and a few days after there are grass and flowers. A like swift transformation is within the limits of possibility for any of us, and—blessed be God! within the experience of a good many of us. There is no reason why it should not be that of each of us, as well as of this Apostle.

Then there is one other thought that I would suggest, viz., that the man who is led through consciousness of sin and experience of uninterrupted love which is forgiveness, is thereby led into a higher and a nobler life. Peter's bitter fall, Peter's gracious restoration, were no small part of the equipment which made him what we see him in the days after Pentecost—when the coward that had been ashamed to acknowledge his Master, and all whose impulsive and self-reliant devotion passed away before a flippant servant-girl's tongue, stood before the rulers of Israel, and said: 'Whether it be right in the sight of God to hearken unto you more than unto God, judge ye!' The sense of sin, the assurance of pardon, shatter a man's unwholesome self-confidence, and develop his self-reliance based upon his trust in Jesus Christ. The consciousness of sin, and the experience of pardon, deepen and make more operative in life the power of the divine love. Thus, the publicans and the harlots do go into the Kingdom of God many a time before the Pharisees. So let us all be sure that even our sins and faults may be converted into stepping stones to higher things.

III. Lastly, notice the deep silence in which this interview is shrouded.

I have already pointed to the occupations of that Resurrection day as bearing on their face the marks of veracity. It seems to me that if the story of the Resurrection is not history, the talk between the denier and the Master would have been a great deal too tempting a subject for romancers of any kind to have kept their hands off. If you read the apocryphal gospels you will see how eager they are to lay hold of any point in the true gospels, and spin a whole farrago of rubbish round about it. And do you think they could ever have let this incident alone without spoiling it by expanding it, and putting all manner of vulgarities into their story about it? But the men who told the story were telling simple facts, and when they did not know anything they said nothing.

But why did not Peter say anything about it? Because nobody had anything to do with it but himself and his Master. It was his business, and no one else's. The other scene by the lake reinstated him in his office, and it was public because it concerned others also; but what passed when he was restored to his faith was of no concern to any one but the Restorer and the restored. And so, dear friends, a religion which has a great deal to say about its individual experiences is in very slippery places. The less you think about your emotions, and eminently the less you talk about them, the sounder, the truer, and the purer they will be. Goods in a shop-window get fly-blown very quickly, and lose their lustre. All the deep secrets of a man's life, his love for his Lord, the way by which he came to Him, his penitence for his sin, like his love for his wife, had better speak in deeds than in words to others. Of course while that is true on one side, we are not to forget the other side. Reticence as to the secret things of my own personal experience is never to be extended so as to include silence as to the fact of my Christian profession. Sometimes it is needful, wise, and Christlike for a man to lift the corner of the bridal curtain, and let in the day to some extent, and to say, 'Of whom I am chief, but I obtained mercy.' Sometimes there is no such mighty power to draw others to the faith which we would fain impart, as to say, 'Whether this Man be a sinner or no, I know not; but one thing I know, that whereas I was blind now I see.' Sometimes—always—a man must use his own personal experience, cast into general forms, to emphasise his profession, and to enforce his appeals. So very touchingly, if you will turn to Peter's sermons in the Acts, you will find that he describes himself there (though he does not hint that it is himself) when he appeals to his countrymen, and says, 'Ye denied the Holy One and the Just.' The personal allusion would make his voice vibrate as he spoke, and give force to the charge. Similarly, in the letter which goes by his name—the second of the two Epistles of Peter—there is one little morsel of evidence that makes one inclined to think that it is his, notwithstanding the difficulties in the way, viz., that he sums up all the sins of the false teachers whom he is denouncing in this: 'Denying the Lord that bought them.' But with these limitations, and remembering that the statement is not one to be unconditionally and absolutely put, let the silence with regard to this interview teach us to guard the depths of our own Christian lives.

Now, dear brethren, have you ever gone apart with Jesus Christ, as if He and you were alone in the world? Have you ever spread out all your denials and faults before Him? Have you ever felt the swift assurance of His forgiving love, covering over the whole heap, which dwindles as His hand lies upon it? Have you ever felt the increased loathing of yourselves which comes with the certainty that He has passed by all your sins? If you have not, you know very little about Christ, or about Christianity (if I may use the abstract word) or about yourselves; and your religion, or what you call your religion, is a very shallow and superficial and inoperative thing. Do not shrink from being alone with Jesus Christ. There is no better place for a guilty man, just as there is no better place for an erring child than its mother's bosom. When Peter had caught a dim glimpse of what Jesus Christ was, he cried: 'Depart from me, for I am a sinful man, O Lord!' When he knew his Saviour and himself better, he clung to Him because he was so sinful. Do the same, and He will say to you: 'Son, thy sins be forgiven thee;

Daughter, thy faith hath made thee whole. Go in peace, and be whole of thy plague.'

THE TRIUMPHANT END

'And as they thus spake, Jesus Himself stood in the
midst of them, and saith unto them, Peace be unto you.
37. But they were terrified and affrighted, and
supposed that they had seen a spirit. 38. And He said
unto them, Why are ye troubled? and why do thoughts
arise in your hearts? 39. Behold My hands and My feet,
that it is I Myself: handle Me, and see; for a spirit
hath not flesh and bones, as ye see Me have. 40. And
when He had thus spoken, He shewed them His hands and
His feet. 41. And while they yet believed not for joy,
and wondered, He said unto them, Have ye here any
meat? 42. And they gave Him a piece of a broiled fish,
and of an honeycomb. 43. And He took it, and did eat
before them. 44. And He said unto them, These are the
words which I spake unto you, while I was yet with
you, that all things must be fulfilled, which were
written in the law of Moses, and in the prophets, and
in the psalms, concerning Me. 45. Then opened He their
understanding, that they might understand the
scriptures, 46. And said unto them, Thus it is written,
and thus it behoved Christ to suffer, and to rise from
the dead the third day: 47. And that repentance and
remission of sins should be preached in His name among
all nations, beginning at Jerusalem. 48. And ye are
witnesses of these things. 49. And, behold, I send the
promise of My Father upon you: but tarry ye in the
city of Jerusalem, until ye be endued with power from
on high. 50. And He led them out as far as to Bethany;
and He lifted up His hands, and blessed them. 51. And
it came to pass, while He blessed them, He was parted
from them, and carried up into heaven. 52. And they
worshipped Him, and returned to Jerusalem with great
joy: 53. And were continually in the temple, praising
and blessing God.'—LUKE xxiv. 36–53.

There are no marks of time in this passage, and, for anything that appears, the narrative is continuous, and the Ascension might have occurred on the evening of the Resurrection. But neither is there anything to forbid interpreting this close of Luke's Gospel by the fuller details contained in the beginning of his other treatise, the Acts, where the space of forty days interposes between the Resurrection and the Ascension. It is but reasonable to suppose that an author's two books agree, when he gives no hint of change of opinion, and it is reasonable to regard the narrative in this passage as a summary of the whole period of forty days. If so, it contains three things,—the first appearance of the risen Lord to the assembled disciples (vs. 36–43), a condensed summary of the teachings of the risen Lord (vs. 44–49), and an equally compressed record of the Ascension (vs. 50–53).

I. The proofs of the Resurrection graciously granted to incredulous love (vs. 36–43). The disciples were probably assembled in the upper room, where the Lord's Supper had been instituted, and which became their ordinary meeting–place (Acts i.) up till Pentecost. What sights that room saw! There, when night had come, they were discussing the strange reports of the Resurrection, when, all suddenly, they saw Jesus, not coming or moving, but standing in the midst. Had He come in unnoticed by them in their eager talk? The doors were shut. How had this calm Presence become visible all at once?

So little were they the enthusiastic, credulous people whom modern theories which explain away the Resurrection assume them to have been, that even His familiar voice in His familiar salutation, tenfold more significant now than ever before, did not wake belief that it was verily He. They fled to the ready refuge of supposing that they saw 'a spirit.' Our Lord has no rebukes for their incredulity, but patiently resumes His old task of instruction, and condescends to let them have the evidence of two senses, not shrinking from their investigating touch. When even these proofs were seen by Him to be insufficient, He added the yet more cogent one of 'eating before them.' Then they were convinced.

Now their incredulity is important, and the acknowledgment shows the simple historical good faith of the narrator. A witness who at first disbelieved is all the more trustworthy. These hopeless mourners who had forgotten all Christ's prophecies of His Resurrection, and were so fixed in their despair that the two from Emmaus could not so far kindle a gleam of hope as to make them believe that their Lord stood before them, were not the kind of people in whom hallucination would operate, as modern deniers of the Resurrection make them out to have been. What changed their mood? A fancy? Surely nothing less than a solid fact. Hallucination may lay hold on a solitary, morbid mind, but it does not attack a company, and it scarcely reaches to fancying touch and the sight of eating.

Note Luke's explanation of the persistent incredulity, as being 'for joy.' It is like his notice that the three in Gethsemane 'slept for sorrow.' Great emotion sometimes produces effects opposite to what might have been expected. Who can wonder that the mighty fact which turned the black smoke of despair into bright flame should have seemed too good to be true? The little notice brings the disciples near to our experience and sympathy. Christ's loving forbearance and condescending affording of more than sufficient evidence show how little changed He was by Death and Resurrection. He is as little changed by sitting at the right hand of God. Still He is patient with our slow hearts. Still He meets our hesitating faith with lavish assurances. Still He lets us touch Him, if not with the hand of sense, with the truer contact of spirit, and we may have as firm personal experience of the reality of His life and Presence as had that wondering company in the upper room.

II. Verses 44–49 are best taken as a summary of the forty days' teaching. They fall into stages which are distinctly separated. First we have (ver. 44) the reiteration of Christ's earlier teaching, which had been dark when delivered, and now flashed up into light when explained by the event. 'These are my words which I spake,' and which you did not understand or note. Jesus asserts that He is the theme of all the ancient revelation. If we suppose that the present arrangement of the Old Testament existed then, its present three divisions are named; namely, Law, Prophets, and Hagiographa, as represented by its chief member. But, in any case, He lays His hand on the whole book, and declares that He, and His Death as sacrifice, are inwrought into its substance. 'The testimony of Jesus is the spirit of prophecy.' Whatever views we hold as to the date and manner of origin of the Old Testament books, we miss the most pregnant fact about them if we fail to recognise that they all point onwards to Him.

Another stage is marked by that remarkable expression, 'He opened their mind.' His teaching was not, like ours, from without only. He gave not merely instruction, but inspiration. It was not enough to spread truth before the disciples. He did more; He made them able to receive it. He gives no lesser gifts from the throne than He gave in the upper room, and we may receive, if our minds are kept expectant and in touch with Him, the same inward eye to see wondrous things out of the Word.

Verse 46, by its repetition of 'and He said,' seems to point to another stage, in which the teaching as to the meaning of the Old Testament passes into instructions for the future. Already Jesus had hinted at the cessation of the old close intercourse in that pathetic 'while I was yet with you,' and now He goes on to outline the functions and equipment of the disciples in the future period of His absence. As to the past sufferings, He indicates a double necessity for them,—one based on their having been predicted; another, deeper, based on the fitness of things. These sufferings made the preaching of repentance and forgiveness possible, and imposed on His followers the obligation of preaching His name to all the world. Without the Cross His servants would have no gospel. Having the Cross, His servants are bound to publish it everywhere.

The universal reach of His atonement is implied in the commission. The sacrifice for the world's sin is the sole ground of remission of sin, and is to be proclaimed to every creature. Mark that here the same word is employed in connection with proclaiming Christ's Death as in John's version of this saying (John xx. 23), which is misused as a fortress of the priestly power of absolution. The plain inference is that the servant's power of remission is exercised by preaching the Master's death of expiation.

The ultimate reach of the message is to be to all nations; the beginning of the universal gospel is to be at Jerusalem. The whole history of the world and the Church lies between these two. By that command to begin at Jerusalem, the connection of the Old with the New is preserved, the Jewish prerogative honoured, the path made easier for the disciples, the development of the Church brought into unison with their natural sentiments and capacities.

The spirit of the commandment remains still imperative. 'The eyes of a fool are in the ends of the earth.' A wise and Christlike beneficence will not gaze far afield, and neglect things close at our doors. The scoff at the supporters of foreign missions, as if they quixotically went abroad when they should work at home, has no point even as regards Christian practice, for it is the people who work for the distant heathen who also toil for home ones; but it has still less ground in regard to Christian conceptions of duty, for the Lord of the harvest has bidden the reapers begin with the fields nearest them.

The equipment for work is investiture with divine power. A partial bestowment of the Spirit, which is the Father's promise, took place while Jesus spoke. 'I send' refers to something done at the moment;

but the fuller clothing with that garment of power was to be waited for in expectancy and desire. No man can do the Christian work of witnessing for and of Christ without that clothing with power. It was granted as an abiding gift on Pentecost. It needs perpetual renewal. We may all have it. Without it, eloquence, learning, and all else, are but as sounding brass and a tinkling cymbal.

III. Verses 50–53 give us the transcendent miracle which closes the earthly life of Jesus. We cannot here enter on the large questions which it raises, but must content ourselves with simply pointing to the salient features of Luke's condensed account. The mention of the place as 'over against Bethany' recalls the many memories of that village where Jesus had found His nearest approach to a home, where He had exercised His stupendous life-giving power, whence He had set out to the upper room and the near Cross. His last act was to bless His followers. He is the High-priest for ever, and these uplifted hands meant a sacreder thing than the affectionate good wishes of a departing friend. He gives the blessings which He invokes. His wish is a conveyance of good.

The hands remained in the attitude of benediction while He ascended, and the last sight of Him, as the cloud wrapped Him round, showed Him shedding blessing from them. He continues that attitude and act till He comes again. Two separate motions are described in verse 51. He was parted from them,—that is, withdrew some little distance on the mountain, that all might see, and none might hinder, His departure; and 'was carried up into heaven' by a slow upward movement, as the word implies. Contrast this with Elijah's rapture. There was no need of fiery chariot or whirlwind to lift Jesus to the heavens. He went up where He was before, returning to the glory which He had with the Father before the world was. The end matches the beginning. The supernatural birth corresponds with the supernatural departure.

We have to think of that Ascension as the entrance of corporeal humanity into the divine glory, as the beginning of His heavenly activity for the world, as the token of His work being triumphantly completed, as the prophecy and pledge of immortal life like His own for all who love Him. Therefore we may share the joy which flooded the lately sorrowful disciples' hearts, and, like them, should make all life sacred, and be continually in the Temple, blessing God, and have the deep roots of our lives hid with Christ in the glory.

CHRIST'S WITNESSES

'Ye are witnesses of these things. 49. And, behold, I
send the promise of My Father upon you: but tarry ye
in the city of Jerusalem, until ye be endued with
power from on high.'—LUKE xxiv. 48, 49.

Luke's account of the Resurrection and subsequent forty days is so constructed as to culminate in this appointment of the disciples to their high functions and equipment for it, by the gift of the Holy Spirit. The Evangelist has evidently in view his second 'treatise,' and is here preparing the link of connection between it and the Gospel. Hence this very condensed summary of many conversations lays stress upon these points—the fulfilment of prophecy in Christ's life and death; the world-wide destination of the blessings to be proclaimed in His name; and the appointment and equipment of the disciples.

The same notes are again struck in the beginning of the Acts of the Apostles. The same charge to the disciples, when viewed in connection with Christ's life on earth, may be considered as its end and aim; and when viewed in connection with the history of the Church, as its foundation and beginning. So that we are following in the line plainly marked out for us by the Evangelist himself, when we take these words as containing a charge and a gift as really belonging to all Christians in this day as to the little group on the road to Bethany, to whom they were first addressed on the Ascension morning. There are, then, but two points to be looked at in the words before us; the one the function of the Church, and the other its equipment for it.

I. The task of the Church.

Now, of course, I need not remind you that there is a special sense in which the office of witness–bearing belonged only to those who had seen Christ in the flesh, and could testify to the fact of His Resurrection. I need not dwell upon that further than to remark that the fact that the designation of the first preachers of the Gospels was 'witnesses' is significant of a great deal. For witness implies fact, and the nature of their message, as being the simple attestation to the occurrence of things that truly happened in the earth, is wrapped up in that name. They were not speculators, philosophers, moralists, legislators. They had neither to argue nor to dissertate, nor to lay down rules for conduct, nor to ventilate their own fancies. They were witnesses, and their business was to tell the truth, the whole truth, and nothing but the truth. All doctrine and all morality will come second. The first form of the Gospel is, 'How that Jesus Christ died for our sins according to the Scriptures, and that He was raised again the third day, according to the Scriptures.' First, a history; then a religion; then a morality; and morality and religion because it is a history of redemption.

These early Christians were witnesses in another sense. The very existence of the Church at all was a testimony to that supernatural fact without which it could not have been. We are often told in recent years that the belief in the Resurrection grew slowly up amongst the early Christians. What became of the Church whilst it was growing? What held it together? How comes it that the fate of Christ's followers was not the fate of the followers of Theudas and other people that rose up, 'boasting themselves to be somebody,' whose followers as a matter of course, 'came to nought' when the leader was slain? There is only one answer. 'He rose again from the dead.' Else there is no possibility of accounting for the fact that the Church as a distinct organisation survived Calvary. The Resurrection was no gradually evolved hardening of desire and fancy into fact, but it was the foundation upon which the Church was built. 'Ye'—by your words and by your existence as a community—'are the witnesses of these things.'

But that is somewhat apart from the main purpose of my remarks now. I desire rather to emphasise the thought that, with modifications in form, the substance of the functions of these early believers remains still the office and dignity of all Christian men. 'Ye are the witnesses of these things.'

And what is the manner of testimony that devolves upon you and me, Christian friends? Witness by your lives. Most men take their notions of what Christianity is from the average of the Christians round about them. And, if we profess to be Christ's followers, we shall be taken as tests and specimen cases of the worth of the religion that we profess. 'Ye are the Epistles of Christ,' and if the writing be blurred and blotted and often half unintelligible, the blame will be laid largely at His door. And men will say, and say rightly, 'If that is all that Christianity can do, we are just as well without it.' It is our task to 'adorn the doctrine of Christ,' marvellous as it may seem that anything in our poor lives can commend that fairest of all beautiful things—and to commend it to some hearts. Just as some poor black–and–white engraving of a masterpiece of the painter's brush may, to an eye untrained in the harmony of colour, be a better interpretation of the artist's meaning than his own proper work, so our feeble copies of the transcendent splendour and beauty may suit some purblind and untrained eyes better than the serener and loftier perfection which we humbly copy. 'We are the witnesses of these things.' And depend upon it, mightier than all direct effort, and more unusual than all utterances of lip, is the witness of the life of all professing Christians to the reality of the facts upon which they say they base their faith.

But beyond that, there is yet another department of testimony which belongs to each of us, and that is the attestation of personal experience. That is a form of Christian service which any and every Christian can put forth. You cannot all be preachers, in the technical sense. You cannot all be thinkers and strong champions, argumentative or otherwise, for God's truth. But I will tell you what you all can be. You can all say, 'Come and hear all ye; and I will declare what He hath done for my soul.' It does not take eloquence, gifts, learning, intellectual grasp of the doctrinal side of Christian truth for a man to say, as the first preacher of Christ upon earth said, 'Brother! we have found the Messias.' That was all, and that was enough. That you can say, if you *have* found Him, and after all, the witness of personal experience of what faith in Jesus Christ can make of a man, and do for a man, is the strongest and most universal weapon placed in the hands of Christian men and women. There is nothing that goes so far as that, if it be backed up by a life corresponding, which, like a sounding–board behind a man, flings his words out into the world'; 'Whether this man be a sinner or no I know not'; 'I leave all that talk about heights and depths of argument and controversy to other people, but this one thing I know'—not I *think,* not I *believe,* not I am disposed to come to the conclusion that—but 'this one thing I *know,* that whereas I was blind now I see.' There is no getting over that! 'Ye are the witnesses of these things.' And do not be ashamed of your function, nor slothful nor cowardly in its discharge.

May I say a word here about the grounds on which this obligation to witness rests for us? If Jesus Christ had never said, 'Go ye into all the world and preach the Gospel to every creature,' it would not have made a bit of difference as to the imperative duty that is laid upon all Christian men; for that arises, not from that command, which only gives voice to a previous obligation, but it flows, from the very nature of things, from the message that we receive from our links with other men and from the constitution and make of our own natures.

It flows directly from the gift that we have received. There are plenty of truths which, *per se,* carry with them no obligation to impart them. But any truth in which is wrapped up the possible happiness of another man, any truth which bears upon moral or spiritual subjects, carries with it the strongest obligation to impart it. We have such large insights into God and His love as the Gospel gives us, not that we may eat our morsel alone, or merely sun ourselves in the light, and expatiate in the warmth of the beams that come to us, but that we may share them with all around: 'God, who commanded the light to shine out of darkness hath shined into our hearts,' that we may 'give the light of the knowledge of the glory of God in the face of Jesus Christ.'

The obligation arises from the links that knit us all together. 'Am I my brother's keeper?' Why, the question answers itself. If he is *your* 'brother,' you are certainly *his* 'keeper.' And you cannot shuffle off the obligation by any irrelevant pitting of one field of Christian work against another; still less by any criticism, hostile or friendly, as it may be, of the methods of Christian work, or of the parity and elevation of the character and motives of the workers. Humanity is one, linked by a mystic chain, and every link of it should thrill by a common impulse; and through all the members there should circulate a common life. That great thought is one of the gains that the Gospel has brought us, and in the presence of it and our indebtedness and obligation to every man, woman, and child that bears the form of man, all geographical limits to Christian witnessing seem supremely absurd and incongruous. You cannot get rid of your obligation by saying, 'I do not care about foreign missions, I go in for home ones.' And you cannot get rid of it by chiming in an ignorant second to the talk that has been going on lately, carping at or criticising methods of work. It would be a very strange thing if we had hit all at once, in the very beginning of an enterprise, upon the best of all possible methods; and it would be a very strange thing if the mission–field is the only one where there are no lazy workers and selfish motives and unworthy occupants of high places. All that is true about home as it is about other places. But grant it all, and back comes the obligation based upon the nature of the truth that we have received, upon our links with our brethren, and upon our loyalty to our Master, and it peals into the ears of every Christian man and woman: 'Thou art a witness of these things'; and 'to this end wert thou born again, that thou mightest bear witness to the truth.'

Ah, brethren! the issues of faithfulness to that high function are sweet and blessed and wonderful. A witnessing Christian will be a believing Christian; for there is no surer way to deepen my own convictions about any moral or spiritual truth than to constitute myself their humble servant to proclaim them. Whosoever is a believer should be an apostle, and if he is an apostle he will be tenfold a believer. There is nothing which will give a man a firmer grasp of the Gospel for his own soul than when he finds that, ministered by his humble efforts, it produces in other hearts the same effects which he finds it working upon himself. There is no page in the great book of the evidences of the truth of Christianity more conclusive than that which in the last century has been written by the experience of Christian missions. Let the objectors, Jannes and Jambres, who withstood Moses, let them do the same with their enchantments, and then we will discuss the questions of the truth of the Gospel with them.

Nor need I do more than remind you of the highest of all blessed issues which is yet to come. 'Be thou faithful unto death and I will give thee a crown of life.' Alas! alas! how many of us professing Christians will have to stand at last without that 'crown of rejoicing' which they wear who, by their poor work and witness, have won some souls to the Master. Do you, Christian men, contemplate entering heaven alone, or bringing your sheaves with you? It will be sad to stand with hands empty then, because they were idle in the days of the seed–basket and the reaping–hook, whilst those that sowed and those that reaped shall rejoice together. 'Ye are the witnesses of these things': see to it that you do your work.

II. And now, secondly, and briefly, note the equipment of the witnesses for their task.

Our Lord here distinguishes two stages in the endowment. Then and there they receive the gift of the Divine Spirit, as is more fully recorded in John's account of these last days, but that gift, rich and precious as it was, was not yet the full bestowment which they needed for their task. That came on the day of Pentecost. Mark the vivid and picturesque word which our Lord here employs: 'Until ye be *clothed* with power from on high.' That divine gift coming down as a vesture, wraps and covers and hides their own weakness, their own naked and poor personality.

I can only say a word or two about this matter. The same collocation of ideas—a witnessing Spirit by whose indwelling energy the Christian community becomes witnesses, is found (and has been explained at length by me in former discourses) in the farewell words of our Lord in the upper chamber. 'The Spirit of Truth which proceedeth from the Father, He shall bear witness of Me, and ye also shall bear witness because ye have been with Me from the beginning.'

I need only remark here that the only power by which Christians can discharge their work of witnessing in the world is the power which clothes them from above. The new life which Jesus Christ brings and gives to us is the only life which will avail for discharging this office. Our self–will, the old life of nature, with all its dependence upon ourselves, is nought in reference to this task. But when that divine spark enters into men's hearts, then natural endowments are heightened into supernatural gifts, and new forces are developed, and new powers are bestowed and the earthen vessel is filled with new treasure. Without it—and there is a great deal of so–called Christian witnessing to–day without it—noise, advertising, skill in getting up externals, and all the other unworthy methods which Christian churches sometimes stoop to adopt, are powerless, as they ought to be. You may accomplish a great deal by fussy activity which calls itself Christian earnestness, and has not God's Spirit in it. But it is no more growth than are what the children call 'devil's puff–balls' which they find in the fields in these autumn mornings; and it will go up in poisonous, brown dust like these when it is pricked.

The one condition of Christian churches doing their Christian work is that they shall be clothed and filled with God's Spirit. Do not let us rely on machinery; do not let us rely on externals; do not let us rely on advertising tricks which might do very well for a cheap shop, but are all out of harmony with the work that we have to do; but let us rely on this, and on this alone. Holding converse with God and Christ, we shall come out of the secret place of the Most High with our faces glowing with the communion, and our lips on fire to proclaim the sweetnesses that lie within the shrine.

One word more and I have done. This clothing with the Spirit, which is the only fitness of the Church for its witnessing work, is only to be won by much solitary waiting. 'Tarry ye,' or as in the original it stands even more vividly, 'Sit ye still in the city ... till ye be clothed.' It is because so many Christian workers are so seldom alone with Christ that so much of their work is nought, and comes to nought. To draw apart from outward activity into the solitary place, and sit with Him, is the only means by which we can keep up the freshness of our own spirits, and be fit for His service. Mary was being trained for Martha's work when she sat at Christ's feet; but Martha could not do hers without being 'troubled and careful,' because she was more accustomed to the work than to the communion that would have made it light.

So, Christian friends, behold your task and your equipment. I beseech you, who call yourselves Christ's servants, to lay to heart your plain and unavoidable obligations. If you have found Jesus, you are as truly and as individually bound to proclaim Him as if a definite and direct divine command sounded in your ears. Your possession of the Gospel as the food of your own souls binds you to impart it to all the famished. The call to witness comes as straight to you as it did to the young Pharisee on the road to Damascus when he heard 'Saul! Saul!' called from the sky.

May you and I answer as he did, 'Lord! what wilt Thou have *me* to do!'

THE ASCENSION

'And He led them out as far as to Bethany, and He
lifted up His hands, and blessed them. 51. And it
came to pass, while He blessed them, He was parted
from them, and carried up into heaven.'
—LUKE xxiv. 50, 51.

'And when He had spoken these things, while they
beheld, He was taken up; and a cloud received Him
out of their sight.'—ACTS i. 9.

Two of the four Evangelists, viz., Matthew and John, have no record of the Ascension. But the argument which infers ignorance from silence, which is always rash, is entirely discredited in this case. It is impossible to believe that Matthew, who wrote as the last word of his gospel the great words, 'All power is given unto Me in heaven and in earth ... lo! I am with you alway....' was ignorant of the fact which alone makes these words credible. And it is equally impossible to believe that the Evangelist who recorded the tender saying to Mary, 'Go to My brethren, and say unto them I ascend to My Father, and your Father,' was ignorant of its fulfilment. The explanation of the silence is to be sought in a quite different direction. It comes from the fact that to the Evangelists, rightly, the Ascension was but the prolongation and the culmination of the Resurrection. That being recorded, there was no need for the definite record of this.

There is another singular point about these records, viz., that Luke has two accounts, one in the end of his gospel, one in the beginning of Acts; and that these two accounts are obviously different. The differences have been laid hold of as a weapon with which to attack the veracity of both accounts. But there again a little consideration clears the path. The very places in which they respectively occur might have solved the difficulty, for the one is at the end of a book, and the other is at the beginning of a book; and so, naturally, the one regards the Ascension as the end of the earthly life, and the other as the beginning of the heavenly. The one is all suffused with evening light; the other is radiant with the promise of a new day. The one is the record of a tender farewell, in the other the sense of parting has almost been absorbed in the forward look to the new phase of relationship which is to begin. If Luke had been a secular biographer, the critics would have been full of admiration at the delicacy of his touch, and the fineness of keeping in the two narratives, the picture being the same in both, and the scheme of colouring being different. But as he is only an Evangelist, they fall foul of him for his 'discrepancies.' It is worth our while to take both his points of view.

But there is another thing to be remembered, that, as the appendix of his account of the Ascension in the book of the Acts, Luke tells us of the angel's message;—'This same Jesus ... shall ... return.' So there are three points of view which have to be combined in order to get the whole significance of that mighty fact: the Ascension as an end; the Ascension as a beginning; the Ascension as the pledge of the return. Now take these three points.

I. We have the aspect of the Ascension as an end.

The narrative in Luke's gospel, in its very brevity, does yet distinctly suggest that retrospective and valedictory tone. Note how, for instance, we are told the locality—'He led them out as far as Bethany.' The name at once strikes a chord of remembrance. What memories clustered round it, and how natural it was that the parting should take place there, not merely because the crest of the Mount of Olives hid the place from the gaze of the crowded city; but because it was within earshot almost of the home where so much of the sweet earthly fellowship, that was now to end, had passed. The same note of regarding the scene as being the termination of those blessed years of dear and familiar intercourse is struck in the fact, so human, so natural, so utterly inartificial, that He lifted His hands to bless them, moved by the same impulse with which so often we have wrung a hand at parting, and stammered, 'God bless you!' And the same valedictory hue is further deepened by the fact that what Luke puts first is not the Ascension, but the parting. 'He was parted from them,' that is the main fact; 'and He was carried up into heaven,' comes almost as a subordinate one. At all events it is regarded mainly as being the medium by which the parting was effected.

So the aspect of the Ascension thus presented is that of a tender farewell; the pathetic conclusion of three long, blessed years. And yet that is not all, for the Evangelist adds a very enigmatic word: 'They returned to Jerusalem with great joy.' Glad because He had gone? No. Glad merely because He had gone up? No. The saying is a riddle, left at the end of the book, for readers to ponder, and is a subtle link of connection with what is to be written in the next volume, when the aspect of the Ascension as an end is subordinate, and its aspect as a beginning is prominent. So regarded, it filled the disciples with joy. Thus you see, I think, that without any illegitimate straining of the expressions of the text, we do come to the point of view from which, to begin with, this great event must be looked at. We have to take the same view, and to regard that Ascension not only as the end of an epoch of sweet friendship, but as the solemn close and culmination of the whole earthly life. I have no time to dwell upon the thoughts that come crowding into one's mind when we take that point of view. But let me suggest, in the briefest way, one or two of them.

Here is an end which circles round to, and is of a piece with, the beginning. 'I came forth from the Father, and am come into the world; again, I leave the world, and go unto the Father.' The Ascension corresponds with, and meets the miracle of, the Incarnation. And as the Word who became flesh, came by the natural path of human birth, and entered in through the gate by which we all enter, and yet came as none else has come, by His own will, in the miracle of His Incarnation, so at the end, He passed out from life through the gate by which we all pass, and 'was obedient unto death, even the death of the Cross,' and yet He passed likewise on a path which none but Himself has trod, and ascended up to heaven, whence He had descended to earth. He came into the world, not as leaving the Father, for He is 'the Son of Man which is in heaven,' and He ascended up on high, not as leaving us, for He is 'with us alway, even to the end of the world.' Thus the Incarnation and the Ascension support each other.

But let me remind you how, in this connection, we have the very same combination of lowliness and gentleness with majesty and power which runs through the whole of the story of the earthly life of Jesus Christ. Born in a stable, and waited on by angels, the subject of all the humiliations of humanity, and flashing forth through them all the power of divinity, He ascends on high at last, and yet with no pomp nor visible splendour to the world, but only in the presence of a handful of loving hearts, choosing some dimple of the hill where its folds hid them from the city. As He came quietly and silently into the world, so quietly and silently He passed thence. In this connection there is more than the picturesque contrast between the rapture of Elijah, with its whirlwind, and chariot of fire and horses of fire, and the calm, slow rising, by no external medium raised, of the Christ. It was fit that the mortal should be swept up into the unfamiliar heaven by the pomp of angels and the chariot of fire. It was fit that when Jesus ascended to His 'own calm home, His habitation from eternity,' there should be nothing visible but His own slowly rising form, with the hands uplifted, to shed benediction on the heads of the gazers beneath.

In like manner, regarding the Ascension as an end, may we not say that it is the seal of heaven impressed on the sacrifice of the Cross? 'Wherefore God also hath highly exalted Him, and given Him a Name, which is above every name; that at the Name of Jesus every knee should bow.' We find in that intimate connection between the Cross and the Ascension, the key to the deep saying which carries references to both in itself, when the Lord spoke of Himself as being lifted up and drawing all men unto Him. The original primary reference no doubt was to His elevation on the Cross, 'as Moses lifted up the serpent.' But the final, and at the time of its being spoken, the mysterious, reference was to the fact that in descending to the depth of humiliation He was rising to the height of glory. The zenith of the Ascension is the rebound from the nadir of the Cross. The lowliness of the stoop measures the loftiness of the elevation, and the Son of Man was glorified at the moment when the Son of Man was most profoundly abased. The Cross and the Ascension, if I might use so violent a figure, are like the twin stars, of which the heavens present some examples, one dark and lustreless, one flashing with radiancy of light, but knit together by an invisible vinculum, and revolving round a common centre. When He 'parted from them, and was carried up into heaven,' He ended the humiliation which caused the elevation.

And then, again, I might suggest that, regarded in its aspect as an end, this Ascension is also the culmination and the natural conclusion of the Resurrection. As I have said, the Scripture point of view with reference to these two is not that they are two, but that the one is the starting point of the line of which the other is the goal. The process which began when He rose from the dead, whatever view we may take of the condition of His earthly life during the forty days of parenthesis, could have no rational and intelligible ending, except the Ascension. Thus we should think of it not only as the end of a sweet friendship, but as the end of the gracious manifestation of the earthly life, the counterpart of the Incarnation and descent to earth, the end of the Cross and the culmination of the Resurrection. The Son of Man, the same that also descended into the lowest parts of the earth, ascended up where He was before.

Now let us turn to the other aspect which the Evangelist gives, when He ceases to be an Evangelist, and becomes a Church Historian. *Then* he considers

II. The Ascension as a beginning.

Expositions Of Holy Scripture

The place which it holds in the Acts of the Apostles explains the point of view from which it is to be regarded. It is the foundation of everything that the writer has afterwards to say. It is the basis of the Church. It is the ground of all the activity which Christ's servants put forth. Not only its place explains this aspect of it, but the very first words of the book itself do the same. 'The former treatise have I made ... of all that Jesus began both to do and teach'—and now I am to tell you of an Ascension, and of all that Jesus continued to do and teach. So that the book is the history of the work of the Lord, who was able to do that work, just because He had ascended up on high. The same impression is produced if we ponder the conversation which precedes the account of the Ascension in the book of Acts, which, though it touches the same topics as are touched by the words that precede the account in the Gospel, yet presents them in a different aspect, and suggests the endowments with which the Christian community is to be invested, and the work which therefore it is to do, in consequence of the Ascension of Jesus Christ. The Apostle Peter had caught that thought when, on the day of Pentecost, he said, 'He, being exalted to the right hand of the Father, hath shed forth this which ye see and hear,' and throughout the whole book the same point of view is kept up. 'The work that is done upon earth He doeth it all Himself.'

So there is in *this* narrative nothing about parting, there is nothing about blessing. There is simply the ascending up and the significant addition of the reception into the cloud, which, whilst He was yet plainly visible, and not dwindled by distance into a speck, received Him out of their sight. The cloud was the symbol of the Divine Presence, which had hung over the Tabernacle, which had sat between the cherubim, which had wrapped the shepherds and the angels on the hillside, which had come down in its brightness on the Mount of Transfiguration, and which now, as the symbol of the Divine Presence, received the ascending Lord, in token to the men that stood gazing up into heaven, that He had passed to the right hand of the Majesty on high.

Thus we have to think of that Ascension as being the groundwork and foundation of all the world–wide and age–long energy which the living Christ is exercising to–day. As one of the other Evangelists, or at least, the appendix to his gospel, puts it, He ascended up on high, and 'they went everywhere preaching the word, the Lord also working with them, and confirming the word with signs following.' It is the ascended Christ who sends the Spirit upon men; it is the ascended Christ who opens men's hearts to hear; it is the ascended Christ who sends forth His messengers to the Gentiles; it is the ascended Christ who, to–day, is the energy of all the Church's powers, the whiteness of all the Church's purity, the vitality of all the Church's life. He lives, and therefore, there is a Christian community on the face of the earth. He lives, and therefore it will never die.

So we, too, have to look to that risen Lord as being the power by which alone any of us can do either great or small work in His Church. That Ascension is symbolically put as being to 'the right hand of God.' What is the right hand of God? The divine omnipotence. Where is it? Everywhere. What does sitting at the right hand of God mean? Wielding the powers of omnipotence. And so He says, 'All power is given unto Me'; and He is working a work to–day, wider in its aspects than, though it be the application and consequence of, the work upon the Cross. He cried there, 'It is finished!' but 'the work of the ascended Jesus' will never be finished until 'the kingdoms of this world are become the kingdom of our God and of His Christ.'

There are other aspects of His work in heaven which space will not allow me to dwell upon, though I

389

cannot but mention them. By the Ascension Christ begins to prepare a place for us. How could any of us stand in the presence of that eternal Light if He were not there? We should be like some savage or rustic swept up suddenly and put down in the middle of the glittering ring of courtiers round a throne, unless we could lift our eyes and recognise a known and loving face there. Where Christ is, I can be. He has taken one human nature up into the Glory, and other human natures will therefore find in it a home.

The ascended Christ, to use the symbolism which one of the New Testament writers employs for illustration of a thought far greater than the symbol—has like a High Priest passed within the veil, 'there to appear in the presence of God for us.' And the intercession which is far more than petition, and is the whole action of that dear Lord who identifies as with Himself, and whose mighty work is ever present before the divine mind as an element in His dealings, that intercession is being carried on for ever for us all. So, 'set your affection on things above, where Christ is, sitting at the right hand of God.' So, expect His help in your work, and do the work which He has left you to carry on here. So, face death and the dim kingdoms beyond, without quiver and without doubt, assured that where the treasure is, there the heart will be also; and that where the Master is, there the servants who follow in His steps will be also at last.

And now there is the third aspect here of

III. The Ascension as being the pledge of the return.

The two men in white apparel that stood by gently rebuked the gazers for gazing into heaven. They would not have rebuked them for gazing, if they could have seen Him, but to look into the empty heaven was useless. And they added the reason why the heavens need not be looked at, as long as there is the earth to stand on: 'For this same Jesus whom ye have seen go into heaven shall so come in like manner as ye have seen Him go.' Note the emphatic declaration of identity; 'this *same* Jesus.' Note the use of the simple human name; 'this same *Jesus*,' and recall the thoughts that cluster round it, of the ascended humanity, and the perpetual humanity of the ascended Lord, 'the same yesterday, and to–day, and for ever,' Note also the strong assertion, of visible, corporeal return: 'Shall so come in *like* manner as ye have seen Him go.' That return is no metaphor, no mere piece of rhetoric, it is not to be eviscerated of its contents by being taken as a synonym for the diffusion of His influence all over a regenerated race, but it points to the return of the Man Jesus locally, corporeally, visibly. 'We believe that Thou shalt come to be our Judge'; we believe that Thou wilt come to take Thy servants home.

The world has not seen the last of Jesus Christ. Such an Ascension, after such a life, cannot be the end of Him. 'As it is appointed unto all men once to die, and after death the Judgment, so Christ also, having been once offered to bear the sins of many, shall appear the second time, without sin unto salvation.' As inevitably as for sinful human nature judgment follows death, so inevitably for the sinless Man, who is the sacrifice for the world's sins, His judicial return will follow His atoning work, and He will come again, having received the Kingdom, to take account of His servants, and to perfect their possession of the salvation which by His Incarnation, Passion, Resurrection, and Ascension, He wrought for the world.

Therefore, brethren, one sweet face, and one great fact—the face of the Christ, the fact of the

Cross—should fill the past. One sweet face, one great fact—the face of the Christ, the fact of His Presence with us all the days—should fill the present. One regal face, one great hope, should fill the future; the face of the King that sitteth upon the throne, the hope that He will come again, and 'so we shall be ever with the Lord.'

END OF VOL. II.

CPSIA information can be obtained
at www.ICGtesting.com
Printed in the USA
LVHW060146191222
735316LV00037BD/744